W9-BVK-146

The **Rough Guide** to

Chile

written and researched by

Melissa Graham and Andrew Benson

with additional contributions by
Anna Khmelnitski, Shafik Meghji and Charlotte Turner

ROUGH
GUIDES

www.roughguides.com

BABYLON PUBLIC LIBRARY

Contents

Adventure sports
colour section
following p.152

Chilean wildlife
colour section
following p.376

◄◄ Vicuña near Putre ◄ Volcán Parinacota

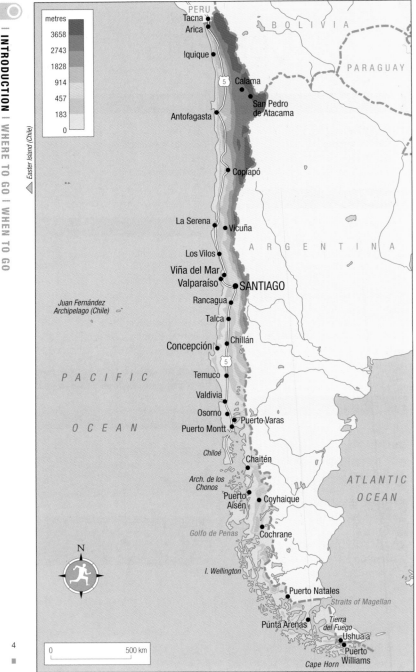

Introduction to
Chile

A long, narrow sliver of land, clinging to the edge of a continent, Chile has often drawn attention to itself for its wholly implausible shape. Seen in the pages of an atlas, the country's outline strikes you as aberrant and fantastical; 4300km in length (the equivalent of Norway to Nigeria), and with an average width of just 175km, the very idea of it seems absurd. Once you're on Chilean soil, however, these boundaries make perfect sense, and visitors quickly realize that Chile is a geographically self-contained unit. The Andes, the great mountain range that forms its eastern border, are a formidable barrier of rock and ice that cuts the country off from Argentina and Bolivia. The Atacama Desert, a thousand-kilometre stretch of parched wasteland, separates it from Peru to the north. And to the west, only a few islands dotted in the Pacific Ocean break the waves that roll onto Chile's coast from Australasia.

All this has created a country distinct from the rest of South America and one that defies many people's expectations of an Andean country. It is developed, relatively affluent, and – with the exception of the infamous military Pinochet regime of the 1970s and 1980s – boasts a long tradition of political stability and orderly government. It is, without doubt, one of the safest and most relaxing South American countries to travel in. Its buses are comfortable and run on time. Its people are polite, respectful and discreet. And, by regional standards, its police are honest and relatively non-corrupt.

5

◄ Barrio Bellavista in Santiago

Fact file

- One of Chile's most outstanding features is its shape – a long thin strip 4300km in length that takes in an extraordinary diversity of terrains.

- Some **16.7 million people** live in Chile, around one third of them in Santiago. It has a fairly homogenous mestizo population of mixed Spanish and indigenous ancestry. Very few indigenous groups remain, only the Mapuche of the Lake District and Aisén (numbering around 600,000), the smaller population of Aymara in the far north (around 48,000), Rapa Nui on Easter Island (around 4000), Yámana (around 1700) and Kawéskar (around 2600) in Patagonia and Tierra del Fuego.

- Chile is **one of the most developed countries in Latin America**, with the steadiest growth in the region. According to figures produced by Transparency International, a nongovernmental organization associated with the United Nations, Chile also has the lowest level of corruption in Latin America, and is less corrupt than a number of wealthier countries such as France and Japan.

- Although known throughout the world for its infamous military dictatorship during the 1970s and 1980s, Chile has a long history of parliamentary democracy, and is today probably the **most politically stable country in South America**.

Above all, though, it is for its remote and dizzyingly beautiful landscapes that visitors head to Chile. With its population of sixteen million largely confined to a handful of major cities, and a land area three times greater than the UK's, much of Chile is made up of vast tracts of scarcely touched wilderness – places where you can be days from the nearest tarred road, and where it's not unusual to stumble upon steaming hot springs, gleaming white salt flats or emerald lakes, and have them all to yourself. Few countries, moreover, can match the astounding contrasts of scenery you'll find here, ranging from the driest desert in the world to immense ice fields and glaciers. Spread between these extremes is a kaleidoscope of panoramas, taking in sun-baked scrubland, lush vineyards and orchards, virgin temperate rainforest, dramatic fjords and bleak Patagonian steppes. Towering over it all is the long, jagged spine of the Andes, punctuated by colossal peaks and smouldering volcanoes.

You can experience this wilderness in whatever style you choose – Chile is not a developing country, and you don't have to slum it while you're here. There are plenty of modest, inexpensive

accommodation options and camping facilities up and down the country, while those on a more generous budget will find increasing numbers of luxurious, beautifully designed lodges in spectacular locations, particularly in the south. Whatever your budget, you'll probably want to take advantage of the numerous possibilities for outdoor activities, whether it be jeep rides, bird watching, skiing, horse trekking, wine tours, hiking, volcano climbing, sea kayaking, white-water rafting or fly-fishing – all offered by a large number of local outfitters, and comprehensively detailed in this guide. If you have less active plans

> **Chile is, without doubt, one of the safest and most relaxing South American countries to travel in**

in mind, you can sit back and take in Chile's scenery from various ferry rides in the south, on reasonably priced flights or on organized tours from most of the main cities. However you do it, you won't be disappointed.

Where to go

Given Chile's great size, and the huge distances that separate the main attractions, it's important to give careful thought to your itinerary before you go. If you want to experience both the northern and southern extremes, you should invest in a LAN air pass (Ⓦwww .lanchile.com), unless you're prepared to spend many hours sitting on a bus, or are in the country for an extended period. Otherwise, most visitors with just two or three weeks to play with tend to choose between heading north or south from Santiago, even then singling out a few chosen targets, rather than trying to fit everything in. Something else to bear in mind is that, on the whole, Chile's cities are not that exciting, and are best used as a jumping-off point to get out into the backcountry. In light of this, you should seriously consider renting a vehicle for at least part of your trip, as public transport to some of the most beautiful areas, including many national parks, is non-existent. We discuss each region's highlights in greater detail in the chapter introductions; what follows is a brief summary of attractions in each area.

Santiago, though boasting some fine monuments, museums and restaurants, with its ceaseless noise and traffic and heavy pollution, is not a destination city like Río or Buenos Aires, and two or three days here is enough for most visitors. The capital is handy for visiting some of the country's oldest **vineyards**, while a string of splendid beaches as well as

Altiplano driving

The south of Chile may have the monopoly on outdoor activities, but the north offers one of South America's most exciting adventures: driving across the altiplano. Shared with neighbouring Argentina, Bolivia and Peru, the altiplano is a high plateau connecting the eastern and western

▲ The vast Altiplano

ranges of the Andes, sitting at an altitude of up to 4500m. Beautiful and desolate in equal measure, it's a land of bleak, sunburnt plains dotted with gleaming white salt flats, turquoise lakes and snow-capped volcanoes. Huddled in their shadows are the tiny, semi-abandoned villages of the indigenous Aymara, who've herded llamas and alpacas up here for many centuries. You can visit the altiplano on organized tours from Chile's northern cities, but far and away the best way to do it is by renting a sturdy 4WD, loading it up with a tent, a stove and gallons of fuel and water, and heading up solo – an experience that allows you to truly appreciate the wilderness, the solitude and the sheer majesty of the place. Naturally, this is a serious journey and you'll need to take sensible precautions; for more on driving through the altiplano, see Basics, p.38, and El Norte Grande chapter.

the quirky port city of **Valparaíso** and the fashionable seaside resort of **Viña del Mar** both sit on its doorstep.

North of Santiago, highlights include the handsome colonial city of **La Serena**, the lush, deeply rural **Elqui Valley**, and another succession of idyllic **beaches** along the dazzling fringe of the **Norte Chico**, a region that mostly comprises semi-arid landscapes and brittle vegetation. At the northern edge of this region, the tidy little city of **Copiapó** serves as a springboard for excursions to the white sands and turquoise waters of **Bahía Inglesa**, one of the country's most attractive seaside resorts, and east into the cordillera, where you'll find the mineral-streaked volcanoes of **Parque Nacional Nevado de Tres Cruces** and the radiant **Laguna Verde**. Further north, the barren **Atacama Desert**, stretching over 1000km into southern Peru, presents an unforgettable, if forbidding, landscape, whose sights number ancient petroglyphs (indigenous rock art), abandoned nitrate ghost towns and a scattering of fertile, fruit-filled oases. Up in the Andes, the vast plateau known as the **altiplano**, as high and remote as Tibet,

> **Few countries match the astounding contrasts of scenery, from the driest desert in the world to immense glaciers**

9

Chile's regions

Administratively, Chile is divided into fifteen regions, numbered one to fifteen, with the exception of region XIII, which does not exist, and with the addition of the Metropolitan region. We've listed each region by number and name below, followed by the regional capital in parentheses.

I	Tarapacá (Iquique)
II	Antofagasta (Antofagasta)
III	Atacama (Copiapó)
IV	Coquimbo (La Serena)
V	Valparaíso (Valparaíso)
VI	Libertador General O'Higgins (Rancagua)
VII	Maule (Talca)
VIII	Bionbío (Concepción)
IX	Araucanía (Temuco)
X	Los Lagos (Puerto Montt)
XI	Aisén (Coyhaique)
XII	Magallanes y Antártida Chilena (Punta Arenas)
XIV	Los Ríos (Valdivia)
XV	Arica and Parinacota (Arica)

encompasses snow-capped volcanoes, bleached-white salt flats, lakes speckled pink with flamingoes, grazing llamas, alpacas and vicuñas, tiny whitewashed churches and native Aymara communities. The best points to head for up here are **Parque Nacional Lauca**, reached from the city of Arica, and **Parque Nacional Volcán Isluga**, near Iquique.

▶ Rodeo in the Central Valley

► Castro palafitos in Chiloé

South of Santiago, the chief appeal of the lush **Central Valley** is its swaths of orchards and vineyards, dotted with stately haciendas, while further south, the famous, much-visited **Lake District** presents a picture-postcard of perfect, conical volcanoes (including the exquisite **Volcán Osorno**), iris-blue lakes, rolling pastureland and dense native forests, perfect for hiking. A short ferry ride from Puerto Montt, at the southern edge of the Lake District, the **Chiloé** archipelago is a quiet, rural backwater, famous for its rickety houses on stilts, old wooden churches and rich local mythology. Back on the mainland, south of Puerto Montt, the **Carretera Austral** – a 1000-kilometre long unpaved "highway" – carves its way through virgin temperate rainforest and past dramatic fjords, one of which is the embarkation point for a 200-kilometre boat trip out to the sensational **Laguna San Rafael glacier**. Beyond the Carretera Austral, cut off by the **Campo de Hielo Sur** (Southern Ice Field) lies **Patagonia**, a country of bleak windswept plains bordered by the magnificent granite spires of the **Torres del Paine** massif, Chile's single most famous sight, and a magnet for hikers and climbers. Just over the easily crossed border in Argentina are two of the region's star attractions: the **Fitz Roy Sector** in the north of the **Parque Nacional Los Glaciares**, a favourite for trekkers, and, to the south, the awe-inspiring **Glaciar Perito Moreno**. Across the Magellan Strait, **Tierra del Fuego**, shared with Argentina, sits shivering at the bottom of the world, a remote land of a harsh, desolate beauty.

Finally, there are Chile's two Pacific possessions: remote **Easter Island**, famed for its mysterious statues and fascinating prehistoric culture; and

the little-visited **Isla Robinson Crusoe**, part of the Juan Fernández Archipelago, Chile's largest marine reserve, sporting dramatic volcanic peaks covered with dense vegetation and a wealth of endemic wildlife.

When to go

The **north** of the country can be comfortably visited at any time of year, though if you're planning to rent a 4WD and tour the altiplano, note that the unpredictable weather phenomenon known as the **Bolivian Winter** (or *invierno altiplánico*) can produce heavy, sporadic rainfall between December and February (the height of summer), washing away roads and disrupting communications.

In the **centre** and **south** of the country, you should avoid the months of June to September (unless you plan to go skiing), when heavy snowfall often blocks access to the mountains, including many national parks. The peak summer months are January and February, but as accommodation rates and crowds increase in equal measure, you'd be better off coming in November, December or March, when the weather is often just as good.

Climate

	Jan	Feb	Mar	Apr	May	Jun	Jul	Aug	Sep	Oct	Nov	Dec
Antofagasta												
Max (°C)	24	24	28	21	19	18	17	17	18	19	21	22
Max (°F)	75	75	82	70	66	64	63	63	64	66	70	72
Min (°C)	17	17	16	14	13	11	11	11	12	13	14	16
Min (°F)	63	63	61	57	55	52	52	52	54	55	57	61
rainfall (mm)	0	0	0	0	0	3	5	4	0	3	0	0
Arica												
Max (°C)	26	27	25	24	22	19	18	18	19	20	22	24
Max (°F)	79	80	78	75	71	67	65	65	66	69	72	76
Min (°C)	20	20	19	17	15	14	14	14	15	15	17	18
Min (°F)	68	68	66	63	60	58	57	58	59	60	62	65
rainfall (mm)	1	0	0	0	0	0	0	3	0	0	0	2
Punta Arenas												
Max (°C)	15	14	12	10	7	5	4	6	8	11	12	14
Max (°F)	59	57	54	50	45	41	39	43	46	52	54	57
Min (°C)	7	7	5	4	2	1	-1	1	2	3	4	6
Min (°F)	45	45	41	39	36	34	30	34	36	37	39	43
rainfall (mm)	38	23	33	36	33	41	28	31	23	28	18	36
Santiago												
Max (°C)	29	29	27	23	18	14	15	17	19	22	26	28
Max (°F)	84	84	81	73	64	57	59	63	66	72	79	82
Min (°C)	12	11	9	7	5	3	3	4	6	7	9	11
Min (°F)	54	52	48	45	41	37	37	39	43	45	48	52
rainfall (mm)	3	3	5	13	64	84	76	56	31	15	8	5
Valdivia												
Max (°C)	23	23	21	17	13	11	11	12	14	17	18	21
Max (°F)	73	73	70	63	55	52	52	54	57	63	64	70
Min (°C)	11	11	9	8	6	6	5	4	5	7	8	10
Min (°F)	52	52	48	46	43	43	41	39	41	45	46	50
rainfall (mm)	66	74	132	234	361	550	394	328	208	127	125	104

things not to miss

It's not possible to see everything Chile has to offer in one trip – and we don't suggest you try. What follows is a selective taste of the country's highlights: outstanding scenery, picturesque villages and dramatic wildlife. They're arranged in five colour-coded categories, which you can browse through to find the very best things to see and experience. All highlights have a page reference to take you further into the guide, where you can find out more.

01 Parque Nacional Torres del Paine Page **431** • Without a doubt, this spectacular park is what draws most visitors to southern Chile, and it does not disappoint even after all the photos and build-up.

02 **Laguna Verde** Page **193** • Massive active volcanoes surround these richly hued waters, making for an almost surreal landscape – the perfect spot to enjoy the bubbling lakeside hot springs.

04 **Pisco Elqui** Page **181** • Take a tour of a distillery, followed by a taste of a pisco sour, Chile's national cocktail.

03 **Teleférico over Santiago** Page **101** • Dangle high above the sprawling capital, surrounded by the snow-capped Andes.

05 **Termas de Puyuhuapi** Page **397** • Isolated and largely inaccessible, the resort here is home to steaming hot springs, and is one of the great getaways along the Carretera Austral.

06 **Valparaíso** Page **133** • This perched city drapes over a jumble of steep hills around a wide bay.

07 Paragliding in Iquique
Page 220 • Soar over Iquique, one of South America's top paragliding destinations, and enjoy incredible views of the giant sand dune of Cerro Dragón far below.

08 Churches of Chiloé
Page 368 • The archipelago's beautiful wooden churches rise over the heart of almost every small village.

09 San Rafael glacier
Page 394 • Embark on an exhilarating boat ride alongside this stunning ice formation.

10 **Bahía Inglesa** Page **195** • Dip into calm waters and soak up rays on the relatively unspoilt beach.

11 **Tracking Pablo Neruda** Pages **99, 140** & **147** • The Nobel Prize-winning poet is one of Chile's best-known literary exports. Visit any of the three houses he lived in: La Chascona in Santiago, La Sebastiana in Valparaíso, or the museum on Isla Negra.

12 **Hiking Volcán Villarrica** Page **316** • Take a guided hike up this active volcano, the focal point of a park with excellent opportunities for trekking and camping.

13 **The night sky** Page **180** • Chile's northern skies are the most transparent in the southern hemisphere, as testified by the many international observatories stationed here. Head to the Elqui Valley's Cerro Mamalluca observatory to play astronomer and gaze up at the stars.

14 **Penguins** Page **424** • Head to the thriving sanctuaries at Isla Magdalena and Seno Otway for an up-close look at penguins.

15 **Valle de la Luna** Page **217** • Trek across this aptly named moonscape, just south of San Pedro de Atacama.

17 **Lapis lazuli** Page **62** • For a lovely Chilean souvenir, pick up jewellery made from lapis, the cool blue stone mined throughout the country and sold in local crafts markets.

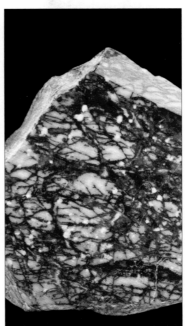

16 **Chinchorro mummies** Page **243** • Gape at these prehistoric, remarkably intact mummies, pulled from a seven-thousand-year-old burial site near Arica.

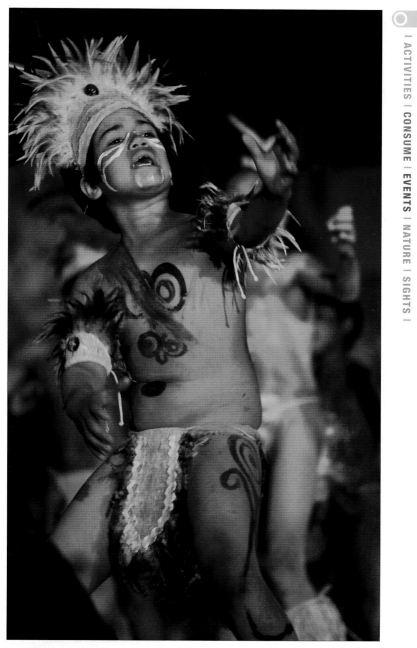

18 **Tapati, Easter Island** Page **466** • Partake in the remote island's liveliest festival, complete with traditional dancing, woodcarving and surfing competitions, all amidst the mysterious moai stone statues.

19 **Rodeos and huasos** Page **257** • Witness expert horsemanship and a slice of national culture at the rodeos in the Central Valley.

20 **Fly-fishing** Page **398** • The gin-clear rivers of the Carretera Austral feature some of the world's best spots for fly-fishing.

21 **Southern Patagonia** Page **413** • Explore the tip of the Americas, where the country splinters into granite towers, glaciers and fjords.

22 **Curanto** Page **362** • In Chiloé, tuck into this delicious concoction of shellfish, smoked meat and potato dumplings, traditionally cooked in a pit in the ground.

23 **Parque Nacional Lauca** Page **254** • Behold Chile's highest national park, with altitudes between 4000 and 6000m, herds of llamas, remote geysers and altiplano lakes.

24 **Sea lions in the Beagle Channel** Page **458** • If you make it all the way down to Tierra del Fuego, a trip through the Channel to see these delightful creatures is a near requisite.

Basics

Basics

Getting there

Nearly everyone flies into Chile, arriving at Santiago's modern international airport, though some will travel by land from a neighbouring country and even fewer will arrive on a ship. Note that relatively few airlines have scheduled flights to Santiago (not to be confused with namesake cities in Spain, Cuba, Dominican Republic and elsewhere), and prices have risen recently as fuel costs have rocketed.

Airfares always depend on the **season**. You'll pay the highest fares in December to February, and June to August, the southern and northern hemisphere's summer holiday months. Fares drop slightly during the "shoulder" months – March and November – and you'll get the best prices during the low seasons: April, May, September and October. Note also that flying on weekends ordinarily adds around ten percent to the round-trip fare; price ranges quoted below assume midweek travel.

Air passes

LAN offers special coupon **air passes**, called **Visit Chile**, available to anyone who's not a resident of Chile, flying into the country on a LAN or Iberia flight only. These must be bought outside the country and can be used for most internal, mainland flights. The price is US$359 for the first three coupons, then from US$116 for each additional coupon. You must buy at least three to start but the number of coupons you buy is unlimited. You cannot fly the same route in the same direction twice and all coupons must be used up within 12 months. In view of all these restrictions and the fact that you may find promotional fares in Chile, you might not find the air pass worth it. If you plan to visit Easter Island, note that your flight there from Santiago will also be far cheaper if the ticket is bought in conjunction with a LAN international flight (see p.30), but Visit Chile coupons cannot be used.

Flights from the US and Canada

While US travellers are not exactly spoiled for choice, they shouldn't find it too hard to get a fairly convenient flight to Santiago. Several airlines offer daily **non-stop flights**, and typical APEX fares from the US are US$900 (low season) or US$1000 (high season) from Miami or the New York region, at least half as much again from California or the Mid-West; you can also stop over in Panama or Lima. There's even less choice if you're flying from Canada to Chile, though you shouldn't have much problem finding a connecting flight with a US carrier or with LAN via Newark, Miami or Los Angeles. Sample fares from Toronto are Can$1200 (low season)/Can$1500 (high season); fares are about twenty percent more from Vancouver.

Approximate **flying times** from the US to Santiago are: from Miami, 8 hours; from LA, 13 hours; and from the New York area, 10 hours. Approximate flying times from Canada to Santiago are: from Toronto, 11 hours; from Vancouver, 16 hours or more.

Flights from the UK and Ireland

Several airlines offer regular scheduled flights from London to Santiago de Chile; a few airlines also offer flights from Dublin. None of them is direct, and as a rule you'll have to choose between flying **via another European or Latin American city** or **via the US** (the latter trips can be marginally cheaper, but are usually longer). In general, high-season fares cost upwards of £900. In addition to fares, it's also worth paying attention to the routings used by the different airlines; even the shortest and most convenient routings via Madrid or Buenos Aires entail a total travelling time of over 16 hours. Apart from trying to minimize the length of the flight, another reason to scrutinize the routings is that many airlines allow you to break your journey and take stopovers on the way – sometimes for free, sometimes for a surcharge. Interesting potential stopovers include Buenos Aires (Air France and Aerolíneas Argentinas), Bogotá (Avianca) and São Paulo and Rio (British Airways and Varig) in South America; Newark, Boston, Chicago, Miami, Dallas and Washington (American, Continental and United) in the US; and Madrid (Iberia, LAN) and Paris (Air France) in Europe.

Flights from Australia, New Zealand and South Africa

Although there are only a couple of airlines that fly to Santiago, the going is pretty straightforward – all follow the same route across the Pacific and cost much the same – with Qantas, Air New Zealand, Air Tahiti, LAN and Aerolíneas Argentinas offering several flights a week between them via Auckland, Papeete and/or Easter Island (LAN only). As total **flying time** is around twenty hours, you may want to take advantage of the free stopover allowed each way.

Tickets purchased direct from the airlines can often work out more expensive than a round-the-world (RTW) fare. Travel agents offer the best deals and have the latest information on limited special offers, such as free stopovers and fly-drive/accommodation packages. Flight Centres and STA (which offer fare reductions for ISIC card-holders and under 26s) generally offer the lowest fares and can also assist with visas.

Airfares vary throughout the year and depend on both the season (defined as high from December to February, and low the rest of the year) and duration of stay (tickets are available for 21 days, 45 days, 90 days, 6 months and one year, with 45- and 90-day tickets the best value. Seat availability on most international flights out of Australia and New Zealand is often limited, so it's best to book several weeks ahead.

Most **Australian** flights are out of Sydney (you'll pay the same from Melbourne, Canberra and Brisbane, but expect to pay ten percent more from Cairns, Adelaide and Hobart, and twenty percent more from Perth and Darwin). The **lowest fares** for 45-day tickets cost upwards of Aus$2000

depending on season, with 90-day tickets costing at least twenty percent more.

Flights out of **New Zealand** generally leave from Auckland, with 45-day fares starting at NZ$1600, while the best 90-day deals will come to at least NZ$2200.

There are currently just two routes out of South Africa to South America: flying from Johannesburg via Cape Town to Buenos Aires with Malaysian Airlines, or from Johannesburg to Sao Paulo with South African Airways. It is cheaper to buy the main flight separately – expect to pay between R7,000 and R8,000 – and then book your flight on to Chile.

Round-the-World flights

If Chile is only one stop on a longer journey, you might want to consider buying a Round-the-World (RTW) ticket. Some travel agents can sell you an "off-the-shelf" RTW ticket that will have you touching down in about half a dozen cities (Santiago is on many itineraries). Alternatively, you can have a travel agent assemble a RTW ticket for you; in this case the ticket can be tailored to your needs but is apt to be more expensive. Figure on around £1600 or US$2400 for a RTW ticket that includes a stopover in Santiago de Chile.

Trains

Chile has **international rail links** between Arica and Tacna in Peru and from Calama to Uyuni and Oruro in Bolivia. However, at the time of writing, the route to Bolivia had been suspended with no official date set for it to start running again.

Buses

There are several good roads **connecting Chile with Argentina** – from Santiago or Valparaíso to Mendoza via Los Andes; from Osorno and Puerto Montt to Bariloche and from Puntas Arenas to Río Gallegos – all of which are served by buses. There are other routes, including the Ruta 41 from La Serena, one of the most dramatic, that leads over the mountains from the Elqui Valley before joining other roads to San Juan. The route only opens in the warmer months between October or November to April. It's

Six steps to a better kind of travel

At Rough Guides we are passionately committed to travel. We feel strongly that only through travelling do we truly come to understand the world we live in and the people we share it with – plus tourism has brought a great deal of **benefit** to developing economies around the world over the last few decades. But the extraordinary growth in tourism has also damaged some places irreparably, and of course **climate change** is exacerbated by most forms of transport, especially flying. This means that now more than ever it's important to **travel thoughtfully** and **responsibly**, with respect for the cultures you're visiting – not only to derive the most benefit from your trip but also to preserve the best bits of the planet for everyone to enjoy. At Rough Guides we feel there are six main areas in which you can make a difference:

- Consider what you're contributing to the **local economy**, and how much the services you use do the same, whether it's through employing local workers and guides or sourcing locally grown produce and local services.
- Consider the **environment** on holiday as well as at home. Water is scarce in many developing destinations, and the biodiversity of local flora and fauna can be adversely affected by tourism. Try to patronize businesses that take account of this.
- Travel with a purpose, not just to tick off experiences. Consider **spending longer** in a place, and getting to know it and its people.
- Give thought to how often you **fly**. Try to avoid short hops by air and more harmful night flights.
- Consider **alternatives to flying**, travelling instead by bus, train, boat and even by bike or on foot where possible.
- Make your trips **"climate neutral"** via a reputable carbon offset scheme. All Rough Guide flights are offset, and every year we donate money to a variety of charities devoted to combating the effects of climate change.

worth noting that all Andean routes, even the road to Mendoza, can be blocked by snow from April onwards. A decent road and regular buses link Chile to Peru from Arica through to Tacna. You can also catch buses from Arica to La Paz in Bolivia (page 000). The reasonable road takes you through the stunning scenery of the Lauca National Park, but it does mean travelling from sea level up to 4500m in just a few hours so take plenty of water and expect to feel pretty uncomfortable.

Airlines, agents and operators

Online booking

Ⓦ www.expedia.co.uk (in UK), Ⓦ www.expedia.com (in US), Ⓦ www.expedia.ca (in Canada)
Ⓦ www.lastminute.com (in UK)
Ⓦ www.opodo.co.uk (in UK)
Ⓦ www.orbitz.com (in US)

Ⓦ www.travelocity.co.uk (in UK), Ⓦ www.travelocity.com (in US), Ⓦ www.travelocity.ca (in Canada) Ⓦ www.travelocity.co.nz (in New Zealand)
Ⓦ www.travelonline.co.za (in South Africa)
Ⓦ www.zuji.com.au (in Australia)

Airlines

Aerolíneas Argentinas US ☎ 1-800/333-0276, Canada ☎ 1-800/688-0008, UK ☎ 0800/096 9747, New Zealand ☎ 09/379 3675, Australia ☎ 02/9234 9000; Ⓦ www.aerolineas.com.
Air Canada Canada ☎ 1-888/247-2262, UK ☎ 0871/220 1111, Republic of Ireland ☎ 01/679 3958, Australia ☎ 1300/655 767, New Zealand ☎ 0508/747 767; Ⓦ www.aircanada.com.
Air France US ☎ 1-800/237 2747, Canada ☎ 1-800/667-2747, UK ☎ 0870/142 4343, Australia ☎ 1300/390 190, South Africa ☎ 0861/340 340; Ⓦ www.airfrance.com.
Air New Zealand New Zealand ☎ 0800/737 000, Australia ☎ 0800/132 476, UK ☎ 0800/028 4149, Republic of Ireland ☎ 1800/551 447,

US ⓣ1800/262/1234, Canada ⓣ1800/663/5494; ⓦwww.airnewzealand.co.nz.
Air Tahiti Nui US ⓣ1-877/824/4846, Australia ⓣ1-1300/732 415 or 1/02/9244 2788, New Zealand ⓣ09/308 3360, UK & Ireland ⓣ0870/066 2050; ⓦwww.airtahitinui-usa.com
American Airlines US ⓣ1-800/433 7300, UK ⓣ020/7365 0777, Republic of Ireland ⓣ01/602 0550, Australia ⓣ1800/673 486, New Zealand ⓣ0800/445 442; ⓦwww.aa.com.
British Airways US & Canada ⓣ1-800/AIRWAYS, UK ⓣ0844/493 0787, Republic of Ireland ⓣ1890/626 747, Australia ⓣ1300/767 177, New Zealand ⓣ09/966 9777, South Africa ⓣ114/418 600; ⓦwww.ba.com.
Continental Airlines US & Canada ⓣ1-800/523-3273, UK ⓣ0845/607 6760, Republic of Ireland ⓣ1890/925 252, Australia ⓣ1300/737 640, New Zealand ⓣ09/308 3350, International ⓣ1800/231 0856; ⓦwww.continental.com.
Copa Airlines US ⓣ1-800/FLY-COPA, UK ⓣ0870/241 4126, Australia ⓣ02/9959 3922; ⓦwww.copaair.com.
Delta US & Canada ⓣ1-800/221-1212, UK ⓣ0845/600 0950, Republic of Ireland ⓣ1850/882 031 or 01/407 3165, Australia ⓣ1300/302 849, New Zealand ⓣ09/977 2232; ⓦwww.delta.com.

Mexico
Peru
Bolivia
Ecuador & Galapagos
Brazil
Argentina
Columbia
Cuba
Suriname
Guyana
The Carribean
Carefully Crafted Tours
CHILE
High Quality Cultural Group Tours for the Discerning Traveller
• Informative, knowledgeable tour leaders
• Over 130 countries worldwide
• All tours are fully escorted
ADVENTURESABROAD
info@adventures-abroad.co.uk
www.smallgroup.travel
0114 247 3400
ABTA
ABTA No.W3508

TRIPSWORLDWIDE
Tailor-made exclusively for you
CHILE
0117 311 4400
www.tripsworldwide.co.uk
info@tripsworldwide.co.uk
ABTA
ABTA No.C0965

Iberia US ⓣ1-800/772-4642, UK ⓣ0870/609 0500, Republic of Ireland ⓣ0818/462 000, South Africa ⓣ011/884 9255; ⓦwww.iberiaairlines.co.uk.
LanChile US & Canada ⓣ1-866/435-9526, UK ⓣ0800/977 6100, Australia ⓣ1800/211 572 or 02/9244 2333, New Zealand ⓣ09/308 3352, South Africa ⓣ11/781 2111; ⓦwww.lan.com.
Lufthansa US ⓣ1-800/3995-838, Canada ⓣ1-800/563-5954, UK ⓣ0871/945 9747, Republic of Ireland ⓣ01/844 5544, Australia ⓣ1300/655 727, New Zealand ⓣ0800-945 220, South Africa ⓣ0861/842 538; ⓦwww.lufthansa.com.
Malaysia Airlines US ⓣ1-800/5529-264, UK ⓣ0871/423 9090, Republic of Ireland ⓣ01/6761 561, Australia ⓣ13 26 27, New Zealand ⓣ0800/777 747, South Africa ⓣ11/880 9614; ⓦwww.malaysiaairlines.com.
South African Airlines ⓣ11/978 1111, US & Canada ⓣ1-800/722-9675, UK ⓣ0870/747 1111, Australia ⓣ1300/435 972, New Zealand ⓣ09/977 2237; ⓦwww.flysaa.com.
United Airlines US ⓣ1-800/864-8331, UK ⓣ0845/844 4777, Australia ⓣ13 17 77; ⓦwww.united.com
Varig US & Canada ⓣ1-800/468-2744, UK ⓣ020/7660 0341; ⓦwww.varig.co.uk.

"MY FAVOURITE THING ABOUT CHILE? THE LANDSCAPE"

Tamsin Butler, Journey Latin America

With first-hand experience of every country in Latin America, our consultants offer a wealth of insight into the real essence of this unforgettable destination. Whether it's a tailor-made holiday or a small group tour, we know the places you'll love

Talk to one of our specialists

020 8622 8470

www.journeylatinamerica.co.uk

JOURNEY LATIN AMERICA

Qantas US & Canada ☎ 1-800/227-4500, UK ☎ 0845/774 7767, Republic of Ireland ☎ 01/407 3278, Australia ☎ 13 13 13, New Zealand ☎ 0800/808 767 or 09/357 8900, South Africa ☎ 11/441 8550; ⓦ www.qantas.com.

Agents and operators

ebookers UK ☎ 0871/223 5000, Republic of Ireland ☎ 01/431 1311; ⓦ www.ebookers.com, www.ebookers.ie. Low fares on an extensive selection of scheduled flights and package deals.
North South Travel UK ☎ 01245/608291, ⓦ www.northsouthtravel.co.uk. Friendly, competitive travel agency, offering discounted fares worldwide. Profits are used to support projects in the developing world, especially the promotion of sustainable tourism.
Trailfinders UK ☎ 0845/058 5858, Republic of Ireland ☎ 01/677 7888; ⓦ www.trailfinders.com. One of the best-informed and most efficient agents for independent travellers.
STA Travel US ☎ 1-800/781-4040, UK ☎ 0871/2300 040, Australia ☎ 134 782, New Zealand ☎ 0800/474 400, South Africa ☎ 0861/781 781; ⓦ www.statravel.com. Worldwide specialists in independent travel; also student IDs, travel insurance, car rental, rail passes, and more. Good discounts for students and under-26s.

Specialist tour operators

In the US and Canada

Adventure Center ☎ 1-800/228-8747, ⓦ www.adventurecenter.com. Hiking and "soft adventure" specialists offering a twelve-day "Discover Chile" tour.
Adventures Abroad ☎ 1-800/665-3998 or 360/755-9925, ⓦ www.adventures-abroad.com. Adventure specialists offering two-week tours to Patagonia, and very long trips throughout Argentina and Chile.
Adventures on Skis ☎ 1-800/908-5000 or 970/429-3099, ⓦ www.ski.com. Offers package trips to Portillo, Chile's top ski resort.
Anglatin, Ltd ☎ 1-800/918-8580 or 503/534-3720, ⓦ www.anglatin.com. Offers ten-day tours of Patagonia and the Lake District and a few educationally oriented packages such as the ten-day "Wine and Cuisine" tours.
Ecosummer Expeditions ☎ 1-800/465-8884 or 250/674-0102, ⓦ www.ecosummer.com. A British Columbia–based company offering expeditions and kayaking and trekking holidays in South America and elsewhere.
Holidaze Ski Tours ☎ 1-800/526-2827 or 732/280-1120, ⓦ www.holidaze.com. Skiing in South America during the northern summer.

20% DISCOUNT FOR ROUGH GUIDE READERS

Learn a language with

ROUTLEDGE
COLLOQUIALS

The ideal way to get the most out of your holiday, year after year.

'Undoubtedly the best series of... language courses on the market.'
– *Waterstone's Booksellers*

- self-taught courses for beginners - easy and fun to use
- over 70 languages from Afrikaans to Zulu
- learn the language the way it's spoken by native speakers
- communicate confidently by the end of each course

And take the next step with Colloquial 2s for intermediate learners

To claim your **20% discount** on all Colloquial packs (containing a book and CD), just visit **www.routledge.com/colloquials**, search for your language of choice and enter the discount code **RG09**

For a full list of the 70 languages offered visit **www.routledge.com/colloquials** or email **colloquials@routledge.com** for a free catalogue.

Routledge
Taylor & Francis Group

Mountain Travel–Sobek ☎1-888/831-7526, ⓦwww.mtsobek.com. Trips include a "Patagonia Explorer" adventure package.

Nature Expeditions International
☎1-800/869-0639, ⓦwww.naturexp.com. The sixteen-day Chile tour takes in Torres del Paine and the Atacama desert.

REI Adventures ☎1-800/622-2236, ⓦwww.rei.com/adventures. Climbing, cycling, hiking, cruising, paddling and multi-sport tours, such as trekking in Patagonia.

Wilderness Travel ☎1-800/368-2794, ⓦwww.wildernesstravel.com. Specialists in hiking, cultural and wildlife adventures. Offers include sixteen days in Patagonia plus an Iguazú Falls extension.

Worldwide Quest Adventures ☎1-800/387-1483, ⓦwww.worldwidequest.com. Their name is self-explanatory. Their packages include an eight-day "Wine Route by Bike" and an eleven-day "Voyage to Antarctica".

In the UK

Austral Tours ☎020/7233 5384, ⓦwww.latinamerica.co.uk. Small company offering a seventeen-day tour in northern and southern Chile, plus tailor-made itineraries. Especially good at organizing special-interest holidays based around wine tours, fishing, trekking or archeology.

Dragoman ☎01728/861 133, ⓦwww.dragoman.co.uk. Extended overland journeys in purpose-built expedition vehicles; shorter camping and hotel-based safaris, too.

Exodus ☎0845/240 5550, ⓦwww.exodus.co.uk. Adventure tour operator taking small groups for specialist programmes, including walking, biking, overland, adventure, and cultural trips. Among its long tours is a month-long exploration of Patagonia.

Explore Worldwide UK ☎0870/333 4001, Ireland (c/o Maxwell's Travel) ☎01/677 9479; ⓦwww.explore.co.uk. Small-group tours, treks, expeditions and safaris. Offers three-week tours of the fjords and Patagonia, with accommodation mostly in small local hotels. Some supplements for single travellers.

Intrepid Travel ☎020/3147 7777, ⓦwww.intrepidtravel.com. Small-group tours with the emphasis on cross-cultural contact and low-impact tourism.

Journey Latin America ☎020/8747 3108, ⓦwww.journeylatinamerica.co.uk. Specialists in flights, packages and tailor-made trips to Latin America, with excursions and cruises in Chile.

Kuoni Travel ☎01306/74 7002, ⓦwww.kuoni.co.uk. Flexible package holidays to Chile and elsewhere; good family offers.

Tucan Travel ☎020/8896 1600, ⓦwww.tucantravel.com. Group holidays in southern Chile and Argentina, plus a range of overland expeditions in South America.

Wildlife Worldwide ☎020/8667 9158, ⓦwww.wildlifeworldwide.com. Tailor-made trips for wildlife and wilderness enthusiasts.

World Expeditions ☎0845/130 6982, ⓦwww.worldexpeditions.co.uk. Australian-owned adventure company offering trips around Latin America and the world. All expeditions are graded by difficulty. Challenging trips available for hardcore adventurers; special offerings for over-fifty travellers.

In Australia and New Zealand

Adventure Associates Australia
☎1-800/222/141, ⓦwww.adventureassociates.com.au. Long-established operator with tours and cruises to Antarctica and South America.

Adventure Travel Company New Zealand ☎039/355 9131, ⓦwww.adventuretravel.co.nz. Adventure tours including South America.

Adventure World Australia ⓦwww.adventureworld.com.au; New Zealand ⓦwww.adventureworld.co.nz. Agents for a vast array of international adventure travel companies that operate trips to South America.

Austral Tours Australia ☎03/9370 6621, ⓦwww.australtours.com. Central and South American specialist covering the region from Ecuador to Easter Island and Tierra del Fuego.

Classic Safari Company Australia ☎1300/130 218 or 02/9327 0666, ⓦwww.classicsafaricompany.com.au. Luxury, tailor-made safaris to India, Africa and South America.

Contours Australia ☎03/9328 8488, ⓦwww.contourstravel.com.au. Specialists in tailored city stopover packages and tours, including self-drive tours through the Lake District and a ten-day budget tour of Patagonia using local buses and cheap to mid-range hotels.

South America Travel Centre Australia ☎03/9642 5353, ⓦwww.satc.com.au. Large selection of tours and city accommodation packages throughout the region.

World Expeditions Australia ☎02/8270 8400, ⓦwww.worldexpeditions.com.au, New Zealand ☎09/368 4161, ⓦwww.worldexpeditions.co.nz. Offers a number of adventure walking holidays. Based in Sydney but also branches in Adelaide, Auckland, Brisbane, Melbourne and Perth.

Getting around

Travelling in Chile is easy, comfortable and, compared to Europe or North America, inexpensive. Most of the population travels by bus, and it's such a reliable, affordable option that you'll probably do likewise. However, internal airlines, catering primarily to business passengers, are handy for covering long distances in a hurry and last-minute flights can be quite reasonable. The country has a good road network with a low volume of traffic away from the major towns, which makes driving a fast and relatively stress-free way of getting around. In recent years Chile's rail network has fallen into decline and only an ever-shrinking service operates south of Santiago. South of Puerto Montt there are limited ferry services that provide a slow but scenic way of travelling as far as Puerto Natales.

By air

Chile is a country of almost unimaginable distances (it's more than 5000km by road from Arica to Punta Arenas), which makes **flying** by far the quickest and most convenient way of taking in both its northern and southern regions in a single trip. Despite the limited competition between LAN and the other airlines that serve the country's numerous regional airports, scheduled fares are quite high, though you can find good promotions from time to time.

Far and away the leading airline is **LAN /Lan Express** (☎5262000, in regions ☎600/5262000, in the US ☎1-866/435-9526; ⓦwww.lan.com), which besides offering the widest choice of domestic flights,

is Chile's principal long-haul carrier and the only one with flights to Easter Island. The **special fares** for selected flights, available with two- to three-days' notice through the LAN website, are exceptionally good value; a round-trip ticket from Santiago to Puerto Montt, for instance, can be as little as CH$35,000, compared to the normal fare of over CH$95,000 return. See p.27 for details of LAN's **Visit Chile air pass**, which can only be bought outside Chile.

With more limited routings but usually lower prices, reliable newcomers **Sky Airlines** ☎600/600/2828, from outside Chile ☎0056/2353-3169; ⓦwww.skyairline.cl) offer welcome competition.

Air taxis and regional airlines operate regular services to smaller destinations

Distance chart in kilometres

Cities	Antofag.	Arica	Calama	Iquique	La Serena	Pto Natales
Antofag asta		700	205	493	899	4750
Arica	700		596	301	1600	5453
Calama	205	596		387	1104	4957
Iquique	492	301	387		1391	5244
La Serena	899	1600	1104	1391		3853
Pto Natales	4750	5453	4957	5244	3853	
Pto Varas	2360	3058	2562	2849	1458	2501
Pto Montt	2377	3078	2582	2869	1478	2481
Pta Arenas	4502	5203	4707	4993	3603	254
Santiago	1361	2062	1566	1853	462	3285
Temuco	2038	2739	2243	2530	1139	2608
Valdivia	2202	2903	2407	2694	1303	2479
V. del Mar	1311	2012	1516	1803	412	3404

between Puerto Montt and Puerto Williams, but they are susceptible to weather delays and won't fly without a minimum number of passengers (usually six people). Two companies also fly out from Santiago to Isla Robinson Crusoe, 650km off the mainland – for more details, see p.484.

Main domestic airports

Antofagasta ℡ 55/269077
Arica ℡ 58/211116
Balmaceda ℡ 67/272126
Calama ℡ 55/363004
Copiapo ℡ 52/214088
Iquique ℡ 57/426350
La Serena ℡ 51/271877
Puerto Montt ℡ 65/294161
Punta Arenas ℡ 61/219131
Santiago ℡ 2/6901752
Temuco ℡ 45/554801
Isla de Pascua ℡ 32/1002372029

Getting into town

Getting between Chile's airports and its city centres is fast, hassle-free, and inexpensive. Most of the main airports have dedicated **bus services** into the centre, or **minibus transfers** that drop off passengers at their hotels (at a cost of around CH$5000). The smaller airports, without these services, are always well stocked with taxis and tend to be only a few kilometres outside the city centre (with Puerto Montt and Iquique being notable exceptions), keeping the cost of a taxi ride down. Only Santiago has flights leaving and departing at really antisocial hours, served by 24-hour minibus transfers.

By bus

Chile's **long-distance buses** offer an excellent service, far better than their European or North American counterparts – thanks mainly to the enormous amount of legroom, frequent departures and flexible itineraries – you can stop a bus at nearly any point of the route. Facilities depend less on individual companies than on the class of bus you travel on, with prices rising according to comfort level. A **pullman** (not to be confused with the large bus company of the same name) or **clásico** contains standard semi-reclining seats; a **semicama** has seats with twice the amount of legroom and that recline a good deal more; and a **salon cama**, at the top of the luxury range, has wide seats (just three to a row) that recline to an almost horizontal position à la first class on an airplane. Most companies offer a choice of all three types of bus, particularly on their longer journeys. All buses have chemical toilets and most supply food at the stops and soft drinks during the ride. Some overnight services include meals or snacks, while others stop at restaurants where set meals might be included in the ticket price. Videos, piped music and bingo games are also common in-transit attractions (or irritations). Check out the locations of video screens first and seat yourself appropriately.

Pto Varas	Pto Montt	Pta Arenas	Santiago	Temuco	Valdivia	V. del Mar
2360	2377	4502	1361	2038	2202	1311
3058	3078	5203	2062	2739	2903	2012
2562	2582	4707	1566	2243	2407	1516
4849	2869	4994	1853	2530	2694	1803
1458	1478	3603	462	1139	1303	412
2501	2481	254	3285	2608	2479	3404
	20	2313	996	319	190	1115
20		2337	1016	339	210	1135
2313	2337		3141	2464	2335	3260
996	1016	3141		677	841	119
319	339	2464	667		164	796
190	210	2335	841	164		961
1115	1135	3260	119	796	961	

Thanks to the intense competition and price wars waged between the multitude of bus companies, **fares** are extremely low. As a rule of thumb, reckon on CH$1000 per hour travelled on standard inter-city buses, CH$800 per hour on local routes and at least CH$1500 per hour in the luxury long-distance buses. It always pays to compare fares offered by the different companies serving your destination, as you'll almost certainly find one offering a special deal. This price comparing is easily done at the central terminal used by long-distance buses in most cities, where you'll find separate booking offices for each company (though Tur Bus and Pullman Bus, the two largest companies, often have their own separate terminals close to the main terminal). Some towns, however, don't have a **central terminal**, in which case buses leave from their company offices, which are normally clustered in the town centre.

Owing to the popularity of bus travel, you should try to buy your ticket at least a few hours in advance, and preferably the day before travelling, especially if you plan to travel on a Friday. An added advantage of buying ahead is that you'll be able to choose a seat away from the toilets, either by the aisle or window and, more importantly, the side of the bus you sit on. Even with air conditioning, seats on the sunny side can get extremely hot, and you may find yourself peeking at the scenery through a curtain. There is little reason to buy a round-trip ticket unless you are travelling at peak season. The price is rarely different, and even when you have a return portion you should go to the bus counter to reconfirm your seat.

When it comes to **boarding**, make sure that the departure time written on your ticket corresponds exactly to the time indicated on the little clock on the bus's front window, as your ticket is valid only on the bus it was booked for. Your luggage will be safely stored in lockers under the bus and the conductor will issue you a numbered stub for each article. Soon after departure – and while Chilean buses do not always leave punctually, you should never bank on a late departure – the conductor will check your ticket and leave you with a stub that must be kept until the end of your journey.

Be warned that if you're travelling north of Santiago on a long-distance route, or crossing an international border, the bus and all luggage may be searched by Ministry of Agriculture officials at checkpoints (often at regional frontiers or major junctions), and all sandwiches, fresh fruit and vegetables will be destroyed – while you stand waiting, even in the cold night air.

Local buses, colectivos and taxis

Local buses, often called micros, connect city centres with residential outskirts, and with nearby villages. These buses are often packed, and travelling with a large rucksack can be a problem, particularly if your journey coincides with students going to or from college, or with market day. Buses sticking to the confines of the town or city usually drive up and down the principal thoroughfares, and around the central square – the main points of the route and final destination are displayed on the inside of the front window, but it always helps to carry a street map and be able to point to your intended destination. Buses that leave the city for the countryside normally depart from their own *terminal rural*, which is usually next door or close to the Mercado Municipal (market building).

For some journeys, a faster alternative is provided by **colectivos**, which are shared taxis operating along a set route with fixed fares, normally only slightly more expensive than the local buses. Most *colectivos* look exactly like normal taxis (apart from being all black, not black and yellow) and have their route or final destination marked on a board on the roof, but in some cities, *colectivo* services are operated by bright yellow cars, often without a roof-board.

Taxis are normally black with a yellow roof, and in the bigger cities can be flagged down quickly on the street. Alternatively, you can usually find them on or near the central square, as well as outside bus terminals and train stations. As Chilean taxi drivers are often eager to charge foreigners too much, it's worth checking to see that the meter has been turned on before you start a journey and, if possible in Spanish, get an estimate for the fare to the nearest 500 pesos. Fares are clearly shown in the windscreen – but there is no limit to what the driver can charge, as long as it corresponds to the advertised price. Nearly all taxis will have similar signs – one saying 150 pesos (which is the starting price) and another saying 80 or 90 pesos, the fee per 200-metre increments. At tourist hotels beware of taxis that put two signs for 150 in the window and thus charge double.

By car

While Chile's towns and cities are linked by plenty of buses, most visitors are here for the country's wilderness areas, which are often difficult, and sometimes impossible, to reach on public transport. Many remote attractions are visited by tour companies operating out of the nearest major city, but for more independence, your best bet is to **rent a vehicle**. To do this, you need to be at least 21 years old and have a major credit card so you can leave a blank voucher as a guarantee. You're allowed to use your national driver's licence, but you're strongly advised to bring, in addition, an **international licence**. Chile's *carabineros* (police officers), who frequently stop drivers to check their documents, are often suspicious of unfamiliar foreign licences and are always happier when dealing with international ones. Traffic regulations in Chile are rarely enforced, except for speeding on the highways. The **speed limit** is 50km per hour or less in urban areas and 100km per hour on highways, and radar speed traps are commonplace. If an oncoming vehicle flashes its headlights, you're being warned of *carabineros* lurking ahead. If you do get pulled over, exercise the utmost courtesy and patience, and under no circumstances do or say anything that could possibly be interpreted as bribery.

Rental outlets and costs

Several international car-rental companies have offices throughout Chile, including Hertz, Avis and Budget. In addition to these, you'll find an abundance of local outlets which are often, but by no means always, less expensive than the international firms. The cost of car rental is much higher in Chile than in North America, and more on a par with European prices. Rates can vary quite a lot from one company to another, and it's always worth phoning as many as possible to compare prices. **Basic saloon cars** go from around US$350 to US$450 per week, while a 4WD **jeep** or **pick-up** truck can cost anything from US$500 to US$800-plus per week (less for non-4WD). Most outlets have lower rates if you're renting for a month or longer. Make sure that the price they quote includes IVA (the 18-percent Chilean value added tax), insurance and unlimited mileage. Your rental contract will almost certainly be in (legal and convoluted) Spanish – get the company to take you through it and explain everything. In most cases your liability, in the event of an accident, is normally around the US$500 mark; costs over this amount will be covered in total by the company.

Car rental agencies

Avis US ☎1-800/331-1212, Canada ☎1-800/879-2847, UK ☎0844/581 8181, Republic of Ireland ☎021/428 1111, Australia ☎13 63 33 or 02/9353 9000, New Zealand ☎09/526 2847 or 0800/655 111, South Africa ☎11/923 3660; ⓦwww.avis.com.
Budget US ☎1-800/527-0700, Canada ☎1-800/268-8900, UK ☎0870/156 5656, Australia ☎1300/362 848, New Zealand ☎0800/283 438; ⓦwww.budget.com.
Dollar US ☎1-800/800-3665, Canada ☎1-800/229 0984, UK ☎ 0808/234 7524, Republic of Ireland ☎1800/515 800; ⓦwww.dollar.com.
Europcar US & Canada ☎1-877/940 6900, UK ☎0845/758 5375, Republic of Ireland ☎01/614 2800, Australia ☎1300/131 390; ⓦwww.europcar.com.
Hertz US & Canada ☎1-800/654-3131, UK ☎0870/040 9000, Republic of Ireland ☎01/870 5777, Australia ☎13 30 39, New Zealand, ☎0800/654 321, South Africa ☎21/935 4800; ⓦwww.hertz.com.
National US ☎1-800/227-7368, UK ☎0870/400 4588, Australia ☎0870/600 6666, New Zealand ☎03/366 5574; ⓦwww.nationalcar.com.
Thrifty US & Canada ☎1-800/847-4389, UK ☎01494/751 540, Republic of Ireland ☎1800/515 800, Australia ☎1300/367 227, New Zealand ☎0800/737 070; ⓦwww.thrifty.com.

Driving in towns

Just about all Chilean towns are laid out on a grid plan, which makes navigating them pretty easy. However, the country is obsessed with **one-way traffic** systems, and you'll find that many streets in even the smallest towns are one-way only, the direction of traffic alternating with each successive street. The direction is usually indicated by a white arrow above the street name on each corner; if in doubt, look at the direction of the parked cars. **Parking** is normally allowed on most downtown streets (but on one side only), and around the Plaza de Armas (central square). You'll invariably be guided into a space by a wildly gesticulating *cuidador de autos* – a boy or young man who will offer to look after your car (quite unnecessarily) in return for a tip, normally of a couple of hundred pesos or so. In larger towns there's a small half-hourly charge for parking on the street, administered by eagle-eyed traffic wardens who slip tickets under your wipers every thirty minutes then pounce on you to collect your money before you leave (a small tip is expected, too). If you can't find a space to park in, keep a look-out for large "estacion-amiento" signs by the pavement, indicating private car parks, normally at around CH$500–600 an hour.

Driving on highways

The **Panamerican** highway, which runs through Chile from the Peruvian border to the southern tip of Chiloé, is known alternately as Ruta 5, la Panamericana, or el longitudinal, with sur (south) or norte (north) often added on to indicate which side of Santiago it's on. Thanks to a multi-billion dollar modernization project, it is quickly becoming a divided highway, with two lanes in each direction and a toll booth every 30km. This is undoubtedly a major improvement over most single-lane highways in Chile, which are prone to head-on collisions involving buses and trucks.

Backcountry and altiplano driving

You'll probably find that many places you want to get to are reached by dirt road, for which it's essential to rent a suitable vehicle, namely a **jeep** or **pick-up truck**. On regular dirt roads you rarely need a 4WD vehicle. The 2WD Chevrolet LUV pick-up is manufactured in Chile, and there are thousands of these trucks for rent and parts are readily available. For **altiplano driving**, however, you should pay extra to have 4WD (with the sturdiest tyres and highest clearance), as you can come across some dreadful roads, hundreds of kilometres from the nearest town. Make sure, too, that you take two spare tyres, not one, and that you always carry a funnel or tube for siphoning, and more than enough petrol. (Work it out yourself then add lots – don't rely on what they say in the rental shop). Also pick up several 5-litre water jugs for a driving trip in the altiplano – it may be necessary for either the passengers or the engine at some point. It can be difficult to navigate in the altiplano, with so much open space and so few landmarks – a good tip is to make a careful note of your kilometre reading as you go along, so you can chart your progress over long roads with few markers. A compass is also helpful. Despite this tone of caution, it has to be emphasized that altiplano driving is among the most rewarding adventures that Chile offers.

Finally, a general point on **tyre punctures**. This is such a common occurrence in Chile that even the smallest towns have special workshops (bearing signs with a tyre painted white) where they are quickly and cheaply repaired.

Hitching

While we don't recommend hitching as a safe way of getting about, there's no denying that it's widely practised by Chileans themselves. In the summer it seems as though all the students in Chile are sitting beside the road with their thumb out, and in rural areas it's not uncommon for entire families to hitch a lift whenever they need to get into town. For backpackers, the large number of pick-up trucks on the road means there's a better chance than normal of being given a lift, as these vehicles have plenty of room to ditch your packs (and yourselves) in the back. Overseas tourists are much more likely to be given a lift if they identify themselves as such, as nearly everyone in Chile can trace their ancestry back to one European country or another, and many are keen to share their heritage with visitors from the fatherland. In general, you'll have a much better chance of getting a lift on a quiet rural road than on the Panamericana, where no one wants to stop for fear of being overtaken by slow-moving lorries. On the Panamericana, your best bet is to get a lift from someone parked at a busy servicentro (fast-food/petrol station complex).

By train

Some fifty years ago, Chile possessed a huge network of **railways**, particularly in the far north where hundreds of kilometres of lines transported the region's nitrate ore down to the ports to be shipped abroad. Now that the nitrate days are over, no national railway lines operate north of Santiago, and what lines are left south of the capital are in ramshackle condition, unable to compete with the speed, low fares and punctuality offered by buses. Today only three daily trains pull out of Santiago's grand Estación Central, heading for Chillán, Concepción and Temuco. The daytime trains offer two standards of compartment – economía and salón – while the overnight trains to Temuco and Concepción offer the added choice of cama and dormitorio, the latter in two-berth cabins in a classic 1920s carriage.

Cycling

Considering the vast distances involved in a trip through Chile, **cycling** might not be the obvious mode you'd choose to do it. However, with the right amount of time and energy, travelling by bike can be incredibly rewarding. Your time is your own and you won't find yourself stuck to rigid timetables or restricted to visiting destinations only served by public buses.

It is essential that you equip yourself with the right kit. Supplies in Chile can be unreliable so it's best to bring as much as you can from home. A good, sturdy mountain bike is a must, along with the usual locks and chains, strong racks, repair kit, lights, waterproof panniers, coats and over-trousers. All equipment and clothes should be packed in plastic to protect from dust and moisture. Your major problem will be getting hold of **spare parts** when you need them. Chileans are not great cyclists, so bike shops tend to be found only in Santiago and a few major cities. Your best bet is to visit such a shop,

Addresses

These are nearly always written with just the street name (and often just the surname, if the street is named after a person) followed by the number; for example, Prat 135. In the case of avenues, however, the address usually starts with the word *avenida*, eg Avenida 21 de Mayo 553. Buildings without a street number are suffixed by s/n, short for *sin número* ("without a number").

befriend the owner, and if you get into difficulty, call for parts to be sent as cargo on a long-distance bus. When on the road, bear in mind that long stretches are bereft of accommodation options and even the most basic services, so you must be completely self-sufficient and prepared for a long wait if you require assistance. Some bus companies will not transport bicycles unless you wrap frame and wheels separately in cardboard. When you enter the country, you may well find that customs officials enter details of your bicycle in your passport to prevent you from selling it.

The main danger when cycling on Chile's roads are other drivers. Make sure you stand out in the traffic by wearing bright colours, good reflective gear and lights when the vision is poor. It goes without saying that you should **wear a helmet**; it's actually illegal to ride in Chile without one. Before you set off get your hands on one of the many good guidebooks available on long-distance cycling. Alternately contact the **Cyclists Touring Club** in the UK (T0844/736/8450, Wwww.ctc.org.uk) for more information and advice.

By ferry

South of Puerto Montt, where the mainland breaks up into an archipelago, a network of ferries operates through the fjords, inlets and channels of Chile's far south, providing a far more scenic and romantic alternative to flights and long-distance buses. Two ferries in particular are very popular with tourists: one from Puerto Montt to Chacabuco and the San Raphael glacier, the other between Puerto Montt and Puerto Natales. The two main ferry companies are **Navimag** and

CTP, both privately run. Both companies' ships transport cargo, vehicles and passengers, and are functional rather than luxurious. In addition to these two main routes, there are ferry links with Quellón on Chiloé, and with Chaitén, on the Carretera Austral, as well as a number of shorter routes forming a bridge along various points of the Carretera Austral (full details given on p.383). There's also a ferry trip across Lago Todos Los Santos, in the Lake District, connecting Petrohué with Peulla, near the Argentine border, operated by **Andina del Sud** (see below and p.345).

Ferry companies

Andina del Sud ⓦwww.andinadelsud.com. Varas 437, Puerto Montt ⓣ65/257797, ⓕ299015; Del Salvador 72, Puerto Varas ⓣ65/232811, ⓕ232511. **Navimag** ⓦwww.australis.com. Angelmó 2187, Puerto Montt ⓣ65/432300, ⓕ276611; Pedro Montt 308, Puerto Natales ⓣ61/411642; Magallanes 990, Punta Arenas ⓣ61/200200, ⓕ225804; Av El Bosque Norte 0440, 11th floor, Las Condes, Santiago ⓣ2/442 3120, ⓕ2/203 5025.

TransMarChilay ⓦwww.transmarchilay.cl. Angelmó 2187, Puerto Montt ⓣ65/270000, ⓔtransporte@tmc.cl.

Main ferry routes

Petrohué–Peulla, across Lago Todos Los Santos Five hours; daily crossings (year-round) with Andina del Sud. See p.345.

Puerto Montt–Chacabuco Twenty-four hours; one sailing per week with Navimag (year-round) and TransMarChilay (year-round). See p.353 & p.349.

Puerto Montt–Chacabuco–Laguna San Rafael Five days, four nights (returning to Puerto Montt); one sailing per week with Navimag (year-round) and two, three or four with TransMarChilay (year-round). See p.353 & p.394.

Puerto Montt–Chaitén Ten hours; one sailing per week with Navimag (Jan–Feb); three or four per week with TransMarChilay (year-round). See p.353 & p.383.

Puerto Montt–Puerto Natales Four days, three nights; one sailing per week with Navimag (year-round). See p.353 & p.425.

Quellón–Chaitén Five hours; three sailings per week with Navimag (Jan–Feb). See p.375 & p.383.

Accommodation

On the whole, the standard of accommodation in Chile is not that great and many visitors feel that prices are high for what you get, especially in mid- and upper-range hotels. Bottom-end accommodation starts at around US$15 for a double room, while you'll have to pay around US$40 for a double room with private bath in a decent mid-range hotel, and anything from US$70 for a smart, upmarket hotel. There's usually a wide range to choose from in the major tourist centres and the cities on the Panamericana, but in more remote areas you'll invariably have to make do with basic *hospedajes* (modest rooms, often in family homes). Most places include a small breakfast – bread roll, jam and instant coffee – in the price of the room, but you shouldn't always count on this, as some will charge extra for breakfast, and others won't serve it at all.

Note that the price of accommodation in the main tourist centres increases dramatically in **high season** – January and February – particularly in seaside resorts, where it can as much as double. Outside high season it's always worth trying to negotiate a discount, wherever you are. A simple *"¿tiene algo un poco mas económico?"* ("do you have anything a little cheaper?") or *"¿me puede dar un descuento?"* ("could you give me a discount?") will often get you a lower price on the spot. It's rarely necessary to make reservations, unless you've got your heart set on a particular hotel or *residencial*, in which case it can be a good idea to phone a few days in advance – especially if you plan to stay at the weekend, even more so if it's within striking distance of Santiago.

Note that room rates are supposed to be quoted inclusive of IVA (a Chilean goods and services tax of 18 percent), but you should always check beforehand (*¿está incluido el iva?*). Many mid- and most upper-range hotels give you the opportunity to pay for your accommodation in US dollars (with credit card), which exempts you from paying IVA. However, hotels are not eager to offer this discount – they need to be reminded forcefully. Often, though, if they can't take off IVA, they'll offer you a discount of ten percent if you pay cash.

Hotels

Chilean hotels are given a one- to five-star rating by Sernatur (the national tourist board), but this only reflects facilities and not standards, which vary widely from hotel to hotel. In practice, then, a three-star hotel could be far more attractive and comfortable than a four-star and even a five-star hotel; the only way to tell is to go and have a look, as even the room rates aren't a reliable indication of quality.

In general, **mid-range hotels** fall into two main categories: large, old houses with spacious, but sometimes tired, rooms; and modern, purpose-built hotels, usually with smaller rooms, no common areas and better facilities. You'll always get a private bathroom

with a shower (rarely a bath), hot water and towels, and either an ancient colour TV or cable TV with dozens of English-language channels. As the price creeps up there's usually an improvement in decor and space, and at the upper end of the price range you can expect room service, a mini-bar (*frigobar*), a private safe, a hotel restaurant, private parking and sometimes a swimming pool. The standards of **upmarket hotels** can still vary quite dramatically, however – ranging from stylish, contemporary city hotels or charming haciendas to grim, impersonal monoliths catering for businessmen. Finally, a word of note on **motels**, which are usually not economical roadside hotels, but places where couples go to have sex. Motel rooms are rented for three hours at very reasonable rates. Though you may get a few strange stares showing up with your backpack, they are a cheap and usually perfectly safe escape for a few hours.

Residenciales

Residenciales are the most widely available, and widely used, accommodation option in Chile. As with hotels, standards can vary enormously, but in general *residenciales* offer simple, modestly furnished rooms, usually off a corridor in the main house, or else in a row arranged around the backyard or patio. They usually contain little more than a bed (or up to four single beds), a rail for hanging clothes and a bedside table and lamp, though some provide additional furniture (perhaps a writing desk and chair) and a few more comforts such as a TV or a thermos for making tea or

Accommodation price codes

Prices are for the cheapest **double room** in high season. In lodging places at the lower end of the scale, **single travellers** can expect to pay half this rate, but mid- and upper-range hotels usually charge the same for a single as for a double. Note that the price of accommodation in many tourist centres drops significantly outside January and February. Rough US equivalents are given according to the exchange rates around the time of publication.

❶ CH$5000 and under (US$9 and under)
❷ CH$5001–10,000 (US$10–18)
❸ CH$10,001–15,000 (US$19–28)
❹ CH$15,001–25,000 (US$29–46)
❺ CH$25,001–35,000 (US$47–65)
❻ CH$35,001–50,000 (US$66–93)
❼ CH$50,001–75,000 (US$94–140)
❽ CH$75,001–150,000 (US$141–280)
❾ CH$150,001 and over (US$281 and over)

coffee. Most, but not all, have shared baths – note that you'll usually have to light the water heater (*calefón*) to get hot water each time you take a shower. Where places differ is in the upkeep or "freshness" of the rooms: some of the really cheap rooms are dank and damp, with peeling paint and saggy beds, while others, though still very simple, have good bed linen, walls that are painted every summer, and a clean, swept, feel to them. Some of the slightly more expensive *residenciales* are very pleasant, particularly the large, nineteenth-century houses with waxed wooden floorboards and floor-to-ceiling windows that open onto balconies. While some *residenciales* cater exclusively to tourists, many, especially in the mining towns of the north, fill mainly with workmen, so you can't always expect to meet fellow travellers where you're staying.

Hospedajes and casas de familia

The distinction between a *residencial* and an *hospedaje* or *casa de familia* is often blurred. On the whole, the term **hospedaje** implies something rather modest, along the lines of the cheaper *residenciales*, while a **casa de familia** (or *casa familiar*) offers, as you'd expect, rooms inside a family home – sometimes just four or five rooms left vacant by grown-up children, other times in an extension added onto the main house. It's nothing like staying with a family, however, and the relationship between the guest and the owner is no different from that in a *residencial*. *Casas de familia* don't normally have a sign at the door, and if they do it usually just says "Alojamiento" ("lodging"); more commonly, members of the family might go and meet tourists at the bus station, handing out photo-copied fliers or cards. These places are perfectly safe and you shouldn't worry about checking them out, though it's always wise to see a room before committing yourself to staying there. Sometimes you'll find details of *casas de familia* at tourist offices, as well; the one in Valparaíso hands out a long printed list of them.

Cabañas

Cabañas are very popular in Chile, and you'll find them in tourist spots up and down the country, particularly by the coast. They are basically holiday chalets and are geared towards families, usually with a fully equipped kitchen area, a sitting/dining area, one double bedroom and a second bedroom with bunks. They range from the very rustic to the distinctly grand, complete with daily maid service. They're often quite expensive at full rate (at least US$60) and the price is normally the same for two people as it is for four. That said, as they're used predominantly by Chileans, their popularity tends to be limited to January and February and sunny weekends, and outside these times demand is so low that you can normally get a very good discount. If there are just two of you, you have a particularly strong case for arguing the price down. Many *cabañas* are in superb locations, right by the ocean, and it can be wonderfully relaxing to self-cater for a few days in the off-season – cooking the fresh fish you bought in the local market and sipping your cabernet on the veranda looking out to sea.

Refugios

Many of the ranger stations in the national parks have a limited number of bunk beds available for tourists, at a charge of around US$8 per person. Known as **refugios**, these places are very rustic – often a small, wooden hut – but they usually have flushable toilets, hot running water, clean sheets and heavy woollen blankets. Some of them, such as those at the Salar de Surire and Lago Chungará, are in stunning locations; conditions in these places can be very inhospitable, however, and there's no doubt that a *refugio* offers a good deal more comfort and shelter than camping. Most *refugios* are open year-round, but if you're travelling in winter or other extreme weather conditions it's best to check with the regional forestry (Conaf) office in advance. While you're there, you can reserve beds in the *refugio*, as the Conaf staff will radio their colleagues and let them know when you're arriving. This is highly advisable if you're relying solely on the *refugio* for accommodation, but if you're travelling with a tent as a back-up, it's not really necessary to book ahead.

Hostels

Hostels are increasingly banding together to provide a link among Chile's major cities. What was until recently a score of isolated bargain spots is now starting to resemble a highly developed hostelling operation such as the one, for example, in New Zealand. Unfortunately, news on the ground tends to be **word of mouth**, as new spots are being organized monthly – often by Europeans who have travelled the world and are now seeing the business and personal opportunities in becoming a hostel owner in Chile. For the latest updates, the best information is found on the Web. Try one of the major search engines like Google, type in "hostelling and Chile", and then start sorting your way through the increasing number of options.

Hostels in Chile also tend to be among the best informal networks for information about **day-trips**. The hostels are often closely linked to local outdoor guides, horse-trekking operations or local fishermen only too glad to rent their equipment for a modest fee.

Youth hostel associations

In the US and Canada

Hostelling International-American Youth Hostels ☏ 301/495-1240, ⊛ www.hiayh.org. Annual membership for adults (18–54) is $28, for seniors (55 or over) is $18, and for under-18s or groups of ten or more, is free. Life memberships are $250.

Hostelling International Canada ☏ 613/237-7884 or 613/237-7868, ⊛ www .hihostels.ca. Rather than sell the traditional 1- or 2-year memberships, the association now sells one Individual Adult membership with a 28- to 16-month term. The length of the term depends on when the membership is sold, but a member can receive up to 28 months of membership for just $35+tax. Membership is free for under-18s and you can become a lifetime member for $175.

In the UK and Ireland

Hostelling International Northern Ireland ☏ 028/9032 4733, ⊛ www.hini.org.uk. Adult membership £15; under-25s £10; family £25; lifetime £75.

Irish Youth Hostel Association ☏ 01/830 4555, ⊛ www.irelandyha.org/www.anoige.ie. Annual membership €20; under-18s €10; family €40; lifetime €100.

Scottish Youth Hostel Association ☏ 01786/891 350, ⊛ www.syha.org.uk. Annual membership £9, for under-16s free; lifetime £90.

Youth Hostel Association (YHA) ☏ 01629/592 700, ⊛ www.yha.org.uk. Annual membership £15.95; under-26s £9.95; lifetime £210.

In Australia and New Zealand

Youth Hostels Association Australia ☏ 02/9261 1111, ⊛ www.yha.com.au. Adult membership rate AUS$42 (under-26s, AUS$32).

Youth Hostelling Association New Zealand ☏ 0800/278 299, ⊛ www.yha.co.nz. Adult membership NZ$40 for one year, NZ$60 for two and NZ$80 for three; under-18s free.

Camping

There are plenty of opportunities for **camping** in Chile, though it's not always the cheapest way to sleep. If you plan to do a lot of camping, equip yourself with the annual camping guide published by Turistel, which has details of every campsite in Chile. Published only in Spanish, this guide is titled **Turistel Rutero Camping** and has maps, prices and information. Even those who don't speak Spanish will find plenty of helpful information, ranging from trail maps to cabins. Official campsites range from plots of land with minimal facilities to swanky grounds with hot showers and private barbecue grills. The latter, often part of holiday complexes in seaside resorts, can be very expensive (around CH$15,000), and are usually only open between December and March.

It's also possible to camp wild in the countryside, but you'll really need your own transport if you plan to do this in remote areas. You should also bear in mind that most national parks don't allow camping outside designated areas, to protect the environment. Instead they tend to have either rustic camping areas administered by Conaf (very common in northern Chile), costing about CH$5,000 per tent, or else smart, expensive sites run by concessionaires (more common in the south) that charge about CH$20,000 for two to four people. As for beaches, some turn into informal, spontaneously erected campsites in the summer months; on others, camping is strictly

Selecting a stove

If you plan to camp in Chile, an important consideration is the type of **stove** you bring. The best sort is probably the basic Camping Gaz model, as butane cylinders are widely available in hardware stores (*ferreterías*) and general stores in most Chilean cities, and there's less that can go wrong with them, though butane gas can fail or burn low at high altitudes. White gas (*bencina blanca*) is more difficult to come by, though it's often available in hardware shops and supermarkets. Stoves that take unleaded petrol are liable to clog up with impurities contained in Chilean petrol, so you should always carry spare parts with you. Multi-fuel stoves are a good alternative, though, again, always carry a couple of spare generators in case of clogging.

forbidden and you'll be moved on by *carabineros* if you try. If you do end up camping wild on the beach or in the countryside, do bury or pack up your excrement, and take all your refuse with you when you leave. Note that butane gas and sometimes Camping Gaz are available in hardware shops in most towns and cities. If your stove takes white gas, you need to buy *bencina blanca*, which you'll find either in hardware stores or, more commonly, in pharmacies.

For details of **camping in Chile's national parks**, see p.61.

Eating and drinking

Chile boasts a vast range of quality raw produce, but many restaurants lack imagination, offering the same limited menu of fried chicken, boiled beef and fried fish, usually served with chips or mashed potatoes. That's not to say, however, that you can't eat well in Chile. One notable exception to the general dreariness of Chilean restaurant food is the country's superb fish and seafood. Other alternatives include the various traditional dishes, often called *comida típica* or *comida criolla*, still served in old-fashioned, family-oriented restaurants known as *picadas*. Furthermore, most cities have a couple of upmarket "international" restaurants, where the staple meats and fishes are prepared more elaborately and imaginatively, with varying degrees of success.

On the whole, eating out in Chile tends to be very inexpensive. In simple, local restaurants you can expect to pay around CH$3000–5000 for standard main courses. If you're aiming to keep costs way down, you can resort to the many **fast-food outlets** spread throughout the country, specializing in hot dogs, burgers and cheap pizzas. You could also head for the **municipal markets** found in most towns; besides offering an abundance of cheap, fresh produce, they are usually dotted with stalls selling basic bargain meals of soup or fried meat and rice. The best trick is to join the Chileans and make your main meal of the day lunch, when many restaurants offer a fixed-price *menú del día*. It is always much better value than the à la carte options. Many travellers only figure this out after several weeks of overspending. Learn how to ask for the "menú", and the same food is instantly available for half-price.

As for the other meals of the day, **breakfast** at most *residenciales* and hotels is usually a disappointing affair of toasted rolls, jam and tea or coffee, though if your hosts are inclined to pamper you, this will be accompanied by ham, cheese and cake. The great tradition of *onces* – literally "elevenses" but served, like afternoon tea, around 5 o'clock – is a light snack consisting of bread, ham, cheese and biscuits when taken at home, or huge fruit tarts and cakes when out in a *salon de té*. Except during annual holidays or at weekends, relatively few Chileans go out to dinner, which leaves most restaurants very quiet through the week. Note, also, that most places don't open before 8 or 9pm for dinner.

Fish and seafood

Chile's fish and seafood rank among the best in the world. To sample the freshest offerings, head to one of the many **marisquerías** (fish restaurants), particularly those along the coasts of the Litoral Central and Norte Chico.

A note of caution: you should never collect shellfish from the beach to eat unless you know for sure that the area is free of red tide, an alga that makes shellfish toxic, causing death within a few hours of consumption (see p.67). There is little danger of eating shellfish contaminated by red tide in restaurants.

Meat dishes

Chileans are also tremendous carnivores, with beef featuring prominently on most restaurant menus and family dinner tables. The summertime **asado** (barbecue) is a national institution, giving Chilean men, who normally never lift a fork in the kitchen, the chance to roll up their sleeves and demonstrate their culinary prowess. Always slow, leisurely affairs, accompanied by lots of Chilean wine, *asados* take place not only in back gardens, but also in specially equipped picnic areas that fill to bursting on summer weekends. In the south, where the weather is less reliable, large covered grills known as *quinchos* provide an alternative venue for grilling; animals such as goats are often sliced in half and cooked in *quinchos* on long skewers, Brazilian-style. The restaurant equivalent of an *asado* is the **parrillada** – a mixture of grilled steaks, chops and sausages (in the best places cooked over charcoal), sometimes served on a hot grill by your table. Following beef in the popularity stakes is **chicken**, which is usually served fried, but can also be enjoyed oven- or spit-roasted. Chilean chickens are nearly all corn-fed and are delicious when well cooked. Succulent, spit-roasted chicken is widely available and inexpensive in Arica, in the far north, owing to the locally based chicken breeding industries. In central Chile, *pollo al coñac* is a popular, and very tasty, chicken casserole, served in large clay pots with brandy and cream. Pork chops also feature on many restaurant menus, but lamb (*cordero*) is hardly ever available, except in the Lake District, where it's a local speciality.

Traditional food

There's a wide range of older, traditional dishes – usually a fusion of indigenous and Hispanic influences – that are still very much a part of Chilean home cooking and can, with a little luck and effort, be found in the small, old-fashioned restaurants that survive in the hidden corners of town or out in the countryside. Though recipes vary from region to region, depending on the local produce available, there are a few core staples, including sweetcorn and potatoes. **Sweetcorn** forms the basis of two of the most traditional Chilean dishes: **humitas** – mashed corn, wrapped in corn husks and steamed – and **pastel de choclo**, a pie made of mince or chicken topped by pureed sweetcorn and sugar and then baked in the oven. The **potato**, meanwhile, is such an important staple in the Chilean diet that it has acquired its own mythology and folklore (see box, p.46).

Another great traditional dish (or snack) is the **empanada**, as symbolic as the national flag, although it was introduced by the Spanish and is popular throughout South America. Baked or fried, large or small, sweet or savoury, empanadas (which are not unlike Cornish pasties) can be filled with almost anything, but the most traditional filling is *pino*, a mixture of minced beef, loads of onions, a slice of hard-boiled egg, and an olive, with the pit. (Beware, as this is a good way to leave a tooth in Chile!)

Also very typical are **soups** and **broths**. There are numerous varieties, of which the most famous, cropping up as a starter on many a set meal, is **cazuela**. Named after large Spanish saucepans, cazuela is celebrated as much for its appearance as for its taste, with ingredients carefully chosen and cooked to retain their colour and texture: pale yellow potato, orange pumpkin, split rice, green beans, peas and deep yellow sweetcorn swimming in stock, served in a large soup plate with a piece of meat on the bone surrounded by a layer of animal fat, and sprinkled with parsley and coriander. Other favourite one-pot broths include **caldillo**, very similar to cazuela but with fish instead of meat, and **escabechado**, a stew made with fish steaks that have been fried then soaked in vinegar. Doubtless because it is so economical, offal enjoys a long (though waning) history in Chilean cookery – slaughtermen in Santiago's original Matadero Municipal were given all the offal from the results of their daily labour, which formed the basis of a traditional stew, caldo de Matadero, while further south, the area around Rancagua is still famous for its roadside vendors with their bowls of cold pigs' trotters and knuckles.

Potatoes

The **potato**, a staple in the Chilean diet, has long been the subject of numerous traditions and superstitions. Nowhere is this truer than in Chiloé, where potatoes must be sown during a waning moon in August or September, unless large *macho* specimens are required for seeds, in which case they are sown at the full moon. Neighbours help each other in every aspect of cultivation, a communal labouring tradition known as a **minga**. There are three main *mingas*: *quechatún*, the turning of the earth; *siembra de papa*, the planting; and *cosecha* or *sacadura*, the harvest.

Amongst the mythology and traditional customs associated with the potato are "magic stones" (*piedras cupucas*), which are found on Cerro Chepu, a hill near Ancud in Chiloé. Believed to have been hidden by witches (*brujos*), these porous silicone stones are carefully guarded until the potato plants bloom, and then the flowers are placed on them and burnt as a sacrifice.

Another potato myth holds that a small silver lizard, *el Lluhay*, feeds on potato flowers, and anyone who can catch one is guaranteed good fortune. Still another maintains that a maggot, *la co–ipone*, that lives in the potato root ball will prevent babies from crying when placed under their pillows.

Popular and traditional ways of eating potatoes include:

Chuchoca Mashed potato mixed with flour and pig fat, plastered onto a long, thick wooden pole (*chuchoquero*) and cooked over an open fire.

Colao Small cakes made from potato, wheat, pork fat and crackling, cooked in hot embers.

Mallo de papas Potato stew.

Mayo de papas Peeled, boiled potatoes mashed with onions, chillies, pepper and pig fat.

Mayocan A potato, seaweed and dried-shellfish stew traditionally eaten for breakfast.

Milcao Small cakes of grated and mashed potato that are steamed like dumplings, baked or deep fried.

Pan de papas Baked flat round cakes of mashed potato mixed with flour, eggs and pig fat.

Papas rellenas Sausage-shaped rolls of mashed potato mixed with flour and filled with meat or shellfish.

Pastel de papas A baked dish with alternating layers of mashed potato and meat or shellfish topped with more potato.

Fast food

All of Chile's towns are well endowed with greasy-spoon cafés and snack bars – usually known as *fuentes de soda* or *schoperías* – serving draught beer and cheap fast food. This usually consists of **sandwiches**, which are consumed voraciously by Chileans of all ages and social standing – indeed, one variety, the **Barros Luco** (beef and melted cheese) is named after a former president who is said to have devised the combination. **Barros Jarpa** (ham and cheese) is another dietary staple. The choice of fillings is firmly meat-based, with most options revolving around **churrasco** – a thin cut of griddle-fried beef, rather like a minute steak.

Chile is also the unlikely home of a variety of **hot dogs**. Sitting all by itself in a bun, the hot dog is simply called a *vienesa*, but it's called an *especial* when mayonnaise is squeezed along the top, and the addition of tomato, sauerkraut and avocado makes it a *dinámico*. The most popular version is the *italiano* – tomato, mayonnaise and avocado, which together resemble the colours of the Italian flag. It is not until the sausage is buried under extra sauerkraut and chopped tomato that it becomes completely *completo*.

Drinking

Soft **fizzy drinks** (*bebidas*) can be found everywhere in Chile, particularly Coca-Cola, Sprite and Fanta. Bottled **mineral water**, too, is widely available, both with fizz (*con gas*) and without (*sin gas*). **Coffee**, in Chile, is usually instant Nescafé, although in the upmarket restaurants and city cafés it's increasingly easy to find good, real coffee (ask for *café de grano*). **Herbal teas** are widely available and come in countless flavours, some of which are internationally recognizable, while others are made from native plants. The most popular varieties are manzanilla (camomile), menta (mint) and boldo (a fragrant native plant). Where Chile really comes into its own, though, is with the delicious, freshly squeezed **fruit juices** (*jugos naturales*) available in many bars, restaurants and roadside stalls, especially in the fruit-producing regions of the Central Valley, and a few northern oases like Pica. Another home-grown drink is **mote con huesillo**, sold at numerous roadsides throughout the Central Valley and Lake District in summer. *Mote* is boiled or soaked barley grain, and *huesillos* are sun-dried peaches, though this sweet, gooey drink can be made with any fresh soft fruit.

Chilean **beer** doesn't come in many varieties, with Cristal and Escudo dominating the choice of bottled lagers, and Kunstman the only speciality brand to make a national mark.

There's always a good selection of **wine**, on the other hand, though the choice on restaurant lists is usually limited to a handful of producers and in no way reflects the vast range of wines produced for export. Regarded as the Chilean national drink, **pisco sour** is a tangy, refreshing aperitif made from pisco (a white brandy created from distilled Moscatel grapes, freshly squeezed lemon juice and sugar. You may also come across a number of **regional specialities**, including *chicha de manzana* (apple cider), made at home by every *huaso* in the Central Valley. Further south, in the Lake District, a traditional element of many drinks is *harina tostada* (toasted maize flour), used by the Mapuche since pre-Spanish days. Today it's still common to see Mapuche sitting around a table with a large jug of frothy coffee-coloured liquid, which is dark beer mixed with *harina tostada*. The flour is also mixed with cheap wine made from dessert grapes, among other drinks, and is usually stocked by the sackful at local Lake District bars.

The media

Media output in Chile is nothing to get excited about. If you know where to look, journalistic standards can be high but you might find yourself turning to foreign TV channels or papers if you want an international view on events. The print media is of rather shoddy quality. The five major dailies include just a tiny amount of international news. TV is worse, dominated by soap operas, half-naked adolescent dance shows and game shows – though the daily weather slot is an unexpected highlight, as it zooms down the length of Chile, with excellent graphics representing the different geographical features. The radio is of a similar standard to the television, though some of the very rural stations provide a fascinating insight into local communities.

Newspapers and magazines

The Chilean **press**, resistant to government interference, has managed to uphold a strong tradition of editorial freedom ever since the country's first newspaper, *La Aurora*, was put together by an anti-royalist friar on an imported printing press in 1812, during the early days of the independence movement. One year before *La Aurora* folded in 1827, a new newspaper, *El Mercurio*, went to press in Valparaíso. It has been in continuous publication ever since, making it the longest-running newspaper in the Spanish-speaking world. Emphatically conservative, and owned by the powerful Edwards family in Santiago, *El Mercurio* is considered to be the most serious of Chile's dailies, but still has a minimal coverage of international news. The other major daily is *La Tercera*, which tends to be more sensationalistic. The liberal-leaning *La Nación*, the official newspaper of the state, prints a decent Sunday edition.

In addition to these two main newspapers, Chile produces a plethora of racy **tabloids** such as *La Segunda* (also part of the Edwards empire), as well as ¡Hola!-style clones, including *Cosas* and *Vanidades*. For a more edifying read, try the selection of *Private Eye*-style satirical papers, such as *The Clinic* and the weekly magazine *Siete más 7*, which provide the best examples of Chile's free press culture.

In Santiago you'll find a wide range of **foreign papers** on offer, while in the south the *Diario Austral* (another Edwards product) usually has at least a brief section on international news, as well as useful listings of regional festivals and events.

Television

Almost every household in Chile owns a television, which tends to be permanently switched on. The cult of the television is also very much in evidence in bars, cafés and the less expensive restaurants, which are often dominated by screens in the corner of the room. Cable TV is widespread, offering around eighty channels that frequently show US films and popular series like *Friends* and *Cheers* in English with Spanish subtitles, most commonly on the Cinecanal, Cinemax and Sony channels. CNN is always on offer (as is the omnipresent MTV) and BBC World is widely available.

Of the five terrestrial channels (curiously numbered 4, 7, 9, 11 and 13), top choice is Channel 7, the state-owned Televisión Nacional, which makes the best programmes in Chile, including decent documentaries. Among the others are the Universidad Católica (good documentaries from the BBC) and Megavisión (lots of talk shows and Mexican soaps) and Red Televisión (mainly dubbed American movies). Lunchtime and evening **news coverage** – shown on Channels 7, 9, 11 and 13 – invariably starts with football highlights followed by bloody road accidents no matter what earth-shattering events have occurred in the rest of the world. Otherwise, soap operas, game shows and talent contests predominate, reaching an excruciating climax with Sábado Gigante, a truly dreadful talent contest where Chileans compete against one another. Popping up in endless commercials, peering down from advertising billboards and plastered over food packaging, the show's indefatigable and larger-than-life compere, Don Francisco, is an international institution whose popularity reaches its zenith every other December when he hosts the Teletón event, which raises money for disabled children. If you happen to be in Chile during this event, you will see flocks of people at midnight rushing to donate pesos at the supermarkets. It is a rare demonstration of national solidarity, and the Chileans take the Teletón very seriously.

Radio

There is a compulsive Chilean habit, particularly prevalent amongst the owners of the country's quietest rural bars, of turning the radio on as soon as you walk through the door. Outside towns and cities, radio reception is quite poor. News stations are very rare, and when the reception is good you can hear the pages of newspapers being turned as a monotone voice reads one article after another, interrupted periodically by voiced-over jingles promoting democracy or government institutions.

An old-fashioned Chilean institution in this age of instant worldwide communications is the local radio station, providing remote rural communities with their sole **message service**. Sitting in a quiet backwoods bar, locals bend an ear for news of family and friends and catch up on the latest developments of ongoing sagas that could easily be scripts for a soap opera.

To find local frequencies for English-language news on either the VOA or Radio Canada, check out their websites, which offer local radio information and list all the service frequencies around the world: Voice of America ⓦwww.voa.gov; Radio Canada ⓦwww.rcinet.ca;. Unfortunately, the BBC has stopped broadcasting its World Service in Chile and can only be listened to via the internet ⓦwww.bbc.co.uk/worldservice.

Festivals

Most of Chile's festivals are held to mark religious occasions, or to honour saints or the Virgin Mary. What's fascinating about them is the strong influence of pre-Spanish, pre-Christian rites, particularly in the Aymara communities of the Far North and the Mapuche of the south. Added to this is the influence of colourful folk traditions rooted in the Spanish expeditions of exploration and conquest, colonization and evangelism, slavery and revolution.

In the altiplano of the **Far North**, Aymara herdsmen celebrate Catholic holy days and the feasts of ancient cults along with ritual dancing and the offering of sacrificial llamas.

In **central Chile**, you'll witness the influence of colonial traditions. In the days of the conquest, an important ingredient of any fiesta was the verbal sparring between itinerant bards called *payadores*, who would compose and then try to resolve each other's impromptu rhyming riddles. The custom is kept alive at many fiestas in the Central Valley, where young poets spontaneously improvise *lolismos* and *locuciones*, forms of jocular verse that are quite unintelligible to an outsider. These rural fiestas always culminate in an energetic display of cueca dancing, washed down with plenty of wine and chicha – reminiscent of the entertainment organized by indulgent hacienda-owners for their peons.

In the **south**, the solemn Mapuche festivals are closely linked to mythology, magic and faith healing, agricultural rituals, and supplications to gods and spirits. Group dances (*purrún*) are performed with gentle movements; participants either move round in a circle or advance and retreat in lines. Most ceremonies are accompanied by mounted horn players whose four-metre-long bamboo instruments, trutrucas, require enormous lung power to produce a note. Other types of traditional wind instruments include a small pipe (lolkiñ), flute (pinkulwe), cow's horn (kullkull) and whistle (pifilka). Of all Mapuche musical instruments, the most important is the sacred drum (kultrún), which is only used by faith healers (machis).

Major festivals

For more on altiplano fiestas and ceremonies, see p.236.

January

20 *San Sebastián* Spaniards brought the first wooden image of San Sebastián to Chile in the seventeenth century. After a Mapuche raid on Chillán, the image was buried in a nearby field, and no one was able to raise it. The saint's feast day has become an important Mapuche festival, especially in Lonquimay, where it's celebrated with horse racing, feasting and drinking.

February

1–3 *La Candelaria* This has been celebrated throughout Chile since 1780, when a group of miners and muleteers discovered a stone image of the Virgin and Child while sheltering from an inexplicable thunderstorm in the Atacama. Typical festivities include religious processions and traditional dances. **End of the month** *Festival Internacional de la Canción* This glitzy and wildly popular five-day festival is held in Viña del Mar's open-air amphitheatre, featuring performers from all over Latin America and broadcast to most Spanish-speaking countries in the world.

April

Easter *Semana Santa* (Holy Week) Among the nationwide Easter celebrations, look out for Santiago's solemn procession of penitents dressed in black habits, carrying crosses through the streets, and La Ligua's parade of mounted *huasos* followed by a giant penguin. **First Sunday after Easter** *Fiesta del Cuasimodo* In many parts of central Chile, *huasos* parade through the streets on their horses, often accompanied by a priest sitting on a float covered in white lilies.

May

3 *Santa Cruz de Mayo* Throughout the altiplano, villages celebrate the cult of the Holy Cross, inspired in the seventeenth century by the Spaniards' obsession with crosses, which they carried everywhere, erected on hillsides and even carved in the air with their fingers. The festivities have strong pre-Christian elements, often including the sacrifice of a llama. **13** *Procesión del Cristo de Mayo* A huge parade through the streets of Santiago bearing the *Cristo de Mayo* – a sixteenth-century carving of Christ whose crown of thorns slipped to its neck during an earthquake, and which is said to have shed tears of blood when attempts were made to put the crown back in place.

June

13 *Noche de San Juan Bautista* An important feast night, celebrated by families up and down the country with a giant stew, known as the *Estofado de San Juan*. In Chiloé, an integral part of the feast are roasted potato balls called *tropones*, which burn the fingers and make people "dance the *tropón*" as they jig up and down, juggling them from hand to hand. **29** *Fiesta de San Pedro* Along the length of Chile's coast, fishermen decorate their boats and take the image of their patron saint out to sea – often at night with candles and flares burning – to pray for good weather and large catches.

July

12–18 *Virgen de la Tirana* The largest religious festival in Chile, held in La Tirana in the Far North, and attended by over 80,000 pilgrims and hundreds of costumed dancers (see p.232). **16** *Virgen del Carmen* Military parades throughout Chile honour the patron saint of the armed forces; the largest are in Maipú, on the southern outskirts of Santiago, where San Martín and Bernardo O'Higgins defeated Spanish Royalists in 1818.

August

21–31 *Jesús Nazareno de Caguach* Thousands of Chilotes flock to the archipelago's tiny island of Caguach to worship at a two-metre-high figure of Christ, donated by the Jesuits in the eighteenth century.

September

18 *Fiestas Patrias* Chile's Independence Day is celebrated throughout the country with street parties, music and dancing.

October

First Sunday *Virgen de las Peñas* Each year, numerous dance groups and more than 10,000 pilgrims from Chile, Peru, Bolivia and Argentina make their way along a tortuous cliff path to visit a rock carving of the Virgin in the Azapa valley, near Arica. There are many smaller festivals in other parts of Chile, too.

November

1 *Todos los Santos* (All Saints' Day) Traditionally, this is the day when Chileans tend their family graves. In the north, where Aymara customs have become entwined with Christian ones, crosses are often removed from graves and left on the former bed of the deceased overnight. Candles are kept burning in the room, and a feast is served for family members, past and present.

2 *Día de los Muertos* (All Souls' Day) A second vigil to the dead is held in cemeteries, with offerings of food and wine sprinkled on the graves. In some Far North villages, there's a tradition of reading a liturgy, always in Latin.

December

8 *La Purísima* Celebrated in many parts of Chile, the festival of the Immaculate Conception is at its liveliest in San Pedro de Atacama, where it's accompanied by traditional Aymara music and dancing.

23–27 *Fiesta Grande de la Virgen de Andacollo* More than 100,000 pilgrims from all over the north come to Andacollo, in Norte Chico to worship its Virgin and watch the famous masked dancers (see p.169).

Spectator sports

The Chileans are not a particularly exuberant people (especially compared to their Argentine neighbours) and the country's entertainment scene sits firmly on the tame side of the fence. That said, passions are roused by several national enthusiasms – chiefly football and rodeo, which at their best are performed with electrifying skill and theatricality. Local and national fiestas provide other opportunities for the Chileans to let their hair down, and usually include a good deal of flag-waving, dancing, singing, drinking and eating of empanadas. If your Spanish is good, you'll also be entertained by the characteristic fast-thinking humour evident throughout Chilean culture, from the teasing jokes of young waiters and bar staff to the sophisticated word play that peppers the country's theatre, music and literature.

Football

El *fútbol* reigns supreme as Chile's favourite sport, and the top *futbolistas* are modern-day folk heroes whose exploits are frequently splashed across the front pages of the newspapers.

Introduced by British immigrants in the early 1800s, football in Chile can trace its history back to the playing fields of the Mackay School, one of the first English schools founded in Valparaíso, and its heritage is reflected in the names of the first clubs: Wanderers, Everton, Badminton, Morning Star and Green Cross.

Everton and Wanderers are still going strong, but the sport is now dominated by the Santiago teams of Colo Colo, Universidad Católica and Universidad de Chile. Matches featuring any of these teams are guaranteed a good turn-out and a great atmosphere. There's rarely any trouble, with whole families coming along to enjoy the fun. In Santiago (unquestionably the best place to watch a match), tickets to see the main teams cost around CH$3000–6000 (US$5–10) at the bottom end, going up to CH$40,000 (US$60) for the most expensive seats. If you can't make it to a match, you'll still see plenty of football on the huge TVs that dominate most cafés and bars, including European games shown on cable channels (you may notice, too, that widespread exposure to English football has led many young Chileans to refer to an Englishman as a *húligan* rather than a gringo).

Football hardly has a season in Chile. In addition to the league games played between March and December, there are numerous other competitions of which the Copa de Libertadores is the most important. So you'll be able to catch the action whatever time of year you visit.

Horse racing

There are two very different types of horse racing in Chile: conventional track racing, known as *hípica*, and the much rougher and wilder *carreras a la chilena*. Hípica is a sport for rich Santiaguinos, who don their tweeds and posh frocks to go and watch it at the capital's Club Hípico and Hipódromo Chile, which have races throughout the year. The most important of these are the St Leger at the Hipódromo Chile on December 14, and the Ensayo at the Club Hípico on the first Sunday in November.

Carreras a la chilena are held anywhere in the country where two horses can be found to race against each other. Apart from the organized events that take place at village fiestas, these races are normally a result of one *huaso* betting another that his horse is faster. Held in any suitable field, well away from the prying eyes of the *carabineros*, the two-horse race can attract large crowds (who bet heavily on the outcome) and enterprising local families (who set up food and drink stalls). After a track is marked out with a piece of string, both horses and riders mill around, giving each other the evil eye for an hour or more. When the race begins, the tension is palpable as the two men and their beasts pit their strength and skill against each other, and the crowd is frozen in silence until the winner crosses the finishing post, whereupon it breaks out into loud, raucous whooping.

Rodeo

Rodeos evolved from the early colonial days when the cattle on the large estancias had to be rounded up and branded or slaughtered by *huasos* (Chilean "cowboys" or horsemen). The feats of horsemanship required to do so soon took on a competitive element, which eventually found an expression in the form of rodeos. Even though ranching has long declined in Chile, organized rodeos remain wildly popular, with many free competitions taking place in local stadiums (known as **medialunas**) throughout the season, which runs from September to April. Taking in a rodeo not only allows you to watch the most dazzling equestrian skills inside the arena, but also to see the *huasos* decked out in all their traditional gear: ponchos, silver spurs and all. Added to this, the atmosphere is invariably loads of fun, with lots of whooping families and excited kids, and plenty of food and drink afterwards. For a fuller account of rodeos, see the box opposite.

Cueca

Huasos are also the chief performers of **cueca**, Chile's national dance – a curious cross between thigh-slapping English morris dancing and smouldering Sevillanas. Its history can, in fact, be traced to the African slave dances, which were also the basis of the Brazilian samba and Peruvian zamacueca, and were introduced to Chile by a battalion of black soldiers in 1824. During the War of Independence, Chileans adopted their own forms of these dances known as la Chilena, la Marinera and el Minero, which eventually became a national victory dance known simply as the cueca. Although there are regional variations, the basic elements remain unchanged, consisting of couples strutting around each other in a courtship ritual, spurs jingling and handkerchiefs waving over their heads. The men are decked out in their finest *huaso* gear, while the women wear wide

The Chilean huaso

"Of the many cowboys of the Americas, none remains as shrouded in mystery and contradiction as Chile's *huaso*", says Richard Slatta in *Cowboys of the Americas*. Certainly the *huaso* holds a special place in Chile's perception of its national identity and has become a potent symbolic figure over the years. But the definition and identity of the *huaso* is somewhat confused and subject to multiple, wildly differing interpretations. The one you're most likely to come across as a traveller is that of the "gentleman rider", the middle-class horseman who, while not a part of the landed elite, is a good few social rungs up from the landless labourer. This is the *huaso* you'll see in *cueca* performances (see opposite) and at rodeos, mounted on a fine-blooded steed and dressed in richly woven ponchos, silk sashes, high-heeled Cordova-leather boots and large silver spurs. This version of the *huaso* has evolved from a Spanish archetype – the dignified country gentleman and his horse – imported, along with cattle and horses, by the conquistadors. While not exactly a fiction, these gentlemen riders (labelled "postcard huasos" by Slatta) are, nonetheless, part of a romanticized image of the Chilean countryside and a far cry from the much larger and perhaps more authentic group of *huasos* who carried out the real horse-work on the land. More akin to the Argentine gaucho and the Mexican *vaquero*, this other type of *huaso* was a landless, badly paid and poorly dressed ranch-hand who worked on the large haciendas during the cattle round-up season. His prototype developed during the early years of the colony with the creation of the immense landed estates and the introduction of livestock breeding, and by the eighteenth century was a fundamental cog in the rural economy. Despite the harsh reality of his lifestyle, the lower-class *huaso* is also the victim of myth-making, frequently depicted as a paragon of virtue and happiness – loyal to his master, honest, hard-working and at one with the land.

All types of *huasos*, whatever their social status, were renowned for outstanding **horsemanship**. One visiting Englishman in the nineteenth century described, with astonishment, the skilful Chilean cowboys who could "throw their lasso at full speed and entangle and secure the wildest animal". They were also marvelled at for their practice of training their horses to stop dead in their tracks at a single command, a technique known as *la sentada*. A skill mastered by *huasos* in the southern Central Valley (and borrowed from Argentine gauchos) was that of the *bolas* – three stones or metal balls attached to long leather straps, that were hurled at animals and wrapped around their legs, bringing them to the ground. *Huasos* also developed a whole host of equestrian games and contests including the *juego de cañas* (jousting with canes), the *tiro al gallo* (a mounted tug-of-war) and *topeadura* (a side-by-side pushing contest). Today these displays have a formal outlet in the regular **rodeos** (see opposite) that take place throughout the Central Valley. As for the working *huaso*, you'll still come across him in the back roads of rural central Chile, herding livestock, often wearing a broad-rimmed *huaso* hat and occasionally a bright poncho.

skirts and shawls. In the background, guitar-strumming musicians sing romantic ballads full of patriotic sentiments. If you are going to a fiesta and want to take part in a cueca, remember to take along a clean white handkerchief.

Outdoor activities

Chile offers an enormous range of outdoor activities, including volcano-climbing, skiing, surfing, white-water rafting, fly-fishing and horse-riding. Although Chile's tourism industry was traditionally geared towards Argentine holidaymakers who come to lie on the beaches, an increasing number of operators and outfitters are wising up to the potential of organized adventure tourism, offering one- or multi-day guided excursions.

Many of these companies are based in Pucón, in the Lake District, with a good sprinkling of other outfitters spread throughout the south. There are fewer opportunities for outdoor activities in the harsh deserts of the north, where altiplano jeep trips and mountain biking are the main options. If you plan to do any adventurous activities, be sure to check that you're covered by your travel insurance, or take out specialist insurance where necessary. For more information on outdoor activities, see also the *Adventure sports* colour section.

Rafting and kayaking

Chile's many frothy rivers and streams afford incomparable rafting opportunities. Indeed, the country's top destinations, the mighty **Río Bío Bío** and the **Río Futaleufú** entice visitors from around the globe. Rafting trips generally range in length from one to eight days and, in the case of the Bío Bío, sometimes include the option of climbing 3160-metre Volcán Callaquén. Prices are normally around US$100 for a day's rafting, US$350 for a three-day trip (with all camping equipment and food provided), going up to US$1500–2000 for all-inclusive ten-day packages, with added excursions. In addition to these challenging rivers, gentler alternatives exist on the **Río Maipo** close to Santiago, the **Río Trancura** near Pucón, and the **Río Petrohue** near Puerto Varas. The Maipo makes a good day-trip from Santiago, while excursions on the last two are just half-day affairs and can usually be arranged on the spot, without advance reservations. In general, all rafting trips are extremely well organized, but you should always take great care in choosing your outfitter – this activity

can be very dangerous in the hands of an inexperienced guide.

Chile's white-water rapids also offer excellent **kayaking**, though this is less developed as an organized activity – your best bet is probably to contact one of the US-based outfitters that have camps on the Bío Bío and Futaleufú (see p.402 for contacts). **Sea kayaking** is becoming increasingly popular in Chile, generally in the calm, flat waters of Chile's southern fjords, though people have been known to kayak around Cape Horn. Note that the Chilean navy is very sensitive about any foreign vessels (even kayaks) cruising in their waters, and if you're planning a trip through military waters, you'd be wise to inform the Chilean consulate or embassy in your country beforehand.

Hiking

For the most part, Chile is a very empty country with vast tracts of wilderness offering potential for fantastic hiking (and concealing no dangerous animals or snakes). Chileans, moreover, are often reluctant to stray far from their parked cars when they visit the countryside, so you'll find that most trails without vehicle access are blissfully quiet. However, the absence of a national enthusiasm for hiking also means that, compared to places of similar scenic beauty like California, British Columbia and New Zealand, Chile isn't particularly geared up to the hiking scene, with relatively few long-distance trails (given the total area) and a shortage of decent trekking maps. That said, what is on offer is superb, and ranks among the country's most rewarding attractions.

Where to hike

For those who want to plan a trip around a few hikes, we refer you to the following accounts in the *Guide*:

The **north** of Chile, with its harsh climate and landscape, isn't really suitable for hiking, and most walkers head for the lush native forests of Chile's **south**, peppered with waterfalls, lakes, hot springs and volcanoes. The best trails are nearly always inside **national parks** or reserves, where the *guardaparques* (rangers) are a good source of advice on finding and following the paths. They should always be informed if you plan to do an overnight hike (so that if you don't come back, they'll know where to search for you). The majority of trails are for half-day or day hikes, though some parks offer a few long-distance hikes, sometimes linking up with trails in adjoining parks. The level of path maintenance and signing varies greatly from one park to another, and many of the more remote trails are indistinct and difficult to follow. Hardly any parks allow wild **camping**, while the few others that now allow it have a series of rustic camping areas that you're required to stick to – check with the *guardaparque*. If you do camp (and this is the best way to experience the Chilean wilderness) note that **forest and bush fires** are a very real hazard. Take great care when making a campfire (having checked beforehand that they're allowed). Also, never chop or break down vegetation for fuel, as most of Chile's native flora is endangered.

By far the most popular destination for hiking is **Torres del Paine** in the far south, which offers magnificent scenery but fairly crowded trails, especially in January and February. Many quieter, less well-known alternatives are scattered between Santiago and Tierra del Fuego, ranging from narrow paths in the towering, snow-streaked central Andes to hikes up to glaciers off the Carretera Austral.

If you go hiking, it's essential to be well prepared – always carry plenty of water, wear a hat and sun block for protection against the sun and carry extra layers of warm clothing to guard against the sharp drop of temperatures after sundown. Even on day hikes, take enough supplies to provide for the eventuality of getting lost, and always carry a map and **compass** (*brújula*), preferably one bought in the southern hemisphere or adjusted for southern latitudes. Also, make a conscious effort to help preserve Chile's environment – where there's no toilet, bury human waste at least 20cm under the ground and 30m from the nearest river or lake; take away or burn all your **rubbish**; and use specially designed **eco-friendly detergents** for use in lakes and streams.

Climbing

The massive Andean cordillera offers a wide range of climbing possibilities. In the Far North of Chile, you can trek up several volcanoes over 6000m, including Volcán Parinacota (6330m), Volcán Llullaillaco (6739m) and Volcán Ojos del Salado (6950m). Although ropes and crampons aren't always needed, these ascents are suitable only for experienced climbers, and need a fair amount of independent planning, with only a few companies offering guided excursions.

In the central Andes, exciting climbs include Volcán Marmolejo (6100m) and

Volcán Tupungato (6750m), while in the south, climbers head for Volcán Villarrica (2840m) and Volcán Osorno (2652m), both of which you can tackle even with little mountaineering experience.

Throughout Chile there's a lot of tedious-bureaucracy to get through before you can climb. To go up any mountain straddling an international border (which means most of the high Andean peaks), you need advance **permission** from the **Dirección de Fronteras y Límites** (DIFROL), Fourth Floor, Bandera 52, Santiago (℡2/671 4110, ℻697 1909). To get this, write to or fax DIFROL with the planned dates and itinerary of the climb, listing full details (name, nationality, date of birth, occupation, passport number, address) of each member of the climbing team, and your dates of entry and exit from Chile. Authorization will then be sent or faxed to you on a piece of paper that you must present to Conaf before ascending (if the peak is not within a national park, you must take the authorization to the nearest *carabineros* station). If your plans change while you're in Chile, you can usually amend the authorization or get a new one at the *Gobernación* of each provincial capital. You can also apply through a Chilean embassy in advance of your departure, or print and send a form from their website. There's further information on climbing in Chile on the Web at ⓦwww.escalando.cl or www.trekkingchile.com.

Fly-fishing

Chile has an international, and well-deserved, reputation as one of the finest fly-fishing destinations in the world, counting Robert Redford, Jane Fonda, Ted Turner, Michael Douglas, Jimmy Carter and George Bush Sr among those to have fished its pristine waters, which are teeming with rainbow, brown and brook trout, and silver and Atlantic salmon. These fish are not native, but were introduced for sport in the late nineteenth century; since then, the wild population has flourished and multiplied, and is also supplemented by generous numbers of escapees from local fish farms. The fishing season varies slightly from region to region, but in general runs from November to May.

Traditionally, the best sport-fishing was considered to be in the Lake District, but while this region still offers great possibilities, attention has shifted to the more remote, pristine waters of Aisén, where a number of classy fishing lodges have sprung up, catering mainly to wealthy North American clients. Fishing in the Lake District is frequently done from riverboats, while a typical day's fishing in Aisén begins with a ride in a motor dinghy through fjords, channels and islets towards an isolated river. You'll then wade upstream to shallower waters, usually equipped with a light six or seven weight rod, dry flies and brightly coloured streamers. Catches weigh in between 1 and 3kg – but note that many outfitters operate only on a catch and release basis, so don't count on being able to cook them for your supper.

Costs range from a reasonable US$70 per person for a day in the more visited waters of the Lake District (including full equipment hire and boat transport), to around US$400 per day to fish the scarcely touched waters of Aisén with top-notch guides. You may also need to get yourself a licence (CH$6300

Useful climbing contacts

American Alpine Club 710 Tenth St, Suite 100, Golden, CO 80401, US ℡303/384-0110, ⓦwww.americanalpineclub.org. A good source of pre-trip advice.
British Mountaineering Council 177–179 Burton Rd, Manchester M20 2BB, UK ℡0161/445 6111, ⓦwww.thebmc.co.uk Produces a very useful information sheet on mountaineering, and also provides specialist insurance for members.
Federación de Andinismo Almirante Simpson 77, Providencia, Santiago ℡2/222 0888, ⓦwww.feach.cl. This friendly organization runs mountaineering courses, sells equipment, can put you in touch with guides and offers knowledgeable, helpful advice. It also helps out foreigners trying to arrange climbing authorization.

for the whole country), widely available at town halls and specialist fishing shops, though many outfitters supply this as part of the package. To find out more about fly-fishing in Chile, contact the government agency **Servicio Nacional de Pesca** at Yungay 1737, Fourth Floor, Valparaíso, Chile (☏32/214371, ℻259564), or consult the excellent website ⓦwww.flyfishchile.com.

Skiing

Chile offers the finest and most challenging **skiing** in South America. Many of the country's top slopes and resorts lie within very easy reach of Santiago, including **El Colorado**, **La Parva**, **Valle Nevado** and world-renowned **Portillo**. A bit further south, but no less impressive, stands the popular **Termas de Chillán**.

Horse-trekking

Exploring Chile's dramatic landscapes on horseback is a highly memorable experience, though organized treks for tourists are only slowly taking off. The best possibilities are **around Santiago**, and in the **Central Valley**, where riding has been a way of life for centuries, and horses are sleek, fit and strong. Here, groups of riders make their way up to remote mountain passes, framed by soaring, jagged peaks, sloping pastures, and clear rivers. In addition to the spectacular scenery, you can also expect to see condors and other birds of prey circling around the peaks. Trips are usually from three to seven days, guided by local *arrieros*, who herd cattle up to high pastures in springtime and know the mountain paths intimately. You normally spend about five or six hours in the saddle each day; a lingering *asado* (barbecue), cooked over an open fire and accompanied by plenty of Chilean wine, will be part of the pleasure. At night, you sleep in tents transported by mules, and you'll be treated to the most breathtaking display of stars.

The only disadvantage of riding treks in the central Andes is that, due to the terrain, you're unlikely to get beyond a walk, and cantering is usually out of the question. If you want a faster pace, opt for the treks offered by some companies in Patagonia, where rolling grasslands provide plenty of opportunity for gallops – though the weather can often put a dampener on your trip.

Most outfitters only offer a few multi-day trips between December and March, and these need to be booked well in advance, as demand often exceeds supply. Casual, one-day riding trips, however, can be arranged on the spot in many Central Valley mountain villages for around CH$20,000 a day. Conaf rangers can often help you find an *arriero* for the day, especially in Monumento Nacional El Morado, Reserva Nacional Río de los Cipreses and Reserva Nacional Altos del Lircay.

Mountain biking

For most of Chile's length, there are extremely good and little-used dirt roads perfect for **cycling** – although the numerous potholes mean it's only worth attempting them on a **mountain bike**. For a serious trip, you should bring your own bike or buy one in Santiago – **renting** a bike of the quality required can be difficult to arrange. An alternative is to go on an organized biking excursion, where all equipment, including tents, will be provided. Note that during the summer, cycling in Patagonia and Tierra del Fuego is made almost impossible by incessant and ferociously strong winds. For information on popular mountain bike routes, see the *Adventure sports* colour section.

Surfing

Chile does not spring to mind as a major surfing destination, but its beaches are pulling in an increasing number of in-the-know enthusiasts from North America, who come to ride the year-round breaks that pound the Pacific shore. By unanimous consent, the **best breaks** – mainly long left-handers – are concentrated around Pichilemu, near Rancagua, which is the site of the annual National Surfing Championships (quite a small affair). Further north, the warmer seas around Iquique and Arica are also increasingly popular with visiting surfers.

Adventure tourism operators and outfitters

Below is a selection of operators and outfitters for various outdoor activities. The list is by no means comprehensive, and new companies are constantly springing up to add to it – you can get more details from the relevant regional Sernatur office.

All-rounders

Altue Active Travel General Salvo 159, Providencia, Santiago ☎2/235 1519, ⓔinfo @altue.com, ⓦwww.altue.com. Reliable, slick operation whose options include rafting the Río Maipo, Aconcagua and Ojos del Salado expeditions, and three- to seven-day horse treks.

Azimut 360 General Salvo 159, Providencia, Santiago ☎2/235 1519, ⓔinfo@azimut360.com, ⓦwww.azimut360.com. Franco-Chilean outfit with a young, dynamic team of guides and a wide range of programmes, including mountain biking in the altiplano, Aconcagua expeditions, and climbs up Chile's highest volcanoes.

Cascada Expediciones Don Carlos 3219, Las Condes, Santiago ☎2/232 9878, ⓔinfo @cascada.travel, ⓦwww.cascada.travel. One of the early pioneers of adventure tourism in Chile, with a particular emphasis on activities in the Andes close to Santiago, where it has a permanent base in the Cajón del Maipo. Programmes include rafting and kayaking the Río Maipo, horse treks in the high cordillera, hiking and one-day mountain biking excursions

Sportstour Av El Bosque Norte 500, 15th Floor, Santiago ☎2/549 5260, ⓔmailbox@sportstour.cl, ⓦwww.sportstour.cl. This well-run operation offers balloon rides and flights, among other tours.

Climbing

See also Azimut 360 and Altue Active Travel in "All-rounders" above for details of tours up Volcán Osorno and Volcán Villarrica.

Concepto Indigo Ladrilleros 105, Puerto Natales ☎61/413609, ⓔindigo@entelchile.net, ⓦwww.conceptoindigo.com. A range of mountaineering and ice-climbing programmes in the Torres del Paine region, plus mountaineering courses. A very good company.

Mountain Service Paseo Las Palmas 2209, Providencia, Santiago ☎2/234 3439. An experienced, specialist company, dedicated to climbing Aconcagua, the major volcanoes and Torres del Paine.

Fly-fishing

For a list of guides and lodges on and around the Carretera Austral, see chapter 8.

Bahía Escocia Fly Fishing Lago Rupanco ☎64/1974731, ⓔcontact@puntiagudolodge .cl, ⓦwww.puntiagudolodge.cl. Small, beautifully

located lodge with fly-fishing excursions run by a US–Chilean couple. Can also book with English-run Travellers in Puerto Montt ☎65/262099, ⓔgochile @entelchile.net.

Cumilahue Lodge PO Box 2, Llifen ☎2/1961601, ⓔadrian@anglingtours.com, ⓦwww.anglingtours .com. Very expensive packages at a luxury Lake District lodge run by Adrian Dufflocq, something of a legend on the Chilean fly-fishing scene.

Off Limits Adventures Av Bernado O'Higgins 560, Pucón ☎45/442681, ⓔoffflimits .cl, ⓦwww.offlimits.cl. Half-day and full-day excursions, plus fly-fishing lessons. One of the more affordable options.

Horse-trekking

See also Altue Active Travel and Cascada Expediciones in "All-rounders", opposite.

Chile Nativo ☎2/7175961, ⓔinfo@chilenativo .com, ⓦwww.chilenativo.com. Dynamic young outfit specializing in five- to twelve-day horse-trekking tours of the region, visiting out-of-the-way locations in addition to the Parque Nacional Torres del Paine.

Hacienda de los Andes Río Hurtado, near Ovalle ☎53/691822, ⓔinfo@haciendalosandes.com, ⓦwww.haciendalosandes.com. Beautiful newly built ranch in a fantastic location in the Hurtado valley, between La Serena and Ovalle, offering exciting one- to four-day mountain treks on some of the finest mounts in the country.

Pared Sur Juan Esteban Montero 5497, Las Condes, Santiago ☎2/2073525, ⓔparedsur @paredsur.cl, ⓦwww.paredsur.cl. In addition to its extensive mountain-biking programme, Pared Sur offers a one-week horse trek through the virgin landscape of Aisén, off the Carretera Austral.

Rancho de Caballos Casilla 142, Pucón ☎09/83461764, ⓔchile@rancho-de-caballos.com, ⓦwww.rancho-de-caballos.com. Ranch offering a range of treks from three to nine days.

Ride World Wide Staddon Farm, North Tawton, Devon, UK ☎01837/82544, or 01837/82179, ⓔinfo@rideworldwide.com ⓦwww .rideworldwide.com. UK-based company that hooks up with local riding outfitters around the world. In Chile, it offers a range of horseback treks from eight days to two weeks in the central cordillera, the Lake District and Patagonia. Groups are limited to six or eight people.

Terracotta Excursions Agustinas 1547, departamento 705, Santiago ☎2/698 8121, ⓔterracot@intercity.cl. Run and guided by a Santiago woman, this young company is an alternative to the more traditional, slightly macho *huaso* outfits. It offers a range of treks from one to eight days in the Andes and coastal mountains near Santiago.

Kayaking

Al Sur Expediciones Aconcagua corner of Imperial, Puerto Varas ☎65/232300, ⓔalsurexpediciones@gmail.com, ⓌwWw.alsurexpeditions.com. One of the foremost adventure tour companies in the Lake District, and the first one to introduce sea kayaking in the fjords south of Puerto Montt.

Bío Bío Expeditions (see White-water rafting below). This rafting outfitter also rents out kayaks to experienced kayakers, who accompany the rafting party down the Bío Bío or Futaleufú.

¡ecole! Urrutia 592, Pucón ☎45/441675, ⓔtrek@ecole.cl, Ⓦwww.ecole.cl. Ecologically focused tour company offering, among other activities, sea kayaking classes and day outings in the fjords south of Puerto Montt, and around Parque Pumalín, from its Puerto Montt branch.

Expediciones Chile Gabriela Mistral 296, Futaleufú ☎65/721386 or 2/570 9885, ⓌwWw.exchile.com. River kayaking outfitter catering to all levels of experience, especially seasoned paddlers. Operated by former Olympic kayaker Chris Spelius.

Onas Patagonia Blanco Encalada 211, Puerto Natales ☎61/614300, ⓔreservas@onaspatagonia.com, Ⓦwww.onaspatagonia.com. Sea kayaking excursions in the remote, bleak waters of Patagonia.

Mountain biking

See also Azimut 360 and Cascada Expediciones in "All-rounders" opposite.

Pared Sur Juan Esteban Montero 5497, Las Condes, Santiago ☎2/207 3525, ⓔparedsur@paredsur.cl, Ⓦwww.paredsur.cl. Pared Sur has been running mountain bike trips in Chile for longer

than anyone else (over twelve years). It offers a wide range of programmes throughout the whole country.

Skiing

Full details of the resorts near Santiago are given in Chapter 1.

Sportstour Av El Bosque Norte 500, 15th Floor, Santiago ☎2/549 5260, Ⓕ2/549 5290, ⓔmailbox@sportstour.cl, Ⓦwww.sportstour.cl. Among a wide-ranging national programme, including hot-air balloon rides and flights on cockpit biplanes and gliders, this travel agent offers fully-inclusive ski packages at the resorts near Santiago, and the Termas de Chillán ski centre.

White-water rafting

See also Cascada Expediciones and Altue Expediciones, listed opposite.

Bío Bío Expeditions PO Box 2028, Truckee, CA 96160, US ☎562/196 4258, ⓔ-info@bbxrafting.com, Ⓦwww.bbxrafting.com. Headed by Laurence Alvarez, the captain of the US World Championships rafting team, this experienced and friendly outfit offers ten-day packages on the Bío Bío and Futaleufú, plus one- to three-day excursions down the latter. Trips can be booked in Chile by Aquamotion, Imperial 0699, Puerto Varas (☎65/232747), in the UK by Adrift at 140–142 High St, Wandsworth, London SW18 4JJ (☎020/8874 4969) and in New Zealand by Adrift, PO Box 310, Queenstown (☎03/442 1615).

Trancura O'Higgins 211-C, Pucón ☎45/401189, Ⓦwww.trancura.com. Major southern operator with high standards and friendly guides, offering rafting excursions down the Río Trancura (one day) and the Bío Bío (three days).

National parks and reserves

Some eighteen percent of Chile's mainland territory is protected by the state under the extensive Sistema Nacional de Areas Silvestres Protegidas (National Protected Wildlife Areas System), which is made up of thirty national parks, thirty-eight national reserves and eleven natural monuments. These inevitably include the country's most outstanding scenic attractions, but while there are provisions for tourism, the main aim is always to protect and manage native fauna and flora. Given Chile's great biodiversity, these vary tremendously from one region to another, and park objectives are as varied as protecting the flamingo populations of the altiplano lakes to monitoring glaciers off the southern fjords. Other important functions include preventing poaching (for instance of vicuñas in the altiplano) and guarding against forest fires. All protected areas are managed by the Corporación Nacional Forestal, better known as Conaf, established in 1972 as part of the Ministry of Agriculture.

Definitions and terms

National parks (*parques nacionales*) are generally large areas of unspoilt wilderness, usually featuring fragile endemic ecosystems. They include the most touristy and scenically beautiful of the protected areas, and often offer walking trails and, less frequently, camping areas. **National reserves** (*reservas nacionales*) are areas of ecological importance that have suffered some degree of natural degradation; there are fewer regulations to protect these areas, and "sustainable" commercial exploitation (such as mineral extraction) is allowed to take place. **Natural monuments** (*monumentos naturales*) tend to be important or endangered geological formations, or small areas of biological, anthropological or archeological significance. In 1976, two tree species, the araucaria and alerce, were awarded the status of natural monument.

In addition to these three main categories, there are a small number of **nature sanctuaries** (*santuarios de la naturaleza*) and **protected areas** (*areas de protección*), usually earmarked for their scientific or scenic interest. It is not difficult for the government to change the status of these areas, and it has been known for national parks to be downgraded so that their resources could be commercially exploited. In addition to these state-owned parks,

there are several important private initiatives, including **Parque Pumalín** (see p.381), just south of Puerto Montt, with some of the most luxuriant native forest in the country, and the **Cañi Reserve**, just outside Pucón.

Park administration

The administration of Chile's protected areas is highly centralized with all important decisions coming from **Conaf's head office** in Santiago. This is a good place to visit before heading out of the capital (for the address, see p.83), as you can pick up brochures and basic maps of all the parks and buy several publications on native flora and fauna. In addition, each regional capital has a Conaf headquarters, which is useful for more practical pre-visit information, such as road conditions and hiking possibilities. The parks and reserves are staffed by Conaf **guardaparques** (park wardens), who live in rustic ranger stations (called *guarderías*); they're easily identifiable by their green uniforms and green peaked caps bearing the Conaf symbol. Chilean *guardaparques* are almost always friendly, enthusiastic and dedicated to their job, despite working extremely long hours under difficult conditions for little pay. They're often out of their stations all day, patrolling the park for poachers or other hazards or monitoring the various programmes set up to recuperate declining wildlife populations or flora with conservation problems. Most parks are divided into several areas, known as "sectors" (*sectores*), and the larger ones have a small *guardería* in each sector.

Visiting the parks

No permit is needed to visit any of Chile's national parks; you simply turn up and pay your **entrance fee**, which is usually between CH$1000 and CH$3500, though some parks are free. Ease of **access** differs wildly from one park to the next – a few have paved highways running through them, while others are served by appalling dirt tracks that are only passable for a few months of the year. Typically, though, parks are reached by rough, bumpy dirt roads. Getting to them often involves renting a vehicle or booking transport through a local tour company, as around two-thirds of Chile's national parks can't be reached by public transport.

Arriving at the park boundary, you'll normally pass a small hut (called the Conaf control) where you pay your entrance fee and pick up a basic map (usually photocopied and of poor quality). Some of the larger parks have more than one entrance point, served by different access roads. The main ranger station is always separate from the hut, sometimes just a few hundred metres away, and at times several kilometres. The station contains the rangers' living quarters and administrative office, and often a large map or scale model of the park, marking all the trails. The more popular parks also have a **Centro de Información Ambiental** attached to the station, with displays on the park's flora and fauna and, in high season, slide shows and talks (*charlas*). A few parks now have **camping** areas. These are often rustic sites with basic facilities, run by Conaf, which charges around CH$5000–10,000 per tent. In other parks, particularly in the south, Conaf gives licences to concessionaires, who operate campsites and *cabañas*, which tend to be very expensive. Some of the more remote national parks, especially in the north, have small **refugios** attached to the ranger

MAJOR PARKS & RESERVES

stations – these are usually rustic, stone-built huts (from CH$5000 per person) containing around eight to ten bunk beds, hot showers and gas stoves. Some of these are in stunning locations, such as the *refugios* overlooking the Salar de Surire, and the ones with views across Lago Chungará to Volcán Parinacota, though sadly the *refugios* are increasingly unreliable (closed, overbooked or dirty).

Shopping

While the handicrafts (*artesanía*) produced in Chile are nowhere near as diverse or colourful as in neighbouring Peru or Bolivia, you can still find a range of beautiful souvenirs that vary from region to region, usually sold in *ferias artesanales* (crafts markets) on or near the central squares of the main towns. As for day-to-day essentials, you'll be able to locate just about everything you need, from sun block to contact lens solution, in the main towns up and down the country.

Artesanía and other souvenirs

The finest and arguably most beautiful goods you can buy in Chile are the items – mainly jewellery – made of **lapis lazuli**, the deep-blue semi-precious stone found only in Chile and Afghanistan. The best place to buy these is in the Bellavista area of Santiago: note that the deeper the colour of the stone, the better its quality. Though certainly less expensive than lapis exports sold abroad, they're still pricey. A reasonable-quality choker, for instance, can cost anything from CH$30,000 (US$55).

Most *artesanía* is considerably less expensive. In the **Norte Grande**, the most common articles are hand-knitted alpaca sweaters, gloves and scarves, which you'll find in altiplano villages like Parinacota, or down in Arica and Iquique. The quality is usually fairly low, but they're inexpensive and very attractive all the same. In the **Norte Chico**, you can pick up some beautiful leather goods, particularly in the crafts markets of La Serena. You might also be tempted to buy a bottle of pisco there, so that you can recreate that pisco sour experience back home – though you're

probably better off getting it at a super-market in Santiago before you leave, to save yourself carting it about. The **Central Valley**, as the agricultural heartland of Chile, is famous for its *huaso* gear, and you'll find brightly coloured ponchos and stiff straw hats in the numerous working *huaso* shops. The highlight in the **Lake District** is the traditional Mapuche silver jewellery, while the **far south** is a good place to buy chunky, colourful knitwear.

A range of these goods can also be bought in the major crafts markets in **Santiago**, notably Los Dominicos market. Also worth checking out are Santiago's little **flea markets** (see p.115), where you can pick up wonderful objects like old South American stirrups and spurs, pre-War of the Pacific maps and English bric-à-brac left over from the nitrate era.

Hard **haggling** is neither commonly practiced nor expected in Chile, though a bit of bargaining is in order at many markets, particularly when buying *artesanía*. It's also worth trying to bargain down the price of hotel rooms (of whatever category), especially outside the peak months of January and February.

Living and/or working in Chile

There are plenty of short-term work opportunities for foreigners wanting to stay-on a while in Chile; the difficultly lies in obtaining and maintaining a work visa. You can only apply for a work permit once you have a firm job offer, and so many arrive on a tourist visa and later apply for the permit once they've found work.

If you're pre-planning a longer stay, consult the websites of the **Overseas Jobs Express** (Ⓦwww.overseasjobs.org; free membership to international jobseekers) and the **International Career and Employment Center** (Ⓦwww.internationaljobs.org; US$26 for six weekly publications, half-price for students, recent graduates and volunteers). Both are good resources listing a wide range of internships, jobs and volunteer opportunities in different parts of the world.

Many students come to Chile taking advantage of semester or **year-abroad programmes** offered by their universities. The majority study in Santiago where there's a large exchange student community. Go to Ⓦwww.studyabroad.com for links and listings to study programmes worldwide.

Teaching English

Demand for native-speaking English teachers in Chilean cities is high and makes **language teaching** an obvious work option. Though it can be competitive, it's relatively easy to find work either teaching general English in private language schools or business English within companies. A lucky few get by with minimal teaching experience, but with an **EFL** (English Language Teaching)/**TEFL** (Teaching English as a Foreign Language) qualification you're in a far better position to get a job with a reputable employer. **CELTA** (Certificate in English Language Teaching to Adults) courses are among the best and you can qualify before you leave home or even while you're abroad. The standard rate for teaching in Chile (with the appropriate quali-fication) is between US$8–12 per hour, though with experience you can expect a bit more. The most lucrative work is private, one-to-one lessons which are best sought

through word-of-mouth or by putting an ad. The British Council website (Ⓦwww .britishcouncil.org/work/jobs.htm) has a current list of teaching vacancies.

Volunteering

Opportunities for work need not be limited to language teaching. You can easily become a **volunteer** in Chile, but you'll often have to pay for the privilege. Many organizations target people on gap-years (at whatever stage in their lives) and offer placements on both inner city and environ-mental projects. For low- or no-cost volunteer jobs have a look at Steve McElhinney's excellent website Ⓦwww .volunteersouthamerica.net.

Study and work programmes

From the US and Canada

AFS Intercultural Programs US ☎1-800/AFS-INFO, Canada ☎1-800/361-7248, UK ☎0113/242 6136, Australia ☎1300/131 736, NZ ☎0800/600 300, SA ☎11/447 2673, international enquiries ☎1-212/807-8686, Ⓦwww.afs.org. Intercultural exchange organization with programmes in over 50 countries.

Amerispan US ☎1-800/879-6640, Ⓦwww .amerispan.com. Highly rated educational travel company that specializes in language courses but also runs volunteer programmes all over Latin America.

Council on International Educational Exchange (CIEE) US ☎1-800/40-STUDY or 1-207/553-4299, Ⓦwww.ciee.org. Leading NGO offering study programmes and volunteer projects around the world.

Earthwatch Institute US & Canada ☎1-800/776-0188, UK ☎01865/318 838, Australia ☎03/9682 6828; Ⓦwww.earthwatch.org. Scientific expedition project that spans over 50 countries with environmental and archeological ventures worldwide.

From the UK and Ireland

British Council ☎020/7930 8466, ⓦwww
.britishcouncil.org. Produces a free leaflet which
details study opportunities abroad. The website has
a list of current job vacancies for recruiting TEFL
teachers for posts worldwide. It also publishes a book,
Year Between, aimed principally at gap-year students
detailing volunteer programmes, and schemes abroad.

Rainforest Concern UK ☎020/7229 2093,
ⓦwww.rainforestconcern.org. Volunteering
opportunities protecting threatened habitats in South
and Central America. The Chilean project is based in
the Nasampulli Reserve in the south of the country.
Raleigh International UK ☎020/7183 1270,
ⓦwww.raleigh.org.uk. Volunteer projects for
young travellers.

Travel Essentials

Costs

Chile is an expensive country compared to
most of South America. Accommodation
prices are usually around US$15 per night
for a bottom-end double room, US$40 for a
mid-range double with private bath, and
anything from US$70 and up per room in a
smart, attractive hotel. Eating out can be
pricey in the evening, especially in big cities
and more sophisticated restaurants, but a
typical beef steak and French fries plus
mineral water in an ordinary local restaurant
still only costs around US$7. You can save
money by having the set lunch menus
offered in most restaurants, usually at very
reasonable prices, though this can get rather
repetitive after a while.

Thankfully transport is still relatively
inexpensive, with long-distance buses
offering particularly good value – for instance,
the 2000-kilometre-journey from Santiago to
Arica costs around US$45. In general, then,
you'll need to allow at least US$200 a week
to get by on a tight budget; at least US$350
a week to live a little more comfortably,
staying in mid-range hotels and eating in
restaurants most days; and from US$700 a
week to live in luxury, staying in the more
upmarket hotels and eating in the best
restaurants.

The most widespread hidden cost in Chile
is the **IVA** (Impuesto al Valor Agregado), a
tax of eighteen percent added to most
goods and services. Although most prices
include IVA, there are many irritating exceptions – some tourist shops, for instance,
quote prices without IVA, and even some

restaurants have a discreet "prices do not
include IVA" at the bottom of their menu.
Hotel rates sometimes include IVA and
sometimes don't; as a tourist, you're
supposed to be exempt from IVA if you pay
for your accommodation in US dollars. Car
rental is almost always quoted without IVA,
which really jacks the end price up. If in
doubt, you should always clarify whether a
price quoted to you, from souvenirs to room
rates, includes IVA.

Once obtained, various official and quasi-
official **youth/student ID cards** soon pay for
themselves in savings. Full-time students are
eligible for the International Student ID Card
(ISIC), ⓦwww.isiccard.com). You only have
to be 26 or younger to qualify for the International Youth Travel Card.

Crime and personal safety

Chile is one of the safest South American
countries to travel in, and violent crime
against tourists is rare. The kind of sophisticated tactics used by thieves in neighbouring
Peru and Bolivia are extremely uncommon in
Chile, and the fact that you can walk around
without being gripped by paranoia is one of
the country's major bonuses.

Tipping

It's customary to leave a ten percent
tip in restaurants – service is rarely
included in the bill. You are not,
however, expected to tip taxi drivers.

That's not to say, of course, that you don't need to be careful. On the contrary, opportunistic pickpocketing and petty thieving is rife in Santiago and major cities such as Valparaíso, Arica and Puerto Montt, and you should take all the normal precautions to safeguard your money and valuables, paying special attention in bus terminals and markets – wear a money belt, and keep it tucked inside the waistband of your trousers or skirt, out of sight, and don't wear flashy jewellery, flaunt expensive cameras or carry a handbag. It's also a good idea to keep photocopies of your passport, tourist card, driving licence, air tickets and credit card details separate from the originals – whether it's safer to carry the originals with you or leave them in your hotel is debatable, but whatever you do, you should always have some form of ID on you, even if this is just a photocopy of your passport.

Chile's police force, the **carabineros**, has the whole country covered, with stations in even the most remote areas, particularly in border regions. If you're robbed and need a police report for an insurance claim, you should go to the nearest *retén* (police station), where details of the theft will be entered in a logbook. You'll be issued a slip of paper with the record number of the entry, but in most cases a full report won't be typed out until your insurance company requests it.

Emergency telephone numbers

Air rescue 138 (for mountaineering accidents)
Ambulance 131
Carabineros 133
Coast Guard 137
Fire 132
Investigaciones 134 (for serious crimes)

Electricity

220V/50Hz is the standard throughout Chile. The sockets are two-pronged, with round pins (as opposed to the flat pins common in neighbouring countries).

Entry requirements

Most foreign visitors to Chile do not need a visa. The exceptions are citizens of countries including Cuba, Russia, all Middle Eastern countries, except Israel, and all African counties, except for South Africa. But check with your local Chilean consulate. If you do

need one, you'll have to submit an application to your consulate, along with your passport and a full written itinerary. Remember that you will need a multiple entry visa if you plan to leave Chilean territory and re-enter it.

Visitors of all nationalities are issued with a **tourist entry card** (Tarjeta de Turismo) on arrival in Chile, which is valid for ninety days, and can be extended once for an additional ninety days. It will be checked by the International Police at the airport or border post when you leave Chile – if it's expired you won't be allowed to leave the country until you've paid the appropriate fine at the nearest *Intendencia* (up to US$100, depending on the number of days past the expiry date). If this happens when you're trying to fly out of the international airport in Santiago, you'll have to go back downtown to Moneda 1342 (Mon–Fri 9am–1pm; ☎2/672 5320).

If at any time during your stay in Chile you lose your tourist card, you should ask for a duplicate immediately, either from the Fronteras department of the Policía Internacional, General Borgoño 1052, Santiago (☎2/698 2211) or from the Extranjero's department of the Intendencia in any provincial capital (addresses are listed below). There's no charge for replacing lost or stolen cards.

If you want to **extend** your tourist card, you've got two choices. You can either pay US$100 at the Intendencia of Santiago or any provincial capital, or you can simply leave the country and re-enter, getting a brand-new ninety-day Tarjeta de Turismo for free. The latter option is usually far cheaper and certainly more interesting – from Santiago, for instance, you could take the very scenic seven-hour bus ride to Mendoza in Argentina – and there are many other opportunities for border crossing up and down Chile.

Note that your tourist card does not allow you to undertake any **paid employment** in Chile – for this, you need to get a work visa before you enter the country, which can either be arranged by your employer in Chile or by yourself on presentation (to your embassy or consulate) of an employment contract authorized by a Chilean public notary. You can't swap a tourist card for a work visa while you're in Chile, which means that legally you can't just go out and find a job – though

Arrival tax

Chile levies an **arrival tax** for **US, Canadian, Australian and Mexican** citizens in reciprocation of similar taxes levied on Chilean citizens arriving in these countries. This means you must pay **US$100, US$55, US$34 or US$15 respectively** upon arrival at Santiago or Easter Island airports (check with a Chilean consulate for the latest amount). However, the payment is valid for the lifetime of the passport and is not levied upon crossing land borders.

many language schools are happy to ignore the rules when employing language teachers. Other points to note are that **under-18s** travelling to Chile without parents need written parental consent authorized by the Chilean Embassy, and that minors travelling to Chile with just one parent need the written, authorized consent of the absent parent.

Chilean embassies and consulates abroad

Australia

Embassy 10 Culgoa Circuit, O'Malley, Canberra ACT 2606 ℡ 02/6286 2098, Ⓔ chileau @embachile-australia.com, Ⓦ www .embachile-australia.com.
Consulate Level 18, National Mutual Building, 44 Market St, Sydney 2000 ℡ 02/9299 2533, Ⓔ cgsydney@optusnet.com.au.

Canada

Embassy 50 O'Connor St, suite 1413, Ottawa, ON K1P 6L2 ℡ 613/235-4402, Ⓔ echileau@chile.ca, Ⓦ www.chile.ca.
Consulates 2 Bloor St W, #1801, Toronto, ON M4W 3E2 ℡ 416/924-0106; 1010 Sherbrooke St W #710, Montréal, PQ H3A 2R7 ℡ 514/499-0405; 1185 W Georgia St, #1250, Vancouver, BC V6E 4E6 ℡ 604/681-9162.

New Zealand

Embassy 19 Bolton St, Wellington ℡ 04/471 6270, Ⓔ echile@embchile.co.nz, Ⓦ www.embchile.co.nz.
Consulates 51 Grotto St, Onehunga, Auckland ℡ 09/622 4610, Ⓔ pbex@ihug.co.nz. PO Box 359, Christchurch ℡ 03/366 5096, Ⓔ petert@cecc.org.nz.

South Africa

Embassy 169 Garsfontein Rd Ashlea, Delmondo Office Park Block C, Gardens, Pretoria ℡ 012/460 1676, Ⓔ chile@iafrica.com
Consulates 1st floor Westquay Building, Westquay Rd, Waterfront, Cape Town ℡ 021/421 2344,

Ⓔ chilecpt@cybersmart.co.za; 67 Venice Rd, Durban ℡ 031/312 8608, Ⓔ timhammond@pixie .co.za

UK

Embassy and Consulate 12 Devonshire St, London W1N 2DS ℡ 020/7580 1023, Ⓔ embachile@embachile.co.uk, Ⓦ www.chile .embassyhomepage.com.

US

Embassy 1732 Massachusetts Ave NW, Washington, DC 20036 ℡ 202/785-1746, Ⓔ politico @embassyofchile.org, Ⓦ www.chile-usa.org.
Consulates 1732 Massachusetts Ave, Washington, DC 20036 ℡ 202/530-4104; Public Ledger Building, Suite 1030, Chestnut & Sixth sts, Philadelphia, PA 19106 ℡ 215/829-9520; 1300 Post Oak Blvd, Suite 1130, Houston, TX 77056 ℡ 713/621-5853; 875 N Michigan Ave, Suite 3352, Chicago, IL 60611 ℡ 312/654-8780; 800 Brickell Ave Suite, Miami, FL 33131 ℡ 305/373-8623; 866 United Nations Plaza Suite 601, New York, NY 10017 ℡ 212/980-3366; 870 Market St #1058, San Francisco, CA 94102 ℡ 415/982-7662.

Gay and lesbian travellers

Although Chile has progressed a long way in terms of attitudes to sexual and gender issues since the return to democracy, society remains extremely **conservative**, and homosexuality is still a taboo subject for many Chileans.

Outside Santiago – with the minor exceptions of some northern cities such as La Serena and Antofagasta – there are no gay venues, and it is advisable for same-sex couples to do as the locals do and remain discreet, especially in public. Machismo is deeply ingrained and mostly unchallenged by women, despite a growing feminist movement. That said, gay-bashing and other homophobic acts are rare and the government has passed anti-discrimination legislation. It has also been considering legalizing civil unions (without full marriage status or adoption rights) for homosexuals.

Health

Chile is a fairly risk-free country to travel in as far as health problems are concerned. No inoculations are required, though you might want to consider a hepatitis-A jab, as a precaution. Check, too, that your tetanus boosters are up-to-date. Most travellers experience the occasional stomach upset while adjusting to unfamiliar micro-organisms in the food and water, however. Sunstroke is also quite common, especially at high altitudes.

Chile is well endowed with **pharmacies** (*farmacias*) – in Santiago and other major cities, you'll find one on just about every street corner, and even smaller towns usually offer at least a handful to choose from. If you need to see a **doctor**, your best bet is to make an appointment at the outpatient department of the nearest hospital, usually known as a *clínica*. The majority of *clínicas* are private, and expensive, so it's essential to ensure that your **travel insurance** provides good medical cover.

Rabies, though only a remote risk, does exist in Chile. If you get bitten or scratched by a dog, you should seek medical attention *immediately*. The disease can be cured, but only through a series of stomach injections administered before the onset of symptoms, which can appear within 24 hours or lie dormant for months, and include irrational behaviour, fear of water and foaming at the mouth. There is a vaccine, but it's expensive and doesn't prevent you from contracting rabies, though it does buy you time to get to hospital.

Note that Chile's **shellfish** should be treated with the utmost caution. Every year, a handful of people die in Chile because they inadvertently eat bivalve shellfish contaminated by red tide, or *marea roja*, algae which becomes toxic when the seawater temperature rises. The Chilean government monitors the presence of *marea roja* with extreme diligence and bans all commercial shellfish collection when the phenomenon occurs. There is little health risk when eating in restaurants or buying shellfish in markets, as these are regularly inspected by the health authorities, but it's extremely dangerous to collect shellfish for your own consumption unless you're absolutely certain that the area is free of red tide. Note that red tide affects all shellfish, cooked or uncooked.

Anyone travelling in Chile's northern altiplano, where altitudes commonly reach 4500m – or indeed anyone going higher than 3000m in the cordillera – needs to be aware of the risks of **altitude sickness**, locally known as *soroche* or *apunamiento*. This debilitating and sometimes dangerous condition is caused by the reduced atmospheric pressure and corresponding reduction in oxygen that occurs around 3000m above sea level. **Basic symptoms** include breathlessness, headaches, nausea and extreme tiredness, rather like a bad hangover. There's no way of predicting whether or not you'll be susceptible to the condition, which seems to strike quite randomly, affecting people differently from one ascent to another. You can, however, take steps to avoid it by ascending slowly and allowing yourself to acclimatize. In particular, don't be tempted to whizz straight up to the altiplano from sea level, but spend a night or two acclimatizing en route. You should also avoid alcohol and salt, and drink lots of water. The bitter-tasting coca leaves chewed by most locals in the altiplano (where they're widely available at markets and village stores), can help ease headaches and the sense of exhaustion.

Although extremely unpleasant, this basic form of altitude sickness is essentially harmless and passes after about 24 hours (if it doesn't, descend at least 500m). However, in its more serious forms, altitude sickness can be dangerous and even life-threatening. One to two percent of people travelling to 4000m develop HAPO (high-altitude pulmonary oedema), caused by the build-up of liquid in the lungs. Symptoms include fever, an increased pulse rate, and coughing up white fluid; sufferers should descend immediately, whereupon recovery is usually quick and complete. Rarer, but more serious, is HACO (high-altitude cerebral oedema), which occurs when the brain gets waterlogged with fluid. Symptoms include loss of balance, severe lassitude, weakness or numbness on one side of the body and a confused mental state. If you or a fellow traveller display any of these symptoms, descend immediately and get to a doctor; HACO can be fatal within 24 hours.

In many parts of Chile, **sunburn** and **dehydration** are threats. They are obviously more of a problem in the excessively dry climate of the north, but even in the south of the country, it's easy to underestimate the strength of the summer sun. To prevent sunburn, take a **high-factor sunscreen** and wear a wide-brimmed hat. It's also essential to drink plenty of fluids before you go out, and always carry large quantities of water with you when you're hiking in the sun. As you lose a lot of salt when you sweat, add more to your food, or take a rehydration solution.

Another potential enemy, especially at high altitudes and in Chile's far southern reaches, is **hypothermia**. Because early symptoms can include an almost euphoric sense of sleepiness and disorientation, your body's core temperature can plummet to danger level before you know what has happened. Chile's northern deserts have such clear air that it can drop to -20°C (-4°F) at night, which makes you very vulnerable to hypothermia while sleeping if proper precautions aren't taken. If you get hypothermia, the best thing to do is take your clothes off and jump into a sleeping bag with someone else – sharing another person's body heat is the most effective way of restoring your own. If you're alone, or have no willing partners, then get out of the wind and the rain, remove all wet or damp clothes, get dry, and drink plenty of hot fluids.

Medical resources for travellers

US and Canada

CDC ☎1-800/311-3435, ⊛www.cdc.gov/travel. Official US government travel health site.
International Society for Travel Medicine ☎1-770/736-7060, ⊛www.istm.org. Has a full list of travel health clinics.
Canadian Society for International Health ☎613/241-5785, ⊛www.csih.org. Extensive list of travel health centres.

UK and Ireland

Hospital for Tropical Diseases Travel Clinic ☎0845/155 5000 or 020/7387 4411, ⊛www.thehtd.org.

MASTA (Medical Advisory Service for Travellers Abroad) ☎0870/606 2782 or ⊛www.masta-travel-health.com for the nearest clinic.
Travel Medicine Services ☎028/9031 5220.
Tropical Medical Bureau Republic of Ireland ☎1850/487 674, ⊛www.tmb.ie.

Australia, New Zealand and South Africa

Traveller's Medical and Vaccination Centre ☎1300/658 844, ⊛www.tmvc.com.au. Lists travel clinics in Australia, New Zealand and South·Africa.

Insurance

You'd do well to take out an insurance policy before travelling to cover against theft, loss and illness or injury. Before paying for a new policy, however, it's worth checking whether you are already covered: some all-risks home insurance policies may cover your possessions when overseas, and many private medical schemes include cover when abroad. After checking out the possibilities above, you might want to contact a **specialist travel insurance company**, or consider the travel insurance deal we offer (see box). A typical travel insurance policy usually provides cover for the loss of baggage, tickets and – up to a certain limit – cash or cheques, as well as cancellation or curtailment of your journey. Most exclude so-called dangerous sports unless an extra premium is paid: in Chile this can mean scuba-diving, white-water rafting, windsurfing and trekking, though probably not kayaking or jeep safaris. If you take medical coverage, ascertain whether benefits will be paid as treatment proceeds or only after you return home, and if there is a 24-hour medical emergency number. When securing baggage cover, make sure that the per-article limit will cover your most valuable possession. If you need to make a claim, you should keep receipts for medicines and medical treatment, and in the event you have anything stolen, you must obtain an official statement from the police.

Internet

Chile is one of the most wired Latin American nations, surpassed perhaps only by Argentina. Cybercafés are everywhere, though many are haunts for adolescents playing nasty games. Broadband (*banda ancha*) access is quite common in cities, much less so in more remote places. Internet access typically costs about CH\$250 for 15 minutes, and connection is now pretty fast even in the more remote parts of the country; if it's not, demand your money back and try somewhere else.

Travelling with children

Families are highly regarded in Latin American societies, and Chile is no exception. Travelling children are popular and they and their parents can expect special treatment and friendly attention.

Chile's **restaurants** are well used to catering for children and will happily provide smaller portions for younger mouths. In hotels, you should try to negotiate cheaper rates. The main health hazards to watch out for are the heat and sun. Very high factor suncream can be difficult to come by in remote towns so it is best to stock up on **sunblock** at pharmacies in the bigger cities. Always remember that the sun in Chile is fierce, so hats and bonnets are essential; this is especially true in the south where the ozone layer is particularly thin. **High altitudes** may cause children problems and, like adults, they must acclimatize before walking too strenuously above 2000m. If you intend to travel with babies and very young children to high altitudes, consult your doctor for advice before you leave.

Long-distances buses charge for each seat so you'll only pay less if a child is sat on your knee. On **city buses** however, small children often travel for free but will be expected to give up their seat for paying customers without one. Airline companies generally charge a third less for passengers under 12 so look out for last-minute **discount flights** – they can make flying an affordable alternative to an arduous bus ride.

As for **attractions**, there are a number of activities in parts of the country that children will love. Santiago has a few interactive museums specifically aimed towards children. The best is the *Museo Interactivo Mirador*, Punta Arenas 6711 (Mon 9.30am–1.30pm, Tues–Sun 9.30am–6.30pm; ☎2/280/7800, Ⓦwww.mim.cl) with numerous exhibits relating to Chile's history as well as art and craft workshops, music rooms and funny mirrors. Chile's **ski resorts**, in particular Portillo, are very family-orientated. Special

deals often allow children to ski free for a week and also provide off-piste activities to entertain younger visitors during their stay.

Mail

The Chilean **postal service** is very reliable for international mailings, but can be surprisingly erratic for domestic mailings. A letter from Santiago takes about five days to reach Europe, a little less time to reach North America and usually no more than a couple of weeks to more remote destinations. Allow a few extra days for letters mailed from other towns and cities in Chile. Do not send any gifts to Chile using regular post; theft is extremely common for incoming shipments. For important shipping to Chile try express services such as Fed Ex and DHL.

Post offices are marked by a blue Correos sign, and are usually on or near the Plaza de Armas of any town; postboxes are blue, and bear the blue Correos symbol.

Maps

No two **road maps** of Chile are identical, and none is absolutely correct. The bulk of errors lie in the representation of dirt roads: some maps mark them incorrectly as tarred roads, some leave out a random selection of dirt roads altogether, and some mark them quite clearly where nothing exists at all.

You'll find a number of reliable country maps, including the **Rough Guides'** detailed, waterproof Chile map. The comprehensive **TurisTel** map is printed in the back of its guides to Chile and also published in a separate booklet. Sernatur produces a good fold-out map of the whole of Chile, called the Gran Mapa Caminero de Chile, on sale at the main office in Santiago, and an excellent map of the north, called the Mapa Rutero Turístico Macroregión Norte, free from Sernatur offices in Santiago and the north (ask, as they're rarely on display). Other useful maps include **Auto Mapa's** Rutas de Chile series, distributed internationally. Outside of Chile, also look for the **Reise Know-How Verlag** and **Nelles Verlag** maps of Chile, which combine clear road detail along with contours and colour tinting.

You can pick up free and usually adequate street plans in the tourist office of most cities, but better by far are those contained in the Turistel guidebooks, with a map for practically every town and village you're likely to want to visit. Bookshops and kiosks sell street-indexed maps of Santiago, but the most comprehensive A–Z of Santiago appears in the back of the CTC phone directory.

The best ones to use for **hiking** are the new series of **JLM** maps (©jmattassi @interactiva.cl), which cover some of the main national parks and occasionally extend into neighbouring Argentina. They're produced in collaboration with Conaf and are available in bookshops and some souvenir or outdoor stores.

Money

The basic unit of currency is the peso, usually represented by the $ sign (and by CH$ in this book, for clarity). Many hotels, particularly the more expensive ones, accept US dollars cash (and will give you a discount for paying this way; see p.40). Apart from this, you'll be expected to pay for everything in local currency. You may, however, come across prices quoted in the mysterious "UF". This stands for *unidad de fomento* and is an index-linked monetary unit that is adjusted (every minute) on a daily basis to remain in line with inflation. The only time you're likely to come across it is if you rent a vehicle (your liability, in the event of an accident, will probably be quoted in UFs on the rental contract). You'll find the exchange rate of the UF against the Chilean peso in the daily newspapers, along with the rates for all the other currencies.

You should have a back-up source of funds, preferably **traveller's cheques**. These should always be in US dollars, and though most brands are accepted, it's best to be on the safe side and take one of the main brands such as American Express, Citibank or Thomas Cook. You will have to change them in a **casa de cambio** (exchange bureau), usually for a small commission. Keep the purchase agreement and a record of cheque serial numbers safe and separate from the cheques themselves. If they're lost or stolen, the issuing company will expect you to report the loss forthwith to their office; most companies claim to replace lost or stolen cheques within 24 hours.

Credit and debit cards can be used either in **ATM**s or over the counter. MasterCard, Visa and American Express are accepted just about everywhere, but other cards may not be recognized. Make sure you have a personal identification number (PIN) that's designed to work overseas. A compromise between traveller's cheques and plastic is **Visa Travel-Money,** a disposable pre-paid debit card with a PIN that works in all ATMs that take Visa cards. For more information, check the Visa TravelMoney website at ⓦhttp://international .visa.com/ps/products/vtravelmoney/

Opening hours and holidays

Most **shops and services** are open Monday through Friday from 9am to 1pm and 3pm to 6 or 7pm, and on Saturday from 10 or 11am until 2pm. Supermarkets stay open at lunchtime and may close as late as 11pm on weekdays and Saturdays in big cities. Large shopping malls are often open all day on Sundays. **Banks** have more limited hours, generally Monday through Friday from 9am to 2pm, but *casas de cambio* tend to use the same opening hours as shops.

Museums are nearly always shut on Mondays, and are often free on Sundays. Many tourist offices only open Monday through Friday throughout the year, with a break for lunch, but in summer (usually between Dec 15 and March 15) some increase their weekday hours and open on Saturday and sometimes Sunday; note that their hours are subject to frequent change. Post offices don't close at lunchtime on weekdays and are open on Saturdays from 9am to 1pm.

February is the main holiday month in Chile, when there's an exodus from the big cities to the beaches or the Lake District, leaving some shops and restaurants closed. February is also an easy time to get around in Santiago, as the city appears half-abandoned.

Phones

Using **phonecards** is a very practical way to phone abroad, and it's worth stocking up on them in major cities, as you can't always buy them in small towns and villages. Alternatively there are dozens of call centres or **centros de llamadas** in most cities, and some of them

Major holidays

January 1 New Year's Day (Año nuevo)

Easter with national holidays on Good Friday, Easter Saturday and Easter Sunday are the climax to Holy Week (Semana Santa)

May 1 Labour Day (Día del Trabajo)

May 21 Combate Naval de Iquique. A Remembrance Day celebrating the end of the War of the Pacific after the naval victory at Iquique

June 15 Corpus Christi

June, last Monday San Pedro and San Pablo

August 15 Assumption of the Virgin

September 18 National Independence Day (Fiestas Patrias), in celebration of the first provisional government of 1810

September 19 Armed Forces Day (Día del Ejército)

October 12 Columbus Day (Día de la Raza), marking the discovery of America

November 1 All Saints' Day (Todos los Santos)

December 8 Immaculate Conception

December 25 Christmas Day (Navidad)

---

offer cheap rates. Another convenient option is to take along an **international calling card**. Generally billed to your home phone account or credit card, these are very handy and easy to use, but are usually two or three times more expensive than buying a Chilean phonecard or using a *centro de llamadas*. This service is offered in the US and Canada with AT&T, MCI, Sprint, Canada Direct and other North American long-distance companies; in the UK and Ireland, with British Telecom (☎0800/345144, ⓦwww.chargecard.bt.com), AT&T and NTL (☎0500/100 505); in Australia, Telstra Telecard or Optus Calling Card; and in New Zealand, Telecom NZ's Calling Card.

If you want to use your **cell phone** in Chile, you'll need to ask your service provider whether it will work abroad, and the rate per minute. If your phone provider at home offers Chile coverage, you may get charged extra for this depending on your existing package. For many reasons, the use of a foreign cell in Chile is often unreliable. You are also likely to be charged exorbitantly for incoming calls when abroad (these calls are free when you have a cell phone from Chile).

If you truly need a cell phone and are visiting Chile for more than three weeks – buy one. You can usually buy mobile phones that use prepaid phonecards for as little as US$50. Avoid buying one at airports where they cost significantly more. Minutes can then be bought as necessary. The main operators are Movistar, Entel and Claro and you'll find several branches of each in the larger cities.

Time

From the end of October to late March, Chile observes Daylight Saving Time and is three hours behind GMT (Greenwich Mean Time). The country is four hours behind GMT the rest of the year.

Tourist information

Chile's government-run tourist board is called **Sernatur** (short for Servicio Nacional de Turismo). There's a large and very helpful office in Santiago (see p.83), plus branches in every provincial capital in Chile. They produce a huge amount of material, including themed booklets on camping, skiing, national parks, beaches, thermal springs and so on; for some reason these are often kept out of sight, so you'll have to specifically ask to see everything they've got. In smaller towns you're more likely to find a municipal **Oficina de Turismo**, sometimes attached to the Municipalidad (town hall) and usually with a very limited supply of printed information to hand out. If there's no separate tourist office it's worth trying the Municipalidad itself – they sometimes stock a few maps and leaflets, and at the very least can deliver over-the-counter advice.

Calling home from abroad

Note that the initial zero is omitted from the city code when dialling numbers in the UK, Ireland, Australia and New Zealand from abroad.

US and Canada international access code + 1 + area code.

Australia international access code + 61 + city code.

New Zealand international access code + 64 + city code.

UK international access code + 44 + city code.

Republic of Ireland international access code + 353 + city code.

South Africa international access code + 27 + city code.

Another source of information is the excellent series of TurisTel guidebooks, published annually by the Chilean phone company CTC, and available at numerous pavement kiosks in Santiago, and CTC offices in Chilean cities. They come in three volumes, covering the north, the centre and the south, and give extremely detailed information on even the tiniest of places, with comprehensive street plans and road maps. The English translation, available at many kiosks, suffers from infrequent updating.

Tourist offices and government sites

Australian Department of Foreign Affairs ⓦwww .dfat.gov.au, ⓦwww.smartraveller.gov.au.

British Foreign & Commonwealth Office ⓦwww .fco.gov.uk/en.

Canadian Department of Foreign Affairs ⓦwww .dfait-maeci.gc.ca.

Irish Department of Foreign Affairs ⓦwww .foreignaffairs.gov.ie.

New Zealand Ministry of Foreign Affairs ⓦwww .mft.govt.nz.

US State Department ⓦwww.travel.state.gov.

Other useful websites

Chilean Patagonia ⓦwww.chileaustral.com. Easy-to-use site dedicated to tourism in Chilean Patagonia, including city guides, national parks, hotels, weather forecasts and lots more.

El Mercurio ⓦwww.emol.com. The long-established, rather conservative daily newspaper, online in Spanish.

Chip Travel ⓦwww.chiptravel.cl. First-rate site (partly funded by the government) with a vast range of useful information, from bus timetables to nightlife listings. Make this your first stop.

Chile Hotels ⓦwww.chile-hotels.com. A long list of Chilean hotels, with online booking facilities, plus brief descriptions of the towns and cities.

LAN ⓦwww.lan.com. Check out timetables and fares on the Lan national flight network.

South American Explorers ⓦwww.saexplorers .org. Excellent site belonging to the long-established non-profit organization providing services for scientists, explorers and travellers in South America. Offers travel advisories and warnings, trip reports, a bulletin board and sensibly indexed links with other sites.

Turismo Chile ⓦwww.turismochile.cl. Descriptions of the major attractions in each region, with some historical and cultural background.

Travellers with disabilities

Chile makes very few provisions for people with disabilities, and travellers with mobility problems will have to contend with a lack of lifts, high curbs, dangerous potholes on pavements and worse. However, Chileans are courteous people and are likely to offer assistance when needed. Spacious, specially designed toilets are becoming more common in airports and the newer shopping malls, but restaurants and bars are progressing at a slower pace. New public buildings are legally required to provide **disabled access**, and there will usually be a full range of facilities in the more expensive hotels. It is worth employing the help of the **local tourist office** for information on the most suitable place to stay. Public transport on the other hand is far more of a challenge. Most bus companies do not have any dedicated disabled facilities so, given that reserved disabled parking is increasingly common, travelling with your **own vehicle** might be the easier option.

Guide

Guide

Santiago and around

CHAPTER 1 # Highlights

* **Plaza de Armas** Gaze at the colonial architecture surrounding Santiago's lively central plaza – or sit on a bench and just take in the hustle and bustle. See p.88

* **Museo Chileno de Arte Precolombino** This exquisite collection of artefacts from dozens of pre-Hispanic civilizations features fine tapestries, intricate ceramics and dazzling gold jewels. See p.91

* **Mercado Central** At lunchtime the city's busy marketplace is an excellent place to sample fresh fish or seafood. See p.98

* **Bellavista** The traditional bohemian quarter offers great theatres, restaurants and bars, as well as one of poet Pablo Neruda's homes, with its eclectic art collection. See p.99

* **Cerro San Cristóbal** Ride the elevator to the top of this steep hill where, on a clear day, you have great views of the snow-capped Andes towering over the city. See p.99

* **Andean skiing** Skiers and snowboarders will delight in the four world-class ski areas near Santiago; for day-trips the slopes just east of the city are great while longer stays are best spent at the world-famous Portillo resort. See p.124

▲ Plaza le Armas

Santiago and around

S et on a wide plain near the foot of the Andes, **Santiago** boasts one of the most dazzling backdrops of any capital city in the world. The views onto the towering cordillera after a rainstorm clears the air are magnificent, especially in winter, when the snow-covered peaks rise behind the city like a giant white rampart against the blue sky. Unfortunately, such vistas are few and far between, as these same mountains prevent winds from shifting the air trapped over the plain, leaving it thickly polluted with diesel fumes and dust. As a result, Santiago is frequently covered by a dense blanket of **smog** through which the Andes can be only dimly perceived – a smudged, tantalizing shadow of their real selves. The worst time for smog is between May and July.

The city itself is a great, sprawling metropolis of five million people – a third of Chile's population. It's divided into 32 autonomous *comunas*, most of them squat, flat suburbs stretching from the centre ever further out. The historic centre of Santiago, in contrast, is compact, manageable, and, while not exactly beautiful, has a pleasant, enjoyable atmosphere. Part of the appeal comes from the fact that it's so green: tall, luxuriant trees fill the main square and line the riverbank, and there are many meticulously landscaped parks. Above all, though, it's the all-pervading sense of energy that makes the place so alluring, with crowds of Santiaguinos constantly milling through narrow streets packed with shoe-shiners, fruit barrows, news kiosks and sellers of everything from coat hangers to pirated DVDs.

Architecturally, the city is a bit of a hotchpotch, thanks to a succession of earthquakes and a spate of undisciplined rebuilding in the 1960s and 1970s. Ugly office blocks and dingy *galerías* compete for space with beautifully maintained colonial buildings, while east of the centre Santiago's economic boom is reflected in the glittering new office buildings and international hotels of the *comunas* of Vitacura, Providencia and Las Condes. These different faces are part of a wider set of contrasts – between the American-style shopping malls in the barrios altos, for example, and the shabby, old-fashioned shops in the historic centre; between the modish lounge bars and the greasy *fuentes de soda*; and, in particular, between the well-heeled, sharp suited-professionals and the scores of street sellers scrambling to make a living. It's not a place of excesses, however: homelessness is minimal compared to many other cities of this size, and there's no tension in the air or threat of violence.

Most travellers stay here for just a few days before launching into far-flung trips to the north or south, but if you've time to spare you'd do well to use Santiago as a base while exploring the surrounding region. With the **Andes** so close and so accessible, you can be right in the mountains in an hour or two. In winter people go **skiing** for the day, with special buses laid on to and from the resorts; in warmer months the **Cajón del Maipo** offers fantastic trekking,

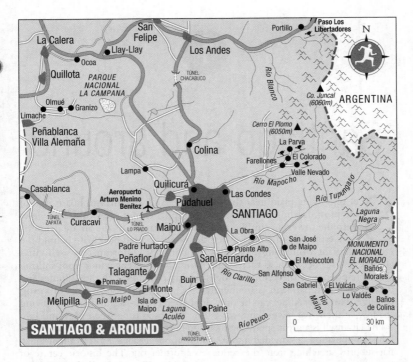

SANTIAGO & AROUND

horseback riding and white-water rafting. Heading west towards Valparaíso (see p.131) you'll also find good hiking opportunities in the arid coastal mountains of **Parque Nacional La Campana**. Nearby villages can provide a relaxing antidote to Santiago's constant din, like **Los Andes** to the north, or **Pomaire** to the west. Still more tempting are the many **vineyards** within easy reach of Santiago. There are also a number of excellent **beaches** less than two hours away by bus – for more on these, see Chapter Two.

Santiago

How much time you spend in **SANTIAGO** depends on the length of your stay in the country. It's by no means the highlight of Chile, and if time is really short a couple of days should suffice before you head off to the spectacular landscapes north or south of the city. That said, Santiago is the cultural, economic and educational hub of Chile, and the best place to come to grips with the country's identity. Dipping into Santiago's vibrant theatre and music scene, getting a sense of its history in the city's museums, and checking out its varied restaurants will really help you scratch beneath the surface and get the most out of your time in this kaleidoscopic country.

The **telephone code** for Santiago is ☏2. Telephone numbers that begin with 9 are mobile phones. When calling from a fixed line to a mobile, dial "09" plus the number. For mobile to mobile calls, begin with just "9". For more telephone information see p.70.

Some history

Some seven years after Francisco Pizarro conquered Cuzco in Peru, he dispatched **Pedro de Valdivia** southwards to claim and settle more territory for the Spanish crown. After eleven months of travelling, Valdivia and his 150 men reached what he considered to be a suitable site for a new city, and, on February 12, 1541, officially founded "Santiago de la Nueva Extremadura", wedged into a triangle of land bounded by the Río Mapocho to the north, its southern branch to the south and the rocky Santa Lucía hill to the east. A native population of **Picunche** was scattered around the region, but this didn't deter Valdivia from getting down to business: with great alacrity the main square was established and the surrounding streets were marked out with a string and ruler, a fort was built in the square (thus named "Plaza de Armas") and several other buildings were erected. Six months later they were all razed in a Picunche raid.

The town was doggedly rebuilt to the same plans, and Santiago began to take on the shape of a new colonial capital. But nine years after founding it, the Spaniards, in search of gold, shifted their attention to Arauco in the south, and Santiago became something of a backwater. Following the violent Mapuche uprising in 1553, however, the Spaniards were forced to abandon their towns south of the Bío Bío, and many returned to Santiago. Nonetheless, growth continued to be very slow: settlers were never large in number, and what opportunities the land offered were thwarted by strict trade restrictions imposed by Spain. Moreover, expansion was repeatedly knocked back by regular **earthquakes**.

Santiago started to look like a real capital during the course of the eighteenth century, as trade restrictions were eased, more wealth was created, and the population increased. However, it wasn't until after independence in 1818 that expansion really got going, as the rich clamoured to build themselves glamorous mansions and the state erected beautiful public buildings such as the Teatro Municipal and the congress building.

As the city entered the twentieth century it began to push eastwards into the new barrio alto and north into Bellavista. The horizontal spread has gone well beyond these limits since then, gobbling up outlying towns and villages at great speed; Gran Santiago now stretches 40km by 40km. Its central zones have shot up vertically, too, particularly in Providencia and Las Condes, where the showy high-rise buildings reflect the country's rapid economic growth over the past decade. Despite this dramatic transformation, however, the city's central core still sticks to the same street pattern marked out by Pedro de Valdivia in 1541, and its first public space, the Plaza de Armas, is still at the heart of its street life.

Arrival

Santiago is undoubtedly one of the easiest and least intimidating South American capitals to **arrive** in. Connections from the airport, bus terminals and train station to the centre of the city are frequent and straightforward, and while you should take normal precautions, you're unlikely to be hassled or feel threatened while you're finding your feet.

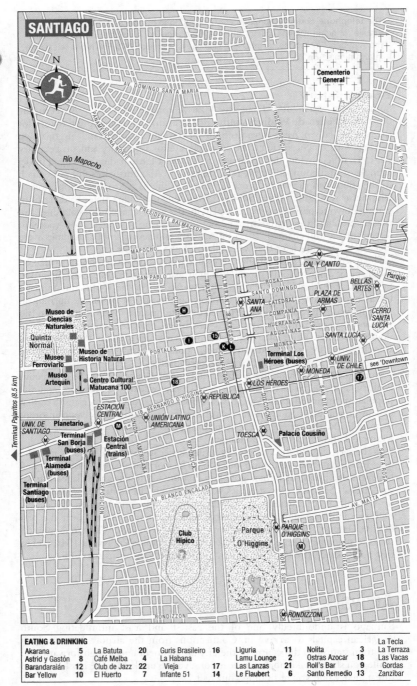

SANTIAGO

N

Cementerio General

Río Mapocho

AV. DOMINGO SANTA MARÍA

AV. FERMÍN VIVACETA

AV. INDEPENDENCIA

PANAMERICANA NORTE

AV. PRESIDENTE BALMACEDA

MAPOCHO

SAN PABLO

CAL Y CANTO

Parque

BELLAS ARTES

ROSAS

SANTO DOMINGO

PLAZA DE ARMAS

CATEDRAL

SANTA ANA

COMPAÑIA

HUÉRFANOS

AGUSTINAS

MONEDA

SANTA LUCÍA

CERRO SANTA LUCÍA

UNIV. DE CHILE

see 'Downtown'

Museo de Ciencias Naturales

Quinta Normal

Museo Ferroviario

Museo de Historia Natural

Museo Artequin

Centro Cultural Matucana 100

Terminal Los Héroes (buses)

MONEDA

MATUCANA

MAIPÚ

AV. PORTALES

BRASIL

CUMMING

ALMIRANTE BARROSO

CIENFUEGOS

BANDERA

LOS HÉROES

SAN DIEGO

LIB. BERNARDO O'HIGGINS

REPÚBLICA

ESTACIÓN CENTRAL

UNIÓN LATINO AMERICANA

TOESCA

Palacio Cousiño

UNIV. DE SANTIAGO

Planetario

Terminal San Borja (buses)

Estación Central (trains)

Terminal Alameda (buses)

Terminal Santiago (buses)

UNIÓN AMERICANA

EXPOSICIÓN

AV. BLANCO ENCALADA

Club Hípico

Parque O'Higgins

PARQUE O'HIGGINS

AV. MATTA

SANTA ROSA

SAN DIEGO

AV. NORTE SUR

RONDIZZONI

RONDIZZONI

Terminal Pajaritos (8.5 km)

EATING & DRINKING

Akarana	5	La Batuta	20	Guris Brasileiro	16	Liguria	11	Nolita	3	La Tecla
Astrid y Gastón	8	Café Melba	4	La Habana		Lamu Lounge	2	Ostras Azocar	18	La Terraza
Barandaraián	12	Club de Jazz	22	Vieja	17	Las Lanzas	21	Roll's Bar	9	Las Vacas
Bar Yellow	10	El Huerto	7	Infante 51	14	Le Flaubert	6	Santo Remedio	13	Gordas
										Zanzibar

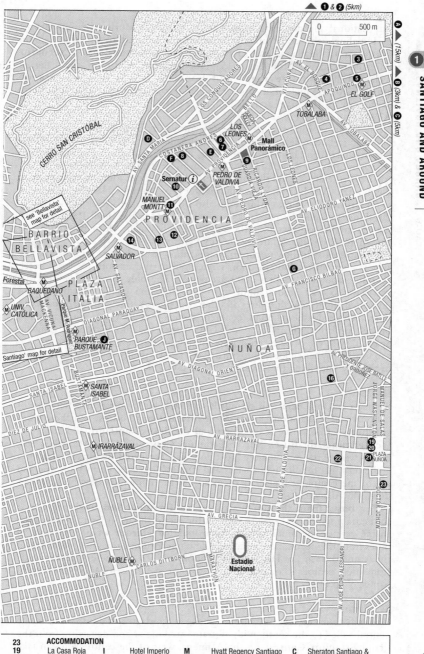

▲ ❶ & ❷ (5km)

❶ A
▲ (15km)
▲ ❶ (3km) & ❸ (5km)

0   500 m

CERRO SAN CRISTÓBAL

❷

❸
❹
❺
EL GOLF
TOBALABA

LOS
LEONES
Mall
Panorámico
❻
❼
❽
ⓔ
❾

see 'Bellavista'
map for detail

BARRIO
BELLAVISTA

Sernatur ⓘ
❿
PEDRO DE
VALDIVIA

MANUEL
MONTT
⓫

PROVIDENCIA

Forestal
BAQUEDANO

UNIV.
CATÓLICA

PLAZA
ITALIA

⓮
⓭
⓬

SALVADOR

ⓓ

ⓕ

ⓖ

AV. FRANCISCO BILBAO

DIAGONAL PARAGUAY

Santiago' map for detail

PARQUE
BUSTAMANTE
ⓙ

ÑUÑOA

AV. DIAGONAL ORIENTE

SANTA
ISABEL

SANTA ISABEL

DIEZ DE JULIO

⓰

AV. IRARRÁZAVAL

IRARRÁZAVAL

⓳
⓴
㉑
PLAZA
ÑUÑOA

㉒
㉓

AV. GRECIA

ÑUBLE
CARLOS DITTBORN

Estadio
Nacional

ÑUBLE

By air

International and domestic **flights** arrive at Arturo Merino Benítez airport in Pudahuel (the commune it is sometimes referred to as), some 26km northwest of Santiago. The smart international terminal has a **Sernatur** information desk (Mon–Sat 8.15am–8pm; ☎601 9320) in the baggage reclaim hall, with **free maps and booklets**. Nearby there's a **casa de cambio**, Afex, which offers poorer exchange rates than options in the centre of the city. In the main arrivals hall, there's another Afex *cambio* and several **ATMs** on each level.

The cheapest way to get to the city centre is by **bus**, with two companies offering frequent services from just outside the arrivals gate. The blue Centropuerto bus has the edge, being cheaper and more frequent (6am–11.30pm; every 10min; CH$1400); it drops you off at **Los Héroes** on the Alameda (the city's main thoroughfare), where you can join the metro or flag down a taxi. Tur Bus (5.30am–midnight; every 30min; CH$1600) takes you to **Terminal de Buses Alameda**, also on the Alameda. Both buses call at the domestic and international terminals, travel via the small **Pajaritos** bus station in the southwest of the city, and will usually drop passengers off anywhere along their route to the city centre.

A couple of **minibus companies**, operating from the row of desks by the airport exit, offer door-to-door services from the airport to your hotel, charging around CH$4000–5000 per person. The only disadvantages are that you have to wait around until the bus is full, and you'll probably get an unwanted city tour as they drop off other passengers before you reach your own hotel. Alongside the minibus counters there's a desk where you can book official airport **taxis**, which cost CH$13,000–15,000. If you bargain (in Spanish) with the private taxi drivers touting for business outside the exit, you can usually pay much less, approximately CH$8500 to any centrally located part of the city, but taking these taxis is at your own risk.

By bus

Santiago has four main bus terminals serving a highly developed network of national and international buses. Most **international buses**, and those from **southern Chile**, arrive at the **Terminal de Buses Santiago** (also known as the **Terminal de Buses Sur** or **Estación Central**) on the Alameda, a few blocks west of the train station. Next door, the **Terminal de Buses Alameda** is the terminal for all Pullman Bus and Tur Bus journeys. From both, you can get to the centre by metro, or catch any of the numerous taxis hurtling east down the Alameda.

Most **buses from the north** arrive at the **Terminal San Borja**, right next to the train station and again handy for the metro (Estación Central) and buses to the centre. The much smaller **Terminal los Héroes** serves a mixture of buses from the north and south, and a few international ones; it's just north of the Alameda (near Los Héroes metro station) and is a short and cheap taxi ride from most central accommodation. For more details, see "Moving on from Santiago", p.117.

By train

The only train services in Chile are between Santiago and destinations in the central valley to the south, with all trains arriving at and departing from the grand **Estación Central** on the Alameda, west of the centre. You can take the metro or a taxi into the centre from right outside the station.

Information

The main sources of tourist information are **Sernatur**, the national tourist board, the **Oficina de Turismo** run by the Municipalidad de Santiago, and **Conaf**, the national parks administration.

Sernatur

The **Sernatur** office is east of the city centre at Avenida Providencia 1550, between Manuel Montt and Pedro de Valdivia metro stations (Mon–Fri 9am–6pm, Sat 9am–2pm; ☎731 8336, ⓦwww.sernatur.cl). It offers a range of free booklets on Santiago's attractions, accommodation and restaurants, and the staff, usually English-speaking, can answer most questions about services and facilities in the city. It's also a good place to stock up on information on the rest of Chile, with lists of accommodation in all the other regions, as well as some themed booklets on subjects like wine circuits, national parks, ski centres and beaches; you have to ask for them, though, as they're usually kept out of sight. Be persistent in your information requests, as staff tend to palm off the nearest brochure instead of the most appropriate.

Oficina de Turismo

Far more conveniently located – in the Casa Colorada, just off the Plaza de Armas at Merced 860 – but less helpful is the **Oficina de Turismo** (Mon–Thurs 10am–6pm, Fri 10am–5pm; ☎632 7783, ⓦwww.municipalidaddesantiago.cl); it has free maps and a range of booklets (including the useful *Historical Heritage of Santiago* and *Walking around Santiago*).

Conaf

For information on Chile's national parks, visit **Conaf** at Presidente Bulnes 265 (Mon–Thurs 9.30am–5.30pm, Fri 9.30am–4.30pm; ☎663 0125, ⓦwww .conaf.cl).

City transport

You'll probably spend most time in the city centre, which is entirely walkable, but for journeys further afield public transport is inexpensive, safe and abundant. For trips along the main east–west axis formed by the Alameda and its extensions, the **metro** is quickest. The city and suburbs are also served by thousands of **buses**, while **colectivos** offer a quick way out of the centre into surrounding districts. Regular **taxis** are numerous and inexpensive, and in many cases the most convenient way to get about.

The metro

Santiago's spotless **metro** system (Mon–Fri 6.30am–11pm, Sat, Sun & public holidays 8.30am–10.30pm; ⓦwww.metro.cl) is modern, efficient and safe, though packed solid at rush hour. Many stations are decorated with huge murals, and often offer free wi-fi access. Of the five **lines**, #1 is the most useful (and crowded) running east–west under the Alameda and Avenida Providencia. Line #2 runs north–south from Vespucio Norte down to Lo Ovalle, crossing Line #1 at Los Héroes, and is useful for visiting Palacio Cousiño, Parque O'Higgins and the Franklin market. Line #4 (somewhat confusingly there's no Line #3) runs from Tobalaba in Las Condes to Plaza de Puente Alto, while the shorter Line #4A

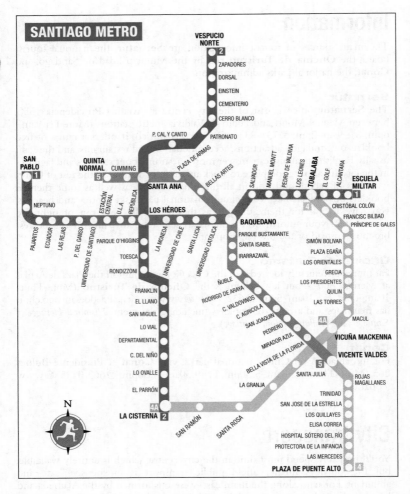

SANTIAGO METRO

connects La Cisterna to Vicuña Mackenna; these two lines mainly travel through residential areas. Line #5 runs from the Quinta Normal in a southeasterly direction, via Plaza de Armas and Bellas Artes, to outlying Bellavista de La Florida – not to be confused with the hip Bellavista neighbourhood in central Santiago.

Fares are the same for any length of journey, but fall into two different price brackets according to the time of day: the peak rate (Mon–Fri 7am–8.59am & 6pm–7.59pm) is CH$420, the off-peak rate (the rest of the time) is CH$380. If you're staying in the city for a while, buy a **Tarjeta Bip!** card (CH$1200, plus however much credit you want to add on to it), a rechargeable multi-trip ticket from which each journey's fare is deducted until it runs out. It gives you slightly cheaper travel, less waiting in ticket queues and is also used on the buses.

Buses

Santiago has one of the highest densities of **buses** in the world, a network it has recently overhauled. The new buses no longer take cash; you must have a

Tarjeta Bip! card (see opposite) to ride them (single journeys cost CH$380), making them considerably less convenient than the metro. Buses are useful for going east or west, along the Alameda – as a general rule, buses displaying Estación Central will take you west, while those displaying Providencia or Apoquindo are going east.

Taxis and colectivos

Santiago has more **taxis** than New York City, and in the centre you'll have no trouble flagging one down. Sometimes you'll have to track down a taxi rank and, away from commercial areas, you may have to phone for one. Taxis are black with yellow roofs and have a small light in the top right-hand corner of the windscreen that's lit to show the cab is available. Fares are relatively low and displayed on the window – usually CH$200 when the meter's started and CH$80–120 every 200m; you're not expected to tip. Drivers are allowed to charge much more at night, so first check the rate on the window before you begin the journey and try to verbally confirm an estimate to your location. **Scams** are frequent, and include drivers taking extra-long routes, and rip-offs on large bills. Be firm and pay with exact change (you supply the small bills), and most drivers will be more honest. Taxi drivers aren't tested on their knowledge of the city's streets in order to get a licence; if you're going somewhere out of the way, it's best to check where it is beforehand (there's a good A–Z in the back of the yellow pages).

Santiago's **colectivos** (shared taxis) look like ordinary taxis except they're black all over and cram in as many as four passengers at a time. They travel along fixed routes, mostly from the centre out to the suburbs; a sign on the roof indicates the destination. Plaza Baquedano (usually called Plaza Italia) is the starting point for many *colectivo* routes. Prices vary along the route, but *colectivos* generally cost around CH$400–500.

Accommodation

There's plenty of **accommodation** in Santiago to suit most budgets, though *really* inexpensive places are scarce and tend to be rather squalid. Most of the city's low-price rooms are small, simple and sparsely furnished, often without a window but usually fairly clean. Moving up a notch or two you'll find more comfort in many of the small, moderately priced hotels, though you need to choose carefully as some of them can be dismal. Upmarket hotels are abundant, especially in Providencia, ranging from good-value independent outfits to luxurious international chains. Prices in Santiago don't usually fluctuate much during the course of the year, although a few hotels charge more in summer (Nov–Feb). The prices listed are for the cheapest double room in high season. At the lower end of the scale, single travellers can expect to pay half this rate, but mid- and upper-range hotels usually charge the same rate for a single as for a double. Non-resident foreigners are exempt from the 19 percent tax on hotel rooms if they pay in a foreign currency (typically US dollars).

Central Santiago

East of the Plaza de Armas is the tidier, better-restored section of the historic centre, with the easiest walking access to most of the central attractions: the art museums, markets, Cerro Santa Lucía, Bellavista, Parque Forestal and Cerro San Cristóbal. There are some good budget places and many mid- and upper-range options.

Andes Hostel Monjitas 506, Bellas Artes metro ☎632 9990, ⓦwww.andeshostel.com. Funky hostel with tidy six-bed dorms (CH\$8500), swish marble bathrooms, roof terrace and bar area with big-screen TV and pool table. There are also a few private rooms. ❹

Che Lagarto Tucapel Jiménez 24, Los Héroes metro ☎699 1493, ⓦwww.chelagarto.com. Part of a growing South American chain of hostels, *Che Lagarto* has a sociable atmosphere and plenty of organized events. There are large, clean six-bed dorms (CH\$7000) and a handful of rooms with private baths. ❸

City Hotel Compañía 1063, near Plaza de Armas metro station ☎695 4526. While staff can be curt, and the rooms a little sparsely furnished, some nice Art Deco touches give this hotel a 1930s feel, which combined with the price and central location make it a good choice. Try to get a room with a view of the Cathedral. ❹

Crowne Plaza Santiago Alameda 136, Baquedano metro ☎638 1042, ⓦwww.ichotelsgroup.com. *Crowne Plaza* offers all of the comfort and facilities you would expect from a member of the InterContinental group – at a steep price (doubles around US\$350). The en-suites in this looming sand-coloured tower boast king-size beds, and those on the upper, eastern side have unobstructed views of the Andes. ❾

Hotel Galerias San Antonio 65, Universidad de Chile metro ☎470 7400, ⓦwww.hotelgalerias.cl. Large, classy establishment boasting quality en-suites with double-glazed windows to minimise road noise; there's also an outdoor pool, bar with extensive wine list and regular art shows in the lobby. ❽

Hostel Plaza de Armas Compañía 960, apartment 607, Plaza de Armas metro ☎671 4436, ⓦwww.plazadearmashostel.com. This hidden gem, on the sixth floor of a building hidden within an alleyway filled with fast food joints, has a prime location right on the Plaza de Armas. There are bright six-bed dorms (US\$10–15), a colourful if compact double (❹), ample communal space and a terrace with fine views.

Hotel Montecarlo Victoria Subercaseaux 209, Universidad Católica metro ☎633 9905, ⓦwww.hotelmontecarlo.cl. This small, quiet hideaway is only two blocks from the Alameda, near the art museums and the lively Barrio Lastarria neighbourhood. The architecture has distinct modernist influences and unusual interior design. Ask for a room with a view of the *cerro*. ❺

Hotel París París 813, Universidad de Chile metro ☎664 0921, ⓔcarbott@latinmail.com. Good-value budget hotel offering a range of rooms, with shared and private baths and TVs; the older ones sometimes lack outside windows so unless pesos are really tight, opt for one in the newer annexe. ❸–❹

Hotel Plaza San Francisco Alameda 816, Universidad de Chile metro ☎639 3832, ⓦwww.plazasanfrancisco.cl. Following an extensive 2008 renovation, this 5-star is now the most luxurious downtown top-end choice: the en-suites are large and handsome with tubs and easy chairs; there's also an indoor pool, mini art gallery and quality restaurant. ❽

Residencial Londres Londres 54, Universidad de Chile metro ☎633 9192, ⓦwww.lula.cl. The rooms at this aged townhouse, a long-standing traveller favourite, have marble floors, pastel-coloured walls and high ceilings; however, some of the baths have mould and the lack of heating means it gets chilly during the winter. ❸–❹

Vegas Hotel Londres 49, Universidad de Chile metro ☎632 2514, ⓦwww.hotelvegas.net. A national monument, in the quiet París-Londres neighbourhood, the Vegas is an excellent mid-range choice, with spacious en-suites, friendly service and thoughtful touches like secondhand novels in various languages and a collection of umbrellas for use on rainy days. ❺

West of the historic centre: Barrio Brasil and Barrio República

From the Plaza de Armas west all the way to Santiago's bus terminals is the more run-down - and sometimes seedy – part of central Santiago. But the area's growing in popularity, especially among students, thanks to its university campuses and ever-increasing supply of cool cafés, restaurants and bars. West of the Norte-Sur highway, both north and south of Alameda, is Santiago's original upper-class neighbourhood, and it still has beautiful, old architecture. These barrios, Brasil to the north and República to the south, are mainly residential and convenient to the bus terminals and the airport. For hotels in these barrios, the centre is just a short metro ride away.

La Casa Roja Agustinas 2113, Barrio Brasil, República metro ☎696 4241, ⓦwww .lacasaroja.cl. This relaxed Aussie-owned hostel has clean eight-bed dorms (CH$7000), some overpriced doubles (❹), a small pool and pleasant gardens. There are regular BBQs and live music events.

🏃 **Happy House Hostel** Catedral 2207, Barrio Brasil, Ricardo Cumming metro ☎688 4842, ⓦwww.happyhousehostel.cl. A bit more expensive than the other hostels, but well worth it: this wonderfully restored early twentieth-century townhouse has stylish eight-bed dorms (CH$11,000), beautiful, airy private doubles (❺) that put many mid-range hotels to shame, bar, terrace and pool table.

Hotel Imperio Av Lib Bernardo O'Higgins 2876, Estación Central metro ☎592 6000, ⓦwww .hotelimperio.cl. A functional, well-equipped 80-room hotel on the Alameda: while the rooms are now beginning to show their age, they are decorated in warm, soothing colours and remain very good value. ❺

Hotel Majestic Santo Domingo 1526, Santa Ana metro ☎690 9400, ⓦwww .hotelmajestic.cl. Although it is part of the Best Western chain, the decor inside is a pastiche of the British Raj. The comfortable rooms, however, are more conservative; there's also an outdoor pool and excellent Indian restaurant (the latter a real rarity in Chile). It's a 15min walk to Plaza de Armas. ❻

Hotel Tokyo Almirante Barroso 160, Los Héroes metro ☎698 4500, ⓦwww.hoteltokyo.cl. Tucked away on a little side street just west of the Panamerican highway, the *Tokyo* has straightforward, slightly tatty en-suites with cable TV. Pieces of antique furniture and Japanese collectables decorate the place, and you can take breakfast in the flower garden. ❹

Providencia

The glitzy commercial heart of Santiago, Providencia has a number of pricey hotels, as well as a few quiet and good-value lodgings off the beaten path. It offers a wide range of restaurants and bars, particularly in hip Bellavista, plus some interesting architecture, although the Suecia section, a common gringo hangout, is filled with rowdy dancehalls and occasionally bothersome drunks.

Hotel Orly Pedro de Valdivia 027, Pedro de Valdivia metro ☎231 8947, ⓦwww.orlyhotel.com. Welcoming and cosy, *Orly* almost seems out of place in the heart of Providencia. The immaculate en-suites have wood fittings, colourful throws, mini fridges and cable TV. An excellent choice. ❻–❼

Hotel del Patio Pio Nono 61, Baquedano metro ☎732 7571, ⓦwww.hoteldelpatio.cl. Part of the Patio Bellavista complex (see p.99), this is a chic boutique hotel: the en-suites are a little tight but wooden floors, cool marble bathrooms, flat-screen TVs and lamps shaped like exotic fruits more than compensate. ❻–❼

Hyatt Regency Santiago Av Kennedy 4601, around seven blocks north of Escuela Militar metro ☎950 1234, ⓦwww.santiago.grand.hyatt.com. More a complex than a hotel – there's a pool, tennis courts, gym, spa, restaurants and bar – this distinctive cylindrical 5-star is the most luxurious in Santiago. Opulent en-suites (from US$300) have perks like Bang & Olufsen TVs. The major drawback is the location in a sterile residential neighbourhood, within walking distance of nothing but the Parque Arauco shopping mall. ❾

El Patio Suizo Condell 847, Parque Bustamante metro ☎474 0634, ⓦwww.patiosuizo.com. Pretty Swiss-owned hotel with a handful of modern rooms, bordering on the minimalist; the more expensive ones have private baths and their own access to the garden. It's very popular, so make sure you book ahead. ❹–❺

Sheraton Santiago and San Cristóbal Tower Santa María 1742, around 1km from Pedro de Valdivia metro ☎233 5000, ⓦwww .starwoodhotels.com. Two hotels in one, but rooms (US$190–300) in the *San Cristóbal Tower* are significantly better and only a little more expensive than those in the original 1970-built *Sheraton*. Nestled right into the side of Cerro San Cristóbal, the property offers impressive views, spacious rooms, ample green areas, a huge pool and a patio. It's all a bit removed from everything, however. ❾

🏃 **Vilafranca Petit Hotel** Pérez Valenzuela 1650, Pedro de Valdivia metro ☎235 1413, ⓦwww.vilafranca.cl. A charming eight-room B&B, in a 1940s-era home, on a peaceful residential street: each room is unique, but all are supremely tasteful, service is personalised, black and white photos of historic Santiago cover the walls, and there's a sunny patio area. ❻

Las Condes and east

Las Condes has become Santiago's burgeoning top-end hotel neighbourhood, with easy access to three major ski centres and the airport. The city's two largest shopping centres and many art galleries are also nearby, but central attractions are not within walking distance and there are no particularly close metro lines.

La Posada del Inglés Camino a Farellones 15201 ☎ 217 4105, ⓦ www.chile-hotels.com /laposada. An excellent choice if you want to spend all day on the mountain and hit the town at night – but don't want to pay for slopeside lodging. On the road winding up to the ski slope, but still 30km away, this is a British-run, lovely old house with great views of El Arrayán valley and the mountains. It has homely rooms and an outdoor terrace with two pools. The trendy El Arrayán neighbourhood, with bars, restaurants and nightclubs, is within walking distance. Follow

Av Las Condes to the edge of town; at the petrol station just before Plaza San Enrique, follow signs to Farellones, a right turn. ⓖ
Regal Pacific Av Apoquindo 5680 ☎ 377 6000, ⓦ www.regal-pacific.com. A handsome, small 5-star hotel, opposite the Manquehue shopping centre, frequented by Latin American skiers and Asian businessmen. The classically styled rooms are a little unexciting for the price but have excellent Andean views. There's a health centre with Jacuzzi and sauna, curvaceous pool and a restaurant headed by an acclaimed chef. ⓗ

The City

Santiago isn't a city that demands major sightseeing, and you can get round many of its attractions on foot in two to three days. A tour of the compact core, centred on the bustling **Plaza de Armas**, should include visits to the **Palacio de la Moneda**, the excellent **Museo Chileno de Arte Precolombino**, and the evocative **Museo Colonial**, followed by a climb up **Cerro Santa Lucía**. Less strenuous options would be lunch at the intriguing **Mercado Central**, or just sitting in the plaza with an ice cream and a book.

North of downtown, on the other side of the Río Mapocho, it's an easy funicular ride up **Cerro San Cristóbal**, whose summit provides unrivalled views for miles around. At its foot, **Barrio Bellavista** is Santiago's "Latin Quarter", replete with small cafés, *salsatecas* and restaurants. This is where you'll find a house in which **poet Pablo Neruda** lived, now a wonderful museum filled with objects he collected around the world. West of the centre, the once glamorous barrios that housed Santiago's moneyed classes at the beginning of the twentieth century make for rewarding, romantic wanders, and contain some splendid old mansions, including the sumptuous **Palacio Cousiño**. Moving east into the barrios altos of Providencia and Las Condes, the tone is newer and flasher. Apart from shiny malls, there's less to draw you out here, with the notable exception of the highly enjoyable arts and crafts market at **Los Dominicos**.

Plaza de Armas

The **Plaza de Armas** is the centre of Santiago and the country, both literally – all distances to the rest of Chile are measured from here – and symbolically. It was the first public space laid out by Pedro de Valdivia when he founded the city in 1541 and quickly became the nucleus of Santiago's administrative, commercial and social life. This is where the young capital's most important seats of power – the law courts, the governor's palace, and the cathedral – were built, and where its markets, bullfights (no longer allowed), festivals and other

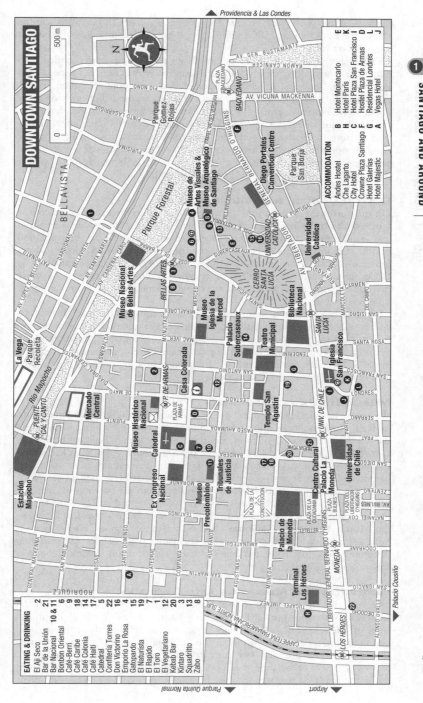

DOWNTOWN SANTIAGO

▲ Providencia & Las Condes

N

0   500 m

ACCOMMODATION

Andes Hostel	B
Che Lagarto	H
City Hotel	C
Crowne Plaza Santiago	F
Hotel Galerías	G
Hotel Majestic	A
Hotel Montecarlo	E
Hotel París	K
Hotel Plaza San Francisco	I
Hostel Plaza de Armas	D
Residencial Londres	L
Vegas Hotel	J

EATING & DRINKING

El Ají Seco	2
Bar de la Unión	21
Bar Nacional	10 & 11
Bonbon Oriental	6
Café-Berri	9
Café Caribe	18
Café Colonia	14
Café Haití	17
Catedral	5
Confitería Torres	22
Don Victorino	16
Emporio La Rosa	4
Gatopardo	15
El Naturista	19
El Rápido	7
El Toro	1
El Vegetariano	12
Kebab Bar	20
Kintaro	3
Squadritto	13
Zabo	8

La Vega

Estación Mapocho

Mercado Central

Parque Recoleta

Río Mapocho

PUENTE CAL Y CANTO

Parque Forestal

BELLAVISTA

Parque Gomez Rojas

AV. GEN. BUSTAMANTE

RAMÓN CARNICER

PLAZA BAQUEDANO

AV. VICUÑA MACKENNA

Museo Nacional de Bellas Artes

Museo de Artes Visuales & Museo Arqueológico de Santiago

Diego Portales Convention Centre

Parque San Borja

Museo Histórico Nacional

Casa Colorada

Museo Iglesia de la Merced

Palacio Subercaseaux

Teatro Municipal

CERRO SANTA LUCIA

Biblioteca Nacional

Universidad Católica

Ex Congreso Nacional

Catedral

PLAZA DE ARMAS

Museo Precolombino

Tribunales de Justicia

Templo San Agustín

Centro Cultural Palacio La Moneda

Iglesia San Francisco

SANTA LUCIA

Palacio de la Moneda

Terminal Los Héroes

Universidad de Chile

LOS HÉROES

MONEDA

UNIV. DE CHILE

CARRETERA PANAMERICANA NORTE SUR

AV. LIBERTADOR GENERAL BERNARDO O'HIGGINS

▲ Palacio Cousiño

▼ Providencia & Las Condes

◀ Parque Quinta Normal

◀ Airport

◀ Parque Quinta Normal

89

public activities took place. Four and a half centuries later, this is still where the city's pulse beats loudest. Half an hour's people watching here is perhaps the best introduction to Santiago.

These days the open market space has been replaced by flower gardens and numerous trees; palms, poplars and eucalyptus tower over benches packed with Peruvian job hunters, giggling schoolchildren, gossiping old men, lovers, tourists, indulgent grandmothers and packs of uniformed shop girls on their lunch break. Thirsty dogs hang around the fountain; shoe-shiners polish the feet of dour businessmen clutching *El Mercurio*; and ancient-looking chess players hold sombre tournaments inside the bandstand. Against this is a backdrop of constant noise supplied by street performers, singers and howling evangelical preachers. Meanwhile, a constant ebb and flow of people march in and out of the great civic and religious buildings enclosing the square.

Correo Central and Municipalidad

On the northwest corner of the Plaza de Armas stands the candyfloss-coloured **Correo Central**, whose interior, with its tiered galleries crowned by a beautiful glass roof, is every bit as impressive as its elaborate facade. It was built in 1882 on the foundations of what had been the Palacio de los Gobernadores (governors' palace) during colonial times, and the Palacio de los Presidentes de Chile (presidential palace) after independence. Now given over to more mundane affairs, this is where you can come to send postcards home and pick up poste restante.

In the same block, on the northeast corner of the square, is the pale, Neoclassical edifice of Santiago's **Municipalidad**. The first *cabildo* (town hall) was erected on this site back in the early seventeenth century and also contained the city's prison. Several reconstructions and restorations have taken place since then, most recently in 1895. A curious feature is that the basement is still divided into the original cells of the old prison, now used as offices.

Museo Histórico Nacional

Wedged between the Correo and the Municipalidad is the splendid **Palacio de la Real Audiencia**, an immaculately preserved colonial building that's borne witness to some of Santiago's most important turns of history. Built by the Spanish Crown between 1804 and 1807 to house the royal courts of justice, it had served this purpose for just two years when Chile's first government junta assembled here to replace the Spanish governor with its own elected leader. Eight years later it was the meeting place of Chile's first Congress, and the building was the seat of government until 1846, when President Bulnes moved to La Moneda. The Palacio's grand old rooms, arranged around a large central courtyard, today house the **Museo Histórico Nacional** (Tues–Sun 10am–5.30pm; CH$600, free on Sun), crammed with eclectic and often fascinating relics of the past, including furniture, sewing machines and ladies' clothes – all of it fun to look at, but too chaotic to be really illuminating.

Cathedral and Museo de Arte Sagrado

The west side of the square is dominated by the grandiose stone bulk of the **Catedral Metropolitana** (Mon–Sat 9am–7pm, Sun 9am–noon). A combination of Neoclassical and Baroque styles, with its orderly columns and pediment and its ornate bell towers, the cathedral bears the mark of **Joaquín Toesca**, who was brought over from Italy in 1780 to oversee its completion. Toesca went on to become the most important architect of colonial Chile, designing many of Santiago's public buildings, including La Moneda. This is actually the fifth church to be built on this site; the first was burnt down by Picunche just months after Valdivia had it built, and the others were destroyed by earthquakes in 1552, 1647 and 1730. Inside, take a look at the main altar, carved out of marble and richly embellished with bronze and lapis lazuli. Note also the intricately crafted silver frontal, the work of Bavarian Jesuits in the sixteenth century.

You'll find more examples of the Jesuits' exquisite silverwork in the **Museo de Arte Sagrado** (Mon–Sat 9am–7pm, Sun 9am–noon) tucked away behind the main body of the cathedral. To find the entrance, go down the passage belonging to the bookshop next door to the cathedral. A gate at the bottom takes you back into the cathedral grounds and into one of Santiago's most evocative courtyards, where languid palm trees brush against crumbling colonial architecture. From here, signs point to the three rooms containing the museum's collection of religious paintings, sculpture, furniture and silverwork, including a finely crafted silver lectern and tabernacle. These two pieces aside, none of it is as impressive as the stuff in the Museo Colonial in the Iglesia San Francisco (see p.96), but still makes for a rewarding browse.

Casa Colorada - Museo de Santiago

Just off the southeast corner of the plaza, at Merced 860, you'll find the **Casa Colorada**, built in 1769 and generally considered to be Santiago's best-preserved colonial house. With its clay-tiled roof, its row of balconied windows giving onto the street and its distinctive, deep-red walls, the two-storey mansion certainly provides a striking example of an eighteenth-century town residence. The house is built around two large patios, one of which you walk through to get to the **Museo de Santiago** (Mon–Fri 10am–5.45pm, Sat 10am–4.45pm, Sun 11am–1.45pm; CH$500, free on Sun), which occupies five of the Casa Colorada's rooms. This rather humble museum is dedicated to the history of the city from pre-Columbian to modern times, which is illustrated mainly by scale models, maps and paintings. None of it is very slick, however, and there's no English commentary.

Museo Chileno de Arte Precolombino

A stone's throw from the southwest corner of the Plaza de Armas, on the corner of Compañía and Bandera, stands the beautifully restored 1807 Real Casa de la Aduana (the old royal customs house) which now houses the **Museo Chileno de Arte Precolombino** (Tues–Sun 10am–6pm; CH$2000, free on Sun; ℡688 7348, ⒲www.precolombino.cl). Unquestionably Chile's best museum, it brings together over three thousand pieces representing some one hundred pre-Columbian peoples of Latin America. The collection spans a period of about ten thousand years and covers regions from present-day Mexico down to southern Chile, brilliantly illustrating the artistic wealth and diversity of Latin America's many cultures. One of the keys to understanding the beauty of this collection is that the items were selected primarily on the basis of their artistic merit, rather than on their scientific or anthropological significance.

The museum's rooms take you on a north-to-south geographical tour of different areas of Latin America, starting with **Mesoamérica**, corresponding to present-day Mexico, Guatemala, Honduras, El Salvador and parts of Nicaragua; moving on to the **Area Intermedia**, covering what is now Ecuador, Colombia, Panama, Costa Rica and Nicaragua; followed by the **Andes Centrales**, or central Andean region (today's Peru and western Bolivia); and ending in the **Andes del Sur** (Chile itself and parts of Argentina).

Area Mesoamérica

Walking through the large double doors off the hall, you'll find yourself in the room devoted to items from **Mesoamérica**. Right in front of you is one of the most startling pieces in the museum: a statue of **Xipé-Totec**, the god of Spring, represented as a man covered in the skin of a monkey, exposing both male and female genitalia. At the time of the Spanish conquest, the cult of Xipé-Totec was widespread throughout most of Mesoamerica, and was celebrated in a bizarre ritual in which a young man would cover himself with the skin of a sacrificial victim and wear it until it rotted off, revealing his young, fresh skin and symbolizing the growth of new vegetation from the earth.

Another eye-catching object, further up the room on the left, is the elaborately ornamented **incense burner**, used by the Teotihuacán culture (300–600 AD) to pray for rain and good harvests. The face carved in the middle represents a rain god, and when the incense was burning, the smoke would escape from his eyes. Standing at the far end of the room, by the exit, a huge slab of stone features **bas-relief carvings** depict a hulking, armed warrior with two small figures at his feet. It originally formed part of an immense Maya structure, built between 600 and 900 AD.

Area Intermedia

In this region the continent's oldest pottery was produced, along with some exquisite goldwork. Pottery made its first appearance in the Americas around 3000 BC on the coast of Ecuador, where it was created by the agricultural and fishing communities of the Valdivia culture. Among the museum's best examples of **Valdivia pottery** is the gorgeous little female figurine with a big, round belly and childlike face, thought to have been used for fertility rites carried out at harvest time. Note also the wonderful **coca-leaf-chewing figures** known as *coqueros*, carved with a telltale lump in their mouth by the Capulí culture (500 BC–500 AD). As well as pottery, this *sala* contains some beautiful **gold objects**, such as the miniature, finely worked carvings produced by the Veraguas and Diquis cultures (700–1550 AD) featuring images of frightening monsters and open-jawed, long-fanged felines.

▲ Figures from the Museo Chileno de Arte Precolombino

Area Andes Centrales

The next room is distinguished by its **masks** and **copper figurines**, many of which were retrieved from ancient graves. Among the collection are examples of the highly expressive work of the Moche culture (100 BC–800 AD), including copper figurines and masks, now a gorgeous jade-green colour, and a series of polished ceremonial pots decorated with images of animals, faces and houses. The room also features some noteworthy **textiles**. Hanging by the door as you go in is a fragment of painted cloth depicting three human figures with fanged jaws – this is the oldest textile in the museum, produced by the Chavín culture almost 3000 years ago, and still in astonishingly good condition.

Area Andes del Sur

The final room contains treasures from modern Chile and northwest Argentina. Among the most striking pieces on display are the huge **ceramic urns** of the Aguada culture (600–900 AD), painted with bold geometric designs incorporating fantastic, often feline, images. Look out too for the wooden and stone **snuff trays**, carved by the San Pedro people of northern Chile between 300 and 1000 AD, and used with small tubes to inhale hallucinogenic substances. The curious thing on the wall that looks like a grass skirt is a relic from the Inca, who made it all the way down to central Chile during their expansion in the fifteenth century. Known as a **quipú**, it consists of many strands of wool attached to a single cord, and was used to keep various records – such as of taxes collected – by means of a complex system of knots tied in the strands.

Ahumada, Huérfanos and around

The southeast corner of downtown Santiago contains the city's busiest pedestrian thoroughfares, Ahumada and Huérfanos, and a miscellany of attractions. Running south from the west side of the Plaza de Armas to the Alameda, **Paseo Ahumada** is a seething mass of people at every moment of the day. Walking down, you'll pass sombre doorways leading into labyrinthine shopping arcades, *confiterías* serving preposterously large cream cakes and, between Agustinas and Moneda, the famous **Café Caribe** and **Café Haiti** (see p.105). Take a moment to pop into the **Banco de Chile**, between Huérfanos and Agustinas; its vast hall, polished counters and beautiful old clock have changed little since the bank opened in 1925.

Paseo Huérfanos crosses Ahumada at right angles, one block south of the plaza, and is lined with numerous banks and cinemas. Several places of interest are dotted amongst the shops, office blocks and *galerías* of the surrounding streets. You could start with the **Basilica de la Merced**, a towering, Neo-Renaissance structure on the corner of Merced and Mac Iver, with a beautifully carved eighteenth-century pulpit. Attached to the church is a small **museum** (Tues–Fri 10am–2pm & 3–6pm; CH$1000) where, among the usual crucifixes and other religious paraphernalia, you'll find a collection of Easter Island artefacts, including a wooden **rongo rongo tablet**, carved in the undeciphered Easter Island script – one of just 29 left in the world.

From here, head south for two blocks and turn right at Agustinas, where you'll find the dazzling white facade of the **Teatro Municipal**, a splendid French-style Neoclassical building, all arches and columns and perfect symmetry. This has been the capital's most prestigious venue for ballet, opera and classical music since its inauguration in 1857. It's worth asking to have a look around inside; the main auditorium is quite a sight, with its sumptuous red upholstery and crystal chandeliers. See p.112 for ticket information.

Standing opposite the theatre, and mirroring its cool, smooth whiteness, is the **Mansión Subercaseaux**, built at the beginning of the twentieth century for one of Santiago's wealthiest families, and now occupied by a bank. A little further along, at the corner of Agustinas and Estado, loom the green walls and yellow columns of the **Templo de San Agustín**, dating from 1608 but extensively rebuilt since then. The chief interest within its highly decorative interior is the wooden carving of Christ, just left of the main altar as you face it. Known as the *Cristo de Mayo*, it's the subject of an intriguing local legend. The story goes that the crown of thorns around the figure's head slipped down to its neck during the 1647 earthquake, and that when someone tried to move the crown back up to its head, the carved face of Christ began to bleed, and the ground started to shake. For this reason, the crown has remained untouched ever since, still hanging around the neck.

La Moneda, the Ex Congreso Nacional and the Tribunales de Justicia

The best approach to the **Palacio de la Moneda** is from the northern side of the vast, paved Plaza de la Constitución, three blocks east and south of the Plaza de Armas. From here you can appreciate the perfect symmetry and compact elegance of this low-lying Neoclassical building, spread across the entire block. The inner courtyards are open to the public.

It was built between 1784 and 1805 by the celebrated Italian architect Joaquín Toesca for the purpose of housing the royal mint. After some forty years it became the residential palace for the presidents of Chile, starting with Manuel Bulnes in 1848 and ending with Carlos Ibáñez del Campo in 1958. At this point it stopped being used as the president's home, but it continues to be the official seat of government. One ceremony worth watching is the **changing of the guard**, held in front of the palace at 10am on alternate days. In front of the Justice Ministry is one of Chile's few monuments to President Salvador Allende, with his arm outstretched.

The **Centro Cultural Palacio La Moneda** (Plaza de la Ciudadania 26; daily 9am–9pm, exhibitions 10am–7.30pm; CH$600, free on Sun; ☎ 355 6500, Ⓦ www.ccplm.cl), on the Alameda side of the Palacio de la Moneda, opened in 2006 as an early part of Chile's 2010 bicentennial celebrations. This flagship underground art gallery and cultural space has a vast modernist concrete central hall, which houses ever-changing exhibitions. The permanent displays in the adjacent galleries feature an eclectic array of artwork, jewellery, pottery, textiles and photography from across Chile (none of the exhibits are signed in English, however). There's also an art cinema, film archive, craft store, bookshop and branch of *Confiteria Torres* (see p.106).

North of Plaza de la Constitución, at the corner of Morandé and Compañía, are another couple of impressive public buildings. The most beautiful, from the outside, is the white, temple-like **Ex Congreso Nacional**, set amidst lush gardens. This is where Congress used to meet, until it was dissolved on September 11, 1973, the day of the coup d'état. In 1990, following the end of the military regime, a new congress building was erected in Valparaíso; since this one currently houses the Cancillería (foreign ministry), unfortunately public access to the inside is extremely limited.

On the southern side of Compañía, spanning the whole block, is the Tribunales de Justicia, an imposing Neoclassical building housing the highest court in Chile, the Corte Suprema. You'd never guess it from the outside, but this austere building conceals one of the most beautiful interiors in the city. Topped by a stunning glass-and-metal vault three floors above, the hall is flooded with natural light. If you want to take photos, you need to get permission from the *secretaría* on the first floor.

Along the Alameda

Officially the Avenida del Libertador Bernardo O'Higgins, Santiago's most vital east–west artery is universally known as the **Alameda**, a poplar-lined avenue used for strolling and recreation, and found in many Latin American cities. This one began life as *La Cañada* (or "channel"), when a branch of the Mapocho was sealed off shortly before independence, and a roadway was created over the old riverbed. A few years later, when the Supreme Director Bernardo O'Higgins decided that Santiago required an alameda, La Cañada was deemed the best place to put it: "There is no public boulevard where people may get together for honest relief and amusement during the resting hours, since the one known as Tajamar, because of its narrowness and irregularity, far from being cheerful, inspires sadness. La Cañada, because of its condition, extension, abundance of water and other circumstances, is the most apparent place for an alameda." Three rows of poplars were promptly planted along each side, and the Alameda was born, soon to become *the* place to take the evening promenade.

Since those quieter times the boulevard has evolved into the city's biggest, busiest, noisiest and most polluted thoroughfare, made up of a sea of vehicles moving as one organic mass, all screeching brakes, frenetic horns and choking fumes. Still, it's an unavoidable axis and you'll probably spend a fair bit of time on it or under it: the main metro line runs beneath it, and some of Santiago's most interesting landmarks stand along it.

Cerro Santa Lucía and Barrio Lastarria

The lushly forested **Cerro Santa Lucía** is the most imaginative and exuberant piece of landscaping in Santiago. Looking at it now, it's hard to believe that for the first three centuries of the city's development this was nothing more than a barren, rocky outcrop, completely ignored despite its historical importance – it was at the foot of this hill that Santiago was officially founded by Valdivia, on February 12, 1541. It wasn't until 1872 that the city turned its attention to Santa Lucía once more, when the mayor of Santiago, Vicuña Macstetenna, enlisted the labour of 150 prisoners to transform it into a grand public park.

Quasi-Gaudíesque in appearance, with its swirling pathways and Baroque terraces and turrets, this is a great place to come for panoramic views across the city, even when they're veiled behind a layer of smog. If slogging up the steps doesn't appeal, there's a free lift on the western side of the park, by the junction with Huérfanos. Up on the terrace is another branch of the Municipalidad de Santiago's **Oficina de Turismo** (Mon–Thurs 10am–6pm, Fri 10am–5pm; ☎664 4216, ⓦwww.municipalidaddesantiago.cl). While it's always busy and safe by day, several muggings have been reported in the Cerro Santa Lucía after dark.

Immediately west of the hill stands the massive **Biblioteca Nacional**, one of the largest libraries in Latin America (and handy for its free loos inside), while to the east, set back from the Alameda, is the quiet, arty **Barrio Lastarria** neighbourhood centred on **Plaza Mulato Gil**, at the corner of Merced and Lastarria. This small cobbled square is enclosed by old buildings housing artists' workshops, galleries, an antiquarian bookshop, a bar-restaurant and the **Museo de Artes Visuales**, Jose Victorino Lastarria 307 (Tues–Sun 10.30am-6.30pm,

CH$1000, free on Sun), which features some of the best new sculptures, painting and photography by Chile's emerging artists. It also houses the small but well-stocked **Museo Arqueológico de Santiago**, with hats, bags, jewellery, baskets and other items from all over the country, some dating back to 1000 BC. The rest of the neighbourhood is well known for its sparkling restaurant scene (see p.106), which offers a more intimate, quiet side to the usual ruckus of Santiago.

Iglesia San Francisco and Barrio París-Londres

Looking west from the Biblioteca Nacional, you can't miss the **Iglesia San Francisco**, with its towering red walls jutting out into the street. This is the oldest building in Santiago, erected between 1586 and 1628 and the survivor of three great earthquakes. Take a look inside at the **Virgen del Socorro**, a small polychrome carving (rather lost in the vast main altar) brought to Chile on the saddle of Pedro de Valdivia in 1540 and credited with guiding him on his way, as well as fending off Indian attackers by throwing sand in their eyes. For all its age and beauty, the most remarkable feature of this church is its deep, hushed silence; you're just metres from the din of the Alameda but the traffic seems a million miles away.

The monastery adjacent to the church houses the **Museo Colonial** (Tues–Sat 10am–1.30pm & 3–6.30pm, Sun 10am–2pm; CH$700), where you'll find a highly evocative collection of paintings, sculpture, furniture, keys and other objects dating from the colonial period, most of it religious and a good deal of it created in Peru, the seat of colonial government. Note the immense eighteenth-century **cedar door** of the first room you come to off the cloisters; carved into hundreds of intricately designed squares, this is one of the museum's most beautiful possessions. Inside the room, you'll find another arresting sight: a gigantic painting of the **genealogical tree of the Franciscan Order** consisting of 644 miniature portraits.

If you turn left as you leave the museum, you'll find yourself on Calle Londres, which intersects Calle París to form **Barrio París-Londres**, tucked behind the Iglesia San Francisco on what used to be the monastery's orchards. These sinuous, cobbled streets lined with refurbished mansions, stylish hotels and busy hostels, look like a tiny piece of Paris's Latin Quarter. Created in 1923 by a team of architects, the barrio is undeniably attractive but feels incongruous to its surroundings; it's also odd the way it's made up of just two streets, and simply stops at the end of them. There is, however, a darker side to the area: the seemingly innocuous building at Calle Londres 38/40 was used as a detention and torture centre under the Pinochet regime. Tiles laid out in front carry the names of some of the political prisoners held here, while the walls are covered with graffiti and slogans. The fate of the building, still undecided, remains an emotive and controversial subject.

From Universidad de Chile to Los Héroes

Back on the Alameda, walking west, you'll come to the yellow-washed walls of the **Universidad de Chile**, a fine French Neoclassical building dating from 1863. Opposite is the **Bolsa de Comercio**, Santiago's stock exchange, housed in a flamboyant, French Renaissance–style building that tapers to a thin wedge at the main entrance. One block further along you reach Plaza Bulnes, flanked by the **tomb** and massive **equestrian statue of Bernardo O'Higgins** to the south (often chained off to keep the public away), and to the north by the grey stone outline of the **Palacio de la Moneda** (see p.94), sitting with its back to the Alameda.

As you continue west past the 128m telecommunications tower known as the **Torre Entel**, the focus of New Year's Eve fireworks displays, you enter what was once the preserve of Santiago's moneyed elite, with several glorious mansions built around 1900 serving as reminders. The first to look out for is the French-style **Palacio Irarrázaval**, on the south side of the Alameda between San Ignacio and Dieciocho; built in 1906 by Cruz Montt, it now belongs to the Círculo Español and houses an old-fashioned restaurant. Adjoining it at the corner of Dieciocho, the slightly later and more ornate **Edificio Iñíguez**, by the same architect in league with Larraín Bravo, houses the institutional *Confitería Torres* (see p.106) – its original home was demolished to make way for the new edifice – said to be where the "national" sandwich, the Barros Luco, was invented in honour of a leading politician. Then check out the 1917 **Palacio Ariztía**, headquarters in Santiago for the nation's deputies, a little further on in the next block; a fine copy of an Art Nouveau French mansion, again by Cruz Montt, it is set off by an iron-and-glass door canopy. Next door, the late-nineteenth-century **Palacio Errázuriz**, the oldest and finest of these Alameda mansions, is now the Brazilian Embassy. Built for Maximiano Errázuriz, mining mogul and leading socialite, it is a soberly elegant two-storey building in a Neoclassical style – the architect was Italian Eusebio Chelli. You're now standing opposite the triumphant **Monumento a los Héroes de la Concepción**, an imposing statue which borders the junction of the Alameda with the Avenida Norte Sur (the Panamericana); this is where metro Lines #1 and #2 intersect at Los Héroes station.

A detour to Palacio Cousiño
Take Line #2 to Toesca, one stop south of Los Héroes, for a highly recommended detour to the **Palacio Cousiño** (Tues–Fri 9.30am–1.30pm & 2.30–5pm, Sat & Sun 9.30am–1.30pm; CH$2100) at Dieciocho 438 (turn left out of Toesca station). This was and remains the most magnificent of the historic palaces, the one that dazzled Santiago's high society by the sheer scale of its luxury and opulence. It was built between 1870 and 1878 for Doña Isidora Goyenechea, the widow of Luis Cousiño, who'd amassed a fortune with his Lota coal mines and Chañarcillo silver mines. All the furnishings and decoration were shipped over from Europe, especially France, and top European craftsmen were brought here to work on the house. The first floor was burnt to ashes in 1968, but the ground floor remains totally intact, and provides a wonderful close-up view of late-nineteenth-century craftsmanship at its best: Italian hand-painted tiles; Bohemian crystal chandeliers; mahogany, walnut and ebony parquet floors; a mosaic marble staircase; and French brocade and silk furnishings are just a few of the splendours of the palace. Visitors must take the 30–45-minute guided **tour** (included in the entry fee), available in Spanish or English.

West to Estación Central
West of Los Héroes, the Alameda continues its path through the once-wealthy neighbourhoods that were abandoned by Santiago's well-heeled a few decades ago, when the moneyed classes shifted to the more fashionable east side of town. After falling into serious decline, these areas are finally coming into their own again, as a younger generation has started renovating decaying mansions, opening up trendy cafés and bookshops and injecting a new vigour into the streets. One of the most beautiful of these neighbourhoods, on the northern side of the Alameda, between Avenida Brasil and Avenida Ricardo Cumming, is **barrio Concha y Toro**, a jumble of twisting cobbled streets leading to a tiny

round plaza with a fountain in the middle. Further north you'll find **barrio Brasil**, one of the liveliest of the newly revived neighbourhoods, centred on the large, grand Plaza Brasil, full of children playing at the amusing cement sculpture playground and among the old silk-cotton and lime trees.

A few blocks west stands one of the Alameda's great landmarks: the stately **Estación Central**, featuring a colossal metal roof that was cast in the Schneider-Creuzot foundry in France in 1896. It's the only functioning train station left in the city, with regular services to the south. Right opposite is the **Planetarium** Av O'Higgins 3349 (shows Fri 7pm, Sat & Sun 11am, noon, 3.30pm, 5pm; CH\$2000; ☎718 2910, ⓦwww.planetariochile.cl), which puts on high-tech audiovisual shows with astronomical themes.

Along the Río Mapocho

Besides the Alameda, the other major axis binding the old city is the **Río Mapocho**, filled with the muddy brown waters from the melted snow of the Andes. There are few historic buildings along here, as frequent flooding deterred riverside development until the Mapocho was canalized in 1891. Nonetheless, several city landmarks stand out, including the flamboyant **Mercado Central**, the **Estación Mapocho** and the elegant **Palacio de Bellas Artes**. Construction of a highway that will run under the riverbed is ongoing.

Mercado Central and Feria Municipal La Vega

If you follow Calle Puente north from the Plaza de Armas you'll reach the **Mercado Central** (Sun–Thurs 6am–4pm, Fri 6am–8pm, Sat 6am–6pm), close to the river's southern bank. This huge metal structure, prefabricated in England and erected in Santiago in 1868, contains a very picturesque fruit, vegetable and fish market that warrants a place on everyone's itinerary. The highlight is the fish stalls, packed with glistening eels, sharks and salmon, buckets of salt-crusted oysters, mussels and clams, and unidentifiable shells out of which live things with tentacles make occasional appearances. The best time to come here is at lunchtime, when you can feast at one of the many **fish restaurants** dotted around the market; the cheapest are on the outer edge, while those in the centre are pretty touristy and pricier, but more atmospheric.

Alternatively cross the river and, by way of the sweetly perfumed **Mercado de Flores**, head for the gargantuan **Feria Municipal La Vega**, set a couple of blocks back from the riverbank opposite the Mercado Central. There's no pretty architecture here, and few tourists; just serious shoppers and hundreds of stalls selling the whole gamut of Central Valley produce, from cows' innards and pigs' bellies to mountains of potatoes and onions, at a fraction of the price charged in the Mercado Central. La Vega is mainly wholesale, and the quantities of fresh fruit on display here are simply breathtaking: table after table piled high with raspberries, grapes, pears, apples, kiwis, plums, nectarines and peaches – all dappled by the sunlight poking through the awnings. There is also a gallery of economical **seafood restaurants**, popular with locals and rarely visited by tourists. Few have alcohol licences, but if you ask for an "iced tea" ("*te helado*") you'll be served either white wine in a Sprite bottle or red wine in a Coca-Cola bottle.

Estación Mapocho

Just west of the Mercado Central, right by the river, is the immense stone and metal **Estación Mapocho**, built in 1912 to house the terminal of the Valparaíso–Santiago railway line. With train service long discontinued, the station is now used as a cultural centre, housing exhibitions, plays and throbbing concerts. You can walk in and have a look inside, worth it if only for the view of its great copper, glass and marble roof. One of the continent's most important book fairs is also held here during the last week of November. This **Feria Nacional del Libro** features appearances by authors such as Isabel Allende, Salvador's bestselling niece.

Parque Forestal neighbourhood

The **Parque Forestal**, stretching along the southern bank of the Mapocho between Puente Recoleta and Puente Pío Nono, was created at the end of the nineteenth century on land that was reclaimed from the river after it was channelled. Lined with long rows of trees and lampposts, it provides a picturesque setting for the **Palacio de Bellas Artes** (Tues–Sun 10am–6.50pm; CH$600, free on Sun), built to commemorate the centenary of Chilean independence. The *palacio* houses the **Museo de Bellas Artes**, featuring predominantly Chilean works from the beginning of the colonial period onwards, and the **Museo de Arte Contemporáneo**. The quality of the work is mixed, and none of the paintings equals the beauty of the building's vast white hall with its marble statues bathing in the natural light pouring in from the glass-and-iron ceiling.

Barrio Bellavista and Cerro San Cristóbal

Originally – and sometimes still – known as *La Chimba*, which means "the other side of the river" in Quichoa (the language of the Inca), **Barrio Bellavista** grew first into a residential area when Santiago's population started spilling across the river in the nineteenth century. Head across the Pío Nono bridge at the eastern end of the Parque Forestal and you'll find yourself on Calle Pío Nono, the main street of Bellavista. Nestling between the northern bank of the Mapocho and the steep slopes of Cerro San Cristóbal, Bellavista is a warren of quiet, leafy streets lined with idiosyncratic restaurants, steeped in a village-like atmosphere. Now a centre for restaurants, pubs, dancing and lofts, it has a reputation for being the capital's bohemian quarter, thanks in part to the fact that Pablo Neruda lived here, along with several other artists, writers and intellectuals. Many of the restaurants are small and atmospheric, and on Thursday, Friday and Saturday nights the district becomes one of Santiago's main dining (see p.107 for restaurants) and going-out centres. Another attraction is the evening handicraft market that spreads along the length of Pío Nono at weekends and is a good place to come for gifts or souvenirs. You might also be tempted by the dozens of lapis lazuli outlets running along Avenida Bellavista, between Puente Pío Nono and Puente del Arzobispo, but be warned that this semi-precious stone is not cheap, and there are few bargains to be found. **Patio Bellavista** (Sun–Wed 10am–2am, Thurs–Sat 10am–4am), Pio Nono 73, is a complex of cafés, restaurants, bars, ice-cream parlours, craft and wine stores, and a bookshop with a good stock of travel guides and trekking maps. There's no metro in Bellavista itself, but it's a short walk from Baquedano station.

La Chascona

Tucked away in a tiny street at the foot of Cerro San Cristóbal – at Marquéz de la Plata 0192 – you'll find **La Chascona**, the house the poet Pablo Neruda shared with his third wife, Matilde Urrutia, from 1955 until his death in 1973 (March–Dec Tues–Sun 10am–6pm; Jan–Feb 10am–7pm; guided tour CH$3000 in Spanish, CH$3500 in English; reserve a place in advance; ⊕737 8712, Ⓦwww.fundacionneruda.org). It was named *La Chascona* ("tangle-haired

BELLAVISTA

CERRO SAN CRISTÓBAL

Parque Jardín Zoológico

PLAZA CAUPOLICAN

La Chascona (Pablo Neruda's home)

CHUCRE MANZUR

CRUCERO EXETER

Centro Cultural Mori

NUEVA DARDIGNAC

EATING & DRINKING

Amorio	6
Bar Dos Gardenias	9
El Caramaño	2
La Casa en el Aire	7
Étniko	4
Galindo	11
Ky Resto-Bar	1
Off The Record	8
El Perseguidor	5
Todos Empanadas	10
Venezia	3

DARDIGNAC

Capilla Liceo Alemán

Patio Bellavista

Hotel del Patio

Parque Gómez Rojas

BELLAVISTA

Escuela de Derecho, Universidad de Chile

Parque Forestal

Río Mapocho

COSTANERA ANDRÉS BELLO

AV. LIB. GENERAL O'HIGGINS

PLAZA BAQUEDANO

BAQUEDANO

AV. PROVIDENCIA

Parque Forestal

0   200 m

woman") by Neruda, as a tribute to his wife's thick red hair. Today it's the headquarters of the Fundación Neruda, which has painstakingly restored this and the poet's two other houses – La Sebastiana in Valparaíso (see p.140) and Isla Negra, about 90km down the coast (see p.147) – to their original condition, opening them to the public.

This house, split into three separate sections that climb up the hillside, is packed to the rafters with objects collected by Neruda, illuminating his loves, enthusiasms and obsessions. Beautiful African carvings jostle for space with Victorian dolls, music boxes, paperweights and coloured glasses; the floors are littered with old armchairs, stools, a rocking horse, exotic rugs and a sleeping toy lion. There are numerous references to Neruda's and Matilde's love for each other, such as the bars on the windows, in which their initials are entwined and lapped by breaking waves, and the portrait of Matilde by Diego Rivera, which has the profile of Neruda hidden in her hair. The third and highest level houses Neruda's library, containing more than nine thousand books, as well as the diploma he was given when awarded the Nobel Prize for Literature in 1971, and a replica of the medal.

Cerro San Cristóbal

A trip up to the summit of **Cerro San Cristóbal** is one of the highlights of a stay in Santiago, particularly on clear, sunny days when the views over the city and to the Andes are quite stunning. The hill is, in fact, a spur of the Andes, jutting into the heart of the capital and rising to a peak of 860m, a point that's marked by a giant 22m-high statue of the *Virgen de la Inmaculada*. The easiest way to get up is to take the **funicular** from the station at the north end of Pío Nono in Bellavista (Mon 1–8pm, Tues–Sun 10am–8pm; CH$1400 return, CH$2500 return including cable-car trip, see below). It stops first at the dismal **zoo** and then continues up to the Terraza Bellavista, where you get out. From here it's a short but steep walk up to the huge white Virgin, where you'll be rewarded with fine views over Santiago's suburbs vanishing into hazy mountains. If you are fortunate enough to be in Santiago after a rain in the winter months, this view includes rows of snowy mountain peaks. Back down at Terraza Bellavista, a path leads west to the **teleférico** (cable car) station known as Estación Cumbre (joint ticket with funicular; see above). This mini-gondola contraption provides hair-raising ski-lift-style rides to Estación Tupahue, then descends to Estación Oasis at the foot of the hill (and a long walk from anywhere).

For an afternoon picnic and **swimming** in the summer months, there is no better place in Santiago than the two huge pools atop the hill. The jointly run Piscina Tupahue and Piscina Antilén (mid-Nov to mid-March Tues–Sun 10am–7pm; CH$5000) offer cool, clean swimming and, at 736m above the city, wonderful views. A *colectivo* from the bottom of the hill costs around CH$400 one-way.

Parque Quinta Normal and its museums

About 1km north of the Estación Central, the **Parque Quinta Normal** is perhaps the most elegant and peaceful of Santiago's parks. It was created in 1830 as a place to introduce and acclimatize foreign trees and plants to the city – Chileans from the nineteenth century onwards have been very fond of filling their public squares with a variety of different trees, many of them

▲ Cable car above Santiago

imported from abroad. Today the park is packed with some beautifully mature examples: Babylonian willows, Monterey pine, cypress, Douglas fir and poplars, to name just a few. Additional attractions include a pond with rowing boats for hire, and four **museums**. The best way to get here is to take the metro to Estación Central, then a bus or taxi up Avenida Matucana. Often deserted during the week, the park is packed on summer weekends.

Museo Nacional de Historia Natural

The grand, Neoclassical building near the park entrance on Matucana houses the **Museo Nacional de Historia Natural** (Tues–Sat 10am–5.30pm, Sun April–Aug noon–5.30pm, Sept–March 11am–6.30pm; CH$600, free on Sun; ☎680 4600, ⓦwww.mnhn.cl). Founded in 1830 and occupying its present building since 1875, this is the oldest natural history museum in Latin America and still one of the most important. It's worth a visit for the colossal skeleton of a blue whale mounted in the vast entrance hall, and for the notable Easter Island collection on the second level, featuring a *moai*, an upturned topknot or hat, and the famous Santiago Staff, inscribed with the mysterious, undeciphered *rongo rongo* script (see p.469). Otherwise, a lack of funds has forced the museum to concentrate more on its role as an academic centre than as a place to inform and entertain the public, and the remaining displays amount to moth-eaten dioramas of Chilean landscapes and a roomful of stuffed birds.

Museo de Ciencia y Tecnología

A short distance west of the natural history museum is the **Museo de Ciencia y Tecnología** (Mon–Fri 9.30am–5.30pm, Sat–Sun 11am–6pm; CH$650). Far more modern and high-tech than the natural history museum, it's geared primarily towards kids, demonstrating the basic principles of physics with entertaining, hands-on gadgets and displays.

Museo Ferroviario

Follow the road down towards the southern park gate, on Avenida Portales, and you'll reach the shiny black steam engines belonging to the outdoor **Museo Ferroviario** (Tues–Fri 10am–5.30pm, Sat–Sun 11am–5.30pm, guided tours available Sat & Sun mornings; CH$750; ☎681 4627). The museum consists of fourteen pristine locomotives dating from 1893 to 1940, including a splendid Kitson-Meyer, manufactured in England in 1909 and shipped over to Chile, where it served the famous trans-Andean service from Los Andes to Mendoza in Argentina until 1971.

Museo Artequín

The wildly colourful glass and metal building standing opposite the park's Avenida Portales entrance was originally the Chilean pavilion in the Universal Exhibition in Paris, 1889. It now contains the engaging **Museo Artequín** (Tues–Fri 9am–5pm, Sat–Sun 11am–6pm; CH$800; ☎681 8687) – short for Arte en la Quinta – which aims to bring people, especially schoolchildren, closer to art by exposing them to reproductions of the world's greatest paintings in a relaxed, less intimidating environment. They're all here, from El Greco and Delacroix through to Andy Warhol and Jackson Pollock.

Parque O'Higgins

Perhaps the best reason to come to the spacious **Parque Bernardo O'Higgins**, a couple of kilometres southeast of the Quinta Normal, is to soak up the Chilean family atmosphere, as it's one of the most popular green spaces in the city. It was originally the Parque Cousiño, commissioned by Luis Cousiño, the entrepreneurial millionaire, in 1869, and *the* place to take your carriage rides in the late nineteenth century. These days working-class families and groups of kids flock here on summer weekends to enjoy the picnic areas, outdoor pools (very crowded), roller rink, basketball court and the gut-churning rides of **Fantasilandia**, an outdoor amusement park (Aug–Nov 9: Sat, Sun and public holidays noon–7pm; at other times only open for group bookings; CH$6500–6900). It's easy to reach via public transport; take Line #2 to the Parque O'Higgins station, then walk three blocks. The park also features **El Pueblito**, a collection of adobe buildings typical of the Chilean countryside and housing several cheap restaurants, some craft stalls and a handful of small museums. The best of these is the **Museo del Huaso** (Tues–Fri 10am–5pm, Sat & Sun 10am–2pm), dedicated to the Chilean cowboy, or horseman, with displays of spurs, saddles, ponchos and hats, and a big photo of Pope John Paul II decked out in a poncho when he visited the museum in April 1987 (he came to offer Mass at the chapel next door). There's also a tiny shell museum, an insect museum and a not very exciting aquarium. See p.257 for more on Chile's *huasos*.

Los barrios altos: Providencia, Las Condes and beyond

The barrios east of the city centre spreading into the foothills of the Andes are home to Santiago's moneyed elite; the farther you go and higher you get, the richer the people, bigger the houses and higher the gates. It's hard to believe that up until the beginning of the twentieth century there was virtually no one here; it was for its isolation and tranquillity that the Sisters of Providencia chose to build their convent on what is now Avenida Providencia in 1853. (By the way, the parallel street running in the other direction, Av 11 de Septiembre, takes its name from the date of the 1973 military coup, not the 2001 terrorist attacks in the United States.) Later, following a slow trickle of eastbound movement, there was a great exodus of wealthy families from their traditional preserves west of the city over to the new barrio alto in the 1920s, where they've been entrenched ever since.

The barrio you're most likely to visit is Providencia, home to Sernatur, various adventure tourism and skiing outfits and a thriving nightlife scene. Further east in Las Condes the atmosphere is more residential, and apart from a few notable exceptions such as Los Dominicos market, there's less to pull you out here. If you've access to a car, however, it can be quite fun to drive around the fabulously wealthy uptown barrios like El Arrayán and La Dehesa. You could even just sit on a bus to the end of Avenida Las Condes to watch the Andes get closer and closer and feel the city creep higher and higher.

Providencia

You can walk east along the Alameda to the centre of **Providencia** in about twenty or thirty minutes from the Universidad Católica, or else you could take the metro (to Manuel Montt, Pedro de Valdivia or Los Leones, depending on which stretch you want to get to). Providencia takes its name from its oldest building, the yellow-washed **Iglesia de Nuestra Señora de la Divina Providencia**, founded in 1853 – the interior is disappointingly dull. Opposite, occupying a former fruit and vegetable market, is **Sernatur** (see p.257), and a few blocks east of here you're into the commercial heart of the barrio, with its stylish stores and elegant cafés. Bland and faceless for some, Providencia is nonetheless convenient for its modern retail, buzzing nightlife and compact size.

Las Condes

As you move east to **Las Condes**, the shops and office blocks gradually thin out into a more residential district, punctuated with the occasional large shopping mall, such as **Alto Las Condes**, Av Kennedy 901 (daily 10am–10pm). A free shuttle bus runs twice daily from most major hotels to the mall and back (T229 1383 for times). In addition, most of the buses running along the Alameda displaying "Las Condes" in the front window will stop near the mall.

The best overall collection of arts and crafts is found at **Pueblito de los Dominicos** market, Apoquindo 9085 (daily: summer 10.30am–8pm; winter 10am–7pm), a large, lively and expensive craft fair held in a mock village. Follow Avenida Apoquindo 4km past the Escuela Militar metro stop to the end. You'll find a wide range of beautiful handicrafts – made in workshops on site and sold at the stalls – as well as antiques, books, fossil shark teeth, a decent restaurant, and a quiet respite from the noise and grime of the city. Chilean sculptor Elias Rivera (in Stand 81) offers a fascinating collection of stone carvings. Next door is the **Iglesia Los Dominicos**, built by Toesca in the late eighteenth century; the church is usually locked, but you can admire its attractive colonial architecture from the gardens between 4pm and 8pm on weekdays. Buses marked "Apoquindo" come here from all along the Alameda, or you can take the metro out to Estación Militar then get a *colectivo* (under the bridge next to the station).

Eating

Santiago could make a serious bid for the title of fast-food capital of the world, with a proliferation of uninviting international and domestic **chains** spread around the city. Even so, those are often more inviting than the hundreds of tacky **fuentes de soda** offering beer, TV and high-cholesterol snacks – such as the *completo*, an avocado, tomato, sauerkraut and mayonnaise-slathered hot dog. Add to these the numerous stand-up **snack bars** on the south side of the Plaza de Armas, and you've got a comprehensive picture of the budget food scene in Santiago. For not much more you can eat more heartily and healthily in some of the old-fashioned **bars** or local **picadas** (inexpensive canteens), which serve Chilean standards like *pastel de choclo*, *humitas* and *cazuela*.

Nonetheless, there's also an enormous choice of **restaurants**, from the humble to the outstanding, offering many different types of cuisine including Asian, Middle Eastern, Spanish, Peruvian, French and Italian. Some are modestly priced but the majority are fairly expensive, although at **lunch time** many offer a good-value fixed-price **menú del día** or **menú ejecutivo**. For this reason a lot of restaurants, particularly downtown, tend to be packed at lunch time but fairly quiet (sometimes empty) in the evening, at least during the week. In most places there's no need to **book ahead**; where it's advisable, we've included a phone number. Most places are open Monday to Saturday for lunch and dinner, and close on **Sunday**. Exceptions are noted.

Santiago is not a café city, but there are a number of **coffee shops** catering to the great tradition of *onces* (afternoon tea). The influence of Chile's German immigrants is very much in evidence here, with many places serving delicious *küchen* and strudel.

Cafés and budget eateries

You don't have to resort to the ubiquitous, multinational burger chains to eat without spending too much in Santiago. This list includes a couple of **sandwich bars**, ideal for a low-cost snack, plus a couple of **Japanese** eateries (often good budget options in Santiago unlike elsewhere). You'll also find a curious and eclectic range of **cafés**, from homely coffee shops full of weary housewives to trendy, US-owned chains serving Seattle-style coffee and baguettes. An unusual (and not particularly politically correct) feature of the city is the tradition of **stand-up coffee bars**, known as *cafés con piernas*, of which there are dozens; they're staffed by micro-skirted or scantily dressed waitresses serving inexpensive, generally decent coffee. While mainly patronized by bored men from the offices, there is no taboo against women entering, and plenty of people do go just for the coffee, which is often better than anywhere else.

El Aji Seco San Antonio 528, historic centre. A hectic Peruvian joint, popular with families, serving sizeable portions of ceviche, fried chicken, seafood and *lomo saltado* (a heaped plate of beef, onions, tomatoes, chips and rice), which you can wash down with an Inca Cola. Mains CH$2800–6000.

Bar Nacional Bandera 317 and Paseo Huérfanos 1151, historic centre. This unpretentious stalwart of the Santiago dining scene has two branches, and serves simple Chilean staples (CH$3500–6500) with the minimum of fuss.

Bar de la Unión Nueva York 11, near the Bolsa, historic centre. Old wooden floors, shelves of dusty wine bottles and animated, garrulous old men make this an atmospheric place to pop in for a cheap glass of wine or a leisurely lunch. The food's tasty (lots of fish), good value (set lunch CH$2300) and generously portioned.

Bonbon Oriental Merced 355, Barrio Lastarria. Photos of regular customers cover the walls of this tiny Middle Eastern café, which serves proper cardamom-scented Arabic coffee, falafel sandwiches (CH$1500–2000) and sticky-sweet baclavas; there's also a sister joint a few doors down.

Café Caribe Ahumada 120, historic centre; one of several branches. Traditional *café con piernas* where members of Chile's ageing business class stand around for what seems like hours, ogling the waitresses and talking on their mobile phones. Coffee from CH$1000.

Café Colonia Mac Iver 161, historic centre. Matronly waitresses in German costume serve the best cakes, tarts, *küchen* and strudel (all from CH$500 per slice) in Santiago. This cute little café has been going for over fifty years and remains a perennial favourite with Santiago's housewives.

Café Haiti Ahumada 140, historic centre, one of several branches. Another of the timewarp *café con piernas*; casual, stand-up cafés serviced by tightly clad waitresses – but the coffee (from CH$1000) is not to be sniffed at.

Emporio La Rosa Merced 291, Barrio Lastarria. Hands-down the best place for a freshly made croissant or *pain au chocolat* (CH$1000) in Santiago – be warned: you're unlikely to find one left after midday – this café-deli also has wildly inventive ice-cream flavours, such as chocolate and basil. It's a popular student hangout in the evening. Open daily.

Galindo Corner of Constitución and Dardignac. Busy at all hours for hearty dishes like beef casserole and *loganiza* (spicy sausage) and chips. During the summer the tables spill out onto the street – something that has invited many nearby copycats – but the young bohemian crowd remains loyal to this classic Bellavista hang-out. Mains CH$3100–5300. Open daily.

Kebab Bar La Bolsa 67, historic centre. This tiny restaurant serves up excellent Greek salads, fresh fruit juices, and thick meat sandwiches spiked with Middle Eastern flavours. Mains around CH$3000. Closed Sat and Sun.

Kintaro Monjitas 460, historic centre. A busy – particularly at lunch time – Japanese canteen serving a delicious range of sushi, sashimi, tempura and yakisoba (meals CH$3000–5000). If you sit at the counter you can even watch the chefs at work.

Las Lanzas Humberto Trucco 25, Plaza Ñuñoa. This traditional bar-restaurant, with tables spilling onto the pavement, is *the* classic drinking spot in Ñuñoa. They also offer a range of fish dishes at amazingly low prices (from CH2500).

El Rápido Bandera 371, historic centre. For more than 80 years El Rápido has lived up to its name, with a brisk turnover in empanadas (from CH$800), sandwiches and soups. Call out your order as you enter and by the time you reach the counter your food will be waiting for you.

Roll's Bar Guardia Vieja 208, Providencia. Hidden behind the forbidding black exterior is an excellent and extremely good-value sushi joint – they have a large selection for under CH$5000. It turns into a DJ bar on weekend evenings.

La Tecla Doctor Johow 320, south side of Plaza Ñuñoa. A curvaceous piano keyboard design on the outside, shaded courtyard garden, some of the city's best pancakes, potent cocktails and vaguely Spanish-French fare (set lunch CH$3200) make *La Tecla* a great choice. Closed Sun evening.

Todos Empanadas Pio Nono 153, Bellavista. There are 31 types of empanada (CH$800) here, from the savoury (such as salmon) to the sweet (like apple), which you can take away or eat on the plastic chairs and tables outside.

Restaurants

Most of Santiago's **restaurants** are concentrated in six areas: the historic centre, Barrio Lastarria, Bellavista, Barrio Brasil, Providencia, and El Bosque Norte. The first three more or less comprise central Santiago, and thus are most accessible, but the others are conveniently on the metro line and not too terrible a trek. There are also some imaginative places springing up around Plaza Ñuñoa in the southeast part of town, and Vitacura (see p.108).

Perhaps the most memorable place for lunch is the Mercado Central (see p.98), whose central hall is lined with *marisquerías*, the most famous and expensive being *Donde Augusto*. Alternatively follow the locals to the cheaper joints across the river in the Feria Municipal La Vega.

Historic centre

Confitería Torres Corner of Alameda and Dieciocho, near Los Héroes. Open since 1879, this is one of the oldest restaurants in Santiago. While the food is a little overpriced (mains around CH$6500), the dark, wood-panelled walls, the old, tarnished mirrors and the sagging chairs provide a fabulous atmosphere. At weekends there's live music from around 10.30pm. There's also a chic modern branch at the Centro Cultural Palacio La Moneda, which, unlike its older sister, is open on Sunday.

La Habana Vieja Tarapaca 755, between Santa Rosa and San Francisco ☎638 5284, ⓦwww.lahabanavieja.cl. Large hall containing a restaurant, small dancefloor and a stage, best at the weekend when there's live salsa music, Cuban "son" and bolero. The menu includes Cuban staples like cassava, yellow rice and black beans, and fried plantains. Mains CH$3900–4700.

Barrio Brasil

Interesting, off-beat cafés, restaurants and bars are springing up all the time in Barrio Brasil, with seafood a particular speciality of the area. Reservations at weekends are recommended for both the establishments listed below.

Las Vacas Gordas Cienfuegos 280 ☎697 1066. This superior steakhouse has earned a well-deserved reputation for top-quality meat (CH$5000–10,000) – try the melt-in-the-mouth Wagyu beef or the flavoursome entrecote. Service is sharp, and the large, airy dining room has a pleasantly relaxed ambiance.

Ostras Azocar General Bulnes 37 ☎681 6109. Complimentary oysters and a glass of wine await you at this long-established seafood restaurant, which has been serving king crab, lobster, squid and more since the 1940s. The house speciality is baked razor clams in a cheese sauce. Sadly the waiting staff can be slack. Mains CH$6000–12,000.

Barrio Lastarria

Reservations are recommended here in the evenings, as many of the restaurants have fewer than ten tables. Parking is easy, and the barrio is just a two-minute walk from the Universidad Católica metro stop. This neighbourhood generally is safe, but the Santa Lucia park around the hill is not a good place to go after midnight.

Don Victorino Lastarria 138 ☎639 5263. The food (pastas, fish and meat; mains CH$4800–6000) is not the best on this street, but it's one of the prettiest and most intimate places to dine, especially at the tables next to the little fountain on the terrace. Closed Sat lunch and Sun dinner.

Gatopardo Lastarria 192 ☎633 6420. Sturdy oak trunks dominate the dining room at this Mediterranean restaurant, whose CH$6000 set lunch includes a trip to the salad bar, main course, desert, Pisco sour, glass of wine and a coffee. Stick with the mainstream dishes as the more exotic options can be a fusion step too far. Closed Sat lunch and Sun.

Squadritto Rosal 332, on east side of Cerro Santa Lucía ☎632 2121. Superb and pricey Italian food (the risottos are a particular highlight) in a stylish, somewhat formal environment. Mains from CH$7000. Closed Sat lunch and Sun.

Zabo Plaza Mulato Gil de Costa, just off Lastarria. This Japanese cocktail bar is a great place for an early evening drink, people-watching and a teriyaki, temaki, sushi or sashimi snack (CH$3000–6000). Sit outside in the cobbled courtyard or in the intimate bar area, which is decorated with giant lanterns.

Bellavista

Bellavista – particularly Calle Constitución, which runs parallel with the area's main drag, Pio Nono – is the epicentre of Santiago's eating-out scene, with a wide range of excellent, and often innovative, restaurants.

Amorio Constitución 181 ☎777 1454. You can dine on octopus with a sake dressing, ostrich carpaccio or rainbow trout with basil pesto at this enticing refurbished nineteenth-century townhouse, which is owned by two Chilean TV stars and forms part of the Mori Cultural centre. Mains CH$6900–9500. Open Tues–Sat, and Sun lunch.

El Caramaño Purisima 257 ☎737 7043. Graffiti-covered walls, soft live guitar music, amiable waiters, excellent, wallet-friendly Chilean food like *pastel de choclo*, and frequently a free aperitif make this a stand-out choice. Mains CH$2900–4900.

Étniko Constitución 172, at Lopez de Bello ☎732 0119. The blue neon-lit, Japanese-inspired interior draws a cool 20s–30s crowd; there are more than 40 types of sushi and sashimi (from CH$2000 per item) and it turns into a bar-club at night. Try the knockout sake-based cocktails. You have to ring the doorbell to enter.

Off the Record Antonia López de Bello 0155 ☎777 7710. While the moderately priced food – mainly Chilean fare (around CH$5000) – varies in quality, the informal setting and lively feel more than compensate. If you come on a Monday evening, you'll have to fight for a seat: local authors and artists give talks or performances that attract an often impassioned crowd. Open daily.

🏃 **El Toro** Loreto 33 ☎737 5937. An effortlessly trendy restaurant with an appealing whimsical air – pots of crayons are left on each table so that you can doodle while you wait for your food – and an array of tempting dishes such as shrimp crepes and crab gratin. Mains CH$4500–6100. Open daily.

Venezia Pío Nono 200. One of the oldest restaurants in the city (it was founded in the 1870s) and a former haunt of Pablo Neruda, this old-fashioned bar/*picada* has a family atmosphere that gives it more charm than many of its smarter, newer rivals. The food is mainly grills, sandwiches and other traditional snacks. Mains CH$4000–6000.

Providencia and Ñuñoa

Conveniently located on the metro, Providencia offers many lunch and dinner options. Nearby, though less accessible, Ñuñoa has trendier eateries, often with good music thrown in.

Astrid y Gastón Antonio Bellet 201, Providencia ☎650 9125. Highly regarded fusion restaurant (although some contend it's lost a little of its sparkle in recent times). The owners' Peruvian origins show through in the menu, but you can also find European (particularly Spanish) and Asian influences. The Catalan-inspired tuna in a honey sauce, wine list and delicate soufflés are all standouts. Reserve at least two weeks in advance. Mains CH$8000–12,000.

Barandaraián Manuel Montt 315, Providencia ☎236 6854. Some of the best Peruvian food in Santiago is served here: ceviche, sea bass and the more leftfield choice of Patagonian lamb in a coriander sauce are all on offer (CH$4000–6000), and there are good lunch deals. It's three blocks from the Manuel Montt metro. There's also a newer branch in Patio Bellavista.

🏃 **Le Flaubert** Orrego Luco 125 ☎231 9424. This exemplary Chilean-French bistro has a select, ever-changing menu marked up on chalkboards. Dishes could include country pate, rabbit and *tarte tartin*, and you can eat in the lovely garden patio or the refined dining room. Mains cost around CH$6000 and there's a set lunch for CH$5800. A shop at the front sells home-made cheeses and preserves. Open daily.

Guris Brasileiro Los Leones 3093, Ñuñoa. Lively Brazilian *churascaria* – an all-you-can-eat meat restaurant that's perfect for carnivores with big appetites. Waiters circulate constantly with all manner of chargrilled beef, chicken, pork and fish, and there's also an endless supply of sides, salads and desserts. CH$9900 for men, CH$7100 for women, plus drinks.

Infante 51 J.M. Infante 51, Providencia ☎264 3357. Outstanding restaurant where simple but refined fish, seafood and lamb dishes are served in a converted villa, with a quiet patio at the back. The Basque chef brings a touch of San Sebastián sophistication to fish (such as orange roughy) from Juan Fernández or even as far away as Rapa Nui. Mains CH$6000–10,000.

Liguria Av Providencia 1373. Portraits, film posters, flower designs and football pennants adorn the walls of this legendary Santiago restaurant-bar, which has outdoor tables, a bar area with stools, main dining area and several back rooms, so you can normally find a seat. The food varies between steaks, pot roasts and Italian dishes (CH$4500–7200). There are two other branches, but this is the best.

Santo Remedio Roman Diaz 152 ☎235 0984. The idiosyncratic decor has a surreal edge – including high-backed wooden chairs and a zebra print sofa – and the food is billed as "an aphrodisiacal experience", with couscous, curries, pasta and teriyaki chicken all featuring on the menu. It's also *the* place for a Sunday night out, as well as a good stopover for drinks any night of the week. Mains CH$5600–7500. Open daily.

La Terraza Jorge Washington 58, Plaza Ñuñoa. A mellow restaurant-bar with a vine-covered terrace and an Italian-flavoured menu of meat, fish, pastas and snacks (mains CH$4000–5500). It attracts a youngish, fashionable crowd, particularly at weekends.

El Bosque Norte and Vitacura

These two exclusive neighbourhoods lie beyond the end of the metro line. As you'd expect, restaurants here tend to be more about money than taste, but those listed below are worth the extra outlay (including the taxi fare).

Akarana Reyes Lavalle 3310 ☎231 9667. This hugely popular New Zealand restaurant offers everything from hearty lamb dishes to creations made with Chile's wealth of seafood, including squid and tuna (mains CH$8700–9800): try the crispy-skinned duck leg stuffed with chestnuts and cranberries. Friendly owner Nell serves tables herself, bringing a homely touch to this charming spot. Open daily.

Cafe Melba Don Carlos 2898 ☎232 4546. Brunch (CH$4000–5000), complete with eggs Benedict and fresh coffee, is a Sunday ritual for many expats. *Melba* also offers free internet access and English-language message boards. Open daily for breakfast and lunch.

Nolita Isidora Goyenechea 3456 ☎232 6114. Self-consciously aping the style of the eponymous New York district, *Nolita* produces top-quality, artfully presented Italian cuisine (mains CH$7000–8000), with the seafood dishes (notably the shellfish platter) and the desserts both outstanding. Open Mon–Sat, and Sun lunch.

Zanzibar Monseñor Escriva de Balaguer 6400, inside the Borde del Río complex ☎218 0120. One of Santiago's most beautiful restaurants, with a host of dining rooms, including a rooftop Moroccan-style tented lounge. Astride the Río Mapocho and a glider port, the restaurant offers plenty of sights from its rooftop. Monthly full-moon parties feature belly dancers, body painting and a collection of fine global dishes (CH$8000–11,000). Highly recommended, even if does take a 25min taxi ride to get here.

Drinking, music and nightlife

Santiago is no Buenos Aires or Rio. It is not a seven-nights-a-week party town, and compared to other Latin American capitals can seem rather tame. That said, Thursdays, Fridays and Saturdays are lively, and huge, buzzing crowds pour into the streets and bars of the nightlife *zonas*. These fall into

▲ Barrio Bellavista's outdoor bars

three main areas – Bellavista, Providencia and Ñuñoa – each with a distinct flavour and clientele. In addition, **the historic centre of Santiago** is seeing a renaissance, as young people turn apartments into lofts and old bars into trendy hangouts, while **Barrio Brasil** also boasts a growing number of cool, idiosyncratic bars, particularly around Plaza Brasil.

Bellavista, a short walk from Baquedano metro, is the most picturesque of the nightlife zones, with its colourful night-time market running the length of the main street. Though a number of loud discos are on Pío Nono, the area is characterized by its small, informal restaurants, many of them putting on live music after 11pm, usually guitar music, *boleros* or Latin. It is generally a safe area, though keep an eye for drunks from around 2am to 6am on Saturday and Sunday mornings.

Providencia is packed with bar-restaurants (notably *Liguria*, see opposite) that at weekends draw huge crowds of professional types, including expats and foreign visitors. The after-work crowd ensures it's fairly lively during the week too. There are also dozens of dispiriting, cheesy American-style bars, particularly around the junction of Suecia and Holley, which should be avoided.

Ñuñoa, a residential neighbourhood popular with artists and families, is very different again. The restaurants are centred on Plaza Ñuñoa, but there are some spectacular exceptions that are worth hauling the map out for. This is where you'll find Santiago's main "underground" scene; the bars and cafés lining the main square are filled with nonchalant students in ripped black jeans and leather jackets. Ñuñoa also has a couple of good live music venues, including a jazz club. The area is often overlooked by travellers and this is a mistake; once you find it, coming back is easy either by bus or a CH$4000–4500 cab ride from most central parts of Santiago.

These are the main areas for drinking and listening to music, though you'll find a number of other places scattered around the city – in Las Condes, for example. When it comes to dancing, Santiago's **nightclubs** are more widely dispersed, some of them quite a drive away. The ones we've listed below are

Santiago's vegetarian restaurants

Chilean food revolves firmly around meat and fish, and vegetarians will quickly tire of the few meat-free staples such as *humitas* (corn mash in corn husk) and *empanadas de queso* (baked or fired dough with a chunk of cheese in the middle). Santiago does, however, offer a handful of good **vegetarian restaurants** serving modern, imaginative veggie food at low prices. Popular with office workers, these places are packed at lunch time.

El Huerto Orrego Luco 054, Providencia. The best veggie restaurant in Santiago, with a mouthwatering range of inventive, seasonal dishes; Greek salad, gazpacho, calzone and a toothsome cheesecake all feature on the menu. Next door to the main restaurant is a café section, which has a more limited menu but is good for a sandwich and a juice. Mains CH$5000. Open Mon–Sat, and Sun lunch.

El Naturista Moneda 846, near Estado, historic centre. The original pioneer of vegetarian food in Santiago, this large, inexpensive restaurant attracts a huge, frenetic crowd at lunch time; the salad featuring Andean supergrain quinoa is well worth sampling. If there's no room, try the stand-up bar on the ground floor. Mains around CH$3000.

El Vegetariano Huérfanos 827, in a *galería* (arcade) near the corner with San Antonio, historic centre. Aim to get a table on the raised level, where you can tuck into Spanish omelette, veggie burgers and crepes (CH$2000–3000) under a stained-glass roof. Leave room for desserts like lemon pie and banana split.

all reasonably central, easily reached by taxi (and some of them on foot). The club scene is notoriously difficult to pin down – places drift in and out of fashion, and open and close in an apparently random manner. The ones below should be reliable, but it's a good idea to seek advice from locals (bar staff are usually helpful). Prices at the most fashionable clubs are high, up to CH$10,000 per person, affordable only to the most affluent young Chileans.

When mega-famous bands or singers play in Santiago, they usually perform in places like the Santiago Arena (Beaucheff 1204, Parque O'Higgins ☎478 7900, ⓦ www.arenasantiago.cl). This is quite rare, however, and most South American and national bands play in smaller, more intimate **venues**. For details of who's playing where and when, check the listings section (under "*Recitales*") of Friday's *El Mercurio* or *La Tercera del Día*, or visit *La Feria del Disco* at Ahumada 286, where performances are advertised and tickets are sold at the Ticketmaster counter. Another source of information is the English-language *Revolver* (ⓦ www.revolver-magazine.com), part of the *Santiago Times* newspaper. Excellent national bands to see live are classics Inti Illimani and Las Jaivas. Newer acts worth catching include Los Bunkers and Natalino.

As you make your plans for the night, bear in mind that at the weekend things don't liven up until quite late in Santiago – from around 10 or 11pm in restaurants, and from about midnight to 1am in clubs.

Also be aware that prostitution is very common here: at least a dozen highly publicized brothels thrive throughout Santiago, and newspapers run pages of advertisements for "saunas".

Bars and live music venues

Santiago's **bars** range from dusty, mahogany-panelled corner bars full of ancient regulars to ultra-trendy spaces selling designer beers. They are often good places to catch up on some musical entertainment too. **Live music** in Santiago ranges from romantic folk songs to Britpop covers, and you'll find venues everywhere from the historic centre to bohemian Ñuñoa, in bars, jazz clubs and special concert venues. The historic **Estación Mapocho** (see p.98) occasionally hosts concerts by stars such as Joan Manuel Serrat and David Byrne; check Ⓦwww .estacionmapocho.cl for details.

Bar Dos Gardenias Antonia López de Bello 199, Bellavista. A chilled-out and welcoming Cuban bar, with the obligatory Che picture, live Latin music and refreshing drinks. There's a sister café at no. 104.

Bar Yellow General Flores 47–51, Providencia. A softly-lit, seductive bar whose expert staff mix a mean selection of cocktails for a sophisticated crowd of patrons.

La Batuta Jorge Washington 52, Plaza Ñuñoa Ⓦwww.batuta.cl. There's a wonderful grungy atmosphere at this dark, packed bar-dance club, which hosts rock bands, hip hop groups and heavy metal outfits.

Café-Berri Rosal 321, historic centre. Small, understated bar hidden away on a little street east of Santa Lucía that's well worth checking out. Friendly Basque staff and a loyal local following give this place a great atmosphere, even during the week.

La Casa en el Aire Antonia López de Bello 0125. Named after Neruda's poem *Voy a hacerte una casa en el aire*, this bar-café is one of the nicest places in Bellavista to enjoy a drink and live folk music, with occasional poetry recitals thrown in. There's also a newer, less atmospheric branch in Patio Bellavista.

Catedral Corner of Merced and Jose Miguel de la Barra, historic centre. This second-floor bar is a swish, modern space with a roof terrace ideal for a summer evening. There's a good menu of drinks, and a small selection of dishes – like *moules et frites* – if you get peckish. Mains CH$8000–9000.

Club de Jazz José Pedro Alessandri 85, a block south of Plaza Ñuñoa. Relaxed and friendly, with loads of atmosphere and invariably an excellent line-up of Chilean and international jazz musicians. Live music Thursday, Friday and Saturday.

Ky Resto-Bar Av Peru 631, Bellavista. From the outside this old house appears to have been abandoned, but once inside you find a beautifully renovated bar-restaurant kitted out with an eclectic array of knick-knacks. It's great for a late-night drink or a Thai-Malaysian meal (mains around CH$6500).

Lamu Lounge Monseñor Escriva de Balaguer 6400, inside the Borde del Río complex, Vitacura ☎218 0116. This lounge bar draws a hip, slightly older 30s crowd with its stripped-back design, white cube-like seats and Asian and African motifs. If you want a table at the weekends, you'll need to reserve in advance.

El Perseguidor Antonia López de Bello 126, Bellavista Ⓦwww.elperseguidor.cl. Acts at *El Perseguidor* play more contemporary and experimental jazz than at *Club de Jazz*; check the website to see who's performing.

Nightclubs

Santiago's nightclubs tend to be the preserve of the city's more affluent classes, and are well out of most young people's price range. In addition to the clubs listed below, *La Batuta* (listed under "Live music venues", above) and *La Habana Vieja* (listed under the "Eating" section, p.106) are popular places to go dancing. Cover charges range from CH$3000–10,000.

Blondie Alameda 2879, north side, near ULA metro. A popular student hangout close to the university with loud music (lots of techno and Britpop) and dancing.

Club La Feria Constitución 275, Bellavista Ⓦwww.clublaferia.cl. The best place in town for electronica, spun by an illustrious cast of Chilean and international DJs.

Laberinto Vicuña Mackenna 915, near Irarrázaval. Very stylish, contemporary club spread over the various levels, galleries and passages of an old converted warehouse. Plays a mixture of house, indie and rock to cool young things in designer threads.

La Maestra Vida Pío Nono 380, Bellavista. One of Santiago's oldest *salsatecas* and popular with dancers of all ages (including a few ageing Latin American revolutionaries), giving it a friendly vibe – there's no need to feel shy about practising your salsa here.

Gay Santiago

Santiago is the only city in Chile with anything resembling an organized gay community. The more progressive social background and the political sea change of the past few years have resulted in a far more relaxed attitude towards gay and lesbian issues than was found after the restoration of democracy. The gay scene, such as it is (do not expect San Francisco or London's Soho), centres around **Bellavista**, consisting of a small collection of bars, restaurants, discos and saunas; up-to-date information about these can be found on Ⓦ www.santiagogay.com. Chile's Gay Pride Parade takes place in September, and there is a gay and lesbian film festival every January or February at the Cine Arte Alameda (see opposite).

Bokhara Pío Nono 430. A legendary, multi-storey disco with a mixed gay and lesbian crowd, and shows featuring drag artists and Brazilian dance troupes. The queues to get in, however, can be long.

Bunker Bombero Nuñez 159. This somewhat gloomy refurbished theatre is one of the most popular gay clubs in Santiago, thanks mainly to its dance and techno music policy. There's a cavernous back room, filled with large crowds at weekends, and it's also busy on Thursdays, when there's no entrance charge. Closed Sun and Mon.

Capricho Español Purísima 65. Spanish and international cuisine (such as garlic olives in an herb mayonnaise) served by an all-male wait staff in an atmospheric, neo-colonial building. Try to grab the cow-print sofa on the terrace. Free passes to *Bokhara* are often handed out.

Farinelli Bombero Nuñez 68. This gay version of a *café con piernas* (the waiters wear nothing but sequin waistcoats and G-strings), lays on shows every evening, some of them hilarious comic drag acts requiring a decent level of Spanish to fully appreciate. Reasonably priced drinks and ice creams, inevitably including a suggestive banana split.

Friend's Bombero Nuñez 365. This aptly named welcoming pub offers cabaret shows and strippers from 9pm onwards. Open Tues–Sat.

The arts and entertainment

Chile is noted in Latin America for the quality and range of its **theatre**, and Santiago is of course the best place to see it. Performances are staged in the many theatres and cultural centres dotted about the city, and take in everything from time-honoured classics to contemporary and experimental works. **Classical music** is performed in a number of venues, including theatres, cultural centres and churches; check out the cheap midday concerts held from around June to December at the Teatro Municipal. This is the most prestigious venue in Santiago for music, **dance** and **opera**, and although it tends to be fairly conservative in its repertoire, it occasionally puts on innovative new productions, usually from abroad. **Cinema** is very popular in Santiago, with a concentration of movie theatres on Huérfanos, in the historic centre, and several newer, modern ones in Providencia, Las Condes and Ñuñoa. Most films shown are mainstream US imports, usually in the original version with Spanish subtitles, but there are a number of **arts cinemas** showing non-commercial films and old movies.

Although all the Friday newspapers include comprehensive details of **what's on** at the weekend, none gives descriptions or synopses to help you work out what you're interested in. The best is probably *La Tercera*'s Friday supplement, though many Santiaguinos prefer the "*Wikén*" section that comes with Friday's *El Mercurio*. Increasingly, websites have current movie schedules (try Ⓦ www.cinehoyts.cl or www.cinemark.cl). The daily papers also give cinema listings for that day.

Most entertainment in Santiago is quite affordable, with theatre and concert tickets commonly going for CH$3000 to CH$5000. Even the Teatro Municipal offers inexpensive ballet and opera (from around CH$2000 for national productions and from CH$15,000 for international productions) though the better seats are considerably more expensive (as much as CH$60,000–70,000 for international opera).

Cinemas

Most of the best cinemas are in the eastern portion of the city. **Huérfanos** is the main cinema street in the historic centre of Santiago. You will find latest Hollywood features in the modern facility at Hoyts (Huérfanos 735).

Mainstream

Cinemark Theatres Av Kennedy 9001, Mall Alto Las Condes. Twelve-screen, modern facility offering Hollywood's latest.

Cine Hoyts Huérfanos 735 ⊕ 600/500 0400. The most modern and comfortable theatre in central Santiago.

Cine Hoyts La Reina Av Ossa 655/Simón Bolívar 5840 ⊕ 600/500 0400, ⓦ www.cinehoyts.cl. Chile's largest movie complex, with sixteen screens, including two or three reserved for non-commercial art films or recent Chilean releases. The best overall cinema in Chile, but way out in La Reina, an eastern suburb. You'll probably need a taxi or car to get here.

Arts cinemas

For art-house films – known as *cine arte* – try the following:

AIEP Miguel Claro 177 ⊕ 570 4000, ⓦ www.aiep .cl. University cinema screening off-beat European documentaries and art films.

Centro Cultural Matucana 100 Matucana 100, near Estación Central ⊕ 682 4502, ⓦ www.m100 .cl. Runs regular film seasons (recent subjects include Ken Loach and Martin Scorsese), often in English. Also has art exhibitions and concerts.

Centro de Extensión de la Universidad Católica Alameda 390 ⊕ 354 6516, ⓦ www.puc .cl/extension. Especially good for older films,

often presented as part of themed programmes. Many free showings for students with ID.

Cine Arte Alameda Alameda 139, near Plaza Baquedano ⊕ 633 9564. Comfy, well-arranged seats and a fast-changing, wide-ranging choice of foreign films.

Cine Arte Normandie Tarapacá 1181, in the historic centre ⊕ 697 2979. Has a reputation for showing obscure contemporary European films.

Theatre

We've listed some of the main theatres below, but quality performances are staged in many different venues, including various multipurpose cultural centres and sometimes in the open-air amphitheatre of the Palacio de Bellas Artes. While there is wide range of shows, audiences are generally pretty small. Check the weekend listings, and keep an eye out for anything involving Paz Bascuñan, Cristián Campos, Willy Semler or Lillian Ross as director. The best time to experience Chilean theatre is in January, when Santiago hosts "*Santiago a Mil*" (ⓦ www.stgoamil.cl), an enormous international **festival of theatre** (plus dance and other arts). During the rest of the year, many theatres are only open Thursday to Saturday. Ticket prices are usually reasonable, from CH$3500 to CH$6000. Entertaining children's theatre is widely available on Saturday and Sunday afternoons.

Centro Cultural Mori Constitución183 ⊕ 777 6246, ⓦ www.centromori.cl. A cutting-edge theatre, dance and arts venue in the heart of Bellavista.

Sala Galpón 7 Chucre Manzur 7 ⊕ 735 5484. This reputable venue has a consistently strong line-up

of edgy Chilean performances featuring both top actors and up-and-comers.

Teatro Alcalá Bellavista 97 ⊕ 732 7161, ⓦ www .teatroalcala.showare.cl. Bellavista theatre with top actors and great performances practically guaranteed. Some of Chile's top performances are shown here.

Teatro Bellavista Dardignac 0110 ☎735 2395.
This long-established and reliable Bellavista
theatre usually stages modern foreign plays, often
comedies.
Teatro San Gines Mallinkrodt 76 ☎738 2159. Top
Chilean productions are staged here, as are fine
children's shows on weekend afternoons. Tickets
are expensive.
Teatro de la Universidad Católica Jorge
Washington 26 ☎205 5652. Operated by the
university, this venue offers classic shows and
Chilean adaptations of international works. Located
on Plaza Ñuñoa.

Classical music, dance and opera

In addition to the three main venues listed below, classical music concerts are
also performed in many churches (often for free) and cultural centres – look
under "*música selecta*" in the listings papers. Traditionally, the season lasts from
March to December.

Teatro Municipal Agustinas 749 ☎463 1000,
Ⓦwww.municipal.cl. Santiago's most prestigious
performing arts venue, offering a menu of classical
concerts, ballet and opera in a splendid old building.
Teatro Oriente Pedro de Valdivia, between
Costanera and Providencia ☎231 2173. Here you
can enjoy classical music performed by Fundación
Beethoven and visiting theatre and musical
groups. Information and tickets at 11 de
Septiembre 2214, oficina 66.
Teatro Universidad de Chile Providencia 043
☎634 5295, Ⓦwww.teatro.uchile.cl. Another
established venue for ballet and classical music,
featuring both national groups (principally the
Orquésta Sinfónica de Chile) and foreign artists
on tour.

Shopping and markets

Santiago is a curious place to go **shopping**. The historic centre is packed
with small, old-fashioned shops dedicated to weird and wonderful things like
panty girdles and industrial-sized food processors, as well as an astonishing
number of pharmacies. One of the first things that strikes you about these
shops is that everything's kept behind the counter, with no opportunity for
browsing or touching.

Another oddity about shopping in the centre of the city is the warren of
arcades, or *galerías*, most of them gloomy and uninviting, that seem to lurk
behind every other doorway. Providencia and Las Condes, on the other hand,
sport a slick array of fashionable boutiques and modern, American-style malls –
better shopping, perhaps, but far less interesting.

Don't miss the fish stalls at the Mercado Central (see p.98) – where
you can often sample produce on the spot – and the enormous variety
of fruit at the Feria Municipal La Vega (see p.98), also a great place to
people-watch.

For the best selections of **wine** in Santiago, try *The Wine House*, Av Vitacura
2904 (☎232 7257) and *Vinoteca*, Isidora Goynachea 2966 (☎269 5659, Ⓦwww
.lavinoteca.cl). *Vinos CyT*, Alonso de Córdova 2391, Vitacura (☎576 5480,
Ⓦwww.vinoscyt.com), a new shop opened by the Concha y Toro vineyard,
offers books on Chilean wine, tastings and special sales.

Crafts, knitwear and
lapis lazuli
Avenida Bellavista between Puente Pío Nono and
Puente del Arzobispo. A string of workshops and
salesrooms selling jewellery and other objects
made of lapis lazuli.
Los Dominicos market next to Iglesia Los
Dominicos in Las Condes. Excellent market with
over 200 stalls selling knitwear, ceramics, glass
objects, books, antiques and lots more; see
p.104 for details on how to get here and
opening times.

Feria Santa Lucía opposite Cerro Santa Lucía. Fairly large market selling crafts, clothes and lapis lazuli.
Patio Bellavista Pio Nono 73. Upmarket collection of craft and jewellery shops. Alternatively try the more economical cluster of stalls nearby on the corner of Pio Nono and Santa Maria.

Books, magazines and CDs
Feria del Disco Ahumada 286. One of the best places to buy Chilean and world music. The Ticketmaster counter at this branch is a good place to check about upcoming concerts.
Feria del Libro Huérfanos 623 ☎ 639 6621. Largest bookshop in Santiago, with an excellent choice of Spanish-language novels, reference books and maps. Very little English-language materials, however, which are generally expensive and hard to come by in Chile.
Libreria Australis Providencia 1652, in courtyard next to *Phone Box Pub*, near Sernatur. A decent selection of English-language travel guides and maps.
Librería Inglesa Huérfanos 669, local 11. Fairly good choice of Penguin paperbacks and other English-language books; very expensive.
Libro's San Antonio 236, local 815, and Pedro de Valdivia 039, Providencia. A small range of English-language paperbacks and an impressive selection of magazines, including *The Face*, *Wired*, *GQ* and *Gramophone* (plus a few bizarre titles, including *Tattoo Magazine*).
Paisajes de Chile Patio Bellavista, Pio Nono 73. The place to go to for travel guides (including *Rough Guides*) and maps for trekkers and drivers.

Shopping malls
Alto Las Condes Av Kennedy 9001, Las Condes. Huge, modern shopping mall with 240 shops. Connected to central Santiago by a free shuttle bus (☎ 229 1383 for times). Daily 10am–10pm.
Arauco Outlet Mall Américo Vespucio 399. Low-cost clothes direct from the manufacturer.

Shuttle buses from Ecuador metro station. Daily 10am–1pm.
La Dehesa El Rodeo, La Dehesa. Small, very upmarket shopping centre. Mon–Sat 10am–9pm, Sun 11am–9pm.
Parque Arauco Av Kennedy 5413, Las Condes. Gets insanely busy at weekends as this is regarded as the best mall in town (it also has some unexpectedly good restaurants). Frequent shuttle buses from Estación Militar metro. Mon–Sat 10am–9pm, Sun 11am–9pm.

Flea markets and antiques
Anfiteatro Lo Castillo Candelería Goyenechea 3820, Vitacura. About twenty serious, expensive antiques dealers on the ground floor. Mon–Fri 10am–2pm & 4–8pm, Sat 10am–2pm.
Anticuarios de Mapocho in the red warehouse at Brasil and Matucana, near Parque de los Reyes. Lots of antique furniture, musical instruments, books and bric-à-brac. A wonderful place to browse. Daily 10am–mid-afternoon.
Franklin Market near Franklin metro. Enormous and very lively market running the length of two parallel streets, Franklin and Bío Bío. There's a lot of rubbish at the bottom end, near the metro, but if you walk about five blocks up to the junction with Victor Manual, there's a great flea market on the Franklin side, and lots of antiques stalls off Bío Bío. Sat & Sun 9am–afternoon.

Food and drink
Confites Larbos Estado 26. A beautiful, old-fashioned shop selling fine wines, spirits and fancy foodstuffs (including small packets of Earl Grey teabags, very useful if you're sick of the Chilean variety).
The Wine House Av Vitacura 2904 ☎ 232 7257. This constantly improving store offers good service and advice on quality wines, both Chilean and European.

Listings

Airlines Aerolíneas Argentinas, Moneda 756 ☎ 639 3922; Air France, 6th floor, Alcantara 44 ☎ 290 9300; Alitalia, Office 21, Av El Bosque Norte 0107 ☎ 378 8230; American Airlines, Huérfanos 1199 ☎ 679 0000; British Airways, 3rd floor, Isidora Goyenechea 2934 ☎ 330 8600; Copa Airlines, Office 703, Fidel Oteiza 1921 ☎ 200 2100; Iberia, 8th floor, Bandera 206 ☎ 870 1070; LAN, Agustinas 640 ☎ 600/526 2000; Lloyd Aero Boliviano, Moneda 1170 ☎ 688 8680; Lufthansa, 16th floor, Moneda 970 ☎ 630 1655; Pluna, 9th floor, Av El Bosque Norte 0177 ☎ 707 8000; Swiss, Office 810, Av Barros Errázuriz 1954 ☎ 244 2888; United Airlines, Tenderini 171 ☎ 337 0000; Varig, 9th floor, Av El Bosque Norte 0177 ☎ 707 8000.
Airport information ☎ 6901 752.

American Express To change traveller's cheques and cash, collect mail, get emergency cash and travel advice, including bookings and confirmations, go to Blanco Viajes, General Holley 148 ☎636 9110 or 636 9100. For card replacements and renewals, go to American Express, 10th floor, Isidora Goyenechea 3621 ☎350 6855.

Banks, cambios and ATMs ATM machines can be found all over the historic centre, especially along Moneda, on Huérfanos between Ahumada and Mac Iver, on Miraflores and along Alameda itself, as well as in Providencia. Most banks are open only from 9am–2pm. Many commercial establishments (particularly pharmacies) all over the city also have ATMs in the entryway; look for the maroon and white Redbanc sign. The best place to change cash and traveller's cheques is the cluster of change houses on Agustinas between Ahumada and Bandera. There is also a cluster of change houses on Pedro de Valdivia Norte, including Mojakar S.A., Pedro de Valdivia 059 ☎378 9900 (charges a commission for changing traveller's cheques; closed Sat). Few Chilean banks are useful for changing dollars, but Citibank (many branches, including Huérfanos 770, Ahumada 40, Teatinos 180 and La Bolsa 64) charges no commission for changing US dollars into pesos.

Bike rental La Bicicleta Verde, Santa Maria 227, office 12 (☎570 9338, 🌐www.labicicletaverde .com), rents bikes and arranges cycle tours (CH$15,000–30,000), including a recommended one that looks at sights associated with Pinochet's coup; Lys, Miraflores 537 (☎633 7300, 🌐www.lys .cl), also runs guided excursions into the Andes on mountain bikes.

Car rental Automóvil Club de Chile ☎431 1117, 🌐www.automovilclub.cl; Avis, airport and San Pablo 9900 ☎690 1382, 🌐www.avis.com; Budget, Francisco Bilbao 1439 ☎362 3200, 🌐www.budget.com; Chilean Rent a Car, Bellavista 0183 ☎&℻737 9650; Diamond, airport ☎211 2682 and Manquehue Sur 841 ☎212 1523; Dollar, Av Kennedy 8292 ☎202 5510, 🌐www.dollar.com; Lys, Miraflores 537 ☎633 7300; Rosselot, airport and Bilbao 2045 ☎381 3695, 🌐www.rosselot.cl.

Embassies Argentina, Miraflores 285 ☎633 1076; Australia, Isidora Goyenechea 3621 ☎550 3500; Austria, 3rd floor, Barros Errázuriz 1968 ☎223 4774; Belgium, Office 1103, Providencia 2653 ☎232 1070; Brazil, Alonso Ovalle 1665 ☎6982486; Canada, 12th floor, World Trade Centre, Nueva Tajamar 481 ☎652 3800; France, Condell 65 ☎470 8000; Germany, Agustinas 785 ☎463 2500; Israel, San Sebastián 2812

☎750 0500; Italy, Clemente Fabrés 1050 ☎470 8400; Netherlands, Apoquindo 3500 ☎756 9200; New Zealand, Office 703, El Golf 99 ☎290 9800; Peru, Av Andrés Bello 1751 ☎235 6451; South Africa, 16th floor, Av 11 de Septiembre 2353 ☎231 2862; Spain, Av Andrés Bello 1895 ☎235 2754; UK, Av El Bosque Norte 0125 ☎370 4100; US, Av Andrés Bello 2800 ☎232 2600.

Emergencies Ambulance ☎131; fire department (*bomberos*) ☎132; police (*carabineros*) ☎133.

Football matches Safe, albeit rowdy, matches held Mar–Dec; most games are on Saturday and Sunday. The National Stadium, Campo de Deportes, Av Grecia, is in Ñuñoa. Don't hang around after matches, as hooliganism can be a problem. The main Santiago teams are Colo Colo, Universidad Católica, Universidad de Chile, Unión Española and Palestino.

Hospitals Clínica Las Condes, Lo Fontecilla 441 ☎210 4000; Clínica Indisa, Av Santa María 1810 ☎362 5555; Clínica Las Lilas, Eliodoro Yánez 2087 ☎410 6666; Clínica Santa María, Av Santa María 0410 ☎410 2000; Clínica Universidad Católica, Lira 40, in the historic centre of the city ☎369 6000.

Internet Most hostels and hotels provide computers with internet access and often free wi-fi (the latter you can also access at central metro stations). There are also dozens of internet cafés all across the city, especially in commercial areas. A couple of convenient places in the historic centre are: Isi Net, Londres 30 (CH$500 per hr), and Ciber Café, Merced 333 (CH$700 per hr); the latter is a little more expensive but also more peaceful, and you can get a decent coffee while you surf.

LAN Pedro de Valdivia, at Av Providencia 2006 ☎600/526 2000, 🌐www.lan.com. This central office for the LAN airline offers tours as well as dealing with seat assignments, itinerary changes and lost luggage.

Language courses Recommended places offering Spanish-language courses include: BridgeChile, Los Leones 439 ☎233 4356, 🌐www.bridgechile.com; Centro Chileno Canadiense, Office 601, Luis Thayer Ojeda 191 ☎334 1090, 🌐www.canadiense.cl; Instituto Chileno Británico, Miraflores 123 ☎413 2000, 🌐www.britanico.cl; Instituto Chileno Norteamericano, Moneda 1467 ☎677 7070, 🌐www.norteamericano.cl; Polyglot-Mitford Instituto de Idiomas, Guardia Vieja 181 ☎233 3143, 🌐www.polyglot-mitford.com.

Laundry These laundry chains have branches all over town, the most central being: Sandrico, local 2B, Huérfanos 632, *galería* La Merced

Moving on from Santiago

Sitting in the middle of the country, Santiago is the unrivalled **transportation hub** of Chile. All national transport networks lead to and from the capital, and most journeys between the north and south of Chile, including those by **air**, involve a change or at least a stop here. There are plenty of flights out of Santiago's **Aeropuerto Arturo Merino Benítez** (℡690 1752) to all the major cities in the country. It's best to reserve your seat as far in advance as possible, as the cheaper fares tend to get booked up long before the flight; a travel agent should be able to give you a rundown all the different options.

There are **train** services to the south, with regular daily connections to Chillán, Curico, Talca, Rancagua and San Fernando. All trains leave from the **Estación Central** on Alameda (℡689 6070), next to the metro stop of the same name.

By far the greatest majority of transport services are provided by **buses**, run by a bewildering number of private companies. These operate out of **four main terminals**.

The **Terminal de Buses Santiago**, more often known as **Terminal de Estación Central** (℡376 1755), just west of the Universidad de Santiago metro station, is the largest (and most chaotic) of the terminals, with more than a hundred bus companies operating out of here. Services **south** down the Panamericana from this terminal are provided by all the major companies, including Andimar (℡779 3810), Cóndor Bus (℡680 6900), (℡764 5231), Inter Sur (℡779 6312) and Tas Choapa (℡779 4694). Buses to the **coastal resorts** of the Litoral Central are run by Cóndor Bus (℡680 6900) and Pullman Bus (℡779 2026), though you can also get to these destinations from the Alameda and San Borja terminals (less frequent services from the latter).

Terminal de Buses Alameda (℡270 7500) is used only by Tur Bus (℡270 7500) and Pullman Bus (℡560 3781), Chile's two largest and most comprehensive bus companies.

Terminal San Borja (℡776 0645), a modern station, at the back of a shopping mall behind the Estación Central (from the metro, follow the signs carefully to exit at the terminal). This is the main departure point for buses to the **north** of Chile, particularly for long-distance buses going to Iquique and Arica. There are several regional buses, as well, and some services to the coastal resorts. Bus companies going north include Elqui Bus (℡778 7045), Pullman Bus (℡560 3821) and Tas Choapa (℡778 6827). Tur Bus (℡778 7338) also runs services to the Litoral.

The fourth terminal **Los Héroes** (℡420 0099; metro Los Héroes), is located on Tucapel Jiménez, just north of the Plaza de Los Héroes; the most **central** of the bus terminals, it hosts a mixture of northbound, southbound and international buses. It is used by eight companies: Buses Ahumada (℡696 9798), Cruz del Sur (℡696 9324), Fenix (℡696 9321), Flota Barrios (℡696 9311), Los Héroes (℡441 0343), Libac (℡698 5974), Pullman del Sur (℡673 1967) and Tas Choapa (℡696 9326).

The much smaller **Pajaritos** terminal (℡250 3464), next to the metro station of the same name at General Bonilla 5600, around 12km west of the centre, is useful for travelling to and from the airport, as it allows you to bypass the city-centre traffic.

The main bus companies serving **international destinations**, mostly out of **Estación Central** and **Los Héroes**, are Ahumada (℡778 2703), Cata (℡779 3660), Chilebus (℡779 2429), El Rápido (℡779 0316), Ormeño (℡779 3443), Pluma (℡779 6054), Pullman del Sur (℡779 5243) and Tas Choapa (℡779 4925). While you can normally turn up and buy a **ticket** for travelling the same day, it's better to buy it a day or more in advance, especially at weekends. For travel on the days around Christmas, New Year's Eve and Easter, you should buy your ticket at least a week ahead.

☎5574243; Astra, Av Providencia 1604
☎2641946.

Maps Topographical maps on all parts of Chile
are available at the Instituto Geográfico Militar,
Calle Dieciocho 369, near Toesca metro (☎410
9463, ⊛www.igm.cl). You'll also find a good
section of road maps for sale at the Fería del
Libro, Huérfanos 623 (☎639 6621). For tourist
and walking maps, go to Sernatur, Av Providencia
1550 (☎731 8310). See also "Books, magazines
and CDs" section (p.115).

Newspapers There are numerous newspaper
kiosks around town; those at the corner of
Huérfanos and Ahumada sell a reasonable range of
foreign newspapers, including *Die Welt*, the
Financial Times, *The New York Times*, the *Miami
Herald* and a good selection of other European and
Latin American newspapers.

Mountain climbing and outdoor equipment
Several outdoor equipment stores have opened in
the El Bosque Norte neighbourhood, especially on
Encomenderos. Also try Patagonia Sport, La
Dehesa mall, La Dehesa (☎216 8420), and
Federación de Andinismo de Chile, Almirante
Simpson 77 (☎222 0888), which has a range of
mountaineering and camping equipment. The
highly recommended La Cumbre, Av Apoquindo
5258 (☎220 9907, www.lacumbreonline.cl), run
by friendly Ivo and Katja, has world-class boots,
eyewear and climbing accessories as well as a
small library of books about exploring the Andes.
Basic fishing equipment is available at Escamas,
Av Brasil 121, just off Alameda (☎671 0285).
Fly-fishing equipment and information is
available at ⊛www.flyshop.cl.

Pharmacies There's an abundance of pharmacies all over the historic centre, and smaller
commercial areas always have at least one.
Farmacias Ahumada (☎222 4000) has a number
of 24hr branches, including Portugal 155, in the
historic centre, and El Bosque 164, Providencia;
they'll deliver to your hotel for a small charge.

Post offices Correo Central, Plaza de Armas 559
(Mon–Fri 8.30am–7pm, Sat 8.30am–1pm). Other
branches at Moneda 1155, near Morandé; Local
17, Exposición 57 Paseo Estación; Av 11 de
Septiembre 2092. Federal Express, Av Providencia
1951 ☎231 5250, and San Camilo 190 ☎361
6081, ⊛www.fedex.com; DHL, Suecia 072 ☎232
7539; UPS, Unión Americana 221 ☎685 0707,
⊛www.ups.com.

Swimming pools Tupahue, near the Tupahue
teleférico station on Cerro San Cristóbal (mid-Nov

to mid-March, Tues–Sun 10am–7pm; CH$5000;
☎776 6666), is large and beautiful, but
expensive. Piscina Antilén, also on Cerro San
Cristóbal (mid Nov to mid March Tues–Sun
10am–7pm; CH$5000; ☎232 6617), is in the
same mould but harder to reach by public
transport. Parque O'Higgins (mid Nov to mid
March, Mon–Fri 1.30–6.30pm, Sat–Sun 11am–
7pm; CH$2000; ☎556 9612) has a large outdoor
pool that is much more affordable but gets quite
crowded. There is also an Olympic-size pool in
Parque Araucano, behind Parque Arauco shopping
centre near Escuela Militar metro (☎212 4376).
For an indoor pool, try Centro de Natación
Patricia Thompson, Bilbao 2342 (CH$3500;
☎204 4096), but call first to find out when it's
open for free swimming.

Telephone centres Entel's biggest branch is at
Morandé, between Huérfanos and Compañía
(☎&⨎360 9447); it's a/c, quiet, has plenty of
phones and internet access. You can also send
and receive faxes here.

Train information ☎600/585 5000,
⊛www.efe.cl.

Travel agents There are countless travel agents
in the historic centre, among them: Andina del
Sud, 2nd floor, Av El Golf 99 (☎484 8444,
⊛www.andinadelsud.com), very friendly and
professional, good for international flights and
package holidays inside and outside Chile; Andy
Tour, Agustinas 1056 (☎671 6592), for good-
value packages in South America, especially to
Peru and Argentina; Chile Information Project
(CHIP; ☎737 5649, ⊛www.chiptravel.cl), Av
Santa Maria 227, runs human-rights tours
looking at the legacy of Pinochet's 17-year
regime, as well as more general city tours; Liz
Caskey (☎6322015, ⊛www.lizcaskey.com) runs
culinary and wine tours of Santiago and beyond;
Rapa Nui, 9th floor, Huérfanos 1160 (☎672
1050), mainly for international flights (not Easter
Island specialists as the name suggests). There
are plenty in Providencia as well, including:
Santiago Adventures, Guardia Vieja 255, office
403, Providencia (☎244 2750, ⊛www
.santiagoadventures.com), a well-respected,
comprehensive agency; Turismo Cocha, Av El
Bosque Norte 0430 (☎464 1000), one of Chile's
largest and most prestigious chains; Turismo
Tajamar, Orrego Luco 023 (☎336 8000), national
and international packages, member of the
Chilean Association of Travel Agencies. All the
above offer city tours and regional excursions.

Around Santiago

Santiago is close to some fine, and frequently overlooked, attractions, from national parks and thermal springs to sleepy villages and lush vineyards.

The obvious main attraction is the **Andes**, with the **Cajón del Maipo** providing good access into the cordillera, leading to the small but spectacular **Monumento Nacional El Morado**. In winter, **skiing** is a terrific possibility, the several excellent resorts are just a ninety-minute drive from the capital and increasingly offer year-round activities like hiking and mountain biking. **Wineries** are another of the area's highlights, with some of Chile's oldest and most famous vineyards within easy striking distance, often offering tours and tastings.

Towards the coast, **Parque Nacional La Campana** offers excellent hiking and requires a couple of days to be fully enjoyed, while **Pomaire**, to the east of the capital, is a picturesque village known for its inexpensive ceramics, country cooking and small-town ambience. North of Santiago, head for the colonial town of **Los Andes**, surrounded by picturesque villages and mountain scenery. All these destinations are served by frequent buses; details are given in the text and in "Travel details" on p.127.

Cajón del Maipo

The **CAJÓN DEL MAIPO** is a beautiful river valley carved out of the Andes by the Río Maipo. Served by a good paved road (for 48km of its 70km length) and punctuated by a string of hamlets offering tourist facilities, it's one of the most popular weekend escapes from the capital. The potential for outdoor adventures is enormous, with organized **hiking**, **rafting**, and **mountain biking** trips.

Start at the mouth of the *cajón*, just 25km southeast of Santiago, at Las Vizcachas. Here the scenery is lush and gentle, and as you climb into the valley you'll pass vineyards, orchards, roadside stalls selling locally produced fruit, and signs advertising home-made *küchen*, *miel* (honey) *pan amasado* (fresh oven-baked bread) and *chicha* (cider). Twenty-five kilometres on, you reach the administrative centre of the valley, **SAN JOSE DE MAIPO**. It's quite attractive, with single-storey adobe houses and an old, colonial church. If you want to **stay**, try the homely *Residencial Inesita*, Comercio 19321 (☎861 1012; ❹). Drivers should note that this is the last place along the road where you can fill up with petrol. There are no banks or ATM machines in the valley, so bring cash.

Getting to Cajón del Maipo is easy from Santiago: **buses** to San José de Maipo run every 10–20 minutes from Avenida Concha y Toro, outside Las Mercedes metro station; several daily buses go as far as El Volcán, and there are less frequent services to Baños Morales (daily mid-Dec to Feb; weekends only March to mid-Dec). From Plaza Italia, Tursmontaña (☎850 0555) runs **minivans** to Baños Morales; call ahead for reservations. Most departures are early morning. Share taxis and minibuses connect San José de Maipo with San Alfonso and other places in the *cajón*. For private vehicles the road is fine until San Gabriel, where it may be filled with rocks and landslides. Weekend traffic can be horrendous, with two- to three-hour backups. To avoid the traffic, make sure you enter the *cajón* well before 10am and leave before 3pm (or, if necessary, late at night).

San Alfonso

Some 15km beyond San José is **SAN ALFONSO** (1100m altitude), a lovely place to head if you just want to unwind for a few hours in beautiful mountain scenery. For longer stays, it offers a good choice of **accommodation**: *Hostería Los Ciervos*, by the roadside (T861 1581, F861 1581; ⑤) has a gorgeous, flower-filled terrace and a little swimming pool, while *Residencial España*, next door (T861 1543, F861 1543; ③) is simpler, but very clean, with an excellent restaurant. Down by the river, the highly recommended former nineteen-century horse ranch 🦌 *Cascada de las Animas* (T861 1303, Wwww .cascada.net), set in a park, has log cabins (CH$44,000 for one sleeping four people), cosy doubles (④–⑤) in a renovated 1930s building and camping areas (from CH$6000 per person) as well as a fabulous outdoor pool, a **restaurant** overlooking the steep river gorge and a good **bar**, *La Tribú*. Open year-round, it offers **horse-riding** trips into the Andes, **kayak lessons** and **whitewater rafting** down the Maipo. You can also arrange rafting through Altué Expediciones in Santiago (T232 1103, Wwww.altue.com). There's a good ninety-minute walk from here up to the 20-metre **waterfall** (called the "Cascada de las Animas") on the other side of the river; ask at the complex's reception for permission to cross the bridge.

Towards Baños Morales

Moving on from San Alfonso, the scenery becomes increasingly rugged and wild as you climb higher into the Andes. By the time you reach **San Gabriel**, 50km from the start of the valley road at Las Vizcachas, the steep walls of the valley are dried-out reds and browns – you are at 1300m. This uninteresting village marks the end of the asphalt road, which continues as a very poor dirt track for another 20km to Lo Valdés. To carry on, you have to go through a *carabineros* (police) checkpoint, so make sure you've got all your driving

▲ Wines From Vina Concha Y Torro

Wine tours near Santiago

Santiago is within easy reach of some of the oldest **wineries** in Chile, several of which offer tours and tastings. Those by the Río Maipo, in particular, are beautifully located, with large swaths of emerald-green vines framed by the snow-capped cordillera and bright-blue skies. Harvesting takes place in March, and if you visit during this month you'll see the grapes being sorted and pressed – a real extravaganza of colours and smells. If you want to visit a vineyard you should book at least a day beforehand. We've listed four, relatively easily reached wineries below; most are accessible by public transport. All the tours include free tastings.

Viña Concha y Toro Virginia Subercaseaux 210, Pirque ☏476 5269, ⊛www .conchaytoro.com. Bilingual tours available daily 10am–7pm; CH$6000. This handsome vineyard was founded in 1883 by Don Melchor Concha y Toro, and in 1994 became the first-ever winery to trade on the New York Stock Exchange. Take the metro to Tobalaba station, from where it's a short taxi ride to the vineyard.

Viña Cousiño Macul 7100 Av Quilin ☏351 4175, ⊛www.cousinomacul .com. 45min tours in English and Spanish available Monday to Friday at 11am and 3pm; the Saturday 11am tours are in Spanish only; CH$5000. Chile's oldest winery dates from 1550, when wine was shipped to Peru. Much of this winery was ripped up in 2003 to make way for a US$2 billion housing development, and new vineyards were planted near the town of Buin, but the main estate and park still make a nice quick trip from central Santiago. Driving directions: take Americo Vespucio south to the Quilin roundabout, head towards the mountains on Avenida Quilin and look for the sign at 7100. Otherwise, take the metro to Quilin station and then take a taxi or walk 30min east along Avenida Quilin.

Viña Santa Carolina 2228 Av Tiltil, Macul ☏450 3137, ⊛www.santacarolina .com. One hour standard tours and 1hr 30min "Icon" tours (which include more tastings, and more expensive wines, than on the normal tour) both available Monday to Friday at 4.30pm; CH$7000 (standard), CH$15,000 (Icon). Just twenty minutes from the centre; take the metro to Rodrigo de Araya and walk west, towards the mountains, for 3–5min. If you are driving, take Avenida Vicuña Mackenna south, turn right on Rodrigo de Araya, and the vineyard is about 200 yards along, on the left.

Viña Undurraga, old road to Melipilla, Km 34 ☏372 2850, ⊛www.undurraga .cl. Bilingual tours available Monday to Friday at 10am, 11.30pm, 2pm and 3.30pm, and Saturday to Sunday at 10am, 11.30pm and 1pm; CH$7000. Still run by the Undurraga family, the vineyard was established in 1885, complete with mansion and park. It's a large, modern winery, and you're likely to be shown around by someone who's directly involved in the wine-making. Take a bus to Talagante from Terminal San Borja (every 15min; 30min), and ask the driver to drop you off at the vineyard.

documents and passport with you. Unless you're in a 4WD you should expect to go *very* slowly from this point onwards. **El Volcán**, at Km 56, is as far as the telephone lines go up the valley – it has a public phone, but little else, as the village was practically wiped out by a landslide some years ago. By now the scenery is really dramatic as you snake between 4000-metre-high mountains coloured with jagged mineral-patterns of violet, cream and blue.

About 12km on, a short track branches left across a rudimentary bridge to **BAÑOS MORALES**, the site of an uninviting thermal pool. Despite its spectacular location, this is quite a grim little village, with lukewarm pools and a half-finished, slightly derelict feel. It is, however, the closest base to the beautiful, jagged-peaked **Monumento Nacional El Morado** and offers a number of

residenciales, although none of them is that great: the just commendable *Pensión Díaz* (☎861 1496; ❷) is the only one that stays open all year. If your budget allows it, head instead for the secluded and very comfortable *Refugio Lo Valdes* (☎9/220 8525, ⓦwww.refugiolovaldes.com; ❺), an Alpine-style hotel at Lo Valdés, about 1km beyond the fork to Baños Morales. From here the road deteriorates into an even poorer track, but continues for another 11km to **Baños de Colina**, a series of natural thermal pools carved into the mountainside; for all their remoteness they can get horribly crowded in summer weekends, but otherwise are blissfully empty. This is also the embarkation for multi-day **horse treks** into the Andes. Up to week-long excursions often leave in packed caravans that snake into the mountains. For less arduous trips, many locals rent horses by the hour or afternoon (around CH$5000 an hour).

Monumento Nacional El Morado and the Cajón del Morado

A path from the bus stop in Baños Morales crosses a bridge and leads to the Conaf hut at the entrance to **MONUMENTO NACIONAL EL MORADO** (Oct–April daily 8.30am–6pm; CH$1500); here you should get the latest hiking and climbing information as landslides, snowmelts and the glaciers change the terrain from year to year. For more good trekking and hiking information, check in at the **Lo Valdés Mountain Centre**, in the little town of Lo Valdés by the side of the road (☎246 3113). The park's single 8km trail follows the Río Morales through a narrow valley that ends at the glacier that feeds the river. Towering above the glacier, and visible from almost all points along the trail, is the magnificent silhouette of El Mirador del Morado (4320m) and, just behind, El Morado itself (5060m). Apart from the first half-hour, the path is fairly level and not hard going, though you may find yourself feeling breathless as you gradually climb in altitude. About 5km beyond the Conaf hut – after roughly two to three hours of hiking – you reach a small **lake**, Laguna de Morado, where there is free camping, a toilet and water pump. Once past the lake, the path is less defined, but it's easy enough to pick your way through the stones to the black, slimy-looking **glacier** 3km beyond, at an altitude of 2500m. Don't enter the tempting ice caves – they are not stable. Unless you are camping, this is a good place for day-trekkers to turn around and head back.

An alternative way to arrive is on **horseback**; guided rides (from CH$12,000) depart from Baños Morales or outside the Conaf hut. There are also guided riding treks up the neighbouring **CAJÓN DEL MORADO**, which runs parallel to the Río Morales, a few kilometres east, and leads to a huge glacier towering over a chocolate-coloured lake full of great chunks of ice. If you plan to walk, make sure you have a good map and a compass, and have a word with the Conaf ranger first, as the route isn't obvious. For information on other guided trips to the park, contact Turismo Arpue (☎211 7165), Terra Incógnita (☎202 8761, ⓦwww.terraincognita.cl) or Manzur Expeditions (☎777 4284).

Pomaire

Back in the other direction, some 50km southwest of Santiago, the dusty, quaint village of **POMAIRE** was one of the *pueblos de indios* created by the Spanish in the eighteenth century in an attempt to control the native population. Its inhabitants quickly built up a reputation for their **pottery**, and to this day Pomaire devotes itself almost exclusively to this craft. The village consists of one long street packed with dozens of workshops selling a vast range of pots, bowls and Chilean kitchenware that the English vocabulary has no words for. Another draw is the chance to see the potters at work (except on Mondays, their day off), as they shape the clay by hand at the wheel.

Pomaire has also built up a reputation for its good, traditional **restaurants** (some of them specializing in giant 1.5-kilo empanadas); *Los Naranjos*, on main drag Roberto Bravo, near the signposted Casa Colorada, and *San Antonio*, on the street of the same name, are especially recommended. To get here from Santiago, **Buses Melipilla** runs regular services from Terminal San Borja; ask to be set off at the side road to Pomaire (one hour from Santiago along Ruta 78, one and a half hours via Talagante). From here, *colectivos* and taxis run into the village, or you can walk it in about half an hour.

Los Andes

There's nothing wildly exciting about **LOS ANDES**, but this old colonial town, with its narrow streets and lively main square, makes a convenient base for day-trips to the ski resort of Portillo (see p.124). Eighty kilometres north of Santiago, on the international road to Mendoza, Argentina, it's set in the beautiful Aconcagua valley; the first ridge rises to 3500m and then soars to 6959m Aconcagua, the highest peak outside the Himalayas, just across the border in Argentina. The surrounding region is very fertile, and as you approach Los Andes from Santiago you'll pass vineyards and numerous peach and lemon orchards. About 10km short of the town, the **Santuario de Santa Teresa de los Andes** is a huge, modern church built in 1987 to house the remains of **Santa Teresa**, who became Chile's first saint when she was canonized in 1993. Her shrine attracts thousands of pilgrims each year, especially on July 13, her feast day.

You can find out more about the saint in the **Monasterio del Espíritu Santo**, a simple brick building on Avenida Santa Teresa in Los Andes, where she lived until her death in 1920, at the age of nineteen. A small museum upstairs (Tues–Sun 10am–6.30pm; CH$600) exhibits an assortment of memorabilia, including photos and clothes. Almost opposite, the **Museo Arqueológico** (Tues–Sun 10am–6.30pm; CH$600) has an impressive collection of pre-Columbian pottery, petroglyphs and skulls, and an astonishing mummy from the Atacama Desert. Six blocks east, on the corner of Freire and Rancagua, **Cerámica Cala** is worth a stop. This family-run business sells pretty, hand-painted ceramics to retailers throughout Chile.

Other than this, the best thing to do in Los Andes is hang out in one of the cafés lining the square and watch the world go by or, if you're feeling energetic, climb **Cerro de la Virgen**, the hill rising behind the town. It takes about an hour to reach the top following the path from the picnic site on Independencia. The views are wonderful, especially just before sunset, when the whole valley is bathed in a clear, golden light.

Practicalities

Frequent **buses** for Los Andes run out of Terminal Los Héroes in Santiago, dropping you at the bus station on Membrillar, one block east of the main square; most of them stop at the Santuario de Santa Teresa en route. There's a helpful **Oficina de Turismo** (Mon–Fri 9am–2pm & 3–5pm) next door to the Municipalidad at Esmeralda 526. If you want to **stay**, options include *Residencia Italiana* at Rodríguez 76 (℡34/423544; ❸–❹), an attractive old house with straightforward, pleasant rooms with shared bath, and *Hotel Plaza*, at Esmeralda 367 (℡34/421169, ℻426029; ❺) with well-equipped, but dowdy, rooms off the square, a pool and popular **restaurant** serving traditional fare. The French-owned *Comédie Française*, at Papudo 375, serves good-value French food, with live music at weekends.

Skiing near Santiago

Santiago is only ninety minutes from some of the best **skiing** in South America. You don't need equipment to take advantage of this – rental skis, clothes and transport to the slopes are easily arranged – and the runs are close enough to the capital to make day-trips perfectly feasible. **Sunshine is abundant and** queues for lifts are practically nonexistent during weekdays. The season normally lasts from mid-June to early-October, with snow virtually guaranteed from mid-July to the first week in September. The most expensive and crowded periods of the year are the Chilean winter vacation, during the last weeks of July, and the national holidays the week of September 18. There are various options for day-trips from Santiago: either the two-hour highway drive to Portillo near the Argentine border, or the ninety-minute serpentine road to the service village of **Farellones**, where three resorts are increasingly linked together.

Farellones itself, sitting high in the Andes at the foot of Cerro Colorado, is a straggling collection of hotels and apartments. It's connected by paved roads to the ski resorts of El Colorado (4km north), La Parva (2km further on), and chic resort Valle Nevado (a winding 14km east). **El Colorado** – also reached from Farellones by ski lift – has fifteen lifts and twenty-two runs, covering a wide range of levels. Elevations range from 2430m to 3333m. The resort's base is known as Villa El Colorado, and includes several apart-hotels, restaurants and pubs. Neighbouring **La Parva** has moderate terrain, huge areas of backcountry skiing and an aged but classy feel. The skiing here is excellent, with some very long intermediate cruising runs and a vertical drop of nearly 1000m. The resort has thirty pistes and fourteen lifts, but limited accommodation facilities, as most people who come here have their own chalet or rent one. **Valle Nevado**, connected to both El Colorado and La Parva by ski runs, is a luxury resort with first-class hotels and some very good restaurants. It has twenty-seven runs, eight lifts and is the clear favourite for snowboarders.

Set just off the international road from Los Andes, 7km short of the border with Argentina, **Portillo** is a classy place, with no condominiums and just one hotel – the restored 1940's *Hotel Portillo* (℡361 7000, ⊛www.skiportillo.com; ❻–❾), perched by the shores of the Laguna del Inca. This all-inclusive resort offers the most relaxing, hip ski scene in South America. Being farther from Santiago (149km), the hotel is designed for weekend or week-long bookings, with an extensive range of package deals. While most rooms are expensive, there are a wide variety of options, including the bunks in the Octagon Lodge (US$190 per person) and simpler dorms in the Inca Lodge (US$100 per person). The rates include full-board and use of the outdoor heated pool and disco. Expect an eclectic crowd of Brazilians, Argentines and famous actors and business leaders. The ski-runs at Portillo are world-class, and off-piste options are endless. Elevation ranges from 2510m to 3350m. There are twelve lifts, as well as extensive snow-making equipment. Portillo is avidly kid-friendly and its ski school is routinely ranked one of the world's best.

Parque Nacional La Campana

Set in the dry, dusty mountains of the coastal range, **PARQUE NACIONAL LA CAMPANA** (daily 9am–5.30pm; CH$1500) is a wonderful place to go hiking and offers some of the best views in Chile. From the 1880m-high summit of Cerro La Campana you can see the Andes on one side and the Pacific Ocean on the other – in the words of Charles Darwin, who climbed the mountain in 1834, Chile is seen "as in a map". Another draw is the chance to see a profusion of **Chilean palms** in their natural habitat; this

All of the resorts described above have ski schools with English-speaking instructors, and equipment rental outlets.

Practicalities

The least expensive way to go skiing is to stay in Santiago and head up for the day. A number of **minibus** companies offer daily services to the resorts during the ski season, including Ski Total (☎246 0156, ⓦ www.skitotal.cl), which also rents out equipment, goggles and clothes. It's based at office 46 in the lower-ground level of the Omnium shopping mall at Apoquindo 4900, four blocks east of Estación Militar metro. Buses leave 8am–8.30am daily for El Colorado, La Parva (return ticket to either CH$9000) and Valle Nevado (CH$9500), and on Wednesdays and Saturdays to Portillo (CH$16,000); buses start to return from the resorts at 5pm. You can also book hotel pick-ups to and from Portillo (CH$20,000–36,000) and El Colorado, La Parva and Valle Nevado (CH$16,000–27,000). Ski and snowboard equipment rental starts at CH$16,000.

If you intend to drive up yourself, note traffic is only allowed up the road to Farellones until noon, and back down to Santiago from 2pm onwards; tyre chains are often required but seldom used; they can be rented on the way up. Each resort has its own **lift ticket**; high season CH$29,500, low season CH$22,000.

If you want to stay, you've got several **accommodation** options. At Farellones you could try the sociable *Refugio Alemán* (☎264 9899, ⓦ www.refugioaleman .cl; ❹–❼ half-board), with its dorms, private en-suites, restaurant-bar, pool table and lounge with log fire. The best place to stay in El Colorado is *Hotel Posada de Farellones* (☎201 3704, ⓦ www.farellones.cl; ❻), which has upmarket en-suites, a Jacuzzi and good restaurant. Prices include half-board and transport to the slopes. The only commercial place to stay in La Parva is *Condominio Nueva La Parva* (☎264 1574; ❼). For **rentals by the week** it is much more economical to negotiate with private owners – one broker is Cecilia Wilson Propiedades, Apoquindo 5555, Office 905 (☎207 3700). Valle Nevado's hotels are all very upscale, and include the grand *Hotel Valle Nevado* (☎206 0027, ⓦ www .vallenevado.com; ❾); classy en-suites (peak season doubles US$980 half-board) and heliskiing is on offer. Ski Total (see above) can give advice on accommodation, and make bookings for you. Your only lodging option in Portillo is *Hotel Portillo* (see opposite).

All of the ski resorts have their **administrative offices in Santiago**: El Colorado is at the Omnium, Office 47, Av Apoquindo 4900, Las Condes (☎363 0559, ⓦ www .elcolorado.cl); La Parva is at Av El Bosque Norte 177, Las Condes (☎339 8482, ⓦ www.skilaparva.cl); Valle Nevado is at Av Vitacura 5250, Las Condes (☎477 7000, ⓦ www.vallenevado.com); and Portillo is at Renato Sanchez 4270, Vitacura (☎263 0606, ⓦ www.skiportillo.com).

native tree was all but wiped out in the nineteenth century, and the Palmar de Ocoa, a grove in the northern section of the park, is one of just two remaining places in the country where you can find wild palms. You can also expect to see eagles and giant hummingbirds and, if you're lucky, mountain cats and foxes.

The park is located 110km northwest of Santiago, and about 60km east of Valparaíso. It's divided into three "sectors" – Ocoa, Granizo and Cajón Grande – each with its own entrance and Conaf control. **Sector Ocoa**, on the northern side of the Park, is where you'll find the palm trees – literally thousands of them. **Sector Granizo** and **Sector Cajón Grande** are both in the south of the park, close to the village of **Olmué**; this is the part to head for if you want to follow Darwin's footsteps and climb **Cerro La Campana**. While it's possible to get to Parque Nacional La Campana on a day-trip from Valparaíso,

---

Hiking in Parque Nacional La Campana

There are about a dozen very scenic **walks** in the park, most of them along good, well-maintained trails and many of them interconnected. The maps given away at the Conaf hut are very useful. If you plan to do some serious walking, try to get hold of a more detailed **map** from Sernatur before you come. If you're on a day-hike you must get back to the Conaf control before it closes (5.30pm); if you plan to camp in the park, inform the *guardaparque* when you sign in. Finally, there aren't many water sources along the trails so bring plenty of **water** with you. Also bring **sunblock**; the summer sun combined with the high altitude make it easy to get burned.

Sector Granizo
The well-marked 9km **Sendero el Andinista** up Cerro La Campana is the most popular and most rewarding trek in the park. It's quite hard going, especially the last ninety minutes, when it's more a climb than a hike, but the views from the top are breathtaking – and this is where Darwin climbed. Allow at least four and a half hours to get up and three to get down. **Sendero Los Peumos** is a pretty, 4km walk (about three hours) up to the Portezuelo Ocoa, through gentle woodland for the first half, followed by a fairly steep climb. Three paths converge at the Portezuelo; you can either go back the way you came; take the right-hand path (Sendero Portezuelo Ocoa; see below) down through the Cajón Grande to that sector's Conaf control (about three hours); or follow the left-hand path (Sendero El Amasijo) through Sector Ocoa to the northernmost park entrance (another four hours; best if you're camping as there's no accommodation at the other end).

Sector Cajón Grande
The **Sendero Portezuelo Ocoa**, also known as **Sendero Los Robles**, is a 7km trail (about three hours) through beautiful woods with natural *miradores* giving views down to the Cuesta La Dormida. From the Portezuelo Ocoa, at the end of the path, you can link up with other paths as described above.

Sector Ocoa
Sendero La Cascada makes a lovely day-hike through lush palm groves to a 35m-high waterfall, most impressive in early spring. The 8km path is mainly flat; allow about seven hours there and back. It has eight well-marked *estaciones* that describe local flora. **Sendero El Amasijo** is a 7km trail (3hrs) following the Estero Rabuco (a stream) through a scenic canyon before climbing steeply to the Portezuelo Ocoa. Most walkers make this a cross-park trek, continuing to Granizo or Cajón Grande (see above). Fast, fit walkers should be able to do it in a day, but it's more relaxing if you camp overnight.

Viña or even, at a push, from Santiago, you should count on spending a couple of nights here. There are **camping** (CH$6000 per site) areas in all three sectors, and plenty of **accommodation** in Olmué (see below).

Getting to the park

To get to **Sector Granizo** and **Sector Cajón Grande** you should aim for the gateway village of **Olmué**, reached via a long, roundabout route from Santiago, but far more directly from Valparaíso. There are direct **buses** from both directions: from Santiago, Pullman runs hourly buses (1hr 30min–2hr) out of the San Borja and Alameda terminals; from Valparaíso's Playa Ancha, Ciferal Express has regular services almost to the park entrance. If you're coming from Santiago **by car**, the quickest route is via Casablanca, Villa Alemana and Limache. Don't be tempted to take the short route from Tiltil to Olmué across the Cuesta La Dormida – this is very scenic but unsuitable unless you're in a 4WD. From Olmué it's a further 9km to the park; regular buses (every 15min) run from the main square to **Granizo**; the last bus stop is a fifteen-minute walk from the Conaf hut in Sector Granizo, and a forty-minute walk from Sector Cajón Grande.

Sector Ocoa is approached on a gravel road branching south from the Panamericana about halfway between Llaillay and Hijuelas; coming from Llaillay, it's the left turn just before the bridge across the Río Aconcagua. Any northbound bus along the Panamericana will drop you at the turn-off, but from here it's a 12km hike to the park entrance, with minimal hitching opportunities.

Accommodation in Olmué

A lovely village in a fertile valley, **Olmué** has a good choice of **places to stay**, many of them with pools. *Centro Turístico La Campana*, Blanco Encalada 4651 (T 33/441515, W www.campana.cl; ❹), has a motel feel; pink buildings house clean, slightly gaudy en-suites, and there's a garden, pool and children's play area. A step-up in class, *Hostería El Copihué*, Portales 2203 (T 33/441544, W www .copihue.cl; ❻–❼) has a nice pool, beautiful gardens full of vines and flowers and a good restaurant. About halfway along the road to the park, *Hostería Aire Puro*, Av Granizo 7672 (T 33/441381; ❹–❺) has well-equipped *cabañas*, great views from its restaurant, and the obligatory pool.

Travel details

Buses (Domestic)

Santiago to: Ancud (4 daily; 18hr 30min); Antofagasta (hourly; 19hr); Arica (hourly; 30hr); Calama (hourly; 22hr); Caldera (10 daily; 12hr 30min); Castro (4 daily; 11hr 50min); Chañaral (every 2hr; 13hr 30min); Chillán (20 daily; 5hr); Concepción (every 30min; 6hr); Concón (every 30min; 2hr); Copiapó (hourly; 11hr 15min); Coquimbo (hourly; 6hr 10min); Curicó (every 30min; 2hr 45min); Iquique (hourly; 24hr); Isla Negra (every 30min; 2hr); La Ligua (every 2hr; 2hr 30min); La Serena (hourly; 6hr 30min); Los Andes (every 15min; 1hr 20min); Los Angeles (every 30min; 8hr); Los Lagos (3 daily; 12hr 30min); Los Vilos (hourly; 3hr 15min); Maitencillo (4 daily; 2hr 45min); Olmué (hourly; 1hr 30min–2hr); Osorno (hourly; 13hr); Ovalle (hourly; 5hr 30min); Papudo (4 daily; 3hr); Pucón (8 daily; 12hr); Puerto Montt (hourly; 14hr); Puerto Varas (every 2hr; 13hr 30min); Rancagua (every 15min; 1hr–1hr 30min); San Fernando (every 15min; 1hr 30min); Santa Cruz (every 30min; 2hr); Talca (20 daily; 3hr 30min); Talcahuano (hourly; 8hr); Taltal (1 daily; 18hr 30min); Temuco (hourly; 10hr); Valdivia (every 2hr; 12hr); Vallenar (hourly; 9hr 30min); Valparaíso (every 15min; 1hr 30min–1hr 45min); Vicuña (3 daily; 8hr); Villarrica (8 daily; 11hr 30min); Viña del Mar (every 15min; 1hr 30min–1hr 45min); Zapallar (3 daily; 3hr 30min).

Buses (International)

Santiago to: Asunción (3 weekly; 30hr); Bariloche (1 daily; 16hr); Buenos Aires (1–2 daily; 22hr); Córdoba (1–2 daily; 16hr); Lima (2 weekly; 48–50hr); Mendoza (9–12 daily; 7hr); Montevideo (1 weekly; 28hr); Rio de Janeiro (4 weekly; 65hr); São Paulo (4 weekly; 62hr).

Trains

Santiago to: Chillán (4–7 daily; 4hr 30min); Curicó (4–7 daily; 2hr 30min); Linares (4–7 daily; 3hr 30min); Parral (4–7 daily; 3hr 50min); Rancagua (15–19 daily; 1hr 5min–1hr 20min); San Fernando (15–19 daily; 1hr 40min–1hr 55min); Talca (4–7 daily; 2hr 50min).

Flights

Santiago to: Antofagasta (16 daily; 1hr 50min–3hr 40min); Arica (4 daily; 2hr 50min–3hr 40min); Balmaceda (for Coyhaique; 2 daily; 4hr 45min); Calama (10 daily; 1hr 50min–2hr 10min); Concepción (11 daily; 1hr); Copiapó (5 daily; 1hr 20min); Easter Island (7 weekly; 5hr 40min); Iquique (11 daily; 1hr 30min–4hr); La Serena (4 daily; 1hr); Puerto Montt (11–13 daily; 1hr 45min–3hr 15min); Punta Arenas (2–3 daily; 3hr 25min–4hr 30min); Temuco (5–6 daily; 1hr 25min).

Valparaíso, Viña and the Central Coast

CHAPTER 2 # Highlights

* **Valparaíso** Chile's most remarkable city sits precariously on a dozen hills above a huge bay, with a quirky set of antique elevators that haul you up to panoramic lookouts. See p.133

* **Isla Negra** Chilean poet Pablo Neruda came here for inspiration and wrote many of his Nobel Prize-winning poems while gazing out at his favourite beach. See p.147

* **Quinta Vergara** A taste of exotic nature amidst all the beaches, this Viña park features all manner of subtropical trees and rare plants, plus a museum of fine art. See p.151

* **Reñaca** Enjoy daytime sunbathing or night-time clubbing at this leading seaside resort, packed in summer with the young party crowd. See p.155

* **Zapallar** With some of the best seafood in the region, soothingly empty beaches and opulently stylish houses, this eternally fashionable coastal resort is one of the pearls of the "Chilean Riviera". See p.156

▲ Zapallar

Valparaíso, Viña and the Central Coast

Of Chile's 4000km-plus **coastline**, the brief central strip between Santo Domingo and Los Vilos is the most visited and developed. Known as the Litoral Central and rather optimistically promoted as the "Chilean Riviera", this 250km-stretch boasts bay after bay lined with gorgeous, white-sand beaches, and a string of coastal resort towns.

Valparaíso ("Valpo" for short) and **Viña del Mar** (or "Viña") sit next to each other near the middle of the strip. They are geographical neighbours, but poles apart in appearance and atmosphere. Viña is Chile's largest beach resort and one of the ritziest. With its high-rise condominiums, casino, and seafront chain restaurants, as well as the northern beaches in nearby Reñaca where bronzed sunbathers laze until sunset and then go clubbing all night, Viña typifies modern hedonism. Valparaíso, on the other hand, has far more personality, with ramshackle, brightly-painted houses spilling chaotically down the hills to the sea, but no decent beaches. For stretches of sand, you'll need to head south or north to find anything from disco-packed pleasure grounds to tiny, secluded coves.

Closest to Santiago, via the toll highway ("Autopista del Sol" or Ruta 78), are the resorts **south of Valparaíso**, which are busier and more developed – especially Algarrobo and Cartagena, once quiet havens for holidaymakers, now horrific clusters of high-rise towers. Further south towards **Quintay** and **Rocas de Santo Domingo**, there's an almost uninterrupted string of *cabañas*, villas and small, rather unpleasant resorts. Even so, along this section the development tends to be more low-key and small-scale, and it's still possible to find places with charm and a soul, especially where Pablo Neruda found them, such as **Isla Negra** – though it, too, is fast being swallowed up by rampant development. **San Antonio**, Chile's second port and the only place on the Litoral south of Valparaíso that doesn't rely on tourism for its livelihood, is nonetheless another nasty blot on the horizon that's best avoided.

Heading **north of Viña** is quite a different story; you leave most of the concrete behind at **Concón**, and from **Horcón** up, the coast begins to look more rugged and feels distinctly wild and windswept by the time you reach **Maitencillo**, where brown, sandstone cliffs tower above a huge, white beach. The stretch from here to **Papudo** is easily the most beautiful of the Litoral, as the road clings to the cliff edge, giving views down to empty coves and

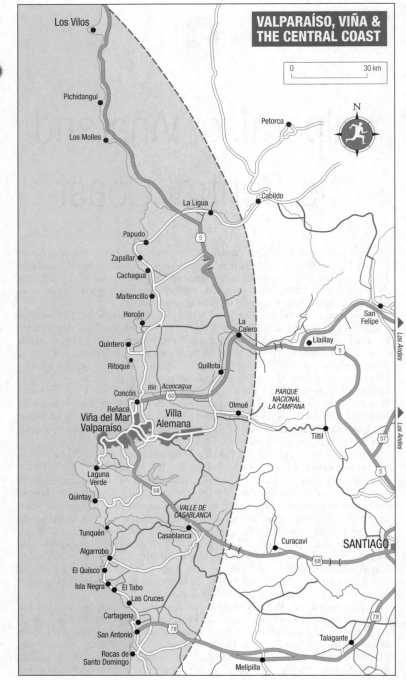

thundering surf. Not even the new villas and second-home complexes that have sprung up along here in the last few years have managed to spoil **Zapallar**, the most architecturally graceful of all the resorts, or Papudo, a small fishing town dramatically hemmed in by steep, green hills. Two more popular resorts lie further to the north, off the Panamericana as it thrusts into the deserts of the Norte Chico: **Los Vilos** and **Pichidangui**.

Note most Chileans take their annual holiday in February, when all the resort towns, large and small, are unbearably crowded. They also get busy on December and January weekends, but outside these times are remarkably quiet. November and March are probably the **best months** to be here, as the weather is usually agreeable and the beaches virtually deserted, especially midweek. This coast is prone to **fog** or cloudy weather, even in the summer; temperatures in Valpo can be considerably lower than in Santiago. From April to October **accommodation rates** are considerably lower, sometimes half of what is listed in our price guide, and even in November, December and March you should be able to negotiate a midweek discount. Some, but not all, beaches are safe for **swimming**, though you should definitely stay out of the water if a red flag is displayed; you might also be put off by the frigid **Humboldt current** that sweeps up the Pacific coast from the Antarctic, leaving the water chilly even in the height of summer.

Don't miss out on the exquisite **seafood** available all along the coast; look out for the *picoroco* inside its rock shell, which resembles something out of a sci-fi movie. Finally a word on **transport**: there are frequent daily buses from Santiago to Valparaíso and Viña, and several direct services from the capital to most of the other resort towns. From Valpo or Viña you can catch buses to all the resort towns in the Litoral. The stretch between Algarrobo and San Antonio is also served by regular local buses which are much quicker if you go direct on Ruta 78 rather than via Viña and then heading south. From Horcón to Papudo there are fewer daily local connections – except during summer when buses run fairly frequently. On nearly all routes you can ask your driver to stop anywhere along the coast or highway so you can hop off at some isolated cove.

Valparaíso

Valparaíso es un montón, un racimo
de casas locas

Pablo Neruda

Spread over an amphitheatre of hills encircling a wide bay, **Valparaíso** is perhaps the most memorable city in Chile. Its most striking feature is the array of houses – a mad, colourful tangle of them tumbling down the hills to a narrow shelf of land below. Few roads make it up these gradients and most people get up and down on the city's fifteen "lifts" or *ascensores*, a collection of ancient-looking funiculars that slowly haul you up to incredible viewpoints. The lower town, known as *El Plan*, named after Pedro Montt's reconstruction strategy after the 1906 earthquake, is a series of narrow, traffic-choked streets packed with shops, banks, offices and abandoned warehouses, crowded round the quays and port that once made Valparaíso's fortune.

Some history

The bay was chosen as the site of the new colony's port as early as 1542, when Pedro de Valdivia decided it would "serve the trade of these lands and of Santiago". Growth was slow, however, owing to trading restrictions imposed by the Spanish Crown, but when Latin American trade was liberalized in the 1820s, following independence, Valparaíso started to come into its own. On the shipping route from Europe to America's Pacific Coast, it became the main port of call and resupply centre for ships after they crossed the Straits of Magellan. As Chile's own foreign trade expanded with the silver and copper booms of the 1830s, the port became ever more active, but it was the government's innovative creation of public warehouses where merchants could store goods at low prices that really launched Valparaíso into its economic ascent.

Foreign businessmen, particularly British ones, flocked to the city where they ran trading empires built on copper, silver and nitrate. By the late nineteenth century they had turned Valparaíso into Chile's foremost financial and commercial centre. The city outstripped Santiago in most urban developments, producing its own daily newspaper, banks and stock exchange long before the capital. Even as it prospered, however, Valparaíso continued to be dogged by the kind of violent setbacks that had always punctuated its history, from looting pirates and buccaneers to earthquakes and fires. On March 31, 1866, following Chile's entanglement in a dispute between Spain and Peru, the Spanish admiralty bombarded Valparaíso, wreaking devastation. It took a long time to rebuild the city, but worse was to come. On August 16, 1906, a colossal **earthquake** practically razed the city to the ground, killing over two thousand people. The disaster took a heavy toll on Valparaíso's fortunes, which never really recovered. Eight years later, the opening of the Panama Canal signalled the city's inexorable decline.

Today, Valparaíso wears a rundown, moth-eaten air. Crime and poverty are worse than elsewhere in Chile and at night parts of the town can be dangerous. It also has the highest rate of AIDS in the country as a result of the still rampant sex trade. That said, it's still a vital **working port**, moving thousands of containers annually, and has been the seat of Congress since the return to democracy in 1990. The port underwent a mini-economic boom in the early years of the new millennium, though the city's inhabitants, known as Porteños, do not seem to have benefited enormously. As the capital of Region V, it also has its share of galleries and museums, but the city's chief attractions lie in its crumbling, romantic atmosphere and stunning setting.

Arrival, information and getting around

Buses from Santiago (every 15min from Terminal Alameda) and other major cities pull in at the Terminal Rodoviario on the eastern end of Pedro Montt, opposite the Congreso Nacional – it's about a twenty-minute walk west to the old town centre; plenty of **micros** and **colectivos** also go into the centre from right outside the station. A local **train** service travels to Valparaíso from Viña del Mar.

Information

The municipal authorities have reorganized the **tourist information** structure in Valpo, with mixed results. There are now two information kiosks, in **Muelle Prat** by the port and **Plaza Aníbal Pinto** (both daily 10am–2pm & 2.30–5.30pm; no phone); they are manned by university students who are friendly and generally speak English but can only offer limited information.

2

Tours

There are innumerable tours on offer in Valparaíso; two of the best operators are **Ruta Valparaíso** (☎32/259 2520, ⓦwww.rutavalparaíso.cl) and **Santiago Adventures** (Guardia Vieja 255, Providencia, Santiago; ☎2/244 2750, ⓦwww.santiagoadven tures.com). Tours generally cost from CH$14,000 to CH$50,000, and both companies have bilingual guides. The former runs a range of tours, including ones exploring the city's famous nightlife, the *cerros*, and Pablo Neruda's La Sebastiana and Isla Negra homes. The latter offers similar packages, as well as others that take in the coastal resorts of Zapallar, Cachagua and Quintay.

There's also a branch at the **bus station** (daily 8.30am–5.30pm; no phone). Two Spanish-language **websites** provide useful information about Valparaíso: ⓦwww.valparaisochile.cl and ⓦwww.granvalparaiso.cl.

Orientation and getting around

Countless **micros** run east and west across the city: those displaying "Aduana" on the window take you west through the centre, past the port, while those marked "P. Montt" take you back to the bus station. To climb the hills to the neighbourhoods of the upper town, it's easiest to use the **ascensores**; some bus routes also take you to the upper town, and you can catch **colectivos** at Plazuela Ecuador, at the bottom of Calle Ecuador. **Taxis** are numerous but more expensive than in Santiago.

Accommodation

Valparaíso has an excellent range of **accommodation** to suit all budgets, with new places springing up all the time. If you're on a really short visit it may be easiest to stay near the bus terminal, but you won't get the full Valparaíso experience unless you head up to one of the *cerros*: Alegre and Concepción are by far the most popular, but Bellavista, Cárcel, Playa Ancha and several others are also developing, and provide a less touristy experience. Many places will pick you up at the bus station if you call ahead.

Alojamiento Villa Kunterbunt Quebrada Verde 192, Playa Ancha ☎32/2288873, ⓔvillakunterbuntvalpo@yahoo.de. Outside the centre, but the reward is one of the friendliest welcomes in town and a truly beautiful house – its attic room has windows on all sides and splendid views of the entire city. Take bus #501, #504, #505, #602, #603, #606 or #611 from the bus terminal and ask to be dropped at "Colegio María Auxiliadora", opposite the house. ❷–❸

Brighton Bed & Breakfast Pasaje Atkinson 151, Cerro Concepción ☎32/223513, ⓦwww.brighton .cl. This British-run nine-bed hotel is actually a modern construction but boasts fantastic views and stylish en-suites. While service occasionally lets the side down, the café is a fine spot for drinks; there's live music on Friday and Saturday nights. ❺–❻

Casa Higueras Higuera 133, Cerro Alegre ☎32/249 7900, ⓦwww.hotelcasahigueras.cl. If money is no object, this is the place to stay: stately 1930s-style en-suites (US$238–280), a pool and Jacuzzi with exquisite vistas, and a classy (and pretty reasonably priced) restaurant, open to non-guests. ❽–❾

Casa Latina Papudo 462, Cerro Concepción ☎32/249 4622, ⓦwww.casalatina.cl. This popular B&B is within walking distance of many attractions and features nineteenth-century architecture smartly mixed with contemporary furnishings. ❹–❻

Hostal Caracol Hector Calvo 371, Cerro Bellavista ☎32/239 5817, ⓦwww.hostalcaracol.cl. A clean and friendly hostel, offering pleasant rooms with private facilities, that receives consistently good

135

reports from backpackers. It's located on an up-and-coming cerro, near the Museo a Cielo Abierto. **④**

Hotel Casa Thomas Somerscales San Enrique 446, Cerro Alegre ☎ 32/233 1006, ⓦ www.hotelsomerscales.cl. Each of the eight en-suites at this beautifully restored home of renowned local painter Thomas Somerscales is fitted out with period furniture and artwork, as well as modern comforts. Stunning views, roof terrace and large stained glass window make this one of the most memorable hotels in town. **⑦–⑧**

Hotel Da Vinci Urriola 426, Cerro Alegre ☎ 32/317 4494, ⓦ www.hoteldavincivalparaiso.cl. A cross between an art gallery and a hotel: the

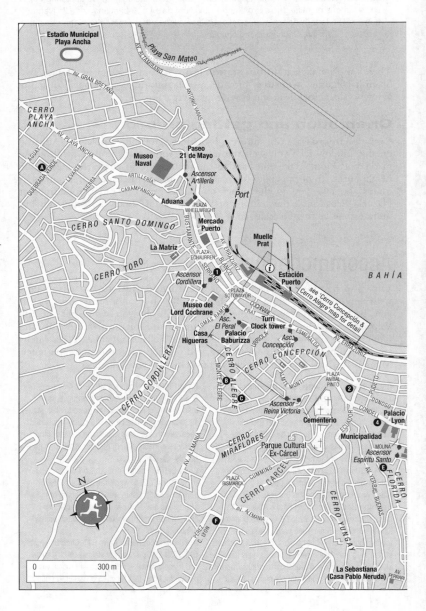

en-suites, some split-level, are set around a central atrium, bathed with light from a towering window, while carefully placed photos and paintings provide a mellow ambience. ❹

Hotel Puerto Valparaíso Chacabuco 2362 ☎&℻ 32/221 7391. Charming hotel dating back to 1902, whose rooms feature evocative black and white photos of Valparaíso, bronze bed frames and dark wood furniture. Those at the front have small balconies, while the ones at the back lack outside windows. ❹

Hotel Ultramar Tomás Pérez 173, Cerro Cárcel ☎32/221 0000, ⓦwww.hotelultramar.cl. Striped, spotted and checked decor – though fortunately not

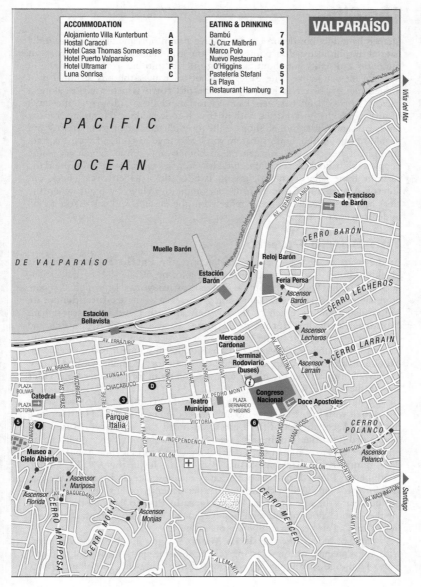

all together – give this thoroughly modern hotel, a refurbished 1907 Italianate townhouse, a unique feel. Rooms with a view are worth the extra. ⑥–⑧ **Luna Sonrisa** Templeman 833, Cerro Alegre ☎ 32/ 273 4117, ⓦ www.lunasonrisa.cl. Minimalist but comfortable rooms, pristine facilities, excellent breakfast with home-made bread and jams, and a sociable atmosphere make this an excellent choice. Staff are very friendly and knowledgeable – the place is owned by a travel writer, so you would expect nothing less. Dorm CH$7500, private rooms ④, apartment ⑥.

The City

Draped languidly but decorously over three dozen hills and arranged around a natural amphitheatre that plunges into the bay, Valparaíso isn't really about museums and sights but about exploring the labyrinthine streets and taking in magnificent panoramas. The eastern end of town near the bus terminal is of limited interest; better to head west to the **old town** which stretches along a narrow strip of land between Plaza Victoria and Plaza Aduana, at the city's historic core. The port district, with its British-style banks and insurance offices, dingy bars and old-fashioned shops, is the most idiosyncratic part of the city and should not be missed. Unfortunately you'll also have to contend with a certain amount of noise, pollution, general shabbiness and crime, which for some people overshadows the city's charms. However, just take a **boat ride** round the harbour (especially at sunset); go up two or three **ascensores**; check out **Cerros Alegre** and **Concepción**; and sample the views by night, when the city's million flickering lights are reflected in the ocean – and you're sure to fall under Valparaíso's spell.

The Barrio Puerto

At the heart of Porteño history and identity, the **Barrio Puerto**, the port neighbourhood, is a good place to start exploring. While safe by day, it gets dodgy at night. The focal point is **Plaza Sotomayor**, a large public square dominated at one end by the imposing grey facade of the **ex-Intendencia de Valparaíso** (now occupied by the navy). At the other end is the triumphant **Monumento de los Héroes de Iquique**, where statues of Arturo Prat and other heroes of the War of the Pacific tower above a crypt housing their tombs (open to the public each May 21). Opposite the monument is the gateway to **Muelle Prat**, the only stretch of the port open to the public. Geared almost exclusively towards tourists, it's the embarkation point for half-hour **boat rides** around the bay (CH$1000).

From the ex-Intendencia, Calle Serrano leads west into the oldest part of the city, dotted with battered shops and dubious-looking sailors' bars. Halfway along the street, **Ascensor Cordillera** takes you up to the red-walled **Museo del Mar Lord Thomas Cochrane** (Tues–Sat 10am–6pm), where you'll find an impressive display of model ships that belonged to Lord Cochrane, and stupendous **panoramic vistas** out to sea. Back in the lower town, Calle Serrano continues to **Plaza Echaurren**, the city's oldest square and very picturesque save for the wine-swilling characters that permanently occupy its benches. Just off the square, the iron structure of the **Mercado Puerto** has a bustling market on the ground floor and several popular, inexpensive fish restaurants upstairs (lunch only). Petty crime can be a problem here.

A couple of blocks east, **Iglesia La Matriz** – a graceful, Neoclassical church with a seventeenth-century carving of Christ inside – sits at the foot of Cerro Santo Domingo surrounded by narrow, twisting streets full of colour, activity and a slightly menacing feel; this is a rough part of town, not to be explored alone or at night. If you continue along Serrano (which becomes Bustamante) you reach Plaza Wheelwright (also known as Plaza Aduana), flanked by the large, colonial-looking **Aduana** building, dating from 1854 and still a working customs house.

The Paseo 21 de Mayo and the Museo Naval

A few steps from Aduana you'll find **Ascensor Artillería**, which takes you up to the **Paseo 21 de Mayo** on Cerro Playa Ancha. Of all the city's viewpoints, this one provides the most spectacular panorama, taking in the whole bay of Valparaíso and sweeping 20km north to the Punta de Concón; on very clear days you can even see the smokestacks at the oil refinery of Ventanas, 45km away. The *paseo* curves around the luxuriant gardens of a former naval school, an impressive whitewashed building that now houses the excellent **Museo Naval y Marítimo** (Tues–Sun 10am–6pm; CH$500). The beautifully presented displays – including paintings, photographs, weapons, uniforms, nautical instruments and personal objects – bring to life some of the central figures in Chile's history, such as Ambrosio O'Higgins, Lord Cochrane and Arturo Prat.

Plaza Sotomayor to Plaza Victoria

Valparaíso's **city centre** is formed by a narrow strip stretching from Plaza Sotomayor in the west to Plaza Victoria in the east. Almost completely devastated by the 1906 earthquake (see p.134), it has evolved into a mixture of ugly, modern blocks and elegant buildings (many former banks or financial institutions) left over from the early twentieth century. Calle Prat, which runs east from Plaza Sotomayor, has some good examples – take a look inside the **Banco Santander** opposite the Turri clock tower, originally the Banco de Londres and dripping with bronze and marble brought over from England. Next door, **Ascensor Concepción** (or Ascensor Turri) provides access to Cerro Concepción, a lovely residential area once the preserve of English businessmen. Further east, **Plaza Aníbal Pinto** is a pretty cobbled square overlooked by a couple of the city's oldest restaurants, including *El Cinzano* (see p.144). From here you can climb up Calle Cumming to **Cerro Cárcel**, where you'll find a collection of **cemeteries**; the names on the graves – Clampitt, Laussen, Van Buren, Matthews, Rivera – provide a fascinating glimpse at the diversity of the city's founders. Nearby is **Parque Cultural Ex-Cárcel** (Mon–Fri 9am–7pm, Sat–Sun 11am–7pm), Castro s/n, a crumbling old prison turned vibrant cultural hub. Murals and graffiti cover the walls, and artists have converted the cells into studios. It's an interesting place to look round, and there are also frequent exhibitions and concerts.

Back at Plaza Aníbal Pinto, the main drag continues along Calle Condell, where you'll find the **Palacio Lyon**, a splendid mansion dating from 1881 (one of the few to survive the earthquake) and now housing the **Museo de Historia Natural** (Tues–Sat 10am–1pm & 2–6pm, Sun 10am–2pm; CH$600, Wed & Sun free). This cash-starved museum tries hard to inform and entertain but its displays look dowdy and outdated. The cellars of the building have been converted into the **Galería Municipal de Arte** (Tues–Sun 10am–7pm), which puts on temporary art exhibitions with excellent oil paintings of the area; the entrance is on Condell, separate from the museum's.

Calle Condell ends at **Plaza Victoria**, a large tree-filled square where most of Valparaíso seems to come to chat and sit in the sunshine. It's flanked, on its

▲ Valparaíso *ascensor*

eastern side, by the gothic-looking **Iglesia Catedral de Valparaíso**, whose simply decorated interior includes a delicate ivory carving of Christ, and most intriguingly, a marble urn (in the crypt) containing the heart of the famous Chilean statesman Diego Portales. If you want to visit the cathedral, ask in the administrative office at the north side of the building, on Chacabuco (Mon–Fri 10am–1pm & 4–6.30pm). From the square, calles Molina and Edwards lead up to the **Museo a Cielo Abierto**, a circuit of narrow streets and passageways painted with seventeen colourful, bold, abstract murals by students and leading local artists, the most memorable being the enormous paintings by Roberto Matta. The increased graffiti destruction of the murals is the most obvious sign, however, that it's worth keeping your wits about you.

La Sebastiana – Neruda's house

Of Pablo Neruda's three houses open to the public (the others being La Chascona, see p.99, and Isla Negra, see p.147), **La Sebastiana** (Tues–Sun 10.10am–6pm; CH$2500), offers the most informal look at the poet, not least because you aren't forced to take a guided tour so you can amble around at your own pace, armed with informative sheets in Spanish and English. Neruda moved into this house in 1961 with Matilde Urrutia, his third wife. Perched high on the aptly named Bellavista hill, giving dramatic views over the bay, it was his *casa en el aire* ("House in the Air") and although he spent less time here than in his other homes, he imprinted his style and enthusiasms on every corner of the house. After the 1973 coup it was repeatedly vandalized by the military but has been meticulously restored by the Fundación Neruda, which opened it as a museum in 1992. Its narrow, sinuous passages and bright colours seem to mirror the spirit of Valparaíso, and the countless bizarre objects brought here by the poet are simply astonishing, from the embalmed Venezuelan Coro-Coro bird hanging from the ceiling of the dining room to the wooden horse in the living room, taken from a merry-go-round in Paris. The house is at Ferrari 692, off Avenida Alemania; to get here, take a short ride in #39 *colectivo* or bus "D" from Plaza Ecuador. If you are staying on *cerros* Alegre or Concepción and don't fancy the 25 minutes' walk, catch Bus "O" from Plaza San Luis at the top of Templeman; it's 5 minutes to La Sebastiana, but if you stay on the bus for the rest of the route you get an inexpensive tour of the city. At the end of the route you can catch a bus back to La Sebastiana.

Cerros Alegre and Concepción

The hilltop residential quarter spread over **cerros Alegre** and **Concepción** is a rambling maze of steep streets and small alleys lined with elegant, brightly painted houses and aristocratic mansions clinging precipitously to the hillside. It grew up as the enclave of Valparaíso's immigrant businessmen, particularly the English, who left street names like Leighton, Templeman and Atkinson, and the Germans, whose influence can be seen in the many half-timbered, shuttered houses. There are two points of access from the lower town; **Ascensor Concepción** (see below), near the Turri clock tower in Calle Prat, takes you

Valparaíso's antiquated lifts

Most of Valparaíso's fifteen **ascensores**, or funicular "lifts", were built between 1883 and 1916 to provide a link between the lower town and the new residential quarters spreading up the hillsides. Appearances would suggest that they've scarcely been modernized since, but despite their rickety frames and alarming noises they've so far proved safe and reliable. What's more, nearly all drop off passengers at a panoramic viewpoint. The *ascensores* operate every few minutes from 7am to 11pm, and cost around CH$100 to CH$300 one-way. Here are a few of the best, from east to west:

Ascensor Barón This *ascensor* has windows on all sides, so you get good views as you go up. Inaugurated in 1906, it was the first to be powered by an electric motor, still in perfect working order. The entrance is hidden away at the back of a clothes market, Feria Persa el Barón, off the seaward end of Avenida Argentina. At the top, you're allowed into the machinery room where you can watch the giant cogs go round as they haul the lift up and down. There's also a display of photos of all of Valpo's *ascensores*.

Ascensor Polanco The most picturesque *ascensor*, and the only one that's totally vertical. It's approached through a cavernous, underground tunnel and rises 80m through a yellow wooden tower to a balcony that gives some of the best views in the city. A narrow bridge connects the tower to Cerro Polanco with its flaking, pastel houses in varying states of repair. Ascensor Polanco is on Calle Simpson, off Avenida Argentina (opposite Independencia).

Ascensor Concepción (also known as Ascensor Turri) Hidden in a small passage opposite the Turri clock tower, at the corner of Prat and Almirante Carreño, this was the first *ascensor* to be built, in 1883, and was originally powered by steam. It takes you up to the beautiful residential area of Cerro Concepción, well worth a visit (see above).

Ascensor El Peral Next door to the Tribunales de Justicio, just off Plaza Sotomayor, this *ascensor* leads to one of the most romantic corners of the city: Paseo Yugoslavo, a little esplanade looking west onto some of Valparaíso's most beautiful houses, and backed by a flamboyant mansion housing the Museo de Bellas Artes. It's worth walking from here to Ascensor Concepción (see map, p.142).

Ascensor Artillería Always busy with tourists, but highly recommended for the stunning vistas at the top, from the Paseo 21 de Mayo. It was built in 1893 to transport cadets to and from the naval school at the top of the hill, now the site of the Museo Naval y Marítimo (see p.139).

CERRO ALEGRE & CERRO CONCEPCIÓN

---- Walking Tour

0   100 m

EATING & DRINKING					ACCOMMODATION			
Barparaíso	2	Café Riquet	4	Gremio	9	Brighton Bed		Hotel Casa	
El Bar Inglés	3	Café Turri	5	Le Filou de Montpellier	11	& Breakfast	A	Thomas Somerscales	E
Café Bijoux	7	El Cinzano	6	Pasta e Vino	8	Casa Higueras	D	Hotel Da Vinci	C
Café con Letras	10	Epif	12	La Piedra Feliz	1	Casa Latina	B	Luna Sonrisa	F
				Vinilo	13				

up to **Paseo Gervasoni** on Cerro Concepción, while **Ascensor El Peral** (see p.141), next to the Tribunales de Justicia just off Plaza Sotomayor, ascends to Cerro Alegre's **Paseo Yugoslavo**, one of the most attractive and peaceful parts of town. A good way to explore the area is to walk between the two *ascensores*: see map above for a suggested **walking tour**, which takes you through some narrow alleys and hidden passageways.

Arriving at Paseo Yugoslavo you'll see an extravagant, four-storey mansion right behind the esplanade. This is **Palacio Baburizza**, built in 1916 for a nitrate baron and now the home of the **Museo de Bellas Artes de Valparaíso** (Tues–Sun 10am–6pm), a scarcely visited museum with a collection of nineteenth- and twentieth-century Chilean and European art. It's worth a look for the evocative paintings of an earlier Valparaíso by artists such as Juan Mauricio Rugendas, Alfred Helsby, Thomas Somerscales and, most notably, Juan Francisco González. Less highbrow, and in some ways more rewarding, **Casa Mirador de Lukas** (Tues–Sun 11am–6pm; CH$1000) sits just a few steps from the Ascensor Concepción, at Paseo Gervasoni 448. This little museum pays homage to *El Mercurio*'s great satirist and cartoonist, known simply as Lukas, who possessed a sharp talent for capturing the spirit of his country in the hilarious drawings he produced for the newspaper between 1958 and 1988. There's also an appealing café.

As you're walking around Cerro Concepción, don't miss **Paseo Atkinson**, an esplanade affording great panoramas and lined with pretty houses whose tiny front gardens and window boxes recall their original English owners. From here you can see the tall tower of the **Lutheran church**, a distinctive, green-walled structure built in 1897; a block or so farther away you'll find the towerless **St Paul's Anglican Church** (built in 1858) whose solemn interior contains a huge organ donated by Queen Victoria in 1903.

Around the Congreso Nacional

If you arrive in Valparaíso by bus the first thing that hits you as you emerge from the station is the imposing **Congreso Nacional**, described by Collier and Sater in their *History of Chile* as "half neo-Babylonian, half post-modernist atrocity". It was one of Pinochet's projects, but the dictator relinquished power before it was completed. Its life began on March 11, 1990, when Patricio Aylwin was sworn in as president and Congress resumed its activities after a sixteen-year absence – away from the capital for the first time. Given the inconvenience of its distance from the capital, politicians have repeatedly discussed a plan to return Congress to Santiago and convert the building into a gigantic hotel, but so far no decision has been made. There's little else to hold your interest in this part of town, but one of Chile's best **antique/flea markets** is held every Saturday and Sunday at Plaza O'Higgins, though the prices are fairly high. The lively **flower, fruit and vegetable market** that runs along Argentina on Wednesday and Saturday is also worth a visit. While you're here, seek out **Ascensor Polanco** (see p.141), the most fascinating of the funiculars, reached by a long, underground tunnel and taking you up to a fine look-out tower. It's located on Simpson, off the southern end of Argentina.

Eating, drinking and entertainment

Valparaíso's eating and drinking scene is one of the city's highlights, especially if you catch it in full swing on a Thursday, Friday or Saturday night. Moreover some of Chile's best and most inventive **food** can be found here. Unless otherwise stated, restaurants are open Monday to Saturday; your best bet for a good Sunday meal is to head up to Concepción or Alegre where the more touristy places generally open every day. The city's speciality is its old-fashioned, charming **bar-restaurants** serving *comida típica* to local families, who turn out in their dozens to join in the singing and dancing on weekends, when many places have live *boleros, tangos* or *música folklórica*. There's also a range of younger, hipper **bars**, many with live music and dancing (and usually a cover charge, which tends to include the first drink). These are concentrated in one main area: the relatively safe **subida Ecuador**, climbing up from Plaza Ecuador and lined with cheap bars, pubs and restaurants, where the partying lasts all night.

A second option is the **Barrio Puerto**, mainly along Errázuriz. Keep alert – even during the weekend when there are usually plenty of people going from bar to bar until the early hours of the morning. Most places are closed on Sunday night and tend to be very quiet Monday to Wednesday; at the weekend, bars and restaurants don't start to fill up until after 10pm, and many stay open until 5am or later. Cover charges range from CH$3000–6000.

Valpo is *the place* to go in Chile to ring in the **New Year**, with huge parties and fireworks extravaganzas; be sure arrive by midday on the 30th or you'll get stuck in horrible traffic.

For an evening of culture, check out the programme at the **Teatro Municipal**, on the corner of Pedro Montt and Plaza O'Higgins, which features regular theatre, music and dance performances. Hoyts, Pedro Montt

2111 (☏32/2594709), shows mainstream **films**. You can find art movies at various cultural centres about town; check the back of the newspaper *El Mercurio de Valparaíso* for details.

Cafés, snacks and cheap eats

Bambú Independencia 1792. Good-value vegetarian food like soups, salads, omelettes, soya burgers and tofu concoctions (CH$2000–3000) in a new city centre location.

Café con Letras Almirante Montt 316. Low-key, faintly melancholy café-cum-bookshop, where aged wooden posts prop up the ceiling and black and white photos adorn the walls. It's a good spot for a quiet read and a coffee (CH$1000–1500). Open daily.

Café Riquet Plaza Aníbal Pinto. An old-fashioned café-restaurant seemingly frozen in time: join the local literary and arty set for coffee, snacks and breakfast (CH$2000–5000).

Café Turri Paseo Gervasoni, by upper exit of *ascensor* Concepción. Come for a sundowner and a dessert (CH$2000–4000) rather than a full meal at this touristy spot. However, the real star is the panoramic Valpo view from the outdoor terrace. Open daily.

Epif Grossi 268, Cerro Concepción. Chilled-out vegetarian joint – expect BBQ tofu *burritos* and stuffed portobello mushrooms (CH$1700–2800) – and a worthwhile evening stop-off for a beer or glass of organic wine.

Pastelería Stefani Condell 1608, Plaza Victoria. Exquisite strawberry tarts and other delights, as well as a small stand-up bar where you can wash down your inexpensive cake (CH$500–1000) with a coffee.

Restaurants

Café Bijoux Abato 561, Cerro Concepción. Attractive restaurant with a decorative old cash register, ship's steering wheel and open parasols dotted around. There's a tapas-style menu (CH$2000–4500) ideal for sampling alongside a glass of Valpo's dark and fruity El Puerto beer.

J. Cruz Malbrán Condell 1466, up side alley next to the Municipalidad. An extraordinary place, more like a museum than a restaurant, packed to the gills with china, old clocks, musical instruments, crucifixes and more. It also claims to have invented the *chorrillana* (steak strips, onions, eggs and a mountain of French fries), which is not to be missed.

Le Filou de Montpellier Almirante Montt 382, Cerro Concepción. A delightful little piece of France in Valpo: postcards of Montpellier and paintings by local artists decorate the place,

while the ever-changing CH$7500 set menu may include quiche, chicken in Roquefort sauce and profiteroles. Open Tues–Sun for lunch; Fri–Sat dinner too.

Nuevo Restaurant O'Higgins Barroso 506, near Plaza O'Higgins. Carnivores are in for a treat at this hugely popular restaurant, which serves perfectly cooked steaks (from CH$5000). Open Mon–Sat, & Sun lunch.

Pasta e Vino Templeman 352, Cerro Concepción ☏32/249 6107. Widely considered to be Valpo's finest restaurant, *Pasta e Vino* provides an inventive and ambitious take on Italian cuisine – gnocchi with a prawn and caviar sauce for example. The only problem is getting a table, and reservations are vital on the weekend. Mains CH$6000–8000. Closed Sun evening and Mon–Tues.

Restaurant Hamburg O'Higgins 1274. This German–Chilean restaurant is filled to the rafters with nautical memorabilia and serves artery-clogging, seafaring portions of pork chops, breaded chicken, steaks and seafood (CH$4000–6500).

Vinilo Almirante Montt 546, Cerro Concepción. Intimate bistro with a select menu of contemporary Chilean dishes (such as rabbit in white wine), a bizarre mix of abstract and children's artwork and a stack of vintage vinyl. Try *Vinilo's* own Cerro Alegre ale while you're here. Mains CH$4200–6500. Open daily.

Bars and pubs

Barparaíso Errázuriz 1041. Funky bar with a dance area downstairs overlooked by a dimly lit balcony where you can hang out and drink. It plays a mixture of rock, Latin and dance music, and is popular with students.

El Bar Inglés Cochrane 851 (rear entrance at Blanco 870). A long-standing favourite since the early 1900s, and very popular for lunch – though more expensive than its old-fashioned, crumbling decor might suggest. Check out the wall map with listings of incoming boats from all over the world.

El Cinzano Plaza Aníbal Pinto 1182. Hugely popular place with a fantastic weekend atmos-phere when it fills with locals and ageing crooners singing sentimental ballads.

Gremio Pasaje Galvez 173, Cerro Concepción. This ice-cool bar draws a trendy crowd and is a good bet if you're staying on Concepción or Alegre as it's not too far to stumble home from.

La Piedra Feliz Errázuriz 1054, near junction with Blanco. Really mellow place with creaky wooden floors and plenty of tables to sit at and chat. There's live jazz on Tues, *boleros* on Wed and various types of music on the weekends.

🏃 **La Playa** Serrano 567. Sociable spot with a long, mahogany bar, dark wood-panelled walls and posters of Jack Nicholson, James Dean and BB King. There's live evening music at the weekend, when a downstairs dance area is opened up and the crowds don't disperse until 7am.

Listings

Airlines LAN, Esmeralda 1048 ☎600/526 2000.
Banks and exchange The main financial street is Prat, where you'll find plenty of banks with ATMs and *cambios*. Of the banks, the Banco de Santiago is the best for currency exchange. There's also an ATM at the bus station.
Car rental Bert Rent a Car, Victoria 2682 ☎32/221 2885; Rosselot, Victoria 3013 ☎32/235 2365.
Consulates United Kingdom, Blanco 1199, 5th floor ☎32/221 3063. Germany, Blanco 1215, Office 1102 ☎32/225 6749.
Football Santiago Wanderers, Chile's oldest club, plays regular matches in the Estadio Municipal at Playa Ancha.

Hospital Van Buren, Colón and San Ignacio ☎32/225 4074.
Instituto Chileno-Norteamericano Esmeralda 1069. Free films and cultural guides.
Internet Centro de Llamadas, Pedro Montt 2368 (CH$600 per hr); Internet Cerro Alegre, Urriola 678, Cerro Alegre (CH$400 per hr).
Post office Prat 856.
Telephone offices Entel, Pedro Montt 1940 and Condell 149, opposite the Municipalidad; Telefónica, Plaza Victoria and Sotomayor 55. Also cheap call centres around the bus station.

South of Valparaíso

The coastal resorts **south of Valparaíso** are among the busiest and most developed in the Litoral Central. A trail of seaside towns, full of busy hotels, *cabañas* and *marisquerías*, are linked by numerous *micros* and *colectivos*. Most sit on long, overcrowded beaches – in the summer, that is; in the winter they are forlorn and abandoned, often lost in marine fog. The majority of the main resorts, such as sprawling Algarrobo, El Tabo and Cartagena, are overrun with ugly apartment blocks and jam-packed with noisy vacationers. If you're looking for a peaceful beach holiday, head instead to **Quintay** or the exclusive **Rocas de Santo Domingo**. You can also take a **wine tour** in the Casablanca Valley. By far the major attraction along the whole seaboard, however, is the fabulous **Isla Negra**, site of Pablo Neruda's extraordinary house, now a museum.

Moving on from Valparaíso

Intercity (every 15min **to Santiago**) and **international buses** leave from Terminal Rodoviario (☎32/939646). You can also get buses **up and down the coast** from here, mainly with Sol del Pacífico (☎32/228 1026), Pullman Bus (☎32/225 3125) and Mirasol (☎32/223 5985). To get **to Viña del Mar**, pick up a *micro* on Pedro Montt; they're very frequent and take about 15 minutes, twice that time in bad traffic; alternatively take a train from the station next to Muelle Prat, off Plaza Sotomayor (every 15–30min), or even a boat from Muelle Prat (CH$1000). For more information see "Travel details" on p.158.

Quintay

Secluded and relatively untouched by tourism, the village of **Quintay** makes an ideal day-trip from Valparaíso. It has a scenic cove and series of small beaches, backed by pine and eucalyptus trees, cacti and wild flowers, perfect for an idle wander. A 45-minute walk to the north takes you to Playa Grande, a lovely stretch of golden sand, now sadly marred by building work. There are a few fish restaurants by the harbour – the *Miramar* is the best – as well as a small museum in a former whaling station (erratic opening times; CH$300) and a lighthouse. While you're by the harbour, keep an eye out for the pair of sea otters who pop up whenever the local fishermen bring in the catch. If you want to stay a night, try *Hosteria y Cabañas Bosquemar* (☎32/224 5130; ❸–❹), Jorge Montt s/n, which has four-person cabins. To get here from Valparaíso, five daily buses (fewer at weekends) depart from the corner of 12 de Febrero and Rawson, and frequent *colectivos* from the rank on 12 de Febrero.

Pablo Neruda

The tiny village of **Isla Negra** was put firmly on the map when **Pablo Neruda** moved into a half-built house on the beach in 1939. Born **Neftalí Reyes** in 1904, this son of a local railwayman grew into a tall, pale and impoverished young man who wandered the streets of Santiago dressed in a swirling cape and a wide sombrero, where he made his name in the world of poetry under the pseudonym of Pablo Neruda, going on to become a **Nobel Laureate** in 1971. He published his first collection of poems, *Crepusculario*, in 1923 at his own expense, selling his furniture and pawning the watch given to him by his father to cover the costs. Success came quickly and when, the following year, he published a slim volume of sensual, tormented verses under the title of *Veinte Poemas de Amor y una Canción Desesperada* ("Twenty love poems and a song of despair") he suddenly found himself, at the age of twenty, with one of the fastest-growing readerships on the continent.

Despite the success of *Veinte Poemas*, Neruda still needed to earn a living to fund his writing, and so, aged twenty-four, he began his career as **Chilean consul** in Rangoon, the first of many posts. It seems ironic that this most "Chilean" of poets, whose verses are imprinted with the forests, rain, sea, lakes and volcanoes of southern Chile, and whose countrymen love him as a man of their soil, should have spent so much of his adult life far from his native land. His years in Rangoon, Colombo, Jakarta and Singapore were often intensely lonely, but also coloured with vivid episodes, not least the many sexual adventures he fondly recalls in his autobiography *Memoirs*. The most dramatic of these was his love affair with a woman in Rangoon who called herself **Josie Bliss**. Described by Neruda as his "Burmese panther...a love-smitten terrorist capable of anything", she was a jealous and possessive lover who would sometimes terrorize him with her silver dagger. When he was transferred to Ceylon (now Sri Lanka), he left secretly, without telling her, but she turned up on his doorstep several months later, carrying a bag of rice (believing it grew only in Rangoon) and a selection of their favourite records. Neruda's outright rejection of her was to haunt him for many years, and Josie Bliss makes several appearances in his poems.

During his time in Asia, Neruda's poetry (published in the collection *Residencia en la Tierra*) was inward-looking, reflecting his experience of dislocation and solitude. His posts in Barcelona (1934) and Madrid (1935–36), however, marked a major turning-point in his life and his work: with the outbreak of the **Spanish Civil War**, and the assassination of his close friend, Federico García Lorca, Neruda became

Isla Negra

Since 1939, poet **Pablo Neruda** spent on and off forty years of his life here, enlarging his house and filling it with the strange and beautiful objects he ceaselessly gathered from far-flung corners of the world. The Fundación Neruda, acting on the wishes of the poet's widow, Matilde Urrutia, has transferred Neruda's and Matilde's graves to its garden and operates the house as a **museum** (Tues–Sun 10am–6pm; Spanish-speaking guide CH\$3000, English-speaking guide CH\$3500; reservations must be made in advance; ☎35/461284, ⓦwww .fundacionneruda.org). Inside, the winding passages and odd-shaped rooms are crammed full of fascinating exotic objects like ships' figureheads, Hindu carvings, African and Japanese masks, ships in bottles, seashells, butterflies, coloured bottles, Victorian postcards and a good deal more.

There's little else to Isla Negra save a small, pretty beach that makes for a great picnic spot. If you want to stay you'll find lovely **rooms** at the historic *Hostería La*

intensely committed to active politics. As consul for emigration, he threw himself into the task of providing Spanish refugees with a safe passage to Chile, and at the same time sought to give his poetry a meaningful "place in man's struggle", with *España en el Corazón*. On returning to Chile he became a member of the Communist Party, and was **elected senator** for the Antofagasta and Tarapacá regions, a role he took very seriously, tirelessly touring the desert pampas to talk to the workers. His politics were to land him in serious trouble, however, when newly elected president González Videla, who had enlisted Neruda's help in managing his presidential campaign, switched sides from left to right, and outlawed Communism. When Neruda publicly attacked González Videla, the president issued a warrant for his arrest, and he was forced into hiding. In 1949 the poet was smuggled across a southern pass in the Andes on horseback, and spent the next three years in exile, mainly in Europe.

It was during his years of **exile** that Neruda met the woman who was to inspire some of his most beautiful love poetry: Matilde Urrutia, whom he was later to marry. Neruda had been married twice before: first, briefly, to a Dutch woman he'd met as a young consul in Rangoon; and then for eighteen years to the Argentinian painter, Delia del Carril. The poet's writings scarcely mention his first wife, nor their daughter – his only child – who died when she was just eight years old, but Delia is described as "sweetest of consorts, thread of steel and honey...my perfect mate for eighteen years". It was so as not to wound Delia that *Los Versos del Capitán* – a book of passionate love poems written for Matilde on their secret hideaway in Capri – was published anonymously. Nonetheless, when the order for his arrest was revoked three years after his return to Santiago, Neruda divorced Delia and moved into **La Chascona**, in Santiago, and then to **Isla Negra** with Matilde. Based in Chile from then on, Neruda devoted himself to politics and poetry almost in equal measure. His dedication to both causes found its reward at the same time: in 1970, Salvador Allende, whose presidential campaign Neruda had tirelessly participated in, was elected president at the head of the socialist Unidad Popular. Then, the following year, Neruda was awarded the Nobel Prize for Literature, the second Chilean to attain the honour after Gabriela Mistral (see box, p.182). His happiness was to be short-lived, however. Diagnosed with cancer, and already bedridden, the poet was unable to withstand the shock brought on by the 1973 military coup, which left his dear friend Allende dead. Less than two weeks later, on September 23, Neruda died in Santiago with Matilde at his side.

Candela, C de La Hostería 67 (☎35/461254, ⓦwww.candela.cl; ❺); here you can soak in the ambience of a cosy hotel where Neruda himself once stayed.

Casablanca Valley Wine Route

The Casablanca Valley, famed for its excellent white wines, is accessed via Ruta 68, which connects Valparaíso and Viña with Santiago. **Ruta del Vino Valle de Casablanca** (☎32/274 3933, ⓦwww.casablancavalley.cl), Portales 90, in Casablanca, organizes half- and full-day tours (from US$80–US$110) of the wineries. You can also visit the vineyards independently (a list of all those participating in the Ruta del Vino is available on the latter's website); having your own car makes things a lot easier, but it is possible to visit some using the frequent Valparaíso/Viña–Santiago buses.

Rocas de Santo Domingo

Marking the end of the coast road and the southern extreme of the Litoral Central, **ROCAS DE SANTO DOMINGO** was designed and built from scratch in the 1940s following a nationwide architectural competition. The beach is superb, stretching 20km south of the town, backed by nothing but sand dunes; even in the height of summer you don't have to walk far to escape the crowds. It's also a very popular spot for **windsurfing**. There is just one **hotel** in Santo Domingo, the expensive *Hotel Rocas de Santo Domingo*, La Ronda 130 (☎35/444356, ⓦwww.hotelrocas.cl; ❺–❼); note the cheaper rooms lack views. The sand dunes further south are a perfect place for unofficial **camping**.

Viña del Mar and around

A 15-minute bus ride north of Valparaíso is all it takes to exchange the colourful and chaotic alleys of Valpo for the tree-lined avenues and ostentatious apartment high-rises of **VIÑA DEL MAR**. This is Chile's largest and best-known beach resort, drawing tens of thousands of mostly Chilean vacationers each summer. In many ways, it's indistinguishable from beach resorts elsewhere in the world, with oceanfront condominiums, bars, restaurants and casino. But lurking in the older corners of town are extravagant palaces, elegant villas and sumptuous gardens. Many date from the late nineteenth century when Viña del Mar – then a large hacienda – was subdivided into plots that were sold or rented to the wealthy families of Valparaíso and Santiago who came to spend their summers by the sea. The city also has a pair of **beautiful botanical gardens** with species from around the world and a museum with an important collection of Easter Island art.

In the past five years, Viña has been eclipsed by the host of new restaurants in Santiago and Valpo, and the beaches of La Serena (see p.172) but it's a comfortable, modern beachside city that offers a relaxing escape from the capital.

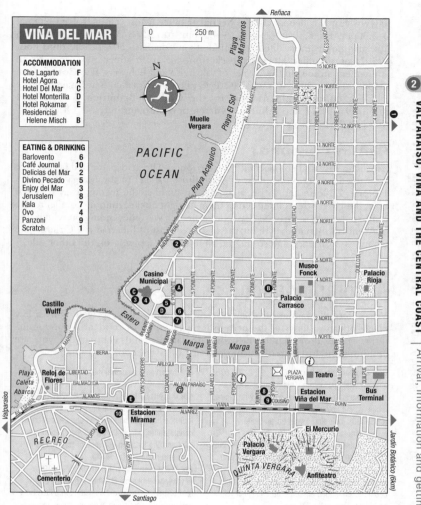

VIÑA DEL MAR

0   250 m

ACCOMMODATION

Che Lagarto	F
Hotel Agora	A
Hotel Del Mar	C
Hotel Monterilla	D
Hotel Rokamar	E
Residencial Helene Misch	B

EATING & DRINKING

Barlovento	6
Café Journal	10
Delicias del Mar	2
Divino Pecado	5
Enjoy del Mar	3
Jerusalem	8
Kala	7
Ovo	4
Panzoni	9
Scratch	1

PACIFIC OCEAN

Arrival, information and getting around

Intercity buses from Santiago (every 15min from Terminal Alameda) and elsewhere arrive at the **bus terminal** at the eastern end of Avenida Valparaíso in the southern part of town. **From Valparaíso** you can travel by boat, train or *micro*: **boats** drop you off at Muelle Vergara; trains stop at the centrally located Miramar and Viña del Mar stations; and **micros** come down Calle Viana and turn into Plaza Vergara.

Information

The **Oficina de Turismo** is just off the northeast corner of Plaza Vergara, next door to *Hotel O'Higgins* (summer: Mon–Fri 9am–9pm, Sat–Sun 10am–9pm; winter: Mon–Fri 10am–2pm & 3–7pm, Sat–Sun 10am–7pm; ☏800/800830,

@ www.visitevinadelmar.cl). The **Sernatur** office (Mon–Thurs 8.30am–2pm & 3–5.30pm, Fri 8.30am–2pm & 3–4.30pm; ☎32/268 3355, @infovalparaiso @sernatur.cl) is more difficult to find: it's at Valparaíso 507, on the third floor (#302) of an office block set back from the main street, next door to an amusement arcade, on the corner of Valparaíso and Echevers. The **Conaf** office (Mon–Fri 9am–2pm; ☎32/232 0210, @valparai@conaf.cl) is at Pasaje 3 Norte 541. For **cultural information**, try the **Chileno–Británico**, 3 Norte 824 (☎32/297 1061), and **Chileno–Norteamericano** institutes, 2 Oriente 385 (☎32/268 6191).

Getting around

Viña is an easy and compact city to get around. The grid-patterned streets here are named simply North, East or West: those parallel to the Marga Marga are 1 Norte, 2 Norte and so on, ascending in number the further away they are from the river. Streets intersecting them at right angles, running parallel to the coast are known as Oriente (East) or Poniente (West) depending on which side of Avenida Libertad they're on; the first street east of Libertad is 1 Oriente, the second is 2 Oriente, and so on, the same system applying on the other side.

Accommodation

Viña offers all manner of places to stay, but most are overpriced. Only a few places offer sea views, as the oceanfront is taken up by residential condominiums. Prices drop significantly outside January and February. If you are coming in high season or during national holidays, book well in advance.

Che Lagarto Diego Portales 131 ☎32/262 5759, @www.chelagarto.com. This reliable, sociable hostel has simple en-suites, doubles with shared facilities and colourful six- to ten-bed dorms (CH$8930), including a women-only one, overlooking a tree-filled garden. ❸–❹

Hotel Agora 5 1/2 Poniente 253 ☎32/269 4669, @www.hotelagora.cl. Fabulous Art Deco-style hotel, on a quiet side street, that wouldn't look out of place in Miami; it has impeccable pastel-shaded en-suites and a stylish yellow and black-tiled lobby. ❻

Hotel Del Mar San Martin 199 ☎32/250 0700, @www.enjoy.cl. Viña's flagship 5-star hotel, a cylindrical building right on the seafront, has a grand Romanesque feel. The exquisite en-suites (from US$250) have balconies, and there's a casino and several restaurants, including the outstanding *Savinya*,

which serves a seasonal menu with international influences. ❾

Hotel Monterilla 2 Norte 65 ☎32/297 6950, @www.monterilla.cl. The en-suites at this intimate boutique hotel have been decorated with considerable flair, while the service is personalised and the location convenient for the city's bars and restaurants. ❼–❽

Hotel Rokamar Viana 107 ☎32/269 0019, @www.hotelrokamar.cl. While the rooms at this refurbished 100-year-old mansion are a little boxy and drab, they are clean, a decent value and have private facilities and cable TV. ❹–❺

Residencial Helene Misch 1 Poniente 239 ☎32/297 1565. The same family has run this *residencial*, situated on a peaceful street, for over 50 years. Rooms are homely and have private baths, but the real highlight is the lovely flower- and bird-filled garden, where you eat breakfast. ❹

The City

Viña del Mar falls into two separate sections, divided by the **Estero Marga Marga**, a dirty lagoon (reclaimed for parking) that cuts through the town to the ocean. South of the Marga Marga is the old part of town, Viña's lively commercial centre with **Plaza Vergara** (also known as **Plaza de Viña**) and **Avenida Valparaíso** at its core. North of the river are the main **beaches** –Viña boasts 3.5km of sandy coast – and most of the tourist **restaurants** and **bars**.

The beaches get very crowded in January and February, but you'll find a number of appealing distractions: the **Quinta Vergara**, an extravagant subtropical park, and the **Jardín Botánico** more than justify the town's sobriquet of Ciudad Jardín ("Garden City"). Handsome old residences include the **Palacio Rioja** and the **Palacio Vergara** (in the Quinta Vergara) which now houses the **Museo de Bellas Artes**. Another worthwhile museum is the **Museo Fonck**, which has a top-notch indigenous and Easter Island collection.

Plaza Vergara and Avenida Valparaíso

Viña's centre is marked by the large, green **Plaza Vergara**, full of tall, stately trees and surrounded by some fine, early twentieth-century buildings including the Neoclassical **Teatro Municipal**, the stately **Hotel O'Higgins**, and the Italian Renaissance-style **Club de Viña**, an exclusive gentlemen's dining club. Ponies and traps hang around the square, on which you can take tours of the town (around CH$8000 for 30min). The south side of the square borders **Avenida Valparaíso**, Viña's main commercial street. Much of the shopping activity occurs in the five blocks between the plaza and Calle Ecuador. There's also a good **feria artesanal** in Pasaje Cousiño, a narrow passage off the south side of the avenue, just west of Plaza Vergara.

Quinta Vergara and the Museo de Bellas Artes

The exceptionally beautiful park **Quinta Vergara** (daily: winter 7am–6pm; summer until 7pm), filled with exotic, subtropical trees and surrounded by wooded hills, sits two blocks south of Plaza Vergara, across the railway tracks. The amphitheatre hosts regular concerts, including the hugely hyped, kitsch **Festival Internacional de la Canción** (International Music Festival) every February. During this time, the traffic and the crowds are out of hand, and booking accommodation ahead is essential.

In the centre of the Quinta Vergara, near the huge and unattractive offices of the *Mercurio* newspaper, sits **Palacio Vergara**, a dazzling, whitewashed Venetian-style palace built in 1906. The palace is now home to the **Museo de Bellas Artes** (Tues–Sun 10am–1.30pm & 3–5.30pm; CH$600), which has a decent collection of Chilean and European paintings, including works by **Rubens**, **Poussin** and **Tintoretto**.

Palacio Rioja and Palacio Carrasco

North of the Marga Marga at Quillota 214 you'll find the **Palacio Rioja**, built in the style of an eighteenth-century French chateau and surrounded by a sumptuous park, all that remains of the once extensive vineyards that gave the town its name. It was built in 1906 for Don Fernando Rioja Medel, a Spanish millionaire who owned the Banco Español among other enterprises. His family lived here until 1956, when the building was acquired by the Municipalidad which now runs it as a reception centre and a **museum** (Tues–Sun 10am–1.30m & 3–5.30pm; CH$600). The entire ground floor is perfectly preserved and provides a fascinating close-up view of early twentieth-century luxury, with its belle-epoque furniture and glittering ballroom. In the summer, the Conservatorio de Música in the basement gives concerts in the palace.

Nearby, at Libertad 250, is the **Palacio Carrasco** (Mon–Fri 9.30am–1pm & 2–6.30pm, Sat 10am–1pm), an elegant, three-storey building designed in a French Neoclassical style

Museo Francisco Fonck

The excellent **Museo Francisco Fonck**, at 4 Norte 784 (Mon–Sat 10am–7pm, Sun 10am–2pm; CH\$1500), has one of Chile's most important **Easter Island collections**, plus some fascinating pre-Hispanic exhibits. It is named after Prussian medic Franz Fonck (1830–1912), who studied botanical and archeological sites in central Chile and left his collections to the state. One of the museum's best pieces stands in the garden, by the entrance: a giant stone *moai*, one of just six that exist outside Easter Island. Inside, the three ground-floor rooms dedicated to Easter Island include wooden and stone carvings of those long, stylized faces (some around five hundred years old), as well as jewellery, weapons, household and fishing utensils, and ceremonial objects.

The beaches and around

Viña's most central beach, and the only one south of the Marga Marga, is **Playa Caleta Abarca**, a sheltered, sandy bay at the eastern end of Calle Viana. Just off the beach, at the foot of Cerro Castillo, you'll find the much-photographed **Reloj de Flores**, a large clock composed of colourful bedding plants and working dials. From here, the promenade continues north past the neo-Gothic **Castillo Wulff**. Built in 1906 for a nitrate and coal baron, the house features a glass-floored passage with waves breaking below. Formerly a museum, it is now closed to the public, though you can always ask for an informal look around.

Just beyond is the **Estero Marga Marga** – follow it inland a couple of blocks to reach the bridge that crosses it. On the other side is the **Casino Municipal**, sitting in the middle of finely landscaped gardens, skirted by the coast road, **Avenida Perú**. A pedestrian promenade runs alongside the ocean but there's no sand here, just a stretch of rocks. A few blocks north, Avenida Perú swerves inland to make way for the long unbroken strip of sand stretching for over 3km towards Reñaca (see p.155). Though effectively one single beach, the different sections are each given their own name: just north of Avenida Perú is **Playa Acapulco**, a 200-metre-long beach that is very popular with locals but a bit hemmed in by high-rises, followed by **Playa El Sol** and **Playa Los Marineros**, where the sea is often too rough for much swimming. Finally there is **Playa Larga**, which has restaurants, showers and parking – it's very crowded in the summer. To get to the beaches, take any of the Reñaca or Concón buses from Puente Libertad (the bridge over the lagoon just north of Plaza Vergara), and get off at 10 or 12 Norte for Playas Acapulco and El Sol or ask the driver to let you off on the coast road for the beaches further north.

Eating, drinking and entertainment

Viña's **restaurants** are among the most varied outside the capital, and while many are geared towards tourists, the quality is usually good, and they offer some welcome alternatives to the *comida típica* you're restricted to in many other towns. Most, however, are fairly expensive. All open daily, unless stated otherwise.

Nightlife tends to be seasonal, reaching a heady peak in January and February when everyone flocks to the clubs and bars of **Reñaca**, a suburb further up the

Adventure sports

If you're looking to experience an adrenaline rush in the great outdoors, you've come to the right place. Chile boasts vast tracts of unspoilt wilderness – much of it preserved within thirty-one national parks – so it's no surprise that *turismo de aventura* has long been a lure for visitors. The country's highly varied landscape, from soaring peaks to flat altiplano, lends itself to a wide range of adventure activities: scale mighty volcanoes, shoot down frothy rapids, ski glistening peaks, all without crowds trailing you.

Skiing in the Andes ▲

Paragliding ▼

Snow sports

Chile features some of the best **skiing** in the southern hemisphere and has the scenery to match. Whether you're carving through fragrant alpine forest or traversing the remote back-country, you can enjoy some of the most impressive vistas in South America.

Conveniently, the finest resorts lie just 40km from Santiago: you can easily ski neighbouring **El Colorado**, **La Parva** and **Valle Nevado** on a day-trip from the capital, while classy **Portillo**, 149km north, lies within comfortable striking distance for a weekend visit. Top ski teams frequently train on Portillo's slopes, where many speed records have been broken. Nowhere else in Chile can match these spots, but the **Termas de Chillán** ski centre, 480km south, isn't too far behind, offering the longest run in South America and steaming thermal pools for après-ski relaxation.

For a fun and much cheaper alternative to the main resorts, head to the fledgling, rustic ski centres dotted along the Andes south of Santiago. These include

Biplane over the Andes ▼

The Andes from the sky

For dizzying, birds-eye vistas of the Andean peaks, climb aboard a **hot-air balloon** or take flight in a **biplane** or **glider**, offered by various tour companies in and around Santiago. You can usually sail the skies throughout the year, due to Chile's relatively stable weather. **Paragliding** also offers the chance to soar above a rolling countryside flanked by magnificent mountains, particularly around Iquique in the north.

Chapa Verde, near Rancagua; Antuco, near Concepción; and El Fraile, near Coyhaique. The Centro de Ski Pucón, on the slopes of Volcán Villarrica, is ideal for families and less experienced skiers, while the exciting slopes of Volcán Osorno, by Lago Llanquihue and Cerro Mirador, near Punta Arenas, draw avid thrill-seekers.

Volcano vertigo

Volcanoes are as defining a feature of Chile's geography as the altiplano plateau in the north or broken coastline in the south. The Andean cordillera, running the entire length of Chile, is loaded with possible slopes to scale, from relatively easy day climbs for novices to challenging peaks for experts. In the Far North rise a series of huge, isolated behemoths over 6000m high that experienced climbers can tackle, including Volcán Parinacota, Volcán Llullaillaco and Volcán Ojos del Salado, Chile's highest peak and the tallest active volcano in the world.

You'll also find several challenging, technical climbs in the central Andes, from Volcán Marmolejo to Volcán Tupungato. In the south lie the relatively diminutive volcanoes of Osorno and Villarrica – ideal for climbers with little or no experience. Further south, the most popular ascents are the giant, vertiginous granite towers – Torre Central (2600m) and Cerro Paine Grande (3248m) – at the heart of Torres del Paine National Park.

River rush

Many world-class rivers cascade down the Andes, providing unforgettable white-water rafting. The once great Bío Bío, on the southern edge of the Central Valley, has been controversially

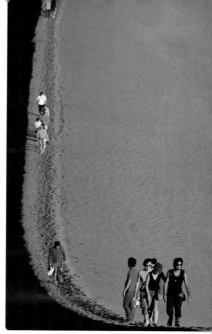

▲ Hiking in El Norte Grande
▼ Trekking in Torres del Paine

tamed by a hydroelectric dam, so now the **Río Futaleufú** – venue of the Rafting World Championships in 2000 – by the Carretera Austral, and the nearby Río Baker, have risen to prominence as Chile's most challenging rivers.

In the Lake District, rivers tumbling from the mountains also make for hair-raising thrills, including the roiling **Río Trancura** and **Río Petrohue**. Closer to Santiago snakes the popular **Río Maipo**, which has exciting waters still accessible for beginners. You can also **kayak** the country's waterways and lakes, although this sector of the industry is less well developed. Perhaps the greatest potential for visitors lies in the burgeoning sport of **sea kayaking**, most often in the calm, protected waters of the southern fjords, or in the Gulf of Ancud near Hornopirén and the northern sector of Parque Pumalín.

Kayaking the Futaleufú River ▲

Hiking the Sendero de Chile ▼

Sendero de Chile

To mark the 2010 **bicentenary** of the founding of the Chilean republic, President Lagos decided to create a monumental icon that united the entire country, and in 2001, the hugely ambitious **Sendero de Chile** (Path of Chile) was born. The idea seems somewhat far-fetched at a glance: to thread a footpath the entire 4320km-length of the country, from the Peruvian border to Cape Horn. To trek the whole of it would be the equivalent of walking from the Scottish borders to Timbuktu. The first section opened in the Conguillío National Park, and since then, stretches have been created throughout the country, but completion isn't projected until at least 2012. For further information, check out the helpful Ⓦwww.senderodechile.cl.

▲ Playa Caleta Abarca

coast (see p.155). During the summer months, *micros* run to and from Reñaca right through the night. In winter, the partying dies out, and the focus shifts back to Viña.

The grand **Teatro Municipal** (☎32/268 1739) puts on theatre, classical music and dance performances, and there's an excellent arts **cinema**, the Cine Arte on the Plaza Vergara (through the passage off the west side of the square).

Restaurants

Delicias del Mar San Martín 459. Smart Basque-influenced *marisquería* with a loyal clientele, relaxed atmosphere and great wine to accompany the crab lasagne, paella or Corvina DiCaprio, the latter dish created to honour the visit of the eponymous Hollywood star. Mains CH$6700–8500.

Divino Pecado San Martín 180 ☎ 32/297 5790. High-class Italian offering mouthwatering dishes like tuna carpaccio, scallops au gratin and chocolate truffle tart; the fish is a particular highlight here. Reservations are necessary at the weekend. Mains CH$6000–8500.

Enjoy del Mar Peru 100. Owned by *Hotel del Mar* and occupying a prime location, *Enjoy del Mar's* outdoor terrace is a wonderful spot for a sandwich, burger (CH$3500–5000), coffee or beer, while crashing waves provide a calming soundtrack.

Jerusalem Quinta 259. Unpretentious Middle Eastern eatery with inexpensive falafels and spiced meatballs (CH$1500–2500) – a welcome alternative to the greasy *fuente de soda* nearby.

Kala Corner 2 Norte and 6 Poniente. Glass-fronted Peruvian restaurant, with cosy leather booths upstairs for evening drinks. Ceviche, *lomo saltado* and a Peruvian take on surf and turf feature on the menu. Mains CH$5000–7500.

Panzoni Paseo Cousino 12B. Delightful Italian joint with a handful of tables, great service and inexpensive pastas (CH$3000–3600) and salads.

Moving on from Viña

Buses **up the coast** (Central Placeres or Sol del Pacífico) don't stop at the bus terminal, but at Libertad (just north of Puente Libertad), with frequent services to Reñaca and Concón, and several daily to Horcón, Maitencillo, Zapallar and Papudo. *Colectivos* also pass this way en route to Reñaca and Concón. To go **down the coast**, your best bet is to catch a bus from **Valparaíso** (see p.133), reached by any *micro* (every 10min) marked "Puerto" or "Aduana" from Plaza Vergara or Arlegui. You can also get to Valparaíso by train (every 15–30min), or by boat from Muelle Vergara. **Intercity buses** leave from the bus terminal on Avenida Valparaíso, two blocks east of Plaza Vergara (**to Santiago** every 15min), along with daily buses **to Mendoza** in Argentina. For more information see "Travel details" on p.158.

You may have to queue at lunchtime, but it's worth the wait. Closed Sun.

Bars and clubs

Barlovento 2 Norte 145. Behind the forbidding concrete exterior is a trendy, upmarket drinking venue; the second-floor lounge with huge windows is the place to head to.

Café Journal Agua Santa and Alvarez. Proximity to Viña's university ensures a healthy crowd of drinkers, who come for the cheap pitchers of beer and to dance the night away.

Ovo Casino Municipal. *The* place to be seen sipping a pisco sour and showing off your fashionable attire; without a doubt, Viña's swishest nightclub.

Scratch Quillota 898. This long-time favourite for dancing, in a new location, draws a university and older crowd; it's packed until sunrise most weekends.

Listings

Airlines LAN, Valparaíso 276 (℡600/526 2000).
Banks and exchange Most banks and *cambios* are on Arlegui and Libertad: of the *cambios*, try Guinaza Cambios, Arlegui 686. For banks, try Banco de Chile, Libertad 1348 and Arlegui 307, and Banco Edwards, Libertad 770.
Bookshops Librería Inglesa, in Galería Paseo del Mar, Valparaíso 554, has English-language fiction.

Car rental Hertz, Quillota 766 (℡32/238 1025); Rosselot, Alvares 762 (℡32/238 2888).
Internet Café Internet, Valparaíso 286 (CH$500 per hr).
Post office Next to the Oficina de Turismo, between Plaza Vergara and Puente Libertad.
Tours Aguitur, Galeriá Fontana, Arlegui 364 Office 223 (℡32/271 1052) is the mainstay Viña tour association.

Jardín Botánico Nacional

Set in a sheltered valley surrounded by sun-baked hills, the Conaf-run **Jardín Botánico Nacional** (Tues–Sun 10am–6.30pm; CH$900) contains three thousand plant species from Chile and other Latin American countries, as well as Europe and Asia. It's just 6km from the centre of Viña but feels far more remote. It's also possible to go **zip-lining** (℡9/255 5117, ⓦwww .canopysuramerica.cl; CH$3000–10,000). The *jardín* is a ten-minute bus ride (#20, eastbound) from Calle Bohn.

North of Viña

North of Viña, the coast road meanders to the small fishing village of **Papudo**, about 75km away, and beyond to the farming town of **La Ligua** from where you can reach the family resort of **Los Vilos**. Hugging the oceanside in some stretches, darting inland in others, the northern coast road is far quieter than its southern counterpart, and very beautiful in parts. **Cachagua** and **Zapallar** are the most exclusive resorts along this coast. Countless local buses head to **Reñaca** and neighbouring **Concón**, but services to the other resorts further north are less frequent; most can also be reached directly from Santiago (see "Travel details" on p.127). Unless you have your own vehicle, the best option is to pick one or two places and head for these, rather than resort-hopping on public transport.

Reñaca

Lively, developed **REÑACA**, 6km north of central Viña, is a 1.5km stretch of coast swamped by bars, restaurants and apartment blocks. The beaches here are amongst the cleanest in the country, and the resort is particularly popular with Chile and Argentina's beautiful young things. **Accommodation** is expensive, with the exception of a pleasant campsite on Santa Luisa 401 (☎32/283 2830; $15,000 per site); it's quite a steep walk from the beach but you can take the Concón bus up and down the hill. Otherwise, you're better off staying in Valparaíso or Viña and travelling here by *micro*. Reñaca's **clubs** are also pricey (cover charges around CH$10,000) but remain resolutely popular throughout the summer season. Every summer a host of new clubs appears, and others disappear, so ask around for the latest.

Concón

CONCÓN, 10km north of Reñaca, is a strange sort of place: part concrete terraced apartment blocks, part elegant villas with flower-filled gardens, and part rundown, working-class fishing village, with six beaches spread out along the bay. When the wind is blowing south, nasty fumes drift over from the nearby oil refinery.

The most interesting bit of town is **La Boca**, the ramshackle commercial centre at the mouth of the Río Aconcagua. The *caleta* here was used to export the produce of the haciendas of the Aconcagua valley in the nineteenth century and is now a bustling fish quay, lined with modest **marisquerías**.

The most popular beaches are the rapidly developing **Playa Amarilla** and **Playa Negra**, south of La Boca, both good for bodyboarding. Concón is an easy day-trip from Viña, but if you want **to stay**, try *Mantagua* (☎32/215 5900, Ⓦwww.mantagua.cl; ❺–❻), which has expensive but well-furnished en-suites, cabins and a well-maintained **campsite** (CH$17,000 per site).

Horcón

The charming and picturesque – if slightly tatty – fishing village of **HORCÓN**, about 30km north of Concón, is a chaotic tumble of houses straggling down the hill to a rocky bay. (En route, you'll pass Quintero, a scruffy, forbidding town with filthy beaches, to be avoided at all costs.) In the summer, Horcón is taken over by artisans on the beach selling jewellery made from seashells and unfeasible numbers of young Chileans who come to chill out for the weekend; this is the hippy alternative to Reñaca. Keep an eye out for the few remaining fisherman who use horses to bring in the day's catch.

The **beach** in front of the village is crowded and uninviting, but a short walk up the main street and then along Avenida Cau-Cau takes you down a steep, rickety staircase to the remote **Playa Cau-Cau**, a pleasantly sheltered beach surrounded by wooded hills. The respected *Caballo de Mar* **restaurant** has been carefully built into the cliffs but a hideous condominium now completely mars the beauty of the area. An hour's walk along the beach north towards Maitencillo takes you to Playa Luna, a nudist beach. In town, try the excellent, good-value *marisquerías* clustered around the fishermen's stalls. You'll find comfortable, fairly tasteful **rooms** at *Hostería Arancibia*, down by the waterfront (☎32/279 6169; ❹).

Maitencillo

Stretching 4km along one main street, **MAITENCILLO** is little more than a long, narrow strip of holiday homes, *cabañas* and hotels along the shoreline. The chief reason for coming here is **Playa Aguas Blancas**, a superb white-sand beach sweeping 5km south of the village, backed by steep sandstone cliffs.

One of the best **accommodation** options at Playa Aguas Blancas is *Cabañas Donde Julián*, Del Mar 78 (T 32/277 1091; ❺) which offers a handful of spacious cabins looking right out to sea; bargain hard outside high season for a discount. *Cabañas Hermansen*, Del Mar 0592 (T 32/277 1028, W www.hermansen.cl; ❻), sits a 5-minute drive north of Aguas Blancas and has great views of the beach, rustic cabins with cute wooden picnic tables, bike rental and switched-on staff. The attached *La Canasta* is the only decent **bar** in the area, attracting surfers from surrounding towns and building up a rowdy crowd during the summer. You'll find excellent, imaginatively prepared **seafood** at ⍟ *El Tubo* (aka *La Pajarera*), a wacky building with great vistas housing a restaurant, pub and ice-cream parlour; it's towards the southern end of Avenida del Mar (and linked by funicular to *Marbella Resort*, an exclusive Club Med-type complex on top of the cliff. Close by is the excellent maritime knick-knack-strewn ⍟ *La Tasca de Altamar*, where the service is extremely welcoming and the fish fabulous – but make sure you save room for the tempting desserts.

Cachagua

CACHAGUA, a short way north of Maitencillo, has a stunning beach, with a wide expanse of pale sand curling round the bay, backed by gentle hills, and is synonymous with Chile's upper crust. It is blessed by a relative lack of holiday homes on the land off the beach, which instead is home to a golf course. Ask for directions to the long staircase from Avenida del Mar down to **Playa Las Cujas**, a tiny, spectacular and often empty beach. Just off the coast, the Isla de los Pingüinos is a **penguin sanctuary** to which local fishermen sometimes offer boat rides for around CH$6000 per person – accept at your peril, for the smell of hundreds of Humboldt penguins can be nauseating.

What little **accommodation** Cachagua offers is up in the village, back from the beach: simple, adequate rooms are rented by Sra Albertina Sepúlveda, at Cachagua 658 (T 33/771044; ❹), and Sra Juana Ormeño, at Nemesio Vicuña 250 (T 33/771034; ❹).

Zapallar

The classiest and most attractive of all the Litoral's resorts, **ZAPALLAR** is a sheltered, horseshoe bay backed by lushly wooded hills where luxurious holiday homes and handsome old mansions nestle between the pine trees. Apart from the beach, you can also stroll along the coastal path around the bay, or walk up Avenida Zapallar, admiring the early-twentieth-century mansions. More strenuous possibilities include hiring a sea-kayak or climbing the 692m-high **Cerro Higuera**.

If you feel like splashing out, the swanky *Hotel Isla Seca* ⍟ (T 33/741224, W www.hotelislaseca.cl; ❼) up by the main road, at the northern end of the bay, offers classically styled **rooms** with balconies, excellent restaurant and magnificent views. *Residencial Villa Alicia*, Moisés Chacón 280 (T 33/741176; ❹) is a good deal simpler but comfortable enough. For **dining** 🍴 *El Chiringuito* (☎33/741024), down by the *caleta* at the southern tip of the bay, serves up legendary seafood – the scallops are absolutely divine. It closes a few days of the week in the off-season.

Papudo

The development in **PAPUDO**, just 10km around the headland, hasn't been as graceful as in Zapallar, and several ugly buildings mar the seafront. However, the steep hills looming dramatically behind the town are undeniably beautiful, and the place has a friendly, local atmosphere. The best beach is the long **Playa Grande**.

Papudo has a wealth of **accommodation** centred mainly around the town square and on Fernández Concha, branching off from it. *Faro Hostal* (☎33/791139; ❹), Fernández Concha 525, has plain rooms with private bath off a sunny passageway, while *Hotel Curande* (☎33/791105, 🌐www.hotelcurande.cl; ❺), Chorrillos 89, offers more comfortable, cosy en-suites. Papudo also has the most offbeat **restaurant** along the entire coast, *El Barco Rojo* (☎33/791488) on Playa Grande, owned by a hip young Parisian who arranges funky jazz and Latin concerts in his restaurant by night. The famous seafood menu is inexpensive and fantastic, and there's an excellent wine list.

La Ligua

The chief appeal of **LA LIGUA**, a bustling agricultural town, is its setting, enfolded by undulating hills that take on a rich honey glow in the early evening sunlight. It is also known for its confectionery: *dulces de La Ligua* – sweet, sugary cakes famous throughout Chile.

In town, the Museo La Ligua at Pedro Polanco 698 (Mon–Fri 9.30am–1pm & 3–8pm, Sat 10am–2pm; CH\$500) features displays like the skeleton and reconstructed burial site of a thirty-year-old Diaguita woman. La Ligua also has a reputation for knitwear; an artisans' market is on the main square.

The infamous La Quintrala of La Ligua

La Ligua was once notorious as the home of one of Chile's darkest figures: Doña Catalina de Los Ríos y Lisperguer, or **La Quintrala**. She was born in 1600, later inheriting the large Hacienda de La Ligua, into a family known for its violent women: Catalina's grandmother had murdered her husband, and her mother whipped one of her stepdaughters to death and attempted to poison the governor of Chile. At 23, Catalina murdered her father by serving him a poisoned chicken. The following year she killed a Knight of the Order of St John (after seducing him). Her bloody tendencies seemed to vanish during her twenty-four-year-marriage to Captain Alonso Campofrío Carvajal – only to return with added fervour when she became a widow at the age of fifty. It was at this point that she embarked on her most brutal period, regularly whipping and torturing her slaves, often to the point of death. In 1660, the Bishop of Santiago appealed to the Real Audiencia (Royal Court) to investigate her behaviour. The inquiry concluded she had murdered 39 people, excluding the murders committed before her marriage. La Quintrala evaded justice to the end however, dying before charges could be brought against her. Today, in La Ligua, her name still strikes fear in the hearts of children.

Pichidangui

North of the Papudo-La Ligua crossroads, the Panamericana follows the coast for some 200km before dipping inland again, towards Ovalle (see p.163). This stretch of highway takes you past a succession of gorgeous, white-sand **beaches** dotted with a few fishing villages and small resorts.

Set 4km back from the Panamericana, 50km beyond the Papudo-La Ligua interchange, is **PICHIDANGUI**, with a lovely beach, up there with Chile's finest: 7km of white, powdery sand fringed by eucalyptus trees, with little beachfront development to spoil the view. *La Rosa Náutica*, at El Dorado 120 (☎53/531133, ⓦwww.rosanautica.cl; ❺–❻), has standard hotel **rooms**, wood cabins and a good **restaurant**. In the eucalyptus woods backing onto the beach are some rustic but comfortable *cabañas* with apricot-coloured interiors at *Bahía Marina* (☎53/531120, ⓦwww.bahiamarina.cl; ❻), plus a **campsite** (CH$10,000 per site).

Buses head to Los Molles and Pichidangui from the capital's Terminal de Buses Santiago (Condor Bus; ☎2/779 3721) and from Valparaíso (Buses La Porteña, which leave from the company's office at Molina 366; ☎32/216568); journeys take around three hours.

Los Vilos

Local legend has it that **LOS VILOS**, 30km north of Pichidangui, takes its name from the Hispanic corruption of "Lord Willow", a British pirate who was shipwrecked on the coast and decided to stay. The town later became notorious for highway robberies. These days it is a great place to spend a couple of days by the sea without paying over the odds. However, it gets incredibly packed in January and February. The town's chief attraction is its long golden **beach**, but there's also a **fish market** on the *caleta* and **Isla de los Lobos**, a 1500-strong seal colony, reached by a five-kilometre jeep track just south of the bay.

The clean, antique-filled *Residencial Vienesa* at Los Vilos 11 (☎53/541143; ❷) is a good-value **place to stay**, while *Hostería Lord Willow*, overlooking the beach at Los Vilos 1444 (☎53/541037; ❹), offers rooms with private bath that are more pleasant but a little overpriced.

From the capital, **buses** to Los Vilos leave from Terminal de Buses Santiago (Condor Bus; ☎2/779 3721) or Terminal San Borja (Tacc-Via Choapa ☎2/778 7570 and Tur Bus ☎2/270 7500).

Travel details

Buses

Valparaíso to: Arica (15 daily; 26hr); Copiapó (6 daily, 11hr); Coquimbo (10 daily; 6hr); Isla Negra (every 15–30min; 1hr 30min); La Serena (16 daily, 6hr); Maitencillo (4 daily; 1hr 40min); Mendoza (Argentina; 1 daily; 8–9hr); Papudo (3–4 daily; 2hr); Puerto Montt (4 daily; 16hr); Quintay (2–5 daily; 45min–1hr); Santiago (every 15min; 1hr 30min–1hr 45min); Temuco (3 daily, 9hr 30min); Viña del Mar (every 15min; 15min); Zapallar (hourly; 1hr 40min).

Viña del Mar to: Arica (2–4 daily; 26hr); Concón (every 15min; 15min); Copiapó (10 daily, 11hr); Horcón (hourly; 1hr); La Serena (12 daily; 6hr); Maitencillo (hourly; 1hr 20min); Mendoza (Argentina; 1 daily; 8–9hr); Papudo (2–3 daily; 1hr 45min); Puerto Montt (4 daily; 16hr); Reñaca (every 15min; 25min); Santiago (every 15min; 1hr 30min–1hr 45min); Zapallar (hourly; 1hr 30min).

3

El Norte Chico

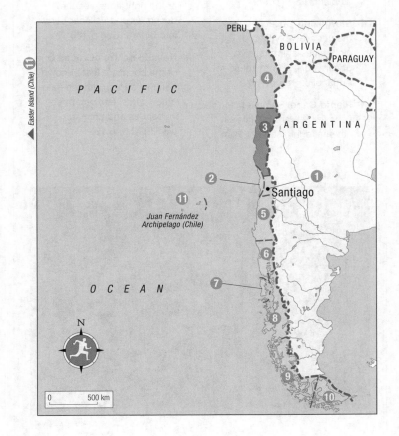

CHAPTER 3 # Highlights

* **Feria Modelo de Ovalle**
  Wander this food market
  and fill your bags with plump
  olives, giant pumpkins, ripe
  tomatoes and very smelly
  cheeses. See p.164

* **La Serena** Chile's second-
  oldest city offers long beaches,
  beautiful churches and a lively
  ambience. See p.172

* **Stargazing** Observe
  the unbelievably limpid
  night skies at impressive
  observatories, from Tololo to
  Andacollo. See p.176

* **Planta Capel** Sample the
  fiery, fruity brandy, Chile's
  national drink, straight from

the barrel at the Elqui Valley's
largest distillery. See p.179

* **Horseriding in the Elqui
  Valley** Pretend you're in the
  Wild West as you trek through
  Chile's untrammelled northern
  plains. See p.183

* **Desierto florido** If you're
  lucky to be in the right place
  at the right time, see the
  desert around Vallenar burst
  into bloom. See p.188

* **Nevado de Tres Cruces** One
  of the country's least-known
  national parks, with emerald-
  green lakes, snow-capped
  volcanoes and plentiful
  wildlife. See p.192

▲ Feria Modelo de Ovalle

El Norte Chico

A land of rolling, sun-baked hills streaked with sudden river valleys that cut across the earth in a flash of green, the **NORTE CHICO**, or "Little North", of Chile is what geographers call a "transitional zone". Its semi-arid scrubland and sparse vegetation mark the transformation from the country's fertile heartland to the barren deserts bordering Peru and Bolivia. From the Santiago perspective, the region is dubbed Norte Chico to distinguish it from the Norte Grande, or Great North (see next chapter). Starting somewhere around the Río Aconcagua, just north of Santiago, it stretches all the way to Taltal, and the southernmost reaches of the Atacama, more than 800km further north.

In between, a series of **rivers** – notably the Choapa, the Limarí, the Elqui, the Huasco and the Copiapó – flow year-round from the Andes to the coast, allowing the surrounding land to be irrigated and cultivated. The result is spectacular: lush, vibrant green terraces laden with olives, apricots and vines snake between the brown, parched walls of the valleys, forming a sensational visual contrast. The most famous product of these valleys is **pisco**, the pale, aromatic brandy distilled from sun-dried grapes and treasured by Chileans as their national drink (a claim vigorously contested by the Peruvians, who consider it their own).

Far more than agriculture, though, it's **mining** that has really shaped the region's growth, giving birth to towns, ports, railways and roads, and drawing large numbers of settlers to seek their fortune here. **Gold** was mined first by the Incas for ritual offerings, and then intensively, to exhaustion, by the Spaniards until the end of the eighteenth century. Next came the great **silver** bonanza of the nineteenth century, when a series of dramatic silver strikes – some of them accidental – set a frenzy of mining and prospecting in motion, propelling the region into its heyday. Further riches and glory came when the discovery of huge **copper** deposits turned the region into the world's largest copper producer from the 1840s to 1870s. Mining is still the most important regional industry, its presence most visible up in the cordillera, where huge mining trucks hurtle around the mountain roads, enveloped in clouds of dust.

The largest population centre – and one of the country's most fashionable seaside resorts – is **La Serena**, its pleasing, colonial-style architecture and lively atmosphere making it one of the few northern cities worth visiting for its own sake. It's also an ideal base for exploring the beautiful **Elqui Valley**, immortalized in the verses of the Nobel laureate Gabriela Mistral, and home to luxuriant vines and idyllic riverside hamlets. Less well-known but even more dramatic, the **Hurtado Valley**, to the south, features virgin trekking territory which can be reached from the unassuming market town of **Ovalle**. Just down the coast from

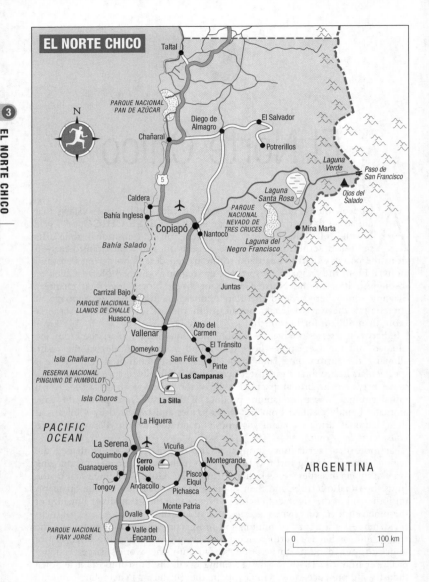

EL NORTE CHICO

Taltal

PARQUE NACIONAL
PAN DE AZÚCAR

N

Diego de
Almagro

El Salvador

Chañaral

Potrerillos

Laguna
Verde

Paso de
San Francisco

Caldera

Laguna
Santa Rosa

Ojos del
Salado

Bahía Inglesa

PARQUE
NACIONAL
NEVADO DE
TRES CRUCES

Copiapó

Nantoco

Mina Marta

Bahía Salado

Laguna del
Negro Francisco

Carrizal Bajo

Juntas

PARQUE NACIONAL
LLANOS DE CHALLE

Huasco

Alto del
Carmen

Vallenar

El Tránsito

Domeyko

San Félix

Isla Chañaral

Pinte

RESERVA NACIONAL
PINGUINO DE HUMBOLDT

Las Campanas

Isla Choros

La Silla

PACIFIC
OCEAN

La Higuera

ARGENTINA

La Serena

Vicuña

Coquimbo

Montegrande

Guanaqueros

Cerro
Tololo

Pisco
Elqui

Tongoy

Andacollo

Pichasca

Monte Patria

Ovalle

PARQUE NACIONAL
FRAY JORGE

Valle del
Encanto

0   100 km

La Serena lies the **Parque Nacional Fray Jorge**, with a microclimate that supports a small, damp cloudforest – rather mangy compared to the great forests of the south but quite extraordinary in this landscape of brittle shrubs and cactus plants. Another botanical wonder is the famous *desierto florido* or **flowering desert**. Occasionally, after heavy winter rains, the normally dry earth sprouts vast expanses of vibrantly coloured flowers. This rare, unpredictable phenomenon, centred on **Vallenar**, occurs on average once every four to eight years.

Skies that are guaranteed cloudless almost year-round and very little air pollution have made the region the obvious choice for some of the world's major **astronomical observatories**. They range from the state-of-the art facility at dazzling-white **Tololo** to the modest municipal installation at **Mamalluca**, near the picturesque village of **Vicuña**, where you don't have to be an expert reserving months in advance to look through the telescope. One of the newest and most accessible is at **Andacollo**.

The Norte Chico also boasts a string of superb **beaches**, some totally deserted and many of them tantalizingly visible from the Panamericana as you enter the region, to the north of Santiago. **Bahía Inglesa** is famous throughout Chile for its turquoise waters, though increasingly prolific algae is turning the bay greener.

Copiapó, the northernmost major city in the region, serves as a useful springboard for excursions into the nearby **desert** or, further afield, up into the high cordillera. Here the **Parque Nacional Nevado de Tres Cruces**, the **Volcán Ojos de Salado** and **Laguna Verde** present some of Chile's most magnificent yet least-visited landscapes: snow-topped volcanoes, bleached-white salt flats and azure lakes. A couple of hours to the north, near the towering cliffs and empty beaches of **Parque Nacional Pan de Azúcar**, a small island is home to colonies of seals, countless pelicans and thousands of penguins.

Bear in mind that, whereas the Norte Grande, Chile's northernmost region, can be visited all year-round, the Norte Chico is at its best in the **summer months** (Oct–March) when the valleys are at their greenest, the coast is likelier to be free of fog and the ocean and sky are pure blue. On the downside, resorts like La Serena and Bahía Inglesa can be horribly overcrowded and overpriced in the high season, especially January.

Ovalle and around

Almost 380km north of Santiago – some 140km beyond Los Vilos – a lone sign points to the little-visited **OVALLE**. The town's main claim to fame is as the birthplace of one of the country's outstanding contemporary writers, Luis Sepúlveda. It's also a good base for exploring the deeply rural **Limarí Valley**, home to a few low-key but worthwhile attractions. To the northeast, a scenic road – an alternative route to Vicuña and the Elqui Valley (see p.178) – winds slowly up into the mountains, passing ancient petrified wood stumps at **Pichasca** and the delightful oasis village of **Hurtado**, which is the main settlement along the dramatic but seldom visited **Hurtado Valley**. If you head west, you'll find a concentration of rock carvings in the **Valle del Encanto**, a hot springs resort at the **Termas de Socos** and the impressive cloudforest reserve of **Parque Nacional Fray Jorge**, attracting an increasing number of visitors.

The Town

The lively **Plaza de Armas**, with expansive lawns, nineteenth-century Phoenix palms and rows of jacaranda, marks Ovalle's centre. Dominating the east side of the square is the white-and-mustard 1849 **Iglesia San Vicente Ferrer**, a large, colonial-style church, with thick adobe walls and a diminutive tower. The streets around the square are narrow, traffic-choked and flanked by typical single-storey adobe houses. One of these streets, Libertad, has a couple of good traditional **leather shops** (opposite *Hotel Roxy*), where you'll find finely crafted belts, wallets, bags and *huaso* (cowboy) gear.

Ovalle's excellent **Museo del Limarí** (Tues–Fri 9am–6pm, Sat & Sun 10am–1pm; CH$600, free Sun) stands on the northeast edge of town in the grand old building that once housed the train station. About a third of the museum's 1800-piece collection of **Diaguita pottery** was damaged, some of it severely, in the 1997 earthquake, but the small amount on display is beautifully restored and shown to great effect in modern cases. Famed for its exquisite geometric designs painted in black, white and red onto terracotta surfaces, the pottery was produced by the Diaguita people who inhabited this part of Chile from 1000 AD until the Inca invasions in the sixteenth century.

Not far from the museum, about ten blocks east of the plaza (take an eastbound *micro* along Vicuña Mackenna), you'll find a huge, ramshackle iron hangar that houses the colourful **Feria Modelo de Ovalle** (Mon, Wed, Fri & Sat 6am–6pm), the largest fresh-produce market in the north of Chile and definitely worth a visit; you can pick up fantastic home-made cheeses (including some alarmingly pungent goat cheeses) as well as delicious dried figs and a vast range of fruit and vegetables.

Practicalities

If you arrive by **bus**, you'll be dropped at either the northern terminal, Terrapuerto Limarí, at Maestranza 443; or at the southern terminal, Medialuna, at Ariztía Oriente 769 (☎53/626612). In general, Tur Bus, Pullman, Tal and Flota Barrios buses stop at the former, while Pullman Carmelito, Covalle, Expreso Norte and Tas Choapa buses at the latter; some stop at both. Most also have offices and stops on the central Avenida Ariztía (known locally as the "Alameda"), three blocks east of the Plaza de Armas.

Much of the **accommodation** has seen better days; a few notable exceptions include the spruce *Hotel Plaza Turismo*, Victoria 295 (☎53/623258, Ⓦwww .hotelplazaturismo.cl; ❺), offering spacious, well-kept rooms in a handsome old building with its own restaurant and parking; and the very similar *Gran Hotel*, at Vicuña Mackenna 210 (☎53/621084, Ⓦwww.yagnam.cl; ❺), albeit minus the restaurant and car park. For something more economical, try *Hotel Roxy*, Libertad 155 (☎53/620080; Ⓔkarimedaire@hotmail.com; ❹), with comfortable if dated rooms ranged around a large, brightly painted patio filled with flowers, chairs and a cage of blackbirds.

Ovalle's **restaurants** tend to limit themselves to the standard dishes you find everywhere else in Chile – which is frustrating, considering this is the fresh-produce capital of the North. However, you will find a few worthwhile spots: *Los Braseros de Angello*, at the corner of Vicuña Mackenna and Santiago, serves delicious if unoriginal fare, including juicy *parrillas*, in pleasant surroundings marred only by the giant TV screen. Otherwise, the *Club Social de Ovalle*, on Vicuña Mackenna at no. 400, has decent fish and seafood; while *El Quijote*, Arauco 294, is an intimate, bohemian sort of restaurant, with political graffiti and poetry on the walls, and an inexpensive menu featuring simple staples like *cazuela* and *lomo*. For snacks, drinks or a meal on Sunday, when everything else is closed, you can do worse than *D'Oscar*, a café-bar on the southeast corner of the Plaza. If in need of real coffee, head to the appropriately named *Café Real*, Vicuña Mackenna 419, round the corner from *Hotel Plaza Turismo*. You'll find several **ATMs** around the plaza.

Monumento Natural Pichasca and Hurtado

Northeast of Ovalle, a first-rate newly paved road climbs through the fertile Hurtado Valley, skirting – 12km out of town – the deep-blue expanse of water formed by the **Recoleta Dam**, one of three that irrigate the Limarí Valley.

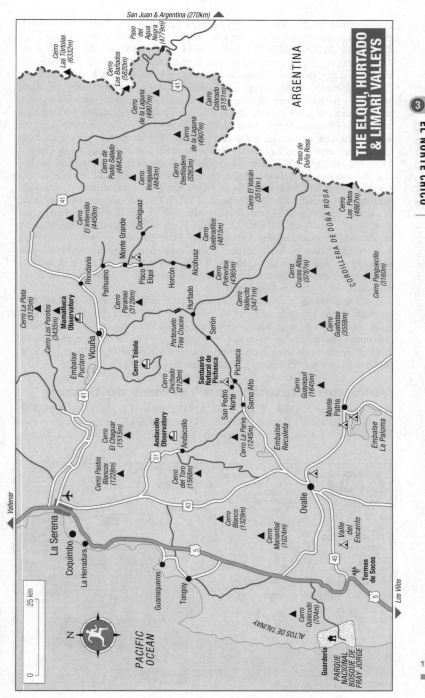

THE ELQUI, HURTADO
& LIMARÍ VALLEYS

San Juan & Argentina (270km) ▲

ARGENTINA

PACIFIC
OCEAN

About 50km up the road, past a string of tiny villages, a side road to San Pedro de Pichasca dips down across the river leading, just beyond the village, to the Conaf-run **MONUMENTO NATURAL PICHASCA** (daily 9am–6pm; CH$1500), the site of a petrified wood, seventy million years old. As you arrive at the parking area, two paths diverge: the right-hand path leads north to a hillside scattered with stumps of **fossilized tree trunks**, some of them imprinted with the shape of leaves; the left-hand, or southern, path leads down to an enormous **cave** formed by an 80-metre gash in the hillside topped by a massive overhanging rock. Archeological discoveries inside the cave point to human habitation some ten thousand years ago. On market days it's possible to get to the turn-off to San Pedro de Pichasca on a rickety **bus** from Ovalle's Feria Modelo (see p.164), but this involves walking 3km from the main road to the site entrance, and then a further 2km to the cave and fossil remains.

Just under 30km further northeast of Pichasca, set amid dramatic mountain scenery, is the traditional oasis village of **HURTADO**, where the main draw, a couple of kilometres outside the village, is a Mexican-style ranch, the *Hacienda Los Andes* (T 53/691822, W www.haciendalosandes.com; 6). Run by an Austro-German couple, the hacienda's main focus is equestrian, offering three-night "horseback adventures", with treks and all meals included, plus transfers to and from La Serena or Ovalle, from US$680 per person. The spacious rooms offer mesmerizing views across the verdant valley, and the hacienda also serves excellent meals.

If you're **driving**, you can visit Pichasca and Hurtado as part of a longer tour through the valley, continuing to Vicuña (see p.178) via a difficult but doable road that fords several mountain streams and crosses several breathtaking mountain passes. You are rewarded by staggering views all the way. A dirt road leading northwards from Samo Alto, about 10km west of Pichasca, leads to Andacollo (see p.169), again through wonderful scenery.

Valle del Encanto and Termas de Socos

The dry, dusty **VALLE DEL ENCANTO** (daily 9am–4.30pm; CH$300) boasts one of Chile's densest collections of **petroglyphs** – images engraved on the surface of rocks – carved mainly by people of the El Molle culture

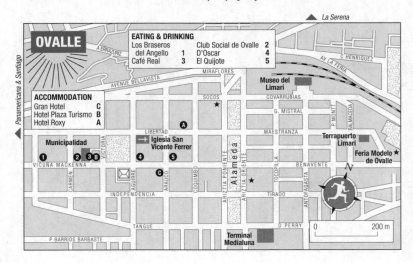

▲ Parque Nacional Fray Jorge

(see p.493) between 100 and 600 AD. Most of the images are geometric motifs or stylized human outlines, including faces with large, wide eyes and elaborate headdresses. A few of the images are very striking, while others are faint and difficult to make out; the best time to visit is around 2–3pm, when the outlines are at their sharpest, unobscured by shadows. Note that you're not allowed to camp in the area. To get here from Ovalle, head 19km west to a heavily potholed dirt road that leads 5km south of Ruta 45 into the ravine.

When you're back on the Panamericana, look for a track just south of the turn-off to Ovalle, which leads 2km to the thermal baths complex of **TERMAS DE SOCOS**, noted for the 22°C (72°F) outdoor pool, surrounded by palm and eucalyptus trees, wicker armchairs and huge potted ferns, and the cubicles containing private bathtubs where you can soak in warm spring water, supposedly rich in medicinal properties. These are free if you're staying at the resort's studiously rustic **hotel** (℡53/198 2505, Santiago ℡2/236 3336, ⓦwww.termasocos.cl; ❼); otherwise, there's a charge of CH$3900 for the baths; the pool is now only open for guests of the hotel. You'll also find a good **campsite** (Sept–April; ⓦwww .campingtermassocos.cl; CH$4000 per person) with its own outdoor pool.

Parque Nacional Fray Jorge

A UNESCO world biosphere reserve since 1977, **PARQUE NACIONAL FRAY JORGE** (daily 9am–4.30pm; CH$1600) sits on the Altos de Talinay, a range of steep coastal hills plunging into the Pacific some 80km west of Ovalle and 110km south of La Serena. It extends over 100 square kilometres, but its focal point, and what visitors come to see, is the small **cloudforest** perched on the highest part of the sierra, about 600m above sea level.

The extraordinary thing about this forest is how sharply it contrasts with its surroundings, indeed with everywhere else in the area. Its existence is the result of **camanchaca**, the thick coastal fog that rises from the ocean and condenses as it meets the land, supporting a cover of dense vegetation – fern, bracken and myrtle trees – normally found only in the south of Chile. Close to the parking area, a one-kilometre path dotted with information panels guides you through a poorly labelled range of plants and trees and leads to the **forest** proper, where a slippery, wooden boardwalk takes you through tall trees dripping with moisture. The whole trail takes less than half an hour to walk.

Practicalities

There's no public transport to the park, so unless you've got a rental car, your best bet is to arrange a trip by **taxi** (try Tasco in Ovalle ℡53/221949, or Pacífico in La Serena ℡51/218000) or take a **tour** from La Serena (see p.178). If you're **driving** here, allow about one and a half hours from Ovalle, a little more from La Serena. The park is reached by a dirt road that branches west from the Panamericana 14km north of the junction with Ruta 45 to Ovalle. From the turn-off, it's 18km to the park entrance, where you pay your fee and register your visit, and then another further 10km to the wood itself along a road that gets rough and extremely steep in some places. Three kilometres beyond the Conaf control there's a **picnic** area, but note that camping is no longer allowed anywhere in the park.

From Ovalle to La Serena

Ovalle is separated from the busy city of La Serena, some 90km north, by a series of gentle valleys and dried-out rivers, punctuated with the occasional abandoned mine or colonial mansion. The most direct, and most scenic, route between the two towns is along Ruta 43, from which a side road branches east to the charming pilgrimage centre of **Andacollo** – a worthwhile detour, especially now that it's home to one of the country's newest observatories, open to the public for evening stargazing. West of Ovalle, the Panamericana turns towards the ocean and skirts a string of small resorts that make a calmer and more attractive beach setting than the built-up coast at La Serena.

Andacollo and around

Enfolded by sun-bleached, rolling hills midway between Ovalle and La Serena, **ANDACOLLO** is a tidy little town of small adobe houses grouped around a long main street. It's been an important gold- and copper-mining centre ever since the Inca mined its hills in the sixteenth century, but is best known as the home of the **Virgen de Andacollo**, a small wooden carving that draws over 100,000 pilgrims to the town each year. Most of them arrive between December 23 and 26 to participate in the Fiesta Grande de la Virgen: four days of music and riotous dancing performed by costumed groups from all over Chile. Many of these dances have their roots in pre-Columbian rituals, such as the *bailes chinos*, recorded in Spanish chronicles around 1580 and thought to have been introduced by the Inca during their occupation in the late fifteenth century. Quieter, less frenetic celebrations take place during the Fiesta Chica on the first Sunday in October.

Even if you miss the fiestas it's still worth coming to check out the two temples erected in honour of the Virgin. Larger and grander is the **Basílica**, which towers over Plaza Pedro Nolasco Videla, the main square, in breathtaking contrast to the small, simple scale of the rest of the town. Built 1873–93, almost entirely of wood in a Roman–Byzantine style, its pale, cream-coloured walls are topped by two colossal 50-metre towers and a stunning 45-metre dome. Inside, sunlight floods through the dome, falling onto huge wooden pillars painted to look like marble. On the other side of the square stands the smaller, stone-built **Templo Antiguo**, dating from 1789. This is where the image of the Virgin stands for most of the year, perched on the main altar, awaiting the great festival when it's transported to the Basílica to receive the petitions and prayers of the pilgrims. Devotees of the Virgin de Andacollo have left an astonishing quantity of gifts here over the years, ranging from artificial limbs and wooden crutches to jewellery, badges, china vases, model boats and exam certificates, all displayed in the crypt of the Templo Antiguo as part of the **Museo del Pelegrino** (Ⓦ www.santuarioandacollo.cl; daily 10am–7pm; donation expected). You can reach Andacollo by bus or *colectivo* from Ovalle (1hr 30min) or La Serena (50min).

The Virgin of Andacollo

The true facts of the story of the **Virgin of Andacollo** – a 90-centimetre carving of the Virgin Mary considered to have miraculous powers – have long been lost in mythology and legend. One popular version has it that the whereabouts of the carving was revealed to an Indian named Collo by a heavenly apparition who urged him to go and seek it crying "¡*Anda, Collo, Anda!*" ("Go, Collo, Go!"). A more credible theory is that the image was taken from La Serena by priests fleeing the city when it was attacked and destroyed by Indians in 1549. They buried the carving in the hills near Andacollo, where it was accidentally discovered by an Indian some time later. Old chronicles tell of a rudimentary chapel erected in Andacollo around 1580, presumably to house the image, and of worship dances held there.

In any event it seems that the image went missing some time in the seventeenth century, prompting Andacollo's parish priest, Don Bernardino Alvarez del Tobar, to organize a collection to pay for a new one to be made. The sum of 24 pesos was duly raised and dispatched to Lima, Peru, where a new image of the Virgin was carved and returned to Andacollo, receiving its inaugural blessing on the first Sunday of October, 1676. The loss of the original image was providential, for the new one turned out to have far greater miracle-working powers than its predecessor. The Virgin's fame spread far and wide, and an intense cult of devotion sprang up. In 1901 the image was recognized as officially "miraculous" by the Vatican, and the Virgin was crowned in a dazzling ceremony attended by five bishops and ten thousand pilgrims.

For a more celestial experience, head to the brand-new **Collowara Observa-tory** (named after the Aymara term for "land of the stars"), some 15km northeast of Andacollo, atop the 1300-metre Cerro Churqui. Built specifically for public use, like that run by the Municipalidad of Vicuña (see p.180), this observatory also features a top-quality Smith-Cassegrain telescope. The two-hour **evening tours** (CH\$3500) start with a high-tech audiovisual talk (in Spanish and English) about the galaxy and other astronomical matters, followed by the opportunity to observe the heavens through one of the telescopes – unless, of course, you're unlucky enough to be here on a cloudy night. You should be at the observatory ticket office at Urmeneta 599 (Mon–Sat 9am–1.45pm & 2.30–5.30pm, Sun 10am–5.30pm; ☎51/432964, ⓦwww.collowara.cl) half an hour before the scheduled visit (7pm, 9pm & 11pm). It's best to make a reservation in advance; minivan transport is provided to and from the observatory.

Tongoy

Some 60km north of the turn-off for Ovalle, a toll-paying side road branches off the Panamericana for **TONGOY**, a popular family resort spread over a hilly peninsula. It has two attractive sandy **beaches**, the Playa Socos, north of the peninsula, and the enormous Playa Grande, stretching 14km south. While there are plenty of hotels, *cabañas* and restaurants, development has been low-key, and the place remains pretty and relatively unspoiled. There's a good choice of **accommodation**. Close to the water's edge on the Costanera Sur at Urmeneta Norte 237 are the *Cabañas Tongoy* (☎51/391902, ⓦwww.cabanastongoy.cl; ⑥), rustic A-framed huts with small gardens, play areas for children and private parking. The *Hotel Panorámico*, Av Mirador 455 (☎51/391944, ⓦwww.hotelpanoramico .cl; ⑥), is crammed with 1950s items including a great TV set and a stand-up hairdryer. On the beachfront at Serena 460, *Yacolen* (☎51/391772; ⑤) offers basic but clean rooms off the yard behind the restaurant, with the two end rooms overlooking the beach, while 500m down Playa Grande, *Ripipal* (☎51/391192; CH\$10,000 per site) is a quiet, year-round **campsite**. Also on the beach, next to the *caleta*, you'll find a row of excellent little **restaurants** serving delicious seafood – try *Negro Cerro* or *La Picada de Veguita*.

There's frequent **transport** to Tongoy from Coquimbo (Colectivos Alfamar; ☎51/323719) and from La Serena (Buses Serenamar; ☎51/212402).

Coquimbo and La Herradura

Spread over a rocky peninsula studded with colourful houses, the busy port of **COQUIMBO** was established during colonial times to serve neighbouring La Serena and became Chile's main copper exporter during the nineteenth century. Despite its undeniably impressive setting, the town has a slightly rough-edged, down-at-heel air, but is useful as an inexpensive base from which to enjoy La Serena's beaches, or for taking public transport to the nearby resorts of Guanaqueros and Tongoy.

Coquimbo's main street, Aldunate, runs parallel to the northern shore of the peninsula, at the foot of the steep hills that form the **upper town**, or Parte Alta. Several stairways lead from Aldunate up to lookout points with sweeping views down to the port and across the bay; if you can't face the climb, take any *micro* marked "Parte Alta". The peak is now crowned with a hideous, concrete "Third Millennium Cross", ablaze at night, which claims to be the only major spiritual monument in the world built at the turn of the millennium (which is just as well if they all looked like this one). The only conceivably redeeming feature is that you can enjoy superb panoramic views of the coast from up here.

Below, the central **Plaza de Armas**, halfway along Aldunate, is slowly being redesigned, with an odd domed structure taking up most of it. North of the square, mostly on Aldunate, you'll find the **Barrio Inglés**, a district with the city's finest houses, many of them carved in wood by English craftsmen during the prosperous mining era. The restored buildings are beautifully lit at night and often double as bars, restaurants or music venues. A couple of blocks north of Aldunate, Avenida Costanera runs along the shore, past the large **port**, the terminal pesquero, and along to the lively **fish market**. This area has been smartened up recently, and makes for a pleasant stroll along the ocean, provided you don't mind the strong whiff of fish.

The southern shore of the peninsula, known as **Guayacán**, has a sandy beach, dominated at one end by a huge mechanized port used for exporting iron. While you're here, take a look at the tall steeple of the nearby **Iglesia de Guayacán**, a prefabricated steel church designed and built in 1888 by Alexandre-Gustave Eiffel, of tower fame, and the **British cemetery**, built in 1860 at the behest of the British Admiralty and full of the graves of young sailors etched with heart-rending inscriptions like "died falling from aloft". (If the cemetery gates are locked, ask in the caretaker's house.)

Guayacán's beach curves south to that of **LA HERRADURA**, which although long, golden and sandy is marred by its proximity to the Panamericana. That said, the night-time views across the bay to the tip of Coquimbo are superb, and if you want to spend a night or two at the seaside, La Herradura makes a convenient, cheaper alternative to La Serena's Avenida del Mar.

Practicalities

Coquimbo's busy **bus terminal** is on the main road into town, near the junction of Videla with Balmaceda. Nearly all the main north–south inter-city buses stop here, as do local buses to coastal resorts like Tongoy and Guanaqueros. You can also get to the resorts, and to Guayacán and La Herradura, by **colectivo** – they pick up behind the bus terminal and throughout the centre of town. There are a couple of *casas de cambio*, Afex, at Melgarejo 1355, and Cambios Maya on Portales 305, plus a couple of **ATMs** on Plaza Prat, on the Plaza de Armas and at Aldunate 822. There's a fair choice of **accommodation** in town, the best being *Hotel Lig*, at Aldunate 1577 (☎51/311171, ✆hotellig@gmail .com; ❹), with bright, comfortable rooms and private parking. *Hotel Iberia*, just off Aldunate at Lastra 400 (☎51/312141, Ⓦwww.hoteliberia.cl; ❹), has spacious rooms, with and without bath, in an attractive old building. For **eating**, go to the little *marisquerías* by the fish market for simple, cheap seafood lunches, or try *Pastissima* at Aldunate 927 for filling, reasonably priced Italian and Chilean fare. Further along you'll find the bizarre but not unattractive pub-restaurant *De Costa a Costa* (named for its 360-degree views enjoyed from the clumsy looking attic), Aldunate 501, serving large helpings of meat and fish with draught beer and live music at weekends. The ♫ *Jazz Club*, one of the best jazz venues in Chile and certainly outside Santiago, showcases home-grown musicians in a fabulous 1920s Barrio Inglés mansion at Aldunate 739.

In **La Herradura**, *Hotel La Herradura*, just off the beach at Av La Marina 200 (☎51/261647; ❹) offers decent rooms at reasonable prices. If you want the best views of the bay, head for *Hotel El Bucanero*, Av La Marina 201 (☎51/265153, Ⓦwww.bucanero.cl; ❻), perched on a jetty projecting into the ocean; here you'll also find La Herradura's plushest **restaurant**, offering good but overpriced seafood and great views across to Coquimbo (best at night). Also looking out to sea, but with more modest prices, is the *Club de Yates*, a little further west along the beach.

La Serena and around

Sitting by the mouth of the Río Elqui, 11km north of Coquimbo, **LA SERENA** is for many visitors their first taste of northern Chile, after whizzing straight up from Santiago by road or air. The city centre is an attractive mix of pale colonial-style houses, carefully restored churches, craft markets tucked away on hidden squares and bustling crowds. Three kilometres away lies Avenida del Mar, a rather charmless esplanade lined with oceanfront aparthotels and *cabañas* that are packed in the summer and gloomily empty out of season.

La Serena is Chile's second-oldest city, with a history chequered by violence and drama. Founded by Pedro de Valdivia in 1544 as a staging post on the way to Peru, it got off to an unpromising start when it was completely destroyed in an **Indian attack** four years later. Undeterred, Valdivia refounded the city in a new location the following year, but La Serena continued to lead a precarious existence, subjected to frequent and often violent raids by pirates, many of them British. Happier times arrived in the nineteenth century, when the discovery of large silver deposits at Arqueros, just north of La Serena, marked the beginning of the region's great **silver boom**. These heady days saw the erection of some of the city's finest mansions and churches, as the mining magnates competed in their efforts to dazzle with their wealth.

It was in the 1940s, when **Gabriel González Videla**, president of Chile and local Serenense, instituted his **"Plan Serena"**, that La Serena developed its signature architectural style. One of the key elements of Videla's urban remodelling scheme was the vigorous promotion of the Spanish colonial style, with facades restored or rebuilt on existing structures and strict stylistic controls imposed on new ones. Unimaginative and inflexible though some claimed these measures to be, the results are undeniably pleasing, and La Serena boasts an architectural harmony and beauty noticeably lacking in most Chilean cities. It's also surrounded by some rewarding places to visit. Close at hand, and with good bus and *colectivo* connections, are the fine beaches at Tongoy (see p.170) and, above all, the glorious **Elqui Valley**, one of the must-sees of the region. Further afield, the cloudforest reserve of **Parque Nacional Fray Jorge** and the penguin and dolphin sanctuary at **Parque Nacional Pinguino de Humboldt** are not served by public transport, but can be visited with several **tour companies** if you don't have your own wheels.

Arrival and information

La Serena's **bus terminal** is a twenty-minute walk south of the centre. There's no direct bus from the terminal into town, but there are plenty of taxis, charging about CH$2000; alternatively, you can flag down a *micro* from the Panamericana, a five-minute walk west. If you've flown in, you'll land at the **Aeropuerto La Florida**, some 5km to the east of town and served by taxis and transfers plus *micros* on the main road (ranging from CH$300–5000).

Sernatur has a well-stocked tourist office on the west side of the Plaza de Armas at Matta 461 (Jan & Feb Mon–Fri 8.45am–8pm, Sat 10am–2pm & 4–8pm, Sun 10am–2pm; March–Dec Mon–Fri 8.30am–5.30pm; ☎ 51/225199, Ⓦ www.turismoregiondecoquimbo.cl). There's also a municipal **Oficina de Turismo** at the bus terminal (Tues–Sat 9.30am–1pm & 3.30–9pm), especially useful for accommodation. For detailed information on Parque Nacional Fray Jorge, Monumento Natural Pichasca and Parque Nacional Pinguino de Humboldt, visit **Conaf** at Cordovez 281 (Mon–Fri 8.30am–2pm; ☎ 51/272798).

Accommodation

You'll find a large choice of budget accommodation and mid- to up-market options in the **centre**. Avenida del Mar, 3km from town, offers only overpriced *cabañas* and hotels.

Hostal Casa Maria Las Rojas 18 ☎51/229282, ⓦ www.hostalmariacasa.cl. Friendly, family-run hostel situated just a block from the bus terminal with rooms off a lovely garden, free internet, shared bathrooms and a communal kitchen. ❸

Hostal Del Mar Cuatro Esquinas at Av del Mar ☎51/225559, ⓦ www.hostaldelmar.cl. Pleasant, well-furnished cabañas with a mid-sized pool, a short walk from the beach. ❻

Hostal Family Home Av El Santo 1056 ☎51/212099, ⓦ www.familyhome.cl. Delightful house that lives up to its name and is conveniently located between the bus terminal and the central plaza; single, double and triple rooms, some en-suite, plus use of kitchen. ❸

Hotel Los Balcones de Aragón Cienfuegos 289 ☎51/221982, ⓦ www.losbalconesdearagon.cl. Smart, upmarket rooms in a fine building with private parking. ❻

Hotel del Cid O'Higgins 138 ☎51/212692, ⓦ www.hoteldelcid.cl. Great hotel run by a Scots-Chilean couple, with a few comfortable rooms around a flower-filled terrace. ❻

Hotel Francisco de Aguirre Cordovez 210 ☎51/222991, ⓦ www.dahoteles.cl. La Serena's plushest hotel, with stylish rooms in a handsome old building, and a poolside restaurant open in summer. ❼

Hotel Londres Cordovez 550 ☎&ⓕ51/219066, ⓦ www.hotellondres.cl. Clean and tidy rooms, some with private bath and others with just a washbasin. ❹

Hotel Pacífico Av de la Barra 252 ☎51/225674, ⓔ reservas@hotelpacifico.cl. Ancient, rambling hotel with clean, basic rooms (some with bath, some without) and friendly staff. ❹

Residencial Suiza Cienfuegos 250 ☎51/216092, ⓔ residencial.suiza@terra.cl. Spotless, well-kept, highly recommended *residencial* with a fresh, modern feel. ❹

Camping

Sol di Mare Parcela 66 ☎51/312531. Lovely, grassy campsite down at the quieter end of the beach. Good facilities and lots of shade. CH$10,000 per site.

The City

La Serena, 2km inland from the northern sweep of the Bahía de Coquimbo, follows the usual grid pattern, with the leafy Plaza de Armas in the centre. It features the noteworthy **Museo Arqueológico**, but the city's main appeal lies in just strolling the streets and squares, admiring the grand old houses, browsing through the numerous craft markets, wandering in and out of its many stone churches and hanging out in the plaza. In the warmer months, hordes of Chilean tourists head for the six-kilometre **beach**, along the Avenida del Mar.

Plaza de Armas

The grand **Iglesia Catedral** dominates the east side of the Plaza de Armas. Its pale walls date from 1844, when the previous church on the site was finally pulled down because of the damage wrought by the 1796 earthquake. Inside, among its more curious features are the wooden pillars, disguised to look like stone. Just off the opposite side of the square, on Cordovez, the pretty **Iglesia Santo Domingo** was first built in 1673 and then again in 1755, after it was sacked by the pirate Sharp.

The two-storey adobe house sitting on the southwest corner of the plaza was, from 1927 to 1977, home to Chile's erstwhile president, Gabriel González Videla, best known for outlawing the Communist party after using its support to gain power in 1946. Inside, a small and rather dull **museum** (Mon–Fri 10am–6pm, Sat 10am–1pm; CH$600) has an eclectic display of photos, objects, documents and paintings relating to the president's life and works, along with a

section on regional history; the temporary art exhibitions, occasionally held here, are often better than the permanent display.

Museo Arqueológico

Entered through an imposing nineteenth-century portico on the corner of Cordovez and Cienfuegos, La Serena's **Museo Arqueológico** (Tues–Fri 9.30am–5.30pm, Sat 10am–1pm & 4–7pm, Sun 10am–1pm; CH$600, Sun free) boasts two outstanding displays, though most of the displays could do with improving.

First is its large collection of **Diaguita pottery**, considered by many to be among the most beautiful pre-Columbian ceramics in South America. The terracotta pieces, dating from around 1000 to 1500 AD, are covered in intricate geometric designs painted in black and white and, in the later phases, red. Starting with simple bowls and dishes made for domestic use, the Diaguita went on to produce elaborately shaped ceremonial pots and jars, often in the form of humans or animals, or sometimes both, such as the famous *jarros patos*, or "duck jars", moulded in the form of a duck's body with a human head.

The museum's other gem is the giant stone statue, or **moai**, from Easter Island, "donated" to La Serena at the behest of President González Videla in 1952. Until recently it stood in a park on Avenida Colo Colo, covered in graffiti and urinated on by drunks. Then, as part of an exhibition of Easter Island art in 1996, it travelled to Barcelona, where it was accidentally decapitated. Tragedy turned to good fortune, however, when the insurance money from the accident paid for a brand-new *sala* to be built for the statue in the archeological museum. This is where you'll find it today, standing on a raised platform against a flattering azure backdrop, the joins at the neck hardly showing.

The rest of downtown

The eye-catching **Museo Mineralógico** (Mon–Fri 9.30am–12.30pm; CH$500), near the university, on Muñoz with Infante, displays a large selection of glittering mineral rocks, many of them mined in the region. Though it's worth a visit while you're in town, note that the similar museum in Copiapó is considerably better.

Of La Serena's numerous **craft markets**, the biggest and best is the bustling **La Recova**, occupying two large patios inside an arcaded building opposite the Iglesia San Agustín. The quality of the merchandise is generally high, and goods include finely worked objects in *combabalita* (a locally mined marble), lapis lazuli jewellery, alpaca sweaters and candied papaya. Backing onto the Panamericana, two blocks west of the Plaza de Armas, the **Parque Japonés Kokoro No Niwa** (Tues–Sun 10am–6pm; CH$600), whose Japanese name means "Garden of the Heart", is an oasis of perfectly manicured lawns, ponds awash with water lilies, ice-white geese and little Japanese bridges and pagodas. Unfortunately, the sense of peace and tranquillity it creates is undermined by the din of the highway.

Avenida del Mar

Stretching 6km round the rim of a wide, horseshoe bay just west of the city, the **Avenida del Mar** is a staid collection of glitzy hotels, tourist complexes and *cabañas* that bulge with visitors for two months of the year and are otherwise empty. In January and February hundreds of cars inch their way up and down the avenue, bumper to bumper, and mostly Chilean tourists pile onto the sandy

---

La Serena's churches

Including Iglesia Catedral and Iglesia Santo Domingo on the Plaza de Armas, a remarkable twenty-nine **churches** dot La Serena, lending an almost fairy-tale look to the city. This proliferation of places of worship dates from the earliest days of the city, when all the religious orders established bases to provide shelter for their clergy's frequent journeys between Santiago and Lima (the viceregal capital). Nearly all the churches are built of stone, which is unusual for Chile, and all are in mint condition.

Standing at the corner of Balmaceda and de la Barra, the **Iglesia San Francisco** is one of La Serena's oldest churches, though the date of its construction is unknown, as the city archives were burnt in Sharp's raid of 1680. Its huge walls are one metre thick, covered in a stone facade carved in fanciful Baroque designs. Inside, the recently restored **Museo de Arte Religioso** contains a small but impressive collection of religious sculpture and paintings from the colonial period. Beautiful for its very plainness, the 1755 **Iglesia San Agustín**, on the corner of Cienfuegos and Cantournet, was originally the Jesuit church but was taken over by the Augustinians after the Jesuits were expelled from Chile in 1767. Its honey-toned stone walls were badly damaged in the 1975 earthquake, but have been skilfully restored. On the northern edge of town, overlooking the banks of the Río Elqui, the seventeenth-century **Capilla de Santa Inés** was constructed on the site of a rudimentary chapel erected by the first colonists and its thick white adobe walls recall the Andean churches of the northern *altiplano*.

beaches, which are clean but spoiled by the horrific high-rise backdrop. While there's no bus or *colectivo* service along the Avenida del Mar, you can take a *micro* headed for Coquimbo from just about any street corner (if in doubt, go to Avenida Francisco de Aguirre) and get off on the Panamericana either at Cuatro Esquinas or Peñuelas, both a short walk from the beach.

Eating, drinking and entertainment

You'll find a wide choice of **places to eat** in downtown La Serena, most of them unpretentious, unexceptional and not too expensive; **cafés** seem to congregate along Balmaceda while **bars** are mostly on O'Higgins. The Avenida del Mar restaurants, on the other hand, tend to be overpriced, though some offer fine views and a lively holiday atmosphere. **Nightlife** downtown is surprisingly quiet, while the pubs and discos by the beach are more seasonal,

---

Observatories around La Serena

Thanks to the exceptional transparency of its skies, northern Chile is home to the largest concentration of astronomical **observatories** in the world. The region around La Serena, in particular, has been chosen by a number of international astronomical research institutions as the site of their telescopes, housed in white, futuristic domes that loom over the valleys from their hilltop locations. Among the research organizations that own the observatories are North American and European groups that need a base in the southern hemisphere (about a third of the sky seen here is never visible in the northern hemisphere).

Some of the observatories offer guided tours, including the impressive **Cerro Tololo** Inter-American Observatory, whose four-metre telescope was the strongest in the southern hemisphere until it was overtaken by Cerro Paranal's Very Large Telescope, the most powerful in the world, located near Antofagasta (see p.208).

Cerro Tololo is 70km east of La Serena, reached by a side road branching south of the Elqui Valley road. Tours take place every Saturday (9.15am–noon & 1.15–4pm) and need to be booked several days in advance (℡51/205200, ℻51/205212, ⓦwww.ctio .noao.edu, ⓔkflores@ctio.noao.edu); quote the registration number of the vehicle you'll be arriving in. You'll be told to collect your visitor's permit from the observatory's offices in La Serena (up the hill behind the university, at Colina El Pino) the day before the tour, but ask to pick it up directly at the observatory gates; alternatively, take a pre-booked tour from La Serena (see box, p.178), which takes care of all the details.

Some 150km northeast of La Serena, reached by a side road branching east from the Panamericana, **La Silla** is the site of the European Southern Observatory's fourteen telescopes, including two 3.6-metre optical reflectors; they are open to the public every Saturday (2–4pm) from January to November, with advance bookings through the observatory's Santiago offices (℡2/2463 3100, ⓦwww.eso.org); you can also contact the observatory directly (℡55/435335). The observatory's La Serena office is at El Santo 1538 (℡51/225387, ℻51/215175).

Thirty kilometres north of La Silla, the Carnegie Institute's observatory at **Las Campanas** contains four telescopes, with two 6.5-metre telescopes under construction as part of its Magellan Project. You can visit on Saturdays (2.30–5.30pm). Contact the observatory's offices in La Serena to make reservations (℡51/207301, ℻51/207308, ⓦwww.lco.cl); they're located next to Cerro Tololo's offices on Colina El Pino.

All of these tours take place during the day and are free of charge but are strictly no-touching; a more hands-on night-time experience is provided by the Municipalidad de Vicuña's small but user-friendly observatory on **Cerro Mamalluca** (see p.180), 5km north of Vicuña and by the newer **Collowara** observatory outside Andacollo (see p.170).

▲ Tololo Observatory

reaching their heady zenith in January and February – *Brooklyn's Corner Pub*, *Kamikaze*, *Tacuba* and *Quinta Ola* are current faves, whilst *Playa Paraíso* and *Kamanga* are the hottest spots by the beach. For a more mellow night out, head to the ☆ *Jazz Club* next to the theatre on the Plaza de Armas. Like its sister club in nearby Coquimbo, this is one of the best jazz venues outside Santiago and is not to be missed. There's a six-screen Cinemark **cinema** at Mall Plaza, next to the bus terminal. The La Recova **market**, at the corner of Cienfuegos and Cantournet, has dozens of good-value *marisquerías* (seafood) on the upper gallery of the handicrafts market, making it a perfect place for lunch.

La Casona del Guatón Brazil 750. Lively, friendly and intimate, this colonial-style restaurant serves the best *parrilladas* in La Serena. Romantic *boleros*, the Latin answer to the waltz, at weekends.

Daniella II Av Francisco de Aguirre 335. Typical Chilean restaurant with friendly service and a traditional menu of local fish and meat dishes like *pastel de jaiba* (a crab and corn pie) and *lomo a lo pobre*.

Hotel Francisco de Aguirre Cordovez 210. If you're around in summer and fancy a splurge, this is the place to come, principally for its glamorous poolside setting. The French-influenced food is toothsome and well-presented.

Rapsodia Prat 470. La Serena's best bet for a good coffee, with tables dotting a little patio under a huge palm. Closed on Sundays.

Tutti Nostra O'Higgins 360. Come to this attractive café-style spot for decent, moderately priced pizzas and also breakfast. At Av del Mar 2100, you'll find an upmarket, seaview branch with outdoor summer seating that draws the crowds with fish and seafood in addition to the tasty pizzas and pasta dishes.

Listings

Airlines LAN, Balmaceda 406 ☎51/210134 or the national number ☎600/526 2000.
Airport information ☎51/200900
Banks and exchange There are plenty of ATMs on or near the Plaza de Armas and the corner of Cordovez and Cienfuegos. For currency exchange, try Cambios Afex, Balmaceda 413; Cambios Fides, Caracol Colonial, Balmaceda 460, Office 7;

Cambios Inter, Balmaceda 431; Euro Cambios, Mall Plaza, Office 3B (daily 10.30am–9pm).
Car rental In addition to the airport, there are many outlets on Av Francisco de Aguirre, including Avis at no. 68 (☎51/545300, ⊛www.avischile.cl); Budget at no. 15 (☎51/218272); Econorent at no. 135 (☎51/220113, ⊛www.econorent.cl); Hertz at no. 225 (☎51/226171, ⊛www.hertz.cl) and

The two most popular day tours from La Serena are to the **Elqui Valley**, taking in Vicuña, Montegrande and Pisco Elqui (also easily reached on public transport), and to the cloudforest reserve at **Parque Nacional Fray Jorge** (see p.167), about two hours' south of the city and not served by public transport. Other favourite destinations include nearby **beaches** such as Guanaqueros and Tongoy; **Andacollo**, an important pilgrimage centre 54km southeast of La Serena (see p.169); the ancient petroglyph site of the **Valle del Encanto**, near Ovalle (see p.166); **Monumento Natural Pichasca**, where you'll find the remains of a "fossilized wood" (see p.166); and, increasingly, the **Reserva Nacional Pinguino de Humboldt**, a penguin and dolphin sanctuary 120km north of La Serena. On Saturdays you can take tours to the international astronomical observatory of **Cerro Tololo** in the Elqui Valley (see box, p.176). The **cost** of most tours ranges from CH\$20,000 to CH\$25,000 per person and a selection of reliable operators is given in the listings below.

Santiago rent a car at no. 660-B (℡51/211951, 🌐www.santiagorentacar.com).
Internet Talinay, Prat 470.
Post office On the west side of Plaza de Armas, on the corner of Prat and Matta.
Taxis 24hr radio taxis ℡51/211455.
Tour operators Best of a mixed bunch are Eco Turismo, Andres Bell 937 ℡51/218970,

🌐ww.eco-turismo.cl; and Talinay Chile, Prat 470 ℡51/218658, 📧talinayexpediciones@gmail.com who also offer mountaineering trips in the Andes and over to Argentina.
Travel agencies For airline tickets, try Viajes Torremolinos at Prat 464 ℡51/226043, 📧torremolinos@atnchile.com.

The Elqui Valley

Quiet, rural and extremely beautiful, the **ELQUI VALLEY** unfolds east from La Serena and into the Andes. Irrigated by canals fed by the Puclara and La Laguna dams, the valley floor is given over entirely to cultivation – of papayas, custard apples (*chirimoyas*), oranges, avocados and, most famously, the vast expanses of grape vines grown to produce **pisco**. It's the fluorescent green of these vines that makes the valley so stunning, forming a spectacular contrast with the charred, brown hills that rise on either side. To get the full visual impact of the valley you need to visit between September and March, but this is a gorgeous region to spend a couple of days at any time of year.

Some 60km east of La Serena, appealing little **Vicuña** is the main town and transport hub of the Elqui Valley. Moving east from here, the valley gets higher and narrower and is dotted with tiny villages like **Montegrande** and the odd pisco distillery. The road from La Serena is paved for 105km as far as **Pisco Elqui**, a very pretty village that makes a great place to unwind for a couple of days. If you really want to get away from it all, head for one of the rustic *cabañas* dotted along the banks of the **Río Cochiguaz**, which forks east of the main valley at Montegrande, or delve beyond Pisco Elqui into the farthest reaches of the Elqui Valley itself. Buses will get you all the way to Horcón but not to the farthest village of all, **Alcohuaz**.

Vicuña and around

VICUÑA, an hour by bus inland from La Serena, is a neat and tidy agricultural town laid out around a large, luxuriantly landscaped square. It's a pleasant, easy-going place with a few low-key attractions, a good choice of places to stay and eat, and a visitor-friendly observatory on its doorstep.

Life revolves firmly around the central **plaza**, which has at its centre a huge stone replica of the **death mask** of Nobel Prize-winning poet **Gabriela Mistral**, the Elqui Valley's most famous daughter. On the square's northwest corner stands the **Iglesia de la Inmaculada Concepción**, topped by an impressive wooden tower built in 1909 – take a look inside at its vaulted polychrome ceiling, painted with delicate religious images and supported by immense wooden columns. Right next door, the eccentric **Torre Bauer** is a bright-red, mock-medieval tower prefabricated in Germany in 1905 and brought to Vicuña on the instructions of the town's German-born mayor, Adolfo Bauer; the adobe building supporting it houses the Municipalidad. Standing on the southern side of the square, the **Museo Entomológico** (Jan–March daily 10am–8pm; April–Dec Mon–Fri 10.30am–1.30pm & 3.30–7pm, Sat & Sun 10.30am–7pm; CH$600) hoards a fascinating collection of horror-movie creepy-crawlies, such as hairy spiders and vicious-looking millipedes, plus exotic butterflies and shells.

Four blocks east of the square, at the end of Calle Gabriela Mistral, the **Museo Gabriela Mistral** (Jan & Feb Mon–Sat 10am–7pm, Sun 10am–6pm; March–Dec Mon–Fri 10am–5.45pm, Sat 10.30am–6pm, Sun 10am–1pm; CH$300) displays photos, prizes, articles and personal objects bequeathed to the city by the poet, along with panels giving an account of her life and works. A few doors down, at no. 683, is the **Solar de los Madariaga** (Jan & Feb daily 10am–7pm; rest of year erratic opening hours; CH$500), an old, colonial-style house preserved as a museum, displaying a modest collection of nineteenth-century furniture and clothes. Just out of town, across the bridge by the filling station, you'll find the **Planta Capel**, the largest pisco distillery in the Elqui Valley. It offers free and very slick guided tours in English and Spanish every half-hour (daily 10am–12.30pm & 2.30–6pm; also during lunch time in summer and on winter holidays and long weekends), with free tastings and the chance to buy bottles and souvenirs at the end.

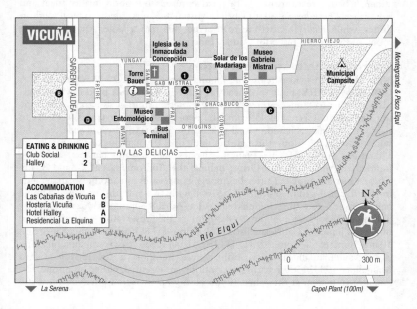

Moving on from La Serena

Inter-city buses operate from La Serena's large, modern bus terminal on El Santo, southwest of the central plaza. From here, there are frequent services to Santiago and all the main cities and towns of the north, plus a few services to regional destinations. Buses for the **Elqui Valley** leave from the Plaza de Abastos on Esmeralda, just south of Colo Colo, about every 30 minutes. To get to **Tongoy**, take a Serenamar bus from the terminal (☏51/323422); the other **coastal resorts** are more easily reached from Coquimbo – to get there, take a *micro* (marked "Coquimbo", of course) from Avenida Francisco de Aguirre or any main south- or westbound street. Two **colectivo** services from La Serena operate from Calle Domeyko, one block south of Iglesia San Francisco: Anserco, at no. 530 (☏51/217567) goes to Andacollo, Vicuña and Ovalle; Tasco, at no. 575 (☏51/224517) goes to Vicuña, Montegrande and Pisco Elqui. From La Florida airport there are daily **flights** to Santiago and Arica.

Practicalities

Buses drop off at the small terminal at the corner of O'Higgins and Prat, one block south of the Plaza de Armas. Vicuña's **Oficina de Turismo** (Mon–Fri 9am–1pm & 2–5.30pm; ☏51/411359) is on the northwest corner of the plaza, beneath the Torre Bauer.

There's plenty of **accommodation**. The friendly *Residencial La Elquina*, at O'Higgins 65 (☏51/209125; ❹), offers rooms with and without bath around a flower-filled patio. The more upmarket *Hotel Halley* at Gabriela Mistral 404 (☏&℻51/412070, ⓦwww.hotelhalley.cl; ❺) comes highly recommended, with large, impeccably decorated rooms in a colonial-style building, and access to a pool. If you prefer a little more independence, *Las Cabañas de Vicuña* on Chacabuco 768 (☏09/937 4834, Ⓔmumanal@yahoo.com; ❺) are modern and homely sleeping up to four with small patios and cable television. Vicuña's top hotel, the *Hostería Vicuña*, at the western end of Gabriela Mistral (☏51/411301, ⓦwww.hosteriavicuna.cl; ❼), is overpriced but has a fabulous pool and one of Vicuña's better **restaurants**, with unadventurous but good-quality meat and fish dishes. The *Club Social*, at Gabriela Mistral 445, serves basic, typical Chilean dishes, while *Halley*, across the road at no. 404, has a large, attractive dining room and is a good place for Sunday lunch.

Cerro Mamalluca observatory

Nine kilometres northeast of Vicuña, the **CERRO MAMALLUCA OBSERVATORY**, built specifically for public use, is run by the Municipalidad de Vicuña and features a 30-centimetre Smith-Cassegrain telescope donated by the Cerro Tololo team. The two-hour **evening tours** (CH$3500) start with a high-tech audiovisual talk on the history of the universe, and end with the chance to look through the telescope. If you're lucky, you might see a dazzling display of stars, planets, galaxies, nebulas and clusters, including Jupiter, Saturn's rings, the Orion nebula, the Andromeda galaxy and Sirius. These tours are aimed at utter beginners, but serious astronomers can arrange in-depth, small-group sessions (US$100) with two months' notice. Assemble half an hour before the scheduled slot (Oct–April 8.30pm, 10.30pm & half past midnight; May–Sept 6.30pm & 8.30pm) at the observatory's administrative office in Vicuña, at Gabriela Mistral 260 (Mon–Fri 8.30am–8.30pm, Sat & Sun 10am–2pm & 4–8pm; ☏51/411352, ℻411255, ⓦwww.mamalluca.org, Ⓔreservas@mamalluca.dm.cl), from where transport is provided to Cerro Mamalluca (CH$1500 return); reservations are essential, either by phone, fax, email or in person at the office. If you have your own transport you must still report to the offices, to confirm and pay for your reservation and to follow the minibus in a convoy.

Montegrande

The picturesque village of **MONTEGRANDE**, 34km east of Vicuña (if you're driving, take the right turn for Paihuano at Rivadavia), features a pretty church whose late-nineteenth-century wooden belfry looms over a surprisingly large square. The childhood home of Gabriela Mistral, Montegrande assiduously devotes itself to preserving her memory: her profile has been outlined in white stones on the valley wall opposite the plaza, and the school where she lived with and was taught by her sister has been turned into a **museum** (Tues–Sun 10am–1pm & 3–6pm; CH$300), displaying some of her furniture and belongings. Just south of the village, her **tomb** rests on a hillside, opposite the turn-off for Cochiguaz. Close by is the wacky **Galería de Arte Zen**, where you can admire esoteric art and have a tarot card reading.

If you need somewhere to eat, *El Mesón del Fraile*, serving predictable fare, beckons opposite the museum. For accommodation – there is none in Montegrande itself – either take the turn-off (from the fork by the Capel plant) for Cochiguaz (see p.184), or continue along the main road to Pisco Elqui, 4km away. Halfway between Montegrande and Pisco Elqui, in a wonderful quiet location with mountain views, is one of the area's best places **to stay**. Stylishly built *El Galpón*, at La Jarilla (☎51/198 2587, ⓦ www.elgalpon-elqui.cl; ❼), is owned by a friendly Chilean who lived for many years in the United States. Each of the rooms has a huge bathroom, TV and a minibar; two- and five-person *cabañas* are also available. The well-kept grounds have an eye-catching swimming pool.

Pisco Elqui and around

PISCO ELQUI was known as La Unión until 1939, when Gabriel González Videla – later President of Chile – cunningly renamed it to thwart Peru's efforts to gain exclusive rights to the name "Pisco". An idyllic village with fewer than nine hundred inhabitants, it boasts a beautiful square filled with lush palm trees and flowers, overlooked by a colourful church with a tall, wooden tower. Locals sell home-made jam and marmalade in the square, and its abundant shade provides a welcome relief from the sun. During **Carnaval**, in the second half of February, the town resounds with folk concerts and other entertainment; on

Getting around the Elqui Valley

Many tour companies in La Serena offer trips to the Elqui Valley, but it's hardly worth taking a tour, as public transport up and down the valley is so frequent and cheap. The two main **bus** companies are Sol de Elqui and Via Elqui (☎51/211707). In **La Serena** they generally use a terminal southeast of the centre at the Plaza de Abastos, on Calle Esmeralda (just south of Colo Colo). But some buses depart from the main terminal, useful if you want to take off for the valley directly – just ask. Daily buses depart every half-hour for **Vicuña**, with about six of these continuing to **Montegrande** and **Pisco Elqui**; one or two a day forge on all the way to Horcón. It might be worth investing in a **day pass**, which costs CH$4000 and is valid for 24 hours, so that you can hop on and off any bus plying the valley as many times as you choose. Tasco **colectivos** (Domeyko 575 ☎51/224517) head from La Serena every half-hour for Vicuña, Montegrande and Pisco Elqui. A *colectivo* is even cheaper than a bus when two or three people are travelling together, but it's not necessarily a more comfortable option.

Possibly even more than its pisco, the Elqui Valley's greatest source of pride is **Gabriela Mistral**, born in Vicuña in 1889 and, in 1945, the first Latin American to be awarded the **Nobel Prize for Literature**. A schoolmistress, a confirmed spinster and a deeply religious woman, Mistral is perceived by Chileans as an austere, distant and even intolerant figure, and yet her poetry reveals an aching sensitivity and passion, and her much romanticized life was punctuated with tragedy and grief.

Lucila Godoy de Alcayaga, as she was christened, was just three years old when her father abandoned the family, the first of several experiences of loss in her life. It was left to her older sister, Emiliana, to support her and her mother, and for the next eight years the three of them lived in the schoolhouse in the village of **Montegrande**, where Emiliana worked as a teacher. At the age of 14, she started work herself as an assistant schoolteacher, in a village close to La Serena, where she taught children by day and workmen learning to read by night. It was here, also, that she took her first steps into the world of literature, publishing several pieces in the local newspaper under the pseudonyms "Alguien" ("Someone"), "Soledad" ("Solitude") and "Alma" ("Soul"). When she was twenty years old, a railway worker, Romelio Ureta, who for three years had been asking her to marry him, committed suicide; in his pocket, a card was found bearing her name.

Although it would seem that his love for her was unrequited, the intense grief caused by Ureta's suicide was to inform much of Mistral's intensely morbid poetry, to which she devoted her time with increasing dedication while supporting herself with a series of teaching posts. In 1914 she won first prize in an important national poetry competition with *Los Sonetos de la Muerte* (Sonnets of Death), and in 1922 her first collection of verse was published under the title of *Desolación* (Desolation), followed a couple of years later by a second collection, *Ternura* (Tenderness). Her work received international acclaim, and in recognition, the Chilean Government offered Gabriela Mistral a position in the consular service, allowing her to concentrate almost exclusively on her poetry; here the parallel with Pablo Neruda is at its strongest. As consul, she spent many years abroad, particularly in the US, but her poems continued to look back to Chile, particularly her beloved **Elqui Valley**, which she described as "a cry of nature rising amidst the opaque mountains and intense blue sky". Her most frequently recurring themes, however, were her love of children and her perceived sorrow at her childlessness.

Though she never gave birth to a child, Gabriela Mistral did serve as a surrogate mother for her adored nephew, **Juan Miguel** or "Yin Yin", who had been placed in her care when he was just nine months old; some say she never really loved anyone else, though she had some very close female friends, including her secretary (it was reported that they had an affair). Once again, though, tragedy struck: at the age of seventeen, Yin Yin committed suicide in Brazil, where she was serving as consul; it has been claimed that he swallowed arsenic because his aunt and adoptive mother was sexually abusing him. In any case, it was a loss from which she never recovered, and for which her Nobel prize, awarded two years later, could do little to console her. Gabriela Mistral outlived her nephew by twelve years, during which she continued to be regaled with international prizes, honorary degrees and other tributes, including the French Legion of Honour. In 1957, she died in New York of cancer of the pancreas at the age of 67, leaving the proceeds of all her works published in South America to the children of Montegrande.

the down side, accommodation gets fully booked then, the campsite bursts at the seams and a generally rowdy ambience pervades, with too many drunken revellers for many people's taste. Down by the main road, the **Pisco Mistral** is Chile's oldest pisco distillery, which today (considerably modernized) produces the famous Tres Erres brand. There are free **guided tours** (daily 10am–7pm) around the old part of the plant, with tastings at the end. You can also visit the 130-year-old private distillery at **Los Nichos**, 4km on from Pisco Elqui (daily 11am–1pm & 3–6pm); if there's no one there, ask in the red house next door.

Pisco Elqui has plenty of good **places to stay**. *Hostal Triskel* on Baquedano (T09/419 8680, Wwww.hostaltriskel.cl; ❸) is a good budget option with simple yet cosy rooms and a peaceful garden. *Hotel Elqui*, on O'Higgins, the main street (T51/198 2523; ❹), offers eight immaculate rooms, some with balconies, in a charming old building with a pool. The friendly, German-run ⚜ *El Tesoro de Elqui*, on Prat (T51/198 2609, Wwww.tesoro-elqui.cl; ❹), offers attractive, spotless *cabañas* with hammocks slung on the verandas and a gorgeous pool. For a real treat, stay up at ⚜ *Los Misterios de Elqui* (T51/451126, Wwww.misteriosdeelqui.cl; ❼), 800m out of town on the road to Alcohuaz. Designer-magazine *cabañas* with fabulous views are spaced comfortably apart among landscaped gardens leading down to a stunning swimming pool; a gourmet chef prepares delicious food in a tastefully decorated restaurant; and horse rides up the valley can be arranged. Pisco Elqui also has three **campsites**, the best being *El Olivo*, just off the main road (no phone; CH$3500 per person), with shade and a small swimming pool. Apart from the one at *Los Misterios*, the best **restaurants** in town are in *Hotel Elqui*, which serves typical Chilean meat dishes on a large, vine-covered patio, and *El Tesoro de Elqui*, where you can tuck into a tasty menu that mixes international and local dishes. Continue the evening at *La Escuela* on Prat, a funky bar where cocktails, snacks and pizzas are offered around an open fire under a billowing tented roof; during the day you can enjoy real coffee, juices, cakes and sandwiches on cowboy-saddle bar stools in its retro café next door. Not to be missed is the wonderful ⚜ *Miraflores* restaurant (T51/285901), a family-run place a couple of kilometres along the road that goes out of town towards Alcohuaz. Here you can feast on excellent roast meats like suckling pig and *bife de chorizo* cooked up on the *parrillada*, whilst savouring mesmerizing views down the valley.

Alcohuaz

Beyond Pisco Elqui, the narrow road leads through increasingly unspoiled countryside and ever deeper into the valley. After 8km you'll pass by the *Pueblo Artesanal de Horcón* (Wwww.pueblodehorcon.cl; Tues–Sat except during holidays – erratic opening hours), which lies just before the sleepy village of the same name (the end of the road for buses from La Serena). Here you can browse among the many stalls for all sorts of local arts, crafts and foods, or just enjoy a fresh juice and a massage by the river. Back on the road, some 15km beyond Pisco Elqui, is the tiny community of **ALCOHUAZ**. Apart from a handsome terracotta-hued church (in sharp contrast to Horcón's, which is sky blue), this remote settlement has little to offer in the way of standard attractions. But it is home to a popular curiosity, the **bee–cure centre** known as Colmenares Alcohuaz, or "Alcohuaz Hives" (T51/978 15331, Enelsoncorreacl@yahoo.cl). People come from throughout the country to treat all kinds of ills by means of apitherapy (bee stings) – after being tested for allergies, of course. You can also buy a variety of excellent bee products such as honey, royal jelly, propolis and creams to treat skin ailments. If you want **to stay** in Alcohuaz, you can choose between two new, unobtrusive *cabaña* complexes: *Valle Hermoso* (T51/270641; ❺) or the slightly more expensive *Refugios La Frontera* (T09/279 8109, Wwww.refugioslafrontera.cl; ❻), which boasts a magical setting by the river willows and its own restaurant, *El Cielo*, where you can sample the region's fresh river prawns.

▲ Pisco Distillery

Along the Río Cochiguaz

Back in Montegrande, a rough, unpaved road branches off the main route, dips down the valley and follows the northern bank of the **RÍO COCHIGUAZ**, a tributary of the Elqui. Rustic *cabañas* dot the riverbank; many offer holistic therapies and meditation classes. The small community of **Cochiguaz**, 12km along the valley, was founded in the 1960s by a group of hippies in the belief that the Age of Aquarius had shifted the earth's magnetic centre from the Himalayas to the Elqui Valley. But don't let this put you off – the multicoloured highland scenery is fabulous and the remoteness and tranquillity of the valley irresistible. If you're walking from the turn-off, you can easily reach the first set of *cabañas*, called *Spa Naturista* (☎51/451067; ❻), 2km from the paved road. A further 3km along, friendly *El Albaricoque* (☎08/543 6288, ✉carmenhurtado74@yahoo.com; ❻) offers rustic *cabañas* in a wood by the river, and tasty vegetarian food. About 13km from Montegrande you'll find luxurious *cabañas* at *Casa del Agua* (☎&ℱ51/321371; ❼) set in fifteen acres of private land spanning both sides of the river. Secluded *Camping Parque Ecológico Río Mágico* at Fundo Victoria (☎08/983 3784; CH$4000 per person) is a great option for campers while at the very end of the road, 18km from Montegrande, *Camping Cochiguaz* (☎51/451154; CH$4000 per person) has 24 sites with picnic tables and offers **horseriding** tours of the valley.

Ruta 41 to Argentina

After Rivadavia – where the right fork leads to Pisco Elqui – **Ruta 41** from La Serena follows first the Río Turbio and then the Río de la Laguna all the way to the **Paso del Agua Negra** (4779m) and the Argentine border, nearly 170km away. Only partly tarmacked, often narrow and hemmed in by imposing mountains, many of them over 4000m high, this road is one of the most dramatic linking the two countries, and is open only from October or November to April. Seventy-five kilometres on from Rivadavia you'll come to the **Complejo Aduanero Junta del Toro**, the Chilean customs post (T51/198 1019; Dec–Apr daily 8am–6pm). The **Argentine border** lies some 95km from the customs post. On the other side of the frontier, the RN 150 winds down to the easygoing market town of Rodeo and hits the adobe-built town of Jachal, from where the RN 40 strikes south to the laid-back provincial capital of San Juan, nearly 270km on from the border post. For more details of these places consult the *Rough Guide to Argentina*.

Vallenar and around

North of La Serena, the Panamericana turns inland and heads via a couple of winding passes (Cuesta Buenos Aires and Cuesta Pajonales) towards the modest town of **VALLENAR**, 190km up the road. There are only a few sporadic signs of habitation in between, and nothing to tempt you off the highway save a detour down a 76-kilometre dirt track (opposite Domeyko) to the **Reserva Nacional Pinguino de Humboldt**, where you can take boat trips (CH$45,000 per boat; Patricio Ortiz is a reliable local guide T51/198 4707) to Isla Chañaral, surrounded by bottle-nosed dolphins, and to nearby colonies of Humboldt penguins. Pushing on to Vallenar, you'll find a busy but somewhat run-down little town that acts as a service centre for local mining and agricultural industries. Founded in 1789 by Governor Ambrosio O'Higgins, who named the city after his native Ballinagh in Ireland, it makes a convenient base for an excursion east into the fertile **upper Huasco Valley**, laced with green vines and small pisco plants, or northwest towards the coast and, in the spring,

---

Pisco

Pisco has been enjoyed by Chileans for more than four centuries, but it wasn't until the 1930s that it was organized into an effective commercial industry, starting with the official creation of a pisco *denominación de origen*. Shortly afterwards, a large number of growers, who'd always been at the mercy of the private distilleries for the price they got for their grapes, joined together to form co-operatives to produce their own pisco. The largest were the tongue-twisting *Sociedad Cooperativa Control Pisquero de Elqui y Vitivinículo de Norte Ltda* (known as "Pisco Control") and the *Cooperativa Agrícola y Pisquera del Elqui Ltda* (known as "Pisco Capel"), today the two most important producers in Chile, accounting for over ninety percent of all pisco to hit the shops.

The basic **distillation technique** is the same one that's been used since colonial times: in short, the fermented wine is boiled in copper stills, at 90°C, releasing vapours that are condensed, then kept in oak vats for three to six months. The alcohol – of 55° to 65° – is then diluted with water, according to the type of pisco it's being sold as: 30° or 32° for *Selección*; 35° for *Reservado*; 40° for *Especial*; and 43°, 46° and 50° for *Gran Pisco*. It's most commonly consumed as a tangy, refreshing aperitif known as **Pisco Sour**, an ice-cold mix of pisco, lemon juice and sugar – sometimes with whisked egg-white for a frothy head and angostura bitters for an extra zing.

Note that the Peruvians also produce pisco and consider their own to be the only authentic sort, maintaining that the Chilean stuff is nothing short of counterfeit. The Chileans, of course, pass this off as jealousy, insisting that their pisco is far superior (it is certainly grapier) and proudly claiming that pisco is a Chilean, not Peruvian, drink. Whoever produced it first, there's no denying that the pisco lovingly distilled in the Elqui Valley is absolutely delicious, drunk neat or in a cocktail. A visit to one of the distilleries in the region is not to be missed – if only for the free tasting at the end.

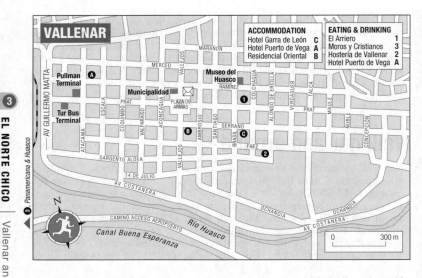

the wild flowers of the **Parque Nacional Llanos de Challe**. The self-appointed "*capital del desierto florido*" (and vigorously promoted as such by the tourist authorities), Vallenar is indeed the best base for forays into the **flowering desert** (see box, p.188), if you're here at the right time. In the town itself, the **Museo del Huasco** at Ramírez 1001 (Mon–Fri 9am–1pm & 3–6pm; CH$450) has some moderately diverting displays on indigenous cultures and photos of the flowering desert.

Practicalities

Vallenar's two main bus terminals are on either side of Prat, some six blocks west of the main square. There is no longer an official tourist office in town; instead an ad hoc information service (⊕51/617475, open weekdays only) is provided in the municipalidad building on the northwest corner of the Plaza de Armas, though don't go expecting much.

Accommodation in Vallenar is on the whole overpriced but there are a few exceptions, including the budget rooms with private bath, set around a quiet patio, at *Residencial Oriental*, Serrano 720 (⊕51/613889; ❷). *Hotel Garra de León*, at Serrano 1052 (⊕&⊕51/613753, ⓦwww.hotelgarradeleon.cl; ❻), offers smart, spacious rooms with air conditioning, cable TV and pristine bathrooms, plus its own car park. Far and away superior, though, is the conveniently located *Hotel Puerto de Vega*, right next to the bus terminal at Ramírez 201 (⊕&⊕51/613870, ⚵ ⓦwww.puertodevega.cl; ❻). It is the only boutique hotel in the whole region, with beautifully decorated rooms and suites, covered parking, a small swimming pool in a tidy garden, an internet connection, afternoon tea with cake and huge, delicious breakfasts.

Of Vallenar's restaurants, the best is *Moros y Cristianos* (⊕51/614600), a stylish place out on the Panamericana by the Huasco turn-off, run by a Lebanese Chilean and serving slightly more interesting meat and fish dishes than the norm. The surprisingly good *Hostería de Vallenar*, at Alonso de Ercilla 848, offers well-cooked Chilean cuisine with imaginative sauces. The tastefully decorated, Chilean-Canadian-run ⚵ *Arriero A*, Prat 1061, dishes up huge *picadas* and juicy Argentine steaks. For pizzas and fast food, try *Il Boccato*, on the east side of the main square. There are no *cambios* in Vallenar, but several ATMs on Prat, between Brasil and Alonso de Ercilla.

The upper Huasco Valley

From Vallenar, a paved road follows the Río Huasco through a deep, attractive valley that climbs towards the mountains. The road weaves back and forth across the river, taking you through dry, mauve-coloured hills and green orchards and vineyards. About 20km from the town, you pass the enormous **Santa Juana dam** which, after a season of heavy rainfall, overflows into a magnificent waterfall that can be viewed close-up from an observation deck. Thirty-eight kilometres from Vallenar, the valley forks at the confluence of the El Carmen and El Tránsito rivers. The right-hand road takes you up the **El Carmen Valley** where, just beyond the fork, you'll find **Alto del Carmen**, a pretty village that produces one of the best-known brands of pisco in Chile; you can visit the Planta Pisquera Alto del Carmen for a free tour and tastings (Feb–May Mon–Fri 9am–noon & 2–6pm, Sat 9am–noon). **Buses** leave Vallenar for Alto del Carmen five times a day, taking one hour. A further 26km up the now unpaved road, **San Félix** has a beautiful setting and a hundred-year-old **pisco plant** that produces high-quality, traditionally made pisco called Horcón Quemado. Guided tours (daily 8am–8pm; free) include a look at the old copper machinery and tastings at the end. There are two rustic **places to stay** in San Félix: *Pensión San Félix* (no phone; ❷), which has a restaurant, and *Pensión La Fortuna* (no phone; ❷).

Parque Nacional Llanos de Challe and the northern beaches

If you have the good luck to be around while the desert's in bloom, head for the **PARQUE NACIONAL LLANOS DE CHALLE** (CH$3500), northwest of Vallenar, for the full impact. This 450-square kilometre swath of coastal plain has been singled out for national park status because of the abundance of **garra de león** – an exquisite, deep-red flower in danger of extinction – that grows here during the years of the *desierto florido*. The park is crossed by an 82-kilometre dirt road branching west from the Panamericana, 17km north of Vallenar, ending at **Carrizal Bajo**, a once-important mining port now home to a tiny fishing community made up of sixteen families. Three buses a week leave Vallenar for Carrizal Bajo; for details, check with the municipalidad in Vallenar (☎51/617475). If you have a 4WD, a tent and a taste for wilderness, follow the very rough track north of Carrizal Bajo up to Puerto Viejo, near Caldera and Copiapó. The deserted **beaches** along this stretch, particularly the northern half, are breath-taking, with white sands and clear, turquoise waters. If you don't have your own transport, you could catch one of the many *micros*, stationed on the corner of Calles Brazil and 14 de Julio, that leave Vallenar for Huasco.

Copiapó

Overlooked by rippling mountains, the prosperous city of **Copiapó** sits in the flat basin of the **Río Copiapó**, some 60km from the coast and 145km north of Vallenar. The valley to the east is the most northerly of Chile's "transverse valleys" and beyond it the transformation from semi-desert to serious desert is complete, and the bare, barren Atacama stretches a staggering 1000km north

The flowering desert

For most of the year, as you travel up the Panamericana between Vallenar and Copiapó you'll cross a seemingly endless, semi-desert plain, stretching for nearly 100km, sparsely covered with low shrubs and *copao* cacti. But take the same journey in spring, and in place of the parched, brown earth, you'll find green grass dotted with beautiful flowers. If you're really lucky and you know where to go after a particularly wet winter, you'll happen upon fluorescent carpets of multicoloured flowers, stretching into the horizon.

This extraordinarily dramatic transformation is known as the **desierto florido**, or "flowering desert"; it occurs when unusually heavy rainfall (normally very light in this region) causes dormant bulbs and seeds, hidden beneath the earth, to sprout into sudden bloom, mostly from early September to late October. In the central strip, crossed by the highway, the flowers tend to appear in huge single blocks of colour (*praderas*), formed chiefly by the purple *pata de guanaco* ("guanaco's hoof"), the yellow *corona de fraile* ("monk's halo") and the blue *suspiro de campo* ("field's sigh"). The tiny forget-me-not-like *azulillo* also creates delicate blankets of baby blue. On the banks of the *quebradas*, or ravines, that snake across the land from the cordillera to the ocean, many different varieties of flowers are mixed together, producing a kaleidoscope of contrasting colours known as *jardines*. These may include the yellow or orange lily-like *añañuca* and the speckled white, pink, red or yellow *alstroemeria*, a popular plant with florists also known as the "Peruvian lily". West, towards the coast, you'll also find large crimson swaths of the endangered *garra de león* ("lion's claw"), particularly in the Parque Nacional Llanos de Challe, near Carrizal Bajo, created especially to protect them. Of course, removing any plant, whole or in part, is strictly forbidden by law.

There's no predicting the *desierto florido*, which is relatively rare – the frequency and intensity varies enormously, but the general phenomenon seems to occur every four to five years. According to local experts, 1997 and 2002 saw particularly memorable displays and some claim that 2004 was also a good year, but spring rainfall has undoubtedly been diminishing. The best **guide** in Vallenar, and a veritable gold-mine of information about the dozens of flower varieties, is Roberto Alegría (☏51/613908, ✉ralegria@terra.cl).

towards the Peruvian border. Just to the north of the city, Arabian–style dunes await exploration.

When Diego de Almagro made his long trek south from Cuzco in 1536, following the Inca Royal Road down the spine of the Andes, it was into this valley that he descended, recuperating from the gruelling journey at the *tambo*, or resting place, where Copiapó now stands. The valley had been occupied and cultivated by the Diaguita people starting around 1000 AD and then was inhabited, beginning around 1470, by the Inca, who mined gold and copper here. Although Spanish *encomenderos* (see p.496) occupied the valley from the beginning of the conquest, it wasn't until 1744 that the city of Copiapó was founded, initially as "San Francisco de la Selva". A series of random silver strikes in the nineteenth century, most notably at Chañarcillo, threw the region into a frenzied boom.

Following a period of decline at the beginning of the twentieth century, Copiapó is once more at the centre of a rich mining industry, revolving around copper, iron and gold. A lively, busy city of some 100,000 inhabitants, it has a fairly compact downtown composed of typical adobe houses, some churches and the odd mansion, with a large, tree-filled square at its centre.

There isn't a great deal to do here, however, and Copiapó's main use to travellers is as a springboard for excursions into the surrounding region – primarily up to the lakes and volcanoes of **Parque Nacional Nevado de Tres Cruces** and nearby **Volcán Ojos de Salado** and **Laguna Verde**, all sitting high in the Andes, or west into the famously beautiful seaside resort of **Bahía Inglesa**, or north to the marine wildlife and coastal scenery of **Parque Nacional Pan de Azúcar**. Closer at hand, the **Río Copiapó Valley** is a popular day-trip and one of the most stunning examples of desert irrigation in Chile. Unlike the more famous Elqui Valley, it's not marred by the nylon windbreakers and protective netting used to protect grape vines from wind damage.

Arrival and information

Copiapó's main **bus terminal**, served by most inter-city buses, is centrally located on the corner of Freire and Chacabuco, three blocks south of Plaza Prat. Next door, also on Chacabuco, is the **Tur Bus terminal**, while one block east, at Freire and Colipí, sits the **Pullman Bus terminal**. The new Desierto de Atacama **international airport** is just over 50km west of the city, at Chamomate, not far from Caldera. There are a few options for getting from the airport to the centre, both the Manuel Flores Salinas **minibus** and Casther **bus** meet arriving planes and both will take you into town for CH$5000; a taxi will set you back CH$12,000–18,000.

A well-organized, helpful **Sernatur** office sits on the north side of Plaza Prat, at Los Carrera 691 (Mon–Fri 8.30am–5.30pm, ☎52/212838, ✉infoatacama @sernatur.cl). **Conaf**, at Juan Martínez 56 (Mon–Fri 9am–1pm & 2.30–5.30pm; ☎52/213404), will give you information on protected areas in this region, including Pan de Azúcar and Nevado de Tres Cruces national parks; it's also a good source of information on road conditions in the altiplano.

Accommodation

Copiapó has an excellent choice of upmarket **hotels** offering the levels of comfort and service you would expect, but rarely get, for the price. Decent mid-priced options, on the other hand, are thin on the ground, but there are plenty of adequate budget rooms. Having said this, it is still advisable to book accommodation in advance, rooms often fill up midweek with out-of-town business-people and miners.

Hotel La Casona O'Higgins 150
☎52/217277, ⓦwww.lacasonahotel.cl. This small, charming and impeccably decorated hotel has an English-speaking owner and serves excellent breakfasts, included in the rate. **⑤**
Hotel Chagall O'Higgins 760 ☎52/213775 ⓦwww.chagall.cl. Modern hotel with an attractive lobby and bar, spacious, new-looking rooms, smart baths, a good restaurant and private parking. **⑦**
Hotel Palace Atacama 741 ☎52/212852, ⓕ52/215079. Reasonable but overpriced rooms with private bath around an attractive patio; try bargaining the rate down. **⑤**

Hotel Montecatini I Infante 766 ☎52/211363, ⓕ52/217021. Bright, spacious rooms falling into two classes: smart, new *ejecutivo* and older but cheaper *turista*, both with private bath. Has its own parking. **④**
Residencial Ben Bow Rodriguez 541 ☎52/217634. Cramped but perfectly fine little rooms, some with private bath. **③**
Residencial Casagrande Infante 525 ☎52/244450. Spacious yet dingy rooms off a shabby central courtyard that are among the cheapest in town. The two rooms off the back patio are the nicest. **②**

The City

The nucleus of Copiapó is the large, green **Plaza Prat**, lined with 84 towering old pepper trees planted in 1880. On the southwest corner of the square stands the mid-nineteenth-century **Iglesia Catedral**, designed by the English architect

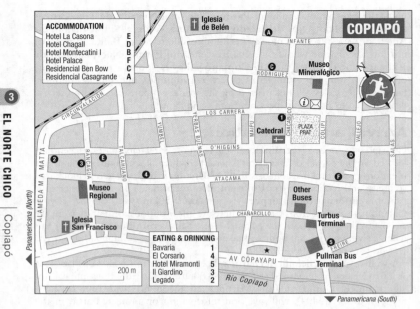

ACCOMMODATION
Hotel La Casona	E
Hotel Chagall	D
Hotel Montecatini I	B
Hotel Palace	F
Residencial Ben Bow	C
Residencial Casagrande	A

Iglesia de Belén

COPIAPÓ

INFANTE

Museo Mineralógico

RODRIGUEZ

LOS CARRERA

Catedral PLAZA PRAT

O'HIGGINS

ATACAMA

Museo Regional

Other Buses

CHAÑARCILLO

Turbus Terminal

Iglesia San Francisco

0   200 m

AV COPAYAPU

Pullman Bus Terminal

Río Copiapó

EATING & DRINKING
Bavaria	1
El Corsario	4
Hotel Miramonti	5
Il Giardino	3
Legado	2

Panamericana (North)

Panamericana (South)

William Rogers, sporting a Neoclassical three-door portico and topped by an unusual tiered wooden steeple. Just off the northeast corner of the square, at the corner of Colipí and Rodriguez, the University of Atacama's **Museo Mineralógico** (Mon–Fri 10am–1pm & 3.30–7pm, Sat 10am–1pm; CH$500) displays a glittering collection of over two thousand mineral samples from around the world, including huge chunks of malachite, amethyst, quartz, marble and onyx; it's a real pity that the museum is so poorly presented, with virtually no explanations or guides of any kind. Five blocks west of the square, at Atacama and Rancagua, the **Museo Regional** (Dec–Feb Mon–Fri 9am–7.30pm, Sat 11am–2pm & 4–7pm, Sun 11am–2pm; March–Nov Mon 2–5.45pm, Tues–Fri 9am–5.45pm, Sat 10am–1pm & 3–5.45pm, Sun 10am–1pm; CH$600) repays a visit, not least for the handsome mansion that houses it, the **Casa Matta**, built in the 1840s for one of Copiapó's wealthy mining barons. The museum's well-presented displays cover the exploration of the desert, the development of mining, the War of the Pacific, pre-Columbian peoples of the region and the Inca road system.

Towering over a tiny square that is the site of a busy Friday market selling fresh produce and household items, the imposing, red-walled 1872 **Iglesia San Francisco** sits one block south and west of the museum. The square's centre is marked by a statue of a rough-clad miner, tools in hand – none other than **Juan Godoy**, the goatherd who accidentally discovered the enormous silver deposits of nearby Chañarcillo in 1832, now honoured in Copiapó as a local legend.

Eating, drinking and entertainment

Copiapó's **restaurants** are, bar a couple of exceptions (see opposite), notably uninspiring, but most of them are moderately priced. For cheap snacks, head for the row of cafés on Chacabuco, opposite the bus terminal – the least insalubrious is *Don Elías*. The **nightlife** scene is not what you'd call swinging, but if you're set on dancing you could try one of the city's **discos**: *Mr Froggy* at Juan Martínez 46 is a perennial favourite.

Restaurants

Bavaria West side of Plaza Prat. Conveniently located branch of the ubiquitous chain serving sandwiches, snacks and meat dishes.

El Corsario Atacama 245. Old-fashioned restaurant with tables around the interior patio of an old adobe house. Offers basic Chilean dishes such as *pastel de choclo* and *humitas*.

Hotel Miramonti Ramón Freire 731, opposite Pullman Bus terminal. This elegant hotel restaurant serves decent but quite expensive Italian food – then spoils it all with appalling music.

Il Giardino Rancagua 341. Pretty, colourful new restaurant with a young chef who prepares tasty fish, salads and pastas. Opens in the evenings and for popular Sunday lunches.

Legado O'Higgins 20. Intimate and friendly, this owner-run restaurant offers pricy yet good-quality meat and fish dinners.

Listings

Airlines LAN, Los Carrera and Colipí, on the northeast corner of the main square ☏52/213512, and nearby Sky Airlines, 526 Colipí ☏52/214640.

Banks and exchange There are several ATMs on the main square, including Corp Banca at Chacabuco 481 and BCI at Chacabuco 449. Intercambios Limitada is the only *casa de cambio* in town, located on the first floor of the Mall Plaza Real off the main square at Colipí 484.

Camping gear Bencina blanca (white gas) and butane gas are available at Ferretería El Herrerito, Atacama 699. Dolomiti, 469 Atacama, has a range of Camping Gaz appliances and other outdoor stuff.

Car Rental Rodaggio, Colipí 127 (☏52/212153, @rodaggio@entelchile.net), has good-value 4x4 jeeps. Most other firms are situated on Ramón Freire, including Carmona at no. 466 ☏52/216030, @carmonarentacar@entelchile.cl; Budget at no. 50 ☏52/216272, @www.budget.cl; and Salfa Rent at no. 330 ☏52/200400, @www.salfa.cl. Hertz is on the opposite side of the highway at Copayapú 173 ☏52/213522, @www.autorenta.cl.

Internet Meg@net at 599 Los Carrera has a good connection for CH$400 per hour.

Post office North side of Plaza Prat at Los Carrera 691.

Around Copiapó

The region around Copiapó features some of the most striking and varied landscapes in Chile. To the east, the **Río Copiapó Valley** offers the extraordinary spectacle of emerald-green vines growing in desert-dry hills, while high up in the Andes, you'll ascend a world of salt flats, volcanoes and lakes,

---

Tours from Copiapó

A handful of companies and individuals offer tours out of Copiapó. Operators come and go, the best providing professional guides, others offering little more than glorified drivers. The main full-day destinations are east into the cordillera, taking in **Parque Nacional Nevado de Tres Cruces** and sometimes **Laguna Verde** and **Ojos de Salado** (see p.191); and north to **Parque Nacional Pan de Azúcar** (see p.197). Half-day trips go north into the **Atacama dunes**, west to the **beaches** around **Bahía Inglesa** (see p.195), or east up the **Copiapó River Valley** (see p.192). Ask at Sernatur in Copiapó for a list of guides.

Maximiliano Martínez of Aventurismo, at Atacama 410 (☏52/316395, @www.aventurismo.cl) has been taking tourists up to Ojos de Salado, Laguna Verde and around for longer than anyone else in the business; trips to Laguna Verde and Laguna Santa Rosa cost around US$75 per person, minimum four. An excellent newcomer is Gran Atacama at Colipí 484, Mall Plaza Real 122 (☏52/219271, @www.granatacama.cl); this highly professional outfit with enthusiastic, informed guides offers half-day excursions or trips lasting a day, several days, a week or more, covering the whole region with a blend of adventure, culture and luxury. A three-night tour of the parks and coast costs around CH$400,000 per person.

encompassed by the **Parque Nacional Nevado de Tres Cruces**, the **Volcán Ojos de Salado** and the blue-green **Laguna Verde**. To the west, **Bahía Inglesa**, near the port of **Caldera**, could be a little chunk of the Mediterranean, with its pristine sands and odd-shaped rocks rising out of the sea. Further south, reached only in a 4x4, the coast is lined with wild, deserted **beaches** lapped by turquoise waters.

Río Copiapó Valley

Despite an acute shortage of rainfall, the **RÍO COPIAPÓ VALLEY** is one of the most important grape-growing areas of Chile. This is thanks mainly to new irrigation techniques that have been developed over the past fifteen years, tapping into the valley's abundance of underground flowing water. The combination of computer-controlled irrigation and a hot, dry climate ensures an early harvest, with the grapes on US supermarket shelves by October. While the Copiapó Valley is not quite as pastoral or picturesque as the Elqui Valley, its cultivated areas provide, more than anywhere else in the north, the most stunning contrast between deep-green produce and parched, dry earth – from September to May, in particular, it really is a sight to behold.

Parque Nacional Nevado de Tres Cruces and around

East of Copiapó, the Andes divide into two separate ranges – the Cordillera de Domeyko and the Cordillera de Claudio Gay – joined by a high basin, or plateau, that stretches all the way north to Bolivia. The waters trapped in this basin form vast salt flats and lakes towered over by enormous, snow-capped volcanoes, and wild vicuña and guanaco roam the sparsely vegetated hills. This is a truly awe-inspiring landscape, conveying an acute sense of wilderness and space. It's easier to fully appreciate it here than around San Pedro de Atacama, for instance, thanks to the general absence of tourists. The number of visitors has started to increase, however, following the creation in 1994 of the new **Parque Nacional Nevado de Tres Cruces**, which takes in a dazzling white salt flat, the **Salar de Maricunga**; two beautiful lakes, the **Laguna Santa Rosa** and **Laguna del Negro Francisco**; and the 6753-metre volcano, **Tres Cruces**.

Close to but not part of the park, by the border with Argentina, the stunning, blue-green **Laguna Verde** lies at the foot of the highest active volcano in the world, the 6893-metre **Volcán Ojos de Salado**. From Copiapó, it's about a three-hour drive to Laguna Santa Rosa, and a six-hour drive to Laguna Verde. Temperatures are low at all times of year, so take plenty of warm gear. There is no public transport to this area – for information on **tours** here see p.191.

Moving on from Copiapó

Copiapó has daily **bus services** to Santiago and Arica and all the major cities in between, as well as to local and regional destinations. **Inter-city** services are offered by all the main companies, including Flota Barrios (☏52/213645), Pullman Bus (☏52/212977), Expreso Norte (☏52/231176) and Tur Bus (☏52/218612). For **Caldera** and **Bahía Inglesa**, Casther (☏52/218889) runs a frequent service (about every 30min) from the corner of Esperanza and Chacabuco, opposite the Líder Hypermarket. Casther also has around seven daily buses up the **Copiapó River Valley**, which is also served by Abarán buses. Alternately you can catch one of the yellow *colectivos* (CH$2,500) that wait on the same corner opposite Líder.

Parque Nacional Nevado de Tres Cruces

The bumpy road up to **PARQUE NACIONAL NEVADO DE TRES CRUCES** (CH$3500) takes you through a brief stretch of desert before twisting up narrow canyons flanked by mineral-stained rocks. As you climb higher, the colours of the scoured, bare mountains become increasingly vibrant, ranging from oranges and golds to greens and violets. Some 165km from Copiapó, at an altitude of around 3700m, the road (following the signs to Mina Marta) reaches the first sector of the park, skirting the pale-blue **Laguna Santa Rosa**, home to dozens of pink flamingos. A track branching north of the road leads to a tiny wooden **refugio** maintained by Conaf on the western shore of the lake. It's a basic but convenient place to camp (no bunk beds, floor space only), with its own private views of the lake backed by the snow-capped **Volcán Tres Cruces**.

Immediately adjacent, the gleaming white **Salar de Maricunga** is Chile's most southerly salt flat, covering an area of over 80 square kilometres. A two- to three-hour drive south from here, past Mina Marta, the park's second sector is based around the large, deep-blue **Laguna del Negro Francisco**, some 4200m above sea level and home to abundant birdlife, including wild ducks and flamingos. Towering over the lake, the 6080-metre **Volcán Copiapó** was the site of an Inca sacrificial altar. Conaf has its park headquarters and a large, comfortable **refugio** (❷) about 4km from the lake; the *guardaparques* are very friendly and take visitors on educational excursions to the lake and around, but if you want to stay over check with Conaf in Copiapó first.

Laguna Verde and Volcán Ojos de Salado

The first, sudden sight of **LAGUNA VERDE** is stupendous. The intense colour of its waters – green or turquoise, depending on the time of day – almost leaps out at you from the muted browns and ochres of the surrounding landscape. The lake lies at an altitude of 4500m, about 250km from Copiapó on the international road to Argentina (follow the signs to Paso San Francisco or Tinogasta). At the western end of the lake, a small shack contains a fabulous **hot-spring bath**, where you can soak and take blissful refuge from the biting wind outdoors. The best place to camp is just outside the bath, where a stone wall offers some protection from the wind, and hot streams provide useful washing-up water. At the lake's eastern end there's a *carabineros* checkpoint, where you should make yourself known if you plan to camp.

Laguna Verde is surrounded by huge volcanoes: Mulas Muertas, Incahuasi and the monumental **OJOS DE SALADO**. At 6893m, this is the highest peak in Chile and the highest active volcano in the world; its last two eruptions were in 1937 and 1956. A popular climb (between Oct and May), it's not technically difficult, apart from the last 50m that border the crater. The base of the volcano is a twelve-kilometre walk from the abandoned *carabineros* checkpoint on the main road, and there are two *refugios* on the way up, one at 5100m and another at 5750m. If you need to arrange transport to the base, or a guide for the ascent, contact Maximiliano Martínez or his son Sebastián at Aventurismo (see p.191). As the volcano sits on the border with Argentina, climbers need to present written permission from the Dirección de Fronteras y Límites plus a Permiso Regional, obtained from the tourist office, to the *carabineros* before climbing up.

Caldera

Just over 70km west from Copiapó, **CALDERA** is a small, easygoing seaside town with a smattering of nineteenth-century buildings, a beach, a pier and a few good fish restaurants. Chosen as the terminus of Chile's first railway by mining and railway pioneer William Wheelwright, it became the country's second-largest port in the last decades of the nineteenth century, when it exported all the silver extracted in the region's dramatic silver boom. Caldera's two ports are still busy – one exporting table grapes, the other exporting copper – but they don't totally dominate the bay, which remains fairly attractive and clean. The town's only landmarks are the Gothic-towered **Iglesia de San Vicente** on the main square, built by English carpenters in 1862, and the former **train station** at the pier, dating from 1850 and looking a little sorry for itself these days. The **pier**, down by the beach, makes for a pleasant stroll and is the starting point for **boat rides** around the bay in summer. Caldera's main **beach** is the sheltered, mid-sized Copiapina, while to the west of the pier, the large, windswept Playa Brava stretches towards the desert sands of the Norte Grande.

Practicalities

Caldera is a one-hour **bus** ride from Copiapó. The most frequent service is provided by Casther; buses leave from the corner of Esperanza and Chacabuco, opposite the Líder Hypermarket, arriving in Caldera at a small terminal at the corner of Cifuentes and Ossa Varas. **Sernatur** has a summer-time kiosk (unfixed hours) on Calle Gana, by the seafront; otherwise, try the Municipalidad on the plaza.

The town has a reasonable spread of **accommodation**. The nicest budget choice is probably *Residencial Millaray*, on the plaza at Cousiño 331 (☎52/315528, ✉rubenhmarre@yahoo.es; ❸), which has simple, airy rooms (some without bath) looking onto a leafy patio. The similarly priced *Hotel Costanera*, on the

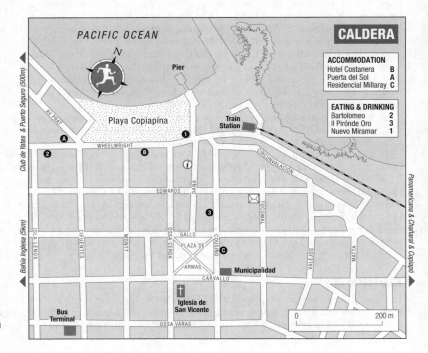

seafront at Wheelwright 543 (T 52/316007, E hotelcostanera@entelchile
.net; ❹) has spacious, clean rooms, some with sea views, and its own parking.
Caldera's best hotel, the *Puerta del Sol*, at Wheelwright 750 (T 52/315205,
E hosteriapuertadelsol@gmail.com; ❺), features a mix of smart and dowdy
rooms, and an attractive outdoor restaurant and pool area.

Many of Caldera's **restaurants** specialize in fish and shellfish. The best in
town is the down-to-earth *Il Pirón de Oro*, Cousiño 218, which serves
imaginatively prepared dishes, including exquisite dressed crab. *Nuevo Miramar*
isn't quite as good (locals claim, disapprovingly, that they use frozen fish), but
has a better location, right on the beach, with wonderful ocean views. Finish off
your evening at *Bartolomeo*, a mellow **pub-café** at Wheelwright 747, which
often has live jazz, folk or blues at the weekend.

There's a **phone office** at Edwards 360, while the **post office** is up the road
at no. 339. The BCI **bank** opposite the *Nuevo Miramar* has an ATM.

Bahía Inglesa and the southern coast

The **beaches** of **Bahía Inglesa** are probably the most photographed in Chile,
adorning wall calendars up and down the country. More than their white,
powdery sands – which, after all, you can find the length of Chile's coast – it's
the exquisite clarity of the turquoise sea, and the curious rock formations that
rise out of it, that sets these beaches apart.

Several beaches are strung along the bay to the north of Caldera, separated
by rocky outcrops: the long Playa Machas is the southernmost beach, followed
by Playa La Piscina, then by Playa El Chuncho and finally Playa Blanca.
Surprisingly, this resort area has not been swamped by the kind of ugly, large-
scale construction that mars Viña del Mar and La Serena, and Bahía Inglesa
remains a fairly compact collection of *cabañas* and a few hotels. While the place
gets hideously crowded in the height of summer, at most other times it's
peaceful and relaxing.

Practicalities

The problem with staying here is that **accommodation** tends to be ridicu-
lously overpriced, but you should be able to bargain the rates down outside
summer. *Cabañas Villa Alegre*, at the corner of Avenida El Morro and Valparaíso
(T 52/315074; ❻), offers humble but well-equipped cabins whilst neighbouring
El Coral (T 52/315331; ❺) has comfortable rooms, two of them with good sea
views, and an excellent, unpretentious fish restaurant. Further along Avenida El
Morro, *Apart-Hotel Rocas de Bahía* (T 52/316005, W www.rocasdebahia.cl; ❼) is
a whitewashed apartment block overlooking the ocean, with a pleasant pool and
a good restaurant. Back from the beachfront, three blocks behind *El Coral* at
Copiapó 100, *Los Jardines de Bahía Inglesa* (T 52/315359, W www.jardinesbahia
.cl; ❺) has smart *cabañas* and a decent restaurant serving Italian-influenced fare.
Camping Bahía Inglesa (T & F 52/315424; CH$18,000 per site) is an expensive
campsite just off Playa Las Machas.

Two **eateries** of note along the seafront are *El Plateado*, the most bohemian
restaurant in town with deck chairs on a sandy terrace serving international
cuisine including flavoursome curries; and, at the end of the promenade, *El
Domo*, a futuristic tent-like cupola, inside which you can try some adventurous
cuisine, or just linger over a real coffee or a drink. Behind the main dome, are
three mini-dome ⅔ *cabañas* (T 52/316168, W www.changochile.cl; ❺), which,
with their huge beds, private bathrooms and proximity to softly crashing ocean
waves, make fantastic places to lay your head for the night.

You can also simply visit Bahía Inglesa for the day from Caldera, just 6km away; plenty of **buses** and **colectivos** (leaving from Caldera's central square) connect the two resorts, and also Copiapó. The best place to catch a *colectivo* back to Caldera is at the crossroads by *Los Jardines de Bahía Inglesa*; be aware that these are few and far between in the off-season.

The southern coast

South of Bahía Inglesa, beyond the little fishing village of Puerto Viejo that marks the end of the paved road, the coast is studded with a string of **superb beaches** lapped with crystal-clear water and backed by immense sand dunes. The scenery is particularly striking around **Bahía Salada**, a deserted bay indented with tiny coves some 130km south of Bahía Inglesa. You might be able to find a tour operator that arranges excursions to these beaches, but if you really want to appreciate the solitude and wilderness of this stretch of coast, you're better off renting a jeep and doing it yourself.

Parque Nacional Pan de Azúcar and around

North of Copiapó and Caldera, the first stop on the Panamericana is **Chañaral**, a drab, uninviting town useful principally as a base for visiting **Parque Nacional Pan de Azúcar**, 30km up the coast, with towering cliffs, unspoilt wildlife and fine beaches. Back on the highway, four hundred empty kilometres stretch north to the city of Antofagasta (see p.208), broken only by the small, neglected fishing town of **Taltal**, 135km on from Chañaral.

Chañaral

Sitting by a wide, white bay and the Panamericana, **CHAÑARAL**, 167km north of Copiapó, is a rather sorry-looking town of houses staggered up a hillside, with more than its fair share of stray dogs. Originally a small *caleta* used for shipping out the produce of an inland desert oasis, it still serves chiefly as an export centre, these days for the giant El Salvador copper mine, 130km east in the cordillera. Despite efforts to clean it up, Chañaral's huge beach remains contaminated with the toxic wastes deposited by the mine.

You can visit the **Parque Nacional Pan de Azúcar** from Chañaral, although it is preferable to visit the park as a day-trip from Copiapó. Many north–south buses make a stop in the town; those that don't will drop you off if you ask. **Accommodation** choices are quite limited, such as the basic but clean and bright *Hotel Jiménez* on the main street at Merino Jarpa 551 (☎52/480328; ❸; all with cable TV, some with private bath), and the marginally better-value *Residencial Sutivan* at Comercio 365 (☎52/489123; ❸), with comfortable rooms at the back looking down to the ocean. By far the nicest place to stay is the *Hostería Chañaral* (☎52/480050, ✉hosteriachanaral@yahoo.com; ❺) with well-maintained rooms off a pleasant, plant-filled garden with private baths and plenty of hot water. There's also an internet connection, a games room and the town's most decent restaurant serving good seafood. Other than here, options for **eating** are uninspiring: try *Nuria* on the main square, opposite the church, or the busy *El Rincón Porteño* at Merino Jarpa 567; both serve basic Chilean staples like fried fish and *lomo con papas* (steak and chips).

Parque Nacional Pan de Azúcar

Home to two dozen varieties of cactus, guanacos and foxes, and countless birds, **PARQUE NACIONAL PAN DE AZÚCAR** is a 40-kilometre strip of desert containing the most stunning coastal scenery in the north of Chile. Steep hills and cliffs rise abruptly from the shore, which is lined with a series of pristine sandy beaches, some of them of the purest white imaginable. Though bare and stark, these hills make an unforgettable sight as they catch the late afternoon sun, when the whole coastline is bathed in rich shades of gold, pink and yellow. The only inhabited part of the park is **Caleta Pan de Azúcar**, 30km north of Chañaral, where you'll find a cluster of twenty or so fishermen's shacks as well as the Conaf information centre and a campsite (see p.198). Opposite the village, 2km off the shore, the **Isla Pan de Azúcar** is a small island sheltering a huge collection of marine wildlife, including seals, sea otters, plovers, cormorants, pelicans and more than three thousand Humboldt penguins; you can (and should – it's well worth it) take a boat trip out to get a close look at the wildlife. The island's distinctive conical silhouette gives the park its name "sugarloaf". For fabulous panoramic views up and down the coast, head to **Mirador Pan de Azúcar**, a well-signposted lookout point 10km north of the village; the different varieties of cactus are fascinating and you may have the place all to yourself – unless you're joined by a curious grey fox or guanaco. More difficult to reach, and less rewarding, **Las Lomitas** is a 700-metre-high clifftop about 30km north of the village; it's almost permanently shrouded in mist and is the site of a large black net, or "fog catcher", that condenses fog into water and collects it below.

Practicalities

There are two **access roads** to the park, both branching off the Panamericana: approaching from the south, the turn-off is at the north end of Chañaral, just past the cemetery; from the north, take the turn-off at Las Bombas, 45km north of Chañaral. Both roads are bumpy but passable in a car. There is no **public transport** to the park, but Chango Turismo (☎52/481107, ⓔchangoturismo @hotmail.com) runs a **bus** (CH$3000) to Caleta Pan de Azúcar from Chañaral;

▲ Parque Nacional Pan de Azúcar

it leaves at 9am and 3pm from opposite the Pullman Bus terminal, at Freire 493, and returns from the park at 10am and 5pm (phone to confirm times). Chango Turismo also runs guided **jeep tours** to all the sights in the park for CH$25,000 per person. Alternatively you could get a **taxi** (between CH$10,000–15,000 each way from Chañaral; worth it if there are several in your group), or you can also come on a **day-trip** from Copiapó.

The **Conaf information centre** (daily 8.30am–12.30pm & 2–6pm, Jan–Feb 8am–12.30pm & 2–9pm), near the village, offers maps, leaflets and souvenirs. This is where you pay your park fee (CH$3500). **Camping** areas are available on the beaches around the village (CH$10,000 per site), as well as two beautifully located *cabañas* (⑤) on a secluded beach to the north. At Playa Piqueros, further south, a couple of concessions offer camping along the beach – *Camping Los Piqueros* (CH$3500 per person) has the most facilities and also few simple *cabañas*. Rough camping is not allowed in the park. A small shop in the village sells basic foods, fish and water but you are advised to bring most things yourself. There's also a little café on the water's edge serving fried fish, rice and empanadas. **Boat trips** to the island depart from the *caleta* and cost CH$5000 per person (minimum ten people) or CH$50,000 per boat trip. It takes about ninety minutes to do the circuit; the best times are around 7 or 8am and 6pm, when the penguins come out to eat. Ask in the village for Segundo Lizana, Manuel Carasco or Alex Guerra who all offer the same trip at the standard price.

Travel details

Buses

Chañaral to: Antofagasta (15 daily; 5hr); Arica (5 daily; 15hr); Calama (10 daily; 8hr); Chuquicamata (2 daily; 8hr 20min); Copiapó (10 daily; 2hr); Iquique (8 daily; 11hr); La Serena (10 daily; 6hr); Mejillones (2 daily; 5hr 40min); Ovalle (10 daily; 9hr); Santiago (16 daily; 14hr); Taltal (2 daily; 2hr 30min); Tocopilla (2 daily; 8hr); Vallenar (14 daily; 4hr).

Copiapó to: Antofagasta (15 daily; 7hr); Arica (11 daily; 16hr); Calama (12 daily; 9hr 30min); Caldera (every 30min; 1hr); Chañaral (10 daily; 2hr); Iquique (12 daily; 13hr); La Serena (20 daily; 4hr); Ovalle (6 daily; 5hr 30min); Santiago (22 daily; 12hr); Vallenar (10 daily; 1hr 45min); Valparaíso (6 daily; 12hr).

La Serena to: Antofagasta (15 daily; 11hr); Arica (8 daily; 18hr); Calama (14 daily; 12hr 30min); Chañaral (7 daily; 6hr); Copiapó (20 daily; 4hr); Iquique (9 daily; 16hr); Montegrande (6 daily; 2hr 20min); Ovalle (18 daily; 1hr); Pisco Elqui (6 daily; 2hr 30min); Santiago (every 30min; 7hr); Vallenar (15 daily; 2hr 20min); Valparaíso (8 daily; 7hr); Vicuña (every 30min; 1hr 30min).

Ovalle to: Andacollo (4 daily; 2hr); Antofagasta (10 daily; 11hr); Arica (1 daily; 19hr); Calama (13hr); Chañaral (10 daily; 7hr); Copiapó (10 daily; 5hr); Iquique (2 daily; 19hr); La Serena (18 daily; 1hr); Los Vilos (6 daily; 2hr); Santiago (15 daily; 6hr); Vallenar (5 daily; 4hr).

Vallenar to: Alto del Carmen (5 daily; 1hr); Antofagasta (10 daily; 9hr); Calama (10 daily; 11hr); Caldera (3 daily; 3hr); Chañaral (10 daily; 3hr 30min); Copiapó (10 daily; 1hr 45min); Iquique (2 daily; 14hr); La Serena (15 daily; 2hr 20min); Ovalle (5 daily; 4hr); Santiago (26 daily; 9hr 30min).

Flights

Note that some of these routes require stopovers; the travel times listed include stopovers.

Copiapó to: Antofagasta (4 daily; 1hr 15min); Arica (2 daily; 2hr 35min); Calama (1 daily; 1hr 20min); Iquique (2 daily; 2hr); Santiago (6 daily; 1hr 15min). **La Serena** to: Antofagasta (1 daily; 1hr 15min); Santiago (3 daily; 1hr).

El Norte Grande

CHAPTER 4 # Highlights

✱ **Chuquicamata** Visit one of the world's biggest open-pit copper mines near Calama. See p.209

✱ **Valle de la Luna** Watch the setting sun heighten the textures and deepen the colours of the valley's sweeping dunes and undulating rock formations. See p.217

✱ **The Salar de Atacama** Explore the vast salt flats of the Atacama Desert, the driest place on Earth – parts of it never, ever see rain. See p.219

✱ **El Tatio** At 4300m, pools of boiling water send clouds of steam into the air at the crack of dawn. See p.220

✱ **Humberstone** Wander around an abandoned nitrate factory – an eerily well-preserved ghost town stranded in the desert. See p.228

✱ **The Pintados geoglyphs** Discover these mysterious, indigenous images, the largest collection of geoglyphs in South America. See p.228

✱ **Lauca and Isluga parks** Trek through a landscape of mineral baths, cobalt lakes, sparkling salt flats and spongy bogs at dizzying altitudes. See p.245 & p.233

✱ **Altiplano wildlife** Thousands of llamas and alpacas, vicuñas and vizcachas, flamingoes and condors – a photographer's dream. See p.245

▲ Salar de Atacama

El Norte Grande

Stretching away between the ocean and the great wall of the Andes, a seemingly endless belt of tawny sand, rock and mountain unfurls itself, more absolute and terrifying in its uncompromising aridity than the Sahara. The first glimpse of a strange land usually elates; but the sight of this grim desert oppresses the mind with a sense of singular desolation...It is only when the rays of the rising or setting sun kindle its sombre surface into the most gorgeous and improbable pink, purple, blue, crimson and orange that we feel the compelling fascination which all deserts exert.

Stephen Clissold, *Chilean Scrapbook*

Austerely beautiful, inhospitably arid and overwhelmingly vast, the **NORTE GRANDE** of Chile – sometimes referred to as the "Far North" – occupies almost a quarter of the country's mainland territory but contains barely five percent of its population. Its single most outstanding feature is the **Atacama Desert**, stretching all the way down from the Peruvian border for over 1000km; the driest desert in the world, it contains areas where no rainfall has been recorded – ever. With a few exceptions the landscape of this desert is not one of Arabian golden sand dunes, but rather of bare rock and gravel spread over a wide *pampa* or plain, almost shockingly barren – alleviated only by crinkly mountains that glow bronze at twilight. To the west, the plain is lined by a range of coastal hills that drop abruptly to a narrow shelf of land where most of the region's towns and cities – chiefly prosperous **Antofagasta**, lively **Iquique** and colourful **Arica** – are scattered, hundreds of kilometres apart. East, the desert climbs towards the cordillera, which rises to the **altiplano**: a high, windswept plateau composed of lakes and salt flats ringed with snow-capped volcanoes, forming a fabulous panorama.

It seems almost inconceivable that such a hostile land can support life, but for thousands of years El Norte Grande has been home to indigenous peoples who've wrested a living either from the sea or from the fertile oases that nestle in the Andean foothills. The excessive dryness of the climate has left countless relics of these people almost perfectly intact – most remarkably the **Chinchorro mummies** (see box, p.244), buried on the desert coast near Arica some seven thousand years ago. It wasn't until the nineteenth century that Chile's more recent inhabitants – along with British and German businesses – turned their attention to the Atacama, when it became apparent that the desert was rich in **nitrates** that could be exported at great commercial value. So lucrative was this burgeoning industry that Chile was prepared to go to war over it, for most of the region at that time in fact belonged to Bolivia and Peru. The **War of the Pacific**, waged against Bolivia and Peru between 1878 and 1883, acquired for Chile the desired prize, and the desert pampas went on to yield enormous

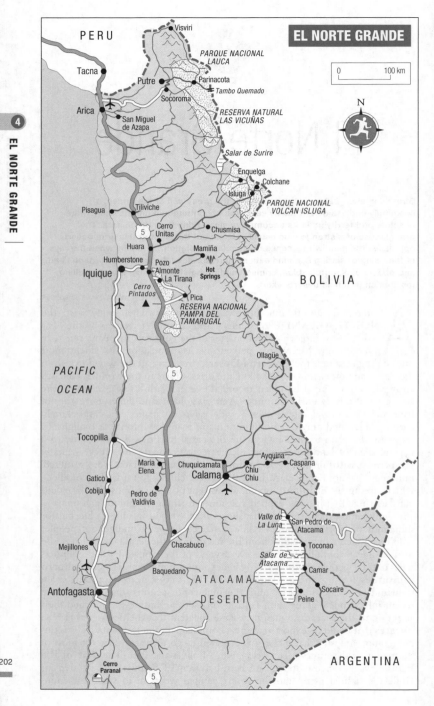

EL NORTE GRANDE

0   100 km

N

PERU

Tacna

Visviri

PARQUE NACIONAL
LAUCA

Putre   Parinacota
                   Tambo Quemado
      Socoroma

Arica

San Miguel
de Azapa

RESERVA NATURAL
LAS VICUÑAS

Salar de Surire

Enquelga
          Colchane
      Isluga

PARQUE NACIONAL
VOLCAN ISLUGA

Pisagua   Tiliviche

Cerro
Unitas   Chusmisa

Huara   Mamiña

Humberstone Pozo
Iquique   Almonte
             La Tirana

BOLIVIA

Hot
Springs

Cerro
Pintados   Pica

RESERVA NACIONAL
PAMPA DEL
TAMARUGAL

PACIFIC
OCEAN

Ollagüe

Tocopilla

Maria   Chuquicamata
Elena   Chiu
             Calama   Chiu

Ayquina
          Caspana

Gatico
Cobija   Pedro de
           Valdivia

Mejillones

Chacabuco

Valle de   San Pedro de
La Luna   Atacama

Toconao

Salar de
Atacama   Camar

Baquedano   ATACAMA

DESERT   Socaire

Antofagasta   Peine

ARGENTINA

Cerro
Paranal

5

revenues for the next three decades. With the German invention of synthetic nitrates at the end of World War I, Chile's industry entered a rapid decline, but a financial crisis was averted when new mining techniques enabled low-grade **copper**, of which there are huge quantities in the region, to be profitably extracted. Today, this mineral continues to play the most important role in the country's economy, accounting for forty percent of Chile's exports and making it the world's leading copper supplier.

Formidable and desolate as it is, the region contains a wealth of superb attractions, and for many constitutes the highlight of a trip to Chile – particularly European travellers, who will find nothing remotely like it back home. The Pacific seaboard is lined by vast tracts of stunning **coastal scenery**, while inland the **desert pampa** itself impresses not only with its otherworldly geography, but also with a number of fascinating testimonies left by man. One of these is the trail of decaying nitrate **ghost towns**, including **Humberstone** and **Santa Laura**, easily reached from Iquique. Another is the immense images known as **geoglyphs** left by indigenous peoples on the hillsides and ravines of the desert – you'll find impressive examples at **Cerro Pintados**, south of Iquique, **Cerro Unitas**, east of Huara, and **Tiliviche**, between Huara and Arica.

As you journey towards and up into the cordillera, you'll come across attractive **oasis villages**, some – such as **Pica** and **Mamiña** – with **hot springs**. Up in the Andes, the altiplano is undoubtedly one of the country's highlights, with its dazzling **lakes**, **salt flats and volcanoes**, its abundance of **wildlife** and its tiny, whitewashed villages inhabited by native Aymara. The main altiplano touring base – and, indeed, one of the most popular destinations in the whole country, for Chileans and foreigners alike – is **San Pedro de Atacama**, a pleasant oasis 315km northeast of Antofagasta, where numerous operators offer excursions to the famous **El Tatio geysers** and the haunting moonscapes of the **Valle de la Luna**. Further north, the stretch of altiplano within reach of Iquique and Arica boasts wild vicuña and spectacular scenery, preserved in **Parque Nacional Lauca** and several adjoining parks and reserves. The towns and cities of the Far North tend to be dreary and uninviting, but serve as unavoidable departure points for excursions into the hinterland.

Many of the region's attractions can be reached by **public transport**, though in order to explore the region in depth you'll need to book some tours or, better still, rent a 4WD vehicle. Whatever your mode of transport, don't underestimate the distances involved in getting to most points of interest, particularly in the altiplano. It makes sense to isolate a few chosen highlights rather than try to see everything, which would be interminably time-consuming.

You can visit the Far North at any time of year, but be aware that tour operators are at their busiest in July and August when most visitors from the northern hemisphere come and visit. Also bear in mind the **Bolivian Winter**, when sporadic heavy rains between December and February in the altiplano can wash roads away and seriously disrupt communications and access. Moreover, despite that, this is a busy period because it's the prime vacation time for Chileans.

Antofagasta and around

Many tourists bypass the decidedly lacklustre desert city of **ANTOFAGASTA** altogether, but as the regional capital it offers a variety of useful facilities – including banks, *cambios* and car-rental firms – and is a major transport hub.

A Bolivian town until 1879, when it was annexed by Chile in the War of the Pacific, Antofagasta is Chile's fifth largest and most rapidly growing city. It's also one of the most prosperous, serving as an export centre for the region's great mines, most notably Chuquicamata (see p.209). Sitting on a flat shelf between the ocean and the hills, Antofagasta has a compact downtown core, made up of dingy, traffic-choked streets that sport a few handsome old public buildings, and a modern stretch along the coastal avenue. On the way north, or as you head out to the airport, stop off at **La Portada**, an iconic natural arch of rock looming out of the sea.

South of the city centre the busy coastal avenue runs past a couple of tiny, coarse-sand **beaches**, first at the Balneario Municipal, then, much further south, at the Playa Huascar – take *micro* #103 from Washington, near the square. In this direction lie one of the city's most curious sights, the **Ruinas de Huanchaca**, vestiges of a disused silver refinery.

Arrival and information

If you're arriving by **bus**, you'll be dropped at one of several terminals, most within easy walking distance of downtown accommodation. The two main stations, where Tur Bus and Pullman operate, sit at opposite corners of Bolívar and Latorre. Coming in by **air**, you'll arrive at the Aeropuerto Cerro Moreno, 25km north of the city, right on the Tropic of Capricorn. From here, regular *colectivos* and infrequent *micros* head to the centre or you can take a minibus directly to your accommodation (they await every arrival).

For **tourist information**, head for the **Sernatur** office at Prat 384, on the ground floor of the Intendencia at the corner of the central plaza (Mon–Fri 8.30am–5.30pm; ℡&Ⓕ 55/451818–20, Ⓔinfoantofagasta@sernatur.cl). For details on the protected areas around San Pedro de Atacama, which lies within this region, visit the regional **Conaf office** at Av Argentina 2510 (Mon–Fri 9am–1pm & 2.30–5.30pm; ℡55/383320).

Accommodation

You'll find an abundance of **accommodation** in Antofagasta, but the range tends to jump from cheap and basic to expensive (and not necessarily good-quality), with very few mid-priced options in between. Most places are in the downtown core, with the mostly expensive hotels, catering primarily to business travellers, on the coastal avenue.

Casa El Mosaico C-18, Huascar Beach ℡9/9380743, Ⓦwww.chilegreentours.com. Near the beach, an easy bus ride south of the town centre. Best rooms are the upstairs' doubles with balconies and beds made from recycled train-track sleepers; downstairs are two cheaper, dormitory-style rooms. Canadian/Swiss-Chilean owners go out of their way to make your stay memorable offering diving trips, art classes, fresh fish dinners and more. ❷–❹

Frontera Hotel Bolívar 558 ℡55/281219. Best mid-range choice, offering spotless, modern rooms with private bath and cable TV. Some rooms can be noisy. ❹

Holiday Inn Express Av Grecia 1490, south of the centre ℡800/808080 or 55/228888. Modern,

super-clean American chain hotel, with pool and parking – a good place to pamper yourself if the desert is getting to you. It's connected to the centre by plenty of *micros*. ❼

Hotel Antofagasta Balmaceda 2575 ℡55/268259, Ⓕ55/264585. Large, venerable hotel overlooking the ocean, with well-furnished but overpriced rooms. ❽

Hotel Ciudad de Ávila Condell 2840 ℡55/221040. Simple, no-frills accommodation; most rooms have private bath and external windows. ❸

Hotel Colón San Martín 2434 ℡55/261851, Ⓕ55/260872. Clean, fairly comfortable rooms with private bath. ❺

Marzal Hotel Prat 867 ☎ 55/268063, ℗ 55/221733. Modern hotel offering spacious rooms with private bath and parking. ❺

Residencial El Cobre Prat 749 ☎ 55/225162. Huge *residencial* with 58 rooms, some airy and light, others dark and dingy. ❷

The City

In Antofagasta's centre sprawls the large, green **Plaza Colón**, dominated by a tall clock tower whose face is supposedly a replica of London's Big Ben – one of many tangible signs of the role played by the British in Antofagasta's commercial development. The city's administrative and public buildings, including the Neo-Gothic Iglesia Catedral, built between 1906 and 1917, surround the square. A couple of blocks northwest towards the port, along Bolívar, you'll find the magnificently restored nineteenth-century offices and railway terminus of the former Antofagasta and Bolivia Railway Company, complete with polished wooden verandas and dark-green stucco walls (but with no public access). Opposite, at the corner of Balmaceda and Bolívar, sits the 1866 customs house, or **Aduana**, the oldest building in the city. Inside, the Museo Regional (Tues–Sat 9am–5pm, Sun 11am–2pm; CH$600; ⓦ www.dibam.cl) houses an impressive mineral display downstairs

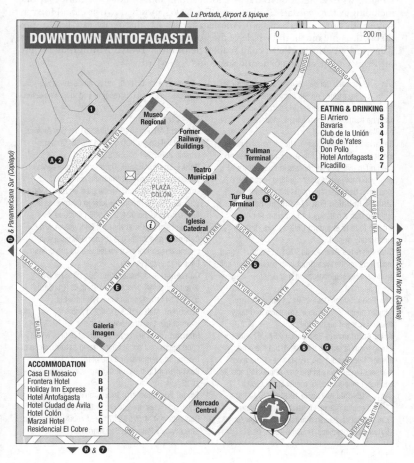

▲ La Portada, Airport & Iquique

DOWNTOWN ANTOFAGASTA

0   200 m

EATING & DRINKING
El Arriero	5
Bavaria	3
Club de la Unión	4
Club de Yates	1
Don Pollo	6
Hotel Antofagasta	2
Picadillo	7

Museo Regional

Former Railway Buildings

Pullman Terminal

Teatro Municipal

PLAZA COLÓN

Tur Bus Terminal

Iglesia Catedral

Galeria Imagen

Mercado Central

ACCOMMODATION
Casa El Mosaico	D
Frontera Hotel	B
Holiday Inn Express	H
Hotel Antofagasta	A
Hotel Ciudad de Ávila	C
Hotel Colón	E
Marzal Hotel	G
Residencial El Cobre	F

D & Panamericana Sur (Copiapó)

Panamericana Norte (Calama)

and, upstairs, a collection of clothes, furniture and general paraphernalia dating from the nitrate era. Also worth a visit is the **Galería del Arte Imagen** (Mon–Sat 10am–1pm & 5–9pm; free), a few blocks south of the plaza at Uribe in an old building that's seen better days. Run by a friendly señora, it's filled with an eclectic jumble of nineteenth-century antiques, lapis lazuli ornaments and colourful painting by local artists. At the opposite end of town, at the corner of Ossa and Maipú, the huge, pink-and-cream Mercado Central sells fresh food and *artesanía*.

Eating, drinking and entertainment

Antofagasta's **restaurants** tend to be busy and lively, with a couple of classy establishments standing out among the grill houses and pizzerias. On the coast just west of the town centre is the town's shiny new Mall Plaza, Balmaceda 2355, home to several newer eating establishments. Among these are the usual American fast-food outlets, but also a few more sophisticated options such as the trendy *Spell Café*, a cut above the rest with its Argentine-inspired menu, excellent Italian coffee and outdoor seating looking out to the ocean. The nightlife scene, thanks mainly to the number of university students around town, is surprisingly vibrant, with some good **bars** to choose from and a choice of **dance spots** including *X3*, *Kamikaze*, *El Sótano* and *Era 2000's*, mostly down at Playa Huascar, way south of town (take a taxi). Antofagasta also has that rarity in Chile, a **gay disco**, the only one in the whole of the north: *Underboys* is at Av Edmundo Pérez Zujovic 4800 (the northern coast road). The modern **Teatro Municipal** lies just off Plaza Colón, at the corner of Sucre and San Martín.

El Arriero Condell 2644. Two brothers play old jazz tunes on the piano every night at this inviting, Spanish-inn-style spot, complete with hanging hams. Try the excellent, moderately priced *parrilladas*.

Bavaria Sucre and Latorre. The same pine decor, the same grilled meat, the same indifferent service you find in every other *Bavaria* in the country. At least you know what you're getting – and the food's not bad, after all, nor is it expensive.

Club de la Unión Prat 474. The attractive building has a balcony and efficient service, but the food is standard Chilean fare, though moderately priced.

Club de Yates Balmaceda 2701 at Sucre. Elegant restaurant on the waterfront with ocean views and an expensive seafood-based menu, more imaginative than most.

Don Pollo Santos Ossa 2594 at Sucre. A very popular place serving up inexpensive and tasty chicken roasted on the spit.

Hotel Antofagasta Balmaceda 2575. The indoor dining room is empty and bland, but the outdoor terrace, overlooking the sea, is one of the most pleasant lunch spots in the city. Appetizing snacks and main meals at quite moderate prices.

Picadillo Av Grecia 1000 ☎55/247503. Popular oceanside restaurant offering the likes of beef carpaccio marinated in ginger for starters, and delicious, unusual sushi, plus

inventive desserts; both music and service are faultless. Reservations recommended at weekends.

Listings

Airlines LAN, Prat 445 ☎55/265151; Sky Airlines, General Velásquez 890 ☎55/459090; Comet, Washington 2548 ☎55/286507.

Banks and exchange There are several ATMs on the central square and the main commercial streets, including Prat, Washington and San Martín. You can change the major foreign currencies at Ancla, Baquedano 524, and US$ cash and traveller's cheques at Nortour, Baquedano 474.

Camping gas White gas (*bencina blanca*) and butane gas available at Andesgear on the ground floor of the Mall Plaza.

Car rental Avis, Baquedano 364 ☎55/563140, ✉antofagasta@avischile.cl; Budget, P.A. Cerda ☎55/214445, ✉antofagasta@budget.cl; Econorent, Maipú 363 ☎55/251745, ✉antofagasta@econorent.cl.

Internet There are several internet outlets with good prices and connections along Latorre, close to the Tur Bus terminal and the plaza.

Post office On the central square, at Washington 2613.

Travel agencies and tours You'll find many travel agencies downtown, including Nortour, Baquedano 474 ☎55/227171, ✉nortour@nortour .tie.cl; Viajes Palanisa, San Martín 2457

Moving on from Antofagasta

All the main **bus** companies offer services from Antofagasta up and down the **Panamericana**, and to **Calama**. There's a municipal central terminal at Argentina 1155, from where several companies operate, including Carmelita, Libac and Ramos Cholele, but many companies operate instead out of their own separate terminal, including: Frontera, Antofagasta 2041 ☏55/824269; Corsal, Condell 2746 ☏55/253377; Condor Bus, Bolivar 468 ☏55/262899; Géminis, Latorre 3055 ☏55/263968; Pullman Bus, Latorre 2805 ☏55/268838; Tur Bus, Latorre 2751 ☏55/220240. Direct **flights** go from Antofagasta to Calama, Iquique, Arica, La Serena, and Santiago and Sky Airlines has three weekly flights to Arequipa, Peru (see "Listings", opposite, for airlines). To get to the airport from downtown, take a taxi (CH\$10,000–12,000), or call Aerobus (☏55/262727) to order a minibus transfer (CH\$3500) to pick you up from your hotel or wherever.

☏55/561120, ✉patricia.alanis@entelchile.net; and Turismo Fenix, Washington 2562 ☏55/495141, ✉operadoresfenix@hotmail.com. For tours into the desert and along the coast, as well as scuba diving, tandem paragliding and trips to Cerro Paranal, try the excellent Chile Green Tours, run by the knowledgeable and enthusiastic owner of Casa El Mosaico ☏9/9380743, ⦿www.chilegreentours.com.

Ruinas de Huanchaca and La Portada

These remains of an old Bolivian silver refinery sit on a hilltop a short distance inland, 3km south of the city centre by the Universidad del Norte. The **RUINAS DE HUANCHACA** were built to process the silver brought down from the Potosí mine (at that time the most important silver mine in South America), before being shipped out of Antofagasta. Looking at the square and circular walls of the complex from below, you'd be forgiven for thinking they were ruins of a pre-Columbian fortress. Sadly, access to the site is limited, so you may have to make do with viewing it from the outside. To get there, take *micro* #2, #3, #4 or #10 from Prat.

A huge eroded arch looming out of the ocean, **La Portada** sits 16km north of Antofagasta along the coast road. Declared a national monument in 1990, the arch has become something of a regional symbol, and its picture graces postcards and wall calendars all over Chile. The upkeep of the site, however, is a disgrace: makeshift signs quite rightly warn you not to approach the crumbling cliffs or descend the rickety steps to the unsafe beach, while the nearby bar-restaurant and shops are often closed, even in high season, lending the place a sadly abandoned air.

To get here, take *micro* #15 from the Terminal Pesquero, or take one of the Mejillones-bound minibuses leaving from Bazar Acuario, at Latorre 2733, Bazar Mariela at Latorre 2727, or Bazar Mejillones, Latorre 2715 – all near the Tur Bus terminal. If you're driving, follow the coast road north and take the turn-off to Juan López, from where La Portada is well signed.

Cerro Paranal observatory

A little under two hours south of Antofagasta, perched on **Cerro Paranal** at 2644m above sea level, is the latest result of international space-watching one-upmanship, the **European Southern Observatory** (ESO). While you have to be a recognized researcher to stand any chance of looking through its **Very Large Telescope** (VLT), currently one of the world's strongest, on certain weekends you can visit the dazzling site, set among suitably lunar, and even Mars-like, landscapes of reddish rock. In fact, NASA tested the Mars Pathfinder rover in the nearby Atacama Desert. To get here, head south from Antofagasta on the Panamericana (Ruta 5); the unpaved turn-off 24km south of the Mina Escondida crossroads leads due south over a mountain pass to the observatory.

The European Southern Observatory

The ESO belongs to a multinational European space research agency and, rivalling US counterparts such as the CTIO at Cerro Tololo near Vicuña, currently holds the record for the **world's most powerful telescope**. Meanwhile the VLT – strictly speaking a set of four 8.2-metre telescopes, each weighing 430 tonnes, whose combined might enables observers to see objects as small as humans on the Moon – has been fully operational since 2001. It's housed in a futuristic-looking set of four trapezoidal cylinders dramatically located on the barren Cerro Paranal, which averages 330 clear nights a year. A luxurious 120-room residence (for scientists only), complete with a cafeteria and an indoor garden (both open to the public), stands nearby.

The observatory is open to the public on the last two weekends of every month except December. Visits last a couple of hours and should be booked well in advance, as numbers are limited (Jan–Nov last two weekends of the month, Sat & Sun 2pm; free; ☎55/435335, Ⓦwww.eso.org); the observatory receives some five thousand visitors annually. Remember to take warm clothing, as it is very cold inside the observatory. If you do not have your own transport, you can join an **organized tour** from Antofagasta; Chile Green Tours (see listings p.207) runs occasional trips (CH$15–20,000 per person, depending on numbers).

Another extremely powerful observatory in the region, the Atacama Large Millimeter Array (ALMA), a joint US, European and Japanese venture will come into operation in 2009. The ALMA will comprise 64 radio-telescopes using millimetre radio waves rather than the VLT's optical-infrared and will be positioned 5000m above sea level at a site east of San Pedro de Atacama.

The ESO is also planning a so-called "Overwhelmingly Large Telescope" (an ironic reference to the names "Very Large" and "Extremely Large" already applied to telescopes and with the appropriate acronym of OWL), possibly in the same site as the ALMA. If funded, the 100-metre optical near-infrared telescope would be operational around 2015.

The nitrate pampa

Northeast of Antofagasta, the vast *pampa salitrera*, or **NITRATE PAMPA**, pans across the desert towards the cordillera – it's not the prettiest landscape in the world, a mass of scruffy plains that look as though they have been ploughed, fertilized and then left for fallow. If you take this road towards Iquique, you can either branch off for Calama and San Pedro de Atacama, or continue north, passing close to the last remaining nitrate *oficinas* (or plants) at Pedro de Valdivia and María Elena. Between 1890 and 1925 there were over 80 *oficinas* here, extracting the nitrate ore and sending it down to the ports by railroad. Some of them are still standing, abandoned and in ruins, including Chacabuco, crumbling in the desert heat. Two highways cross the pampa: the Panamericana, heading due north, and Ruta 25, branching off northeast to the mining city of Calama.

The former skirts **Pedro de Valdivia** and **María Elena**, both of which can be reached on public transport. Although you can find basic accommodation if you look hard enough (mainly in María Elena), you may as well forge on if you can; these are desperately soulless places to spend the night.

The Chug Chug geoglyphs

The Panamericana is crossed by a lateral road, Ruta 24, 107km north of the Carmen Alto junction. This is connected to Tocopilla, 60km west, and Chuquicamata, 66km east. Just short of 50km along the road for Chuquicamata, a sign points north to the **CHUG CHUG GEOGLYPHS**, reached by a thirteen-kilometre dirt road that's just about passable in a car. These consist of some three hundred images spread over several hills, many of them clearly visible from below, including circles, zoomorphic figures, human faces and geometric designs. It's an impressive site, and certainly deserves a visit if you're driving in the area.

Calama and Chuquicamata

Sitting on the banks of the Río Loa, at an altitude of 2250m, **CALAMA** is a modern and rather bland town, whose chief role is as a service centre and residential base for **Chuquicamata**, the massive copper mine 16km north. It's a convenient place for sorting out money or doing laundry, and many visitors end up spending a night here on their way to or from San Pedro de Atacama, the famous oasis village and tourist centre 100km east.

Calama began life as a *tambo*, or resting place, at the intersection of two Inca roads – one running down the Andes, the other connecting the altiplano with the Pacific – and both Diego de Almagro and Pedro de Valdivia visited on their journeys into Chile. It was never heavily populated by pre-Hispanic peoples, who preferred nearby Chiu Chiu, with its less saline water supply. The town took on a new importance, however, as the stop on the Oruro–Antofagasta railway in 1892, and its future was sealed with the creation of the Chuquicamata copper mine in 1911. Today its busy streets are built around a surprisingly small and laid-back central core.

Check out the **Parque El Loa**, where you'll find the **Museo Arqueológico** (Tues–Fri 10am–1pm & 3–7.30pm, Sat & Sun 3–7pm; CH$500), with a mini reconstruction of Chiu Chiu's church and displays on local pre-Columbian history. To get to the park, take a *colectivo* – #5, #18 #80 – on Vicuña Mackenna at the corner of Latorre, or *micros* #1b, #1c or #1d from Vivar at Mackenna.

Practicalities

Arriving by **bus** you'll be dropped at your bus company's office, generally near the city centre; there's no single terminal. Tur Bus has a terminal of its own, inconveniently more than a kilometre north of town – a taxi will charge CH$2500–3000 to the city centre. Some companies drop off at the shopping mall, also north of the centre.

If you're **flying** to Calama you'll land at the Aeropuerto El Loa, 5km south of the centre – the only way into town from here is by taxi (CH$5000). **Trains** from Bolivia pull in at the conveniently located station, three blocks east of the plaza. At the municipal **Oficina de Turismo** opposite the Municipalidad, Latorre and Vicuña Mackenna (Mon–Fri 8am–1pm & 2–6pm; ☎55/531707),

you can get maps and other basic information, but not much else.

Calama has a wide range of **accommodation**, but many places are overpriced owing to the mining clientele. Nonetheless, local hotels can get fully booked during the San Pedro tourist seasons. Beware of overbooking and always call or send an email to confirm if possible. Good budget choices include *Residencial Toño*, at Vivar 1970 (℡55/341185; ❸), offering very simple rooms, some with bath, and *Hotel El Loa*, Abaroa 1617 (℡55/341963; ❸), with lots of basic but comfortable singles out the back, and a few doubles and triples in the main house. *Hotel El Mirador*, at Sotomayor 2064 (℡55/340329, ⓦwww .hotelmirador.cl; ❻), is a lovely, small hotel with spacious rooms – including one with a Victorian cast-iron bath – and attractive furnishings. At the top end of the scale, the overpriced *Park Hotel*, at Camino al Aeropuerto 1392 (℡55/319900, ⓦwww.parkplaza.cl; ❽), boasts elegant decor, a good restaurant and a swimming pool.

Most of Calama's **restaurants** offer reasonably priced, but not particularly inspiring fare. *Terramater*, just off Sotomayor, is an unlikely exception, with a more imaginative menu than most and a great wine list. Another good choice is the friendly and unpretentious *Restaurant Mariscal*, just a short walk from the plaza, that serves good, yet pricey, fish and seafood dishes. *Bavaria*, on the plaza, is part of a nationwide chain offering decent if predictable mid-price meat dishes and sandwiches from its downstairs café and upstairs restaurant.

You'll find plenty of **ATMs** on Sotomayor, as well as a *cambio* around the corner called Moon Valley at Vivar 1818. A number of companies **rent cars**: Avis, Aeropuerto (℡55/563153); Econorent, Latorre 2507 (℡55/341076); First, Antofagasta 2168 (℡55/556482); and Hertz, Granaderos 1416 (℡55/340018).

Chuquicamata

One of the world's largest open-pit copper mines, **CHUQUICAMATA** (16km north of Calama) produces 600,000 tonnes per year – outstripped only by Mina Escondida, 200km southeast of Antofagasta, whose capacity exceeds 800,000 tonnes. Carved out of the ground like a giant, sunken amphitheatre, the massive mine dwarfs everything within it, making the huge trucks carrying the ore up from the crater floor – whose wheels alone are an incredible 4m high – look like tiny, crawling ants. Its size is the result of some ninety years of excavation, and its reserves are predicted to last at least until the middle of the twenty-first century. Along with all of Chile's large-scale copper mines, or "*grandes minerías*" as they're called, Chuquicamata belongs to Codelco, the government-owned copper corporation. Codelco also used to maintain an adjacent company town, complete with its own school, hospital, cinema and football stadium, but the nine thousand workers and their families who lived there have now been moved to Calama, making way for further excavation.

As a result, the whole area is now an industrial site and visits can be arranged only with the official **guided tour** (Mon–Fri 1.30pm; free, but donations to a children's charity supported by the mine are welcomed) that leaves from the former school in the abandoned town. It is important to book ahead at the tourist information office in Calama, or directly by telephone (℡55/322122) or email (ⓔ visitas@codelco.cl). Regular yellow *colectivos* (20min; CH$1500) leave for Chuquicamata from Calle Abaroa, on Calama's main plaza. The tours last 1 hour 30 minutes and take place almost entirely on a bus, though you're allowed to get out at the viewpoint looking down to the pit – wear sensible shoes and clothing that covers most of your body. The rest of the tour takes you round the machinery yards and buildings of the plant, which you see from the outside only.

San Pedro de Atacama and around

The little oasis village of **SAN PEDRO DE ATACAMA** (100km southeast of Calama), with its narrow dirt streets and attractive adobe houses, has transformed itself, since the 1990s, into *the* tourism centre of Chile. Sitting at an altitude of 2400m between the desert and the altiplano, or *puna* (the high basin connecting the two branches of the cordillera), this has been an important settlement since pre-Hispanic times, originally as a major stop on the trading route connecting the llama herders of these highlands with the fishing communities of the Pacific. Later, during the nitrate era, it was the main rest stop on the cattle trail from Salta in Argentina to the nitrate *oficinas*, where the cattle were driven to supply the workers with fresh meat.

The large numbers of Chilean tourists and hordes of gringos here can come as quite a shock if you have just arrived from more remote parts of northern Chile. San Pedro has recently begun to lose some of its charm and is lined with overpriced, trendy-looking hotels with questionable cleanliness and poor service. Luckily, you will find exceptions (see reviews, p.213).

Moving on from Calama

Most visitors are in Calama on their way to San Pedro with regular bus connections (around ten a day) provided by several companies, including Tur Bus at Balmaceda 1802 (℡55/341472) and Buses Frontera, at Antofagasta 2041 (℡55/318543) with the most frequent services, and Buses Atacama, Abaroa 2106 (℡55/316664). Note that the first bus is at 7.30am and the last around 8.45pm. The inter-city bus companies all have ticket offices on Balmaceda: Tur Bus and Flota Barrios share 1852 (℡55/345883); Expreso Norte is at 1902 (℡55/347250); and Pullman Bus at 1802 (℡55/364411). LAN, Latorre 1726 (℡55/341477) and Sky Airlines, Latorre 1499 (℡55/310190) offer regular flights out of Calama to Santiago and the main northern cities.

Finally, there's the famously no-frills 20-hour **train** to Uyuni in Bolivia, base for the spectacular Salar de Uyuni. At the time of writing, the service had been suspended and, though it is likely to re-open, no date has been set. In the meantime, there are several quicker, slightly more comfortable buses to Uyuni – the journey takes about 8 hours and leaves on Monday and Thursday with Buses Frontera (CH$16,000) and on Monday, Wednesday, Thursday and Sunday with Buses Atacama (CH$7000).

SAN PEDRO DE ATACAMA

▲ Ⓐ (250m)   ▲ Pukará de Quitor   ▲ El Tatio

★ Buses Gemini
Food stalls
★ Buses Atacama 2000

TurBus Terminal
★ Buses La Frontera
LICANCABUR

Museo Arqueológico
GUSTAVO LE PEIGE

Artesanía
Municipalidad
Hospital

Calama
Valle de la Luna

GUSTAVO LE PEIGE

Ⓒ Ⓘ Ⓓ
Ⓔ
Ⓖ

PLAZA
Casa Incaica

Ⓕ Iglesia de San Pedro
Les Copains
Estrella del Sur
Cordillera Traveller ⓶

Azimut 360

Ⓗ Ⓘ
⑩ @ ⑨ ⑧
⑦
Cosmo Andino
Vulcano

CARACOLES
⑤ ⑥
Ⓚ

DOMINGO ATIENZA
TOCOPILLA
TOCONAO

Customs Post & Argentina

Ⓙ

PALPANA
PALANA

N

EATING & DRINKING

Adobe	7
Babalu	8
Blanco	4
Café Etnico	2
Café Export	3
La Casona	9
Las Delicias de Carmen	1
La Estaka	5
Paacha	10
Tierra Todo Natural	6

ACCOMMODATION

Awasi	L
Camping Los Perales	K
Casa de Don Tomás	M
Explora	N
Hostal Katarpe	G
Hostal Sonchek	D
Hostal Takha Takha	H
Hostal Vilacoyo	B
Hostería San Pedro	J
Hotel Altiplánico	A
Hotel Kimal	I
Hotel Tambillo	E
Hotel Terrantai	F
Residencial Chiloé	C

0 ————— 100 m

▼ Ⓛ, Ⓜ & Ⓝ (250m)

Arrival, information and orientation

Several **bus** companies have regular services from Calama to San Pedro (for details see box, p.211); they all have different drop-off points, all of which sit a couple of blocks off the main square, mostly along Licancabur. Head to the plaza for the **post office** or the **Oficina de Turismo** (Mon–Fri, 10am–1.30pm & 3–7.30pm, Sat 10am–2pm ☏ 55/851420, Ⓔ sanpedrodeatacama@gmail.com, Ⓦ www.sernatur.cl); if it's closed, try the Municipalidad, also on the square, but do not expect very much help.

San Pedro's main street is **Caracoles**, which is where you'll find the biggest concentration of accommodation, eating places and services. Early in the new millennium, Calle Antofagasta was renamed Gustavo Le Paige and all houses in the village were given a number, but the changes have still not quite sunk in. Fortunately, as San Pedro is a very small place, you should always be able to find your destination without much difficulty. Note that there are no banks in the village and, although there are two **ATMs**, electricity in the desert can be temperamental so it is advisable to bring funds before you arrive. You can change money at a number of *cambios* and most tour agencies will also exchange cash. Many but by no means all restaurants and hotels accept credit cards, so check first.

Accommodation

There are loads of places offering **rooms** in San Pedro, including a number of comfortable *residenciales* plus some classy, upmarket places for those on a far more generous budget. Recently, more and more of the latter have sprung up, often with a now hackneyed pseudo-native architectural style – lots of adobe, stone walls and thatched roofs – but mercifully, there have been no high-rises. A wonderful alternative, especially for those on a smaller budget, is provided by a new scheme of *albergues turísticos*, rural guesthouses in the villages of Peine and Socaire. Most have double rooms, some with private bath (❷–❹), and they usually serve breakfast and occasionally other meals. For details and bookings contact Red Licanhuasi (Ⓦwww.licanhuasi.cl).

You'll also find a few **campsites** within easy reach of the village centre; the best is listed below. If you're travelling alone and arrive at a busy time, you may have difficulty finding a **single room** in many *residenciales* and will probably be asked to share with another traveller.

Hotels

Awasi Tocopilla 4 ☎55/851460, Ⓦwww .awasi.cl. This special place is exclusive, without being stuffy. Eight rooms each come with a guide and vehicle for guests to handpick the shape of their stay. The staff is young and friendly, the food outstanding and comfort is paramount. Relax and be spoiled. ❽

Casa de Don Tomás Tocopilla s/n ☎55/851055, Ⓕ55/851175, Ⓦwww.dontomas.cl. Rustic, well-established hotel with spacious rooms, a pool, good breakfasts and a friendly welcome. Located away from the buzz of central San Pedro, 300m south of the crossroads with Caracoles. ❼

Explora Ayllu de Larache ☎2/2066060, Ⓦwww.explora.com. Located outside the village, in a world of its own, this Chilean chain resort offers its usual high standards of comfort, gastronomy and professional service in a beautiful setting. Mostly packages of at least three nights. ❾

Hostal Katarpe Domingo Atienza ☎55/851033, Ⓦwww.katarpe.cl. Good-value, comfortable rooms, all with private bath and fluffy towels. ❻

Hostal Sonchek Gustavo Le Peige 170 ☎55/851112, Ⓔsoncheksp@hotmail.com. Great-value hostel run by a personable Slovenian-Chilean couple with cosy rooms, communal kitchen and garden. Those with private bathrooms are particularly attractive. ❸

Hostal Takha-Takha Caracoles ☎55/851038. Small but tidy and quiet rooms giving onto a pleasant garden. A good bet for singles. ❹

Hostal Vilacoyo Tocopilla 386 ☎55/851006. Very friendly, homely hostel with rooms set around a relaxing hammock-strewn courtyard. Kitchen and shared bathrooms are spotless. ❸

Hostería San Pedro Solcor ☎55/851011, Ⓕ55/851048, Ⓦwww.diegodealmagrohoteles.cl. Well-maintained, comfortable accommodation – mostly in little bungalows – and a fantastic swimming pool. The restaurant is good, too. ❽

Hotel Altiplánico Domingo Atienza 282, ☎55/851212, Ⓦwww.altiplanico.cl. Gorgeous hotel complex in typical San Pedro adobe-style, with fantastic views, tasteful decor, comfortable en-suite rooms, a swimming pool (albeit odd-looking), internet access, a café-bar and bicycle rental. Located in a calm spot 250m from the centre, on the way to the Pukará de Quitor. ❽

Hotel Kimal Domingo Atienza ☎&Ⓕ55/851030, Ⓦwww.kimal.cl. Spacious, light and very attractive rooms, combining contemporary, spartan architecture with plants and warm rugs. ❽

Hotel Tambillo Gustavo Le Paige s/n ☎&Ⓕ55/851078, Ⓦwww.hoteltambillo.cl. Reasonably priced hotel offering fresh, clean rooms around a grim patio, and a dependable water supply. ❻

Hotel Terrantai Tocopilla 411 ☎55/851045, Ⓕ55/851037, Ⓦwww.terrantai.com. Modern, stylish but slightly snobbish hotel with bare stone walls and minimalist wooden furniture. For most of the year it offers only packages of two or three nights with all meals and excursions included. ❽

Residencial Chiloé Domingo Atienza ☎55/851017. Simple rooms kept very clean by the friendly owner. ❸

Camping

Camping Los Perales Tocanao ☎55/851570. Best campsite in San Pedro (around CH$3500 per person), a short distance south of the plaza, with lots of trees, water and an outdoor kitchen.

The Village

The focus of San Pedro is the little **plaza** at its centre, dotted with pepper trees and wooden benches. On its western side stands the squat white **Iglesia de San Pedro**, one of the largest Andean churches in the region. It's actually San

Pedro's second church, built in 1744, just over one hundred years after the original church was erected near the present site of the archeological museum. The bell tower was added towards the end of the nineteenth century, and the thick adobe walls surrounding the church rebuilt in 1978. Inside, religious icons look down from the brightly painted altar, among them a stern-looking Saint Peter, the village's patron saint. Overhead, the sloping roof is made of rough-hewn planks of cactus wood and gnarled rafters of reddish algarrobo timber, bound together with leather straps.

Opposite the church, on the other side of the square, sits San Pedro's oldest building, the lopsided **Casa Incaica**, now a souvenir store, dating from the

▲ San Pedro de Atacama

earliest days of the colony; the roof seems to be in imminent danger of collapse. A narrow alley full of **artesanía** stalls, where you can buy alpaca knitwear and other souvenirs, links the square to the main bus stops to the north.

Don't miss the excellent **Museo Arqueológico Gustavo Le Paige** (daily 9am–6pm; CH$2000), just off the northeast corner of the square. Named after the Belgian missionary-cum-archeologist who founded it in 1955, the museum houses more than 380,000 artefacts gathered from the region around San Pedro, of which the best examples are displayed in eight "naves" arranged around a central hall. Charting the development, step by step, of local pre-Columbian peoples, the displays range from Neolithic tools to sophisticated ceramics, taking in delicately carved wooden tablets and tubes used for inhaling hallucinogenic substances, and a number of gold and silver **ritual masks** worn by village elders during religious ceremonies.

Eating, drinking and entertainment

Thanks to the steady flow of young travellers passing through town, San Pedro boasts a lively **eating and drinking** scene. Just about every restaurant offers a fixed-price evening meal, with several choices of main course, usually including a vegetarian option; despite fierce competition, prices are notably higher than in other parts of the country. For much cheaper, filling set meals of *cazuela* followed by a main of meat or fish with rice, try one of the handful of good restaurants by the taxi rank at the top end of Licancabur. As with the accommodation, you'll see a definite "San Pedro look" among local restaurants, with a predilection for "native-style" adobe walls, wooden tables with benches, faux rock-paintings and other wacky decorations, and trendy staff who, more often than not, are working migrants from cities in the south. Many eating places double up as bars, sometimes with live music, while a couple of places also have **dancing**. Partying in San Pedro reaches a climax on **June 29**, when the village celebrates its saint's day with exuberant dancing and feasting.

Adobe Caracoles 211. Bustling outdoor restaurant with a roaring fire lit every night. Uncomfortable seats and pricey food but warm atmosphere and wi-fi.

Babalu Caracoles 160. Small *heladería* offering home-made ice creams that quench the thirst. Daily-changing flavours include pisco sour, chirimoya and lip-smackingly good fruits of the forest.

Blanco Caracoles s/n. White minimalist-chic adobe: this newcomer certainly stands out from the crowd, and, it's arguably the best restaurant in town. The select, sophisticated menu – try the *lomo salsa de vainilla* – and great wines will not disappoint.

Café Etnico Tocopilla s/n. Argentine-run restaurant and bar with great-value lunches and dinners, funky ambience and book swap. The friendly, helpful owner is full of information on things to do in the area and beyond.

Café Export Caracoles and Tocanao. Real coffee, snacks and sandwiches in a building and patio with striking decor, including Valle de la Luna–inspired tables, hand-crafted using adobe.

La Casona Caracoles s/n. Informal, busy restaurant with a very elegant dining room inside a large, colonial-style house. The fire-lit bar out the back is a great spot for after-dinner drinks.

Las Delicias de Carmen Calama s/n. Quiet spot serving delicious, reasonably priced soups and pastas, as well as freshly baked empanadas and sweeter treats (try the delicious lemon meringue pies) on a lovely patio behind the main building. Closed in the evening and on Sundays.

La Estaka Caracoles 259. Rustic restaurant-bar with young waiters and waitresses, open from breakfast-time until 1am. Very popular, though not cheap.

Paacha Domingo Atienza s/n, in *Hotel Kimal*. Moderately priced restaurant with an attractive interior, good food and regular performances by Andean folk bands.

Tierra Todo Natural Caracoles 46. Excellent little café specializing in wholesome home-made food, including wholemeal bread, pizzas, empanadas, fruit pancakes, yoghurt, fantastic salads and cakes. One of the earliest places open for breakfast.

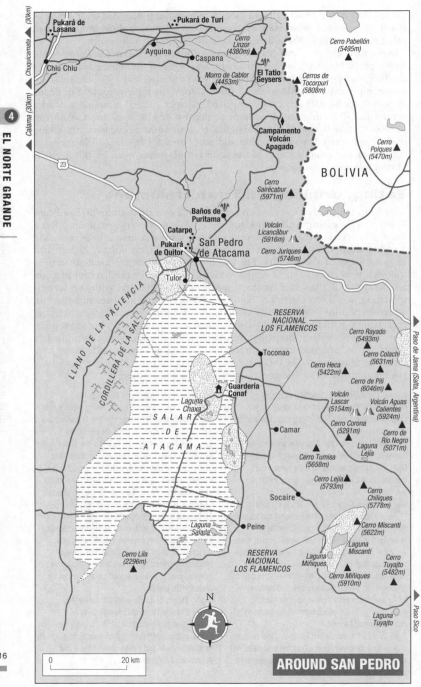

Pukará de Lasana

Pukará de Turi

Chuquicamata (30km)

Calama (30km)

Ayquina

Chiu Chiu

Caspana

Cerro Linzor (4380m)

El Tatio Geysers

Morro de Cablor (4453m)

Cerros de Tocorpuri (5808m)

Cerro Pabellón (5495m)

Campamento Volcán Apagado

Cerro Polques (5470m)

BOLIVIA

Cerro Sairécabur (5971m)

Baños de Puritama

Catarpe

Volcán Licancábur (5916m)

Pukará de Quitor

San Pedro de Atacama

Cerro Juriques (5746m)

Tulor

RESERVA NACIONAL LOS FLAMENCOS

LLANO DE LA PACIENCIA

CORDILLERA DE LA SAL

Toconao

Cerro Rayado (5493m)

Cerro Colachi (5631m)

Paso de Jama (Salta, Argentina)

Cerro Heca (5422m)

Cerro de Pili (6046m)

Volcán Lascar (5154m)

Volcán Aguas Calientes (5924m)

Guardería Conaf

Laguna Chaxa

SALAR

DE

ATACAMA

Camar

Cerro Corona (5291m)

Cerro de Río Negro (5071m)

Laguna Lejía

Cerro Tumisa (5658m)

Cerro Lejía (5793m)

Socaire

Cerro Chiliques (5778m)

Peine

Laguna Salada

Cerro Miscanti (5622m)

RESERVA NACIONAL LOS FLAMENCOS

Laguna Miscanti

Cerro Tuyajto (5482m)

Cerro Lila (2296m)

Laguna Miñiques

Cerro Miñiques (5910m)

N

Laguna Tuyajto

Paso Sico

0   20 km

AROUND SAN PEDRO

Listings

Banks and exchange There are no banks, but three *casas de cambio*, on Toconao, Caracoles and the other on Caracoles and Licancabur.

Bicycles There are many places that rent bikes in San Pedro. H2O on Caracoles charges CH$4000 per half-day or CH$6000 per day plus a handy map and emergency bike-repair kit.

Internet There are plenty of cyber cafés around the village. Ckausana Yapu, Gustavo Le Paige 181, and internet Equinoccio on Caracoles 362 charge the usual CH$1000 per hour. Alternatively, try *Café*

Sol Inti on Tocopilla 432 where you can check your emails over breakfast or lunch.

Post office On the main plaza on Toconao s/n, opposite the archeological museum.

Swimming pool There's a swimming pool (permanently open) at Pozo Tres, a three-kilometre walk east of the museum along the Paso de Jama.

Car Rental Euro Rent a Car, Palpana 7d, ☎55/555393, ⓦwww.eurorentacar.cl.

Tour companies See box on p.218.

Around San Pedro

The spectacular landscape around San Pedro includes vast, desolate plains cradling numerous **volcanoes** of the most delicate colours imaginable, and beautiful **lakes** speckled pink with flamingoes. You'll also find the largest **salt flat** in Chile, the **Salar de Atacama**, a whole field full of fuming **geysers** at El Tatio, a scattering of fertile **oasis villages**, and several fascinating **pre-Columbian ruins**.

The otherworldliness of this region is reflected in the poetic names of its geographical features – Valle de la Luna (Valley of the Moon), Llano de la Paciencia (Plain of Patience), Garganta del Diablo (Devil's Throat) and Valle de la Muerte (Valley of the Dead), to mention but a few. You might prefer to explore these marvels by yourself, but several companies in San Pedro trip over themselves to take you on guided tours, often a more convenient option – see box on p.218.

Pukará de Quitor

Just 3km north of San Pedro (head up Calle Tocopilla then follow the river), the **PUKARÁ DE QUITOR** (CH$2000) is a ruined twelfth-century fortress built into a steep hillside on the west bank of the Río San Pedro. It has been partially restored, and you can make out the defence wall encircling a group of stone buildings huddled inside. According to Spanish chronicles, this *pukará* was stormed and taken by Francisco de Aguirre and thirty men as part of Pedro de Valdivia's conquest in 1540. Another 4km up the road you'll find the ruins of what used to be an Inca administrative centre at **Catarpe**, but there's little to see in comparison with the ruins of Quitor.

Valle de la Luna

The **VALLE DE LA LUNA** (CH$2000), or Valley of the Moon (about 14km west of San Pedro on the old road to Calama), really lives up to its name, presenting a dramatic lunar landscape of wind-eroded hills surrounding a crust-like valley floor, once the bottom of a lake. An immense sand dune sweeps across the valley, easy enough to climb and a great place to sit and survey the scenery.

The valley is at its best at sunset, when it's transformed into a spellbinding palette of golds and reds, but you'll have to share this view with a multitude of fellow visitors, as all San Pedro tour operators offer daily sunset trips here. A more memorable (but more demanding) experience would be to get up before day breaks and cycle to the valley, arriving at sunrise (see listings for bike rental info). Note that the valley is part of the Conaf-run Reserva Nacional Los Flamencos, and camping is not permitted.

Tours from San Pedro

San Pedro has a high concentration of **tour operators** offering similar excursions into the surrounding altiplano at pretty much the same prices. This can, of course, be a curse as well as a blessing, for it increases tourist traffic in the region to the point where it can be difficult to visit the awe-inspiring landscape of the *puna* in the kind of silence and isolation in which it really ought to be experienced. Some of the tours are responsibly managed but many are not; the astounding environmental damage of late has finally, if belatedly, forced local communities (but not the national authorities) to take action; they now charge entrance fees to each site and do their best to clean up after visits. The **tourist office** keeps volumes of complaints registered by tourists and they are worth consulting to find out which operators to avoid.

Tours usually take place in minibuses, though smaller groups may travel in jeeps. Competition keeps prices relatively low – you can expect to pay from around CH$8000 to visit the Valle de la Luna, CH$15,000 for a tour to the Tatio geysers, and around CH$25,000 for a full-day tour of the local lakes and oases. Don't necessarily choose the cheapest tour, as some companies cram passengers in and offer below-par services, so it may be worth paying a couple of thousand pesos more. Do visit several companies – or their websites, where available – to get a feel for how they operate and to work out which one you prefer. If you don't speak Spanish, check that they can offer guides who speak your language (French, German and English being the most common on offer).

A selection of tour companies is given below with their specialization, if any. If a company does not appear on this list, it doesn't mean it's not worth checking out, it may just be new on the block. Check ⓦ www.sanpedroatacama.com for more information and links. We have not listed any companies about which we, or the local tourist office, have received a large number of complaints (usually concerning reliability of vehicles or lack of professionalism).

Atacama Connection Corner of Caracoles and Calama ⓣ55/851421, ⓔatacamaconnection@entelchile.net, ⓦwww.atacamaconnection.com. Long-running operator offering standard tours.

Cactus Domingo Atienza 419 ⓣ55/332837, ⓔcactustour@hotmail.com.

Cosmo Andino at Caracoles s/n ⓣ55/851069, ⓔcosmoandino@entelchile.net, ⓦwww.cosmoandino-expediciones.cl. Well-established and respected company offering the usual tours, with an emphasis on exploring the countryside on foot. Highly recommended.

Desert Adventure Caracoles s/n ⓣ&ⓕ55/851067, and also Latorre 1815, Calama ⓣ55/344894, ⓦwww.desertadventure.cl. Professional and reliable outfit with enthusiastic and well-informed guides.

Estrella del Sur at Caracoles 238 ⓣ55/852109. Reliable, family-run company offering trips across the border into Bolivia to see the fabulous Salar de Uyuni (covered in the *Rough Guide to Bolivia*).

Rancho Cactus Tocanao 568 ⓣ55/851506, ⓔrancho_cactus@123mail.cl, ⓦwww.rancho-cactus.cl. The place to go for horse treks lasting from a few hours to a couple of days. English and French spoken.

Space Obs at Caracoles 166 ⓣ55/851935, ⓔalain@spaceobs.com, ⓦwww.spaceobs.com. Excellent, highly memorable tours of Northern Chile's night sky led by an enthusiastic and personable French astronomer.

Vulcano Expediciones at Caracoles 317 ⓣ55/851023, ⓔvulcanochile@terra.cl, ⓦwww.vulcanochile.com. The best operator for mountain/volcano ascents, trekking and bike tours.

▲ Valle de la Luna

Tulor

The site of the earliest example of settled habitation in the region, **TULOR**, 9km southwest of San Pedro, (CH$2000), dates from around 800 BC. It was discovered only in the mid-twentieth century by Padre Le Paige, founder of the Museo Arqueológico in San Pedro. Today, the uppermost parts of the walls are exposed, protruding from the earth, while the rest remains buried under the sand. Two reconstructions of these igloo-like houses stand alongside the site.

The Salar de Atacama

The northern edge of this 3000-square-kilometre basin covered by a vast crust of saline minerals lies some 10km south of San Pedro. The largest salt flat in Chile, **SALAR DE ATACAMA** (CH$2000) is formed by waters flowing down from the Andes which, unable to escape from the basin, are forced to evaporate, leaving salt deposits on the earth. It's not a dazzling white like the Salar de Surire (see p.249), or Bolivia's Salar de Uyuni, but it's fascinating all the same – especially when you get out and take a close look at the crust, which looks like coral reef, or ice shards, and clanks when you walk on it. The *salar* contains several small lakes, including **Laguna Chaxa**, home to dozens of flamingoes, and the beautiful **Laguna Salada**, whose waters are covered with floating plates of salt.

The southern oases and lakes

Heading south from San Pedro, on the eastern side of the Salar de Atacama, you enter a region of beautiful lakes and tiny oasis villages. The first oasis, 38km south, is **Toconao**, whose softwater stream enters the village through the **Quebrada de Jérez** (CH$1000), a steep, narrow gorge with figs and quinces growing on its southern banks. Though not as pretty as some of the other villages, Toconao does possess a handsome whitewashed 1750 bell tower, set apart from the main church. Some 35km further south you reach **Camar**, a tiny hamlet with just sixty inhabitants, set amidst lush green terraces. **Socaire**, 15km beyond, is less picturesque, save for its little church set by a field of sunflowers. **Peine**, off a track branching west from the "main road" between Camar and Socaire, has a mid-eighteenth-century church and a large swimming pool, invariably full of squealing children. It is possible **to stay** in Peine and Socaire under the Red Licanhuasi rural guesthouse scheme run from San Pedro (see p.213).

One of the most stunning lakes in the region, **Laguna Miscanti** (near Socaire, 4350m above sea level; CH$2000), boasts brilliant blue waters. Adjacent lies the much smaller **Laguna Miñeques**, whose waters are a deep, dark blue; both lakes are protected areas, part of the Reserva Nacional Los Flamencos. Further south, pastel-coloured **Laguna Tuyajto** is home to dozens of flamingoes and is set against a fabulous backdrop of mineral-streaked mountains, while **Laguna Lejía**, further north, is filled with emerald-green waters tinged white with salt deposits floating on the surface; it, too, is home to large numbers of flamingoes.

The Tatio geysers

Getting to the geysers, 95km north of San Pedro, is quite an ordeal: first, you drag yourself out of bed in the dead of night with no electric lights to see by, then you stand shivering in the street while you wait for your tour company to come and pick you up at around 4am; and finally, you embark on a three-hour journey on a rough, bumpy road. Added to this is the somewhat surreal experience of finding yourself in a pre-dawn rush hour, part of a caravan of minibuses following each other's lights across the desert.

But hardly anyone who makes the trip regrets it. At 4300m above sea level, the **TATIO GEYSERS** (CH$3500) form the highest **geothermal** field in the world. It's essentially a large, flat field containing countless blowholes full of bubbling water that, between around 6 and 8am, send billowing clouds of steam high into the air (strictly speaking, though, geysers spurt water, not steam). At the same time, the spray forms pools of water on the ground, streaked with silver reflections as they catch the first rays of the sun. It's really a magnificent spectacle. Take great care, however, when walking around the field; the crust of earth is very thin in some parts, and serious accidents can happen. You should also remember that it will be freezing cold when you arrive, though once the sun's out the place warms up quite quickly.

There's a swimming pool near the geysers, visited by most tour companies, so remember to take your bathing suit. On the way back, some tour companies also pay a visit to the **Baños de Puritama** (CH$5000), a rocky pool filled with warm thermal water, 60km south of the geysers and run by a local community but owned and maintained by the *Hotel Explora* (see p.213).

Iquique

Dramatically situated at the foot of the 800-metre coastal cordillera, with an enormous sand dune looming precariously above one of its barrios, **IQUIQUE**, 390km north of Calama, is a sprawling, busy and surprisingly cosmopolitan city. The town is also fast gaining a reputation as one of the continent's finest spots for paragliding. Predictably cloudless skies and winds that come in off the Pacific and rise up the dunes create near-perfect conditions; you'll see many enthusiasts swooping down to the beaches, silhouetted by dawn or dusky sunsets. Iquique rivals Arica as the best place to base yourself for a tour of the extreme northern tip of the country. From here, you can easily arrange excursions into the interior, whose attractions include the famous nitrate ghost towns of **Humberstone** and **Santa Laura**, the beautiful hot-springs oases of **Pica** and **Matilla**, and the stunning altiplano scenery of **Parque Nacional Volcán Isluga**.

Some history

Iquique started out as a small settlement of indigenous fishing communities, and during the colonial period became a base for extracting guano deposits from the coast. It continued to grow with the opening of a nearby silver mine in

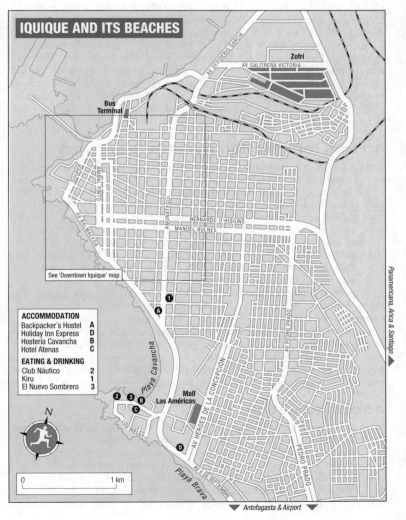

IQUIQUE AND ITS BEACHES

Zofri

AV SALITRERA VICTORIA

AV DESIDERIO GARCÍA

Bus Terminal

SOUPER

ANIBAL PINTO

AV BALMACEDA

AMUNATEGUI

BERNARDO O'HIGGINS

MANUEL BULNES

See 'Downtown Iquique' map

ACCOMMODATION
Backpacker´s Hostel   A
Holiday Inn Express   D
Hostería Cavancha   B
Hotel Atenas   C

EATING & DRINKING
Club Náutico   2
Kiru   1
El Nuevo Sombrero   3

Playa Cavancha

LOS RIELES

Mall Las Américas

AV HÉROES DE LA CONCEPCIÓN

AV PEDRO PRADO

PEDRO PRADO

AV 11 DE SEPTIEMBRE

Playa Brava

N

0   1 km

Panamericana, Arica & Santiago

▼ Antofagasta & Airport ▼

1730, but its population never exceeded one hundred in the eighteenth century, and it wasn't until the great nineteenth-century nitrate boom that it really took off as a city.

Following its transferral to Chilean hands during the War of the Pacific (1878–83), Iquique became the **nitrate capital** of Chile – where the largest quantities of ore were shipped from, and where the wealthy nitrate barons based themselves, building opulent mansions all over the rapidly expanding city. By the end of the nineteenth century, Iquique was the wealthiest and most hedonistic city in Chile – it was said that more champagne was consumed here, per head, than in any other city in the world.

With the abrupt end of the nitrate era after World War I, Iquique's boom was over, and the grand mansions were left to fade and crumble as the industrialists headed back to Santiago. Fishing stepped in to fill the economic gap, at least partially, and over the years Iquique has transformed itself into the world's leading exporter of fishmeal. This is a thriving and prosperous industry, but has the unfortunate effect of filling Iquique's streets with a distinctly unpleasant odour at times, particularly down by the waterfront. On a more positive note, its central square and main avenue conserve some splendid buildings from the **nitrate era**, which, along with the city's beaches, are for many people a good enough reason to visit. Seizing upon this, Iquique authorities have invested in an ambitious restoration scheme aimed at enhancing the beauty of this historic part of the city. Still more people, mainly Chileans, head here for the duty-free shopping at Iquique's **Zona Franca**, or "Zofri".

Arrival, information and city transport

Iquique's main **bus terminal** is in a rather run-down quarter at the northern end of Patricio Lynch, several blocks from the centre – best take a taxi to the centre, or wait for a *colectivo*. **Tur Bus**, however, has its own terminal in a beautifully converted townhouse, proudly sporting a dazzling 1917 vintage black Ford, at the corner of Ramírez and Esmeralda. This saves you a couple of blocks' walk and is in a more agreeable neighbourhood, so don't get out at the main terminal even though Tur Bus buses stop there, too. If you're arriving **by air**, you'll land at Diego Arecena airport, a whacking 40km south of the city. From here, you can get to the centre by bus (Transfer ☎57/310800; CH$4000), *colectivo* or regular taxi (CH$10,000).

For **tourist information**, head for the Sernatur office at Aníbal Pinto 436 (Mon–Fri 9am–5.30pm, Sat 10am–1pm; ☎57/419241, ⓔinfoiquique @sernatur.cl).

Except for fares from the bus terminal and airport, nearly all Iquique's **taxis** function like *colectivos*, with fixed, low prices but flexible routes. This is very handy for shuttling to and from the beach, or even going from your hotel to a restaurant. Find out from Sernatur or your hotel what the going rate is, and confirm this with the taxi driver before you get in.

Accommodation

Iquique is a popular holiday resort and offers an abundance of **accommodation**. You'll find the widest choice in the centre, which is dotted with cheap *residenciales* and smart hotels, while the hotels by the beaches are almost unanimously expensive – but worth it, perhaps, if you want a couple of days by the ocean. Both in the centre and by the beaches, always ask what the "best price" is, as many places will give discounts when pushed. One thing to bear in mind is that, owing to the region's severe water shortage, water supplies are occasionally cut in the busy summer months, sometimes without warning.

Downtown Iquique

Hostal Cuneo Baquedano 1175 ☏ 57/428654, ✉ hostalcuneo@hotmail.com. Small, neat rooms off a leafy patio in an old timber building on the historic stretch of Calle Baquedano. Hospitable and homely. ❹

Hostal Pleamar Latorre 1036 ☏ 57/411840. Small but clean, quiet rooms with private bath and TV, giving onto a covered terrace with tables and chairs. ❸

Hostal Sol del Norte Juan Martínez 852 ☏ 57/421546. Simple but well-maintained rooms (with shared bath) off a long corridor, run by a very friendly señora. ❸

Hotel Arturo Prat Aníbal Pinto 695 ☏ 57/411067, ⑤ 57/423309. Plush city-centre hotel with an elegant period front area containing the reception and restaurant, and modern rooms in tall blocks behind. Also has a small rooftop pool. ❻

Hotel Intillanka Obispo Labbé 825 ☏ 57/311104, ⑤ 57/311105. Friendly and efficiently run hotel offering 30 spacious, light rooms with private bath. Showing its age a little, but very clean. ❹

Hotel Riorsa Vivar 1542 ☏&⑤ 57/423823. Good-quality, tidy rooms with private bath and cable TV. The very helpful owner is also a plus. On the southern edge of town, an easy walk from the beach. ❹

Residencial José Luis Ramírez 402. Bright, airy and fairly large rooms with shared bath – a good budget choice. ❷

The beaches

Backpacker's Hostel Amuñategui 2075 ☏ 57/320223, ✉ vinko@terra.cl. Excellent HI-affiliated hostel offering weekly barbecues, surfboard and wetsuit rental and clean rooms and facilities. CH$5000 per person. ❸

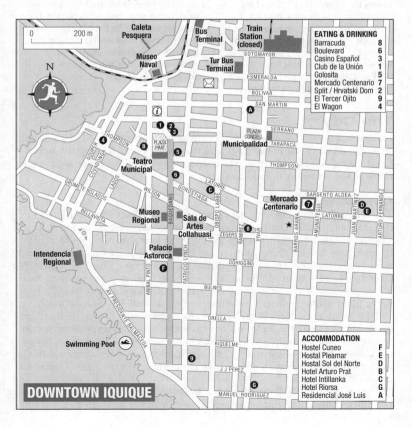

DOWNTOWN IQUIQUE

EATING & DRINKING	
Barracuda	8
Boulevard	6
Casino Español	3
Club de la Unión	1
Golosita	5
Mercado Centenario	7
Split / Hrvatski Dom	2
El Tercer Ojito	9
El Wagon	4

ACCOMMODATION	
Hostel Cuneo	F
Hostal Pleamar	E
Hostal Sol del Norte	D
Hotel Arturo Prat	B
Hotel Intillanka	C
Hotel Riorsa	G
Residencial José Luis	A

▲ Palacio Astoreca

Holiday Inn Express 11 Septiembre 1690 ☎57/433300. Impersonal but immaculate US chain hotel, with a pool, a/c and spacious rooms with ocean views (at the front). Special discounts Fri–Sun. ❼
Hostería Cavancha Los Rieles 250 ☎&℉57/434800. Modern, 80-room hotel with tennis courts, swimming pool, a dining room overlooking the ocean and direct access to the beach. Rooms not as fresh as they could be. ❼
Hotel Atenas Los Rieles 738 ☎&℉57/431100. Grand nitrate-era house with lots of character and beautifully furnished rooms with verandas. A modern annexe out the back has plainer, less expensive rooms. ❺–❻

The City

Iquique falls into two quite distinct areas: **downtown**, lined with shops, services, and old historic buildings, and the modern stretch along the **ocean-front**, given over almost entirely to tourism. The **Zofri** duty-free zone is just north of the centre, in an industrial area.

Downtown

The focus of town is the large, partly pedestrianized **Plaza Prat**, dominated by the gleaming white **Teatro Municipal**, whose magnificent facade features Corinthian columns and statues representing the four seasons – spoiled at night by criminally hideous fairy lights. It was built in 1890 as an opera house and showcased some of the most distinguished divas of its time. These days, productions aren't quite so grand, featuring everything from national ballet to local school concerts. If the programme doesn't appeal, it's still worth taking a look inside (daily 10am–4pm; free) to admire the lavish, if slightly faded, furnishings and the grand proportions of the auditorium. Opposite the theatre, in the centre of the square, the **Torre Reloj** is a tall white clock tower with Moorish arches, adopted by Iquique as the city's symbol. On the northeast corner of the square, the **Casino Español** – formerly a gentlemen's club, now a restaurant – features an extravagant interior with oil paintings depicting scenes from *Don Quijote*; it's definitely worth a visit.

Leading south, **Calle Baquedano** is lined with an extraordinary collection of late nineteenth-century timber houses, all with porches and balconies and fine wooden balustrades, and many undergoing loving restoration. This is the showcase of Iquique's nitrate architecture and has been designated a national monument. The street is pedestrianized from the plaza all the way down to the seafront, using noble materials such as fine stone for the paving and polished timber for the sidewalks. Three buildings are open to the public: the **Sala de Artes Collahuasi** at no. 930 (open every evening till late; free), an impeccably restored building used for temporary art exhibitions, usually of outstanding quality; the **Museo Regional** at no. 951 (Mon–Fri 9am–5.30pm, Sat & Sun 10am–5pm; free), which houses an eclectic collection of pre-Hispanic and natural history artefacts, including deformed skulls and a pickled two-headed shark; and the **Palacio Astoreca** (Mon–Fri 10am–1pm & 4–7pm, Sat 11am–2pm; free; entrance on O'Higgins), a glorious, though deteriorating, mansion featuring a massive wood-panelled entrance hall with a painted glass Art Nouveau ceiling.

A short walk north from Plaza Prat is the **Museo Naval** (Mon–Sat 10am–1pm, Tues–Fri also 4–7pm; CH$200), which displays letters, maps and photos relating to Arturo Prat, hero of the War of the Pacific (see p.501), and, just behind, the **Caleta Pesquera**, or fishermen's wharfs, where the huge, yawning pelicans strutting around the pier make compelling viewing. You can take **boat tours** around the harbour from here, worth it for the views onto the steep desert mountains, rising like huge slabs of chocolate cake behind the city.

The beaches

Two beaches lie within striking distance of the city centre: **Playa Cavancha**, the nearest, most popular, and more sheltered, and **Playa Brava**, larger, less crowded and more windswept, but only suitable for daring surfers. You can just about walk to Playa Cavancha, which begins at the southern end of Amuñategui, but it's far easier, and very cheap, to take one of the numerous taxis constantly travelling between the plaza and the beach; many continue to Playa Brava, as well, for a slightly higher fare. Further south, between Playa Brava and the airport, there's a series of attractive sandy beaches including **Playa Blanca**, 13km south of the centre, **Playa Lobito**, at Km 22, and the fishing cove of **Los Verdes**, at Km 24. You can get to these on the airport bus or *colectivo*.

The Zofri

About 3km north of the centre, located in a large industrial compound, the duty-free shopping complex known as the **Zofri** (Mon–Sat 11am–9pm) is widely touted as one of the great attractions of the north. Thousands of Chileans flock here from up and down the country to spend their money at

---

Tours from Iquique

A number of Iquique tour companies offer one-day circular tours – from around CH$17,000 per person – taking in the nitrate ghost towns of **Humberstone** and **Santa Laura** (see p.228); the geoglyphs of Pintados (see p.228); the oases villages of **Matilla** and **Pica**, with a plunge in Pica's hot springs (see p.230); and the basilica and nitrate museum of **La Tirana** (see p.231). Another standard tour offered by some companies is the highly memorable route up into the cordillera, continuing north across the altiplano and descending in Arica; these excursions take in **Parque Nacional Volcán Isluga** (see p.233), the **Salar de Surire** (see p.249) and **Parque Nacional Lauca** (see p.245). The tour entails three overnight stays, with prices starting around CH$180,000 per person. Recommended companies are given in the Listings section, p.227, under "Tour operators."

Moving on from Iquique

Most **long-distance buses** (including Tur Bus) depart from the Terminal Rodoviario, at the north end of Lynch, but many bus companies also have offices around the Mercado Centenario, including: Buses Carmelita, Barros Arana 841 (℡57/412337); Flota Barrios, Sargento Aldea 987 (℡57/426941); Ramos Cholele, Barros Arana 851 (℡57/411650); and Tur Bus, Barros Arana 825 (℡57/413028). Remember that Tur Bus also has its own impressive terminal at the corner of Ramírez and Esmeralda. There are regular daily buses to **Pica** (with stops at **Matilla** and **La Tirana**) with San Andrés, on the corner of Barros Arana and Sargento Aldea (℡57/413953), and Buses Tamarugal, Sargento Aldea 781 (℡57/412981). The latter also has daily services to **Mamiña** (Mon–Sat 8am & 4pm, Sun 8am only). Yellow *colectivos* for **Pozo Almonte** leave from the side of the market and will drop passengers at **Humberstone**. El Paraíso is a Bolivian company that runs regular buses to Oruro, Cochabamba and La Paz departing from their offices at Esmeralda 939. Buses Géminis, Obispo Labbé 151 (℡57/413315), goes to Salta in Argentina (erratic service), and Oruro and La Paz, in Bolivia. You can **fly** out of Iquique to most of the main cities of northern Chile, plus Santiago de Chile, Santa Cruz and La Paz in Bolivia and Arequipa in Peru.

what turns out, at close quarters, to be a big, ugly mall crammed full of small shops selling electronic items like cameras, watches and domestic gadgets. There's a curious mixture of the upmarket and the tacky, with the latter tending to dominate. The building itself is shabby and old-fashioned, and the bargains aren't really good enough to deserve a special trip. If you do want to check it out, take any *colectivo* marked "Zofri" heading north out of town – the east side of the Plaza or Calle Armuñategui are both good bets for catching one.

Eating, drinking and entertainment

While there's a reasonable choice of **restaurants** in the centre, it's worth coming out to have at least one evening meal by the beach, to see the ocean lit up with coloured lights projected from the promenade. As for entertainment, you'll find several **discotheques** that get very crowded in summer and maintain a gentle buzz during low season. They are nearly all down on the Costanera Sur; leading names to look out for include *Kamikaze*, *Sala Murano* and *Bar T*. Iquique's main **cinema** is at Mall Las Américas on Avenida Héroes de la Concepción (see "Iquique and its Beaches" map).

Restaurants

Downtown Iquique

Barracuda Gorostiaga 601, at Ramírez. Very popular wood-panelled pub serving wine by the glass, pisco sour, foreign beers, tea, coffee, milkshakes and delicious snacks, plus reasonably priced full-blown meals in the evening. Soft jazz music, lovely mellow atmosphere and top-notch service.
Boulevard Baquedano 790. French-style bistro that offers a change from the usual Chilean fare, if you're prepared to pay a little extra. The broad menu includes fish dishes, pizzas, crêpes, pastas, salads and even tagines (a Moroccan speciality of meat or fish cooked with herbs in an earthenware pot).

Casino Español Plaza Prat 584. Huge, fabulous dining room decorated like a mock Moorish palace. The food is unexceptional, and a little overpriced, but this is a must-visit.
Club de la Unión Plaza Prat 278. Uninspired food (typical meat and fish dishes), but the building is spacious and rather grand, with views onto the Teatro Municipal. A good place for an inexpensive lunch.
🏃 **Kiru** Amuñategui 1912. Peruvian restaurant that feels sophisticated and exclusive – there's no sign at the door; just follow the palm-fringed corridor and chill-out music. The chef rustles up fantastic fusion dishes and memorable ceviches. There are plenty of wines and cocktails at the trendy, well-stocked bar.

Mercado Centenario Barros Arana, between Latorre and Sargento Aldea. Cheap fish lunches available upstairs at the ten or so bustling *marisquerías*.

🏃 **El Tercer Ojito** Patricio Lynch 1420. This peaceful garden oasis is the mellowest place to spend a shady afternoon or candle-lit evening. A healthy menu of seafood, salads, sushi, pasta, cocktails, juices and lassis showcases the best ingredients the region has to offer, with the odd Asian or Peruvian twist. Service is impeccable. Be sure to leave room for pudding; the home-made kulfi is superb.

El Wagon Thompson 85. Nitrate-era paraphernalia lines the walls of this warm and friendly restaurant. Take your pick from an extensive menu of imaginative fish and seafood dishes – the spicy *pescado a la Huara-Huara* is particularly good. There's also a great choice of wines and live music on the weekends.

By the beach

Club Náutico Los Rieles 110. First-rate, reasonably priced restaurant with great views from its outdoor terrace, especially at night.

El Nuevo Sombrero Los Rieles 704. Rather formal, expensive restaurant specializing in seafood – invariably served up in rich, roux-based sauces. It's right by the sea, with floor-to-ceiling windows giving great views.

Bars

Golosita Baquedano 696. Little place serving pricey but deliciously thirst-quenching juices made with fruit from the oasis towns.

Split/Hrvatski Dom Plaza Prat, next to *Casino Español*. A little piece of Croatia on the Pacific, with its cosy interior lifted straight from the Dalmatian city it's named for, this friendly place does decent snacks and serves the best espresso around.

Listings

Airlines LAN, Tarapacá 465 ☎57/427600; Sky Airlines, Tarapacá 530 ☎57/415013 or 57/424139 at airport; TAM, Serrano 430 ☎57/390600; Comet, San Martín 385 ☎57/420230.

Banks and exchange Iquique has numerous ATMs, including those at: Banco Santander, Plaza Prat; BCI, Tarapacá 404; Scotiabank, Uribe 530; Corp-Banca, Serrano 343. There are fewer *casas de cambio*, but you could try Afex, on the corner of Serrano and Lynch, downtown, or Fides Ltda, at the Zofri Plaza de Servicios.

Car rental Best value may well be at Stop, at Bulnes 168 ☎57/575316, ⓔrentacarstop @importadorastop.cl. You could also try: Budget, Bulnes 542 ☎57/416095, ⓦwww.budget.cl; Hertz, Aníbal Pinto 1303 ☎57/510432, ⓦwww .autorentas.cl; JR Rent a Car, Arturo Fernández 1591 ☎57/429019, ⓔjrpropuestas@yahoo.es; Autos Procar, Serrano 796 ☎57/470668, ⓕ57/413470.

Internet There are several places both in the centre and near the beach. Centro de Llamadas Diegnito at Tarapacá 401 charges CH$400 per hour; Cyber Café Juan López, on Playa Cavancha at Arturo Prat 950, charges $500.

Post office The main office is at Bolívar 485, a few blocks northeast of Plaza Prat.

Swimming pool There's a fantastic outdoor pool (☎57/544864) overlooking the Pacific at Av Costanera with Riquelme, opposite the Copec station.

Taxis Taxi Aeropuerto Plaza Prat ☎57/413368; Playa Brava radio Taxi ☎57/443460.

Tour operators Avitours, Baquedano 997 ☎57/473775, ⓦwww.avitours.cl; Coki, Orden y Patria 2824 ☎ 57/321289, ⓔcokitouriqq@hotmail .com; Surire Tours, Los Algarrobos 3460 ☎&ⓕ57/445440 ⓔsuriretours@hotmail.com. Longest on the scene is Turismo Lirima, at Gorostiaga 301 (corner of Baquedano) ☎57/391384, ⓔturismolirima@hotmail.com. For information on tours into the cordillera, see box, p.225.

Travel agencies There are numerous travel agents in town, including Iquitour, Patricio Lynch 563, ☎57/428772, ⓔiquitour@gmail.com; Lolo Tour, O'Higgins 1307 ☎&ⓕ57/321551.

Inland from Iquique

Iquique lies within easy reach of many inland sights. Just half an hour away, **Humberstone** and **Santa Laura** are perhaps the most haunting of all the nitrate ghost towns. South of here, close to the Panamericana, **Cerro Pintados** features a dense collection of geoglyphs, among the most impressive in Chile. East of Pintados sits the pretty oasis village of **Pica**, with a lovely thermal pool, while **Mamiña**, further north, is the Norte Grande's hot-springs town *par* *excellence.* You can also visit **La Tirana**, an important pilgrimage centre, famous for its colourful festival in July. Public transport around this area is sporadic but manageable.

Humberstone and Santa Laura

The best-preserved ghost town in Chile, **HUMBERSTONE** (daily 9am–6pm; CH$1000) is a nitrate *oficina* that was abandoned in 1960 and today appeals especially to lovers of industrial architecture. It sits some 45km inland from Iquique, by Ruta 16 just before it meets the Panamericana.

The town began life in 1862 as Oficina La Palma, but was renamed in 1925 in honour of its British manager, James "Santiago" Humberstone, an important nitrate entrepreneur famous for introducing the "Shanks" ore-refining system to the industry. In its time it was one of the busiest *oficinas* on the pampas; today it is an eerie, empty ghost town, slowly crumbling beneath the desert sun. What sets Humberstone apart from the other ghost towns is that just about all of it is still standing – from the white, terraced workers' houses (now in total disrepair) and the plaza with its bandstand, to the theatre, church and company store. The **theatre**, in particular, is highly evocative, with its rows of dusty seats staring at the stage. You should also seek out the **hotel**, and walk through to the back where you'll find a huge, empty **swimming pool** with a diving board – curiously the pool is made from the sections of a ship's iron hull. Located a short distance from the town are the sheds and workshops, with old tools and bits of machinery lying around, and invoices and order forms littering the floors.

At **SANTA LAURA**, about 2km down the road and clearly visible from Humberstone, you'll see only a couple of remaining houses, but the processing plant is quite amazing, seeming to loom into the air like a rusty old dinosaur. As you walk around the site, listening to the endless clanging of machinery banging in the wind, the sense of abandonment is nearly overwhelming.

Pampa del Tamarugal and Cerro Pintados geoglyphs

About 20km south of the junction between Ruta 16 and the Panamericana, the latter passes through the **RESERVA NACIONAL PAMPA DEL TAMARUGAL**, an extensive plantation of wispy, bush-like *tamarugo* trees. These are native to the region and are especially adapted to saline soils, with roots that are long enough to tap underground water supplies. There's a Conaf-run **campsite** here, exactly 24km south of Pozo Almonte, on the west side of the Panamericana. While the *tamarugos* aren't really interesting enough to merit a special trip, you can take a look at them on your way to the far more impressive **CERRO PINTADOS** (daily 9.30am–6.30pm; CH$1000), with the largest collection of **geoglyphs** in South America, situated within the reserve's boundaries. Extending 4km along a hillside, the site features four hundred images (not all of them visible from the ground) of animals, birds, humans and geometric patterns, etched on the surface or formed by a mosaic of little stones around the year 1000 AD. The felines, birds, snakes and flocks of llamas and vicuñas scratched into the rock are thought to have been indicators for livestock farmers. The circles, squares, dotted lines and human figures are more enigmatic, however, and may have had something to do with rituals, perhaps even sacrifices.

Cerro Pintados begins 5km west of the Panamericana, reached by a gravel road that branches off the highway 45km south of Pozo Almonte, almost opposite the turn-off to Pica. There's a Conaf control point 2km along the road, where you pay your entrance fee. If you haven't got your own transport, you should be able to arrange a lift there and back with a *colectivo* from the stand outside Iquique's Mercado Centenario – it's probably not a good idea to hitch

The nitrate boom

Looking around the desert pampa, it's hard to believe that this scorched, lifeless wasteland was once so highly prized that a war was fought over it – and still more difficult to imagine it alive with smoking chimneys, grinding machinery, offices, houses and a massive workforce. But less than a century ago, the Far North of Chile was the scene of a thriving industry built on its vast **nitrate deposits**, heavily in demand in Europe and North America as a fertilizer. Nitrates were first exploited in the Atacama Desert in the 1860s, when the region still belonged to Bolivia (around Antofagasta) and Peru (around Iquique and Arica). From the early stages, however, the Chilean presence was very strong, both in terms of capital and labour – in the 1870s Chileans made up over fifty percent of the workforce in Iquique, and some eighty percent in Antofagasta, and the largest nitrate company, the **Companía de Salitres y Ferrocarril de Antofagasta**, was a Chilean enterprise.

When in 1878 the Bolivian government violated an official agreement by raising export taxes on nitrate (hitting Chilean shareholders, including several prominent politicians), Chile protested by sending troops into Antofagasta. Two weeks later, Chile and Bolivia were at war, with Peru joining in (on the Bolivian side) within a couple of months. The War of the Pacific (see p.597) went on for five years, and resulted in Chile, the undisputed victor, extending its territory by 900km, taking in all of the nitrate grounds. With the return of political stability after the war, the nitrate industry began to boom in earnest, bringing in enormous export revenues for Chile. Foreign – particularly British – investors poured money into companies like the Liverpool Nitrate Company, and a trail of processing plants, known as **oficinas**, sprang up all over the pampa, connected to the seaports by an extensive railroad network.

Each *oficina* sat in the centre of its prescribed land, from where the raw nitrate ore – found just beneath the surface of the earth – was blasted using gunpowder. The chunks of ore, known as *caliche*, were then boiled in large copper vats, releasing a nitrate solution which was crystallized in the sun before being sent down to the ports to be shipped abroad. The plants themselves were grimy, noisy places. William Russell, a British journalist who toured the pampa in 1889, wrote: "The external aspect of the *oficina* was not unlike that of a north country coal or iron mine – tall chimneys and machinery, corrugated iron buildings, offices and houses, the shanties of workmen, a high bank of refuse." It was a hard life for the labourers, who worked long hours in dangerous conditions, and were housed in squalid shacks, often without running water and sewerage. The (mostly British) managers, meanwhile, lived in grand residences, dined on imported delicacies and enjoyed a whirl of social activities – Russell wrote of "picnics, nightly dances and even balls to which the neighbours came from the *oficinas* around, from Iquique and Pisagua below by special train, which conveyed bands of music and armies of cooks, confectioners and waiters". Nitrate provided more than half of the Chilean government's revenues until 1920, by which time the boom was over and the industry in decline.

It was World War I that dealt the first serious blow to the nitrate companies, when the suspension of sales to Germany – Chile's major European buyer – forced almost half the *oficinas* to close down. The final death knell was sounded when Germany, forced to seek alternative fertilizers, developed cheap synthetic nitrates which quickly displaced Chile's natural nitrates from their dominant role in the world market. Most of what was left of the industry was killed off by the World Depression in the 1930s, and today just two *oficinas* – María Elena and Pedro de Valdivia (see p.234) – remain in operation.

and then try walking to the site from the Panamericana, owing to the relentless heat and lack of shade.

Pica and Matilla

As you cross the vast, desert pampa, the neighbouring oases of Pica and Matilla first appear as an improbable green smudge on the hazy horizon. As you get nearer, it becomes apparent that this is not a mirage and you are, indeed, approaching cultivated fields and trees. It's a remarkable sight, and anyone who has not seen a desert oasis should make a special effort to visit. By far the larger of the two oases, **PICA** is a sleepy little town overflowing with lemon and lime trees, bougainvilleas and jasmine. It's the largest supplier of fruits to Iquique – *limas de Pica* are famous throughout the country – and one of the treats of visiting is drinking the delicious *jugos naturales* – orange, mango, pear, guava and grapefruit juices – freshly squeezed in front of you in the little streetside kiosks. The tidy plaza, by the entrance to town, is overlooked by a beautiful pale-coloured **church** dedicated to St Andrew. It has a grand Neoclassical facade and was built in 1880. Pica's real selling point, however, is the **Cocha Resbaladero** (daily 9am–9pm; CH$1000), a gorgeous **hot-springs pool** carved into a rocky hollow with two caves at one end. It's at the far end of Calle Presidente Ibañez, quite a walk from the main part of town, but there are several places to stay up here if you want to be close to the waters. To enjoy the waters in peace, it's best to arrive early before the buses of day-trippers start arriving at midday.

The tiny, pretty village of **MATILLA**, about 5km away, has a beautiful church, albeit more humble than Pica's. You'll also see an eighteenth-century wine press, just off the plaza, used by the Spaniards to produce wine; the roots of grapevines were brought over by the conquistadors. While you're here, try the wonderful *jugos* in the café opposite the church.

Practicalities

The town's friendly **Oficina de Turismo** sits opposite the Municipalidad building just past the main square on the way to the hot springs on Balmaceda 299 (Mon–Fri 8.30am–1.30pm & 3–6pm, Sat–Sun 10.30am–1.30pm & 3–6.30pm). Just a couple of doors down is the post office and there's an internet café on the opposite side of the road. On the main plaza is an ATM and there are several phone centers dotted around it. The nicest place to stay in the centre is *Hotel Los Emilios*, at Lord Cochrane 213, the first right from the plaza as you come into town (☎57/741126; **③**). It offers comfortable rooms with private bath in a handsome old house with a plunge pool in the back garden. Up by the hot springs, you'll find basic but clean rooms in *Residencial El Tambo*, at Ibañez 68 (☎57/741041; **③**), and a few attractive wooden cabañas overlooking the pool at Ibañez 57 (*Sr Medina*, ☎&⑤57/741316; **④**). A ten-minute walk from the centre, signposted off Balmaceda, is an excellent campsite, *Camping Sombre Verde* (☎09/8403 2348; CH$1500 per person), offering great facilities and plenty of trees for shade. As for eating, try *La Viña*, at Ibañez 79, up by the hot springs, or *El Bandio* down in the centre at Balmaceda 319, where good, standard Chilean food is served up in the creaky rooms of an old purple building. For something a bit different *Los Naranjos*, on Barboza 200, is a homely little place with a hearty menu of Andean specialities like llama stew with quinoa. The best fruit-juice stalls are on Ibañez, towards the hot springs, and there's a wonderful shop selling home-made jams and conserves a little further along from the campsite.

La Tirana

Driving back to the Panamericana from Pica, if you take the right-hand (north-bound) road, rather than the left-hand one, you'll pass through the little town of **LA TIRANA**, 10km before you get back to the highway. It's a rather cheerless place, made up of dusty streets and neglected adobe houses, which makes it all the more surprising when you come upon the immense, paved square stretching out before the imposing **Santuario de la Tirana**. This curious church, at once grand and shabby, is made of wood covered in cream-coloured corrugated iron. It's the home of the **Virgen del Carmen**, a polychrome carving that is the object of a fervent cult of devotion. Every year, from July 12 to 18, up to eighty thousand pilgrims come to honour the Virgin and take part in the riotous **fiesta** in which dozens of masked, costumed dancers perform *bailes religiosos*. These dances have their roots in pre-Spanish, pre-Christian times, with an exuberant, carnival feel wholly out of keeping with traditional Catholic celebrations. If you're not around to see them in action, you should at least visit the small **museum** in a wing of the church (Sat & Sun 10am–8pm; CH$100 donation) where many of the costumes and masks are displayed. (Try asking the caretaker to let you in if it's shut.) All **buses** between Iquique and Pica make a stop in La Tirana.

Mamiña

A paved road branches east from the Panamericana at Pozo Almonte and climbs gently through the desert to **MAMIÑA**, 74km away. First impressions of Mamiña are not encouraging; huddled on a hillside overlooking a valley, its narrow streets and crumbling stone houses seem to belong to a forgotten town, left to the mercy of the heat and dust. Continue down the valley, however, and its charms become more apparent as you come upon the fertile terraces emerald with alfalfa, and the little stream running through the gorge (*quebrada*). The real lure here, though, are the **hot springs** for which Mamiña is famous throughout Chile; the delicious bottled mineral water from here is on sale in the region only, as production is small. Unlike Pica, Mamiña doesn't have just one hot spring, but many, and their waters are piped to every house in the village. Furthermore, these waters are not merely hot, but are reputed to cure all manner of afflictions, from eczema and psoriasis to respiratory problems and anxiety. Whatever their medicinal value, there's no doubt that the waters are supremely relaxing to bathe in. This you can do in any of the village's hotels or *residenciales*, usually in your own private *tina*, or bathtub.

There are also a number of public springs, including the **Baños Ipla** (daily 8am–1.30pm & 3–9pm; CH$1000), down in the valley, whose four large *tinas* are filled with hot sulphurous water (45°C/115°F) bubbling up from underground. Nearby, the **Vertiente del Radium** is a little fountain whose radioactive waters are supposed to cure eye infections and, according to legend, restored the sight of an Inca princess. A short walk from here, behind the water-bottling plant, you'll find the mud baths of **Barros Chino** (daily 9am–4pm; CH$1000) where you can plaster yourself in mud (don't let the caretaker do it for you), lie on a wooden rack while it dries, then wash it off in a small thermal pool.

Practicalities

Mamiña is 125km – a two-and-a-half-hour drive – from Iquique. **Accommodation** is centred in two quite separate areas, one on the ridge overlooking the valley, and the other down in the valley, by the Baños Ipla. All are run on a

The Legend of La Tirana

La Tirana is named after an Inca princess whose story is vividly recorded in twelve large panels inside the town's church. It all began in 1535 when **Diego de Almagro** marched south from Cuzco to conquer Chile. He took with him some five hundred Spaniards and ten thousand locals, including Paullo Tupac, an Inca prince, and Huillac Huma, high priest of the cult of the Sun God, who was accompanied by his beautiful 23-year-old daughter, **la ñusta** (the princess). Unknown to Almagro, the party also included a number of **Wilkas**, or high-ranking warriors from the Inca Royal Army. When the party reached Atacama la Grande, the high priest took the opportunity to slip away from the group and flee to Charcas, where he planned to stir up rebellion against the Spaniards. Later, while the group was resting for several days in the oasis of **Pica**, the princess followed her father's lead and escaped from the Spaniards – with a hundred Wilkas and followers – and fled to the *tamarugo* forests which at that time covered much of the pampa. She lost no time in organizing her followers into a fierce and sophisticated army that, for the next four years, waged a relentless war against their oppressors, the Spaniards. Her mission was clear: death to all Spaniards, and to all Indians who had been baptized by them. Before long, this indomitable woman became known far and wide as La Tirana del Tamarugal – the Tyrant of the Tamarugal.

One day, in 1544, La Tirana's army attacked an enemy group and returned to their leader with a prisoner – a certain **Don Vasco de Almeyda**, one of the Portuguese miners established in Huantajaya. Don Vasco was clearly a man of exceptional qualities for, according to the legend, "*Mirarle y enamorarse fue una sola cosa*" – simply to look at him was to fall in love with him. La Tirana, hitherto immovable, fell passionately in love with the foreigner. But according to everything she stood and fought for, he must be sentenced to death. In desperation, she devised a ruse to prolong the prisoner's life: she consulted the stars and her tribe's gods, and claimed that they had ordered her to keep him alive until four moons had passed. For the next four months, La Tirana and her prisoner spent day after day talking to one another in the shade of the *tamarugos*, and a tender love grew up between them. The princess neglected her people and her duties, arousing the suspicion of the Wilkas, who began to keep a secret watch on her. As the fourth month was coming to an end, La Tirana asked her loved one if they would be reunited for eternity in heaven if she too were a Christian. On his affirmative reply, she begged him to baptize her, and bent down on her knees with her arms crossed against her breast. Pouring water over her head, Almeyda began to do so, but before he could finish, the couple were showered with arrows from the bows of the betrayed Wilkas. As she lay dying in the wood, the princess cried, "I am dying happy, sure as I am that my immortal soul will ascend to God's throne. All I ask is that after my death, you will bury me next to my lover and place a cross over our grave." Ten years later, when Padre Antonio Rondon arrived in these parts to evangelize the Indians, it was with astonishment and joy that he discovered a simple cross in a clearing of the wood. The priest erected a humble chapel on the site, which was later replaced by a larger building, and became, in time, the centre of worship in a town that took its name from the beautiful princess who had died there.

full-board basis. Down in "Sector Ipla", you'll find modest rooms at *Inti Raimi* (℡57/413218; ❸), run by a friendly young couple, and *El Tamarugal* (℡57/414663; ❸), whose dining room has lovely views. If you can afford to pamper yourself, try Austrian-run *Los Cardenales* (℡&℻57/517000; ❺), which offers comfortable rooms in a large family house, fabulous *tinas* and a pool; or the *Llama Inn* (℡57/419893, ⓦ www.termasdemamina.cl; ❹), with a bright, sunny dining room, a pool and a beautiful lounge with floor-to-ceiling windows giving stunning views. For a small fee you can **camp** in the yard behind *El Basian*, or in the land belonging to *Inti Raimi*; a better place, however, is by the pool on the track out to Cerro del Inca, about a 30-minute walk from the Ipla baths.

Up to Parque Nacional Volcán Isluga

At the one-horse-town of **Huara**, 33km up the Panamericana from the turn-off to Iquique, a good road branches east into the desert, then climbs high into the mountains, continuing all the way to Oruro in Bolivia. It's paved as far as **Colchane**, on the Chilean side of the border, but the main appeal lies in getting off the tarmac once you're up into the cordillera and heading for the deserted wilderness in and around **Parque Nacional Volcán Isluga**. Here you'll find a remote, isolated landscape of wide plains, dramatic, snow-capped volcanoes and semi-abandoned villages, home to indigenous Aymara herding communities that have been a part of this windswept land for thousands of years. Unlike Parque Nacional Lauca, further north, this region hasn't yet been "discovered", and it's unlikely you'll come across many other tourists. There are a number of attractions on the way up, as well, in particular the weird desert geoglyph known as the **Gigante de Atacama**, in the pampa, and the frozen geysers of **Puchuldiza**, on the lower slopes of the Andes. There's no public transport around this region, so to explore it you must either take an organized tour from Iquique (see p.225), or rent a high-clearance vehicle, preferably 4WD.

Parque Nacional Volcán Isluga

Lying in the heart of the altiplano, **PARQUE NACIONAL VOLCÁN ISLUGA** is named after the towering, snow-capped volcano whose 5500-metre peak dominates the park's landscape. Its administrative centre is in **Enquelga**, a dusty, tumbledown hamlet – 3850m above sea level – home to a small Aymara community. Many of its inhabitants, particularly the women, still dress in traditional, brightly coloured clothes, and live from tending llamas and cultivating potatoes and barley. There's a Conaf *refugio* in the village, with **accommodation** for five people (CH$5500 per person); it's supposed to be open year-round, but sometimes isn't. Two kilometres on from Enquelga, **Aguas Calientes** is a long, spring-fed pool containing warm (but not hot) waters, set in an idyllic location with terrific views of the volcano. The pool is surrounded by pea-green *bofedal* – a spongy grass, typical of the altiplano – and drains into a little stream, crossed every morning and evening by herds of llamas driven to and from the sierra by Aymara shepherdesses. There's a stone changing-hut next to it, and a few **camping** spaces and picnic areas, protected from the evening wind by thick stone walls.

Six kilometres east of Enquelga, still within the park's boundaries, **Isluga** is composed of a hundred or so stone and adobe houses huddled around one of the most beautiful churches of the altiplano. Built some time in the seventeenth century (it's not known when, exactly), it's a humble little church made of thick, whitewashed adobe that flashes like snow in the constant glare of the sun. The main building, containing a single nave, is enclosed by a low wall trimmed with delicate arches; just outside the wall sits the two-tier bell tower with steps leading up to the top, where you can sit and survey the scenery or watch the humming-birds that fly in and out. The church, along with the entire village, remains locked up and abandoned for most of the year – Isluga is a "**ceremonial village**", whose inhabitants come back only for festivals, important religious ceremonies and funerals; the principal fiestas are held February 2 and 3, March 10, Easter week, and December 8, 12 and 21 through 25.

4

In April 1998, regional municipalities from Chile, Bolivia and Peru pledged their commitment to the proposed **Ruta Altiplánica de Integración** – a paved highway stretching 1500km across the altiplano, from San Pedro de Atacama in Chile to Cuzco, Peru. The "altiplano summit" optimistically set the year 2000 as its goal for getting work started, but the multimillion-dollar costs of the project haven't even been calculated yet, let alone raised. Nonetheless, given that it has support from all three governments, the highway is a realistic prospect for the coming decade. If it's built, the road will certainly open up what's currently a remote and largely inaccessible area, and is likely to give an economic boost to the whole altiplano region.

In the meantime, crossing the altiplano's pothole-riddled dirt tracks by jeep is still the road adventure of a lifetime – and should be enjoyed to the full before the arrival of tarmac and increased traffic. Probably the best starting point is Iquique (the ascent in altitude is more gradual in this direction), heading into the cordillera as far as Parque Nacional Volcán Isluga, continuing north across the altiplano to Parque Nacional Lauca, and finally descending in Arica. It's a **700-kilometre journey**, and takes about four to five days at an easy pace. If you do the trip, remember that there's no petrol station once you're off the Panamericana, which means taking it all with you in jerry cans (*bidones*, available in most ironmongers). Always take far, far more than you think you need. Another essential precaution is to take two spare tyres, not just one. For more on 4WD driving, see Basics, p.37.

Colchane and Cariquima

Ten kilometres from Isluga, at the end of the paved road from Huara, at 3730 metres above sea level, **COLCHANE** is a small, grim border town of grid-laid streets and truckers' canteens. Most days, the only reason you might want to come here is for **accommodation** (very basic rooms in *Camino del Inca*, opposite the telephone office; no phone; ➋); emergency **petrol** (*bencina verde*, or unleaded petrol, may be available in Andrés García's backyard, in the street opposite the school, but don't bank on it); or to cross over into **Bolivia** (border control open daily 8am–7pm, sometimes closed at lunch time). Twice a month, however, on alternate Saturdays, Colchane takes on a bit of life and colour as the neighbouring altiplano villagers bring their fresh produce, weavings and knitwear to sell at the **market**.

A far more charming place to stay is **CARIQUIMA**, just 17km south of Colchane. It has picturesque, cleanly swept streets and an old altiplano-style church with a painted interior. Seek out the **crafts cooperative**, housed in a beautifully decorated building along one of the village's few streets; high-quality woollens are sold. Cariquima sits in the lee of the dramatic Nevado Cariquima, while, 5km to the north, is the minute hamlet of **Ancovinto**. There you'll see a forest of giant cacti that sway in the breeze and enjoy fantastic views across the altiplano to Bolivia and the Salar de Coipasa. The unnamed *hostería* (no phone; ➋) has no hot water and you cannot book ahead.

The Panamericana between Iquique and Arica

Some three hundred long, dusty kilometres spread out between Iquique and Arica in a continuous stretch of brown desert hills and dried-up rivers. Most people whizz up here in about four hours without stopping, but there are a couple of interesting places to visit on the way: **Tiliviche**'s nineteenth-century graveyard and pre-Columbian geoglyphs can be explored in an hour or so, while **Pisagua** – a crumbling, evocative nitrate port about an hour's drive west to the coast – is more suitable as a night's stopover.

Pisagua

Eighty kilometres north of the turn-off to Iquique, a poorly paved side road leads 52km down to the once-important, now forgotten town of **PISAGUA**. The final stretch is very steep, giving dramatic views down to the little toy town cowering by the ocean, the only sign of life on this barren desert coast. Pisagua is a funny sort of place, part scruffy, ramshackle fishing town, part fascinating relic of the past. It was one of the busiest and wealthiest ports of the nitrate era, and is still dotted with many grand nineteenth-century buildings, some of them restored and repainted, others decaying at the same slow pace as the rest of the town (which has only about 150 inhabitants today). Most striking is the handsome, white-and-blue timber **clock tower**, built in 1887 and still standing watch from the hillside. The other great monument to the nitrate era is the old **theatre**, a fine wooden building erected in 1892, with a typical nineteenth-century facade featuring tall

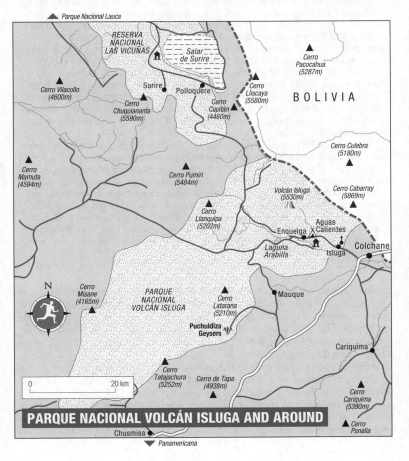

PARQUE NACIONAL VOLCÁN ISLUGA AND AROUND

The Aymara of Chile

The Aymara people are the second-largest indigenous linguistic group of South America (after the Quichoa). The culture flourished around **Lake Titicaca** and spread throughout the high-plain region, known as the altiplano, of what is now Bolivia, Peru and Chile. Today there are around three million Aymara scattered through these three countries, with the Chilean Aymara forming the smallest group, totalling some forty thousand people. Following the big migrations from the highlands to the coast that took place in the 1960s, most of the Aymara people of Chile now live and work in the coastal cities of **Arica** and **Iquique**. At least thirteen thousand Aymara, however, remain in the altiplano of northern Chile, where their lifestyle is still firmly rooted in the traditions of the past thousand years. The main economic activity is llama and sheep herding – which provides wool, milk, cheese, meat, leather and fertilizer – and the cultivation of crops such as potatoes and barley.

Traditionally, the Aymara live in **small communities**, called *ayllu*, based on extended family kinship; there are usually about a hundred people in each village. Their houses are made of stone and mud with rough thatched roofs, and most villages have a square and a small whitewashed church with a separate bell tower – often dating from the seventeenth century when Spanish missionaries evangelized the region.

Nowadays many of the smaller villages, such as Isluga, are left abandoned for most of the year, the houses securely locked up while their owners make their living down in the city or in the larger cordillera towns like Putre. Known as "ceremonial villages" they're shaken from their slumber and burst into life when all their people return for important religious festivals or funerals, usually two or three times a year. Andean **fiestas** are based on a fascinating blend of Catholic and indigenous rites. For instance, the aim of the fiestas is usually to worship the Virgin Mary, but sometimes a llama or lamb will be offered as a sacrificial victim – in some cases after the Virgin herself has put this request to the village *yatiri*, or elder. At the centre of Aymara culture is respect for the life-giving Mother Earth, known as *pachamama*, and traditional ceremonies – involving singing and dancing – are still carried out in some communities at sowing and harvest time.

The Aymara also believe that the tallest mountains looming over their villages contain spirits, or *mallku*, that guard over them, protecting their animals and crops. Once a year, on **May 3** – Cruz de Mayo – the most traditional communities climb up the sacred mountains, where a village elder speaks to the *mallku*, which appears in the form of a condor. It's hard to assess to what extent these long-held beliefs survive only as habit and superstition, and to what extent they remain a fundamental part of the Aymara world view. Today's young Aymara go to local state schools and speak Spanish as their main language, and while traditional lifestyles continue in the altiplano, it's with increasingly closer links with mainstream Chilean life.

wooden pillars, a balcony and a balustrade. You can borrow the key from the *carabineros* and wander inside to take a look at the large, empty stage, the rows of polished wooden seats, and the high ceiling, lavishly painted with cherubs dancing on clouds. The ghostliness of the place is made all the more intense by the monotonous sound of the waves crashing against the building's rear wall, which plunges directly down to the sea.

At the far end of town, next to the *carabineros* station, the village's more recent history is the subject of a haunting **mural** dedicated to the memory of those executed here during the military dictatorship, when Pisagua was used as a concentration camp. A couple of kilometres north, on the edge of the cemetery, the former site of the mass graves is marked by an open pit bearing a simple cross, a scattering of wreaths and a block of stone inscribed with a single line by Pablo Neruda: "Even though a thousand years shall pass, this site will never be cleansed of the blood of those who fell here."

There's a free (and shadeless) **campsite** close to the *carabineros* station, but to really soak up the nitrate-era atmosphere **stay** at ⚑ *Hotel Pisagua* (☎57/731509; ❹ full board), on Calle Videla in what was once the town prison. The guest rooms are in a beautiful wooden building – originally the warders' residence – built around a large patio filled with tall, lush banana plants and squawking parrots. The prison cells, in the adjacent building, are now filled with snooker and ping-pong tables that guests can use. The hotel is also about the only place **to eat** in Pisagua, serving excellent, fresh fish and good breakfasts. There is no public transport here.

Hacienda de Tiliviche

Ten kilometres north of the turn-off for Pisagua, just before the bridge across the Quebrada de Tiliviche, a short track branches left (west) to the **HACIENDA DE TILIVICHE**. At the end of the track you'll find the old *casa patronal*, a charmingly dilapidated house overlooking a yard full of clucking chickens and lethargic dogs. It was built in 1855 for a British nitrate family and remained in British hands until very recently; the current owners have plans to renovate it and turn it into a hotel. Set within the hacienda grounds, on the other side of the stream, stands a nostalgic testimony to the nitrate era: the old **British Cemetery**, enclosed by tall iron railings and a huge, rusty gate – you can borrow the key from the hacienda caretaker. Inside, about a hundred lonely graves stand in the shade of a few *tamarugo* trees at the foot of the desolate mountain that rises over the *quebrada*. This stark desert setting is strikingly at odds with the very English inscriptions on the tombstones ("Thy will be done" and the like). The graves read like a who's who of the erstwhile British business community, including people like Herbert Harrison, the manager of the Tarapacá Waterworks Company and, most famously, **James Humberstone**, the manager of several nitrate *oficinas*.

The southern wall of the *quebrada* also features some of the most impressive **geoglyphs** in Chile. They're best viewed from the pull-in just off the Panamericana, a few hundred metres up from the bridge on the northern side of the *quebrada*. From this vantage point, you can see the images in all their splendour – a large crowd of llamas covering the hillside. All of the llamas are moving in the same direction, towards the sea, and it's thought that the drawings were designed to guide caravans descending from the mountains on their journey towards the coast.

Arica and around

ARICA likes to call itself "*la ciudad de la eterna primavera*" – "City of Everlasting Spring". Chile's northernmost city, only 19km south of the Peruvian border, is certainly blessed with a mild climate, which, along with its sandy beaches, makes it a popular holiday resort for Chileans and Bolivians. Although a lingering sea fog can dampen spirits, in the winter especially, just head a few kilometres inland, and you'll usually find blue skies.

The city's compact, tidy centre sits proudly at the foot of the Morro cliff, the site of a major Chilean victory in the War of the Pacific (and cherished as a symbol of national glory). It was this war that delivered Arica into Chilean hands, in 1883, and while the city is emphatically Chilean today, there's no

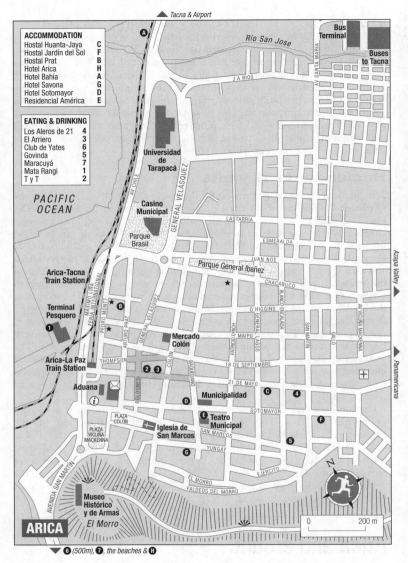

▲ *Tacna & Airport*

ACCOMMODATION
Hostal Huanta-Jaya	C
Hostal Jardín del Sol	F
Hostal Prat	B
Hotel Arica	H
Hotel Bahía	A
Hotel Savona	G
Hotel Sotomayor	D
Residencial América	E

EATING & DRINKING
Los Aleros de 21	4
El Arriero	3
Club de Yates	6
Govinda	5
Maracuyá	7
Mata Rangi	1
T y T	2

Río San Jose

Bus Terminal

Buses to Tacna

J A RIOS

AV SANTA MARIA

Universidad de Tarapacá

PACIFIC OCEAN

Casino Municipal

GENERAL VELASQUEZ

Parque Brasil

LASTARRIA

ESMERALDA

JUAN NOE

Parque General Ibañez

CHACABUCO

Arica-Tacna Train Station

Azapa Valley ▶

Terminal Pesquero

O'HIGGINS

AV VICUÑA MACKENNA

Panamericana ▶

Mercado Colón

Arica-La Paz Train Station

18 DE SEPTIEMBRE

THOMPSON

Aduana

21 DE MAYO

Municipalidad

SOTOMAYOR

PLAZA COLÓN

Iglesia de San Marcos

Teatro Municipal

SAN MARCOS

YUNGAY

PLAZA VICUÑA MACKENNA

EJERCITO

EL MORRO

FALDEOS DEL MORRO

N

Museo Histórico y de Armas

ARICA

El Morro

0   200 m

▼ **6** (500m), **7**, the beaches & **H**

denying the strong presence of *mestizo* and Quichoa-speaking Peruvians on the streets, trading their fresh produce and *artesanía*. This, added to its role as Bolivia's main export centre, makes Arica more colourful, ethnically diverse and vibrant than most northern Chilean cities, although the early years of the new millennium have seen an economic slump, largely due to unrest in Bolivia and difficulties in Peru. The liveliest streets are pedestrianized Calles 21 de Mayo and Bolognesi, the latter clogged with **artesanía stalls**. Far from beautiful, Arica does boast a couple of fine pieces of nineteenth-century architecture, pretty squares filled with flowers and palm trees, and a young, lively atmosphere. It's a pleasant enough place to spend a couple of days – or longer, if you feel like kicking back on the beach. A short taxi ride out of town, in the Azapa Valley, the marvellous **Museo Arqueológico** is one of Chile's best and certainly deserves a visit. A few hours east, up in the cordillera, **Parque Nacional Lauca** has become one of the most popular attractions in the north of Chile. A few of Arica's tour operators will get you there if you don't relish the idea of driving yourself.

Arrival and information

Coming in **by bus**, you'll arrive at Arica's Terminal Rodoviario, which uniquely charges a CH$100 platform fee for all **departures**; make sure to pay this fee at your bus company desk, even if you already have a bus ticket. The terminal is quite a distance from town on Avenida Diego Portales, but you can easily catch a *colectivo* or *micro* into the centre. Arica's Chacalluta **airport** lies 18km north of the city and is connected to the centre by reasonably priced airport taxis (CH$5000) or minibus transfers (CH$2000). For tourist information, head for the **Sernatur** office in a sadly dilapidated old building at San Marcos 101 (March–Nov, Mon–Fri 8.30am–2pm & 3–5.30pm; Jan–Feb, daily 8.30am–8pm; ☎58/254506, ⓦwww.sernatur.cl).

Tours from Arica

Three or four companies in Arica regularly offer **tours** up to **Parque Nacional Lauca** (see p.245). The problem, however, is that the most commonly available tour takes place in a single day, which means rushing from sea level to up to 4500m and down again in a short space of time – really not a good idea, and very likely to cause some ill effects, ranging from tiredness and mild headaches to acute dizziness and nausea. In very rare cases the effects can be more serious, and you should always check that the company carries a supply of oxygen and has a staff member trained to deal with emergencies. Altitude aside, the amount of time you spend inside a minibus is very tiring, which can spoil your experience of what is one of the most beautiful parts of Chile. Therefore it's really worth paying extra and taking a tour that includes at least one overnight stop in Putre; better still is one continuing south to the Salar de Surire (see p.249) and Parque Nacional Isluga (see p.233). However, it's worth noting that availability of these longer tours can be frustratingly scarce during the quieter low season months. One-day trips usually cost around CH$20,000 per person, while you can expect to pay around CH$45–100,000 for a one- or two-night tour, overnighting in Putre, and around CH$180,000 for a three-night tour, sleeping in Putre and Colchane.

Geotours Bolognesi 421 ☎58/253927, Ⓕ58/251675, Ⓔgeotur@entelchile.net. Slick, professional but fairly impersonal company offering mostly one-day tours.

Latinorizons Bolognesi 449 & Thompson 236 ☎&Ⓕ58/250007, ⓦwww.latinorizons .com, Ⓔlatinor@entelchile.net. Friendly Belgian-run company offering a wide range of altiplano tours, including overnight, with a more adventurous feel than most of the others on offer. Extremely reliable and French and English spoken.

Parinacota Expediciones Prat 430 ☎&Ⓕ58/256227. Well-established company offering several options for visiting Parque Nacional Lauca and around, including the usual day-trip, an overnight stop in Putre and a two-night tour taking in the Salar de Surire.

Tierra Expediciones Ⓔinfo@tierraexpediciones.com, ⓦwww.tierraexpediciones .com. Highly recommended newcomer offering specialized tours, such as trekking and photo-safaris, throughout Northern Chile lasting from a couple of days to one month. Run by a very enthusiastic and well-informed Chilean-Swiss couple. English, German and Italian spoken.

The regional **Conaf** office, at Vicuña Mackenna 820 (Mon–Fri 8.30am–
5.30pm; ℡58/201225, ℻58/250750), has basic maps and information on
Parque Nacional Lauca and adjoining protected areas. You can also reserve
beds at the Conaf *refugios* in these areas, if you know exactly when you'll be
arriving (see box, p.247).

Accommodation

Unlike Iquique, Arica has very little seafront accommodation and most places
to stay are situated in and around the town's centre. Here, there's no shortage
of *residenciales*, ranging from the dirt-cheap to the polished and comfortable.
Typically for these parts, however, there's a lack of decent mid-range accommodation. **Camping** options are limited to *El Refugio* (℡58/227545;
CH$8000 per site), a shady, grassy campsite with a pool, 1.5km up the Azapa
Valley, reached by frequent *colectivos*. The valley is a welcome refuge from the
hectic downtown but you won't find much accommodation – try the *Azapa
Inn* (see p.243).

Hostal Huanta-Jaya 21 de Mayo 660
℡&℻58/314605. Clean and pleasant sky-lit rooms
off a leafy corridor, all with private baths. Central, yet
quiet. ❸

Hostal Jardín del Sol Sotomayor 848
℡58/232795, ℮info@hostaljardindelsol.cl. Small,
tidy rooms with private bath off a flower-filled
courtyard with tables, chairs and loungers. Very
friendly, too – great for the price. ❸

Hostal Prat Prat 555 ℡58/251292, ℮info@
residentialprat.com. Spartan but spotless little rooms
with white walls, tiled floors and clean baths – do not
confuse with the *residencial* of the same name. ❸

Hotel Arica Av San Martín 599 ℡58/254540,
℮reservas@hotelarica.cl. Upmarket but rather dated
and overpriced hotel overlooking the ocean, with
pleasant rooms, *cabañas* and a pool. Mediocre food
is served at its expensive *Península* restaurant. ❽

Hotel Bahía Ave Luis Beretta Porcel 2031
℡58/260676, ℮info@bahiahotel.cl,

ⓦwww.bahiahotel.cl. A 15min walk from the
centre, this place has direct access to the beach.
Inexpensive, basic rooms are all glass-fronted with
superb ocean views. Two self-contained beachfront
cabañas are also available. ❸

Hotel Savona Yungay 380 ℡58/231000,
℮reservas@hotelsavona.cl. Low-rise, 70's-style hotel
built around a bright patio garden with a swimming
pool. Tasteless yet comfortable rooms have small
private bathrooms. Bikes available for hire. ❺

Hotel Sotomayor Sotomayor 367 ℡58/585761,
℮reservas@hotelsotomayor.cl. Formerly the *Hotel
San Marcos*, it features clean, airy yet somewhat
dated rooms (disappointing after the beautiful old
Spanish tiles in the lobby) with private bath and
parking. ❹

Residencial América Sotomayor 430
℡58/254148. Good-value budget rooms with an
encouraging odour of furniture polish. Some rooms
have private bath. ❷

The City

In the centre you'll find the small, tree-filled **Plaza Colón**, dominated by the
Iglesia de San Marcos, a pretty white church with a high, Gothic spire and
many tall, arched windows. Designed by Gustave Eiffel, this curious church,
made entirely of iron, was prefabricated in France before being erected in Arica
in 1876. The riveting key used to assemble the structure was kept in a display
case inside the church, but when Chilean troops attacked, it was thrown into
the sea to prevent the invaders from dismantling the church and stealing it as a
war trophy (instead, they took the whole city).

Two blocks west, towards the port, rises another Eiffel-designed building – the
1874 **Aduana** (customs house) with an attractive stone facade of pink and
white horizontal stripes. These days it's used as a cultural centre and puts on
regular photographic and art exhibitions. It looks onto **Parque Baquedano**, a
little square full of palm trees and shady benches, flanked to the south by the
coastal avenue, and on its northern side by the Arica–La Paz **train station**.

Wander inside this large wooden 1913 building and you'll find a couple of shiny black locomotives displayed in an interior patio, and a roomful of nineteenth-century railway paraphernalia (ask a guard to let you in). Nearby, you'll see the smelly but colourful **terminal pesquero**, where inquisitive pelicans wander around the fish stalls.

Arica's most visible feature is the 110-metre-high cliff known as **El Morro**, which signals the end of the coastal cordillera. Steps starting at the southern end of Calle Colón lead you to the top, where sweeping, panoramic views (especially impressive at night) and the **Museo Histórico y de Armas** (daily: 8am–8pm; CH$600) await. Built on top of a former Peruvian fortification, this museum is owned by the army, rather than the government, and has clearly had more money spent on it than most Chilean museums. The exhibits – primarily nineteenth-century guns and military uniforms – are very well displayed, but the theme is rather chauvinistic in tone, the main thrust being the superiority of the Chileans and the inferiority of the Peruvians in the Battle of the Morro, when Chilean forces stormed and took possession of the hilltop defence post.

The beaches

The closest beach to the centre is the popular **Playa El Laucho**, a curved, sandy cove about a twenty-minute walk down Avenida San Martín, south of El Morro. You can also get *micros* down the avenue, which continue to several other beaches, including **Playa La Lisera** and **Playa Brava**, both attractive, and the usually deserted **Playa Arenillas Negras**, a wide expanse of dark sand backed by low sand dunes, with a fish-processing factory at its southern end. Two kilometres north of the centre, **Playa Chinchorro** is a large, clean beach where you can rent jet skis in high season (Dec–March; CH$12,000 for 30min). Further north, **Playa Las Machas** is quieter but more exposed to the wind. To get to **Playa Chinchorro**, take bus #5-A from General Velásquez with Chacabuco.

Eating, drinking and entertainment

You'll find the biggest concentration of **restaurants**, **cafés** and **bars** on the pedestrianized section of 21 de Mayo, the city's main thoroughfare. Arica seems to be the national capital of the **roasted-chicken-on-a-spit** industry – low-cost places serving it dot Maipú, between Baquedano and Colón. The **disco** scene can get quite lively in high season, and even in low season there are a few locales where you'll always find a crowd on a Friday and Saturday night – *Cantaverdi*, Bolognesi 453, is one of the most welcoming spots offering good music, tasty snacks and drinks. Otherwise head out to the Azapa Valley (see p.242) to places like *Sunset* or *Swing*.

Los Aleros de 21 21 de Mayo 736. Traditional Chilean restaurant serving pricey, yet excellent steaks, seafood and other meat dishes. Great quality and service – it's a favourite among locals, and deservedly so.

El Arriero 21 de Mayo 385. Mid-price grill house serving tasty fillet steaks and other meat dishes; often has live folk music at the weekends.

Club de Yates Ex *Isla Alacrán*. Privileged location, on a spur (once an island) projecting into the ocean, with outdoor seating and great views

(especially at night). Serves reasonably priced omelettes, salads and meat and fish dishes. Closed to non-members Sat & Sun.

Govinda Blanco Encalada 200. Tasty, vegetarian set menu lunches that include soup, salad and a main dish. Great for healthy lunches on small budgets.

Maracuyá Av San Martín 0321, Playa La Lisera ☎58/227600. At this smart restaurant (one of Arica's best), sitting dramatically right over the ocean's edge, you're treated to a

Moving on from Arica

You have many different options to head out of Arica. To get up to the altiplano, you can take a bus to Putre or Parinacota with Buses La Paloma, Germán Riesco 2071 (☎58/222710); or to Lago Chungará on any bus to La Paz; you sometimes are asked to pay full fare to La Paz – refuse. From the main bus terminal there are plenty of inter-city buses heading south down the Panamericana, as far as Santiago. You can also catch buses at the main terminal to La Paz, in Bolivia (CH$8000–10,000; 7–8hr), with Pullman (☎58/241972), Cuevas y Gonzales (☎58/241090) or Chile Bus Arica (☎58/222817); or alternatively you can depart from the shabbier International Terminal just opposite on Diego Portales 1002 with Buses Trans Salvador (☎58/246064). Tacna, 55km north in Peru, can be reached easily by *colectivo* (CH$3,000) or regular buses (CH$1500), that also depart from the International Terminal. Tur Bus runs a daily "direct" service to San Pedro de Atacama, leaving around 10pm and arriving in time for breakfast the following day. There are regular flights from Arica to Iquique, Antofagasta, Calama, Copiapó and Santiago, plus Arequipa in Peru.

spectacle of breaking waves as you sample the boldly prepared fish and seafood.

Mata Rangi Terminal pesquero. Tucked inside the fishermen's harbour, a rustic inexpensive place serving unfussy fish and seafood lunches – sit by the window and watch the pelicans eat theirs as you eat yours. Picnic trips to a nearby penguin colony on the owner's boat can also be arranged (ⓦwww.turismomarino.com).

T y T 21 de Mayo 233. With a terrace strategically located on the main drag and a bright, stylish decor, this godsend serves real coffee; excellent breakfasts; a range of sandwiches, snacks and crisp salads; some hot dishes; and delicious cakes (such as raspberry cheesecake) and cookies. It offers a good selection of beers, wines and cocktails, too.

Listings

Airlines LAN, Arturo Prat 391 ☎58/252650; Sky Airlines, 21 de Mayo 356 ☎58/251816 or 290768 at airport.

Banks and exchange Arica has many ATMs – mostly on 21 de Mayo – but only three *casas de cambio*: Yanulaque, Colón 392, Costa Arica, Colón 427 and Zesal, 21 de Mayo 345. There are also several money-changers on the street, at the corner of 21 de Mayo and Colón.

Car rental Budget, Colón 996 ☎58/258911; Hertz, Baquedano 999 ☎58/231487; Klasse, Velásquez 760 ☎58/254498; Cactus, Baquedano 635 ☎58/258353.

Internet Cyber Technicomp, Sotomayor 199, charges CH$300 an hour.

Post office Arturo Prat 305.

Taxis Radiotaxi Chacalluta, Patricio Lynch 371 ☎58/254812; Radio Taxi ☎58/257000.

Tour operators See box, p.239.

Travel agencies Among the numerous travel agencies in town are Mega Tour, 21 de Mayo 260 ☎58/254701; Tacora, Colón 388 ☎58/232786; and Globo Tour, 21 de Mayo 320 ☎58/583372; America Tour Colón 373 ☎58/231845; all of these are good for air tickets, etc. For tours to Parque Nacional Lauca, see box, p.239.

The Azapa Valley

Avenida Diego Portales extends out of Arica's city centre into the green **AZAPA VALLEY**. The far western end of the valley is, for all intents and purposes, a suburb of Arica, crammed as it is with condos and villas, some of which have been converted into trendy discos, along with a couple of good restaurants.

On your way out towards the Azapa Valley, on Calle Hualles, just south of the river, the **Poblado Artesanal** is a replica of an altiplano village, where twelve white houses serve as workshops for artisans selling handicrafts ranging from ceramics and glass to knitwear and leather items; its hours of operation are erratic.

Thirteen kilometres along the road, the outstanding **Museo Arqueológico** (daily: Jan & Feb 10am–7pm; March–Dec 10am–6pm; CH$1000), part of the University of Tarapacá, houses an excellent collection of regional pre-Columbian artefacts, including four extraordinary Chinchorro mummies (see box, p.244) – of a man, a woman and two children – buried over four thousand years ago. Other exhibits include finely decorated Tiwanaku ceramics, ancient Andean musical instruments and snuff trays, and many beautifully embroidered tapestries – look out for the one in Case 11, decorated with images of smiling women – and displays on contemporary Aymara culture. All the pieces are extremely well presented, and there are unusually explanatory leaflets available in several languages, including English, French and German.

In the nearby village of **San Miguel de Azapa**, the only place of interest is the fabulously multicoloured desert **cemetery**, which climbs like a mini-Valparaíso for the deceased towards a dune-like cliff. The colour comes from the artificial flowers laid on the graves. By the entrance sits the morbidly named **restaurant**, *La Picá del Muertito* (the "Little Dead Man's Snack-Bar"), famous for miles around for its first-rate *pastel de choclo*, a sugar-glazed corn-bake containing meat, egg and olives.

The Azapa Valley is also the site of several **geoglyphs**. The most impressive example is **Alto Ramírez**, a large, stylized human figure surrounded by geometric shapes; you can see it, at a distance, from the main road on the way to the museum (ask your *colectivo* driver to point it out to you) or take a detour to get a closer look.

Practicalities

If you want to get away from the pollution of downtown Arica, the Azapa Valley is a pleasant place to **stay**, though options are pretty much limited to the *Azapa Inn* at Guillermo Sánchez 660 (☎58/244517 or 58/225191, Ⓦwww.azapainn .cl; ❻), at the beginning of the valley. Its spacious rooms, many with balconies, are in two-storey blocks spread around luxuriant subtropical grounds with a large swimming-pool; the restaurant serves imaginatively prepared dishes at reasonable prices. The **Club de Huasos** (Km 3.5) is one of several country restaurants, all very popular with families, offering hearty, moderately priced Sunday lunches in the green Azapa Valley.

Colectivos for the Azapa Valley, including the Museo Arqueológico and the nearby geoglyphs, leave from the corner of Lynch and Chacabuco in Arica's centre.

Up to Parque Nacional Lauca

Some 160km east of Arica, **Parque Nacional Lauca** is the perfect microcosm of the Chilean altiplano, offering snow-capped volcanoes, pristine lakes, whitewashed villages and wild vicuña – all conveniently located at the end of a paved highway, just four hours' drive from the city. The journey there takes you through some beautiful and varied scenery, ranging from deep-green vegetation to rippling desert hills. There are several opportunities for overnighting en route to the park, which is strongly recommended to avoid the risk of altitude sickness. Once you're up there, you can head south

Chinchorro mummies

In 1983, while laying a new pipeline near the foot of El Morro, the Arica water company came across a hoard of withered corpses buried a couple of metres beneath the sand. Work immediately ceased and archeologists from the University of Tarapacá were rushed in to assess the scene, which turned out to be a seven-thousand-year-old burial site containing 96 bodies – the largest and best-preserved find, to date, of **Chinchorro mummies**.

The ancient practice of mummification in this region – the oldest known in the world – was first identified in 1917 when **Max Uhle**, a German archeologist working in Arica, discovered a series of highly unusual human remains. The Atacama had already yielded prehistoric bodies naturally mummified by the heat and dryness of the desert, but Uhle realized that these bodies were different – they were, in fact, the result of an elaborate and highly skilled form of **artificial mummification** that had kept them intact for thousands of years. Further excavations revealed similar findings spread along the coast, concentrated between Arica and Camerones, 65km south, and it became apparent that they were relics of an ancient society that archeologists have named the Chinchorro culture. Uhle originally estimated that the Chinchorro people started mummifying their dead some two thousand years ago, but modern radiocarbon dating has established that the practice was well under way by 5000 BC – more than two millennia before the Egyptians began practising mummification.

No one knows exactly where the Chinchorro people came from; some archeologists speculate that they moved down from the north, others that they came from the Andean highlands. What's clear, however, is that by 7000 BC scattered groups of people – possibly extended families – were spread along the coast of Chile's Far North, where they lived on the abundant crabs, clams, mussels, seaweed, pelicans, sea lions and other marine life of the region, supplementing their diet with guanaco and wild berries.

The great simplicity of their hunter-gatherer lifestyle makes the sophisticated techniques they developed to **preserve the dead** all the more extraordinary. The practice involved removing the brain through a hole at the base of the skull, and removing all internal organs, which were probably discarded. After this, the cavities were dried with hot stones or fire and then refilled with straw and ashes. The bones of the arms and legs were replaced with sticks bound into place with reeds, and the skeleton was given extra padding before the body was stitched up. The face was then coated in paste that dried into a hard mask with a sculpted nose and incisions marking the eyes and mouth. The finishing touch was provided by a wig made of human hair that was attached to the skull.

One of the most curious aspects of the Chinchorro mummies is that they probably weren't buried immediately – signs of repeated "repair jobs" on many of them suggest they were kept on display and venerated before being wrapped in their reed shrouds and buried with their funerary offerings. Whether or not this was the case, there's no doubt that the cult of mummification was based on a complex approach to the dead and the afterlife. The Chinchorro culture performed this elaborate process for over three thousand years until, for unknown reasons, the practice died out around 1500 BC, and the era of the oldest known form of artificial mummification came to an end.

across the altiplano to neighbouring **Parque Nacional Las Vicuñas** and the **Salar de Surire**, and if you're feeling really adventurous, continue to **Parque Nacional Volcán Isluga**, descending in Iquique. Remember to take warm clothing with you, as temperatures can drop as low as -20°C (-4°F) at night.

Putre

The busy little mountain town of **PUTRE**, surrounded by a patchwork of green fields and Inca terraces, lies 24km on from Socoroma. At 3500m above sea level, it's a popular overnight stop en route to the higher altitudes of Parque Nacional Lauca – climbers, in particular, like to spend a few days walking in the hills here before attempting the volcanoes in the park. Putre's rustic houses are clustered around a large, green square, overlooked by the Municipalidad, which provides basic **tourist information** (Mon–Fri 8.30am–12.30pm & 3–6pm). Nearby, off the northeast corner of the square, you'll find the **church**, built in 1670 after an earthquake destroyed the original one, which, according to old Spanish chronicles, was clad in gold and silver. The current building, heavily restored in 1871, is considerably more modest, consisting of a small stone chapel and a whitewashed, straw-roofed bell tower. The village observes the Feast of the Assumption, August 15, with a week-long celebration that features much singing and dancing; accommodation is hard to find during this time.

Putre has several options for eating and sleeping. On the main street into town, you'll find small, tidy **rooms** off a sunny backyard at *Residencial Cali*, Baquedano 399 (ⓔhostal_cali@hotmail.com; ❷), and decent, more comfortable rooms with good-sized breakfasts and parking at the newer *Hotel Kukuli*, Baquedano 301 (no phone; ❹), run by the very friendly Libertad. Situated just behind *Kukuli*, *Pachamama* (ⓣ58/228564; ❸) on Lord Cochrane is one of the most relaxed places to stay with simple rooms grouped around a shady courtyard, shared bathrooms, a kitchen and free internet. On the western edges of town, about a ten-minute walk from the plaza, *Hotel Q'antati*, Hijuela 208 (ⓣ58/228916; ❻) is the smartest, and most expensive, place to stay, offering modern heated bedrooms with views out to the valley. Most of Putre's few **restaurants** are dire, with the exception of ☂ *Kuchu Marka* on Baquedano, a cosy place where you can get alpaca stew and other hearty mountain dishes like *picante de conejo* (a sort of rabbit curry) along with an excellent vegetarian option; and *Cantaverdi*, right on the square, serving standard meat and fish dishes, sandwiches and a superb quinoa risotto. Alto Andino Nature Tours, along Baquedano (ⓣ58/300013, ⓕ58/222735, ⓦwww.birdingaltoandino.com, ⓔbeknapton@hotmail.com), is run by an Alaska naturalist who offers wildlife-viewing excursions, specializing in ornithology and marine mammals, in Parque Nacional Lauca and coastal areas; consult the website for more details. She also has a few simple, clean rooms (❹), with heating, cooking and laundry facilities. For informative trips into the altiplano, Alvaro Mamani (ⓔamamaniguia@gmail.com) is a very personable Aymara guide, while local Valentina Alave offers walks to interesting cave paintings 7km from the village – ask at the Municipalidad for more information. Buses La Paloma, Germán Riesco 2071 (ⓣ58/222710; CH$3000), runs regular **buses** to Putre from Arica.

Parque Nacional Lauca

As you continue up the main road, about 4km past the turn-off to Putre a little dirt road on the right leads 3km to the **Termas de Jurasi** – a beautifully situated tin shack containing two large baths of hot thermal water plus a large open-air, concrete pool, along with toilets and changing rooms (open daylight hours, CH$1000). Back on the paved road, a steep 7km up from the turn-off to the springs, at a 4400-metre-high mountain pass, you cross the boundary into **PARQUE NACIONAL LAUCA**. By now the air is thin and cold, and the road is flanked by light-green *bofedal* (highland pasture) where herds of

▲ Parque Nacional Lauca

wild vicuña come to feed in the mornings. Ten kilometres into the park, you reach the Conaf hut at **Las Cuevas**, a good place to stop to check on weather and road conditions and observe the comical antics of vizcachas, cuddly chinchilla-like rodents with curly tails and a spring-like leap. From here the road continues through a wide, green plain filled with grazing llamas and alpacas, passing the turn-off for Parinacota, 19km on from the Conaf hut, and Lago Chungará, a further 18km along the road.

Parinacota

The park's headquarters are in **PARINACOTA** (the name means "flamingo lake" in Aymara), an idyllic *pueblo altiplánico* composed of fifty or so crumbling, whitewashed houses huddled around a beautiful little **church**. Built in 1789, this is one of Chile's most assiduously maintained Andean churches, sporting brilliant white walls and a bright-blue wooden door, trimmed with yellow and green. Like most churches of the altiplano, it has thick stone and adobe walls and a sloping straw roof, and is enclosed within a little white wall incorporating the bell tower into one of its corners. It's usually open in the morning (if not, you can borrow the key from the caretaker – ask at the *artesanía* stalls). Inside, you'll find a series of faded, centuries-old friezes depicting the Stations of the Cross and vivid scenes of sinners suffering in hell. There's also an unusual collection of skulls belonging to former priests, and a magical "walking" table that's kept chained to the wall, for fear it will wander off in the night.

Opposite the church, in the plaza, local women sell alpaca knitwear and other **artesanía** – a sign of life returning to Parinacota, which until recently was virtually depopulated. Many of its houses are still under lock and key for much of the year, their owners returning only for important fiestas and funerals (see box, p.236). The nearby **Conaf** administration centre, housed in a large, chalet-style building, makes a valiant attempt at informing the public about the park and its wildlife, and sometimes offers **camping** space out the back. *Pensión Uta Kala* (☎58/261526, ✉leonel_parinacota@hotmail.com ❷) is the first and only

Conaf refugios

If you are travelling under your own steam but do not fancy camping in the open wilds of the cold, high altiplano, the various **Conaf refugios** (ⓦwww.conaf.cl) dotted around the Parque Nacional Lauca, Parque Nacional Isluga and in between make for excellent places to stay. They have proper beds, some have decent facilities, and they are nearly all located in amazing spots, with views to linger over. The only problem is that in recent years their upkeep has been shoddy and they are sometimes left in a pitiful state by previous visitors. Worst of all, even if you book ahead through the Conaf offices in Arica or Iquique, reservations are not always respected and you might turn up to find no room at the inn.

hostel in town – and it's a good one, with several comfy beds, hot water, heating, meals and splendid views onto fields of grazing llama. Alternatively, some villagers offer very basic **rooms** without hot water (①–②); ask around. You can reach Parinacota by **bus** from Arica with Buses La Paloma, Germán Riesco 2071 (Tues & Fri 11.30am; ☎58/222710).

Lagunas de Cotacotani
A collection of small, interconnected lakes lying in a dark lava field, filled with exquisite jade-green water, the **LAGUNAS DE COTACOTANI** lie about

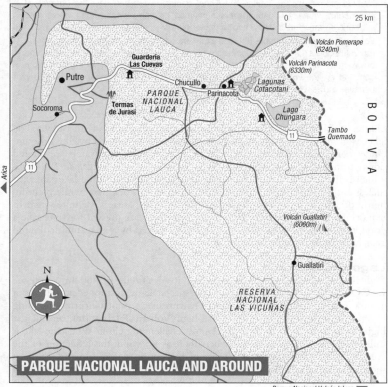

PARQUE NACIONAL LAUCA AND AROUND

Parque Nacional Volcán Isluga ▼

Walks and climbs in Parque Nacional Lauca

Lauca doesn't offer a great many hiking possibilities, and most people are content to just admire the scenery and the wildlife. There are, however, at least three half-day or day **walks** you can do, and many more possibilities for **climbing**. Remember to respect the altitude, and to allow yourself more time to cover distances that you could walk quite easily at lower elevations.

Cerro Choquelimpie No technical experience or equipment is necessary to climb this 5288-metre-high peak, reached in about four hours from the *refugio* at Lago Chungará. From the top, you get views down to the gold mine behind the mountain, and on to Lago Chungará and Volcán Parinacota.

Cerro Guane Guane A slow but straightforward climb up this 5096-metre peak is rewarded by panoramic views over the park. It's suitable for any fit person used to hill-climbing and takes around four hours to the top from the Conaf centre at Parinacota, and two to three hours back down.

Lago Chungará to Parinacota (or reverse) This 18-kilometre walk from the *refugio* at Lago Chungará to Parinacota takes about six hours. Follow the paved highway as far as the *mirador de Lagunas Cotacotani*, then climb down to the lakes, from where a jeep track continues to Parinacota.

Parinacota to Lagunas de Cotacotani A rewarding, not-too-difficult walk, taking about three hours (one way) from Parinacota; ask the Conaf *guardaparque* to point you in the direction of the jeep track you need to follow.

Sendero de excursión de Parinacota An easy, six-kilometre circular walk, marked by blue stones starting behind the Conaf centre, taking you past the *bofedal de Parinacota*, where you can observe numerous grazing alpaca. Good views onto surrounding mountains. Allow two to three hours.

Volcán Parinacota Suitable only for experienced climbers carrying crampons and ropes (though it's not always necessary to use them). Allow two days to get up and down from the base camp (a day's hike from Parinacota), including one night camping on the volcano. Avoid this climb between mid-December and February, because of the weather conditions.

8km east of Parinacota, clearly visible from the paved highway to Bolivia. The lakes were formed by volcanic eruptions and are surrounded by fine dust and cinder cones, further adding to their lunar appearance. The waters are filtered down from Lago Chungará and then continue to the *bofedal de Parinacota*, which is the source of the Río Lauca. On closer inspection the lakes aren't as lifeless as they first appear; many wild Andean geese flock here, while plentiful herds of alpaca graze the soggy marshland. This area is definitely worth exploring as a day hike from Parinacota, but if you are pressed for time take a good look from the *mirador* on the highway, marked by a giant multicoloured *zampoña* (Andean panpipes).

Lago Chungará

Eighteen kilometres on from Parinacota, at an altitude of 4600m, you'll see **LAGO CHUNGARÁ**, a wide blue lake spectacularly positioned at the foot of a snow-capped volcano that rises over its rim like a giant Christmas pudding covered in cream. This is 6330-metre-high **Volcán Parinacota**, one of the highest peaks in Chile and the park's most challenging climb. When the lake is mill-pond calm, in other words when there is no wind, the reflection of the volcano is the most memorable view in the entire region. On the southern shore of the lake, right by the highway, you'll find a small stone **Conaf refugio** with four beds (CH$4500 per person), a kitchen and unbeatable views. **Camping** can be organized through a local company based next door to the refugio (❶–❷). This is unquestionably the best place to stay in the park, allowing you to observe the changing colours of the lake and volcano at different times of day, from the transparent pinks of early morning to the deep blues and gleaming whites of the afternoon.

Reserva Nacional las Vicuñas and the Salar de Surire

Directly south of Parque Nacional Lauca, the **RESERVA NACIONAL LAS VICUÑAS** stretches over 100km south across spectacular altiplano wilderness filled with wild vicuña, green *bofedales*, abandoned Aymara villages, groves of *queñoa* – spindly, rickety-looking trees belonging to a species that miraculously defies the treeline – and sweeping vistas of volcanoes. It's far less accessible than Lauca, with no public transport, which means hiring a high-clearance 4WD vehicle or taking an organized tour. Note that the drive into the reserve involves fording several streams, which are usually very low but can swell dangerously with heavy summer rains – check with Conaf before setting out. You will also have to contend with the huge borax trucks carrying heavy loads and generating bothersome clouds of dust, spoiling your enjoyment of the scenery. The reserve's administrative centre is about a 90-minute drive from Putre, in **Guallatire** (4428m altitude), a pretty hamlet with a traditional seventeenth-century Andean church. There's also an obligatory *carabineros* checkpoint here, and a Conaf *refugio* that is seldom in service. Looming over the village, snow-capped **Volcán Guallatire** puffs wispy plumes of smoke from its 6060-metre peak, while a grassy-banked stream snakes at its foot.

Following the road south of Guallatire, you'll be rewarded, about 40km on, with sudden, dramatic views of the **SALAR DE SURIRE**, a dazzling white salt flat containing several lakes with nesting colonies of three species of flamingo. Originally part of Parque Nacional Lauca, its status was changed to that of national monument in 1983 to allow borax to be mined from its surface. The mining is still going on today, and you can see the mine's enormous trucks driving over the *salar*, dwarfed by its massive dimensions but a nuisance nonetheless. On the west shore of the *salar* there's a Conaf **refugio** with four beds (CH$5500 per person), hot water and a kitchen. It's in a wonderful location with terrific views onto the salt flat, but it is often closed or bookings are not always respected, so do not rely on staying here. Sixteen kilometres further on, skirting the southern edge of the salt flat, **Polloquere** (also known as Aguas Calientes) is the site of several pale-blue pools filled with hot thermal water and with a muddy bottom reminiscent of the Dead Sea, an absolutely stunning place to take a bath, despite the lack of facilities – though be sure to get here in the morning, before the bone-chilling afternoon wind picks up. There are a couple of picnic areas and **camping** spaces here, too, but it's a treacherously exposed site.

Travel details

Buses

Antofagasta to: Arica (4 daily; 10hr); Calama (every hour; 3hr); Caldera (every hour; 6hr); Chañaral (16 daily; 5hr); Chuquicamata (5 daily; 3hr); Copiapó (every hour; 7hr); La Serena (16 daily; 11hr); María Elena (2 daily; 3hr); Mejillones (every 30min; 40min); Santiago (every hour; 20hr); Tocopilla (2hr 40min).

Arica to: Antofagasta (17 daily; 10hr); Calama (5 daily; 10hr); Chañaral (7 daily; 15hr); Copiapó (13 daily; 16hr); Iquique (every 30min; 4hr 30min); La Serena (13 daily; 18hr); Putre (1 daily; 3hr); San Pedro de Atacama (1 daily; 10hr); Santiago (10 daily; 29hr); Vallenar (10 daily; 20hr).

Calama to: Antofagasta (6 daily; 3hr); Arica (6 daily; 10hr); Chañaral (10 daily; 8hr); Chuquicamata (every 30min; 30min); Copiapó (14 daily; 9hr 30min); Iquique (4 daily; 7hr); La Serena (14 daily; 12hr 30min); San Pedro de Atacama (1 hourly; 1hr 30min); Santiago (14 daily; 22hr 30min); Toconao (1 daily; 2hr 30min).

Iquique to: Antofagasta (17 daily; 7hr); Arica (every 30min; 4hr 30min); Calama (3 daily; 7hr); Caldera (12 daily; 12hr); Chañaral (12 daily; 11hr); Chuquicamata (3 daily; 6hr 30min); Copiapó (12 daily; 13hr); La Serena (every hour; 16hr); La Tirana (7 daily; 1hr 40min); Mamiña (2 daily; 2hr 30min); María Elena (3 daily; 5hr); Mejillones (3 daily; 5hr); Pica (7 daily; 2hr); Santiago (every hour; 25hr); Tocopilla (12 daily; 3hr).

Flights

Antofagasta to: Arica (3 daily; 1hr 30min); Calama (3 daily; 35min); Iquique (4 daily; 45min); La Serena (3 daily; 2hr); Santiago (17 daily; 2hr).

Arica to: Antofagasta (1 daily; 45min); Calama (1 weekly; 1hr 20min); Copiapó (1 daily; 1hr 45min); Iquique (4 daily; 20min); Santiago (4 daily; 3hr).

Calama to: Antofagasta (3 daily; 35min); Arica (2 daily; 35min); Iquique (2 daily; 30min); La Serena (2 daily; 3hr); Santiago (5 daily; 2hr direct, 3hr via Antofagasta).

Iquique to: Antofagasta (7 daily; 45min); Arica (3 daily; 35min); Calama (4 weekly; 30min); Santiago (11 daily; 2hr 20min).

The Central Valley

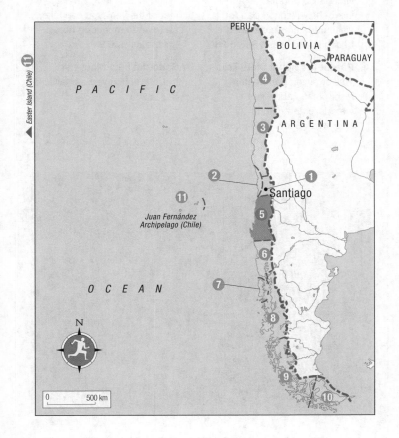

PERU

BOLIVIA

PARAGUAY

PACIFIC

ARGENTINA

Easter Island (Chile)

Santiago

Juan Fernández
Archipelago (Chile)

OCEAN

N

0   500 km

CHAPTER 5

Highlights

✳ **Santa Cruz** Visit classic Chilean haciendas in this pretty wine valley town, then taste your way through some of the world's best red wines on the "Ruta del Vino". See p.263

✳ **Pichilemu and the beaches** Relax at this haven for surfing and other watersports, which also doubles as an inexpensive launch pad for visiting the area's deserted beaches and lakes. See p.265

✳ **Parque Nacional Siete Tazas** This stunning park features lush forests, abundant waterfalls and natural swimming pools. See p.269

✳ **Altos del Lircay** Hiking trails, spectacular views and relatively easy access make one of Chile's few Andean parks perfect for camping trips. See p.272

✳ **Termas de Chillán** Legendary hot springs on the side of a volcano; in the winter, the skiing is excellent, while the rest of the year you can hike, swim and embark on horse treks. See p.279

✳ **Salto del Laja** Marvel at these thundering waterfalls. See p.288

▲ Salto del Laja

5

The Central Valley

Extending south from Santiago as far as the Río Bío Bío, Chile's **CENTRAL VALLEY** is a long, narrow plain hemmed in by the Andes to the east and the coastal range to the west, with a series of gentle ridges and lateral river valleys running between the two. This is the most fertile land in Chile, and the immense orchards, vineyards and pastures that cover the valley floor form a dazzling patchwork of greenery. Even in urban zones, country ways hold sway, and the Central Valley is perhaps the only part of Chile where it is not uncommon to see horse-drawn carts plodding down the Panamericana Highway, the main artery that runs south from Santiago, through Rancagua to Los Angeles in the southern section of the region and beyond. The kernel of the Central Valley lies between the capital and the city of **Chillán**, some 400km south – a region that for over two hundred years constituted the bulk of colonial Chile. It was here that the vast private estates known as estancias, or haciendas, were established, and where the country's most powerful families exercised an almost feudal rule over the countryside, a situation that persisted well into the twentieth century. These days most of the land is controlled by commercial food producers rather than old, moneyed families, but signs of the colonial way of life are still very much in evidence, with grand *casas patronales* lurking behind the adobe walls of the region's back lanes, and endless rows of poplars marking the divisions between the former estates. The people, too, have held on to many of their rural traditions: most farm workers still prefer to get around by horse, and the cult of the *huaso*, or cowboy, is as strong as ever, as can be witnessed at the frequent **rodeos** held in stadiums known as *medialunas*.

Further south, the busy city of **Concepción** guards the mouth of the **Bío Bío**, the mighty river that for over three hundred years was the boundary between conquered, colonial Chile and unconquered **Mapuche territory**, whose occupants withstood domination until 1883. Until recently the river was more famous as a **white-water rafting** destination, but hydroelectric dams tamed the raging torrent. Despite its rich soils having long been incorporated into the production belt of the Central Valley, traces of the frontier still linger, visible in the ruins of colonial Spanish forts, the proliferation of Mapuche place names and the tin-roof pioneer architecture. Beyond the Bío Bío, towards the Lake District, the landscape alters, too, the gently sloping plains giving way to verdant native forests and remote Andean lakes.

Many visitors bypass the Central Valley altogether, whizzing south towards the more dramatic landscapes of the Lake District and beyond. Certainly the agricultural towns dotted along the highway – **Rancagua**, **San Fernando**, **Curicó**, **Talca** and **Los Angeles** – are, on the whole, rather dull, offering little to tempt tourists off the bus or out of their car. But stray a few kilometres off

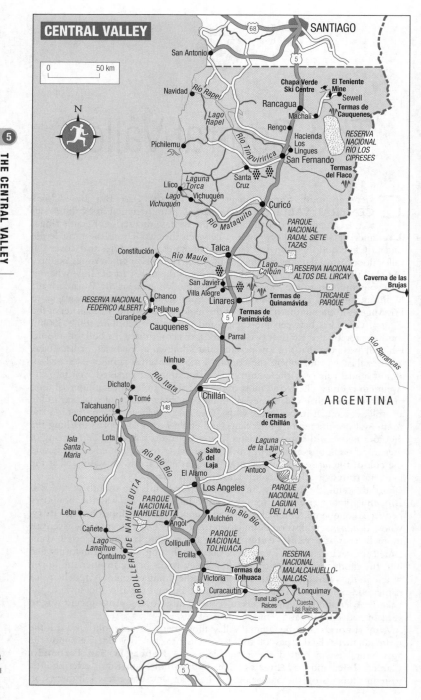

the Panamericana and you'll catch a glimpse of an older Chile impossible to find elsewhere, abounding with pastoral charms. Chief among these are the splendid **haciendas**, the best of which lie near **Santa Cruz**. The region's small, **colonial villages**, with their colourful adobe houses topped by overhanging clay-tiled roofs, are another Central Valley highlight – among the prettiest examples are **Vichuquén**, west of Curicó, and **Villa Alegre**, south of Talca in the Maule Valley, where you can also visit a trail of lush, emerald **vineyards**.

Away from the valley floor, you'll find attractions of a very different nature. To the west, up in the coastal hills, a couple of lakes offer great **watersports** facilities, notably **Lago Rapel**, while further west a number of inviting **beaches** and cheerful seaside towns are scattered down the coast, among them the popular surfer hangout **Pichilemu**. East of the valley, the dry, dusty slopes of the Andes offer excellent **horseriding** and **hiking** opportunities, particularly along the trails of protected areas such as **Reserva Nacional Los Cipreses**, near Rancagua, and **Reserva Nacional Altos del Lircay**, near Talca. After a strenuous day in the mountains, relax in one of the many **hot springs** in the area: the **Termas de Chillán** are at the base of a booming ski and adventure resort. Also rewarding are the beautiful **Termas de Cauquenes**, near San Fernando. The rustic **Termas de Tolhuaca**, southwest of Los Angeles, sit on the edge of the beautifully forested **Parque Nacional Tolhuaca**, and are also handy to one of Chile's more unusual sights: the **Túnel las Raíces**, cutting 4.5km through the cordillera, and the second-longest tunnel in South America. Built between 1929 and 1939, the tunnel was designed to be part of a coast-to-coast railway project that was later shelved, and instead now enables the surfaced road from Curacautín to pass under the mountains on its way to the small logging town of Lonquimay.

Getting down the Central Valley by **public transport** is easy, with hundreds of **buses** ploughing down the Panamericana. Branching off into the cordillera and to the coast normally requires catching a "rural bus" from one of the cities dotted down the highway, though some of the more remote places can only be reached with your own transport. The **train** from Santiago stops at Rancagua, San Fernando, Curicó, Talca and Chillán – slower than the buses, but more leisurely and scenic. The amount of annual rainfall picks up steadily as you head south; by the time you reach the Bío Bío there is a significant amount of rain every month. While winter is never too cold and snowfall is plentiful in the foothills, most visitors come here between October and March.

Rancagua and the Rapel Valley

Zipping down the Panamericana from Santiago, you can reach the prosperous agricultural town of **Rancagua**, 87km south, in about an hour. With a little more time and your own transport, however, the old road from Santiago (signed Alto Jahuel, running east along the highway) makes a far more appealing route, winding its way past estates of vines, fruit trees and old haciendas, half-hidden behind their great adobe walls.

Once in town, you'll find little to hold your interest for more than a few hours – unless your arrival coincides with a **rodeo** – but Rancagua makes a useful jumping-off point for several attractions in the adjacent **Rapel Valley**, including the 40-kilometre-long **Lago Rapel**, the largest artificial lake in Chile. In the opposite direction, a paved highway known as the Carretera del Cobre heads 60km east into the cordillera to the copper mine of **El Teniente** and the **Chapa Verde ski resort**, while a southern fork takes you to the charming **Termas de Cauquenes** and the nearby **Reserva Nacional Río los Cipreses**.

Rancagua

RANCAGUA presents a picture that is to repeat itself in most of the Central Valley towns – large, well-tended central plaza; single-storey adobe houses; a few colonial buildings; sprawling, faceless outskirts. Unusually, however, its square is known not as the Plaza de Armas, but as the **Plaza de los Héroes**. The name honours the patriot soldiers, headed by Bernardo O'Higgins, who defended the city against Royalist forces in 1814, only to be crushed in what has gone down in Chilean history as the "Disaster of Rancagua". In the centre of the square, a rearing equestrian statue celebrates O'Higgins' triumphant return to the city, four years after he had left it in ruins, to present it with a coat of arms depicting a phoenix rising from the ashes. The square's other major monument is the towering, yellow-walled **Iglesia Catedral**.

▲ Panamericana (North) & Medialuna (1km)

RANCAGUA

EATING
Los Antojitos del Charro 2
Reina Victoria 1

ACCOMMODATION
Hotel España B
Hotel Rancagua A
Turismo Santiago C

Panamericana (South) ▼

Rodeos

The Central Valley is the birthplace and heartland of Chilean **rodeo**, whose season kicks off on Independence Day, September 18. Over the following six months, regional competitions eliminate all but the finest horses and *huasos* in the country, who go on to take part in the national championships in Rancagua in late March or early April. Rodeos are performed in *medialunas* ("half moons"), circular arenas divided by a curved wall, forming a crescent-shaped stadium and a smaller oval pen called an *apiñadero*. The participants are **huasos** – cowboys, or horsemen – who cut a dashing figure with their bright, finely woven ponchos, broad-rimmed hats, carved wooden stirrups and shining silver spurs. The mounts they ride in the rodeo are specially bred and trained *corraleros* that are far too valuable for day-to-day work.

A rodeo begins with an inspection of the horses and their riders by judges, who award points for appearance. This is followed by individual displays of horsemanship that make ordinary dressage look tame. In the main part of a rodeo, pairs of *huasos* have to drive a young cow, or *novillo*, around the edge of the arena and pin it up against a padded section of the wall. Rodeos are as much about eating and drinking as anything else, and the canteen and foodstalls by a *medialuna* are a good place to sample **regional food**, gourmet wine and sweet fruity alcohol known as *chicha*. Rodeo events are spread over the course of a weekend and end with music and dancing. This is where you can see the **cueca** (see p.53) being danced at its flirtatious best. For the dates of official rodeos, contact the **Federación de Rodeos** in Santiago (℡2/420 2553) or visit ⓦwww.huasosyrodeos.cl.

One block north of the square, at the corner of Cuevas and Estado, the **Iglesia de la Merced** suffered fewer battle scars, despite being used as O'Higgins' headquarters. Another well-preserved colonial building is the eighteenth-century house occupied by the **Museo Regional de Rancagua** at Estado 685 (Tues–Fri 10am–6pm, Sat-Sun 9am–1pm; CH$600, free Sun and Tues; ℡72/221524, ⓦwww.museorancagua.cl). Inside, three of its rooms maintain the decor and furnishings of that era, while another is crammed with objects and documents relating to the independence movement. Opposite, at Estado 682, the 1812 **Casa del Pilar de Esquina** is a splendid two-storey late-colonial house, recently restored and open to visitors (with a bit of persistence). One block south, on the corner of Cachapoal and Millán, the **Casa de Cultura** (Mon–Fri 9am–1pm & 3–6pm) is more accessible, hosting regular photographic and art exhibits – though the main draw is its rural colonial architecture, including thick foundations made of river boulders mortared with mud. Finally, no account of Rancagua could fail to mention its fame as Chile's **rodeo** capital, hosting the national rodeo championships during the last week of March or the first week of April in its *medialuna* on the northern edge of town (on the corner of Av España and Germán Ibarra). For more information, see box above.

Practicalities

The **bus terminal** is at Salinas 1165 (℡72/225425), with the **train station** (℡72/230361) a couple of blocks south. There's a helpful **Sernatur** office one block east of the Plaza at Germán Riesco 277 (Mon–Fri 8.30am–5.30pm; ℡72/230413, Ⓔinforancagua@sernatur.cl). Conaf's regional office is at Cuevas 480 (Mon–Fri 8.30am-5.30pm; ℡72/204612, Ⓔrancagua.oirs@conaf.cl). Inexpensive **accommodation** is available at the welcoming *Hotel España*, San Martín 367 (℡72/230141, Ⓔnoraberriosf@latinmail.com; ❹), which has small, clean rooms with private bathrooms and TV set around a central patio in a slightly ramshackle colonial-style building. *Hotel Rancagua*, a few blocks north at San

▲ Chilean Rodeo

Martín 85 (☎72/232663, ⓦwww.hotelrancagua.galeon.com; ④–⑤), is probably the best place to stay in town; aim to get one of the more modern en-suites in the extension out the back. It's very popular, so book ahead. The overpriced *Turismo Santiago*, Brasil 1036 (☎72/230860, ⓦwww.hotelsantiago.cl; ⑥), is squarely aimed at the business traveller with comfortable but antiseptic en-suites.

As for **eating**, try 🍴 *Los Antojitos del Charro*, Estado 642, a tiny Mexican joint with orange, yellow and green walls, decorative sombreros and 1980s pop tunes on the radio. The menu has great-value, authentic tacos, burritos and quesadillas (CH\$1500–2900). For something sweet, join the steady stream of shoppers and schoolchildren who head to bustling café *Reina Victoria*, Independencia 667, for coffee, cakes, biscuits and huge tubs of ice cream.

LAN is at Astorga 233-B (☎600/526200). You'll find numerous **banks** with ATMs on Paseo Independencia. For a **casa de cambio**, there's AFEX at Astorga 365 and Campos 363. **Car rental** is available from Weber Rentacar, Membrillar 40, Oficina 2 (☎72/268028). Turismo Dakota, Mujica 605 (☎72/228165, ⓦwww.turismodakota.cl) and Cobretour, Astorga 409 (☎72/232532) can arrange local tours, treks and horseriding. Surf the **web** at Internet del Centro, Independencia 657 (CH\$500 per hr).

El Teniente copper mine and the Chapa Verde ski centre

Sixty kilometres east of Rancagua, **El Teniente** is the largest underground mine in the world, with more than 1500km of tunnels. Local legend has it that its name – "the lieutenant" – refers to a disgraced Spanish officer who, while heading to Argentina to escape his creditors, discovered enormous copper deposits, thus making a fortune and saving himself from bankruptcy. Today the mine belongs to Codelco, the government-owned copper corporation, which also owns the famous Chuquicamata mine in northern Chile.

You aren't allowed to just turn up and visit, but group tours can be arranged in advance by contacting Codelco, Millán 220 in Rancagua (☎72/292000 in Rancagua, ☎2/787 7710 in Santiago, ⓌWwww.codelco.com). The half-day tours (from CH$12,000 per person) include a visit to the abandoned company town of **Sewell** (Ⓦwww.sewell.cl), staggered in dramatic tiers up the mountainside. After this, you don protective gear and go down the shafts to the gloomy underground tunnels. VTS, Manuel Montt 192, Rancagua (☎72/210290, Ⓦwww.vts.cl), also organizes trips to Sewell for a similar price.

A few kilometres north of the mine, and ranging from 2300m to 3100m, is the Codelco-owned **Chapa Verde ski centre** (☎72/217651, Ⓦwww.chapaverde.cl), initially built for the company's miners but now open to the public between July and September. There are no hotels or other accommodation, but check with ski area administration for information on private homes for rent. You can drive up in your own vehicle (4WD is advisable) as long as you call the Ski Club (☎72/217651 or 72/294255) for a permit beforehand. Otherwise, take Codelco's own bus service, Buses El Teniente, at Av Miguel Ramírez 665, Rancagua, next to the Lider Vecino supermarket (departures June–Sept weekdays at 9am, weekends at 8.30am and 9.30am, return trip daily at 4.30pm; CH$4500; times are prone to change so it is worth confirming with the ski centre). Lift tickets (CH$18,000 adult, CH$10,000 children) are sold at Miguel Ramírez 655, the central offices of the ski centre. Full ski and snowboard equipment rental costs from CH$16,000.

Termas de Cauquenes

A couple of kilometres on from the turn-off to El Teniente, you'll come to a southern fork that branches towards **TERMAS DE CAUQUENES**, 6km beyond. Sitting high above the Río Cachapoal, surrounded by the steep foothills of the Andes, this is one of the most beautiful – and the oldest – hot springs resorts in Chile. The centrepiece is the nineteenth-century *sala de baños*, a huge wooden hall with an extremely high ceiling, painted wooden beams, stained-glass windows and marble floor tiles. From the entrance, steps lead down to 24 cubicles containing the *tinas* – the original Carrara marble bathtubs that were installed in 1856, where guests take their hot thermal baths. The water, at a temperature between 42° and 48°C (107° and 118°F), contains magnesium, potassium and lithium among other minerals. It has been revered for its curative properties from the earliest days of the colony when, according to old chronicles, ailing Jesuits were sent here to be cured of their "gout, syphilis, anaemia and many other problems". Over the years, the fame of the springs increased, and they were visited by a number of important figures, including Charles Darwin, Bernardo O'Higgins and the great Argentinean Liberator José de San Martín, who spent a month here after bringing his "Army of the Andes" across to liberate Chile from the Royalists.

As well as the *sala de baños*, there's an old, colonial-style chapel, an outdoor swimming pool and comfortable but unremarkable **rooms** (☎72/899010, Ⓦwww.termasdecauquenes.cl; ❽). Some are a little scruffy, so ask to see a few. Full board and entry to the springs is included in the rates. The **food** – served in an immense dining room with fine river views – is excellent, prepared by the Swiss chefs who own the resort. Day visitors are charged CH$3500 for half an hour in the marble *tinas* and CH$3000 to use the outdoor pool. Buses Termas de Cauquenes runs **buses** to the *termas*, leaving at 11am and 5pm from

Rancagua's Mercado Municipal, returning at 8.30am and 2pm. Confirm times with the hotel before setting out.

Reserva Nacional Río de Los Cipreses

Beyond the Termas de Cauquenes, the road continues for another 14km to the **RESERVA NACIONAL RÍO DE LOS CIPRESES** (daily: March–Nov 8.30am–6pm, Dec–Feb 8.30am–8pm; CH$1700, camping CH$5000; ℡72/297505). A little-visited gem, the reserve encompasses 36 square kilometres of protected land stretched along the narrow canyon of the Río de los Cipreses, with altitudes ranging from 900m to 4900m. It's a great spot for multi-day **hiking** or **horse-riding**, and you may spot rare burrowing parrots, foxes, eagles and condors. There's no public transport so you will need your own car.

At the entrance, a Conaf office provides maps and a diorama of the park. Ask about the trails that offer a look at the parakeets nesting in the cliffs. From the office, a jeep track leads 6km to **Sector El Ranchillo**, a camping and picnic area with a swimming pool. This is the end of the track, and vehicles must be parked. From here, take the left fork just before El Ranchillo, continue past a second gate (locked) and after another 6km you'll reach **Sector Maitenes**, with a few camping spots and running water. Beyond, a trail follows the river along the canyon, passing through forests and with occasional views of high Andean peaks like Cerro El Indio and Cerro El Cotón. Lateral ravines regularly branch out from the river, leading to waterfalls, lakes and "hanging" valleys carved out of the hills by glaciers. These aren't signed, however, so unless you're with an *arriero* (horseman), stick to the main path. Twenty kilometres on from Sector Maitenes, you reach **Sector Urriola**, where there's a rustic *refugio* (1500m) and a few camping areas; count on taking around six or seven hours to get here on foot from Maitenes, and about four or five on horseback. Beyond Urriola, the path continues for a further ten or so kilometres, giving great views onto the 4900-metre-high Volcán Palomo. To hire a **horse**, call the reserve's administration office or visit the corral a couple of kilometres before the reserve entrance.

Lago Rapel

The forty-kilometre-long artificial **LAGO RAPEL** nestles in the low coastal hills southwest of Rancagua. The lake's main attractions are its excellent **water sports facilities**, with speed boats, windsurfers and jet skis available for rent from several hotels and campsites.

Accommodation is often informal, with numerous *residenciales* between Puente El Durazno and El Manzano. *Club Náutico Rapel* (℡72/773 7761, ⓦwww.campingnauticorapel.cl), offers camping (CH$15,000–20,000 per site), as well as a pool and a volleyball court. In a similar vein, *Camping Alemán* (℡09/883 3397, ⓦwww.campingaleman.cl), along the lakeshore 8km west of El Manzano, has campsites (CH$4000 per person) and rustic *cabañas* sleeping four to six people (❹). *Hotel Jardín del Lago* (℡09/743 4420, ⓦwww.jardindellago.cl; ❻), a couple of kilometres further north, provides smart, self-contained, apartment-style accommodation and watersports facilities. Buses Galgo (℡72/511055) runs **buses** to El Manzano from Rancagua's regional terminal every twenty minutes, and Buses Sextur (℡72/231342) has an hourly service.

San Fernando and the Colchagua Valley

Fifty-five kilometres south of Rancagua, **San Fernando** is a busy little town sitting in the 120-kilometre-long valley of the Río Tinguiririca, known locally as the **Colchagua Valley** after the province through which it runs. This is serious fruit-production territory, as signalled by the numerous fruit stalls and large Del Monte factories lining the highway on the approach to San Fernando. The town itself is emphatically agricultural and known throughout the region as *the* place to get your tractor repaired. Forty-one kilometres west is **Santa Cruz**, which boasts the **Hotel Santa Cruz Plaza**, a starting point for several popular excursions and site of a superb restaurant. **Hacienda los Lingues**, a splendid, privately owned hacienda which operates as a hotel and is open for visits, lies 32km south of Rancagua. Still further east, high in the cordillera, the **Termas del Flaco** is an inexpensive option for soaking in hot springs. Around San Fernando, the **Ruta del Vino del Valle de Colchagua** takes in a trail of local vineyards as well as the excellent **Museo de Colchagua**, with historical regional artefacts, and **Hacienda El Huique**, while if you continue to the coast, you'll get to the hip, budget seaside town of **Pichilemu**, popular with surfers.

San Fernando

Surrounded by low, rippling hills washed golden in the sunlight, **SAN FERNANDO** makes for a pleasant amble along its narrow streets. The main commercial artery is Manuel Rodríguez, which, on the corner with Valdivia, has the huge nineteenth-century **Iglesia de San Francisco**, a Neo-Gothic church with a 32-metre-high tower. There is a similar monument, the **Capilla San Juan de Dios**, eight blocks north, on the corner of Negrete and Manso de Velasco. Close by, at the corner of Manso de Velasco and Jiménez, the **Museo Casa Patronal de Lircunlauta** (Tues–Fri 9am–1pm & 3–7pm, Sat & Sun 10am–1pm & 4–6pm; CH\$200) is the oldest building in San Fernando. It was originally the *casa patronal* of the eighteenth-century Hacienda Lircunlauta, whose owner donated 450 "blocks" of land to San Fernando when the town was founded in 1742.

Practicalities

The **bus terminal** (☎72/713912) is on the corner of Avenida Manso de Velasco and Rancagua. There's no Oficina de Turismo, but the Municipalidad at Carampangue and Argomedo provides basic **information**. Three of the better hotels are on Manuel Rodríguez. At no. 968, *Hotel Marcano* (☎72/714759, ⓦwww .hotelmarcano.cl; ❹–❺) has brightly coloured en-suites with big TVs and pictures of Chilean rural scenes. Opposite, at no. 959, *Hotel Español* (☎72/711098; ❺) is a little smarter and marginally more expensive; rooms are neat and tidy, and there's an indoor patio filled with plants and faux Greek statues. Those on a tight budget should head to *Residencial Rahue 2* (☎72/716115; ❸–❹) at no. 1030, a rambling

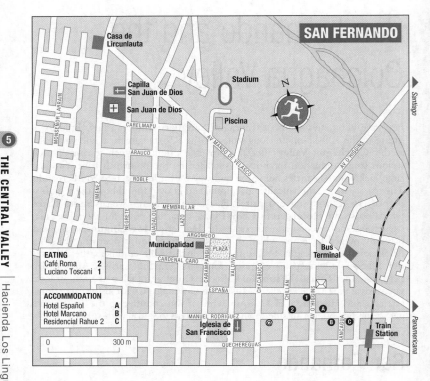

Casa de
Lircunlauta

SAN FERNANDO

Capilla
San Juan de Dios

Stadium

San Juan de Dios

Piscina

N

CARELMAPU

MONSEÑOR LARRAIN

AV MANSO DE VELASCO

AV O'HIGGINS

ARAUCO

ROBLE

JIMENEZ

MEMBRILLAR

GUADALUPE

NEGRETE

LAZO

ARGOMEDO

Municipalidad

PLAZA

Bus
Terminal

CARAMPANGUE

CARDENAL CARO

VALDIVIA

CHACABUCO

EATING
Café Roma   2
Luciano Toscani   1

ESPAÑA

CHILLAN

ACCOMMODATION
Hotel Español   A
Hotel Marcano   B
Residencial Rahue 2 C

MANUEL RODRIGUEZ

Iglesia de
San Francisco

@

AV O'HIGGINS

RANCAGUA

Train
Station

0   300 m

QUECHEREGUAS

Santiago

Panamericana

old house with high ceilings, wicker furniture and slightly gloomy rooms. Those with shared facilities are good value, but the ones with private bathroom are overpriced. *Luciano Toscani*, O'Higgins 661, an appealing trattoria decked out with photos and sketches of vintage motorbikes, is one of the best places to **eat**. Tasty pizzas and pastas and a reasonably priced set lunch (CH\$3900) are on offer, but the service is glacially slow. *Café Roma*, Manuel Rodríguez 815, with its welcoming red-brick interior and a TV tuned to *telenovelas*, is a good spot for a light meal, sandwich, cake or coffee. You can **rent a car** with Alvaro Asenjo at España 911, Office 3 (℡&🖷72/712105). For **tours** and rafting trips, try Mundo Aventura Rafting, Manuel Rodríguez 430 (℡72/721733). **Internet** access is available at Centro de Llamadas, Manuel Rodriguez 746 (CH\$500 per hr).

Hacienda Los Lingues

One of the oldest and best-preserved haciendas in Chile, **Hacienda Los Lingues** (🌐www.loslingues.com; bookings through office in Santiago at Avenida Providencia 1100, Torres de Tajamar C, oficina 205 ℡2/431 0510), lies 20km northeast of San Fernando. It dates from 1599, when King Felipe III of Spain presented it as a gift to the first mayor of Santiago. Since then, the hacienda has remained in the same family and is today presided over by the elderly and redoubtable don Germán Claro-Lira. The main house dates from the seventeenth and early eighteenth century and bears all the hallmarks of the colonial *casa patronal*, including thick adobe walls and an overhanging clay-tiled roof supported by oak pillars that form a "corridor", or covered veranda, around its interior patio.

Inside, look out for the "English Room", with its framed letter from Buckingham Palace, confirming don Germán's wife is, in all likelihood, a very distant relative of the Queen of England. Although it now functions as an exclusive hotel, the hacienda is still, unquestionably, a family home, and the guest bedrooms are liberally decorated with family portraits, old pictures and religious iconography. Outside are sumptuous gardens, a *medialuna* and the stables where thoroughbred Aculeo horses are bred. Rates (⓼–⓽) are high (up to US$150–190), but you can visit on a cultural tour (US$63), which includes lunch and the chance to watch a horse show. Buses for Los Lingues depart from the regional terminal in San Fernando.

Termas del Flaco

Some 107km east of San Fernando, sitting high in the cordillera 1700m above sea level, the **TERMAS DEL FLACO** (Dec–April; CH$1000) are among the cheapest and consequently most-visited thermal baths in the Central Valley. They're reached by a serpentine dirt road that follows the Río Tinguiririca through a beautiful gorge, so narrow in parts that *carabineros* allow traffic to go in only one direction at a time. On Monday through Saturday, traffic can start the trip down between 6am and 2pm, and traffic can start going up between 4pm and midnight; Sunday is variable, so ask the *carabineros* in San Fernando (☏72/711219). You'll need to stay at the baths overnight if you visit during the week. The wild beauty of the cordillera and the feeling of remoteness and solitude are, upon arriving, suddenly interrupted with the appearance of numerous shack-like, tin-roofed houses – almost all of them *residenciales* – crowded around the thermal baths. Nor are these baths particularly attractive, consisting of several rectangular concrete, open-air pools. The waters, however – which reach up to 57°C (135°F) in some pools – are just bliss. If you manage to get here midweek, when there are no crowds (except during high season, Jan & Feb), you can lie back, close your eyes and just relax, without another soul around. You'll find several short treks around the *termas*, including one that leads to a set of dinosaur footprints preserved in the rock.

Accommodation is abundant, with little to distinguish one place from the next, and most operating on a **full-board** basis. *Posada Amistad* (☏72/817227; ⓸), beside the bus stop, offers small, basic rooms around a garden patio, overlooking the baths. It is only open December to February. You'll find more comfort in the roomy wooden *cabañas* at *Hotel Cabaña Las Vegas* (office at Cillero 34, Rancagua ☏72/222478, ⓦ www .termasdelflacohotellasvegas.cl; ⓹–⓺), which has a large dining room with floor-to-ceiling windows looking down to the valley and its own small thermal pool. Buses Amistad (☏72/452007) provides **transport** to the *termas*, with one daily departure from Rancagua and three daily from San Fernando.

Santa Cruz and around

West of San Fernando, the paved road running through the Colchagua Valley to the coast takes you past a couple of glorious **haciendas**, converted into museums,

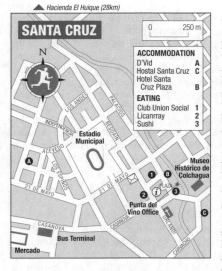

▲ Hacienda El Huique (28km)

SANTA CRUZ

0   250 m

N

ACCOMMODATION
D'Vid   A
Hostal Santa Cruz   C
Hotel Santa
Cruz Plaza   B

EATING
Club Union Social   1
Licanrray   2
Sushi   3

Estadio Municipal

Museo Histórico de Colchagua

Punta del Vino Office

Bus Terminal

Mercado

as well as a trail of **wineries** (see box below). The small, well-preserved town of **SANTA CRUZ**, 40km from San Fernando and connected by half-hourly buses, sits in the heart of this renowned wine-making district. There's a **tourist information** booth (Mon–Fri 10am–1pm & 3–6pm, Sat 10am–2pm) in a mini clock-tower on the Plaza de Armas. Just to the east is the private **Museo de Colchagua**, Errázuriz 145 (summer Tues–Sun 10am–7pm, winter Tues–Sun 10am–6pm; CH$3000; ☎72/821050, ⓦwww.museocolchagua.cl), housed in a splendid, plum-coloured colonial hacienda. Owned by international arms dealer Carlos Cardoen (the so-called "king of cluster bombs"), it has a well-designed if eclectic collection, including fossils, a huge amount of amber, pre-Columbian pottery, relics from the War of the Pacific and memorabilia from the Chilean Independence movement. Among the most evocative exhibits are the shiny black nineteenth-century carriages, steered by ghostly mannequins wearing Victorian capes, and the beautiful old saddles, carved wooden stirrups and silver spurs in the *huaso* display.

La Ruta del Vino del Valle de Colchagua

The Valle de Colchagua lies in the heart of one of Chile's finest wine-making districts. More than a dozen wineries in the area have launched a tour called **La Ruta del Vino del Valle de Colchagua**, operating out of Santa Cruz (see above). Tours (half-day from CH$27,000, full-day with lunch from CH$60,000) run daily and include visits to two to three wineries with multilingual guides and the chance to sample wines at each. Lunch is taken in some of the best restaurants in the valley. Reservations must be made at least 24 hours in advance at the office at Plaza de Armas 298 in Santa Cruz (Mon–Fri 9.30am–6.30pm, Sat–Sun 10am–6.30pm; ☎72/823199, ⓦwww.rutadelvino.cl). Tours can also include a visit to either the Museo de Colchagua or the Hacienda El Huique (see opposite). The best time to take the tour is in late March, when the wineries organize their own Fiesta de la Vendimia (grape-harvest festival). You can also visit the wineries by rail on the touristy **Tren del Vino** (San Antonio 65, third floor, office 309, Santiago, ☎2/470 7403, ⓦwww.trendelvinochile.cl), which runs every Saturday. The CH$62,000 price tag includes transfers to and from Santiago to San Fernando, where a special train takes you on a day-tour of several wineries, a bilingual guide, wine tastings, lunch and folk music entertainment. The following are some of the best wineries to visit independently. The family estate of **Viña Bisquertt** (☎72/821792, ⓦwww.bisquertt.cl) has attractive colonial buildings and antique carriages in its tasting rooms. The compact boutique winery at **Viña Laura Hartwig** (☎72/823179, ⓦwww.laurahartwig.cl) first planted vines in 1979, while the historic **Viu Manent** (☎72/858751, ⓦwww.viumanent.cl) dates from 1935. **Viña Mont Gras** (☎72/823242, ⓦwww.montgras.cl) produces, amongst others, the rare Carmenère wine.

On the edge of the Plaza de Armas sits the impressive *Hotel Santa Cruz Plaza*, Armas 286 (☎72/209600, ⊛www.hotelsantacruzplaza.cl; ❽), also owned by Cardoen. A large and somewhat incongruous casino, attached to the hotel, has recently been opened, boosting room numbers, but reservations are still definitely necessary. There are two swimming pools, a spa with wine-based treatments and the top-class *Las Varietales* restaurant. A more economical option is ✹ *D'Vid* (☎72/825610, ⊛www.dvid.cl; ❹–❺), Alberto Edwards 205. This excellent nine-room B&B is one of the best places to stay in the area – and a relative bargain. The chic modern rooms, most of which are en-suite, have incredibly comfy beds; there's also a lovely communal living room and a small pool. You'll find cheaper accommodation at the motel-like *Hostal Santa Cruz* (☎72/823125, ⊛hostalsantacruz@terra.cl; ❹) at Carvacho 40, which has cramped rooms with shared facilities and bigger en-suites.

A handful of restaurants dot the west side of the Plaza, including *Club Unión Social*, on the north side of the Plaza, which has a relaxing vine-covered terrace, Chilean staples (CH$4500–7000) and more adventurous dishes like eel omelette. *Sushi*, General de Canto 5, on the eastern side of the Plaza, is an approximation of a Japanese restaurant, with pretty authentic food (from CH$4000) and friendly service.

Twenty-four kilometres beyond Santa Cruz, along the road towards the coast, and 6km past the Los Errázuriz bridge, sits the superb **Hacienda El Huique** (Tues–Sun 10am–5pm; CH$1500; ☎72/933083, ⊛www.elhuique.com). One of the Central Valley's loveliest haciendas, it is perfectly preserved, along with all its furniture and outbuildings, and open to the public as a museum. The hacienda's history dates from the seventeenth century, in the colonial period, but the current *casa patronal* was built in the early years of independence, in 1829. Standing alongside, and entered through a huge doorway, is the **chapel**, sporting a 23-metre-high bell tower (Sunday Mass at 11.30am).

Pichilemu

If you continue west towards the coast you'll end up, 87km on from Santa Cruz, at the bustling seaside surfer town of **PICHILEMU**, built around a wide, sandy bay at the foot of a steep hill. The town dates from the second half of the nineteenth century, when Agustín Ross Edwards set out to create a European-style seaside resort. Today Pichilemu wears the charming, melancholy air of a faded Victorian seaside town. From the seafront, a broad flight of identically coloured steps sweeps up the hillside to the splendid **Parque Ross**, planted with century-old Phoenix palms and extravagant topiary. On the edge of the park, jutting out over the hillside, the grand old **casino** – Chile's first but now in disuse – is perhaps the most evocative of Ross's legacies. In contrast, Pichilemu's central streets are crammed with snack bars and *schoperías* catering to the crowds of young surfers who come to ride the waves – among the best in all of Chile. The most challenging surf is at Punta de Lobos, 6km south, where the national surfing championships are held. Look out for the sea lions in the beach's peculiar escarpments.

Frequent **bus** services to Pichilemu are provided by Buses Andimar (☎72/711817) and Buses Nilahue (☎72/229358) from San Fernando and Rancagua. **Arriving** in town by bus, you'll be dropped a couple of blocks north of the main street, Ortúzar. Nearby you'll find the Municipalidad de Pichilemu, at Angel Gaete 365 (Mon–Fri 8.30am–5.30pm; ☎72/841017), where you can pick up **information** on the town. For a local, insider's guide, try the Spanish-language Ⓦ www.pichilemunews.cl.

Cheap **accommodation** is abundant. Near the cross overlooking town, a 15min walk from the centre, *Cabañas Buena Vista* (Ⓣ72/842488, Ⓦ www.343sur .com; ❸) has cabins and an eco-friendly resort: there's composting, recycling and organic eggs for breakfast. Staff can help organize Spanish, surf and kayak classes. Call ahead for a free pick-up from the bus station. *DunaMar*, Comercio s/n (Ⓣ72/841676, Ⓦ www.dunamar.netfirms.com; ❻), 3km south of town, is a modern beach resort boasting rooms with kitsch seaside paintings and balconies with great views, plus a recommended seafood restaurant. Back in town, one of the best-value *residenciales* and *cabañas* is the welcoming, well-kept *Residencial Antumalal* at Joaquín Aguirre 64 (Ⓣ72/841004, Ⓦ www .residencialantumalal.cl; ❸–❹), which has en-suite rooms in luminous blues and pinks. The popular *Hostería La Gloria*, ten blocks south of the seafront at J.J. Prieto 980, is worth the walk for its excellent and inexpensive **seafood**, including tasty *machas a la parmesana* and dressed crab. You'll find many **cheap eats** on Ross and Ortúzar.

For a tiny town, Pichilemu has plenty of **nightlife**, though most of it tends to be surf parties organized at the last minute: try *Disco 127*, Angel Gaete 127, and *Delirious* on Ortúzar.

Curicó and the Mataquito Valley

The Teno and Lontué rivers converge to form the broad Río Mataquito, which meanders west through Chilean wine country towards the Pacific. The manicured town of **Curicó** (54km south of San Fernando) sits in the Mataquito Valley and makes an appealing place to break your journey – en route, perhaps, to the **wineries**, or further west to the **Lago Vichuquén**, near the coast, or the **Siete Tazas waterfalls**, southeast towards the mountains.

Curicó

Prosperous **CURICÓ** is built around one of the most beautiful central **plazas** in Chile, luxuriantly planted with sixty giant Canary Island palms. Standing in their shade, on the northern side of the square, is a highly ornate, dark-green wrought-iron **bandstand**, constructed in a New Orleans style in 1904, while close by an elaborate fountain features a cast-iron replica of *The Three Graces*. In contrast to these rather fanciful civic commissions, the memorial to **Toqui Lautaro** – the Mapuche chief at whose hands Spanish conquistador Pedro de Valdivia came to a grisly end – is a raw and powerful work, carved out of an ancient tree trunk. Standing on the northwest corner of the square, the **Iglesia**

La Matriz makes a curious sight, its grand Neoclassical facade giving onto an empty shell ever since the great 1985 earthquake. Next door, the dignified **Club de la Unión** escaped unscathed, its fine white pillars and balconies still perfectly intact. You can also climb **Cerro Carlos Condell**, the little hill on the eastern edge of town, and survey the scene from its 99m-high summit or take a dip in its public swimming pool.

While you're in town, it's worth making the easy excursion 5km south to the **winery** of Miguel Torres (daily: autumn–winter 10am–5pm; spring–summer 10am–7pm; ☏75/564100, ⓦwww.migueltorres .cl; free 45min tours), the innovative Spanish vintner who revolutionized

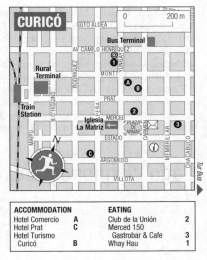

ACCOMMODATION		EATING	
Hotel Comercio	A	Club de la Unión	2
Hotel Prat	C	Merced 150	
Hotel Turismo		Gastrobar & Cafe	3
Curicó	B	Whay Hau	1

Chile's wine industry in the 1980s. There's also the superb *Restaurant Viña Torres* (Mon–Sun 12.30–3.30pm, Fri also 8pm–midnight) which serves dishes like Wagyu beef ravioli (mains CH$8600–9200). To get here, take a bus heading to Molina (every 10min) and ask to be let off outside the *bodega*, which is right next to the Panamericana. Other wine tours are arranged by **Ruta del Vino Valles de Curicó**, which has an office (Mon–Fri 9am–2pm & 3.30–7pm, Sat 10.30am–1pm; ☏75/328972, ⓦwww.rutadelvinocurico.cl) in *Hotel Turismo Curicó* (see below). This route is less developed than that in the Colchagua area, but cheaper (from CH$15,000, plus transport). From March 15 to 20, the **wine festival** in the Plaza de Armas is a celebration of the grape harvest, complete with dances and beauty pageants.

Practicalities

Arriving in Curicó by bus, you generally pull in at either the main **bus terminal** (☏75/328575) on the corner of Camilo Henríquez and Carmen, or the smaller **rural terminal** on O'Higgins, near the **train station** (☏75/310028), which is on Prat, four blocks west of the Plaza de Armas. Tur Bus is inconveniently located a good 20min walk southeast of the Plaza at Manso de Velasco 12. You can get basic **tourist information** in the Municipalidad, opposite the Plaza. Reasonably priced **accommodation** is available at *Hotel Prat*, at Peña 427 (☏75/311069, ✉hotelpratcurico@yahoo.es; ❸–❹). Behind the orange and yellow exterior are carpeted doubles with TVs and cavernous bathrooms; those with shared facilities, however, are not for the claustrophobic. At *Hotel Comercio* (☏75/312443, ⓦwww.hotelcomercio.cl; ❻), Yungay 730, the heated indoor pool and the attractive "superior class" rooms with flat-screen TVs overlooking it are the main draws, although the standard en-suites are also decent. The best place in town, however, is ⚜ *Hotel Turismo Curicó* at Carmen 727 (☏75/310552, ⓦwww.hotelturismocurico.cl; ❻–❼), a surprisingly slick modern hotel with cream and white en-suites, large lounge area complete with giant fireplace, bar and fine **restaurant**. The handsome old *Club de la Unión*, Merced 341, has white pillars and high windows overlooking the Plaza, and is a local favourite for Chilean food (CH$3500–5000). The lime-green walls clash spectacularly with the orange table cloths at *Merced 150 Gastrobar & Café*, Merced 150, but the place still manages to retain a dignified air, and is good for an evening drink, afternoon latte or a set lunch (CH$2500). *Whay Hau*, Yungay 853, has pretty authentic Cantonese fare – fried rice, noodles and stir fries (CH$2000–4000) – and a formal dining room with mini chandeliers.

There are several **ATMs** on Merced, near the Plaza, and you can **change money** at Forex, Carmen 497 and Yungay 649. For **car rental**, head to Rent a Car Curicó, Manso de Velasco 520 (☏75/312297). Centro de Llamadstets, Camilo Henrique 412, provides **internet** access (CH$350 per hr).

Lago Vichuquén and around

West of Curicó, a scenic road follows the northern bank of the Río Mataquito through the fertile river valley. Eighty-five kilometres along the road, just beyond Hualañé village, take the right fork and follow the signs for a further 25km along a dirt road to tiny **VICHUQUÉN**, one of the best-preserved villages in the Central Valley. Most of the brightly painted adobe houses date from the mid-nineteenth century, but Vichuquén's history goes back much further: there was a settlement here long before the arrival of the Spaniards, and it was chosen by the Inca as a site for one of their *mitimaes* – agricultural colonies populated by Quechua farmers brought down from Peru. You'll find relics of the Inca occupation – and a three thousand-year-old mummy – in the **Museo Colonial**, on Calle Rodríguez (daily 10.30am–1.30pm & 4–6pm; CH$550).

Four kilometres beyond you'll reach the southern tip of **Lago Vichuquén**, a long, narrow lake enclosed by deep-green, pine-covered hills. Considerably more upmarket than Lago Rapel, this is a popular holiday destination with Santiago's upper crust, whose beautiful villas line the lakeshore. There are several **places to stay** and **eat**. On the southern shore, in the village of **Aquelarre**, you'll find good food and accommodation at *Hotel Marina Vichuquén* (☏75/400265, ⓦwww.marinavichuquen.cl; ⑥–⑦), which offers smart, spacious rooms with lots of natural light, as well as excellent **watersports facilities**, mountain bikes and horseriding (all available for non-guests, too). Other options are dotted along the winding road that follows the lake's western shore: *Camping Vichuquén* (☏75/400062, ⓦwww.campingvichuquen.cl), just beyond Aquelarre, charges CH$3500–6100 per person and rents out kayaks.

Laguna Torca and Llico

Beyond the northern tip of the lake, the road comes to a junction. The right fork takes you across the rickety Puente de Llico to **RESERVA NACIONAL LAGUNA TORCA** (daily 9.30am–5pm; CH$3000), a marshy man-made lake a couple of kilometres away, preserved as a breeding sanctuary for 106 species of birds, including hundreds of black-necked swans. There's a Conaf office just beyond the bridge, hiding behind the large house with the veranda, and a camping area (Sept–April; CH$8000 for up to six people) in a eucalyptus grove (turn right immediately after the bridge, then first left). Back at the junction, the left fork leads to nearby **LLICO**, a rugged little seaside town perched on the edge of an exposed sandy beach whose turbulent waves attract many surfers – during January and February numerous surf tournaments bring a buzz to this usually quiet beach. **Accommodation** here is much cheaper than at Lago

Vichuquén. Try *Residencial Miramar*, Carrera Pinto 48 (☎75/400032; ❸–❹), right on the beachfront. The en-suite rooms are cramped, but they have balconies and good sea views; there's also a good seafood **restaurant** here.

Parque Nacional Radal Siete Tazas

Of all the natural phenomena in Chile, the **Siete Tazas**, 73km southeast of Curicó, must be one of the most extraordinary. In the depths of the native forest, a crystal-clear mountain river drops down a series of seven waterfalls, each of which has carved a sparkling *taza* ("teacup") out of the rock. The falls are inside **PARQUE NACIONAL RADAL SIETE TAZAS** (April–Nov 8.30am–6pm; Dec–March 8.30am–8pm; CH$1500, camping CH$8000 for up to six), reached by a poor dirt road from the village of Molina, 18km south of Curicó – be sure to fill up with petrol there. Busy on summer weekends, this park is practically empty the rest of the year. Also within the reserve are forests, several hiking trails and the **Velo de Novia** ("Bride's Veil"), a 50m waterfall spilling out of a narrow gorge. For keen hikers, it's also possible to trek from Siete Tazas to Reserva Nacional Altos de Lircay (see p.272), but you'll need to hire a local guide. Conaf has a small hut on the road towards the Siete Tazas, but for more information you need to go to the administrative office (daily: Dec–Feb 9am–8.30pm, March–Nov 9am–7pm; no ☎) at **Parque Inglés**, 9km further east.

Hostería Flor de Canela (☎75/491613; ❹) offers adequate but small and draughty **rooms** with either private or shared facilities, near the administrative office. You can also camp in the area, including at *Radal Eco Adventure*, 1km before the town of Radal, on the right (☎09/333 8719; CH$12,000 for up to five people); they also offer **treks** and a wealth of local information. For more privacy, swimming, horse rides and accommodation ranging from camping (CH$11,000 per site) to cabins (CH$30,000 for up to six people), try *Valle de Las Catas*, a private ranch located inside the park (☎2/535 3649, ⓦwww .sietetazas.cl); it's halfway between Parque Inglés and the Siete Tazas, close to the Puente de Frutillar. You can get to the Siete Tazas on **public transport** from Curicó with Buses Hernández (☎75/491607 or 75/512346), which has one daily bus from April to November and six to seven daily December through March, which is the best time to visit.

Talca and the Maule Valley

The fairly unmemorable town of **Talca**, 67km south on the Panamericana from Curicó, is mainly used as a jumping-off point for several rewarding excursions spread along the valley of the **Río Maule**, which flows into the sea almost 75km west at the industrial port of **Constitución**. The river has been dammed to the east of Talca, resulting in Lago Colbún. It's also where Chile's declaration of independence was signed. Just east of town, the **Villa Cultural Huilquilemu** is a handsome nineteenth-century hacienda, now a museum, while further east, high in the cordillera, the **Reserva Nacional Altos del Lircay** provides trails through dramatic mountain scenery. Further south, you'll find the neighbouring hot springs resorts of **Panimávida** and **Quinamávida** and, down on the valley floor, a proliferation of **vineyards**, many of them conveniently located between the town of **Villa Alegre** and village of **San Javier** on a route served by plenty of local buses from Talca. South from Constitución, a coast road leads to the seaside villages of **Chanco**, **Pelluhue** and **Curanipe**.

Talca

As the capital of Region VII, **TALCA** boasts its fair share of services and commercial activity, mostly centred on the main shopping street, **1 Sur**. Away from the frantic bustle of this thoroughfare, however, the rest of Talca seems to move at a snail's pace, not least the tranquil **Plaza de Armas**, shaded by graceful bougainvilleas, jacarandas and magnolias. Half-hidden beneath their foliage is a handsome 1904 iron bandstand and a number of stone statues plundered from Peru by the Talca Regiment in 1881, following their victories in the War of the Pacific. Standing on the northwest corner of the square, the Neo-Gothic **Cathedral**, built in 1954, is pale grey with a long, thin spire and series of turrets running along each side. It's worth popping inside to look at the delicately coloured stained-glass Belgian windows and the sombre main altar. One block east, on the corner of 1 Norte and 2 Oriente, the **Museo O'Higginiano** is currently closed for refurbishment and not due to reopen until 2010. The museum occupies a handsome colonial house that hosted some of the most important developments of the independence movement. It was here that Bernardo O'Higgins, future "Liberator" of Chile, lived as a child; where the Carrera brothers established the first *Junta de Gobierno* in 1813; and where in 1818, O'Higgins signed Chile's declaration of independence. Southwest at 2 Sur 1772 (near the corner with 5 Oriente), the **Museo Bomberil Benito Riquelme** (Mon–Fri 8.30am–11pm) is crammed full of antique fire engines, hoses and other firefighting equipment.

Practicalities

Most **buses** pull in at the terminal (⊕71/243270) on 2 Sur and 12 Oriente, ten blocks east of the Plaza de Armas; Tur Bus uses its own terminal a couple of blocks to the south. The **train station** (⊕71/226254) is one block west of the bus terminal, at 11 Oriente 1150. To get into the centre, take any *colectivo* or *micro* along 1 Sur (and to get back to the terminals, along 1 Norte). LAN has an office at 1 Sur 1030 (⊕600 526200). There's an extremely helpful **Sernatur** office on the Plaza at 1 Oriente 1150 (Mon–Fri 8.30am–5.30pm; ⊕71/233669, ⓔinfomaule@sernatur.cl), while **Conaf** is on the corner of 2 Poniente and 3 Sur (⊕71/228029).

Talca has numerous **hotels** including, in sharp contrast to most other towns in the region, several excellent economical options. ⚲ *Hostal del Rio* (⊕71/510218, ⓦwww.hostaldelrio.cl; ❹), 1 Sur 411, is the stand-out choice. The freshly painted rooms have modern private baths, and there's a good breakfast, friendly vibe and informed owners. Almost as good is the neighbouring *Hostal del Puente*, next to the river at 1 Sur 407 (⊕71/220930, ⓦwww .hostaldelpuente.cl; ❹), a welcoming place with en-suite rooms set around a patio and attractive gardens. A cheaper option is *Hostal Los Castaños* (⊕71/684531, ⓔloscastanostalca@gmail.com; ❸), a clean, quiet and pleasant

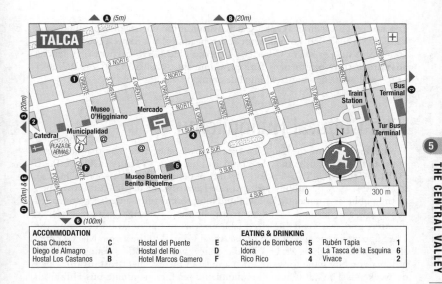

ACCOMMODATION

Casa Chueca	C	Hostal del Puente	E
Diego de Almagro	A	Hostal del Rio	D
Hostal Los Castanos	B	Hotel Marcos Gamero	F

EATING & DRINKING

Casino de Bomberos	5	Rubén Tapia	1
Idora	3	La Tasca de la Esquina	6
Rico Rico	4	Vivace	2

family home; doubles come with TV but share bathrooms. While the en-suites at *Hotel Marcos Gamero* (☎71/223388, Ⓦwww.marcosgamero.cl; ❻), 1 Oriente 1070, are fairly standard for this price range, the eclectic collection of aged record players, etchings and old irons strewn about the place give it a certain charm. The most upscale place is *Diego de Almagro* (☎71/714400, Ⓦwww.diegoalmagrohoteles.cl; ❼), 4 Norte 1011, which has ample en-suites, excellent service, a tiny pool and sauna, but a bland chain-hotel feel.

The German-Austrian guesthouse ⚑ *Casa Chueca*, 4km down the road to Las Ratras (office in Talca at Casilla 143, ☎71/197 0096 or 09/837 1440, Ⓦwww.trekkingchile.com; dorm ❷, private double ❺) is well worth the detour. Surrounded by banana and palm trees, the "Crooked House" offers an abundance of services, amenities and tours, including a pool, intensive Spanish lessons, dance classes and a climbing wall. It's closed June to August. To get here, phone ahead and then catch the Taxutal 'A' bus on 13 Oriente to the *El Toro Bayo* restaurant, an old colonial building at the end of the route, where you'll be picked up. The knowledgeable owners, who run the tour company Turismo Caminante (see p.272), also have a refuge (CH$8000 per person) in the beautiful Melando Valley.

One of the best **places to eat** is the atmospheric *Rubén Tapia*, 2 Oriente 1339 (☎71/215991, Ⓦwww.rubentapia.cl; CH$4000–7000 per main), which prepares rabbit casserole and other regional delicacies. ⚑ *La Tasca de la Esquina*, 1 Poniente 896, has expertly cooked dishes, many with a Spanish slant such as paella, squid ink pasta and tender beef and pork (CH$5500–6500), along with decorative flamenco posters, vintage wine bottles and colourful open fans. *Vivace* (☎71/238337), Isidoro del Solar 50, is a classy Italian with delicious home-made pasta (CH$5000–8000). Just ask them to turn the blaring radio down. For cheaper staples (CH$2000), head for the firemen's canteen, *Casino de Bomberos*, behind the **Museo Bomberil Benito Riquelme** (see opposite). *Rico Rico*, 1 Sur 1240, serves the best ice cream in town (from CH$700). For **drinks**, try *Idora*, Isidora del Solar 97, which has a suave bar with red leather seats.

Talca has several **casas de cambio**, including Casa de Cambio Marcelo Cancino at 1 Sur 898, Oficina 15, and several **ATMs** on 1 Sur, around the plaza.

You can rent a car from Rent a Car Rosselot at the corner of San Miguel and Varoli (☎71/247979). For **internet** access head to Zona Express Internet, 1 Sur 1064 (CH\$400 per hr), or Cibertel, 2 Oriente 1112 (CH\$450 per hr). A general **adventure tour operator** is Turismo Caminante, Casilla 143 (☎71/197 0097 or 09/837 1440, ⓦwww.trekkingchile.com).

Villa Cultural Huilquilemu

Ten kilometres along the San Clemente Highway, the paved road that heads east out of Talca towards the Argentinian border, is **VILLA CULTURAL HUILQUILEMU** (Tues–Fri 9am–1pm & 3–6.30pm, Sat noon–6pm; CH\$500; ☎71/242474). A beautifully restored *casa patronal* built in 1850, it's now open to the public as a museum. Inside, three long rooms off a series of colonnaded courtyards are devoted to religious art, housing paintings, statues, cassocks, furniture and two vivid, life-sized tableaux carved out of wood depicting the Last Supper and the appearance of the Angel Gabriel to the Virgin Mary. There's also an *enoteca*, where several Maule Valley wineries offer tastings of their products; or, buy wine to wash down a meal in the excellent **restaurant**, open on weekends. The Villa Cultural Huilquilemu is a fifteen-minute **bus ride** from Talca on any *micro* heading to San Clemente.

Reserva Nacional Altos del Lircay

As you continue east along the road, a left fork onto a poor dirt road some 30km on from Villa Huilquilemu leads 27km to the mountain village of **Vilches** and from here to the entrance of the **RESERVA NACIONAL ALTOS DEL LIRCAY**, 6km beyond (daily; Mar–Nov 9am–5pm; Dec–Feb 9am–8pm; CH\$3000, camping CH\$8000). This is an extremely beautiful part of the central cordillera, with a covering of ancient native forests and fantastic views onto surrounding mountain peaks and volcanoes streaked with snow. The road is difficult to pass in winter months, so the best time to visit is October through May. The **hiking trails** here are among the best in the region. Close to the entrance, an **information centre** has displays on the park's flora and fauna and the area's indigenous inhabitants, whose traces survive in the **piedras tacitas** (bowls used for grinding corn) carved out of a flat rock face a few hundred metres away along a signed path.

Of the various **trails** inside the reserve, the most popular is to a hilltop viewpoint at 2300m known as **Enladrillado**. From the reserve entrance (get more detailed directions from the *guardaparque*), follow the steep track up the hillside for about 2.5km, then follow the signed turn-off, from where it's a stiff uphill walk of about five hours; count on an eight-hour round-trip. The views from the top are exhilarating, down to the canopy of native *coigües* and *lenga* forests covering the valley beneath, and across to the towering **Volcán Descabezado** and surrounding peaks, made famous by the book and film *Alive*, which told the story of the Uruguayan rugby team whose plane crashed here in October 1972. Sixteen of the forty-five players on board survived the crash and endured 72 days in the mountains, eating the corpses of their teammates, until they were eventually rescued. Up here you'll also find areas of exposed volcanic rock resembling giant crazy paving, giving the spot its name, which translates roughly as "brick paving". The hike from the campsite to

Laguna del Alto, a lagoon inside a volcanic crater, is eight hours round-trip, with great lookout spots along the way.

If you want to explore further, try it on **horseback**: in Vilches, contact don Eladio (☎09/341 8064). The staff at *Refugio Galo* (see below) can also help organize trips, including overnight stays (around US$100). Buses Vilches runs three daily **buses** up to Vilches Alto in the winter and six in the summer (the latter continue on to the reserve entrance).

There's no **accommodation** within the park, though you're allowed to camp wild. But because of wildfire dangers, no campfires are permitted. In Vilches Alto, 7km east of the park, you will find several places to stay and eat, including *Refugio Galo* (☎09/272 1305, ✉galovilches55@gmail.com; ❷), which has basic but decent digs, and the owners are a good source of local information; and *Hostal Alto Vilches* (☎71/235442; ❸–❹) with cabins, a swimming pool, lots of information on local hikes and excursions.

Lago Colbún, the Termas de Panimávida, and Quinamávida and Tricahue Parque

There are various approaches to **LAGO COLBÚN**, Chile's largest artificial reservoir, stretching 40km from east to west. From Talca, drive east and carefully follow signs to stay on Ruta 115, a scenic mountain road to the northern shore of the lake. Lago Colbún was created between 1980 and 1985 when the Río Maule was dammed as part of a huge hydroelectricity project, and it wasn't long before its shores, framed by undulating hills, were dotted with holiday chalets, wooden cabins and mini-markets. The town of Colbún is not actually on the lake, but just west of it.

Accommodation options include *Cabañas Lago Colbún* (☎09/895 6401, ⓦwww.cabanaslagocolbun.cl; ❺) which has sheltered cabins in the woods for up to six people, and a games room, and *Complejo Turístico Valshi*, several kilometres further on (☎09/221 8793, ⓦwww.valshi.cl; ❹), with cabins, camping (CH$7000–10,000 per person) and tranquil surroundings. There are several **campsites**, too, but these are along the **southern shore**, which can be a pain to get to – though two bridges span the lake, access to them is often barred by the hydroelectricity company, which means going back to the Panamericana and driving instead along the southern bank of the Río Maule. This route provides access to **Colbún Alto**, a small village on the southwest shore of the lake, with some well-equipped campsites, including *Camping Pehuenche*, on the lakeshore (☎73/217070 or 09/348 9720; ❸). The village is served year-round by taxis from Linares.

The Río Maule road also leads to a couple of neighbouring hot-springs resorts, 5km south of the town of Colbún. The first one you reach is the **TERMAS DE PANIMAVIDA** (☎73/211743, ⓦwww.termasdepanimavida .cl; ❼), a nineteenth-century hacienda-style building built around numerous courtyards and patios. The gardens are immaculate but the rambling old building has rather gone to seed. It is, however, full of character, especially the distinctly Victorian-looking wing housing the long row of cubicles where guests soak in the thermal waters (not especially hot at 33°C/91°F), mud baths and steam rooms. Five kilometres further south, the **Termas de Quinamávida** (☎73/627100, ⓦwww.quinamavida.cl; ❻) is another labyrinthine hotel, this one featuring a huge indoor thermal pool in addition to the usual *tinas*, mud baths, massage and Turkish baths. The guests all seem eighty if they're a day. Both *termas* can be visited for the day, with use of the waters costing from

CH$4000–6000. You can get here from Santiago on **public transport** with Buses Villa Prat (T2/376 1758).

Around 25km east of Lago Colbún, at the confluence of the Maule and Armerillo rivers, is the village of Armerillo, close to the little-visited and remote **Tricahue Parque**, filled with tree-covered mountains, lakes and the 2000m Picudo Peak. A great way to explore the area is by staying at *Refugio Tricahue* (Wwww.refugio-tricahue.cl; CH$5000 per person); there's no telephone here because of lack of reception. This peaceful 10-bed hostel has a Finnish sauna and pool, and the welcoming owners organize fishing trips, walks, bike tours, swimming in thermal pools and, in the winter, snowshoe hikes. Interbus runs six daily buses to the area from Talca.

San Javier, Villa Alegre and the wineries

Twenty kilometres south of Talca is a massive iron bridge over the Río Maule, followed by the turn-off to **SAN JAVIER**, a bustling little town sitting in the heart of the Maule Valley's wine country. Its main interest lies in its proximity to two dozen local **vineyards**, spread between and around San Javier and the village of **Villa Alegre**, 9km further south, all of which are marked on a map distributed by Sernatur in Talca. The **Ruta del Vino Valle del Maule** includes fifteen wineries, and tours can be arranged through the Ruta del Vino Valle del Maule Enoteca at Villa Cultural Huilquilemu (Mon–Fri 9am–6.30pm, Sat–Sun midday–7pm; T71/246460, Wwww.valledemaule.cl). Half-day tours – including a visit to one to two wineries, tastings, transport, guides and generally a stop at Villa Cultural Huilquilemu – cost CH$20,000–25,000, based on a minimum of two people. Full-day tours cost CH$40,000–50,000 per person, based on a minimum of four people; they involve the same as the half-day tours, but also include visits to more wineries, lunch and a choice of cultural, gourmet, spa or physical (such as horseriding and cycling) activities.

One of the best wineries to visit on your own is **Viña Balduzzi** at Balmaceda 1189 in San Javier (Mon–Sat 9am–6.30pm; T73/322138, Wwww.balduzzi.cl), where you can drop in without a reservation for a 45-minute guided tour (CH$5000) of its *bodegas*. With two hundred acres of vineyards and beautiful grounds featuring an old *casa patronal*, a chapel and a *parque centenario* full of 100-year-old trees, this is a very picturesque example of a Central Valley winery. All the wineries below can also be visited independently, but should be contacted in advance.

A 10-minute journey south from Talca is **Casa Donoso** (T71/341400, Wwww.casadonoso.com; 8), Fundo La Oriental s/n, Camino a Palmira 3.5km, a beautiful nineteenth-century colonial building turned luxurious guesthouse surrounded by more than 123 acres of vineyards. East of Talca is **Viña Calina** (T71/263126, Wwww.calina.com), Camino Las Rastras s/n 7km, a large, modern operation set up in 1994. By contrast the nearby Hugo Casanova (T71/266540, Wwww.hugocasanova.cl), Camino Las Rastras s/n 8km, is much smaller in scale and remains in the hands of the family of its founder, who arrived from northern Italy in the late nineteenth century. On the road west from San Javier to Constitución, **Viña Gillmore** (T73/197 5539, Wwww.tabonko.cl; 8), Camino Constitución 20km, is one of the oldest vineyards in Chile. Also known as Tabontinaja or Tabonko, it has a good set-up for tourists, with tours examining the ecology of its vineyards. There's also a guesthouse – rooms have king- or queen-sized beds and Jacuzzis – and spa. The family enterprise of **Viña J Bouchón** (☎73/197 2708, ⓦwww.jbouchon.cl), founded in 1892 by a Frenchman from the Bordeaux region, is also located on the road to Constitución a little further on from Viña Gillmore.

Continuing south from San Javier you approach **VILLA ALEGRE** through a stunning avenue of trees whose branches meet overhead to form a dense green canopy. A stroll down the village's main street, lined with fragrant orange trees, takes you past grand *casas patronales* in luxurious grounds, and an almost uninterrupted stretch of nineteenth-century adobe houses topped by overhanging clay-tiled roofs. Vineyards here include **Viña El Aromo**, just off the avenue of trees (☎71/265587, ⓦwww.elaromo.cl).

All these wineries are easy to visit on day-trips from Talca, either by taxi or on **public transport**, with Interbus, 13 Oriente 880 (☎71/613146) and Pullman del Sur, 2 Sur s/n (☎71/613147) providing frequent services down the Panamericana, into Villa Alegre, up to San Javier and back to Talca. There are a few **places to stay** in Villa Alegre; try the tranquil *Hotel Colonial Maule* on Cancha de Carreras s/n (☎73/381214, ⓦwww.hotelcolonialmaule.com; ❺), set in an attractive old house. In San Javier there's *Residencial y Restaurante El Aromo*, Cancha de Carreras 2348 (☎73/322797; ❸).

Constitución and the coast

At the mouth of the Río Maule is the busy port of **CONSTITUCIÓN**. Now a popular holiday resort, the occasional foul stench of the local cellulose plant makes it unlikely you'll want to stay too long. Apart from the weird rock formations on the town's grey sand beaches, the main reason you might want to come here is to move on to the 60km of quiet beaches and small fishing towns stretching to the south.

From Talca, Constitución is served by plenty of **buses** and two daily **trains** (going to Talca, the right side of the train has the best views) which pull in opposite each other on the riverside, a few blocks northeast of the plaza. Should you need to **stay** here, head for the fairly smart *Hostería Constitución*, Echeverría 460 (☎71/671450, Ⓕ673735; ❹), perched on the banks of the Maule, which has rooms with private baths, good river views and a decent **restaurant**. A little further afield, 12km south of Constitución on the road to Chanco, is *Casa del Bosque Ruta Verde* (☎09/744 8224, ⓦwww.turismorutaverde.cl; ❸), a pleasant wooden house surrounded by forest; they use solar power and offer horse-riding, hikes, swims in natural pools and boat trips.

Chanco and the Reserva Nacional Federico Albert

From Constitución, a paved road follows the coast as far as the little seaside resort of **Curanipe**, 80km south. You pass extensive pine plantations bordered by grey, empty beaches and sand dunes before reaching **CHANCO**, a tiny village almost fossilized in the nineteenth century, populated by ageing farmers who transport their wheat, beans and potatoes to market on creaky, ox-drawn carts. The village's wonderful sky-blue **church** has images of various saints covering its interior.

On the northern edge of the village, the **RESERVA NACIONAL FEDERICO ALBERT** (daily 8am–6pm; CH$3000; ☎71/242474) is a dense pine and eucalyptus forest planted in the late nineteenth century in an attempt to hold back the advance of the coastal sand dunes – which by then had already usurped much valuable farmland. In the forest there's an attractive **camping** area (CH$8000 per site), while a three-kilometre **path** skirts the edge of the reserve, leading to an enormous sandy **beach** with small kiosks, picnic tables and running water. Camping aside, you can **stay** in the rudimentary *Hostal Mohor* at Av Fuentealba 135 (T73/551026, @juanita_mohor@hotmail.com; ❸), which also serves traditional dishes in its restaurant, or the rather plain but functional *Residencial y Artesania Lucy* at Errázuriz 2671 (T73/197 1145, @residencial_lucy @hotmail.com; ❸). Chanco is served by several daily **buses** from Constitución and Talca, run by Buses Contimar, 2 Sur s/n (T71/244197).

Pelluhue and Curanipe

The pleasant summer seaside resort and popular surfing destination of **PELLUHUE** (11km south of Chanco) is an undisciplined collection of houses strung around a long, curving black-sand beach. You'll find stacks of places to **stay**, including *Cabañas Campomar* (T73/541000, Wwww .cabanascampomar.cl; ❸–❺), about 3km south of town, near the top of a steep hill, which offers log cabins sleeping two to six with ocean views and a pool. The town has an untidy, slightly ramshackle feel to it, however, that doesn't encourage you to stay long, and you'd be better off 7km south in the prettier village of **CURANIPE**. With a backdrop of rolling hills, wheat fields and meadows, Curanipe's dark-sand **beach**, with colourful wooden fishing boats, is a lovely place to hang out, though that's just about all there is do here. You'll find neat, simple **rooms** and a fish **restaurant** at the *Hostería Pacifico*, on Comercio 509 (T73/556016; ❹). There's also an attractive **campsite**, *Los Pinos*, set in pine and eucalyptus woods by the beach. **Buses** Amigo (T73/511992) has services to Pelluhue and Curanipe from Constitución and Chanco. Buses Pullman del Sur (T71/244039) and Interbus (T71/613146) run buses from Talca.

Chillán and the Itata Valley

Back on the Panamericana, a hundred and fifty kilometres – punctuated by the nondescript towns of **Linares** and **Parral** – separate Talca from the busy city of **Chillán**, in the middle of the **Itata Valley**. Though lush and very beautiful, the broad valley is short on specific attractions, which amount to a **naval museum** in the village of Ninhue, 50km northwest of Chillán, and the hot-springs resort and ski centre of the **Termas de Chillán**, 80km east, high in the cordillera.

Chillán

Lively **CHILLÁN** is famous as the birthplace of Bernardo O'Higgins, the founding father of the republic. Unlike most of the towns staggered down

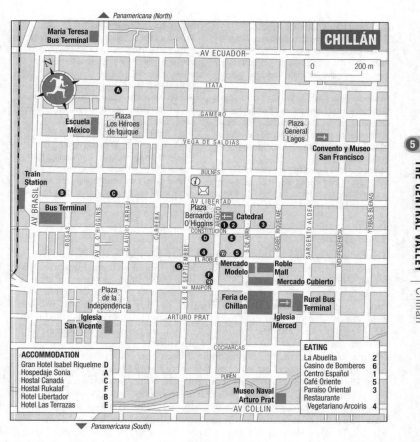

Panamericana (North)

Maria Teresa
Bus Terminal

CHILLÁN

AV ECUADOR

0   200 m

ITATA

GAMERO

Plaza
Los Héroes
de Iquique

Escuela
México

Plaza
General
Lagos

VEGA DE SALDIAS

Convento y Museo
San Francisco

Train
Station

BULNES

Bus Terminal

AV LIBERTAD

Plaza
Bernardo
O'Higgins

Catedral

CONSTITUCIÓN

EL ROBLE

Mercado
Modelo

Roble
Mall

Mercado Cubierto

MAIPON

Plaza
de la
Independencia

Feria de
Chillan

Rural Bus
Terminal

Iglesia
San Vicente

ARTURO PRAT

Iglesia
Merced

COCHARCAS

ACCOMMODATION
Gran Hotel Isabel Riquelme   D
Hospedaje Sonia   A
Hostal Canadá   C
Hostal Rukalaf   F
Hotel Libertador   B
Hotel Las Terrazas   E

PUREN

Museo Naval
Arturo Prat

AV COLLIN

EATING
La Abuelita   2
Casino de Bomberos   6
Centro Español   1
Café Oriente   5
Paraíso Oriental   3
Restaurante
Vegetariano Arcoiris   4

Panamericana (South)

the highway, it is, moreover, a place worth visiting in its own right – principally for its vast **handicrafts market** and fascinating **Mexican murals** – and
not just as a staging post to arrange transport to neighbouring attractions.

Arrival and information

Most **long-distance buses** use the Terminal María Teresa at O'Higgins 010
(☎42/272149), on the northern edge of town. **Local** and **regional buses**
operate out of the centrally located Terminal Rural, Maipón 890, a few blocks
southeast of Plaza Bernardo O'Higgins (☎42/223606). **Trains** pull in opposite
the old bus terminal on Avenida Brasil (☎42/222424), five blocks west of the
Plaza. **Sernatur** is at 18 de Septiembre 455 (Mon–Fri 8.30am–1.30pm &
2.30–6.30pm; ☎42/233272, Ⓔinfochillan@sernatur.cl), with the **Oficina de
Turismo** in the Municipalidad near the Plaza at 18 de Septiembre 590 (Mon–
Fri 9am–1pm & 3–7pm, sporadic hours May–Aug; ☎42/214117). **Conaf** is at
Arrau 738 (☎42/221085).

Accommodation

Chillán's upper- and mid-range hotels cater primarily to business travellers.
Budget accommodation is plentiful, but not of a great standard.

Gran Hotel Isabel Riquelme Arauco 600
ⓣ42/434400, ⓦwww.termaschillan.cl. This pale
salmon-coloured hotel gazes proudly over the
Plaza. While it is undoubtedly the grandest place in
town, the en-suites are a little unexciting and
overpriced. ❼

Hospedaje Sonia Itata 288 ⓣ42/214879. Slightly
ramshackle and chaotic but very friendly digs at
rock-bottom prices. Most rooms have TVs, shared
facilities are clean and home-cooked meals are on
offer. Solo travellers may have to share rooms at
busy times. ❷

Hostal Canadá Libertad 269, second floor
ⓣ42/234515. Here you can stay in the spare rooms
of a welcoming family home; the shared facilities are
spotless and there's a roof terrace to relax on. ❸

Hostal Rukalaf Arauco 740 ⓣ42/233366,
ⓦwww.rukalaf.cl. Solid mid-range hotel right
in the centre frequented mainly by business
travellers, and offering discounts for stays of
several days. ❺

Hotel Libertador Libertad 85 ⓣ42/223255,
ⓦwww.hlbo.cl. The rooms on the second floor are
the best, but all have big bathrooms, cable TV and
paintings of European cities. ❹

🏃 **Hotel Las Terrazas** Constitución 664
ⓣ42/437000, ⓦwww.lasterrazas.cl.
Excellent hotel split between two buildings that
face each other across the street. The airy whitewashed rooms have swish facilities and modern art
on the walls, while a relaxed ambience permeates
the whole place. ❺–❻

The Town

Thanks to periodic earthquakes and regular Mapuche attacks, Chillán has
repeatedly been rebuilt since being founded in 1550. The last major earthquake
was in 1939, and most of Chillán's present architecture dates from just after. It's
not unattractive, with wide avenues and no fewer than five open squares. The
focal one is **Plaza Bernardo O'Higgins**, dominated by a giant, 36-metre
concrete cross commemorating the thirty thousand inhabitants who died in the
1939 earthquake, and the futuristic, earthquake-resistant **cathedral**, built
between 1941 and 1961 in the form of nine tall arches.

A few blocks northwest, the **Escuela México**, a school built with money
donated by the Mexican government following the 1939 disaster, looks out over
leafy **Plaza de los Héroes de Iquique**. On Pablo Neruda's initiative, two
renowned Mexican artists, David Alfaro Siqueiros and Xavier Guerrero,
decorated the school's main staircase and library with fabulous murals (now a
little worn) depicting pivotal figures in Mexican and Chilean history. The
Mexican images, entitled *Muerte al Invasor*, feature lots of barely clothed native
heroes and evil-looking, heavily armed Europeans engaged in various acts of
cruelty. The Chilean tableau is even more gruesome, dominated by the lacerated,
bleeding body of the Mapuche *toqui*, Galvarino, and his bloodthirsty Spanish
captors. The school allows visitors access to the murals (Mon–Fri 10am–1pm &
3–6.30pm) in return for a small donation.

Seven blocks east, on Plaza General Lagos, the 1906 **Convento San
Francisco** is one of the few buildings to have survived the 1939 earthquake,
albeit in a lamentable state of repair. Inside, the **Museo Franciscano** (Tues–
Sun 9am–1pm & 3–6pm; CH$500) contains a collection of colonial furniture,
religious objects and military items brought to the region by members of the
Franciscan order, which arrived in 1585 to convert the Mapuche. Five blocks
south, filling Plaza de la Merced, the daily **Feria de Chillán** is an exuberant
open-air market selling a vast range of fresh produce and *artesanía*, ranging from
knitwear and leather items to jewellery, paintings and secondhand books. A
souvenir-hunter's paradise, the market is especially lively on Saturdays, when it
bulges out of the square and spreads into the surrounding streets. Three blocks
south, tucked away in the Naval Club at Isabel Riquelme 1173, the **Museo
Naval Arturo Prat** (Mon–Fri 10am–noon & 3–5pm) contains a disappointing
collection of model ships (naval fans will be better off skipping this and heading
straight for the museum at Ninhue – see p.280). The **Parque Monumental**

Bernardo O'Higgins (daily: April–Nov 8am–6pm; Dec–March 8am–8pm), a short bus ride south along Avenida O'Higgins, is a handsomely landscaped park featuring a 60m wall covered with a badly faded mosaic depicting the life of the city's most famous son. In a small chapel nearby, O'Higgins' mother, Isabel Riquelme, and his sister, Rosita, are both buried, not far from the site where Bernardo was born.

Eating

For a cheap bite and great, buzzing atmosphere, head to the hectic **Mercado Cubierto** and the slightly more restrained **Mercado Modelo**.

La Abuelita Constitución 635. The best place in Chillán for cakes (around CH$1000) and coffee, served in an attractive *pastelería* with wood furnishings.

Casino de Bomberos Corner of El Roble and 18 de Septiembre. Cheap Chilean cuisine (CH$2000) and plenty of local colour can be found at this no-frills, bustling fire station canteen.

Centro Español Arauco 555. Penguin-suited waiters at this sun-filled Spanish-Chilean restaurant serve signature dish paella with prawns, mussels, scallops, salmon, chorizo, pork ribs and chicken; the huge one-person portion (CH$5000) is easily enough for two.

Café Oriente El Roble 655. Look beyond the unprepossessing location on the edge of a shopping mall and you'll find good coffee, sandwiches and sweet Arabic pastries (CH$1000).

Paraíso Oriental Constitucion 715. Cough medicine-pink tablecloths aside, this popular Chinese spot is good for generous portions of fried rice and noodles (CH$3500–5000), either eat-in or takeaway.

Restaurante Vegetariano Arcoiris El Roble 525. A rainbow sign guides diners into this great vegetarian restaurant, which has an all-you-can-eat lunchtime buffet (CH$4000) and fresh juices. Check out the flyers in the front window for local events.

Listings

Banks and exchange There are several ATMs on Arauco and Constitución. To change traveller's cheques or cash, try AFEX Cambios Schuler, Constitución 608.

Car rental First, 18 de Septiembre 380 ☎42/211218.

Hospital Herminia Martin (☎42/212345), corner of Argentina and Francisco Ramírez.

Internet *Planet*, Arauco 683, 2nd floor (CH$500 per hr); Hi-Net Cyber Café, Arauco 764 (CH$450 per hr).

Post office The main *correo* is at Libertad 505.

Telephone offices Entel is at 18 de Septiembre 746, CTC at Arauco 625.

Travel agencies Alas Tour, Libertad 485, Office 403 ☎42/238301.

Termas de Chillán

The most famous and developed mountain resort south of Santiago is the **Termas de Chillán** (information in Santiago at Pío X 2460, Office 508 ☎2/233 1313, ⓦwww.termaschillan.cl; information in Chillán at Panamericana Norte 3651 ☎42/434200), an all-season tourist complex 80km east of Chillán, nestled at the foot of the 3122m **Volcán Chillán**. Surrounded by glorious alpine scenery, it possesses nine open-air **thermal pools**, **steam baths** inside dripping caves, hot **mud baths**, and state-of-the-art **spa** centre, offering massages, facials, hydro-massages and a range of other treatments. It's often packed with kids and is very family-friendly. The hot baths and spa function year-round, but in winter the emphasis shifts to the resort's excellent **skiing** facilities, which include nine lifts, 28 runs, one of which is 2500m, the longest in South America, and a snowboard park. Summer activities also abound, from hiking and mountain biking to tennis.

There are three types of **accommodation** within the resort itself, all very expensive. Prices vary dramatically throughout the year, with July the most expensive, so consult the resort's website before booking. The large ⚡ *Gran Hotel Termas de Chillán* (☎2/366 8800 in Santiago, ☎42/434200 in Chillan; ❾) is the plushest, a large five-star with spacious en-suites (high season US$2450 for seven nights half-board and lift tickets) in soothing colours, restaurants, bar, casino and its own hot springs. You can also rent out fully furnished apartments (❽) sleeping two to six people. If you don't mind being 7km from the slopes, try the swanky *Hotel Pirimahuida* (❽).

On the way up to the resort you'll pass several **campsites** along the road between 50km and 57km. Further along, between 68km and 75km, a growing number of **lodgings** have sprung up, including *Cabañas Los Nirres* at 71km (☎42/197 3898, ⓦwww.losnirres.cl; dorm CH$15,000, apartments sleeping two to twelve (❸–❻), which has a pool, sauna, games room and bike hire, and *Chillán Youth Hostel* (☎42/243211, ⓔhilastrancas@hostelling.cl; dorm CH$7600) at 73.5km, next to the police station, with four- to six-bed dorms, café and bar. The various accommodation options here are a ten- to fifteen-minute drive from the *termas*.

Additionally, you'll find plenty of well-equipped cabins available for rent; among the best is *Parador Jamón, Pan y Vino*, at 74km (☎42/221306, ⓦwww .paradorjamonpanyvino.cl; ❼), offering pyramid-shaped cabins and cosy apartments, and great, Spanish-accented food. For cabin rentals visit ⓦwww .vallelastrancas.cl and ⓦwww.nevadosdechillan.cl.

During the summer you might consider visiting for the day: use of the hot sulphur pools costs CH$12,000, while the steam baths are CH$20,000; during the ski season (normally June–Sept), **lift tickets** cost from CH$18,000. Linea Azul (☎42/211192) runs a year-round **bus** service to Valle Las Trancas and on to the Termas.

Santuario Cuna de Prat

Naval enthusiasts will not be let down by the splendidly preserved colonial **Hacienda San Agustín de Puñal** (Tues–Sun 10am–6pm; CH$1000) just outside the village of **Ninhue**, 50km northwest of Chillán. Arturo Prat was born here in 1848, and the area is now a shrine to the naval hero, who died in 1879 in the Battle of Iquique while trying to capture a Peruvian ironclad gunship armed only with a sword. Inside the hacienda is a museum devoted to the hero, the **SANTUARIO CUNA DE PRAT**. While the national obsession with the young officer – a thousand Chilean plazas and streets are named after him – continues to mystify outsiders, the museum's collection of polished, lovingly cared-for naval memorabilia and colonial furniture are worth a visit in their own right, and the building they're housed in, with its large interior patio and elegant verandas, is a beautiful example of colonial rural architecture.

Concepción and
the Bío Bío Valley

South of Chillán and the Itata Valley, Chile is intersected by the great **Río Bío Bío**, generally considered the southern limit of the Central Valley. One of Chile's longest rivers, it cuts a 380-kilometre diagonal slash across the country, emptying into the ocean by the large city of **Concepción**, over 200km north of its source in the Andean mountains. For more than three hundred years the Bío Bío was simply "La Frontera", forming the border beyond which Spanish colonization was unable to spread, fiercely repulsed by the native **Mapuche** population.

Today, the Bío Bío Valley, which stretches 400km southwest from the mouth of the Río Bío Bío, still feels like a border zone between the gentle pastures and meadows of central Chile, and the lakes and volcanoes of the south. While the valley floor is still covered in the characteristic blanket of cultivation, dotted with typical Central Valley towns such as **Los Angeles** and **Angol**, the landscape on either side is clearly different. To the west, the **coastal range** – little more than gentle hills further north – takes on the abrupt outlines of real mountains, densely covered with the commercial pine forests' neat rows of trees and, further south, native araucaria trees in their hundreds within **Parque Nacional Nahuelbuta**. Cut off by these mountains, the towns strung down the coast road south of Concepción – such as **Lota**, **Arauco**, **Lebu** and **Cañete** – feel like isolated outposts. To the east, the Andes take on a different appearance, too: wetter and greener, with several outstandingly beautiful wilderness areas like **Parque Nacional Laguna del Laja** and **Parque Nacional Tolhuaca**.

▲ Kayaking on the Río Bío Bío

Concepción

The sprawling, fast-paced metropolis of **CONCEPCIÓN** is the region's administrative capital and economic powerhouse, and Chile's second-largest city, sitting at the mouth of the Bío Bío, 112km southwest of Chillán. Surrounded by some of Chile's ugliest industrial suburbs, Concepción's centre is made up of a spread of dreary, anonymous buildings. This lack of civic splendour reflects the long series of catastrophes that have punctuated Concepción's growth – from the incessant Mapuche raids during the city's days as a Spanish garrison, guarding La Frontera, to the devastating earthquakes that have razed it to the ground dozens of times since its founding in 1551. It does, however, have the energy and buzz of a thriving commercial centre, and the large number of students here at the Universidad Austral de Chile gives the place a young, lively feel and excellent nightlife.

Arrival and information

Most **buses** arrive at Terminal Collao, northeast of the centre at Tegualda 860, just off the Autopista General Bonilla (☎41/286 1533); plenty of *colectivos* and taxis will take you into town. If you arrive with Tur Bus or Linea Azul, you may be dropped at the smaller Terminal Chillancito, also called Terminal Henríquez, off Autopista General Bonilla at Henríquez 2565. **Aeropuerto Carriel Sur** is 5km northwest of the city. **Sernatur** is at Aníbal Pinto 460 (Mon–Fri 8.30am–1.30pm & 3–6pm; ☎41/274 1337, Ⓔnoyarzo@sernatur.cl), with **Conaf** at Barros Arana 215 (☎41/224 8048).

Accommodation

Concepción has several upmarket, business **hotels**, but budget accommodation is hard to find, with no rock-bottom options at all.

Hotel Alborada Barros Arana 457 ☎41/291 1121, Ⓦwww.hotelalborada.cl. The reflective glass exterior, modern lobby, plant-filled walkway and classical music offer no warning that the en-suites will be shockingly pink. You'll either love or hate it. **❼**
Hotel El Araucano Caupolicán 521 ☎41/274 0606, Ⓦwww.hotelaraucano.cl. A stellar – and reasonably priced, especially if you book online – hotel boasting en-suites with flat-screen TVs and tubs. There's an indoor pool, sauna and good restaurant with a terrace over the Plaza. **❼**
Hotel Cecil Barros Arana 9 ☎41/273 9981, Ⓔhotel_cecil@123mail.cl. While the room doors are an unappealing grey, inside everything is clean with mock wood floors and views over Plaza España. It's in the heart of the city's nightlife district, so can be noisy at weekends. **❻**

Hotel Maquehue Barros Arana 786 ☎41/262 9500, Ⓦwww.hotelmaquehue.cl. This 7th-floor hotel offers very good value but dated wood-floored en-suites – bathrooms have bidets and lizard skin-style decor. Some rooms command fine city views. **❹**
Hotel San Sebastián Rengo 463 ☎42/295 6719, Ⓦwww.hotelsansebastian.cl. Rooms at this small, amiable hotel are a little old-fashioned but spotless and have private baths. **❹**
Residencial Central Rengo 673, 2nd floor ☎41/222 7309. The paint on the outside's peeling and the wooden staircase creaks ominously, but inside, this aged townhouse hides large, musty rooms, character-filled communal areas and a warm welcome. **❸–❹**

The City

The city's focal point is the busy **Plaza de la Independencia**, where Bernardo O'Higgins read the Chilean declaration of independence in January 1818. In the centre, a classical column rises above the main fountain, atop which stands a gold-painted statue symbolizing the region's agricultural wealth. On the

CONCEPCIÓN

ACCOMMODATION
Hotel Alborada	C
Hotel El Araucano	D
Hotel Cecil	B
Hotel Maquehue	E
Hotel San Sebastián	F
Residencial Central	A

EATING & DRINKING
Café Rometsch	3
Cantabria	5
Cheng Nan	1
La Fontina di Trevi	6
Restaurant Tradiciones	2
Peruanas	
Treinta y Tantos	4

Train Station

BARRIO ESTACIÓN

PLAZA ESPAÑA

Mural "Historia de Concepción"

Mercado

Parroquia de la Merced

PLAZA DE LA INDEPENDENCIA

Catedral

PLAZA PERÚ

Casa del Arte

University Campus

Parque Ecuador

Galería de la Historia

PAICAVI

ONGOLMO

TUCAPEL

CASTELLÓN

COLO COLO

SAN MARTIN

COCHRANE

CHACABUCO

MAIPU

FREIRE

BARROS ARANA

O'HIGGINS

ANÍBAL PINTO

CAUPOLICÁN

RENGO

LINCOYÁN

ANGOL

SALAS

SERRANO

PRAT

PEDRO AGUIRRE CERDA

JANEQUEO

LARENAS

BELTRÁN MATHIEU

VICTOR LAMAS

PEDRO DE VALDIVIA

200 m

N

western side of the plaza rises the Romanesque-Byzantine **Catedral de la Santísima Concepción**, built between 1940 and 1950 and adorned with faded mosaics by Alejandro Rubio Dalmati. Adjacent to the cathedral is the **Museo de Arte Sagrado** (Caupolicán 441; Tue–Fri 10am–1.30pm & 4–8pm, Sat–Sun 11am–2pm; CH$400), featuring colonial artwork, marble statues, gold-embroidered vestments and religious artefacts.

For a more in-depth introduction to the city, the **Galería de la Historia** (Mon 3–6.30pm, Tues–Fri 10am–1.30pm & 3–6.30pm, Sat–Sun 10am–2pm & 3–7pm) at the southern end of Lincoyán, in Parque Ecuador, has a series of impressive dioramas, some with sound and light effects. Walk up to the far end of the park and on to Calle Larenas, where you'll reach the **Universidad Austral de Chile**, set in splendid, landscaped gardens surrounded by thickly wooded hills. This is Chile's third-largest university and has the curious distinction of being funded by the local lottery. It houses one of Chile's largest national art collections in the **Casa del Arte** (Tues–Fri 10am–6pm, Sat 10am–4pm, Sun 10am–1pm). The bulk of the collection consists of nineteenth-century landscapes and portraits by Chilean artists, but the showpiece is the magnificent mural in the entrance hall, *Presencia de América Latina*, by the Mexican artist Jorge González Camarena in 1964. Dominating the mural is the giant visage of an *indígena*, representing all the indigenous peoples of the continent, while the many faces of different nationalities superimposed on it indicate the intrusion of outside cultures and fusion of races that characterize Latin America. You'll find another mural, though not in the same league, inside the **railway station**, Arturo Prat 501: over 6m long and 4m tall, this massive *Historia de Concepción*, painted by Chilean artist Gregorio de la Fuente was installed in 1964.

At the western end of the Bío Bío estuary, a fifteen-minute taxi ride from the city centre, a large park with several kilometres of footpaths and an extensive collection of native and exotic trees surrounds the **Museo Hualpén** (Tues–Sun 9am–6pm; CH$1500 for parking). A traditional single-storey hacienda houses an eclectic collection of souvenirs from every corner of the globe, picked up by the millionaire industrialist Pedro del Río over three world trips in the nineteenth century.

Sixteen kilometres northeast of Concepción is the industrial city and naval base Talcahuano, where the historic ironclad gunship **Huáscar** is moored. From Calle Chacabuco in Concepción, white buses marked "Base Naval" go from Avenida Collao and O'Higgins right to the entrance of the base, where you need to ask the guard for permission to visit the ship (Tues–Sun 9.30am–noon & 2–5.30pm; CH$1000). The *Huáscar* was built for the Peruvian navy at Birkenhead in 1866 and controlled the naval engagements during the War of the Pacific until 1879, when it was trapped off Cape Angamos, near Antofagasta, and forced to surrender. Kept in an immaculate state of preservation, the *Huáscar* is one of only two vessels of its type still afloat today.

Eating, drinking and nightlife

Concepción has a good range of **restaurants** and boasts the liveliest **nightlife** in the Central Valley, fuelled by the large student population. The **Barrio Estación** is buzzing at night, particularly on Calle Prat and Plaza España, revolving mainly around a string of small restaurants that double up as bars on the weekend evenings. *Loft*, Barros Arana 37, and *Marengo*, Prat 522, are two good places to try. You can also enjoy inexpensive meals at one of the dozens of little *picadas* in the **Mercado Central**, on the corner of Freire and Caupolicán.

Moving on from Concepción

There are direct **buses** to most towns and cities between Santiago and Puerto Montt, most leaving from Terminal Collao. A notable exception is Tur Bus, whose downtown office is Tucapel 530 (☎41/778 7338), and which leaves from both Terminal Collao and Terminal Chillancito (see "Arrival and Information", p.282). If you're heading up the coast to Tomé, take a Costa Azul bus from Chacabuco street (☎41/265 1267). The coastal route south of Concepción to **Cañete**, **Arauco**, **Lebu** and **Contulmo** is served by Los Alces, Salas 1444 (☎41/224 0855) and Buses J. Ewert, Lincoyán 1425 (☎41/222 9212); both companies leave from Prat, near the train station. There are regular **flights** from Concepción to Santiago, Temuco and Puerto Montt. Several minibus companies offer inexpensive door-to-door transfers to the airport, including Airport Service (☎41/223 9371).

Café Rometsch Barros Arana 685. Cavity-inducing ice-cream sundaes, cakes and crepes (CH$2000–3000) are available at this long-standing café, which is decorated with city sketches.

Cantabria Caupolicán 415. Prices are a little steeper here on account of the prime people-watching location, but the good coffee and decadent cakes (CH$2000) make it eminently worthwhile.

Cheng Nan Freire 877. An inexpensive self-service vegetarian joint with wholesome, mainly Chinese, dishes, a few pastas and salads (CH$2000). The food is much fresher at lunchtime.

La Fontina di Trevi Colo-Colo 344. A menu of tasty but standard Italian pizzas and pastas (CH$3500–5000), alongside checked tablecloths and a display of dozens of wine bottles, is the order of the day here. The CH$3500 lunch special is a good choice.

Restaurant Tradiciones Peruanas Barros Arana 337. Waiters in red shirts and large white kerchiefs around their necks serve delicious Peruvian food (CH$4000–5500) like ceviche and *lomo saltado* (steak strips with tomato, onion, chips and rice).

Treinta y Tantos Prat 404. A long-standing student haunt serving more than thirty varieties of inexpensive empanadas (around CH$1000) in a cosy setting with mellow music. Evenings only.

Listings

Airlines Aerolíneas Argentinas, Aníbal Pinto 509, Oficina 201 ☎41/286 1300; American Airlines, Barros Arana 340 ☎41/252 1616; LAN, Barros Arana 600 and Colo-Colo 550 ☎600 526 2000.

Banks and exchange There are many banks with ATMs, mainly on O'Higgins, by the central plaza. To change money, try Cambio Fides and AFEX at Barros Arana 565.

Bicycle repairs Martínez, Maipu 297.

Car rental Avis, Prat 750 ☎41/288 7420; Budget, Chacabuco 117 ☎41/221 2438.

Cinema Cine Arte, O'Higgins 650 ☎42/222 7193.

Consulates Argentina, O'Higgins 420, Oficina 82 ☎41/223 0257; Canada, Caupolicán 245 ☎41/236 7553; UK, Galvarino 692 ☎41/222 5655; Italy, Barros Arana 245 ☎41/222 9506.

Internet *Portal*, Caupolicán 314; *Cyberprint*, Barros Arana 368; both CH$400 per hr.

Hospital San Martín and Lautaro ☎41/223 7445.

Post office Corner of O'Higgins and Colo-Colo.

Shipping Navimag, San Martín 553 ☎41/291 1910.

Telephone centres Entel, Barros Arana 541 and Colo-Colo 487.

Travel agents Turismo Cocha, Oficina 309 ☎41/291 0175; Gestur, Rengo 484 ☎41/222 5975.

The northern beaches

North of Concepción, a series of small towns and golden, sandy bays stretches up the coastline as far as the mouth of the Río Itata, 60km beyond. The first 44km, past Dichato, is paved and served by regular **buses** and **colectivos**. Heading up the road, 12km out of the city centre, you pass through the suburb of **Penco**, where the remains of a Spanish fort, **Fuerte La Planchada**, recall the area's turbulent history.

A couple of gentle hills separate Penco from **Lirquén**, a small industrial harbour used for exporting timber. Its beach is nothing special, but the nearby tangle of narrow streets known as the **Barrio Chino** is full of first-class, excellent-value seafood restaurants, famous throughout the region for their clam dishes and *paila marina*. Beyond Lirquén, the road runs inland for 30km, and the only access to the ocean along here is controlled by *Punta de Parra* (☎41/274 7676, ⓦwww.puntadeparra.cl). It has cabins (CH$28,000 per night, minimum two-night stay) and charges CH$1500 per non-guest for admittance to the powdery white sands. There's a restaurant and a beautiful coastal walk along the old rail tracks to several even more secluded beaches.

Twenty-eight kilometres out of Concepción, the thriving timber centre, textile town and port of **Tomé** is squeezed into a small flat-bottomed valley, its suburbs pushed up the slopes of surrounding hills. Hidden from the drab town by a rocky point is the long, white-sand **Playa El Morro**, with several places to **stay** including *Cabañas Broadway*, Av Werner 1210 (☎41/265 8476; ❹–❺) and *Hotel Althome*, Sotomayor 669 (☎41/265 0807; ❹). The beach, while very attractive, gets dreadfully crowded on summer weekends; a quieter alternative is **Playa Cocholgue**, a fine white beach studded with rocky outcrops, reached by taking the four-kilometre side road off the main coast road as you head out of Tomé. Eight kilometres north, **Dichato** is the most popular beach resort along this part of the coast, with a handful of **accommodation** options spread along the crescent-shaped, coastal avenue, Pedro Aguirre Cerda. Try *Cabañas Asturias*, at no. 734 (☎41/268 3000; ❹), which offers inviting, fully furnished rooms and a **seafood restaurant** with excellent views. Four kilometres north of Dichato, towards the Río Itata, there's a restful **campsite**, *El Encanto* (☎41/265 0462; CH$10,000 per site). Beyond here, the road turns to dirt and passes through dense forests with tracks leading off to a series of isolated, yellow-sand **beaches**, pounded by strong waves. Among the most beautiful of these are **Playa Purda**, 8km north of Dichato, and tiny **Playa Merquiche**, a further 2km north.

The southern coast road and beyond

South of Concepción, a road skirts the ocean, passing through the towns of Coronel, **Lota** and Arauco. This area was deserted until the mid-nineteenth century, when the enormous submarine coal seam – the **Costa del Carbón** – was discovered running off the coast. About 150km south of Concepción, **Lebu** has great beaches, while nearby **Cañete**'s Mapuche museum is worth a visit en route to pretty **Lago Lanalhue**, 51km from Lebu. Rural areas along the coast all the way to Temuco are hotly contested battlegrounds. Intentional forest fires set by Mapuche groups asserting ancestral land claims were once frequent, and travellers were warned to avoid conflict areas where land seizures were taking place, as bloody confrontations with police occurred quite frequently. The issue remains unresolved, but there have been no recently confirmed fires or seizures. Los Alces and Buses J. Ewert have regular **bus** services along this route from Concepción. Accommodation lists are available from the **Lanalhue Tourism Board** (☎41/261 3317, ⓦwww.lanalhueturismo.cl).

Lota

Squeezed into a small valley on the edge of the sea, the soot-streaked town of **LOTA** was the site of Chile's first and largest coal mine, opened by industrialist Matías Cousiño in 1849. Production finally ceased in 1997, and today the ex-colliery is turning its attention to tourism, with hotels, swimming pools and a casino. The town centre, in the lower part of town known as Lota Bajo, does not inspire enthusiasm, though while you're here you should check out the curious **statue of the Virgin**, carved out of coal, in the church on the plaza. Spread up the hillside west of the centre is Lota Alto, containing the former miners' residences, as well as the impressive **Iglesia San Matías**, where the coal baron lies buried. From here it's a short walk to **Parque de Lota** (daily: April–Oct 10am–6pm; Nov–March 10am–8pm; CH$1600), a formal garden laid out by an English landscape gardener in 1862 under the direction of Cousiño's wife, doña Isidora Goyenechea. The park also has colonial homes, a museum containing a motley collection of photographs and colonial possessions (free for visitors to the Parque de Lota, CH$600 just to visit the museum) and actors who dress and speak like characters from the nineteenth century. You can visit the **coal mine** on **tours** (daily 10am–5pm; ☎41/870682) guided by ex-miners, with the choice of going down the 820-metre shaft of the **Chiflón del Diablo** (CH$4000) or to the much deeper **Pique Carlos**, 1500m below ground (CH$6000). Lota makes an easy day-trip from Concepción, with regular **bus services** provided by Buses J. Ewert, leaving from near the train station.

Isla Santa María

From Lota's pier you can take a two-hour boat ride (departures Tues, Thur and Sat at 11am; CH$5000 return; ☎41/287 1322 or 09/565 7253) to **ISLA SANTA MARÍA**, a small, lush island with steep cliffs, rolling hills and a population of about three thousand farmers and fishermen. El Club Aéreo Concepción (☎09/465 4593) flies to the island for around CH$65,000 per person. The island's mild climate and fertile soil have supported small Mapuche communities for hundreds of years. There are secluded bays scattered around the island, with good beaches, sea lion colonies and excellent fishing opportunities. Other activities include boat trips and tractor rides with Juan Carlos Vargas (☎09/742 3228) and **horse rides** with René Guzmán. Simple but acceptable **accommodation** is available at *Hotel Angel de Peredo* at Carlos Cousino 149 (☎41/287 6824; ❹). Since boats **return** to Lota on Mondays, Wednesdays and Fridays at 7.30am, you will need to stay on the island overnight, unless you opt to take the more expensive option and fly back and forth.

Lebu

Seventy-six kilometres south of Lota, a 31-kilometre side road shoots off the highway to the small coastal town of **LEBU**, one of the few places still mining coal in this region. It has huge, unspoiled **beaches**, including **Playa Millaneco**, 3km north, where you'll find several massive caves overgrown with ferns and lichen. Lebu's only other attraction is its pair of bronze cannon on display in the plaza, which were cast in Lima in 1778 and bear the Spanish coat of arms. The best place to **stay** is *Hotel Central*, Pérez 183 (☎41/251 1904; ❹), a building that's over 100 years old, with comfortable, well-maintained rooms and a good **restaurant** that often serves the local speciality – king crab.

Cañete

Back on the highway, 16km south of the turn-off for Lebu, **CAÑETE** is a busy agricultural town perched on a small rise above a bend in the Río Tucapel. Just off the northern end of the main street, commanding fine views over the river valley, the historic **Fuerte Tucapel** was founded by Spanish conquistador Pedro de Valdivia in 1552 and is the site of his gruesome death at the hands of the Mapuche chief Lautaro two years later. Just south of town, 1km down the highway, the **Mapuche Museum** (Jan–Feb Mon–Fri 9.30am–7pm, Sat–Sun 11am–7pm March–Dec Mon–Fri 9.30am–5.30pm, Sat 11am–6pm, Sun 1.30–6.30pm; CH$600; ☎41/261 1093) houses a fine collection of indigenous artefacts, including textiles, silver jewellery, musical instruments and weapons. Perhaps the most striking exhibit is the *ruca* in the museum's garden – a traditional Mapuche dwelling made of wood and straw.

If you want to **stay**, head for *Hotel Alonso de Ercilla*, at Villagrán 641 (☎41/261 1974; ❸) or the slightly more expensive *Hotel Nahuelbuta* at Villagrán 644 (☎41/261 1073; ❸); both have pleasant doubles with private bathrooms. The best place to **eat** is *Club Social* on the plaza, in an unprepossessing building but serving well-cooked meat and fish dishes. From Cañete, a dirt road climbs 46km to Parque Nacional Nahuelbuta (see p.291), while the highway curves south through a lower pass in the Cordillera de Nahuelbuta.

Lago Lanalhue

Ten kilometres out of Cañete, the road reaches the northern shore of **LAGO LANALHUE**, nestled amongst dense pine forests on the western slopes of the coastal range. Its waters are crystal clear and warmer than the Pacific, and its heavily indented shores form numerous peninsulas and bays, some of them containing fine white sand. There are many **places to stay**, including *Cabañas Playa Dorada* (☎09/879 9014, ⓦwww.playadorada.cl; ❹), 12km from Cañete, on the north tip of the lake, which has modern cabins with heating, TV, mini kitchens and ample living and sleeping space. *Cabañas Terrazas del Lanalhue* (☎09/499 5330, ⓦwww.terrazasdellanalhue.cl; ❹), also on the northern side of the lake, 2km from Peleco, has a range of cosy cabins. You can buy basic provisions in the village of **Contulmo**, about 5km along the highway; while you're there, carry on a couple of kilometres around the south shore of the lake to visit the **Molino Grollmus** (officially Jan–April Mon–Sat 10–11am & 6–7pm, but in reality more sporadic; CH$500), an early twentieth-century wooden mill whose gardens contain an impressive collection of *copihues*. Some 44km east of Contulmo, the highway forks, with one branch heading to the town of Angol (see p.291), and the other continuing south to the Panamericana.

Down the Panamericana to the Salto del Laja and Los Angeles

From Concepción, the southern coastal route makes an appealing diversion but if you're in a hurry, take the direct 85km trunk road back to the Panamericana. Some 50km south from there, the first major town you reach is **Los Angeles**; halfway along this route, the Panamericana crosses the Río Laja. Until recently the highway passed directly by the **Salto del Laja**, which ranks among the most impressive waterfalls in Chile. It's still a good break spot on the long drive from Santiago, but beware of old maps that show the highway cruising by the falls. To actually get to the Salto del Laja, you'll need to follow the turn off-signs for the "Salto", which lead to the old highway. From there you will see the falls – cascading almost 50m from two crescent-shaped cliffs down to a rocky canyon.

There are parking spaces around the bridge, and a short path passes through the cabins and campground of the *Complejo Turístico Los Manantiales*

(☎43/314275; ❹) to a closer viewpoint. Other options include the swish en-suites at *Hotel Salto del Laja*, Panamericana Km 480, about 30km north of Los Angeles (☎43/321706, ⓦwww.saltodellaja.cl; ❺–❻), which has sixty acres of parks, delightful swimming holes, Jacuzzis and waterfall views. For low-budget camping, you'll find numerous places convenient to public transport. One kilometre south of the falls, the road east (by the church) holds two year-round campsites, jointly run (CH$7000 for up to five people, cabins CH$25,000). The first, *Salta Chica* (☎43/314772, ⓦwww.turismosaltosdellaja.cl), lies 800m from the highway and is beautiful but noisy. Up the road (1.5km) is *Playa Caliboro* with a mini beach and natural pool. Further south at Km 495, the German-run year-round hotel, *El Rincón* (☎09/441 5019, ⓦwww.elrinconchile.cl; ❹–❺), has regular doubles with private bathrooms and an attractive log cabin in lovely surroundings. It also offers excursions into the practically uninhabited foothills, and Spanish lessons. If you're relying on **public transport**, your best bet is to visit the falls on a short trip from Los Angeles on one of the frequent Buses Bío Bío services to Chillán – they run every half hour in both directions.

Los Angeles

LOS ANGELES is an easy-going agricultural town, pleasant enough but without any great attractions. In the library on the southeast corner of the Plaza de Armas is the **Museo de la Alta Frontera** (Mon–Fri 8am–1.45pm & 2.45–6.45pm), which has a stash of colonial rifles and Mapuche silver ornaments and jewellery. At the north end of Colón, eight blocks from the plaza, is the colonial **Parroquia Perpetuo Socorro**, a church whose handsome colonnaded cloisters enclose a flower-filled garden. Otherwise, the town is really just a jumping-off point for the **Parque Nacional Laguna del Laja** (see below).

Practicalities

The **bus terminal** is on Av Sor Vicenta 2051 (☎43/363035), the northern access road from the Panamericana. You can get **information** from the Oficina de Turismo in the Municipalidad, on the southeast corner of the Plaza de Armas (Mon–Fri 8.30am–1pm & 3–5.30pm; ☎43/409400) and Conaf, Manso de Velasco 275 (☎43/322126). There are numerous **ATMs** on Colon.

If you are on a really tight budget, *Residencial Central* at Almagro 377 (☎43/323381; ❷) has austere, but just about habitable **rooms**. A much better bet is *Hotel Oceano* (☎43/341694, ⓔhoteloceanola@hotmail.com; ❹), Colo Colo 327, which has helpful staff and neat, sunny rooms with clean bathrooms. *Hotel Mariscal Alcázar*, Lautaro 385 (☎43/311725, ⓦwww.hotelalcazar.cl; ❼) boasts modern and well-equipped en-suites, and is the most comfortable in town. The *Club de la Unión*, at Colón 261 – overlooking the Plaza – is one of Los Angeles' best **restaurants**. Appetizing Chilean fare (CH$4000–5500) and a tasty set-lunch menu are on offer. The low-key *Tu Café*, Colo Colo 384, has a good selection of breakfast items, sandwiches and ice creams (CH$2500); it feels a little like dining in someone's living room.

Parque Nacional Laguna del Laja

Set in an otherworldly volcanic landscape of lava flows and honeycombed rock, the **Parque Nacional Laguna del Laja** (daily: April–Nov 8am–6pm; Dec–March 8am–9pm; CH$1000; ☎43/321086) takes its name from the

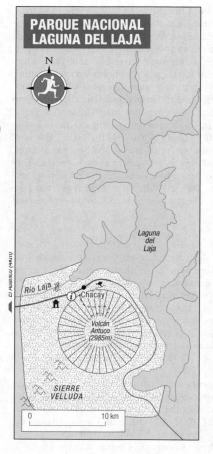

PARQUE NACIONAL LAGUNA DEL LAJA

N

Laguna del Laja

Río Laja

Chacay

Volcán Antuco (2985m)

SIERRA VELLUDA

0   10 km

great green lake formed by the 1752 eruption of **Volcán Antuco** (2985m). The road from Los Angeles, 93km away, is paved for the first 66km to **Antuco**; after that, the road surface is gravel but in decent condition for the 30km to the park entrance.

The park boundary is 4km east of the village of **EL ABANICO**, but the Conaf hut, where you pay your entrance fee, is 12km on from the village (though they're thinking of moving it closer to the park boundary), and the administrative and environmental **Centro de Informaciones**, at Chacay, lies another kilometre beyond the hut. From here, an easy path leads a couple of kilometres to a pair of large, thundering waterfalls, **Salto Las Chilcas** and **Salto del Torbellino**, fed by underground channels from the lake, which emerge here to form the source of the Río Laja. Hikes to the summit are not particularly difficult, but allow four to five hours for the trip up and three hours for the hike down. Wear strong boots as the volcanic rocks will shred light footwear.

The road through the park continues east from the information centre towards the lake, passing a small **ski centre** (5km along the road) with a small restaurant and simple refuge. At this point, the road deteriorates into a terrible dirt track that skirts the southern shore of the lake for 22km, continuing to the Paso Pichachén and the Argentine border. Few vehicles make it along here, so the road serves as an excellent walking trail through the sterile landscape, with changing views of the lake and of the mountains of **Sierra Velluda** in the southwest, which are studded with hanging glaciers. From the administrative centre of Chacay, short trails lead to the Salto Las Chilcas and Salto del Torbellino.

Getting to the park by **public transport** is difficult: from Los Angeles' Terminal Rural, at Villagrán 501, Buses ERS (☎43/322356) has five daily services to El Abanico (fewer at weekends), but from here it's a twelve-kilometre hike to the Conaf office, and another 5km to the lake. You can **stay** in the park at *Cabañas y Camping Lagunillas* (☎43/321086), which has secluded camping areas (CH$7000 per site), four spacious cabins (❺) and a **restaurant** by the banks of the Río Laja. If you don't mind roughing it, contact the park authorities about staying in *Refugio Digeder* (CH$5000 per person) at the base of **Volcán Antuco**.

THE CENTRAL VALLEY

Parque Nacional Laguna del Laja

5

Angol

Sixty-four kilometres southwest of Los Angeles, **ANGOL** is the final major town before Temuco, the gateway to the Lake District, and serves as a useful base for visiting the nearby **Parque Nacional Nahuelbuta**. In the centre of the town's attractive Plaza de Armas a large, rectangular pool is guarded by four finely carved – and comically stereotypical – marble statues of women representing the continents of Asia, Africa, Europe and America. Angol's **Museo de Historia**, on Sepulveda 371 (Mon–Sat 9am–7pm; donation expected), displays the town's historical memorabilia, including interesting photos from the late 1880s. Better, though, is the **Museo Dillman Bullock** (daily 9.30am–1pm & 3–7pm; CH$450) out in the suburbs, 5km south down Avenida Bernardo O'Higgins, reached by *colectivo* from the Plaza de Armas. Within an agricultural college, it has beautifully landscaped gardens and a strange assortment of archeology including pre-Columbian funeral urns, a moth-eaten mummy, Mapuche artefacts and malformed foetuses.

Practicalities

On the Museo Dillman Bullock's grounds is the *Hostal El Vergel* (☎45/712103 or 712403; ❸), Angol's best **place to stay**, with large rooms in an old wooden house, and a good restaurant. In town, at Caupolicán 498, *Hotel Club Social* (☎45/711103, ⓔcshotel@entelchile.net; ❹) offers light, airy rooms, an outdoor pool, aged billiards tables, and a decent **restaurant**. Angol's long-distance **bus terminal** is on the corner of Caupolicán 200 and Chorillos (☎45/711100), one block north of the Plaza; rural services operate from the far end of Lautaro, three blocks east of the Plaza. There's an **Oficina de Turismo** at the fork of O'Higgins and Bonilla (Mon–Fri 8.30am–1pm & 2.30–6pm; ☎45/201556), over the river from the town centre, while **Conaf** is at Prat 191 (☎45/711870).

Parque Nacional Nahuelbuta

From Angol, a dirt road (difficult to pass after rain) climbs 35km west to the entrance of **PARQUE NACIONAL NAHUELBUTA** (daily: April–Nov 8am–6pm; Dec–March 8am–9pm; CH$4000), spread over the highest part of the Cordillera de Nahuelbuta. The park was created in 1939 to protect the last remaining **araucaria** (monkey puzzle) trees in the coastal mountains, after the surrounding native forest had been wiped out and replaced with thousands of radiata pines for the pulp and paper industry. Today it's a 68-square-kilometre enclave of mixed evergreen and deciduous forest, providing

▲ Parque Nacional Nahuelbuta

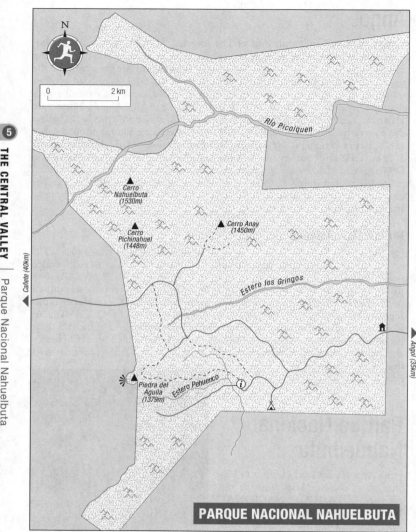

the coastal cordillera's only major refuge for wildlife such as foxes, pumas and *pudús* (pygmy deer). You're unlikely to catch sight of any of these shy animals, though if you look up amongst the tree trunks you may well see large black woodpeckers hammering away. Of the park's trees, star billing goes to the towering araucarias, with their thick umbrellas of curved, overlapping branches covered in stiff pine needles. Some of these trees are over 40m high, and the most mature ones in the park are more than a thousand years old.

You can find out more about the park's flora and fauna at the **Centro de Informaciones**, 5km west along the road from the entrance. From here there are two treks: an interesting, 700-metre interpretative loop through the forest and an easy one-hour, four-kilometre hike (look out for the giant araucaria about five minutes' walk along the path, estimated to be 1800 years old) up to the **Piedra del Aguila**. This craggy rock, at 1450m, offers superb views that on clear days take in the whole width of Chile, from the Andes to the Pacific. At a slightly lower, flatter rock a few metres west, you can enjoy even better views onto the smoking volcanoes of the northern Lake District. To get here by car, take the road through the park to the signed car park, from where it's a twenty-minute walk up to the viewpoint past a series of information panels on the trees. There's another rewarding trek up the gentle slopes of **Cerro Anay**, 4km north of the information centre, reached by a jeep track followed by a short path. Its 1400-metre peak is the best place to take in the whole of the park.

Practicalities

In the summer **Buses** Angol and Buses Nahuelbuta come from Angol's rural terminal and from a stop on the corner of Ilabaca and Caupolicán respectively to Vegas Blancas (25km to the west of Angol) and stop at El Cruce, an hour's walk from the entrance. The park is open all year but expect snow and 4WD conditions June through September. There are two **camping** areas (CH$12,000 per site); bring food, as there's nowhere to buy supplies in the park.

Parque Nacional Tolhuaca

Back on the Panamericana, 40km south of the turn-off to Angol, a detour into the Andean foothills will take you to another area of protected native forest, **PARQUE NACIONAL TOLHUACA** (daily: May–Nov 8am–6pm; Dec–April 8am–9pm; CH$3000), a pristine landscape offering some of the finest hiking in the region. The park covers a long and relatively narrow strip of land stretching through the valley of the Río Malleco, hemmed in by steep, thickly wooded hills. Dominating the bottom of the valley is the wide and shallow **Laguna Malleco**, bordered by tall reeds rich in birdlife, while other attractions include waterfalls, small lakes and hundreds of araucaria trees.

The best **approach** to the park is along the 57-kilometre dirt road (via the village of Inspector Fernández) branching east from the Panamericana, a couple of kilometres north of **Victoria** (a small, ramshackle town of no interest). This leads directly to the Conaf administration on the southeastern shore of Laguna Malleco, where you'll also find **camping** (CH$12,000 per site) and picnic areas. From here, a footpath follows the northern shore of the lake for about 3km, through lush evergreen forest to the **Salto Malleco**, where the lake's waters spill down into the Río Malleco, forming a spectacular 50-metre waterfall. About halfway along this path, another trail branches north, climbing steeply up the hillside before forking in two. The left fork follows the twelve-kilometre **Sendero Prados de Mesacura** across a gentle plain before climbing steeply again through dense forest. The right fork follows the **Sendero Lagunillas** (also 12km), climbing moderately to a group of small lakes near the summit of Cerro Amarillo, from where you get fabulous panoramic views onto the surrounding peaks, including the 2800-metre Volcán Tolhuaca. Both of these are full-day hikes, requiring an early start. Following the flat path along the northern bank of the Río Malleco eastwards, after about 5km you'll reach the trailhead of the eight-kilometre **Sendero Laguna Verde**, which climbs up and around a steep hill to the small, emerald-green Laguna Verde, 1300m above sea level and surrounded by soaring peaks. This makes a good camping spot.

PARQUE NACIONAL TOLHUACA

Río Pichimalleco

(1290m)

SENDERO PRADOS DE MESACURA (1156m)

(1355m)

SENDERO LAGUNILLAS

(1792m)

Las Lagunillas   Laguna Verde

SENDERO LAGUNA VERDE   (1606m)

Río Malleco   Salto del Malleco   Laguna Malleco

0   4 km

Termas de Tolhuaca

▼ Inspector Fernández (57km) & Victoria   Curacautín (33km) ▼

Termas de Tolhuaca

From the Conaf office, a bouncy nine-kilometre dirt road leads to the **TERMAS DE TOLHUACA** (daily 8.30am–6pm; ☎45/881211, ⓦwww.termasdetolhuaca.cl), just outside the park's boundaries. The source of the *termas* is at the bottom of a narrow, rocky canyon, inside a large cave, where bubbling, sulphurous water seeps out of the rocks, and steam vents fill the cave with fumaroles, forming a kind of stone-age sauna. The small pools around the cave are too hot to paddle in, but a little further down the canyon, where the thermal water has mixed with cold stream water, there's a gorgeous natural pool that you can bathe in. The administration operates two **hotels** (❻), one down in the canyon, the other higher up, near a large swimming pool filled with thermal water. The rooms are very simple for the price, but the location (particularly of the lower hotel) is stunning. You can also visit the *termas* for the day (CH$8000). It can get very busy in January and February, especially at weekends, but outside these months the place is blissfully quiet.

The road to Lonquimay

At **Victoria**, a paved road branches east from the Panamericana to the small agricultural town of **Lonquimay**, 115km away, passing the entrance to the **Reserva Nacional Malalcahuello–Nalcas** en route. There's nothing especially appealing about Lonquimay itself, but the road there – running through a narrow valley overlooked by towering volcanoes – is spectacular, particularly the stretch across the **Cuesta de las Raíces**. Fifty-six kilometres out of Victoria, the road passes through the logging town of **Curacautín**, from where a 40-kilometre dirt road branches south to Lago Conguillío, in **Parque Nacional Conguillío** (see p.304). As the northern gateway to the park, Curacautín has its fair share of hotels, but there's more dramatic scenery further along the road, including the 60-metre waterfall, **Salto del Indio**, just off the road, 14km out of Curacautín, and, 7km beyond, the 50-metre **Saltos de la Princesa**. Three kilometres past the falls is the smartly furnished **Termas de Manzanar** hotel (☎45/881200, ⓦwww.termasmanzanar.cl; ❻–❽), where the more expensive en-suites come with Jacuzzis. A full 27km east of town sits the very popular hostel *La Suiza Andina* (☎09/884 9541 or 45/197 3725, ⓦwww.suizaandina.com; ❹–❺), which offers a range of rooms with private facilities and safe. The staff provide hiking information, horse and bike riding and camping (CH$4000 per person). There's also a Swiss restaurant.

Reserva Nacional Malalcahuello-Nalcas

Some 30km west of Curacautín, you'll pass the entrance to the **RESERVA NACIONAL MALALCAHUELLO-NALCAS** (daily: May–Nov 8am–6pm; Dec–April 8am–8pm), with the administrative office just a few hundred metres from the road. The Conaf staff are extremely helpful and friendly, and while there's no official **camping** in the reserve, they often let people camp for free in the gardens by the wardens' house. The attractions here are hiking, fly fishing and horse treks. Hiking trips on the Lonquimay Volcano take about four hours up, one down, and an ice axe and crampons are required. Ask for information at Conaf or the *La Suiza Andina* hostel. Another popular walk is the seven-kilometre **Sendero Piedra Santa**, a trail through different types of vegetation that illustrate the techniques used by Conaf to protect and manage native forest. The trail passes through quite separate areas of evergreen tepa, raulí, coigüe, lenga and the famous araucaria. Parts of the path give excellent views onto 3125-metre **Volcán Llaima**, and 2890-metre **Volcán Lonquimay**. Count on around five hours to complete the trail.

Cuesta de Las Raíces

A couple of kilometres further along the main road from the administration, a gravel road (signed Volcán Lonquimay) branches north, and then forks in two. The left fork leads 4km to a small **Los Arenales ski centre** (☎09/893 0435; ski ticket CH$7500, equipment rental CH$8000, half-day group ski school CH$15,000). Open year-round, it offers overnight accommodation in the form of pricey bunk beds (❹), and there's also a café. From here, the track continues up to a lookout point over **Cráter Navidad**, the gaping hole produced when the volcano last erupted, on Christmas Day 1988. The right fork leads 26km to the village of Lonquimay, across the **CUESTA DE LAS RAÍCES**, part of the volcanic chain that forms the highest peaks in this section of the Andes. This is a beautiful drive, through lush araucaria forests, with birds of prey, such as buzzards, swooping around the tree branches. From the pass at the top, you get an extraordinary view down over the araucarias, spread out below like a vast green carpet.

An alternative route to Lonquimay is through the **Túnel de Las Raíces** (open 24hrs; CH$1000 each way), reached by continuing along the paved road. Built in 1930 as a railway tunnel, in an abortive attempt to connect the Pacific and Atlantic by railroad, this 4.5km tunnel was once the longest in South America, but is only wide enough for traffic to pass through in one direction at a time; be prepared to wait up to an hour for the traffic direction to reverse. Driving through is quite an adventure, as it's constantly dripping with water and littered with potholes and puddles. In winter it's even more dramatic – huge, metre-long icicles hang from the roof, transforming the tunnel into a sort of frozen Gothic cathedral.

Lonquimay

After the excitement of driving through the tunnel or crossing the Cuesta de Las Raíces, the rather sedate little town of **LONQUIMAY**, sitting at the end of the paved road, is something of a let-down. A quiet collection of wooden houses and corner shops, the town boasts only one interesting feature – a bizarre street plan. It's laid out in the shape of a rugby ball, with an elliptical Plaza de Armas. Lonquimay is, however, beautifully located on a flat, fertile plain, to the east of the

Andes. The only part of the country to cross the cordillera, it was claimed by Chile because the Bío Bío rises here, fed by numerous meandering rivers that flow through a 100-kilometre stretch of pampa. There are several places to **stay** in Lonquimay, including *Hostal Follil Pewenche*, Carrera Pinto 110 (☎45/891110; ❸), with good en-suite rooms and a **restaurant** and *Hotel Turismo*, Caupolicán 925 (☎45/891087; ❹), offering neat, sunny rooms with flowery curtains.

Travel details

Buses

Chillán to: Concepción (every 15min; 1hr 30min); Curicó (7–8 daily; 2hr 30min); Los Angeles (every half hour; 1hr 15min); Puerto Montt (9–10 daily; 9hr); Rancagua (10 daily; 3hr 30min); San Fernando (10 daily; 3hr); Santiago (20 daily; 5hr); Talca (12 daily; 2hr); Temuco (10 daily; 3hr).

Concepción to: Cañete (every 30min; 3hr); Chillán (every 15min; 1hr 30min); Contulmo (5 daily; 4hr); Lebu (every 15min; 2hr 20min); Los Angeles (every 30min; 1hr 30min–2hr); Puerto Montt (15 daily; 10hr); Rancagua (5 daily; 5hr); San Fernando (5 daily; 5hr 30min); Santiago (every half hour; 6hr); Talca (11 daily; 3hr 30min); Temuco (every hour; 4hr); Tomé (every 20min; 40min); Valdivia (11 daily; 7hr).

Curicó to: Chillán (7–8 daily; 2hr 30min); San Fernando (every 15min; 40min–1hr); Radal Siete Tazas (summer: 6–7 daily; winter 1 daily; 50min–1hr).

Los Angeles to: Angol (every 30min; 45min); Chillán (every half hour; 1hr 15min); Concepción (every 30min; 1hr 30min–2hr); El Abanico (7 daily; 1hr 30min); Puerto Montt (10 daily; 8hr); Rancagua (5 daily; 4hr 30min); San Fernando (5 daily; 4hr); Talca (15 daily; 3hr); Temuco (20 daily; 2hr).

Rancagua to: Chillán (10 daily; 3hr 30min); Concepción (5 daily; 5hr); Lago Rapel-El Manzano (every 15min; 2hr); Los Angeles (5 daily; 4hr 30min); Pichilemu (16–18 daily: 2hr 30min); Puerto Montt (10 daily; 13hr); San Fernando (every 15min; 50min–1hr 20min); Santa Cruz (15 daily; 1hr 30min); Santiago (every 15min; 1hr–1hr 30min); Talca (every 30min; 2hr); Temuco (10 daily; 7hr); Termas de Cauquenes (2 daily; 1hr 15min).

San Fernando to: Angol (2 daily; 7hr); Chillán (10 daily; 3hr); Concepción (5 daily; 5hr 30min); Curicó (every 15min; 40min–1hr); Lago Rapel-El Manzano (every 15min; 2hr 45min); Los Angeles (5 daily; 4hr); Pichilemu (every 30min; 1hr 40min); Puerto Montt (10 daily; 12hr 30min); Rancagua (every 15min; 50min–1hr 20min); Santa Cruz (every half hour; 35–45min); Santiago (every 15min; 1hr 30min); Talca (every 30min; 1hr 30min); Temuco (10 daily; 6hr 30min); Valdivia (5 daily; 9hr).

Santa Cruz to: Rancagua (15 daily; 1hr 30min); San Fernando (every half hour; 35–45min); Santiago (every half hour; 2hr).

Talca to: Chanco (6 daily; 3hr 30min); Chillán (12 daily; 2hr); Concepción (11 daily; 3hr 30min); Constitución (summer: every 20min, winter 4 daily; 1hr 20min); Curanipe (summer: every hour; winter: 3 daily; 1hr 30min); Los Angeles (15 daily; 3hr); Pelluhue (summer: every hour; winter 3 daily; 1hr 20min); Puerto Montt (9 daily; 11hr 30min); Radal Siete Tazas (2 daily; 1hr 45min); Rancagua (every 30min; 2hr); San Fernando (every 30min; 1hr 30min); San Javier (every 15min; 30min); Santiago (20 daily; 3hr 30min); Temuco (15 daily; 5hr 30min); Vilches Alto (summer: 6 daily; winter 2 daily; 1hr 30min); Villa Alegre (every 15min; 20min).

Trains

Chillán to: Curicó (4–7 daily; 2hr 20min); Rancagua (4–7 daily; 3hr 30min); San Fernando (4–7 daily; 2hr 50min); Santiago (4–7 daily; 4hr 30min); Talca (4–7 daily; 1hr 40min).

Curicó to: Chillán (4–7 daily; 2hr 20min); Rancagua (4–7 daily; 1hr 5min); San Fernando (4–7 daily; 30–40min); Santiago (4–7 daily; 2hr 30min); Talca (4–7 daily; 40min).

Rancagua to: Chillán (4–7 daily; 3hr 30min); Curicó (4–7 daily; 1hr 5min); San Fernando (15–19 daily; 35min); Santiago (15–19 daily; 1hr 5min–1hr 20min); Talca (4–7 daily; 1hr 45min).

San Fernando to: Chillán (4–7 daily; 2hr 50min); Curicó (4–7 daily; 30–40min); Rancagua (15–19 daily; 35min); Santiago (15–19 daily; 1hr 40min–1hr 55min); Talca (4–7 daily; 1hr 10min).

Talca to: Chillán (4–7 daily; 1hr 40min); Constitución (2 daily; 2hr 50min); Curicó (4–7 daily; 40min); Rancagua (4–7 daily; 1hr 45min); San Fernando (4–7 daily; 1hr 10min); Santiago (4–7 daily; 2hr 50min).

Flights

Concepción to: Puerto Montt (2 daily; 1hr 50min); Santiago (11 daily; 1hr); Temuco (2 daily; 35min).

The Lake District

CHAPTER 6

Highlights

✳ **Parque Nacional Conguillío**
Hiking is spectacular in this
Andean park, where fresh
volcano fields mix with
ancient araucaria forests.
See p.304

✳ **Pucón** At the capital of
adventure tourism in the
Lake District, you can climb
smoking Volcán Villarrica,
raft the rapids of the
Trancura or disappear into
the hills on mountain bike
trails. See p.309

✳ **Siete Lagos** Get away from
the crowds by exploring
Andean lakes that have only
recently been opened to
tourists. See p.319

✳ **Valdivia** Find a surprising
mix of European history at
this lively coastal city, where

German breweries and old
Spanish forts are surrounded
by rivers and bays. See p.325

✳ **Lago Todos Los Santos**
Enjoy the spectacular scenery
surrounding its emerald-green
waters as you take a boat ride
towards the Argentine border.
See p.338

✳ **Estuario de Reloncaví** A top
spot for hiking, kayaking or
horse-trekking into the oldest
forests of the Americas,
including the Cochamó Valley,
known as "Chile's Yosemite".
See p.345

✳ **Puerto Varas** The
introduction to Patagonia,
where you can embark on
rafting and fishing expeditions
after gorging on the best food
in the region. See p.346

▲ Parque Nacional Conguillío

6

The Lake District

The landscape gradually softens as you travel south along the Panamericana. This is the **LAKE DISTRICT**, which stretches 339km from **Temuco** in the north to **Puerto Montt** in the south, a region of lush farmland, dense forest, snow-capped volcanoes and deep, clear lakes, hidden for the most part in the mountains.

Until the 1880s, when small farm settlements arrived, the entire region was blanketed in thick forests: to the north, the high, spindly araucaría; on the coast, dense *selva valdiviana*; and to the very south, two thousand-year-old alerces. These forests were inhabited by the tenacious **Mapuche** (literally "people of the land"), who fought off the Inca and resisted Spanish attempts at colonization for 350 years before finally falling to the Chilean Army in the 1880s. This heritage is a badge of honour in today's Chile, and at least half a million of the region's population claim this ancestry, many of whom reside on the extensive indigenous *reducciones* (reservations) throughout the Lake District.

In little over a century since the subjugation of the Mapuche, the German, Austrian and Swiss settlers transformed this region into some of the finest **dairy farmland** in Chile. The efforts of the European settlers opened the area up to travellers, and visitors have been coming here for over a hundred years.

While much of the Lake District's population lives in the main cities of Temuco, Osorno, Valdivia and Puerto Montt, with the exception of Valdivia these are mainly sprawling transportation hubs, with little to offer the visitor. The real action lies in the region's many national parks and around the adventure sports capitals of **Pucón** and **Puerto Varas**, where the options abound for hiking, volcano-climbing, rafting, kayaking, canyoning and horseriding. In the winter, skiing down volcanoes draws an adventurous crowd. Those seeking less strenuous activities can soak in the many thermal springs that are part of the region's volcanic legacy, laze on the black-sand beaches or explore the remote, picturesque towns and villages.

The main cities and popular resorts in the Lake District are served by an excellent network of buses that run up and down the Panamericana. Frequent minibuses connect the main cities with all but the most remote of villages, while within larger cities there are numerous taxis, buses and *colectivos*.

Temuco and around

Once a Mapuche stronghold, **TEMUCO**, 677km south of Santiago, is the largest city in southern Chile, a commercial centre filled with jostling crowds and horn-honking traffic. Most visitors use it solely as a transport hub or as a

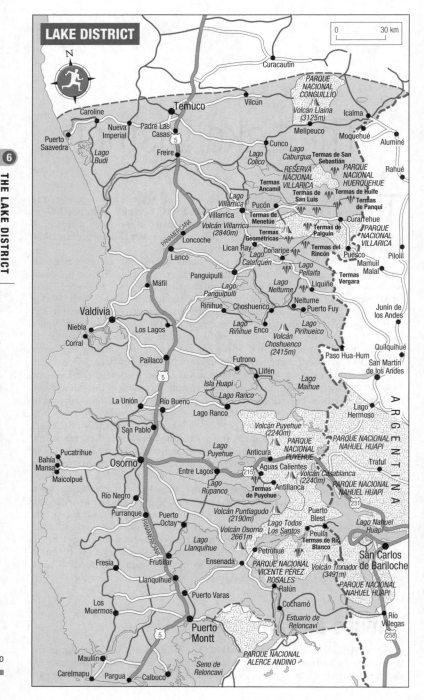

LAKE DISTRICT

0   30 km

N

Curacautín

*PARQUE
NACIONAL
CONGUILLIO*

Vilcún

*Volcán Llaina
(3125m)*

Icalma

Caroline

Temuco

Nueva
Imperial

Padre Las
Casas

Melipeuco

Moquehué

Aluminé

Puerto
Saavedra

*Lago
Budi*

Freire

Cunco

*Lago
Colico*

*Lago
Caburgua*

Termas de San
Sebastián

Rahué

*RESERVA
NACIONAL
VILLARICA*

*PARQUE
NACIONAL
HUERQUEHUE*

Termas
Ancamil

Termas de
San Luis

Termas de Huife

*Lago
Villarrica*

Pucón

Termas
de Panqui

Villarrica

Termas de
Menetúe

Termas de
Palguín

Curarrehue

*Volcán Villarrica
(2840m)*

Loncoche

Termas
Geométricas

Termas del
Rincón

*PARQUE
NACIONAL
VILLARICA*

Lanco

Lican Ray

Coñaripe

Puesco

Piloilí

*Lago
Calafquén*

Máfil

Panguipulli

*Lago
Pellaifa*

Termas
Vergara

Mamuil
Malal

*Lago
Panguipulli*

*Lago
Neltume*

Liquiñe

Valdivia

Riñihue

Choshuenco

Neltume

Puerto Fuy

Junín de
los Andes

Niebla

Los Lagos

*Lago
Riñihue*

Enco

*Lago
Pirihueico*

Corral

Paillaco

*Volcán
Choshuenco
(2415m)*

Quilquihué

Futrono

Paso Hua-Hum

San Martín
de los Andes

Llifén

*Lago
Maihue*

Isla Huapi

Lago Ranco

La Unión

Río Bueno

Lago Ranco

*Lago
Hermoso*

San Pablo

*Volcán Puyehue
(2240m)*

Pucatrihue

*PARQUE
NACIONAL
PUYEHUE*

*PARQUE NACIONAL
NAHUEL HUAPI*

Bahía
Mansa

Osorno

Entre Lagos

Anticura

Traful

Maicolpué

Aguas Calientes

*Volcán Casablanca
(2240m)*

*PARQUE NACIONAL
NAHUEL HUAPI*

Río Negro

*Lago
Rupanco*

Termas
de Puyehue

Antillanca

Purranque

Puerto
Octay

*Volcán Puntiagudo
(2190m)*

Puerto
Blest

*Volcán Osorno
2661m*

*Lago Todos
Los Santos*

Peulla

*Lago Nahuel
Huapi*

Fresia

Frutillar

*Lago
Llanquihue*

Petrohué

Termas de Río
Blanco

San Carlos
de Bariloche

Llanquihue

Ensenada

*PARQUE NACIONAL
VICENTE PÉREZ
ROSALES*

*Volcán Tronador
(3491m)*

Los
Muermos

Puerto Varas

Ralún

*PARQUE NACIONAL
NAHUEL HUAPI*

Cochamó

Río
Vilegas

Puerto
Montt

*Estuario de
Reloncaví*

Maullín

*Seno de
Reloncaví*

*PARQUE NACIONAL
ALERCE ANDINO*

Carelmapu

Pargua

Calbuco

A R G E N T I N A

base for exploring nearby **Parque Nacional Conguillío**. But the city itself has a rich **Mapuche heritage**, particularly evident in and around the colourful **markets**, which are among the best places in the country to hear Mapudungun (the Mapuche language) spoken.

Temuco was founded in 1881, and it was only when the railway from Santiago arrived in 1893 that the city began to prosper. An influx of seven thousand European immigrants from seven different countries formed the farming and commercial nucleus that soon transformed the forested valleys and plains.

Arrival and information

If you're coming from a nearby town by **bus**, you'll be dropped either at the Terminal de Buses Rurales on Pinto and Balmaceda (℡45/210494), or at the Buses JAC terminal at Aldunate and Balmaceda (℡45/210313). The main long-distance bus terminal, Rodoviario Araucario, is at Vicente Pérez Rosales 1609, Sector Pueblo Nuevo (℡45/225005), served by *colectivos* from the city centre and bus #7. Temuco's **airport**, Maquehue, lies six kilometres southwest of town (℡45/554801), and has numerous daily flights to Santiago, as well as twice-daily flights to Concepción, Osorno, and Puerto Montt. There are no buses to downtown, though Transfer Araucanía (℡45/339900) can arrange transfers if you call in advance, and there are plenty of cabs outside.

For general **tourist information**, visit the Sernatur office on the northeast corner of Plaza Aníbal Pinto at Claro Solar 899 (Jan–Feb Mon–Sat 8.30am–7.30pm, Sun 10am–2pm; March–Dec Mon–Thurs 9am–1pm & 3–5.30pm, Fri 9am–1pm & 3–4.30pm; ℡45/312857, ℮infoaraucania@sernatur.cl). There's also a tourist kiosk by the entrance to the Mercado Municipal. For information about the region's **national parks**, including Parque Nacional Conguillío, visit Conaf at Bilbao 931, second floor (Mon–Fri 8.30am–2pm; ℡45/298114).

Accommodation

Temuco is filled with **hotels**, though good budget and mid-range accommodation tends to be scarce. The areas around the rural bus terminal and open-air market are not very safe to wander around after dark.

Hospedaje Aldunate Aldunate 187 ℡45/213548. A clean, basic house with a pleasant communal sitting room, kitchen facilities and basic breakfast included. Some rooms are windowless; dorm accommodation also available. ②–③

Hotel Bayern Prat 146 ℡45/276000 ⓦwww .hotelbayern.cl. This smart hotel has smallish rooms with wi-fi and cable TV and slightly larger, better *ejecutivo* rooms. A good buffet breakfast is included. Cheaper rates if paying in US dollars. ④–⑤

Hotel Don Eduardo Bello 755 ℡45/214133 ⓦwww.hoteldoneduardo.cl. Modern and well-furnished high-rise with comfortable en-suite rooms. Free wi-fi, pleasant staff and cable TV in every room are among the bonuses; airport transfers can be arranged. ④–⑤

Hotel Nicolás Mackenna 420 ℡45/210020 ⓦwww.hotelnicolas.cl. Conveniently located near the Mercado Municipal, this hotel offers plain, clean rooms with wi-fi and cable TV. Staff speak some English and there is a good bar and restaurant. ③–④

Hotel Frontera Bulnes 726 & 733 ℡45/200400 ⓦwww.hotelfrontera.cl. Facing each other across the street are two hotels, the *Clásico* and the *Nuevo*, that share many facilities. The *Nuevo* has the edge, as it's slightly more modern and has a decent restaurant and piano bar. The best rooms have free internet access, but are somewhat overpriced for what they are. ⑤

Hotel Turismo Lynch 563 ℡45/951090 ⓦwww .hotelturismotemuco.cl. This central, three-storey, thirty-room business hotel has gracious English-speaking staff and boasts large and comfortable rooms with modern amenities, with internet on the second floor. The café is a good place for a light meal. ④

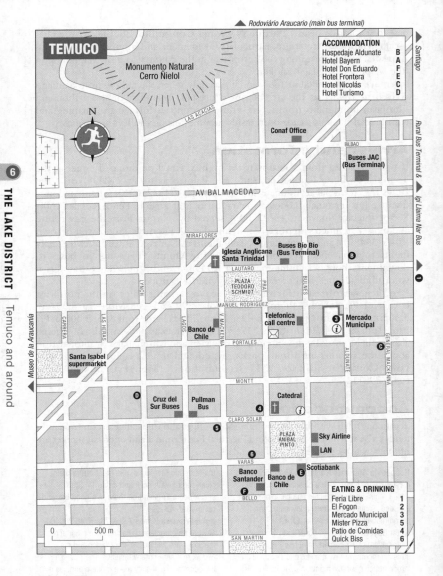

The Town

The diagonal **Avenida Caupolicán** separates the city's quiet and exclusive residential districts to the west and the unattractive maze of shops and offices to the east. Temuco's centre is the relaxing **Plaza Aníbal Pinto**, luxuriant with fine native and imported trees, set off by a large monument depicting the struggle between the Spanish and the Mapuche Indians.

A few blocks northeast of the Plaza, the sprawling **Mercado Municipal** (Mon–Sat 8am–8pm & Sun 8.30am–4pm), built in 1929, is one of the best covered markets in the country, with noisy and pungent butchers' and fishmongers' stalls around the edge, and the inexpensive eateries in the centre surrounded by countless craft stalls selling silver Mapuche jewellery, baskets, musical instruments, woven ponchos and more; the quality tends to vary.

A few blocks northwest of the market lies the **Monumento Natural Cerro Ñielol** (daily 8.30am–8.30pm; CH$700), a densely forested hill with some enjoyable walking trails. On clear days, check out the impressive view from the hilltop **lookout point**. Some say that it was on this hill in February 1881 that a treaty was signed between the Mapuche and the Chilean Army for the peaceful foundation of the future city, an event commemorated by a plaque on a patagua tree. (Most historians, however, maintain that the treaty was signed outside of town.) Take bus #1 from the centre to get here.

Feria Libre and Parque Museo Ferroviario

Out to the east, spread across the two blocks of Avenida Pinto between Barros Arana and Avenida Balmaceda, is Chile's liveliest and most colourful fruit and vegetable market, the **Feria Libre** (daily: summer 8.30am–5pm; winter 8.30am–4pm), its every inch crammed with fresh produce from all over Chile. This is a good place to savour typical local dishes in one of the numerous eateries, and one of the few places you'll see *piñones* (araucaria tree nuts traditionally boiled and eaten by the Mapuche) for sale.

Train buffs should walk the six blocks north to **Parque Museo Ferroviario Pablo Neruda**, on Barros Arana 565, a revamped national railway museum (Tues–Sun 9am–6pm; CH$1000). Among the old rolling stock and machinery are a dozen steam engines built in the US and Europe between 1915 and 1953. These were last fired up in 1972 when Chile's road hauliers went on strike during Allende's presidency. A lavish presidential coach, built in Germany in 1923, is also on display.

Museo Regional de la Araucanía

The **Museo Regional de la Araucanía**, Av Alemania 84 (Mon–Fri 9am–5pm, Sat 11am–5pm, Sun 11am–2pm; CH$500, Sun free), sits ten blocks west of the centre; take bus #1 or *colectivo* #11 from Manuel Montt.

A fine 1920s house with a garden full of stately palms and totem poles, it used to house an impressive collection of silver **Mapuche jewellery**, which has now been returned to various Mapuche families as an act of reparation by the Chilean government. The single room downstairs now has a Spanish-language exhibit on European settlement in the area. Outside there is an intriguing display of black-and-white photographs of present-day Mapuche involved in various daily activities, such as collecting seaweed.

Eating and drinking

You'll find the cheapest set meals at the Mercado Municipal, while Feria Libre is best for filling empanadas and other snacks.

El Fogón Aldunate 288. Though its popularity has somewhat declined, the food at this restaurant is still excellent. Offal, meat and shellfish *parrilladas* are a speciality and cost CH$15,000 for two. If you're brave, try the knockout *chuponao*, a punch made with *aguardiente* (grain alcohol).
Mister Pizza Claro Solar at Vicuña Mackenna. Cheap pizzas and friendly service in a popular place filled with students drinking Kunstmann beer.

Try the pizza with *merkén*, the traditional Mapuche hot spice mix. Mains CH$3500.
Ñam Ñam Portales 855. A lively and inexpensive sandwich bar that also serves basic and very cheap pizzas and main meals.
Patio de Comidas Falabella, fourth floor, in front of Plaza Aníbal Pinto. Take a break from the road at this handy spot with several fast-food eateries serving hot dogs, fried chicken, burgers and empanadas.

QuickBiss Antonio Varas 755. This atypical fast-food restaurant has been revamped but still keeps the unique combination of loud zebra stripes and soft natural woods. It's a great place for vegetarians, with a large self-service counter and a salad bar.

Listings

Airlines LAN, Bulnes 687 ☎600/526 2000; Sky Airlines, Bulnes 655, Oficina 4 ☎45/747300.
Banks and exchange There are numerous banks with ATMs around Plaza Aníbal Pinto. For a decent exchange rate, try Cambio Global, Bulnes 655, Local 1.
Buses Bío Bío, Lautaro 853 ☎45/210599; Flota Erbuc, Miraflores 1149 ☎45/233958; Igi Llaima and Nar Bus, Miraflores 1535 ☎45/407777; Tur Bus, Claro Solar 598 ☎45/230979; Cruz del Sur, Claro Solar 599 ☎45/730320; Pullman, Claro Solar at Lagos ☎45/212137.

Car rental Automóvil Club de Chile, San Martín 0278 ☎45/248903; Avis, San Martín 755 ☎45/237575; Hertz, Bello 792 ☎45/318585.
Hospital Hospital Regional, M.Montt 115 ☎45/212525.
Internet Several internet cafés in the centre along Prat and Mackenna.
Post office Portales 839.
Telephone centres Telefónica del Sur, Bulnes 537.

Parque Nacional Conguillío

The grey peak of Volcán Llaima (3125m) looms over the horizon about 80km east of Temuco. Wrapped around its neck is **PARQUE NACIONAL CONGUILLÍO** (daily 8am–9pm; CH$4000), a park the volcano has been doing its best to destroy with belch after belch of black lava. The latest noticeable eruption was in January 2008, after which the park was partially closed. The northern sector is lush, high forest, with steep cliffs covered in spindly-armed araucaria trees often draped in furry lime-green moss. In the south, however, the volcano has wreaked havoc. The road from Temuco passes over a wide lava flow, consisting of either rolling plains of thin dust or walls of recently congealed spiked rock.

Volcán Llaima is one of the three most active volcanoes on the continent; its last serious eruption was in 1957, though as recently as 1994 a lake, Laguna Arco Iris, was formed by a fresh lava flow that blocked a river. You pass this lake on the road to the park administration office from the south.

The northern route into the park is through the village of **Curacautín** (97km from Temuco), entering the park at sector Laguna Captrén, while the southern road from **Melipeuco** enters at sector Truful-Truful, and from the west, a little-used dirt road runs from the village of Cherquenco past the Llaima ski resort. Conaf's excellent **Centro de Información Ambiental** (daily 9am–1pm & 3–7pm) sits at the heart of the park, to the northeast of

---

Moving on from Temuco

Temuco is served by dozens of buses going up and down the Panamericana, and most of the long-distance buses now leave from the new terminal (taxis to town available for CH$1,500). The Buses JAC terminal is more conveniently located for those wanting to travel to Pucón, Villarrica and around the Siete Lagos area. There's also a regular service up into the mountains at Curacautín, Melipeuco and Parque Nacional Conguillío; local buses use the rural bus terminal on Pinto and Balmaceda. For Argentinian destinations, such as Junín de los Andes, try Igi Llaima and Nar Bus, though for Bariloche you'll have to change buses at Osorno. Temuco's airport has eight daily flights to Santiago as well as service to most other major cities in Chile.

Volcán Llaima, near the wide Lago Conguillío, and sells good trail maps and a number of short excursions.

Exploring the park

The park splits neatly into two main sectors, formed by the volcano's western and eastern slopes. Each has its own seasonal appeal. The **western slopes**, otherwise known as Sector Los Paraguas, shine in winter, boasting a small ski centre, the Centro de Esquí Las Araucarias (T45/562313), with breathtaking views, two drag lifts, three runs and a refuge near the tree line. There's no hiking on the western slopes so in summer the focus shifts to the **eastern slopes**, which form the bulk of the park and are further subdivided around the two main entry points.

Those with sufficient experience, an ice axe and crampons can make the difficult seven-hour **ascent of Volcán Llaima**, but you need permission from Conaf (who will want evidence of your climbing ability). You also must be prepared to deal with crevasses and fumaroles – beware of sulphur fumes at the summit. Aside from that, the park offers a good selection of hikes for all abilities. For incredible views of the Sierra Nevada range through araucaria forest, take the 7km (2.5hr) trail from Playa Linda, at the east end of Lago Conguillío, to the base of the Sierra Nevada. The challenging **Travesía Río Blanco** (5km; 5hr), which crosses a small glacier before continuing into the Sierra Nevada proper, is recommended for very experienced trekkers only. From the western shores of Laguna Verde, the 11km (5hr) **Sendero Pastos Blancos** runs to the Laguna Captrén, traversing spectacular scenery, rewarding you with panoramic views of Sierra Nevada, Lago Conguillío and the Truful-Truful valley. From the Truful-Truful Conaf ranger station, you can take the **Sendero Subtramo Arpehue**, part of the Sendero de Chile, to Laguna Captrén, passing the Andrés Huenupi Mapuche community along the way. The Truful-Truful ranger station is also the starting point for two **short nature trails**: the Cañadón Truful-Truful (900m; 30min) passes by colourful strata, exposed by the Río Truful-Truful's flow, while the Las Vertientes trail (800m; 45min) is characterised by the subterranean springs that rush out of the ground. The Laguna Captrén ranger station is the starting point for the **Sendero Los Carpinteros**, also part of the Sendero de Chile, a fairly easy eight-kilometre, five-hour round-trip that starts from Lago Captrén, which loops around the lagoon before continuing to the administration centre and joining the El Contrabandista trail, which was formerly used by the Pehuenche hunters and cattle rustlers going to and from Argentina. The highlight is an araucaria that's estimated to be fifteen hundred years old.

Less strenuous activities are available in summer; these include guided hikes along the trails, excursions to other parts of the park and talks on native birds and mammals. You can also peruse the excellent displays – the best in Chile – on the geology, flora and fauna of the park at the visitors' centre. The exhibition on volcanism is particularly fascinating; look out for the bullet-shaped pyroclastic rock.

Park practicalities

Getting to the park without your own transport is difficult, though buses will take you as far as the gateway towns. The southern gateway to the eastern section is the tiny village of **Melipeuco**, 91km east of Temuco and 30km south of the park administration. There are hourly buses from Temuco to Melipeuco, but from Melipeuco, you'll have to take a taxi to the park. Nar Bus (T45/257074) runs eight **buses** a day from Temuco (four on Sun).

The northern route into the park is through the village of **Curacautín**, 75km from Temuco and 30km from the administration. There are frequent Buses Flota Erbuc (☎45/233958) services daily from Temuco and from Curacautín, there are twice-daily departures to the park's Laguna Captrén; otherwise you can get a taxi (CH$30,000) to the park. In winter, buses go the 106km from Temuco to the western ski slopes, but off-season, rural buses stop 20km short at the village of **Cherquenco**.

The best trekking and housing outpost is the well-marked Swiss-run hostel *La Suizandina*, at Km 83 from Temuco (☎45/197 3725, ⓦwww.suizandina .com; ❺). Open year-round, it has cabins, a gourmet restaurant and a small hostel with plush dorms and rooms, from which park treks are organized, including a not-difficult ascent of the stunning volcano Volcán Lonquimay, 30km east, northeast of Curacautín.

There are plenty of **places to stay** in the park, all pretty pricey. At Laguna Verde, on the edge of a dense wood, is a complex of expensive five-person *cabañas* called *La Baita Conguillío* (☎45/416410, ⓔlabaita@entelchile.net; ❻). It's also an **activity centre**, co-ordinating trekking and eco-tourism in the summer, and skiing and snow-walking in the winter, with other programmes run year-round. There are similarly priced *cabañas* (❻–❼) near the park administration office by the Los Ñires campsite. The lower-priced *cabañas* are circular huts strapped to trees and quite a novelty, though the bedding provided is useless, so consider bringing a sleeping bag for additional comfort. The *Centro de Ski las Araucarias*, (☎45/562313, ⓦwww.skiaraucarias.cl; ❺), has two comparably priced *refugios: Las Paraguas* and *Pehuén*, the former offering dorms (❷ – bring own bedding), while the latter also has several doubles, some en-suite, some with shared bath. ❹–❺

Camping in the park is expensive. There are about one hundred sites, mainly along the south shore of Lago Conguillío and Lago Captrén, all run by concessionaires charging CH$15,000 per site of up to six people. They're only open from November through April. Wild camping is not allowed.

Lago Villarrica and around

LAGO VILLARRICA, tucked in the mountains some 86km to the southeast of Temuco, is Chile's most visited lake. The reason for its popularity is **Pucón**, a prime outdoor adventure centre. At the other end of the lake from Pucón is **Villarrica**, a functional town with cheap rooms for rent.

The area around Lago Villarrica was first settled by the Spanish in the late sixteenth century, but they didn't have much time to enjoy their new territory, as their towns were sacked by the Mapuche in 1602. Recolonization didn't take place until the Mapuche were destroyed 250 years later. With the arrival of the railroad from Santiago in 1933, the area became one of Chile's prime holiday destinations.

Villarrica

Sitting on the southwestern edge of the lake with a beautiful view of the volcano, **VILLARRICA** is one of Chile's oldest towns, although it may not feel like it – it has been destroyed several times by volcanic eruptions and skirmishes with the Mapuche. Most people drive straight through it on their way to Pucón. Now that the town's last mayor has authorised the building of a highway across Villarica's beaches, it seems likely that the town will receive fewer visitors still.

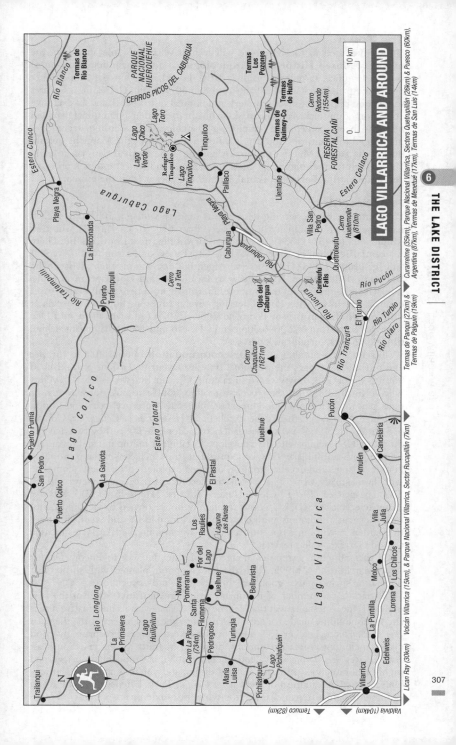

6

LAGO VILLARRICA AND AROUND

0   10 km

Río Blanco

Termas de Río Blanco

PARQUE NACIONAL HUERQUEHUE

CERROS PICOS DEL CABURGUA

Estero Cunco

Termas Los Pozones

Termas de Huife

Lago Toro

Lago Chico

Lago Verde

Refugio Tinquilco

Lago Tinquilco

Tinquilco

Termas de Quimey-Co

Cerro Redondo (1554m)

RESERVA FORESTAL CAÑI

Estero Coilaco

Paillaco

Llentane

Villa San Pedro

Cerro Huelemolle (810m)

Playa Negra

La Rinconada

Lago Caburgua

Peña Negra

Caburgua

Río Caburgua

Quetroleufú

Carileufú Falls

Ojos del Caburgua

Río Pucón

Puerto Trafampulli

Cerro La Teta

Río Trafampulli

Río Liucura

El Turbio

Río Turbio

Río Claro

Cerro Chaquilcura (1621m)

Estero Totoral

Río Trancura

Quelhué

Pucón

Amulén

Candelaria

Lago Colico

San Pedro

Puerto Colico

Puerto Puma

La Gaviota

El Pastal

Los Raulíes

Laguna Las Ranas

Villa Julia

Los Chilcos

Molco

Río Longlong

La Primavera

Lago Huilipilun

Cerro La Plaza (734m)

Nueva Pomerania

Flor del Lago

Quelhué

Bellavista

Lago Villarrica

Lorena

Trailanqui

Santa Filomena

Turingia

Pedregoso

La Puntilla

María Luisa

Pichilafquén

Lago Pichilafquén

Villarrica

Edelweis

N

▶ Lican Ray (30km) ▶ Volcán Villarrica (15km), & Parque Nacional Villarrica, Sector Rucapillán (7km)

▶ Termas de Panqui (27km) & Termas de Palguín (19km)

▶ Curarrelme (35km), Parque Nacional Villarrica, Sectors Quetrupillán (26km) & Puesco (60km), Argentina (87km), Termas de Menetué (17km), Termas de San Luis (14km)

◀ Valdivia (104km)   ◀ Temuco (82km)

The Town

Those interested in the Mapuche will leap at Villarrica's sole attraction, the municipal **Museo Histórico y Arqueológico**, on the main drag, adjacent to the tourist office, at Pedro de Valdivia 1050 (Jan–March Mon–Sat 9am–1pm & 6–10pm; April–Dec Mon–Fri 9am–1pm & 3.30–7.30pm; CH$250). It features some good displays of silver jewellery and musical instruments, and an exclusive collection of unusual Mapuche masks, while in the garden a traditional thatched *ruca* has been constructed employing thatching and wattling techniques unchanged for centuries. You can learn even more about the Mapuche culture during the annual Muestra Cultural Mapuche – the **festival** (late Jan to early Feb), which features traditional crafts, food, music and dance, and pick up crafts year-round at the **Feria Artesanal**, around the corner from the museum.

Practicalities

Long-distance **buses**, serving destinations such as Santiago and Temuco, each have their own terminal: Buses JAC, Bilbao 610 (T45/411447); Tur-Bus, Muñoz 657 (T45/411534); and Pullman, across the street from Tur-Bus. There is a central Terminal de Buses at Valdivia 621; Buses San Martín (T45/411584) and Igi Llaima (T45/412733) serve Argentine destinations such as Bariloche and Junín de los Andes. Rural buses to Licán Ray and Coñaripe, meanwhile, stop across the street from the Buses JAC terminal; from here, small shuttle buses connect the town with Pucón, leaving several times an hour. The excellent **Oficina de Turismo** is at Pedro de Valdivia 1070 (mid-March to mid-Dec Mon–Sat 9am–1pm & 2.30–6.30pm; mid-Dec to mid-March daily 9am–10pm; T45/206619, Eturis@entelchile.net).

Villarrica has a number of good **accommodation** options. At the cheaper end of the scale there's the perpetual traveller favourite, *La Torre Suiza*, Bilbao 969 (T45/411213, Wwww.torresuiza.com; ●), run by two ex-world cyclists who've finally hung up their pedals. It offers double rooms, dorm rooms or tents, plus kitchen access, good breakfast, bike rental, internet access and a book exchange. Mid-range, there's the excellent ✗ *Hostería de la Colina*, Las Colinas 115 (T45/411503, Wwww.hosteriadelacolina.com; ●–●), run by two accommodating US teachers who have developed a fabulous hilltop inn and restaurant featuring a beautiful lake view, large breakfasts (not included in the room rate), book exchange, and excellent tips on outdoor exploration for guests, complete with home-made maps. The wood-panelled rooms have great views and no TVs. The pricier *Hotel El Ciervo*, General Körner 241 (T45/411215, Wwww .hotelelciervo.cl; ●–●), is a converted family house owned by descendants of early German immigrants, with cosy rooms with cable TV and wi-fi, an attractive garden, a swimming pool and a terrace overlooking the lake. Rates include a good German-style breakfast.

Of the numerous campsites along the lake on the way to Pucón, *Du Lac* (Dec–March; T45/214995; ●) is the better option, planted with shrubs that offer some shelter, plus a good café, hot showers, and water sports.

Villarrica has a number of reasonably priced **restaurants**. One of the best options is the ✗ restaurant at the *Hostería de la Colina*, with its imaginative dishes and fantastic home-made ice cream. Gringos tend to congregate at the *Travellers Pub-Restaurant* at Letelier 753, lured by the diverse range of surprisingly good dishes, including vegetarian options, drawn from India, China and Southeast Asia. *El Rey del Marisco*, on Valentín Letelier 1030, has moderately priced and highly recommended fish and seafood dishes, and you're guaranteed a pricey but fantastic Chilean meal of meat at *La Cava de Roble*, Letelier 658, where you can taste imaginative game dishes; the wine list is extensive.

Pucón

On a clear day, you will be greeted by the awe-inspiring sight of **Volcán Villarrica** smouldering in the distance long before the bus pulls into **PUCÓN**, 25 kilometres from Villarrica. This small mountain town has firmly established itself as a top backpacker destination in the last decade. Each November–April season brings scores of hikers, climbers, white-water enthusiasts and mountain bikers looking to climb Volcán Villarrica, brave the Río Trancura rapids or hike in the remote forested corners of the nearby Parque Nacional Huerquehue. A day outdoors is usually followed by eating, drinking and partying in the town's restaurants and bars, or by a soak in the

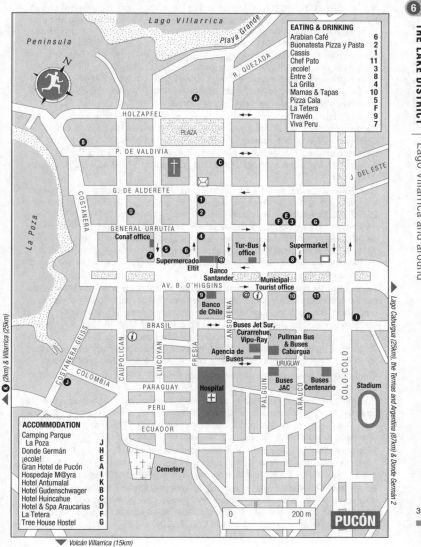

EATING & DRINKING

Arabian Café	6
Buonatesta Pizza y Pasta	2
Cassis	1
Chef Pato	11
¡ecole!	3
Entre 3	8
La Grilla	4
Mamas & Tapas	10
Pizza Cala	5
La Tetera	F
Trawén	9
Viva Peru	7

ACCOMMODATION

Camping Parque La Poza	J
Donde Germán	H
¡ecole!	E
Gran Hotel de Pucón	A
Hospedaje M@yra	I
Hotel Antumalal	K
Hotel Gudenschwager	B
Hotel Huincahue	C
Hotel & Spa Araucarias	D
La Tetera	F
Tree House Hostel	G

PUCÓN

0   200 m

◀ K (2km) & Villarrica (25km)

▶ Lago Caburgua (25km), the Termas and Argentina (87km) & Donde Germán 2

▼ Volcán Villarrica (15km)

There are a multitude of **tour companies** in Pucón, mostly offering the same trips for similar prices. Most companies run **tours of the area**, which take in the Ojos de Caburgua waterfalls and any of the thermal springs at Huife, Palguín, Menetúe and Pozones (CH$10,000–15,000), as well as night-time visits to Termas Los Pozones (CH$12,000) and rather touristy **Mapuche tours**, involving a visit to one of the nearby *reducciones*, where you can watch traditional crafts being made; lunch is often included (CH$15,000). We've picked out a selection of the more established operators, and arranged them according to the tours at which they are best.

Volcán Villarrica This is a full-day excursion, usually leaving at 7am, and prices are around CH$40,000–45,000. Climbing is not possible when the weather is bad, though some operators will still take customers up when it's cloudy, only to turn back halfway. There are several companies Conaf authorizes to climb the volcano: Politur, O'Higgins 335 (☎45/442617, ⓦwww.politur.com); Sol y Nieve, O'Higgins 192 at Lincoyán (☎45/463860, ⓦwww.chile-travel.com/solnieve.htm); Sur Expediciones, O'Higgins 660 (☎45/444030); and Paredón Andes Expeditions (☎45/444663, ⓦwww.paredonexpeditions.com); the latter will take groups no larger than eight people. In winter, companies such as Aguaventura, Palguín 336 (☎45/444246, ⓦwww.aguaventura.com) rent skis and snowboards.

Fishing Both fly-fishing and boat fishing trips can be arranged in the lakes and rivers surrounding the town. Prices for a half-day's fishing on the Río Liucura range from CH$65,000–85,000, but substantial reductions are available for large groups. The better companies include Mario's Fishing Zone, O'Higgins 590 (☎09/760 7280, ⓦwww.flyfishingpucon.com) and Off Limits, O'Higgins 560 (☎45/442681, ⓦwww.offlimits.cl).

Horseriding You can go for a full-day or half-day ride in the mountain wilderness of the Parque Nacional Villarrica. Prices start at about CH$25,000 for a half-day, CH$45,000 for a fullday. *Rancho de Caballos "Palguín Alto"* (☎08/346 1764, ⓦwww.rancho-de-caballos.com), is a German-owned ranch 32km east of Pucón offering a range of treks from three hours to ten days. Centro Ecuestre Huepil Malal (☎09/643 2673, ⓔinfo@huepil-malal.cl), 25km east of Pucón, is run by Rodolfo Coombs, a master rider who offers half-day to five-day horse treks, leaving from the hills east of Pucón, on the way to Lago Caburga.

Rafting The nearby **Río Trancura** offers a popular class II-III run on the lower part of the river, with the more challenging class VI, upper Trancura run made up almost entirely of drop pools. Both of these trips are half-day excursions; some operators allow you to combine the two. Sol y Nieve on Av O'Higgins at Lincoyán (☎45/463860, ⓦwww.chile travel.com/solnieve.htm) is a long-standing reliable operator, as is Aguaventura at Palguín 336 (☎45/444246, ⓦwww.aguaventura.com). Prices for two-three hours rafting range from CH$20,000 for the lower Trancura to CH$25,000 for the upper Trancura.

Skydiving Aguaventura (see above) charges CH$150,000 for a one-hour tandem jump.

Canopy Ziplining tours, involving sliding from treetop platform to platform while attached to a metal cord with a harness, are offered by most companies, but the most reliable operator is Bosque Aventura, Arauca at O'Higgins (☎45/444030, ⓦwww.canopypucon.cl). Outings typically cost CH$12,000–15,000.

Hidrospeeding This exciting sport involves bodyboarding down the Río Liucura rapids (no greater than class III); the half-day excursion, including an hour in the river, costs CH$20,000. Aguaventura (see above) has the guides and the equipment.

Eco-tours The helpful *¡école!*, in association with the Lahuen Foundation, owns and operates a pristine araucaria forest sanctuary called Cañi, home to *pudú*, puma and other wildlife, as well as a wealth of birds, about 30km east of Pucón, where it runs ecologically sensitive tours from around CH$15,000.

many thermal spas surrounding the town. The town gets particularly busy in January and February when Chilean students join forces with international backpackers.

Arrival and information

Pucón doesn't have a main bus terminal. Instead, Buses JAC, Tur-Bus, Pullman and Intersur each have their own purpose-built large terminals. Buses JAC at Palguín 605 (☏45/443963) has regular departures for destinations along the Panamericana, such as Puerto Montt, Puerto Varas, Valdivia, Villarrica and Temuco. Tur-Bus on O'Higgins 910 on the outskirts of town (☏45/443328) has overnight departures to Santiago via Temuco. Buses Caburgua leave for Parque Nacional Huerquehue from the Pullman terminal at Palguín 575. Across the street, Buses Vipu-Ray depart frequently for Villarrica while Jet Sur has a couple of departures daily for Santiago via Temuco. At Palguín and Uruguay, the Agencia de Buses sells advance tickets for Igi Llaima, Tas Choapa and Intersur departures. Buses Centenario from Argentina's Junín de los Andes and San Martín de los Andes stop at Uruguay and Colo Colo, while Igi Llaima and Cóndor stop at Colo Colo and O'Higgins.

The **Cámara de Turismo** has a well-stocked kiosk on the corner of Caupolicán and Brazil (daily 9am–1.30pm & 4–7pm; ☏45/441671, ⓦwww.puconturismo.cl or www.pucononline.cl). The helpful staff at the **Oficina Municipal de Turismo**, O'Higgins 483 (March–Nov daily 8.30am–8pm; Dec–Feb daily 8.30am–10pm; ☏45/293002, ⓦwww.municipalidadpucon.cl), speak some English. For information about national parks, head to Conaf at Lincoyán 336 (Mon–Fri 8.30am–noon & 2–6.30pm; ☏45/443781).

Accommodation

While the competition between budget accommodation keeps prices relatively stable, at the upper end of the spectrum prices double from Christmas to the end of February; book all accommodation in advance in peak season. If you are looking to escape the crowds, head 23km east from Pucón towards Curarrehue, to the welcoming 🏃 *Kila Leufu* (☏09/7118064, ⓦwww.kilaleufu.cl; ❸), a Mapuche farmhouse with a warm family environment where you can enjoy activities such as kayaking, mountain biking and horseriding in the lovely surrounding countryside and eat home-grown food.

Camping Parque La Poza Costanera Roberto Geis 769 ☏45/441435. Large, shaded campsite near the lake with hot showers and cooking facilities, popular with overland expeditions, cycling tourists and backpackers. CH$10,000 per site. ❷

🏃 **Donde Germán** Las Rosas 590 ☏45/442444 ⓦwww.dondegerman.cl. Run by a knowledgeable local rafting guide, this charming wooden chalet has a spacious garden and terrace and offers use of its kitchen, laundry service and free internet to its guests, as well as holding barbecues, renting bikes and arranging tours. The second hostel at Brasil 640 is being completely rebuilt. ❸–❹

¡école! Urrutia 592 ☏45/441675 ⓦwww.ecole.cl. With owners who are deeply involved in conservation projects throughout Patagonia, including the Cañi reserve (see opposite), this excellent *residencial* offers a wealth of fantastic traveller information through its onsite agency (ⓦwww.outdoorexperience.org). The dorms and rooms are comfortable, well-furnished and often booked, so reserve well in advance. ❷–❹

Gran Hotel de Pucón Holzapfel 190 ☏600/7006000, ⓦwww.granhotelpucon.cl. Right on the most popular part of the beach, the *Gran Hotel* is probably the most famous hotel in Chile. It comes with the usual range of amenities that you'd expect from a 4-star hotel, including its own restaurant, tour agency, wi-fi, Jacuzzi, sauna and gym. Focuses largely on multi-day packages. ❾

Hospedaje M@yra at Brasil and Colo Colo ☏45/442745 ⓦwww.myhostelpucon.com. Run by a friendly and helpful proprietress, this popular hostel offers clean dorms and rooms (the latter with cable TV), as well as wi-fi, laundry service and help in arranging all sorts of outdoor activities. ❷–❸

Hotel Antumalal 2km outside Pucón ☎45/441011 ⓦwww.antumalal.com. A quiet refuge, this architectural gem was designed by a student of Frank Lloyd Wright. It is a hotel with class: the service is excellent, as is the restaurant; the views over the lake are picturesque; and both Queen Elizabeth II and Jimmy Stewart have stayed here. Bonuses include a spa with an extensive range of treatments, and numerous tours on offer.❽

Hotel Gudenschwager Valdivia 12 ☎45/442025, ⓦwww.hogu.cl. In 1927, the descendants of one of Villarrica's 1880s settlers opened this hotel as a remote lodge catering for fly-fishermen. It has now been modernized and offers tasteful en-suites with wi-fi, a good restaurant (open in season only) and helpful staff. ❻

Hotel Huincahue Valdivia 375 ☎45/443540, ⓦwww.hotelhuincahue.com. Opulent boutique hotel, its 16 en-suite rooms are flooded with plenty of natural light and come with all expected amenities, such as wi-fi and cable TV. An outdoor

swimming pool is open in the summer and a peaceful atmosphere reigns throughout. ❽–❾

Hotel & Spa Araucarias Caupolicán 243 ☎45/441284, ⓦwww.araucarias.cl. This central hotel has an excellent private museum of Mapuche artefacts and considering that room and *cabaña* rates include pool and sauna access as well as wi-fi and cable TV, it's an absolute bargain. ❺–❻

La Tetera Urrutia 580 ☎45/441462, ⓦwww.tetera.cl. Small guesthouse with cosy rooms, some en-suite. A good book exchange, bright common area and helpful owners who can arrange excursions into the area are all pluses, not to mention an excellent café. ❹

Tree House Hostel Urrutia 660 ☎45/444679 ⓦwww.treehousechile.cl. Run by young, congenial and extremely knowledgeable bilingual hosts who can help organize all manner of outdoor activities, including visits to the nearby Mapuche communities and the volcano climb. The hostel has clean, cosy rooms with good beds, guest kitchen, wi-fi and two friendly resident dogs. Relax in the garden hammocks, join in on an impromptu barbecue or try one of their herbal teas. ❸

The Town

Pucón's wide, tree-lined streets are arranged in a compact grid, with most tour companies, supermarkets, banks and bars located along bustling Avenida O'Higgins, which bisects the town, and restaurants and guesthouses scattered nearby. O'Higgins ends by La Poza, a black-sand beach on the dazzling blue Lago Villarrica, while at the northern end of Calle Lincoyán, you will find Playa Grande, with a multitude of *pedalos*, jet skis and rowing boats for rent.

Eating and Drinking

Pucón's popularity with international travellers is reflected in its cuisine, which is more diverse than in most Chilean towns.

Arabian Café Fresia 354. While it's not the most authentic Middle Eastern food, this restaurant serves up sizeable portions of kofta kebab, stuffed aubergines and chillies, among other dishes. Mains CH$4500.

Buonatesta Pizza y Pasta Fresia 243. Excellent home-made pasta with range of delicious sauces and pizza make this a good lunch or dinner spot. Try the smoked salmon ravioli (CH$4700).

Cassis Fresia at Urrutia. Popular wi-fi-equipped café where travellers linger for hours over coffee, cake and fresh fruit juice.

Chef Pato Av O'Higgins 619A. Reasonably priced and well-cooked Chilean food, as well as decent pasta and pizza. Mains CH$4000.

¡ecole! Urrutia 592. Tasty, inexpensive and imaginative vegetarian dishes served in peace and quiet in a vine-covered courtyard or an attractive

dining room. The vegetable lasagne is superb, as is the curried salmon with quinoa and the homemade bread. Mains CH$4500.

Entre 3 Arauco at O'Higgins. Lively bar popular with local mountain guides has a rooftop patio and the cheapest drinks in Pucón. Beer CH$1200.

La Grilla Fresia 243. Sate all your carnivorous cravings here. While not the cheapest, *La Grilla* is definitely a cut above the rest when it comes to grilled meat; the chef's specials are excellent. Steak CH$6000.

Mamas and Tapas O'Higgins 597. In a large, dimly lit, wooden-and-glass building, a young drinking crowd knocks back seriously strong pisco sours late into the night. Established traveller favourite.

Pizza Cala Lincoyan 361. Immensely popular informal restaurant serving the town's best thincrust pizza. (CH$3500–4500).

La Tetera Urrutia 580. This spot is justifiably famous for the best breakfasts in Pucón and a refreshing selection of teas, including the otherwise unobtainable lapsang souchong, properly made in a pot. They also serve excellent home-made cakes.

 Trawén Fresia at O'Higgins. *The* place for the town's most imaginative cuisine, this

restaurant dishes up such treats as Antarctic krill empanadas, excellent home-made pasta, large, tasty sandwiches and combinations of fresh fruit juices.

Viva Perú Lincoyán 372. New restaurant offering decent Peruvian dishes, such as ceviche and *ají de gallina*, though they could be spicier.

Listings

Airlines LAN, Urrutia 102 (☎45/443516) and Sky Airline, Alderete 590 (☎45/283612) are open from Dec to March only.

Banks and money There are ATMs in banks along O'Higgins and inside the Eltit supermarket. The *casa de cambio* on O'Higgins 261, Local C, offers a good exchange rate.

Bicycle rental Several outlets along O'Higgins.

Books and maps Travelaid, Ansorena 425, Local 4; Expolibros, Ansorena at O'Higgins.

Buses Buses Power, Palguín 550 ☎45/441055; Cóndor Bus, Colo Colo 430 ☎45/443023;

Igi Llaima, Colo Colo 465 ☎45/442061; Intersur, O'Higgins 910 ☎45/443963; JAC, Palguín 605 ☎45/443963; Tur Bus, O'Higgins 910 ☎45/443963.

Car rental Hertz, Fresia 220 ☎45/441664; Pucón Rent A Car, Colo Colo 340 ☎45/443052.

Hospital San Francisco, Uruguay 325 ☎45/441177.

Internet *Trancura*, Palguín at O'Higgins; *Cyber Unid@d*, Ansorena at O'Higgins.

Post office Fresia 183.

Telephone centre Entel, at Ansorena 299.

Lago Caburgua and around

If you want to escape the noise of town for a while, make for the tranquil **LAGO CABURGUA**. Take the international road towards Argentina for 8km, then turn at the signed left, heading northeast. After 17km, hang a left and 500 metres later you will come to the **Ojos de Caburgua** (Eyes of Caburgua), three waterfalls in the forest plunging into a deep pool of crystal-clear water; in hot weather, the air around the Ojos is cool and refreshing. Thousands of years ago, an eruption blocked this southern end of the valley, drowning it, and the water from the lake now flows out through subterranean streams and porous rock until it reappears here. You can drive (parking CH$1500), or request that the bus to Caburga stop (walking in is free). The best time to visit is in the morning, before the crowds gather.

Six kilometres further, the road arrives at the southern end of Lago Caburgua, with allegedly the warmest water of all the Lake District lakes, looking onto a long lake bordered by scrub- and forest-covered craggy peaks. The southern shore of the lake is densely developed with *cabañas* and campsites, but they're mostly hidden behind the trees. Just to the southwest unfolds the pretty white sand **Playa Blanca**, and you can rent paddle boats at Playa Negra, ten minutes southeast of Playa Blanca. If you want to **stay**, a well-appointed, friendly guesthouse, *Landhaus San Sebastian* (☎45/197 2360, ⊛www.landhaus.cl; ❺), sits adjacent to the Ojos de Caburgua. For **camping**, try the shaded *Playa Blanca* (CH$12,000 per site), a large park with plenty of isolated places to pitch a tent and private access to a small, secluded white-sand cove.

Many minibuses and *colectivos* come to the lake area from Pucón, leaving from both the rural bus terminal and the JAC terminal, though the service drops off somewhat in winter.

Parque Nacional Huerquehue

Rising up almost 2000m from the eastern shore of Lago Caburgua are the forest-clad hills and peaks that form the 125-square-kilometre **PARQUE**

NACIONAL HUERQUEHUE (only officially open Jan–March 8.30am–9pm but accessible at other times of year; CH$4000). Crowned by araucaria forests, the horseshoe-shaped **Cerros Picos de Caburgua** (Caburgua Mountains) enclose a dozen breathtakingly beautiful lakes of which the largest four – Tinquilco, Chico, Toro and Verde – are the most visited. At lower altitudes there are mixed forests of *coigüe* (southern beech) and the conifer *mañío*. Where areas of forest have been affected by fire you'll find impenetrable undergrowth of *colihue* and *quila*, types of native Chilean bamboo. The park is home to over eighty **bird** species, including the Magellanic woodpecker, the delightful white-crested *fío-fío* and the red-chested *chucao*, as well as the little Darwin's frog.

The park entrance, 35km from Pucón, is named **El Nido del Aguila** (Eagle's Nest) after a nearby waterfall. From the entrance, the short and pleasant Sendero Ñirrico leads down to Lago Tinquilco through dense bamboo groves before rejoining the main trail. From Lago Tinquilco, there is a worthwhile two-hour hike up **Cerro Quinchol**, rewarding you with excellent views of Lago Caburgua beyond. A steep and more challenging hike continues up Cerro San Sebastián; allow five hours for the climb. The most popular hike is the Sendero Los Lagos, which climbs through dense forest to the beautiful Chico, Toro and Verde lakes from the *Refugio Tinquilco*; allow two to three hours, as the trail is steep in sections and can be muddy. About halfway up there's a pictureque detour to the thundering **Salto Nido del Aguila**, and several scenic viewpoints along the way. Past Lago Chico, the trail splits, the left fork leading to Lago Verde and the right to Lago Toro; the two join up. If you wander off the main trail along the shores of Lago Verde or Lago Toro, you can often have the spot completely to yourself. There's the two-day **Sendero Los Huerquehues** that continues north from this trail (check conditions with Conaf beforehand, as it may be covered in snow even in December); you can camp by Conaf's *Refugio Renahue* (CH$6000 per site). The trail then continues 8km (about 3hr) further, to the remote Centro Termal San Sebastián, a hot spring outside the park's northeastern boundaries. You'll find the *JLM Pucón Trekking Map* useful – it's readily available in Santiago and Pucón.

▲ Landscape around Pucón

Termas around Pucón

Ample amounts of volcanic activity mean that there are more commercialized **hot springs** around Pucón than in any other town in Chile. The facilities on offer vary, but the alleged health-giving properties of the waters are just about the same: bathing in them can benefit arthritis, nervous ailments and mental fatigue. Getting to some of the *termas* without your own car is difficult, though various companies in Pucón run tours to several of the hot springs below. Buses JAC have two buses daily to Huife for CH$2500. Alternatively, you can charter a cab for the day (about CH$40,000) or hire a **colectivo** (from CH$4000 per person each way; minimum of 4 people) and ask the driver to wait for you.

The *termas* are mainly divided into two river valleys, the Río Liucura and the Río Trancura. Here are five of the best, arranged in order of proximity to Pucón.

Termas de Huife From Pucón, drive towards Lago Caburgua and turn right at Km 15, then continue for another 14km beside Río Liucura ⊤45/441222, ⓦwww .termashuife.cl; CH$10,500 a day and an extra CH$4500 to use the indoor hydrotherapeutic pool; open 9am–9pm. A well-designed complex with varied temperature pools, spa with various treatments, a tranquil atmosphere and a first-class swimming pool. It gets busy and entry is restricted, so you'll need to book in high season. Bus transfers from Pucón cost CH$15,000. In addition to the hot springs there is a canopy tour (CH$10,000), where you explore the forest while in harnesses hung from cables suspended high above the ground. There's a good restaurant, and luxurious double-bed *cabañas* (⊤45/449570; CH$132,000 for two) should you wish to stay.

Termas Los Pozones 2km beyond Huife; ⊤45/197 2350; CH$4500 before 6pm, CH$5500 after; open 11am–6am. Simple, shallow pools dug out beside the river and dammed up with stones, with basic wooden changing huts above them. These *termas* are extremely popular with backpackers, and most tours from Pucón come here at night. There is a 3-hour limit on visits.

Termas de Menetúe 5km west of San Luis bridge in the Río Trancura Valley ⊤45/441877, ⓦwww.menetue.com; CH$9500 a day, open 9am–9pm, double cabins CH$87,000; full-board CH$60,000 per person. Set in beautiful gardens near the river, with naturally heated rock pools, spa, sauna and Jacuzzi, a small restaurant and *cabañas*. The swimming pools are open December through April, while the *termas* operate year-round. To get here, head out of Pucón towards Argentina on the international road for 27km then turn left across the Puente (bridge) San Luis and continue west for 5km.

Termas de Panqui 15km further east of Termas de San Luis ⊤45/442040, ⓦwww .termas.cl/panqui/html; CH$7000. A North American reinterpretation of the Andean forest, Panqui concentrates on the more mystical side of the hot springs, and calls itself a "Healing Retreat Centre". There are two thermal pools, a swimming pool, a mud bath, a medicine wheel, and also massages, Reiki and aquatic Shiatsu. You can camp here (CH$6000 per person), or stay in tepees (CH$10,000 per person) or the small hotel (CH$15,000 per person). The vegetarian restaurant serves hearty, healthy meals and there's a chance to join in the full moon celebrations.

Termas de Palguín ⊤45/441968, ⓦwww.termas.cl/palguin/html; CH$4500; 9am–8pm. The most remote *termas* from Pucón are deep in the Quetrupillán sector of the Parque Nacional Villarrica. The waters in the eleven thermal pools here are mineral-rich and are apparently good for respiratory ailments, kidney, heart and digestion problems, rheumatism, gastrointestinal disorders, joint pain, skin disorders, gout, sciatica, asthma and arthritis (just to name a few). There is also a swimming pool and a comfortable hotel here (⊤45/441968; ⓻) that is equipped with all the amenities. To get here by car, drive eighteen kilometres along the Camino International towards Argentina, then turn right after a bridge near the village of Llafenco Alto, and drive thirteen kilometres south down the dirt road.

Park practicalities

Campsites fringe the park entrance. Conaf has its own site near the entrance ((☎45/441480; CH$10,000 per site) with hot showers, picnic tables and cooking facilities, all near a small beach. Alternatively, try *El Rincón* (☎09/646 3025; CH$7000 per site), with ten sites, cold showers, fire pits, and access to a small pier on the lake. The best accommodation is the *Refugio Tinquilco*, on the north-eastern shores of Lake Tinquilco (☎09/539 2728, ⓦ www.tinquilco.cl; ❸). This airy, welcoming hostel offers both en-suite doubles and bunks; pluses include a sauna, use of a kitchen, a comfy lounge area, and large portions of home-cooked food; you can eat meals here even if you're not lodging here.

Buses JAC runs five daily services to the park during peak season between 8.30am and 7pm, while Buses Caburgua runs three buses between 8.20am and 5.05pm from Pucón to the Conaf *guardería* at the entrance (CH$3200 return). If you're driving, take the road to Lago Caburgua and turn right at Km 14, from where it's 16km to the park entrance.

Parque Nacional Villarrica

The centrepiece of the **PARQUE NACIONAL VILLARRICA** (daily: May–Sept 8am–6pm; Oct–April 8am–9pm; CH$4000) is, of course, the **Volcán Villarrica**, just 15km south of Pucón, in all its smoking, snow-capped glory.

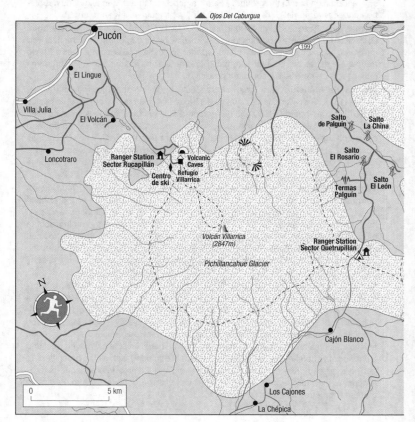

But the park is much more than its most celebrated feature: it stretches 40km to the Argentine border (74km by road), contains two other volcanoes, and is one of the few national parks in the Lake District in which you can camp wild and hike for long distances.

The park divides into three sections: **Rucapillán**, **Quetrupillán**, and **Puesco**. This region was inhabited long before the arrival of the Spanish, and the names of its peaks reflect this: Volcán Villarrica's original Mapuche name, Rucapillán, means "house of the devil", because of its frequent eruptions, while Quetrupillán, the dormant volcano next-door, means "mute devil". Another peak towards the border with Argentina is called Quinquili, or "devil's fang".

Sector Rucapillán

SECTOR RUCAPILLÁN, home to the magnificent **Volcán Villarrica** (2840m), presents a visual contradiction: below the tree line it's a lush forest; above, it's a black waste of lava, dotted with snow and encrusted with an ice-cap. The volcano forms the obvious focal point, standing sentinel over the park, and it's very active – there were sixteen recorded eruptions in the twentieth century, the most recent in 1984. Despite this, it's quite safe to visit, as considerable warning is given before serious activity.

A good road branches off the Pucón–Villarrica road, running up the northern slopes of the volcano. After 7km you reach the **park entrance**, and almost

PARQUE NACIONAL VILLARRICA

Catripulli

Curarruehue

Puelo Bajo

Co Lepe (1477m)

Saltos de Carén   Garén

Las Peinetas

Río Trancura

Sierra Millaillén

ARGENTINA

Cerro Quinquilii (2022m)

PARQUE NACIONAL VILLARRICA

Ranger Station Sector Puesco

Lago Quilleihue

Laguna Blanca

Volcán Quetrupillán (2360m)

Paso Mamuil Malal (1270m)

Laguna Azul

Laguna Abutardes

Volcán Lanín (3776m)

halfway up, 12km from Pucón, is the **ski centre**, run by the *Gran Hotel de Pucón* (late June–mid-Oct; full-day lift ticket CH$18,000 in peak season; check out ⓦ www.skipucon.cl for more details). You can hire cheaper equipment from the agencies in Pucón.

Just under a kilometre after the entrance, a signpost points you to the **Volcanic Caves** (daily: Jan–Feb 9am–9pm; March–Dec 10am–6pm; CH$7000, one-hour Spanish-language tour). A large lava tube, the main cave looks rather like a dragon's lair: the rock walls and ceiling could almost be made of scales. It's dank and wet, but there's a dry path for almost 350m, and electric bulbs so you can see the multicoloured minerals on the walls. The tube hasn't been fully explored and apparently continues for kilometres. Check out the museum exhibits on volcanology and seismology before embarking on the tour.

The main activity in this section of the park is **climbing the volcano**. The path leaves from the ski centre, and it's four hours up to a crater in which, if you're lucky and the gas clears, you'll see bubbling pits of molten rock. If it's not too windy, the chairlift will be running and it's possible to trim an hour off the climb (CH$5000). The route to the top passes over snow, and whilst it doesn't demand technical climbing skills, you do need ropes, ice-axes, sturdy boots and crampons. Gas masks are optional and all equipment is provided by the tour agency you go with.

Conaf keeps a list of companies authorized to guide climbers up the volcano. A maximum of nine climbers are allowed with one guide (fewer in winter), but Conaf will let up to four people a day climb without a guide if they've got professional mountaineering experience and equipment. It all gets very crowded up there in high season, but the view from the top on a clear day is stupendous (though you won't linger for long due to the noxious fumes), followed by a rollicking tobogganing down the side of a volcano along snow slides, using your ice-axe as a brake.

Sector Quetrupillán

SECTOR QUETRUPILLÁN, the middle section of the park, is dominated by the rarely visited majesty of Volcán Quetrupillán (2009m). It's a remote area of wilderness, tucked between two volcanoes and accessible only on foot, by horse or down a 35km dirt road that turns south from the Camino International 18km out of Pucón, climbing through native coigüe and araucaria forest. Here you can find the contemporary hotel at **Termas de Palguín**, with its all-curing waters (see box, p.269), and also four splendid **waterfalls** – Palguín, La China, El León and Turbina, a little way off the main track. La China, at 73m, is the highest, but El León is more spectacular; all are surrounded by native trees and lush vegetation, though this is actually private land and the owners sometimes charge for access. From the *termas*, a terrible track continues for 10km to the Conaf ranger post and the basic Chinay campsite, from where the 23km (12hr) **Sendero Challupen Chinay** skirts around the southern side of Volcán Villarrica, to end at the ski centre. From the ranger station, the **Sendero Los Venados** (15km; 5hr) heads southeast along the south side of Volcán Quetrupillán, passing the tranquil Laguna Azul – a haven for birds, with ancient araucaria trees sweeping almost to its shore – before merging with the Sendero Las Avutardas (17km; 7hr), which finishes in the Puesco sector. From the Quetrupillán Conaf ranger post, the dirt road continues on to Coñaripe; you will need a sturdy 4WD vehicle, even in the summer.

Sector Puesco

East of Quetrupillán, close by the border with Argentina, the third part of the park, **SECTOR PUESCO** is very beautiful, and rather like the Canadian Rockies, with pine forests and craggy mountain sides. The Conaf station is at

Puesco frontier post, where there's nothing else except a customs post and a *hostería*. Around 10km south of Puesco, the **Sendero Momolluco** (13km; approx 12hr) leads southeast from the main road towards Volcán Lanín, before finishing at the remote Laguna Verde. From here, the **Sendero Lagos Andinos** (12km; 5hr) loops back to the main road via Lagunas Huinfiuca, Plato and Escondida, ending at the Laguna Quilleihue, just across the main road.

Right on the border with Argentina (the border runs right through the summit) is **Volcán Lanín**, the least-visited volcano in the park and with no trails. If you intend to trek or climb it, you'll need to get permission from Conaf and DIFROL and you must be *very* careful not to cross into Argentina.

Park practicalities

Hostería Trancura at Puesco has decent *cabañas* (❹) and a campsite (CH$4000). There are also **campsites** near the entrance to Rucapillán (CH$6000), but the only campsite actually in the park is near the Quetrupillán Conaf station (CH$9500).

There's no **public transport** to Sector Rucapillán, though there are dozens of tour buses, and a taxi from Pucón will cost around CH$12,000. In the winter, most tour agencies will take you to the park for CH$6000 per person, leaving Pucón at 9.30am and returning at 4.30pm. To get to Quetrupillán and Puesco, either take one of the local buses that ply the international road, or get on an international bus heading to Junín de los Andes in Argentina and ask to be dropped off. Although you should be able to get off at the Puesco customs post and Conaf station, the nearest you'll get to Quetrupillán will be the hamlet of **Palguín Bajo**, 9km away down a dirt track. If you've got permission, take the same bus to get to Volcán Lanín.

If you plan on doing lengthy hikes, be sure to take plenty of water, as the seasonal streams can't be relied on, as well as the useful *JLM Pucón Trekking Map*, widely available in Pucón. Wild camping is allowed, apart from in the zone east of the border post.

The Siete Lagos

Overshadowed by the popular resort of Pucón, the region known as **SIETE LAGOS** – Seven Lakes – is the next one south of Villarrica. Six of the lakes are in Chile, one (Lago Lácar) in Argentina, and all are linked by rivers in one hydrological system. They offer a mixture of attractive small villages with good tourist facilities, and countless tracks that plunge deep into remote parts of the cordillera.

The Siete Lagos' relative tranquillity owes itself to the area having been largely ignored by the Spanish. Pedro de Valdivia was the first European to visit it in 1551, but apart from a short-lived silver mining enterprise, the Spanish kept away. The Siete Lagos' first settlement, Lican Ray, was a small trading post founded in the late nineteenth century to serve the Pehuenche and Mapuche Indians driven from the pampas by Argentine clearances.

Today the busiest lakes are the largest ones, the relatively warm **Lago Calafquén**, 30km south of Villarrica along a tarred road, and **Lago Panguipulli**, 17km on. The next valley down contains the slightly smaller **Lago Riñihue**, hardly visited and perfect for nature lovers and fishermen. To the east of Calafquén, beside a little-used road into Argentina, lies **Lago Pellaifa**, near a concentration of good *termas*. To the east of Lagos Panguipulli and Riñihue, nestling deep in the

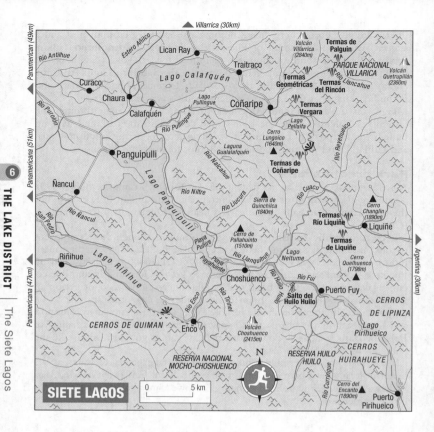

Villarrica (30km)

Panamerican (49km)

Río Antilhue

Estero Añilco

Lican Ray

Traitraco

Volcán
Villarrica
(2840m)

Termas de
Palguin

Curaco

Lago Calafquén

Termas
Geométricas

PARQUE NACIONAL
VILLARICA

Río Llancahue

Volcán
Quetrupillán
(2360m)

Chaura

Lago
Pullingue

Coñaripe

Termas
del Rincón

Río Purulón

Calafquén

Río Pullingue

Termas
Vergara

Panamericana (51km)

Panguipulli

Laguna
Gualalafquén

Río Natcahue

Cerro
Lungoico
(1640m)

Lago
Pellaifa

Río Reyehueico

Termas de
Coñaripe

Ñancul

Río Nancul

Río San Pedro

Lago Panguipulli

Río Niltre

Río Liucura

Río Cuacu

Sierra de
Quinchilca
(1840m)

Cerro
Changlin
(1890m)

Termas
Río Liquiñe

Liquiñe

Argentina (30km)

Panamericana (47km)

Riñihue

Lago Riñihue

Playa
Puñire

Cerro de
Pallahuinto
(1510m)

Río Llanquihue

Lago
Neltume

Termas
de Liquiñe

Cerro
Quelhuenco
(1798m)

Playa
Payahuinte

Choshuenco

Río Hulio

Río Fui

Río Fui

Puerto Fuy

CERROS
DE LIPINZA

Río Enco

Río Trinel

Salto del
Huilo Huilo

Lago
Pirihueico

CERROS DE QUIMAN

Enco

Volcán
Choshuenco
(2415m)

N

RESERVA HUILO
HUILO

CERROS
HUIRAHUEYE

RESERVA NACIONAL
MOCHO-CHOSHUENCO

Río Currifangue

Cerro del
Encanto
(1890m)

Puerto
Pirihueico

SIETE LAGOS

0   5 km

pre-cordillera and surrounded by 2000-metre peaks, are the most remote of the Siete Lagos, **Lago Neltume** and **Lago Pirihueico**, neither of which was accessible by road until thirty years ago and today are rapidly making their way onto the map.

Lago Calafquén and around

The most developed of the seven lakes, **Lago Calafquén** features a paved road for the 30km along its northern shore between the settlements of **Lican Ray** and **Coñaripe**, and a decent dirt road around most of the rest. To the east is tiny **Lago Pellaifa**, created by an earthquake in 1960 that altered the water flow in the region. It's bordered by an international road to Argentina that passes a clutch of thermal springs around the mountain hamlet of **Liquiñe**.

Lican Ray
LICAN RAY, a slightly scruffy holiday town organized around the main Avenida General Urrutia, lies 30km south of Villarrica, on the northernmost point of Lago Calafquén. There are two pleasant black-sand **beaches**: Playa Chica, with a small forested promontory, and Playa Grande, a long strip of dark sand framed by the surrounding hills; you can rent boats on both.

From March through November, the town is pretty much dead, but during the first weekend of January, the whole length of the main street, General Urrutia, is transformed into Chile's **largest outdoor barbecue** (*asado*) in which some three hundred lambs meet their spicy ends. Each year's feast is bigger than the last as the town attempts to break its own world record.

The helpful and friendly **Oficina de Turismo** is on the plaza at Urrutia 310 (daily: Dec–Feb 9am–10pm; erratic hours rest of the year; ☏45/431516). The best **places to stay** include *Hostería Inaltulafquén*, on Playa Grande at Cacique Punulef 510 (☏45/431115 ⓦwww.hotel-refugio.com; ❹), an attractive, slightly shabby house with pleasant rooms, owned by a helpful Canadian couple who organize local tours, and *Hotel Becker*, Manquel 105 (☏45/431553 ⓦwww.hotelbecker-licanray.com; ❺), offering rooms with balconies overlooking Playa Chica and a good restaurant downstairs. One kilometre out of town on the road to Coñaripe is *Cabañas and Camping Foresta* (☏45/431480), an expensive shady campsite in the woods, with sites for six people (CH$12,000), hot showers and easy beach access, and fully-equipped *cabañas* for up to seven (CH$60,000).

Café Ñaños, on Urrutia 105, is a popular and inexpensive restaurant serving meat and fish dishes, as well as large empanadas.

Buses leave from offices around the plaza. Buses JAC runs services to Villarrica every 15 minutes on weekdays; every half and hour on weekends; there are nightly bus services to Santiago in the summer and direct buses to Temuco, and one bus daily goes to Panguipulli.

Coñaripe and Liquiñe

Laid-back **COÑARIPE**, a 21-kilometre drive along the northern shore of Lago Calafquén, has just a couple of good black-sand beaches and a sleepy air. The small image of Christ on the lakeshore by the entrance to town is a memorial to two lava-engulfed victims and a testament to the uncertainty of living in this volcanically unstable area.

For **accommodation**, try the *Hostal Chumay*, Las Tepas 201 (☏63/313287; ❸), a welcoming guesthouse behind the plaza, with rates including breakfast; there's also internet and an excellent restaurant that specializes in seafood.

After Coñaripe there's a junction; the road to the right (south) follows the shore of Lago Calafquén to the town of Panguipulli, while the main road in front (east) climbs through native forest – with superb views of Lago Pellaifa, Volcán Villarrica and Choshuenco – for 22km to the tiny village of **LIQUIÑE**. Overlooked by a church and on the banks of the deep, wide Río Liquiñe, this pretty hamlet is surrounded by mountains and has a climate all of its own: in the summer the 2000-metre peaks trap the heat and it's difficult to believe that you're deep in the southern Andes. The hills around the village are strewn with **thermal springs**.

Coñaripe is served by frequent **buses** from Villarrica, operated by Buses JAC, and Igi Llaima; three buses daily continue on to Liquiñe. There are also less-frequent buses from both Coñaripe (seven in peak season; four in off-season) and Liquiñe to Panguipulli, operated by Buses Pirehueico.

Lago Panguipulli and around

Ten kilometres south of Lago Calafquén is the northern snout of long, thin **Lago Panguipulli**, a lake that stretches 26km southeast into the cordillera. Its western edge is a shore of little bays and hills, its east is cleared forest, the trees long since felled and taken by boat to the neat little town of Panguipulli on the

Termas around Coñaripe and Liquiñe

Around Coñaripe and Liquiñe, deep in the mountainous forest either side of the little-used international road to Argentina, you'll find numerous **thermal springs**, every bit as good as those around Pucón. Here are three of the best, listed in order of proximity to Coñaripe.

Termas Geométricas 12km northeast of Coñaripe ☏02/214 1214, ⓦwww .termasgeometricas.cl; CH$14,000; open 10am–10pm. The most exclusive set of thermal springs in the region, with seventeen smart, slate-covered pools, linked by a series of wooden walkways strung along a half-mile mountain stream amid lush vegetation. Grass-roofed shelters blend into the surroundings but there is no overnight accommodation here.

Termas de Coñaripe 15km southeast from Coñaripe ☏45/411111, ⓦwww .termasconaripe.cl; CH$7000; CH$2000 extra for the indoor pool, open 9am–11pm This popular holiday complex, built from glass and wood, has a good restaurant, serving locally-sourced food including trout from the on-site farm, and first-class accommodation, with full-board double rooms (❾). The *termas* from which the place gets its name have been diverted into four outdoor swimming pools of varying temperatures, one with a slide, and one indoor pool with a waterfall. There's also a spa offering a range of pampering treatments.

Termas Río Liquiñe On the riverbank in the centre of the village ☏63/317377. The *cabañas* (❺) have thermal water piped into private baths, and there's a big, square thermal swimming pool, access to which costs CH$4000.

lake's northwesternmost tip. Thirty years ago, a road was built around the uninhabited eastern shore to the remote Lagos **Neltume** and **Pirehueico**. These beautiful lakes are hardly touched by humanity and difficult to visit, as much of the lakefront is private property.

Panguipulli

The attractive village of **PANGUIPULLI**, bright with colourful roses, dark copper beech trees and manicured lawns, sits amid rolling fields, forests and peaks of grey and purple. You can get here following the southern shore road from Coñaripe (37km), but it's more easily reached via one of two 50- to 60-kilometre spurs from the Panamericana.

Founded in 1885, Panguipulli started life as a trading post for Pehuenche and Mapuche Indians driven off the Argentine pampas. It grew beyond these humble origins in 1903 when a Capuchin mission was established here, and when the railway arrived in 1937, the town became an important timber centre. The trees are gone now, and the boom is over, but Panguipulli remains the administrative hub for the Siete Lagos, with bustling shops, services and accommodation. It's best known today as the **town of roses**, with an estimated fourteen thousand closely pruned rose bushes lining the streets, and a crowd-pulling folk festival, Semana de las Rosas, the last week of January, when the city hosts arts exhibits and concerts.

There's not much to do in Panguipulli except sit on the beach, smell the roses and check out the famous **church** (unpredictable opening hours), around the corner from Plaza Arturo Prat. Built by the Capuchins and envied and copied throughout the Lake District, the church was modelled on traditional chapels around Berne in Switzerland. It's an unexpected sight – a twin-towered latticed confection of yellow, red, brown and white, looking like a massive iced chocolate cake.

Practicalities

Near the church, on Plaza Arturo Prat, you'll find the helpful **Oficina de Turismo** (Jan–Feb daily 9am–9pm; March–Dec Mon–Sat 9am–6pm; ☎63/310436, ⓦwww.panguipulli.cl). There's plenty of **accommodation** here. Try the *Hotel Le Francais* at Martínez de Rozas 880 (☎63/312496; ❹); while there is nothing French about it, the comfortable en-suite rooms have cable TV and wi-fi, and the restaurant serves good lunch-time specials. *Hostal Orillas del Lago*, at Martínez de Rozas 265 (☎63/311710; ❷), by the lake, is a welcoming backpacker favourite with kitchen use available. If you want a bit more luxury, try the friendly *Hostal España*, O'Higgins 790 (☎63/311166, ⓔjhirios@telsur.cl; ❹–❺), more like a family house than a hotel, with large, comfortable en-suite rooms. The nearest **campsite** is the small and well-maintained *Camping El Bosque*, just off the Plaza de Armas and close to the beach (☎63/311489).

Panguipulli's no town for gourmets, but it does have a **cookery school** – *Restaurant La Escuela*, Freire 394 – which, in January and February, opens its doors to the paying public. Apart from this, *Restaurant Girasol* at Martínez de Rozas 663 serves Chilean specialities such as *pollo asado* and *pastel de choclo*, whilst *Gardylafquen*, at Martínez de Rozas 722 also serves decent Chilean standards.

Panguipulli is very wellconnected to the rest of the Lake District. The **bus terminal** is at Gabriela Mistral 1000 (☎63/311055), and there are local and long-distance services heading as far afield as Santiago. Buses Pirehueico (☎63/311497) serves Valdivia and Puerto Montt several times daily, while Buses Lafit (☎63/311647) goes to Choshuenco, Neltume and Puerto Fuy three times daily. Tur-Bus (☎63/311377) runs services to Santiago from its own terminal at Carrera 784.

Choshuenco and around

Turning right from the shore road at the southern end of Lago Panguipulli, 42km from Panguipulli town, you'll pass along a magnificent avenue of trees, which forms an incongruous entrance to the tiny village of **Choshuenco**, formerly a steamer port and now a base for fishermen in the summer and for wild boar hunters in the winter. If you want to stay here, *Hostería Rucapillán*, San Martín 85 (☎63/318220, ⓔrucapi@telsur.cl; ❹) offers heated wooden cabins, a good restaurant and fishing, rafting and boating excursions.

Fifteen kilometres along a dirt road southwest of Choshuenco is **Enco**, a tiny logging camp at the end of Lago Riñihue. From Enco, a nine-kilometre track leads up through the Reserva Nacional Mocho Choshuenco to three ski refuges, maintained by the Club Andino de Valdivia, just above the tree line, which can be used as a base for climbing **Volcán Choshuenco** (2415m). Another 30-kilometre logging track leads to the town of **Riñihue** on the southern shore of the lake, passing through thick forest and along the edges of high cliffs to reveal constantly changing views across the lake. Walkers or cyclists who use it are unlikely to meet another soul. Be warned, though, that temporary bridges cross countless streams which, after even moderate rainstorms, turn long sections of the track into one great sticky bog.

Lago Neltume and Lago Pirehueico

Back on what was the shore road, 5km after the turn for Choshuenco, a gravel road branches left to smallish **LAGO NELTUME**, depositing you on its eastern shore, where much of the waterfront is effectively closed to the public. The other side of the lake is a mountain: the densely forested side of the impressive Cerro Paillahuinte, which rises 1435m straight up from the water. Heading once more towards Argentina, after another 7km you'll reach the waterfalls **Saltos del Huilo Huilo**, a powerful torrent forced through a ten-metre-wide green cleft in the rock to deafening effect; you can walk here from Choshuenco in around three hours.

Six kilometres further on lies **LAGO PIREHUEICO**. Pirehueico means "worm of water" in the local Mapuche language, and there couldn't be a better name for this curving, twisting, snake-like lake, bordered by forest-clad mountains. It's crossed by a **ferry**, from Puerto Fuy in the north to Puerto Pirehueico in the south (March–Dec one daily, departing 1pm and returning at 4pm; 1hr 30min; Jan–Feb thrice daily, departing Puerto Fuy at 8am, 1pm, and 6pm returning at 10am, 3pm and 8pm; CH$20,000 for cars, CH$1500 for passengers; ☎63/197 1585, ⓦwww.panguipulli.cl). The crossing is beautiful and extremely worthwhile, not to mention that it costs far less than the Puerto Varas-Bariloche crossing (see p.348). Hardly anyone stops in either village due to their remoteness, but because of that, the surrounding lakes and forests are home to more wildlife than most of the national parks. If you do find yourself stranded here, an unusual place to stay is the *Montaña Mágica*, near Neltume (☎63/197 2651; ⓞ), a Tolkienesque creation, shaped like a volcano, with water spouting out of the top, containing uniquely shaped wood-panelled rooms; if you are tall, get a room on one of the lower floors. The restaurant serves wild boar, among other delicious offerings.

From Puerto Pirehueico, it's 11km to the **border**, where there is a café and a customs post, open 8am to 8pm, year-round. If you're planning to cross the border in a rental car, bring written authorization from the rental company and ask the rental shop for full paperwork details.

In summer, there are twice-daily **buses** running across the border from Puerto Pirehueico to San Martín de los Andes, or if you're feeling particularly adventurous, there is nothing to stop you from walking the relatively undemanding 50km stretch of gravel road, which follows the northern bank of Lago Lácar all the way to San Martín.

Lago Riñihue

LAGO RIÑIHUE, the beautiful flooded valley to the south of Lago Panguipulli and the last of the Siete Lagos, has been almost completely untouched by tourism. There is no apparent reason why: the tiny village of **Riñihue** on the western shore of the lake was the first to be connected to the railway in 1910; there's a good tar road linking it with the Panamericana, 50km to the west; and the area is well-known by Chileans for producing famous Swiss- and German-style hard cheeses.

The village itself is merely a collection of houses built on the slight rise pushed up by an old, long-melted glacier, with a small village store and a small bar. You'll find few facilities, but one alluring spot to experience the gorgeous outdoors is at the mouth of the Río San Pedro, on the northern shore of the lake, where *Hotel Riñimapu* and its seventeen **rooms** are quietly tucked away (☎63/311388, ⓦwww.rinimapu.cl; ⓞ–ⓞ). It has no TV or internet access, but boasts fifty acres of fields, a tennis court and a prime launch pad for kayakers and rafters. The owner speaks French and English.

Valdivia and around

Fifty kilometres to the west of the Panamericana lies the attractive city of **VALDIVIA**, one of Chile's oldest cities, founded by Pedro de Valdivia as a supply halt on the route to Lima, six days' sail from the Magellan Strait. He chose the confluence of the rivers Calle Calle and Cruces as a suitable location because it was defensible and had access to both the sea and the inland plains,

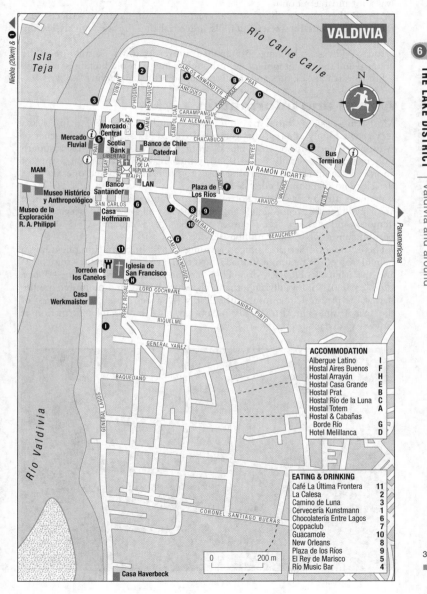

VALDIVIA

Río Calle Calle

Isla Teja

Niebla (20km) & ●

Río Valdivia

MAM

Museo Histórico y Anthropológico

Museo de la Exploración R. A. Philippi

Mercado Fluvial

Mercado Central

Scotia Bank

Banco de Chile

PLAZA LIBERTAD

Banco Santander

Casa Hoffmann

Catedral

LAN

Plaza de Los Ríos

PLAZA DE LA REPUBLICA

Torreón de los Canelos

Iglesia de San Francisco

Casa Werkmaister

Casa Haverbeck

Bus Terminal

Streets: CARLOS ANWANDTER, PRAT, JANEQUEO, CARAMPANGUE, AV ALEMANIA, CAMPOLICÁN, CHACABUCO, G REYES, AV RAMÓN PICARTE, CHACABUCO, VALDIVIA, YUNGAY, O'HIGGINS, CAMILO HENRIQUEZ, PRAT, YUNGAY, LIBERTAD, MAIPÚ, SAN CARLOS, CAMILO HENRIQUEZ, ESMERALDA, BEAUCHEFF, ARAUCO, ANÍBAL PINTO, LORD COCHRANE, PÉREZ ROSALES, RIQUELME, GENERAL YÁÑEZ, BAQUEDANO, GENERAL LAGOS, CORONEL SANTIAGO BUERAS

N

Panamericana

ACCOMMODATION

Albergue Latino	I
Hostal Aires Buenos	F
Hostal Arrayán	H
Hostal Casa Grande	E
Hostal Prat	B
Hostal Río de la Luna	C
Hostal Totem	A
Hostal & Cabañas Borde Río	G
Hotel Melillanca	D

EATING & DRINKING

Café La Última Frontera	11
La Calesa	2
Camino de Luna	3
Cervecería Kunstmann	1
Chocolatería Entre Lagos	6
Coppaclub	7
Guacamole	10
New Orleans	8
Plaza de los Ríos	9
El Rey de Marisco	5
Río Music Bar	4

0   200 m

but it had to be abandoned in 1599 after the Mapuche uprisings. The site was almost immediately pounced on by the Dutch, who wanted to create an enclave on the coast of South America, but was reoccupied by the Spanish in 1645, who realized that such actions threatened the Spanish Empire. To counter the threat, the Viceroy in Peru ordered a string of forts – including Corral and Niebla – to be built. These were strengthened when Britain threatened in 1770, and by the time of the wars of Chilean independence, Valdivia was a formidable redoubt.

After independence there was a great influx of German settlers, who founded shipyards, breweries and mills, industrializing the area quickly leaving lasting legacy.

Today Valdivia is a vibrant, cosmopolitan university town – a mixture of the colonial and the contemporary, even though many of its old buildings are gone – lost to earthquakes, fires and floods throughout the last century.

Arrival and information

Most long-distance buses travelling north-south along the Panamericana service the highly efficient **bus terminal** (☎63/212212) is on the corner of Anwandter and Muñoz, five blocks from the city centre. It has a superb information kiosk (daily 8am–10pm), which maintains a current listing of approved accommodation. Coastal buses to Niebla and beyond operate from the city end of Puente Pedro de Valdivia.

Valdivia's **airport** lies 29km northeast of town in the village of Pichoy. There are daily flights between Valdivia and Santiago as well as weekday services from Temuco and Concepción. Transfer Valdivia (☎63/225533; CH$3000 per person) runs door-to-door minibus service.

There is a good Sernatur office providing tourist **information**, including a helpful map of the region, at Prat 555, next to the river between the cruise boats and the Mercado Fluvial (Mon–Thur 8.30am–5.30pm, Fri 8.30am–4.30pm; ☎63/239060, ✉infovaldivia@sernatur.cl). More helpful and motivated are the staff at the private Codeproval office nearby (Dec–Feb 9am–8pm daily; rest of the year 10am–4pm; ☎63/278100). You can also find useful information at ⓦwww.valdiviachile.cl.

▲ Valdivia waterfront

Accommodation

In January and February, when Valdivia's student population is on holiday, the city has some of the cheapest accommodation in the Lake District, including a plethora of *hospedajes* near the bus terminals, though some are rather run-down.

Albergue Latino General Lagos 1036 ☎63/578319 ⊛http://albergue-latino.blogspot .com. Colourful mansion-cum-hostel under new French-Chilean ownership, offering bright doubles and triples to younger travellers. A relaxed atmosphere, pleasant common area and garden, free breakfast, internet, cable TV and kitchen facilities are all part of the deal. ❷–❸

Hostal Aires Buenos García Reyes 550 ☎63/222202 ⊛www.airesbuenos.cl. Well-run HI-affiliated hostel, bustling with younger travellers, with cheery dorms at their new central location, complete with internet, TV lounge and guest kitchen, as well as friendly staff on hand to help and advise. ❷–❸

Hostal Arrayán Perez Rosales 852 ☎63/527058 or 8/549 7727 ✉macarenapaz26@yahoo.es. Exceptionally welcoming atmosphere, and clean rooms with kitchen privileges, all in a rambling house. ❷–❸

Hostal Casa Grande Anwandter 880 ☎63/202035 ⊛www.hotelcasagrande.cl. Enormous, well-maintained mansion near the bus terminal with a view of the river. Rooms have cable TV; good laundry facilities are a big plus, as is the buffet breakfast and internet access. ❹

Hostal Prat Av Prat 595 ☎63/222020. Overlooking the river, this smart, refurbished hotel with comfortable, if undistinguished, en-suite rooms and cable TV is run by a small, energetic woman who's eager to please and who provides a decent breakfast. ❹

Hostal Río de Luna Prat 695 ☎63/253333, ⊛www.hostalriodeluna.cl. A large, quiet and pleasant guesthouse with airy en-suite rooms overlooking Río Calle Calle, run by friendly staff. Wi-fi and cable TV are amongst amenities offered. ❹

Hostal Totem Carlos Anwandter 425 ☎63/292849 ⊛www.turismototem.cl. Quiet and welcoming guesthouse with clean, spacious, en-suite rooms. Cable TV, internet access, wi-fi and breakfast are included. ❸–❹

Hostal & Cabañas Borde Río Camilo Henríquez 746 ☎63/214069 ⊛www.valdiviacabanas.cl. This guesthouse complex offers both en-suite singles, doubles and triples with colourful bedspreads, cable TV and wi-fi and an attractive common area, and fully-equipped *cabañas* for up to seven people, which are good value for groups. Rooms ❸–❹; *cabañas* ❷–❹.

Hotel Melillanca Av Alemania 675 ☎63/212509 ⊛www.hotelmelillanca.cl. Modern four-star hotel with sizeable rooms and all the expected amenities, including sauna, Wifi, and a good restaurant and bar. ❼

The Town

Unlike most Chilean towns, Valdivia's social centre is not its plaza but its **waterfront**, where the Río Calle Calle and the Río Cau Cau meet the Río Valdivia. Inland from the rivers, to the east, lies the modern concrete town centre. Opposite the town centre, across the Pedro de Valdivia bridge, sits **Isla Teja**.

Ferry tours

Just down from the Mercado Fluvial there are the kiosks and touts of the ferry tour companies, offering to take you down to the **coastal forts**, or upriver to the **wetlands**. The tours on offer vary greatly, so shop around. The **Santuario de la Naturaleza Carlos Anwandter** is visited by both Bahía, with its fleet of four boats (☎63/348727; 3hr; CH$7000, including *onces* and a guide); or Pólux (☎63/249047; 3hr; CH$5000, return only); boats depart at 4pm. Bahía also runs hour-long cruises along the river (CH$4000) and to Isla Teja (CH$5000). The 250-person *Neptuno* (☎63/218952; 5hr; bilingual guide, lunch and *onces* included) runs a large loop behind Isla del Rey, with 35min stops at the Corral and Mancera forts; *Catamaran Marqués de Mancera* (☎63/249191) and *Reina Sofia* (☎63/207120) offer similar services. Tours cost between CH$10,000 and 14,000, and depart at 1.30pm. The 108-person *Orion III* (☎63/225011; 5hr; CH$14,000) is the only boat offering trips that include both Isla Huapi and the two forts.

A haven of tranquillity, the island is home to the **Museo Histórico y Antropológico Maurice van de Maele** and has beautiful views back across the river to the Mercado Fluvial. It's also the site of the large and prestigious Universidad Austral de Chile.

Just south of the bridge to Isla Teja is the **Mercado Fluvial** and Valdivia's fish quay on the riverfront, with fishermen expertly gutting the day's catch and throwing scraps to the clamouring seagulls and the family of sea lions who treat the market as their local takeaway. Opposite, on the other side of the path, vendors sell all types of bright fruit, vegetables and strings of smoked shellfish. Across the road, the **indoor market** features good crafts stalls and inexpensive *marisquerías* (seafood restaurants), which are great places to stop for lunch. Just to the south of the Mercado Fluvial, touts offer ferry tours (see box, p.281).

In the centre of town you can see a couple of squat defensive towers that date from 1774 – **Torreón del Barro** on Avenida Picarte and **Torreón de los Canelos** on the corner of Yerbas Buenas and General Lagos, while north–south **Calle General Lagos** is filled with Valdivia's gems, a series of nobly proportioned nineteenth-century buildings. Take a stroll down the road and peek through the railings at the austere, double-staircased **Casa Werkmaister** (between Cochrane and Riquelme) and at the crinkly gabled **Conjunto Haverbeck** on the way out of town, or the many others between the two. The only one you can actually visit is **Casa Hoffmann**, at Yungay 733 (Tues–Sun 10am–1pm & 3–7pm; free). It was constructed in 1870 as a private residence by Alberto Thater, a German who came to Valdivia in 1857, and has been lovingly restored and furnished in the style favoured by successful merchants during Valdivia's golden years. Temporary art exhibitions are mounted in the upstairs rooms.

On February 9, the city celebrates the founding of Valdivia, and between the second and third Saturday of February all of Valdivia comes out to celebrate "Valdivia Week": the river lights up with a **parade of boats**, and a memorable fireworks show.

Isla Teja

The quiet island is reached via the concrete bridge to the north of the Mercado Fluvial. Turning left from the bridge, and entering Campus Cultura, also on your left, you'll come to Isla Teja's main attraction, the splendidly sited **Museo Histórico y Antropológico Maurice van de Maele** (Mon–Fri 9am–1pm & 3.30–7pm; CH$1250), in an old colonial house surrounded by a veranda. Once owned by Karl Anwandter, founder of Chile's first brewery, it's still furnished with the trappings of nineteenth-century European society, including a double piano, an ornate red-marble fireplace and a magic lantern. Also on display is a fascinating collection of old sepia prints of the first German settlers and the Anwandter family tree. The highlight of the museum is the collection of **Mapuche artefacts**, mainly splendid silverwork and cloth. There are also some lovely old maps of South America on the wall of the stairway, and a room of memorabilia pertaining to British-born Lord Cochrane, who played a decisive role in securing independence for Chile, and his staff.

Next door to the Museo Histórico sits the **Museo de la Exploración R.A. Philippi** (Dec–Feb daily 10am–8pm; March–Nov Tue–Sun 10am–6pm; CH$1800 or CH$2500 for entry to both museums). It's housed in a Jugendstil house that was originally dismantled and then put back together at its current location, and dedicated to the groundbreaking naturalist, with an interesting collection of local flora and fauna. Upstairs you'll find Philippi's study, numerous pickled denizens of the sea and a superb collection of photos of local wildlife, while the ground floor is occupied by larger fauna and colourful beetle and butterfly collections.

Down by the water, housed in Valdivia's old brewery, is the **Museo de Arte Contemporaneo**, or "MAC" (@www.macvaldivia.uach.cl), currently undergoing extensive renovation. When open, MAC doesn't have a permanent collection, but features visiting modern art exhibitions and installations.

Eating and drinking

Café La Ultima Frontera Pérez Rosales 787. A slightly scruffy building conceals this fashionable, bohemian café that serves tasty sandwiches, vegetarian dishes and real coffee.

La Calesa O'Higgins 160 ☎63/225467. This Peruvian-owned, expensive international restaurant is *the* place to splurge. The menu includes international dishes, but the best ones are Peruvian; try the delicious *chupe de corvina*. Open evenings only; closed Sun.

Camino de Luna Costanera Arturo Prat. Moored on a boat just upstream from the bridge to Isla Teja, this is reputedly one of the best restaurants in Valdivia. It's expensive, but the German-Chilean cusine is worth it and the dishes are prepared with finesse and attention to detail.

Cervecería Kunstmann On the road to Niebla ☎63/292969, @www .cerveza-kunstmann.cl. Come hungry, as this restaurant-brewery-museum serves monster portions of smoked meat, sauerkraut and potatoes to accompany its range of beers; try the honey-tinted Miel or the darker Torobayo, and finish off with tasty beer-flavoured ice cream. Mains CH$4500.

Chocolatería Entre Lagos Vicente Pérez Rosales 622–640. A famous chocolate shop, known for its rich cakes, and connected to a *salón de té* that sells giant veggie sandwiches, a wide range of icecreams and fresh-squeezed natural fruit juices.

691 Dance Bar Esmeralda 691. Split-level dance club/bar popular with local students; 2-for-1 drinks from 8pm, though the actionin the basement does not kick off until midnight. Appeals to Latin and pop music lovers.

Guacamole Esmeralda 693. Somewhat gaudy Tex-Mex joint, though the enormous portions of enchiladas and burritos more than make up for the decor. Mains CH$4500.

New Orleans Esmeralda 682. While the dishes may not be authentically Cajun, the portions are generous, the service is excellent and the spicy touch is welcome. Mains CH$5500.

Plaza de los Ríos Arauco 561. Large central shopping mall with a popular and extensive food court featuring typical fast-food branches such as Schopdog, which specializes in hot-dog combos. Meals CH$3000.

El Rey de Marisco Chacabuco at Prat, across the street from the Mercado Fluvial. A homely restaurant popular with locals, offering fresh fish and seafood. *Congrio a la plancha* CH$4500.

Río Music Bar Camilo Henriquez 361. Popular local bar/club, with local DJs appearing on Wednesday and Thursday nights and live Latino pop on weekends. Happy hour until midnight.

Yang Cheng General Lagos 1118. Generic Cantonese cuisine at reasonable prices in a restaurant set behind a small oriental garden; weekday students' lunch a bargain at CH$2000.

Listings

Airlines LAN, Maipú 271, in front of Plaza de la República (☎63/258844).

Banks and exchange There are various banks with ATMs around the Plaza de la República. For *cambios*, try Cambio La Reconquista, Carampangue 325 or Cambio Arauco, Arauco 331, Local 24.

Buses Most companies have offices at the bus terminal, at Muñoz 360 ☎63/212212. Buses JAC ☎63/212925; Cruz del Sur ☎63/213842; Igi Llaima ☎63/213542; Buses Pirehueico

☎63/218609; Tur Bus ☎63/226010; Tas Choapa ☎63/213124 and Bus Norte ☎63/251362.

Car rental Autovald, Rosales 660 ☎63/212786; Hertz, Picarte 640 ☎63/218316.

Hospital Clinica Alemana, Beaucheff 765 ☎63/246100.

Internet *Café Phonet*, Libertad 127.

Telephone centres *Café Phonet*, Libertad 127.

Shopping Arts and crafts at Feria Artesanal Camino de Luna, by the river.

Niebla and Corral

At the mouth of the Río Valdivia, 18km from Valdivia, is the small, spread-out village of **NIEBLA** and its fort (March–Nov Tues–Sun 10am–7pm; Dec–Feb daily 10am–7pm; CH$600, free on Wed). The **Fuerte de Niebla** (or Castillo de la Pura y Limpia Concepción de Montfort de Lemus), was originally built by the Spanish from 1667 to 1672 as part of an extensive line of defences of this key position in their empire, and massively enlarged in the eighteenth century according to the design of the Royal Engineers in Madrid. Today it's been restored and houses a small museum, but the most interesting things are the old features: the powder room, double-walled and well below ground level, the crenellated curtain wall hacked out of the bare rock, and the twelve slightly rusting cannons. The view from up here, high above the sea, is inspiring, and you can appreciate how the fort dominated the mouth of the river far below. Boats arrive here from Valdivia, and *colectivos* run regularly from Yungay near the Mercado Fluvial and cost CH$700.

On the other side of the estuary lies the little village of **CORRAL**; it used to be a thriving port until it was flattened by the 1960 tidal wave. Another Spanish fort, the somewhat dilapidated **Castillo de San Sebastián de la Cruz** (daily 10am–6.30pm; CH$600), constructed in 1645 and reinforced in 1764, with its 21 cannon, is a short walk from the pier.

North along the coast from Corral lie the remains of **Castillo San Luis de Alba de Amargos** (daily 10am–6.30pm; CH$600). It's more ornate than the fort at Niebla, with little, stone-roofed towers to protect those unfortunates who had to keep a look-out for the fall of the shells. From December 15 until the end of February, there's a twice daily re-enactment of an attack by corsairs at 4.30pm and 6.15pm.

The only way across the river is by a half-hour ferry ride – frequent boats leave from the pier at the entrance to Niebla between 9am and 5.40pm (CH$700), some stopping at the small and pleasant **Isla Mancera** with the most intact of the forts, the 1645 **Castillo de San Pedro de Alcántara** (daily 10am–7pm; CH$600). Though the journey is often obscured with *niebla* (rolling fog), quite often you'll catch sight of sea lions and black-necked swans along the way.

Santuario de la Naturaleza Carlos Anwandter

After the 1960 earthquake, the 50km of low-lying land around the Río Cruces north of Valdivia was flooded, forming an extensive delta which has been protected as the **Santuario de la Naturaleza Carlos Anwandter**. This marsh now forms an important breeding ground and resting place for more than ninety species of migrating birds. The importance of this wetland area was officially recognized by UNESCO in 1981, and 48 square kilometres became a protected nature reserve in 1982.

Lago Ranco

Dozens of distant high and rugged mountains surround pretty **LAGO RANCO**, 91km east of Valdivia. The lake is big – the second largest in the region, covering over 400 square kilometres – and is bordered to the west by flat land, and to the east by the rising Andes. Around the lake's edge is a 121-kilometre partially-paved road, passing the village of **Futrono** – gateway to **Isla Huapi**, a Mapuche *reducción* – and leading to **Llifén** on the eastern shore, a compact village with good fishing.

Isla Huapi festival

Two Mapuche communities live on the **Isla Huapi**, and they meet twice a year – at the full moon in January or February and again at the full moon in June. This great council, called **trapëmuwn**, lasts for twenty-four hours. With its origins in the ancient harvest ceremony, *lepún*, the council decides on all community matters. Held in the open, the proceedings are shrouded from the view of outside observers by a thick stockade of branches, which also serve to protect the participants from the elements, but there is enough to see and hear, including **traditional music** and **dancing**. The seemingly interminable debates are periodically broken by the beating of **drums** (*kultrún*) and blowing of **pipes** (*trutru*ca). Take food and drink to sustain you throughout the day.

Futrono and Isla Huapi

FUTRONO, the dusty village on the northern shore of Lago Ranco, is a one-street town with a helpful and well-stocked **Oficina de Turismo** on the corner of the plaza at Balmaceda and O'Higgins (Mon–Fri: mid-March to mid-Dec 9am–1pm & 3–5pm; mid-Dec to mid-March 9am–9pm; ☏63/482636) but little else to offer. The only draw is that the **boats for Isla Huapi**, the Mapuche reserve, leave from here daily (except Sun) in the mornings, returning later the same day; ask at the tourist office for an updated timetable. The crossing costs CH$2000. Futrono is connected to Valdivia by one bus an hour, run by Buses Futrono (☏63/481279); some go on to Llifén; there is no bus station and buses stop in front of a supermarket in the centre of town.

A good place to stay is the centrally located *Hospedaje Futronhué*, Balmaceda 90 (☏63/481265; ❸), with welcoming hosts, clean rooms and reliable hot water. *Don Floro*, at Balmaceda 114, a block from the bus stop, is a popular family-run restaurant where you can fill up on good Chilean standards, such as *lomo a lo pobre*.

ISLA HUAPI, the largest island in the middle of Lago Ranco, is a Mapuche *reducción* and a haven of peace and quiet, with pocket-sized fields, scattered huts and winding tracks just wide enough for the teams of oxen that pull water carts up from the lakeshore. Visitors are made very welcome but you should be sensitive, especially with your camera. There's no official accommodation on the island, though the Futrono tourist office can request that you stay with one of the islanders.

Llifén

Tucked on a ledge between the forest and the lake, **LLIFÉN**, 22km along the northern shore from Futrono, is a remote little place, but it's been a famous **fishing destination** since the 1930s. Most of the **accommodation** here is oriented towards fishermen, and is quite expensive, though *Cabañas y Hostería Licán*, with no formal address, but hard to miss in this small town (☏63/371917; ❸), offers basic rooms and fully-equipped cabins. Twelve kilometres east of town is the *Cumilahue Lodge* (☏02/231 1027; ❾), one of Chile's leading fly-fishing lodges, set in native forest with exclusive river access, run by the grandson of the Frenchman who brought the Cabernet grape to Chile; three-day and six-day packages are available.

Osorno and around

Despite being founded in one of the best defensive positions of all the Spaniards' frontier forts, Osorno was regularly sacked by Mapuche Indians from 1553 until 1796, at which point Chile's governor, Ambrosio O'Higgins, ordered it to be resettled. From tentative beginnings, it has grown into a thriving agricultural city mainly due to the industry of European settlers who felled the forests and began to develop the great dairy herds that form the backbone of the local economy today.

Though Osorno has few attractions for tourists, as the transport hub for the southern Lake District and starting point for the region's main road into Argentina, it has an abundance of public **buses**, making it a snap to visit Osorno's surrounding attractions, such as **Parque Nacional Puyehue**, one of Chile's most-visited national parks.

Arrival and information

Osorno's two **bus terminals** are less than a block from each other on Calle Errázuriz and close to the city centre. The long-distance terminal is at Errázuriz 1400 (⊤64/234149), and the rural terminal is at Mercado Municipal, Errázuriz 1300 (⊤64/232073).

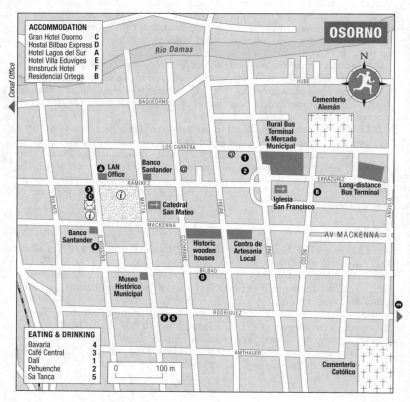

ACCOMMODATION
Gran Hotel Osorno	C
Hostal Bilbao Express	D
Hotel Lagos del Sur	A
Hotel Villa Eduviges	E
Innsbruck Hotel	F
Residencial Ortega	B

EATING & DRINKING
Bavaria	4
Café Central	3
Dalí	1
Pehuenche	2
Sa Tanca	5

OSORNO

Río Damas

HUBE

Cementerio Alemán

BAQUEDANO

Rural Bus Terminal & Mercado Municipal

LOS CARRERA

LAN Office

Banco Santander

ERRÁZURIZ

Long-distance Bus Terminal

RAMÍREZ

MATTA

FREIRE

Iglesia San Francisco

Catedral San Mateo

MACKENNA

AV MACKENNA

Banco Santander

O'HIGGINS

BULNES

COCHRANE

Historic wooden houses

Centro de Artesanía Local

PRAT

COLÓN

ANGULO

BILBAO

Museo Histórico Municipal

RODRÍGUEZ

AMTHAUER

Cementerio Católico

0   100 m

Conaf Office

Seven kilometres from Osorno, Cañal Bajo **airport** (T64/232529) is served by daily LAN flights from Santiago via Temuco and Concepción. Taxis to town cost around CH$3000.

Sernatur's helpful **information office**, O'Higgins 667 (Mon–Fri 8.30am–1pm & 2.30–5.30pm; T64/237575, ⓔinfosorno@sernatur.cl), in the Gobernación building on the west side of the Plaza de Armas, has good city maps and accommodation lists. There are also **information kiosks**: one on the plaza in summer, and another in the long-distance bus terminal. **Conaf** is at Martínez de Rozas 430 (Mon–Thurs 9.30am–1pm & 2.30–5.30pm, Fri 9.30am–1pm & 2.30–4:30pm; T64/234393); the staff are helpful but lack up-to-date information on trail conditions in the nearby national parks.

Accommodation

Osorno's **accommodation** is largely aimed at travelling businessmen, so the mid-range is good but the low end is a bit thin on the ground.

Gran Hotel Osorno O'Higgins 615 T64/232171, ⓔhoteleraustral@telsur.cl. A large rambling 1950s building, with cable TV and spacious though spartan rooms, but those overlooking the Plaza de Armas make up for it with a great view and it's good value. ❺

Hostal Bilbao Express Bilbao 1019 T64/262200, ⓔpazla@telsur.cl. Jolly, welcoming and well-equipped with a restaurant, snug rooms and internet access, this is an excellent deal for the price (❸). Its sister building, *Hotel Bilbao*, Mackenna 1205 (T63/264444), has similar rooms and amenities, but is more expensive (❹).

Hotel Innsbruck Rodríguez 941 T64/242000. Pleasant mid-range hotel with an attractive exterior. The singles and doubles are on the small size, but the price and the location make up for it. ❸–❹

Hotel Lagos del Sur O'Higgins 564 T64/243244 Ⓦwww.hotelagosdelsur.cl. Centrally located and somewhat musty business hotel offering comfortable en-suite rooms with cable TV, a good cafeteria and internet access. Staff can help you rent a car. ❺

Hotel Villa Eduviges Eduviges 856 T64/235023 Ⓦwww.hoteleduviges.cl. This a good option for groups, providing friendly service, clean rooms with cable TV, breakfast in a cheerful dining room and wi-fi. ❸

Residencial Ortega Colón 602 T64/232592. Basic budget option around the corner from the bus station, popular with travellers. Has a large dining area and a small communal lounge; breakfast is included in the rates. Secure parking is available for guests. ❷

The City

What strikes you first about Osorno are its controversial **churches**, such as the **Catedral San Mateo** on the Plaza de Armas, and **Iglesia San Francisco** on Prat, three blocks east. Their modern concrete exteriors are not to everyone's taste.

A block east of the Plaza, Calle Mackenna is lined with a row of **wooden houses**, built between 1876 and 1923, that have been declared national monuments. The prettiest is the two-storey clapboard **Casa Schüller**, with an ornate porch and a hexagonal side tower that sports a weather vane.

One block southwest of Juan Mackenna is the worthwhile **Museo Histórico Municipal**, Matta 809 at Bilbao (Dec–Feb daily 11am–7pm; March–Nov Mon–Fri 9.30am–5.30pm; Sat 3–6pm; CH$500), with displays on the history of Osorno, both before and after European conquest, illustrated with old photographs of Osorno, a collection of daggers and swords from the colonial era, and various Mapuche artefacts. The best natural history exhibits include the bones, teeth and tusks of a mastodon (a prehistoric giant herbivore), and a mummified body, thousands of years old, found near Arica in the north of Chile.

Moving on from Osorno

Osorno is a major transportation hub with buses serving all major destinations along the Carretera Austral from its central Terminal de Buses, while its Terminal de Buses Rurales has frequent departures to Aguas Calientes and Anticura wth Expreso Lago Puyehue. Bariloche, Argentina, is served by Igi Llaima and Cruz del Sur. If you wish to travel to Coyhaique, on the Carretera Austral, Osorno is the starting point for the Queilen Bus and Buses Transaustral departures via Argentina (note that this route does not serve any Argentine destinations).

6 Eating and drinking

Bavaria O'Higgins 743. The *comedor* section of this chain dishes up ample portions of sausages, sauerkraut and potatoes, while the upstairs restaurant offers more sophisticated meat dishes.

Café Central O'Higgins 610. Come here for American breakfasts, hamburgers, sandwiches, real coffee and good service.

Dalí Interior Patio Freire 542, Local 14. This trendy restaurant specializes in well-prepared fish and seafood dishes. All-you-can-eat Wednesday and Friday nights are particularly popular.

Dino's Ramírez 898. Popular chain restaurant specialising in sandwiches and light meals; the lunchtime *menú ejecutivo* is particularly good value (CH$3000).

Mercado Municipal Prat at Errázuruz. By far the best place to find a filling and cheap meal; the market's many *comedores* serve empanadas and large portions of fish and seafood (steer clear of the fried fish, though).

Rehuenche Interior Patio Freire 542, Local 16. Steaks grilled to perfection served in an airy and pleasant dining area. Mains CH$6000.

Restaurant Club de Artesanos Mackenna 634. Inexpensive Chilean food, particularly fish and seafood, served in a hassle-free setting with a relaxed atmosphere, along with the locally produced beer, Märzen.

Sa Tanca Pub Rodríguez 955. Lively pub which doubles as a sushi restaurant/takeaway. The sushi rolls are surprisingly good. Open from 7pm Mon–Fri; from 8pm Sat.

Listings

Airlines LAN, Ramírez 802 ☏64/314909.
Banks and exchange There are banks and ATMs around the plaza. For a *cambio* with good rates, try Cambio Tur, Mackenna 1004.
Bus companies Cruz del Sur ☏64/232777; Tas Choapa ☏64/233933; Buses Pirehueico ☏64/233050; Igi Llaima ☏64/234371; Intersur ☏64/231325; Pullman Sur ☏64/232777; Tur Bus ☏64/234170; Via Tur ☏64/230118; Expreso Lago

Puyehue ☏64/243919.
Car rental Automóvil Club de Chile, Bulnes 463 ☏63/540080.
Hospital Hospital Base, Av Bühler 1765 ☏64/230977.
Internet *Ciber Cochr@ne*, Cochrane at Ramírez.
Shopping You can pick up very good leatherwork in the Mercado Municipal, Errázuriz s/n.
Telephone centre Entel, Ramírez 1107, Local 9.

Parque Nacional Puyehue and around

PARQUE NACIONAL PUYEHUE (daily 8am–9pm; CH$1000; ☏64/197 4572, ⓦwww.parquepuyehue.cl), 81km east of Osorno, is one of Chile's busiest national parks, largely because of the traffic on the international road that runs through its middle. It's part of a massive, 15,000-square-kilometre area of protected wilderness, one of the largest in the Andes: it borders the Parque Nacional Vicente Pérez Rosales to the south, and some Argentine parks that stretch all the way to Pucón's Parque Nacional Villarrica in the north. The land is high temperate rainforest spread over two volcanoes, Volcán Puyehue (2240m)

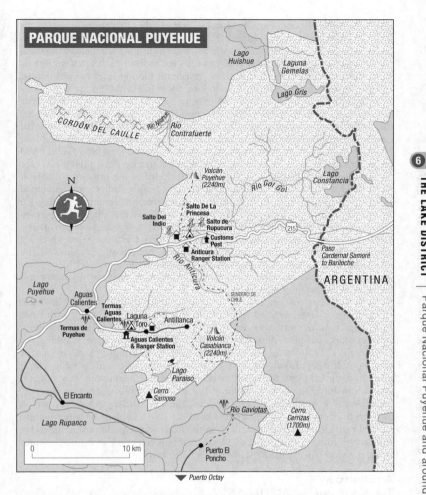

PARQUE NACIONAL PUYEHUE

Lago Huishue

Laguna Gemelas

Lago Gris

CORDÓN DEL CAULLE

Río Nilahue

Río Contrafuerte

Volcán Puyehue (2240m)

Río Gol Gol

Lago Constancia

Salto De La Princesa

Salto Del Indio

Salto de Rupucura

Customs Post

215

Anticura Ranger Station

Paso Cardenal Samoré to Bariloche

Río Anticura

ARGENTINA

Lago Puyehue

Aguas Calientes

Termas Aguas Calientes

SENDERO DE CHILE

Laguna Toro

Antillanca

Termas de Puyehue

Aguas Calientes & Ranger Station

Volcán Casablanca (2240m)

Lago Paraiso

El Encanto

Cerro Samoso

Río Gaviotas

Cerro Cerrizas (1700m)

Lago Rupanco

0   10 km

Puerto El Poncho

Puerto Octay

to the north, and Volcán Casablanca (1990m), on the west slope of which is the Antillanca ski resort.

The park's divided into three sectors: **Aguas Calientes** where the *termas* are, **Antillanca** and **Anticura**, straddling the international road near the Argentine border.

Aguas Calientes

The 47-kilometre road that shoots east from Osorno to **LAGO PUYEHUE** passes through some rich and fertile farmland. As the road nears the lake, passing through the nondescript village of Entre Lagos, you'll see rugged hills and mountains on the horizon, including the spiked pyramid of **Volcán Puntiagudo** (2490m). Around 30km after Entre Lagos, the road forks: the left-hand road heads on to the Anticura section of the Parque Nacional Puyehue and the Argentine border, while the right-hand one leads to the Aguas Calientes section and the Antillanca skiing resort, passing the thermal springs of one of Chile's most famous and fashionable hotels, the ⚿ **Hotel Termas de Puyehue** (reservations ☎02/293 6000, ⊛www.puyehue.cl; ❽). It features sprawling gardens and a plush resort with attractively furnished standard double rooms, surrounded by the main attractions of an Olympic-sized pool and tubs, spa facilities and treatment rooms. The verdant complex also boasts a fine restaurant serving international cuisine and occasionally hosts concerts. The indoor pools (CH$12,000) are open daily 8am–8pm; outdoor pools (CH$8000) operate daily 11am–7pm. Other cheaper hot springs in the area include the pools and resort at *Aguas Calientes* (☎64/236988, ⊛www.puyehue.cl), right at the entrance to the Parque Nacional Puyehue. It has *tinas* (personal bathtubs; CH$9000), double *tinas* (so you can bathe with a friend), a hot outdoor pool that is not the cleanest (pass costs CH$17,500 for up to a week; open 8am–7pm), and a very hot indoor pool (CH$20,000 for up to a week; 8am–8pm); use of the latter is included in the price of a *cabaña* in summer. These *cabañas* (❻–❼) sleep four to eight people and are well-equipped (modern fridges, cookers, *parrillas* on the balcony for barbecuing), but they are somewhat cramped and arranged in a military-style row that offers little privacy. For those who want to stay somewhere more private, try the two **campsites**: scenic, well-sited *Camping Chanleufú* (☎64/197 4533; CH$12,000 for up to six people) includes access to the outdoor pool, tables, fire pits and hot showers; the more informal *Camping Los Derrumbes* (CH$8000 for four people) has no hot water and can be rather dirty. Both campsites fill up to capacity in January and February. Wild camping is also permitted in the national park.

There is a Conaf station and information centre at **AGUAS CALIENTES**, where there's a large, detailed **map of the park** on the wall, along with basic park maps that you can take with you. There are several **walks** in the area, mainly short, self-guided **nature trails**, such as the Sendero Rápidos del Chanleufú, a 1250-metre track alongside the river rapids. There are also a couple of **longer hikes**, such as El Pionero (6km; 90min), a steep climb through dense Valdivian forest that rewards you with a panoramic view of Lago and Volcán Puyehue, before rejoining the road to Antillanca. A two-day trip, Lago Bertín y Antillanca (17km), follows the old road to Antillanca sector, through the dense forest along the banks of the Río Chanleufú. There's a rustic six-bed **refugio** at Lago Bertín, deep in the heart of the park, and the next day you can continue on to Antillanca, 9km further on, returning to Aguas Calientes along the road (there's usually enough traffic to hitch).

Antillanca

The **ski centre** at **ANTILLANCA**, the *Centro Turístico De Ski Antillanca* (☎64/235114, ⊛www.skiantillanca.com), is 18km from Aguas Calientes by road, at the foot of the Volcán Casablanca (also known as Antillanca). This resort is open year round; in summer it's relatively quiet, with excellent views along the cordillera, right across the central plain to the Pacific Ocean, and offers various outdoor activities, such as mountain biking, canoeing, fishing and hikes up the volcano. You can do the latter by yourself, though there is no path; allow seven hours return, giving yourself a little extra time to drink in the spectacular views of the surrounding volcanoes and lakes. Part of the Sendero de Chile, two trails begin at Antillanca: the 25km Las Parras, that runs through native forest to Lago Paraíso, south of the main road, passing the indigenous community of Calfuco, and passing by the tiny Laguna Toro before finishing at the Aguas Calientes Conaf office; and the 50km trail that finishes at Anticura (see opposite). It is also possible to hike south to the eastern shores of Lago Rupanco, timing it so that your arrival coincides with a boat taxi to the southern shore, where you can catch a bus; *Zapato Amarillo* in Puerto Octay (see p.339) has detailed information on this trek.

You can stay in the refuge (④) or in the hotel (⑤). The centre is open all year (ski season July–Aug) and has three T-bar lifts, one chairlift and ski slopes for all skill levels. It also has a restaurant, open-air swimming pool, gymnasium, ski-rental shop and a few apartments that book up quickly. In winter, the resort is extremely popular with locals, and it gets so busy that traffic on the last 8km up to the ski centre is subject to time restrictions (up 8am–noon & 2–5.30pm; down noon–2pm & after 5.30pm); also, bear in mind that car chains are often required if driving here during the winter. Ski day-passes cost around CH$12,000 per day.

Anticura

ANTICURA lies 22km from Aguas Calientes; to get here, head back to the junction by the *Hotel Termas de Puyehue* and then along the international road to Argentina, a pretty stretch with lakes on either side, though mind the potholes. You'll find a number of short **hikes** around the Conaf station, and across the road from the campground, the *cabañas* and the *hostería*; the prettiest is the 850-metre walk to El Salto del Indio (CH$1000), a half-hour loop through a forest of ancient coigüe to some thundering **waterfalls** amidst dense greenery. From the Conaf side, a 1.3km track leads to the single gushing fall of Salto de Pudú, while from the other side of the office, an easy 1.5km ramble leads you to the Miradór del Puma, where you get a great view of Salto Anticura and the Volcán Puyehue beyond. More adventurous is the 50-kilometre trail that goes to Antillanca, part of the Sendero de Chile. The track is well-maintained and signposted and runs through lush ulmo, coigüe and lenga forest, skirting the eastern flank of Volcán Casablanca, affording great views of the neighbouring volcanoes. Some parts of the trail are quite steep, though not technical, and shouldn't present any difficulties to reasonably fit hikers. Halfway along, on the Pampa Frutilla, the trail passes by two pretty little lagoons harbouring a wealth of waterfowl. The trail starts behind the Conaf office in Anticura and takes approximately two days to complete. Another adventurous hike is the 22-kilometre return trail to Volcán Puyehue, which starts 2km west of Anticura, opposite a church, where there's a small Conaf office. The beginning of the path passes over some private property, where you'll have to pay CH$8000 to cross the land either on foot or you can arrange for a guide and horses (El Caulle Expediciones ☎09/641 2000, ⓦwww.elcaulle.com). The fee entitles you to use the basic refuge, which sleeps sixteen; it's a three-hour walk along the trail from the Conaf office. Shortly past the refuge, the trail forks: the right-hand route goes up the volcano for 6km (2hr; no special equipment needed), and from the crater there are views over Lagos Puyehue and Rupanco. The left-hand path leads to a thermal spring next to an icy stream, half a day's walk from the refuge. You can mix the waters and bathe – an amazing experience at night, cooking yourself gently in the waters underneath the stars.

Park practicalities

The only places to stay or eat in the park are at the ski centre, the refuges, the campsite, *cabañas* and hostel in the Anticura section, run by the Mapuche Nalay Mapu community (☎09/259 6770; camping ②) hostel (③); *cabañas* (③) and the *Hotel Termas de Puyehue* and the Aguas Calientes complex. Expresos Lago Puyehue runs numerous daily **buses** from Osorno to Aguas Calientes between 7am and 7pm; two departures daily may continue to Anticura if there is sufficient demand (minimum three people). There is no public transport to Antillanca, but in winter the Club Osorno Andino (☎64/232297) runs between Osorno and the ski area.

The Chilean customs post, Pajaritos (daily: May to mid-Oct 9am–7pm; mid-Oct to April 8am–9pm) is 4km down the road from Anticura, and the Argentine border post, Paso Cardenal Samore, is 44km beyond it.

Lago Llanquihue and around

An immense inland sea of 870 square kilometres, **LAGO LLANQUIHUE** boasts a backdrop for one of the icons of the Lake District, the Mount Fuji-like **Volcán Osorno** (2661m), in all its stunning, symmetrical perfection, surrounded by gently rolling pastures scattered with black and white Friesian cows. The easiest way here from Parque Nacional Puyehue is to travel back to Osorno and then down the Panamericana – you'll spot the lake from the road.

The little villages around Lago Llanquihue have a shared German heritage, but differ greatly in character. **Frutillar Bajo**, on the lake's western shore, is a summer holiday resort beloved by Chileans; **Puerto Octay**, to the north, is a neat little Bavarian-looking town; and **Puerto Varas**, a bustling adventure tourism centre to rival Pucón.

By the time you come to the village of **Ensenada**, on the far eastern shore of the lake, forest has overtaken dairy fields and the land begins to rise as you enter the foothills of the Andes. This forest extends to the border, and is protected by the **Parque Nacional Vicente Pérez Rosales**. The national park is a favourite scenic route into Argentina via the magical green waters of **Lago Todos Los Santos**.

South of Ensenada the road winds its way down through isolated country to the placid calm of Chile's northernmost **fjord**, a branch of the Estuario de Reloncaví. Here you can horse-trek into South America's oldest rainforest – the famous alerce groves found in the valleys above the village of **Cochamó**.

Frutillar Bajo

The Panamericana first approaches Lago Llanquihue at Frutillar Alto, 4km west of **FRUTILLAR BAJO**. Up until the 1980s, apartheid divided Frutillar, with Frutillar Bajo reserved for the German-Chilean population and the mestizo population restricted to Frutillar Alto, forbidden to use the lower town's beaches. That has all changed now, and because it's so popular it gets very crowded here in summer, especially during the last week of January to the first week of February, when the town hosts a **classical music festival** (Ⓦwww .semanasmusicales.cl).

Frutillar Bajo's two main streets, Vicente Pérez Rosales and Avenida Philippi, both run parallel to the coast; most services are located on Philippi. At the bottom of the hill leading from Frutillar Alto, near the junction with Vicente Pérez Rosales, is a beautifully tended garden, an old water mill and several other traditional wooden buildings that make up the worthwhile **Museo Colonial Alemán** (daily: summer 10am–7.30pm; winter Tues–Sun 10am–1.30pm & 3– 6pm; CH$2500). The museum houses a wide variety of household objects and farm machinery used by the earliest immigrants to Llanquihue, but most interesting is a circular barn (*campanario*) outside, that houses a collection of early agricultural machinery. Inside, pairs of horses were once tethered to the central pillar and driven round in circles, threshing sheaves of corn with their hoofs. Further up the hill in the **Casa del Herrero**, the blacksmith's house, you can buy horseshoes with your name stamped on them, and higher up still is the reconstruction of a typical early farmhouse filled with period furniture and decorated with old family photos.

If you cross over the main road by the museum and turn left at the end of Vicente Pérez Rosales, you'll come to a dirt road that leads to the **Reserva Forestal Edmundo Winckler** (Jan–Feb daily 9am–7pm; March–Dec Mon–Sat 9am–4pm; CH$1000), a peaceful detour. Hemmed in by low hills, in an area of perfectly preserved native forest, is an experimental forestry station set up by the Universidad Austral de Chile. An 800m trail loops through the forest, with species of trees, flowers and shrubs labelled along the way.

Practicalities

You'll **arrive** in Frutillar Alto, not Frutillar Bajo, unless you've caught one of the summer minibuses that run directly here from Puerto Montt and Puerto Varas. From Frutillar Alto, you can walk the 4km down to the lakeshore or catch one of the *colectivos* that operate shuttle services (CH$400) along the main street, Carlos Richter. In Frutillar Bajo there's a lakefront **tourist information office**, on Avenida Philippi and O'Higgins (Dec–March daily 9am–9pm; ☎65/420198, ⓦwww.frutillarsur.cl).

Accommodation along the lakeside gets booked up well in advance. *Hospedaje Nohelia*, Philippi 615 (☎65/421310; ❸), offers basic rooms with private bath in a restored old wooden home in front of the lake. The friendly hostess serves a big German-style breakfast. *Hostería Winkler*, Philippi 1155 (☎65/421388; ❹), has cosy, well-maintained double rooms with superb views of the lake; cable TV and free breakfast are included. The newly refurbished *Hotel Frau Holle* at Varas 54 (☎65/421201; ❻) is an attractive colonial house overlooking the lake from a small hill, with superb views, tasteful rooms and a friendly hostess. A short distance from the lake, *Cabañas Edelweiss* at 21 de Mayo 85 (☎65/421573 ⓔedelweiss@surnet .cl; ❸–❹) is a good deal for groups: each of the tidy *cabañas* decorated with deer horns comes fully equipped for five people.

Six kilometres north, in a sheltered bay off the road to Puerto Octay, is the *Playa Maqui Lodge* (☎65/330000, ⓔplayamaquilodge@willnet.cl; ❸). This large, traditional house, built in 1880, sits amid native woods and offers a tranquil escape from the hubbub in town, various outdoor excursions and hearty German-style breakfast.

There's no shortage of places to **eat** in Frutillar; *onces* (afternoon tea) is almost an obligatory ritual. You'll find several cafés along Philippi where you can partake in this custom; one of the best is the *Salón de Té Trayén*, Philippi 963, a good spot to sit and soak up the calories and the views. For reasonably priced set lunches, head for *Tierra del Fuego*, Philippi 1065, in the old Art Deco fire station. Frutillar's *Club Alemán*, at Philippi 741, has excellent service and tasty set lunches; the traditional à la carte menu offers a mixture of German and Chilean dishes. *El Ciervo*, at San Martín 64, is one of the best places to eat in town, delighting the palate with its smoked meats and well-executed game dishes, while the bakery attached to the *hostería Winkler* offers excellent *kuchen*.

Buses leave Frutillar Alto for Puerto Montt every ten minutes, operated by Thaebus (San Pedro 255 ☎65/420120); several buses daily run to Puerto Octay. Cruz del Sur (☎65/421552), Alessandri and Portales, and Tur-Bus (☎65/421390), Diego Portales 150, serve long-distance destinations along the Panamericana.

Puerto Octay and around

Thirty kilometres northeast of Frutillar, around Lago Llanquihue, lies **PUERTO OCTAY**, a friendly little town by the lakeshore, nestling in the crook of some hills. With its needle-steepled church and balconied houses with ornate eaves, it looks as though it's been transplanted to Chile from the Alps. Puerto Octay was the first settlement on Lago Llanquihue and dates from 1852. The town developed into an important port in the days of the lake steamer, and today it's the municipal centre for a vast territory stretching up to Lago Rupanco in the north.

If you're interested in the history of the village, the small and well-organized Museum "El Colono", on the second floor of the 1920 Casa Niklitschek, at Independencia 591 (Dec–Feb Tues–Sun 10am–1pm & 3–7pm; CH$500) focuses on German colonization and is filled with musical instruments, tableware and old photographs. There are plenty of old agricultural machines and stills for making the sweet alcoholic *chicha* drink, a local speciality.

Practicalities

You can reach Puerto Octay from Osorno on Buses Vía Octay, which runs hourly. There are six buses a day from Frutillar and Puerto Montt. Puerto Octay's **Oficina Municipal de Turismo** (Dec–Feb daily 9am–9pm; ☎64/391491, ⓦwww.puertooctay.cl) is next door to the Municipalidad on the Plaza de Armas, and staffed by garrulous volunteers.

As for **accommodation**, Puerto Octay has the atmosphereic *Hotel Haase* at Pedro Montt 344 (☎64/391302, ⓦwww.hotelhaase.cl; ❸), with spacious rooms and a resturant offering hearty meals inside one of Puerto Octay's oldest and most beautiful houses (1894). The posh hotel *Hotel y Cabañas Centinela* (☎64/391326, ⓦwww.hotelcentinela.cl; ❼) on the end of Península Centinela, 5km from Octay, decorated in its original 1913 "High Bavarian" style, boasts spacious, attractive rooms and plush *cabañas* for four-six people with superb lake views. *Zapato Amarillo*, 2.5km north of Puerto Octay (☎64/391575, ⓦwww.zapatoamarillo.cl; doubles ❹, dorm ❷), a destination in itself as much as lodging, has a homely main lodge with grass roof and wooden interior, while an eight-bed dorm, kitchen and communal area are in a separate building. Meals served in the main house include a sumptuous cheese fondue. They also have canoe, bike, sailing boat and climbing gear rentals, internet access and free pick-up in town; the owners speak German and English and can organize a series of excursions to Vicente Pérez Rosales National Park, to Volcán Osorno, or around Lake Rupanco.

For **eating**, the expensive and highly acclaimed restaurant at *Hotel Centinela* serves up fantastic steaks and seafood. Cheaper alternatives in town include *El Fogón de Anita*, on the northern edge of town, one kilometre along the road to Osorno, which serves well-prepared *parrilladas*. Three kilometres out of Puerto Octay on the road to Frutillar is *Tante Valy*, a reasonably priced and very typical German style tea house with cakes (*kuchen*) and tea.

The northern shore

The gravel road continues around Lago Llanquihue, passing beaches, fields and the seemingly deserted villages of **Puerto Fonck** (20km) and **Puerto Klocker** (29km). This was the part of the area that was first settled, and it was here in 1852 that 21 German families were allocated plots to farm. Shortly after Puerto Klocker, there's a turning to the east that leads 20km up the northern slope of Volcán Osorno to an unserviced **refuge** called *La Picada*, but the main road continues around the lake for 36km to **Las Cascadas**, a quiet village with an attractive beach, a couple of houses, a *hospedaje* and a *carabineros* checkpoint; you can camp at the beachfront *Camping Las Cascadas*, with shaded sites and hot showers (CH$6000 per site). Beyond here the scenery changes as the recently paved section of the road narrows and ploughs into dense scrub and forest. The fields have gone, and through the trees you catch glimpses of the volcano towering above you, no longer picturesque but menacing. Beneath the volcano, 4km south of Las Cascadas and 15km north of Ensenada, is **Canopy Lodge** (℡65/300922, Ⓦwww.canopychile.cl; ➎), with ten *cabañas*, a restaurant and a pub. Set amid native forest, this was the first company in Chile to set up a canopy tour for visitors to explore the forest suspended from wires, high above the ground. The exhilarating tours last 2–3 hours and are well worth the CH$25,000. Horse-riding and fishing excursions are also offered. Nineteen kilometres after Las Cascadas, deep in the forest, there's a turning to the east heading up the slopes of Volcán Osorno (see p.342) shortly before you arrive in Ensenada.

Ensenada

Two kilometres before the Ensenada crossroads, you'll pass a local beauty spot. From a car park, a signpost directs visitors to a ten-minute walk through the trees to **Laguna Verde**, an attractive pond near the edge of a lake. Almost immediately after the Laguna Verde car park, the road breaks clear of the forest and you arrive in **ENSENADA**, a small village in a lovely location on the shores of the lake, with a smattering of *hospedajes*, campsites and restaurants stretching pretty much all the way to Puerto Varas. There are some good **accommodation** and eating options here, starting with the venerable *Hotel Ensenada* (℡65/212028, Ⓦwww .hotelensenada.cl; ➐), which has been around for a hundred years and looks like the kind of stylish place that Bonnie and Clyde might have settled down at, with lots of colonial German antiques and large, well-appointed rooms, some with shared bathroom. The restaurant serves simple Chilean fare. The luxurious resort ⚓ *Yan Kee Way Lodge* (℡65/212030, Ⓦwww.yankeewaylodge.com; ➒), at Km 42, hidden away in a beautiful lakeside location, specializes in fly-fishing excursions but also offers a variety of hiking, biking, and boating excursions for non-fishing guests. The resort consists of exclusive *cabañas*, and their restaurant, *Latitud 42°*, is counted amongst the Lake District's finest. Featuring a comprehensive wine list, its impeccable service is complemented by the perfectly executed fusion dishes make from local and organic ingredients only. Non-guests are welcome. For more gourmet dining, try the smoked salmon and traditional *asado* (Chilean barbeque) at the ever-popular *Restaurant Las Tranqueras* on Route 225, Km 41 (℡65/212056). *Cabañas Brisas del Lago* (℡65/212012, Ⓦwww.brisasdellago.cl; ➏) comprises fully-equipped 6-person chalets; the beautiful excellent lakeside and proximity to several good restaurants make this an ideal option for groups. Lovers of the great outdoors may prefer to stay at the ideally located *Camping Montaña* (℡65/212088), not far from the crossroads, with excellent beach access and plenty of facilities, including reliably hot showers.

There are frequent **buses** running to Ensenada from Puerto Varas and Puerto Montt, most continuing on to Petrohué; every half an hour on weekdays; somewhat fewer on weekends.

Parque Nacional Vicente Pérez Rosales and around

PARQUE NACIONAL VICENTE PÉREZ ROSALES (daily: April–Nov 9am–6pm; Dec–March 9am–8pm; CH$1500), Chile's first national park, was established in 1926, and covers an area of 2,510 square kilometers. It is divided

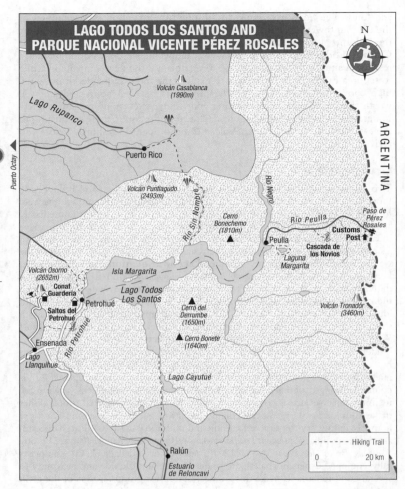

LAGO TODOS LOS SANTOS AND
PARQUE NACIONAL VICENTE PÉREZ ROSALES

N

ARGENTINA

Lago Rupanco

Volcán Casablanca
(1990m)

Puerto Rico

Volcán Puntiagudo
(2493m)

Río Sin Nombre

Cerro
Bonechemo
(1810m)

Río Negro

Río Peulla

Paso de
Pérez
Rosales

Peulla

Customs
Post

Cascada de
los Novios

Volcán Osorno
(2652m)

Conaf
Guardería

Isla Margarita

Lago Todos
Los Santos

Laguna
Margarita

Petrohué

Cerro del
Derrumbe
(1650m)

Volcán Tronadór
(3460m)

Saltos del
Petrohué

Ensenada

Río Petrohué

Cerro Bonete
(1640m)

Lago
Llanquihue

Lago Cayutué

Ralún

Estuario
de Reloncaví

- - - - - Hiking Trail

0   20 km

into three sectors: Sector Osorno, Sector Petrohue and Sector Peulla, and comprises some of the most sensational scenery in the Lake District: the emerald Lago Todos Los Santos, the thundering turquoise waters of the Saltos de Petrohué, and the imposing peaks of the area's main volcanoes: Osorno, Tronador and Puntiagudo. Coupled with the fact that this vast chunk of wilderness provides endless hiking opportunities, it's little wonder that this park is the most visited in the whole of Chile. If you are planning to do any extensive hikinig in the park, you will find it useful to have a copy of the excellent **map** published by JLM, *Ruta de los Jesuitas (No.15)*, available in Puerto Varas and Puerto Montt.

Volcán Osorno

From the turnoff just short of Ensenada, a newly paved 14km road leads up **VOLCÁN OSORNO**. The higher you climb, the more capricious the weather becomes; take care when driving around the hairpin bends due to sudden gusts of ferocious wind. About halfway up the slope you'll come across the signposted Sendero El Solitario (6km; 2hr) leading east through dense forest before emerging on the road to Petrohué, about 1km away from the Saltos de Petrohué. You'll also pass three worthwhile *miradores* along the way, each offering sweeping views of the surrounding area. The best view, however, is from the Conaf station at the top: to the west you can see across Lago Llanquihue, the central plain and across to the sea, and dominating the skyline to the south are the jagged peaks of Volcán Calbuco, which erupted spectacularly in 1893, ripping its summit apart and hurling rocks all the way to the coast. Up here, keeping Conaf company are two *refugios*: the renovated *La Burbuja*, owned by the *Centro de Ski & Montaña Volcán Osorno* (☎65/235114), and the *Refugio Teski Ski Club* (☎09/262 3323), a rustic hut pegged out with wires to prevent it from taking off, with bunkrooms (CH$8000 per person) and a cosy little café with vibrant photographs of Volcán Osorno's deep-blue ice caves. The *Centro de Ski & Montaña Volcán Osorno* has two chairlifts and seven runs open to skiers, though this isn't a skiing destination in the same vein as Portillo near Santiago, but rather a novelty to try while in the area.

You can climb the volcano from *La Burbuja*. It's about five hours to the summit (two to the snowline, three more to the top), and there are many crevasses, so ice equipment is needed and a guide mandatory. Conaf authorizes several companies to guide people up, including AquaMotion and Al Sur (see Puerto Varas, p.349). The strenuous climb is worth it for the views alone.

Petrohué and around

The **Saltos de Petrohué** (daily: summer 8.30am–9pm; winter 9am–6pm; CH$1500), a series of impressive waterfalls formed by an extremely hard layer of lava that has been eroded into small channels by the churning water, lie 10km northeast of Ensenada, off a gravel road that leads through dense forest. Los Enamorados and Carilemu are two marked **nature trails** which make for a pleasant ramble through native flora, while Sendero Saltos leads you straight to the falls.

▲ Volcán Osorno

The volcanic rock in the area was part of a tongue of lava sent this way by Volcán Osorno in 1850, an eruption that diverted the Petrohué River from its old course into Lago Llanquihue. As you drive alongside the river, areas of regenerating forest are clearly visible, and every spring sections of the road are washed away when rain and snow-melt pour down the flanks of the volcano. At the end of the road lies **LAGO TODOS LOS SANTOS**, deep green and stunningly clear, one of the most beautiful in the Lake District – it's also known as Lago Esmeralda (Emerald Lake) because of the intense colour of its water. The lake and the forests that crowd its shores are protected by the Parque Nacional Vicente Pérez Rosales. On the other side of the lake is a road that leads to the Argentine border. This route was first used as a border crossing by Jesuit missionaries in the seventeenth century, in their attempts to convert the Tehuelche Indians on the pampas. The lake's now a twisting, turning, flooded valley, with forested banks and a sense of isolation in the jagged, pine-forested hills.

The sleepy hamlet of **PETROHUÉ** sits on the western shore of Lago Todos Los Santos. The settlement dates from the early twentieth century, when one Ricardo Roth began taking tourists across the lakes between Puerto Varas and Bariloche, a venture that led to the construction of two hotels – *Petrohué* and *Peulla* – and the foundation of Andina del Sud tour company.

In Petrohué you will find a Conaf **Centro de Educación Ambiental** (erratic opening hours), and an attractive black-sand **Playa Larga** – the start of two good hiking trails. A pleasant 5km trail runs along the lakeshore, while **Sendero Los Alerzales** makes for a two-hour (6km) enjoyable hike through dense local forest, at one point crossing over the **Sendero Paso Desolación** which climbs up the northeast side of Volcán Osorno to a height of 1,100m – from where you get a fantastic view of Volcán Tronador and the lake below. Another pleasant five-kilometre walk follows the western shore of the lake, joining the Sendero Los Alerzales at the end of it.

To reach the trailheads of the longer trails, you'll need to rent a **boat** from the dock at Petrohué (CH$45,000–50,000 for up to six people) to get to the starting point. The first trail, the 18km **Termas de Callao** (approximately 11hr), starts from the northern shores of the lake by the Río Sin Nombre (No-Name River). Head up the river – the path is reasonably clear but be sure to always head upwards to the source – and after about three hours of climbing you reach the namesake hot springs and a basic refuge. From here you can either go back down to Lago Todos Los Santos, having asked the boatman to pick you up again, or carry on up to the Laguna Los Quetros and over the pass – another two hours' hike – and then descend to Lago Rupanco, which takes another three hours. From the shores of Lago Rupanco, it's about another hour (west) to Puerto Rico, from where there are buses to Osorno. Sometimes there's a boat-taxi waiting at the point where the trail reaches Lago Rupanco, to take you to the bus stop.

Another picturesque hike of similar length leaves from **Cayutué**, a fishing village down a channel, on the south shore of the lake, and follows the missionaries' route south to Ralún on the Estuario de Reloncaví, passing the tranquil Laguna Cayutué along the way. It's an easy walk along a heavily rutted logging road.

Check with Conaf regarding trail conditions before attempting the longer hikes and avoid wearing dark clothing when hiking, or else you risk attracting the local biting **horseflies** (*tábanos*).

On the edge of Lago Todos Los Santos stands the *Hotel Petrohué* (T65/212025, W www.petrohue.com ❻) with comfortable rooms and four comfortable lakeside *cabañas* that sleep up to four people (❻); full board includes one daily activity, such as rafting, and internet reservations get a ten per cent discount. The Conaf-run *Camping Playa Petrohué* on the beach costs CH$7000 for up to five people. You can also stay in *Hospedaje Küschel* (☎65/277832; ❷) across the river – either in a basic room in the farmhouse, or you can camp (CH$3000 per tent); their smoked trout is delicious. **Buses** JM runs daily to Petrohué from Puerto Montt via Puerto Varas, every thirty minutes or so, less frequently on Sundays.

Andina del Sud offers **tours** on the lake, which provide unsurpassed views of Volcán Osorno, the spiked peak of Volcán Puntiagudo, and highest of all, the glacier-covered Monte Tronador. Day excursions to **PEULLA**, at the far end of the lake, leave at 10.30am (CH$30,000 per person, including transportation from Puerto Varas or Puerto Montt or CH$22,000 from Petrohue). At Peulla, there's little except the border post (daily: Jan–March 8am–9pm; April–Dec 8am–8pm) and the *Hotel Peulla* (☎65/972116, ⓦwww.hotelpeulla.cl; ❽), a refurbished large old wooden building with comfortable rooms and a good, if overpriced, restaurant. Those staying overnight have time to do the moderately difficult yet rewarding 8km climb to **Laguna Margarita** (4hr) or take a stroll to the beautiful **Cascada de Los Novios** waterfall nearby. Argentine customs is 23km east, at Laguna Frías.

The Estuario de Reloncaví

On the way back to Ensenada from Parque Nacional Vicente Pérez Rosales, a southern fork, 1km before the town of Ensenada, will take you 33km along a good road, fringed with large bushes of wild fuchsia and giant rhubarb plants, to the tranquil **ESTUARIO DE RELONCAVÍ**. The fjord, now packed with salmon farming operations, is a good place to escape and unwind or to horse-trek into the **Cochamó Valley**, home to the oldest standing trees in South America. Your first view of the bay comes as you descend to **Ralún**, a village with a couple of stores, the rustic Termas de Ralún across the river (rowboat return CH$4000) and frequent buses to Puerto Montt. The bay is an amazing colour – bright green from one angle, deepest blue from another – and at the far end, standing sentinel over the fjord's exit, is Volcán Yate (2111m).

Ralún sits near the junction of two roads; the road west of the fjord leads to a hydroelectric project, passing the edge of the Parque Nacional Alerce Andino. The other road, along the east side of the fjord, goes through wild, dramatic scenery, with waterfalls crashing underneath snow-capped mountains. This is the beginning of the landscape of the **Carretera Austral**, a pioneering expansion into Southern Chile (see Chapter 8), and there are unmapped trails through virgin forests in these mountains ready to be explored by the adventurous. Many of these trails lead to Argentina, and throughout history the low passes in this area have been used by bandits, missionaries and merchants to crisscross the Andes. One of the most frequently trodden trails into Argentina starts at Puelo, the village at the end of this road, and eventually leads to El Bolsón on the other side of the cordillera.

After 14km, the road reaches **Cochamó**, a beautiful little fishing village flanked with pine-clad hills, which makes a good base for exploring the valley. On the seafront, *Residencial Edicar* (☎65/216526; ❸) has clean rooms with shared bathroom, breakfast included. There's also the small and rustic *Hotel Cochamó*, Catedral 19 (☎65/216212; ❸), with basic rooms, often full of salmon farmers. The best place to stay, however, is the adventure tourism complex *Campo Aventura Eco-Lodge* (Oct–May 15; ☎65/232910, ⓦwww.campo-aventura .com; ❺), 5km south of the village, specializing in multi-day horse-trekking in the Cochamó Valley, hiking, rafting on Río Petrohue and kayaking on the Reloncaví Fjord. Their *La Mesa de los Sabores* restaurant cooks up excellent vegetarian and fish dishes.

Buses Fierro runs several services daily from Puerto Montt to Cochamó via Ralún between 8.15am and 5pm.

Puerto Varas

If you double back to Lago Llanquihue, from Ensenada an excellent tarred road along Lago Llanquihue's southern shore after 47km brings you to **PUERTO VARAS**, a spruce little town with wide streets, grassy lawns and exquisite views of two volcanoes, Osorno and Calbuco. Like Pucón, the reason you come to Puerto Varas is because it's a prime location for all manner of outdoor activities.

Arrival and information

Most long-distance buses pull in at Del Salvador 1093, a couple of blocks away from the town's compact grid centre, with Pullman Bus stopping more centrally

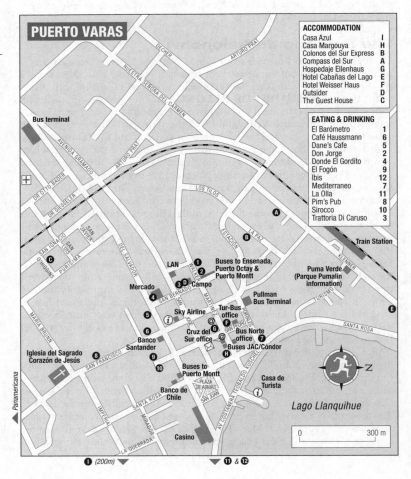

PUERTO VARAS

ACCOMMODATION
Casa Azul	I
Casa Margouya	H
Colonos del Sur Express	B
Compass del Sur	A
Hospedaje Ellenhaus	G
Hotel Cabañas del Lago	E
Hotel Weisser Haus	F
Outsider	D
The Guest House	C

EATING & DRINKING
El Barómetro	1
Café Haussmann	6
Dane's Cafe	5
Don Jorge	2
Donde El Gordito	4
El Fogón	9
Ibis	12
Mediterraneo	7
La Olla	11
Pim's Pub	8
Sirocco	10
Trattoria Di Caruso	3

Bus terminal

Train Station

LAN

Buses to Ensenada, Puerto Octay & Puerto Montt

Puma Verde (Parque Pumalín information)

Mercado

Campo

Pullman Bus Terminal

Sky Airline

Tur-Bus office

Cruz del Sur office

Bus Norte office

Buses JAC/Cóndor

Banco Santander

Iglesia del Sagrado Corazón de Jesús

Buses to Puerto Montt

Banco de Chile

Casa de Turista

Casino

Lago Llanquihue

0   300 m

Panamericana

(200m)

11 & 12

at Portales 318. The efficient **minibuses** that connect Puerto Varas to Ensenada, Petrohué, Frutillar and Puerto Octay stop at a bus shelter at San Bernardo 240, opposite the Esso petrol station, while the Puerto Montt ones also use a shelter in Del Salvador between San Pedro and Santa Rosa. For tourist information, head to **Casa del Turista** on the wharf, Piedraplén s/n, Muelle de Puerto Varas (Feb–Nov daily 9am–1.30pm & 3–7pm, Dec–March daily 9am–10pm; ☎65/237956, ⓦwww.puertovaras.org). **Informatur**, at San José and Santa Rosa (daily: Jan–March 9am–10pm; April–Dec Mon–Sat 9am–2pm & 3–8pm; ☎65/338542, ⓦwww.informatur.com) offers basic info but is often closed in the off-season.

Accommodation

🎄 *Casa Azul* Manzanal 66 at Rosario ☎65/232904, ⓦwww.casaazul.net. Plenty of young international travellers stay at this popular spot, which has smallish rooms. There's a reading room, free internet access, a kitchen, garden and terrace, as well as excellent breakfast with home-made muesli (CH\$2500). Private rooms ❹; dorms ❷

Casa Margouya Santa Rosa 318 ☎65/237640, ⓦwww.margouya.com. Smack in the centre, this vibrant, 24hr hostel is a great spot to meet other travellers. You also get free use of the kitchen, a laundry service and a book exchange. The helpful owners speak English and French and can advise on or arrange all sorts of outdoor activities around the area. ❷–❸

Colonos del Sur Express Estación 505 ☎65/637000, ⓦwww.colonosdelsur.cl. A cheaper sister hotel to the exclusive beachfront accommodation (currently undergoing refurbishment); the spotless three-storey colonial house looms over the centre and has an outdoor pool with panoramic views. ❻

Compass del Sur Klenner 467 ☎65/232044, ⓦwww.compassdelsur.cl. A large traditional house popular with international travellers, with a large kitchen, shared or private rooms, internet access and basic breakfast. The helpful staff can arrange all manner of excursions. ❸–❹

🎿 **Hospedaje Ellenhaus** Walker Martínez 239 ☎65/233577, ⓦwww.ellenhaus.cl. Popular labyrinthine guesthouse with a range of dorms and rooms, with and without bathrooms. German spoken, tours arranged, wi-fi available;

breakfast CH\$1500 extra. A bargain for its central location. ❷–❸

Hotel Cabañas del Lago Pasaje Luis Wellmann 195 ☎65/232291, ⓦwww.hotelcabanasdellago.cl. The plushest hotel in town with a spa overlooking the lake, numerous treatments available, as well as a swimming pool, comfortable rooms equipped with cable TV and wi-fi, and excellent buffet breakfast. ❽

Hotel Weisser Haus San Pedro 252 ☎65/346479. This comfortable German-run hotel stands out due to its extremely helpful service; mid-sized en-suite rooms have cable TV and wi-fi and the German-style breakfast is a bonus. ❻

Outsider San Bernardo 318 ☎65/232910, ⓦwww.turout.com. Excellent little bed and breakfast that offers simple rooms (some with internet), strong showers and storage facilities, all atop the helpful Campo Aventura Tour Operator (see box, p.349) on the ground floor. The staff know the area well and can arrange tours; German and English spoken. ❺

The Guest House Santa Rosa 318 ☎65/232240, ⓦwww.vicki-johnson.com. Beautifully restored mansion, with eight big, sunny rooms, owned by a California transplant. Extras range from yoga and massage to internet access; no TVs. ❺

The Town

Puerto Varas is built on a long bay that curves from southeast to northwest, and the heart of town is clustered around a small pier to the northwest. The town's German colonial architecture gives it a European feel, and notable early-twentieth century private residences include **Casa Kuschel**, on Klenner 299 (1910), Casona Alemana (1914) at Nuestra Señora del Carmen 788 and Casa Angulo (1910) at Miraflores 96.

The thin strip of sandy beach at **Puerto Chico**, at the southeast end of Puerto Varas' long bay, is popular with locals in the summer. Nearby is the rebuilt and gaudy **Casino de Puerto Varas**, for gambling enthusiasts.

Lake crossing into Argentina

If you're Argentina-bound, **a lake crossing** between Puerto Varas and Bariloche allows you to experience the beauty of Chile's **Parque Nacional Vicente Perez Rosales**, and is an excellent alternative to a long bus journey. Starting out at 8am, you are first driven along the banks of Lago Llanquihue to **Petrohué,** before boarding the ferry that takes you across **Lago Todos Los Santos**, a spectacular expanse of clear blue-green. As you sail along the densely forested shores, skirting lovely Isla Margarita, the volcanoes Osorno (2660m) and Puntiagudo (2490m) loom to the north, with the majestic Tronador (3491m) to the east. After going through **Chilean customs** at Peulla, you then cross the Argentine border at **Paso Pérez Rosales**, and get stamped in at tiny Puerto Frías. At this point you'll board the ferry again for the short crossing of Laguna Frías, then transfer by bus to your final nautical leg of the journey – a boat across the stunningly beautiful **Lago Nahuel Huapi**, arriving at your destination around 9pm. At CH$170,000, crossing by lake is significantly pricier than a bus journey, but it's worth it. Book this popular trip in advance with **Turismo Peulla** (Ⓣ65/437127, Ⓦwww.turismopeulla.cl).

Eating and drinking

Barómetro Walker Martínez 584. A revamped pub and restaurant offering well-executed Chilean dishes as well as a wide range of beers, including Kunstmann. Open late. Mains CH$4500.

Café El Barista Walker Martínez 215. A great spot for people-watching, this trendy new café also serves large slices of tasty *kuchen*.

Dane's Café Del Salvador 441. Old-fashioned tea room that serves superb cakes and tarts, and also main meals. Open late.

Don Jorge San Bernardo 240. An unpretentious place popular with locals, with an emphasis on fish dishes. You can't go wrong with the *congrio* (conger eel) prepared in several different ways. Mains CH$4000.

Donde El Gordito San Bernardo 560, inside the market. Busy and popular little eatery serving large portions of inexpensive seafood. Try the *paila marina* (CH$3500).

El Fogón San Pedro 543. Tucked into a corner with a beautiful little garden, this popular newcomer is *the* place for excellent steak and outstanding *centolla* (king crab) dishes. Mains CH$7500.

Ibis Pérez Rosales 1117. Varied menu specializing in fresh seafood dishes served in inviting, contemporary surroundings, a little way along the coastal road.

Mediterráneo Santa Rosa 068. Enjoy Spanish tapas, pasta and tasty vegetarian dishes at this attractive lakefront restaurant with an outdoor deck. Fettucini with abalone is a standout dish (CH$6500).

Imperial 605 Imperial 605 Ⓣ65/233105, Ⓦwww.merlinrestaurant.cl. This renowned restaurant is widely hailed as one of the best in the Lake District and serves outstanding hybrid international cuisine; the fruit and seafood combinations work surprisingly well.

Pim's Pub San Francisco 712. In the summer this bar is packed with plenty of young adventure kayak types and their fans. You can chow on burgers and TexMex, but most come for the extensive list of potent drinks and the 2-for-1 happy hour specials (daily 6–10pm).

La Olla Pérez Rosales 1071. Upmarket and popular fish and seafood restaurant, 5km west of town, dishing up hearty portions of well-executed dishes. The *corvina* dishes In particular are excellent. Mains CH$6500.

Sirocco San Pedro 537. A fine new restaurant with excellent service, offering imaginative dishes made from local ingredients. Try the curried trout on squid Ink risotto. Mains CH$7000.

Trattoria Di Caruso San Bernardo 318. Tuck into the hearty lunch-time pasta specials at this informal Italian restaurant popular with locals.

Listings

Airlines LAN, Av Gramados 560 Ⓣ65/234799; Sky Airline, San Francisco 451.

Banks and exchange There are several banks with ATMs around the Plaza de Armas and along Del Salvador, including Banco de Chile, Del Salvador 210. For a *cambio*, try Inter, Del Salvador 257, Local 11 (in the Galería Real).

The main tours offered by the many companies in Puerto Varas are rafting on the Río Petrohué (grade 3 and 4; from CH$20,000 for a half-day); canyoning (climbing down precipices and waterfalls; CH$30,000 for a half-day); climbing Volcán Osorno (from CH$100,000); hiking in the Parque Nacional Vicente Pérez Rosales (from CH$95,000 for two days on the Termas de Callao trail – see p.344); and horse-riding, generally on the slopes of Volcán Calbuco, through old coigüe forest (from CH$35,000 for a half-day).

Al Sur Expediciones Aconcagua at Imperial ☎65/232300; ⓦwww.alsurexpeditions .com. A good company – one of those authorized by Conaf as guides on Volcán Osorno. In addition to the standard tours above, it offers sea-kayaking to the northern part of Parque Pumalín (CH$650,000 for a six-day trip; see p.386) and rafting trips on the Ríos Petrohué, Puelo and Futaleufú.

Andina del Sud Del Salvador 72 ☎65/232811, ⓦwww.cruceandino.com. Distinguished Lake District tour company which organizes 1–2 day lake crossings into Argentina via Lago Todos Los Santos (see box opposite).

AquaMotion San Francisco 328 ☎65/232747, ⓦwww.aqua-motion.com. A well-respected agent with German- and English-speaking guides, authorized by Conaf to guide up Volcán Osorno. Great for fishing trips but also for canyoning, trekking, horseriding, rafting, canoeing and canopy tours in the Lake District and beyond.

Campo Aventura San Bernardo 318 ☎65/232910, ⓦwww.campo-aventura.com. The place to go for horse-trekking, from one day to ten days into the foothills of Cochamó valley near the Estuario de Reloncaví (see p.345). Run by Lex Fautsch, who has developed a multilingual team. Customized options, like veggie meals, are available and canyoning and rafting are also among activities on offer.

Grayfly San José 192 ☎65/310734, ⓦwww.grayfly.com. Offers fishing trips on Lake Llanquihue or fly-fishing in Río Puelo with camping in the mountains. Custom trips are easily arranged.

Ko'kayak Ruta 225, Km 40, Casilla 896, Ensenada ☎09/310 5272, ⓦwww.kokayak .com. Excellent multilingual rafting and kayaking specialists who run half- to four-day rafting trips in the Lake District, as well as one- or three-day sea kayaking trips, with more challenging twelve-day expeditions to the southern fjords.

Pachamagua ☎09/208 3660, ⓦwww.pachamagua.com. A reliable and professional canyoning specialist arranging all-day, adrenalin-filled excursions; *Casa Margouya* can help organize tours.

Yak Expediciones ☎65/234409 or 09/299 6487, ⓦwww.yakexpediciones.cl. Long-standing operator running multi-day sea-kayaking adventures in Patagonia and beyond, including trips to the northern part of Parque Pumalín (see p.386).

Books El Libro del Capitán, Martínez 417, has a large selection of English and German books, as well as a book exchange.
Bus Buses JAC and Cóndor Bus, Walker Martínez 227-A; Cruz del Sur, Pullman Sur and Bus Norte, Walker Martínez 239-B and San Francisco 1317 ☎65/236969; Tas Choapa, Walker Martínez 230 ☎65/233831; Tur-Bus, San Pedro 210 and Del Salvador 1093 ☎65/233787; Intersur, Walker Martínez 227-B ☎65/236995; Pullman Bus, Portales 318 ☎65/234612.

Hospital Clínica Alemana, Otto Bader 810 ☎65/232336.
Internet *Cibernick*, Walker Martínez 317.
Post office San José 242 at San Pedro.
Shopping Vicki Johnson Fine Food & Gifts, Santa Rosa 318 ⓦwww.vicki-johnson.com, specializes in home-made chocolates and also carries sweaters, jewellery and art; she's a good source for local tips on travel and eating, too. The Feria Artesanal, in the park across from the Plaza de Armas and the Casino, on Del Salvador, features arts and crafts.

Puerto Montt and around

Seventeen kilometres south of Puerto Varas, the Panamericana approaches a large bay with snow-capped Volcán Calbuco and Volcán Osorno towering beyond – the Seno de Reloncaví. On its edge lies the administrative and commercial capital of the Lake District – **PUERTO MONTT**.

Puerto Montt is an important transportation hub, with buses to many Chilean and Argentinian destinations, a busy port, with a billion-dollar-a-year salmon farming industry, fishing and the embarkation point for the long-distance ferry trips. It's also a good place to stock up on supplies if heading south, or to catch up on the latest films at the multiplex cinema inside Mall Paseo del Mar.

Arrival and information

If you're arriving by **bus**, you'll pull in at the terminal, which is on the seafront (Av Portales s/n), six blocks west of the town centre. The **ferry terminal** is a further half-kilometre out of town, southwest towards the suburb of Angelmó. You can take one of the many cabs or *colectivos* that run along the *costanera* both towards the Plaza and towards Angelmó. El Tepual **airport** (T65/486200) is 13km northwest of Puerto Montt; flights are met by the ETM bus company, which will take you to the bus terminal for CH$1700. Puerto Montt's helpful **tourist information office** is on the southeastern corner of the Plaza de Armas (daily: mid-March–mid-Dec Mon–Fri 9am–6.30pm & Sat 9am–1pm; mid-Dec–mid-March 9am–9pm; T65/261823; Wwww.puertomonttchile.cl). Conaf's Patrimonio Silvestre office at Av Portales 1000, 4th floor (Mon–Fri 9am–4.30pm T65/486709) has information on visiting the Alerce Andino, Hornopirén and Vincente Pérez Rosales national parks.

Accommodation

Casa Perla Trigal 312 T65/262104, Wwww .casaperla.com. Simple rooms in a Chilean home packed with antiques and decorations. Pluses here include a garden, internet access and an English-speaking staff. Spanish lessons are available and breakfast is included. ❷–❸

Holiday Inn Express Avenida Costanera s/n, next to Mall Paseo del Mar T65/566000, Wwww .holidayinnexpress.cl. With excellent views of the Seno de Reloncaví, this modern hotel boasts spacious rooms, good shopping facilities next door, a fitness centre and sauna, as well as an excellent buffet breakfast and wi-fi access. ❼

Hospedaje Rocco Pudeto 233 T65/272897, Wwww.hospedajerocco.cl. Clean hostel run by an effusive Argentine hostess offering a dorm, double and quadruple rooms. Guests can use the kitchen and take advantage of the laundry service, internet access (pay extra) and the delicious breakfast. ❸

Hostal Pacífico Juan José Mira 1088 T65/256229, Wwww.hostalpacifico.cl.

This well-cared for, quiet property a short walk uphill from the bus terminal offers modern rooms with cable TV and private bath, friendly and helpful staff and parking. ❹

Hotel Don Luis Quillota 146 at Urmeneta T65/259001, Wwww.hoteldonluis.cl. This central hotel, part of the Best Western chain, offers spacious, comfortable rooms with all modern conveniences. Extras include a gym, sauna and a restaurant serving good fish dishes. ❼

Hotel O'Grimm Guillermo Gallardo 211 at Benavente T65/252845, Wwww.ogrimm.cl. The stone-clad entrance might put some off, but this is a comfortable modern hotel; its en-suite rooms all have Cable TV and wi-fi and there is a popular café/bar downstairs. ❻

Residencial Urmeneta Urmeneta 290 T65/253262. Central guesthouse with clean basic rooms (some windowless), some with shared bathroom, and a friendly hostess. Breakfast CH$2000 extra. ❸–❹

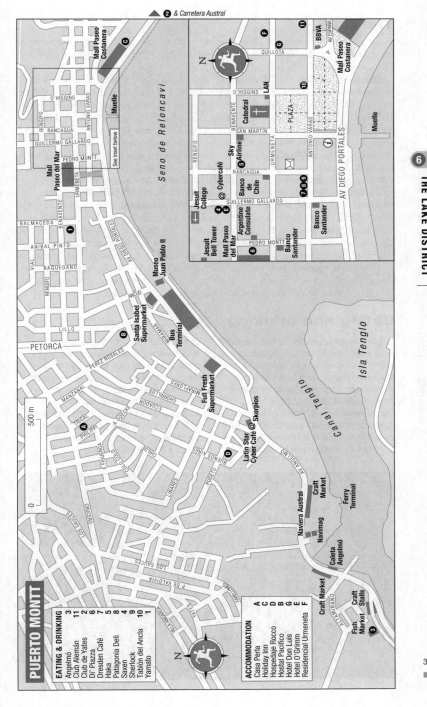

PUERTO MONTT

EATING & DRINKING

Angelmó	3
Club Alemán	11
Club de Yates	2
Di' Piazza	6
Dresden Café	7
Haka	5
Patagonia Deli	8
Saxen	4
Sherlock	9
Tablón del Ancla	10
Yamato	1

ACCOMMODATION

Casa Perla	A
Holiday Inn	C
Hospedaje Rocco	D
Hostal Pacifico	B
Hotel Don Luis	G
Hotel O'Grimm	E
Residencial Urmeneta	F

& Carretera Austral

Mall Paseo Costanera

Seno de Reloncaví

Muelle

See inset below

O'HIGGINS
RENGIFO
RANCAGUA
GUILLERMO GALLARDO
PEDRO MONTT

ANTONIO VARAS

Mall Paseo del Mar

BENAVENTE
URMENETA
BALMACEDA
ANIBAL PINTO
VIAL
BAQUEDANO
RENGIFO
LILLO
PETORCA

AV DIEGO PORTALES

Museo Juan Pablo II

Santa Isabel Supermarket

Bus Terminal

PEREZ ROSALES
MANZANAL
ECUADOR
CHORRILLOS
MIRAFLORES
BUENOS AIRES
PUERTO
CHILOE
EGECKE
EGUREROA
OGO
MELIPULLI
GUECHE
PHILIPPI
BRICAL
CRUCERO
LINARES

Full Fresh Supermarket

Latin Star Cyber Café @ Skorpios

AV ANGELMO

Naviera Austral

Navimag

Caleta Angelmó

Craft Market

Craft Market
Fish Market
Craft Stalls

Ferry Terminal

Canal Tenglo

Isla Tenglo

Muelle

AV DIEGO PORTALES

QUILLOTA
O'HIGGINS
BENAVENTE
SAN MARTIN
URMENETA
RANCAGUA
GUILLERMO GALLARDO
PEDRO MONTT

AV ESPANA
BBVA
Mall Paseo Costanera

LAN
Catedral
PLAZA
Sky Airline
@ Cybercafé
Banco de Chile
Banco Santander
Banco Santander

ANTONIO VARAS

Jesuit College
Argentine Consulate
Jesuit Bell Tower
Mall Paseo del Mar

6

THE LAKE DISTRICT

351

The City

Puerto Montt is strung out along the bay, with the central part of town located on a narrow flat bit along the main Avenida Diego Portales, with much of the city crowding the hills behind it.

Puerto Montt was founded by the same influx of German colonizers that settled Lago Llanquihue to the north, but very little is left of the old city. Next to the bus terminal on Portales 991 is Puerto Montt's museum, **Museo Juan Pablo II** (Mon–Fri 9am–6pm, Sat & Sun 10am–1pm, 2.30–6pm; CH$300). Built to commemorate the pope's visit in 1987, this museum now also has archaeology exhibits and dioramas of the oldest known human settlement of the Americas – **Monte Verde**, on the outskirts of Puerto Montt, where human tools found at the site date to 20,000 BC. This discovery in 1976 challenges the belief that human settlements started in the Bering Straits and migrated south.

A kilometre further west sits the neighbourhood of **ANGELMÓ**, where the *costanera* (coastal road) features an excellent **feria artesanal**, its myriad stalls with wooden and copper souvenirs, woven baskets and furniture, woollen clothing, and lapis lazuli jewellery. On the opposite side of the road are stalls selling country cheeses, honey, bottles of powerful *licor de oro* and strings of smoked shellfish.

Beyond the feria artesanal lies a thriving **fish market**. Angelmó is a combination of many fish retailers and various eateries operated by ebullient mothers and daughters who crowd around the cauldrons, tempting punters by lifting the lids off steaming vats of *curanto* (a seafood extravaganza with sausages).

Eating and drinking

Angelmó (by the fish market). By far the best spot for an inexpensive seafood meal, this collection of no-frills eateries serves up such goodies as *picorocos* (barnacles), *curanto*, *almejas* (razor clams), *erizos* (sea urchins) and *chupe de locos* (abalone chowder). Mains CH$3500.

Club Alemán Antonio Varas 264. An excellent old-fashioned restaurant with a German-influenced menu. Attentive waiters serve tasty dishes, including the enormous seafood platter for two.

Club de Yates Juan Soler Manfredini 200, Pelluco ℡65/284000. On a pier sticking out into the ocean, with a bright neon light on top, the *Club de Yates* is hard to miss. It is one of the best seafood restaurants in Puerto Montt – but expensive. Booking is advisable in the evenings.

Di' Piazza Montt 181. A busy spot popular with locals serving filling pasta dishes, thin-crust pizza and Chilean standards. The lunchtime *menú ejecutivo* (CH$2500) is a bargain.

▲ Puerto Montt feria artesanal

One of the main reasons people travel to Puerto Montt is to catch a **ferry** south. From Puerto Montt you can sail to Chaitén and Puerto Chacabuco on the Carretera Austral, the Laguna San Rafael far in the southern fjords, and Puerto Natales in Patagonia. These ferry trips are almost always fully booked in summer, and you must **reserve ahead**.

The quality of your experience will largely depend on the weather. The seas on these ferry rides are usually calm, because most of the time the ferries are sailing through sheltered fjords, though it can still be windy. The exception is the trip to Puerto Natales, when the ship heads out to the Pacific across the often-turbulent Golfo de Penas. The trips are long, giving you plenty of opportunity to get to know the other passengers, whom you are bound to run into all over Patagonia, and the scenery is absolutely spectacular: wild forests, steep mountains, placid fjords and a wealth of marine life, especially further south.

Navimag Av Angelmó 2187 ℡65/270416, ⍟www.navimag.com. The busiest of Puerto Montt's ferry companies; it's recommended that you book ahead at least a month before travel. Within two weeks before travel, you must pay up front to secure a ticket. Navimag offers several standards of travel, ranging from Class C (a bunk with bedding, a locker for storage and a curtain for privacy; bring own towel) to Class AAA (own room with sea view, en-suite bathroom and private dining with the captain).

There are departures every three or four days to Puerto Chacabuco during peak season and Saturday departures to Laguna San Rafael; it costs from CH$280,000 to CH$950,000 round-trip from Puerto Montt to Laguna San Rafael (5 days, 4 nights), and CH$38,000 (berth) or CH$143,000 (cabin) one-way to Puerto Chacabuco (24hr); to transport a car costs an additional CH$135,000.

The most popular cruise heads all the way down to Puerto Natales; it costs from CH$340,000 to CH$1,660,000 (4 days, 3 nights; price includes full board and informative lectures), sailing from Puerto Montt on Mondays at 4pm and returning from Puerto Natales on Fridays at 6am. To transport a car it's CH$250,000.

Skorpios Av Angelmó 1660 ℡65/275646, ⍟www.skorpios.cl. Upmarket company running expensive, luxury cruises. The *Skorpios II* sails from Puerto Montt every Saturday on a seven-day/six-night journey to the San Rafael Glacier. Single/double cabins per person CH$1,850,000/1,230,000. The *Skorpios III* sails every Sunday from Puerto Natales on a five-day cruise through the fjords, taking in the Pio XI Glacier, among others. Single/double cabins CH$2,890,000/1,810,000.

Naviera Austral Av Angelmó 2187 ℡65/270430, ⍟www.navieraustral.cl. The short-distance *Don Baldo* and *Pincoya* sail to Chaitén on Mondays, Thursdays and Saturdays, usually at night, and from Chaitén to Puerto Montt on Mondays, Thursdays and Fridays, usually at 10am (check online schedule for updates and details); CH$21,500 one way (10hr), CH$86,000 per car. Bear in mind that you must have your own transport because government regulations currently do not allow visitors to stay in Chaitén overnight.

Dresden Café Antonio Varas 488. Attractive, pleasant coffee shop and deli, with sandwiches and generous wedges of cake, where you can watch the world go by.

Haka Rancagua 196 at Benavente. Lively pub-restaurant full of atmosphere that serves international grub and decent drinks, and also hosts live music. Good lunchtime *menú ejecutivo* (CH$3200).

Mall Paseo del Mar on the Costanera near the Plaza de Armas. Cheap Western-style fast food is found In various outlets in this food court, including *Doggis* (hot-dog meals), *Telepizza* and fried chicken.

Patagonian Deli Antonio Varas 486. Trendy, airy café with an extensive crêpe menu; popular spot for light meals and coffee.

Saxen Gallardo 237. Kunstmann beer and German-style meat dishes are on offer here, as well as *kuchen* and *crudos* (beef tartare). Mains CH$4000.

Sherlock Rancagua and Antonio Varas. Cheap Chilean staples including *lomito* and *barros jarpa* as well as good fish dishes are doled out in this atmospheric café-bar, which fills with locals in the evening.

Tablón del Ancla Antonio Varas and O'Higgins. This informal bar-restaurant has intimate booths and serves enormous, cheap sandwiches, burgers and fish and meat dishes. You can also order a three-litre tower of Kunstmann beer that comes with its own tap. The all-you-can-eat buffet on weekday nights (CH$6500; 8–10pm) is worth it.

Yamato Balmaceda 225. An unexpectedly decent Japanese restaurant, serving a good selection of sushi rolls and super-fresh sashimi.

Listings

Airlines LAN, O'Higgins 167 at Urmeneta ☎65/253002, ☎65/278172; SKY, San Martín 189 at Benavente ☎65/437555.
Banks and exchange AFEX, Av Diego Portales 516; La Moneda de Oro, Bus Terminal Oficina 37. There are many banks with ATMs along Antonio Varas and Urmeneta.
Bus The main bus terminal is on Diego Portales. All of the main companies have offices here, including Buses Norte Internacional ☎65/254731; Cruz del Sur is at Antonio Varas 437 ☎65/254731; Queilén Bus ☎65/253468; Pullman Bus ☎65/315561; Río de la Plata ☎65/253841; Tas Choapa ☎65/254828; Cóndor Bus ☎65/312123; Igi

Llaima ☎65/254519; Lit ☎65/254011; Via Bariloche ☎65/253841; Tur Bus ☎65/253329.
Car rental Budget, Antonio Varas 162 ☎65/286277; Hertz, A. Varas 126 ☎65/259585.
Hospital Hospital Regional, Seminario s/n ☎65/261134.
Internet *Latin Star Cyber Café*, Angelmó 1672; *Cybercafé*, Gallardo 218.
Shopping The best crafts are in Angelmó, where you can get a good selection of wood carvings, woollen goods and jewellery. Outdoor equipment is sold at the Mall Paseo Mar. The fish market is a good spot to pick up locally-smoked salmon.
Telephone centre Entel, Pedro Montt 75, Pedro Montt 114.

Travel details

Buses

Osorno to: Aguas Calientes, Puyehue (9 daily; 1hr); Bariloche, Argentina (every 2hr; 5hr plus border formalities); Panguipulli (6 daily; 2hr 30min); Puerto Montt (every 30min; 1hr 30min); Puerto Octay (every hour; 1hr); Puerto Varas (every 30min; 1hr); Santiago (every hour; 10hr); Temuco (every 30min; 3hr); Valdivia (every 30min; 1hr 30min); Coyhaique (4 weekly; 20hr).
Puerto Montt to: Ancud (every 30min; 2hr); Bariloche, Argentina (2 daily; 7hr 30min plus border formalities); Castro (every 30min; 3hr 30min); Frutillar (every 15min; 1hr); Osorno (every 30min; 1hr 30min); Pargua (every 30min; 1hr); Panguipulli (5 daily; 4hr); Puerto Varas (every 15min; 30min); Ralún (2 daily; 2hr 30min); Santiago (every 30min; 14hr); Temuco (every hour; 5hr); Valdivia (every 30min; 3hr); Coyhaique via Osorno (4 weekly; 24hr); Hornopirén (1 daily; 6hr); Futaleufú (1 weekly on Fri; 12hr).
Temuco to: Melipueco (8 daily; 2hr 30min); Osorno (every 30min; 3hr); Panguipulli (every hour; 2hr 30min); Pucón (every 30min; 2hr); Puerto Varas (every hour; 5hr 30min); Santiago (every 30min; 8hr 30min); Valdivia (every 30min; 2hr 30min); Villarrica (every 30min; 1hr 45min).
Valdivia to: Futrono (every 30min; 2hr 30min); Lago Ranco (every 30min; 3hr); Niebla (every

15min; 30min); Osorno (every 30min; 1hr 30min); Panguipulli (every hour; 2hr); Puerto Montt (every 30min; 3hr 30min); Puerto Varas (every 30min; 3hr); Santiago (every hour; 11hr); Temuco (every 30min; 2hr 15min).

Ferries

Puerto Montt to: Chacabuco (4 weekly; 24hr); Chaitén (1–2 weekly; 10hr); Laguna San Rafael (4 weekly, Dec–March; 4–5 days return); Puerto Natales (1–2 weekly; 4 days); Quellón (1–2 weekly; 6hr).

Flights

Osorno to: Santiago (4 daily; 2hr); Temuco (2 daily; 30min).
Puerto Montt to: Bariloche, Argentina (1 weekly; 2hr); Balmaceda/Coyhaique (3 daily; 1hr); Concepción (1 daily; 1hr 45min); Punta Arenas (3 daily; 2hr 10min); Santiago (8 daily; 1hr 30min); Temuco (2 daily; 45min).
Temuco to: Balmaceda (3 daily; 1hr); Osorno (2 daily; 30min); Puerto Montt (2 daily; 45min); Santiago (8 daily; 2hr); Valdivia (1 daily; 1hr 40min).
Valdivia to: Santiago (2 daily; 2hr); Temuco (1 daily; 45min).

Chiloé

✳ **Taste curanto** Dig into Chiloé's national dish, a savoury hotchpotch of meat, seafood and potatoes, traditionally cooked out in the open. See p.362

✳ **Chepu Valley** Explore this tranquil valley's sunken forest in a kayak at dawn, or go penguin-watching. See p.364

✳ **Palafitos in Castro** Slums or shrines? Insalubrious yet picturesque fishermen's houses on stilts, the last remaining in the country. See p.364

✳ **Isla Quinchao** A soothing spot to experience the slow pace of Chiloé's lesser isles. See p.370

✳ **Parque Nacional Chiloé** Explore the remains of the region's once vast forests by hiking its interior trails. See p.371

✳ **Chonchi** Chiloé's most attractive town is proud of its age-old customs celebrated in the Museo de las Tradiciones. See p.374

✳ **Parque Tantauco** A new private nature reserve offering access to pristine and remote corners of southern Chiloé. See p.376

▲ Palafitos in Castro

7

Chiloé

mmediately to the south of the Lake District, the already slim Chilean mainland narrows even further and the straight Pacific coastline splinters into a seemingly never-ending series of islands and inlets continuing all the way down to Cape Horn. The fascinating **CHILOÉ** archipelago, part of a mountain range that sank below the waves following the last Ice Age, is a haven of rural tranquillity. The main island, **Isla Grande**, is South America's second largest (the biggest being Tierra del Fuego). Flanked to the west by the Pacific Ocean, Isla Grande is separated from the Aisén province to the east by the Golfo de Ancud and is sliced in half lengthways by the Panamericana as it tears past the two main towns, **Ancud** and **Castro**, before culminating in the port of Quellón. Castro, the island's colourful capital, makes the best base for exploration. The ideal way to explore Chiloé is to drive or cycle along the islands' minor roads, though most parts of the archipelago are also serviced by regular buses. It's well worth heading west into the densely forested and almost pristine wilderness of **Parque Nacional Chiloé**, while the new protected area of **Parque Tantauco**, to the south of the island, offers even more opportunities to explore unique Chilote wilderness.

To Isla Grande's east are dozens of tiny islands, which are a veritable playground for sea kayakers, most of them uninhabited and practically unreachable. Of the 35 inhabited, the two largest and simplest to visit are **Isla Quinchao** and **Isla Lemuy**.

Chiloé was originally populated by the native Chonos and Huilliche (southern Mapuche), who eked out a living from fishing and farming before the Spanish took possession of the island in 1567. For over three hundred years, Chiloé was isolated from mainland Chile due to the fierce resistance of the Mapuche to European colonists. As a result, the slow pace of island life saw little change. Ancud was the last stronghold of the Spanish empire during the wars of Independence, before the final defeat by the pro-independence forces in 1826. In spite of being used as a stopover during the California Gold Rush, Chiloé remained relatively isolated until the end of the twentieth century, though now it draws scores of visitors with its unique blend of architecture, cuisine and famous myths and legends.

More than 150 eighteenth- and nineteenth-century **wooden churches** and **chapels** dot the land. Chiloé is also one of the few places in the country where you can still see **palafitos**, precarious but picturesque timber houses on stilts, which were once the traditional dwellings of most of the fishermen of southern Chile. Much of the old culture has been preserved, assimilated into Hispanic tradition by a profound mixing of the Spanish and indigenous cultures that

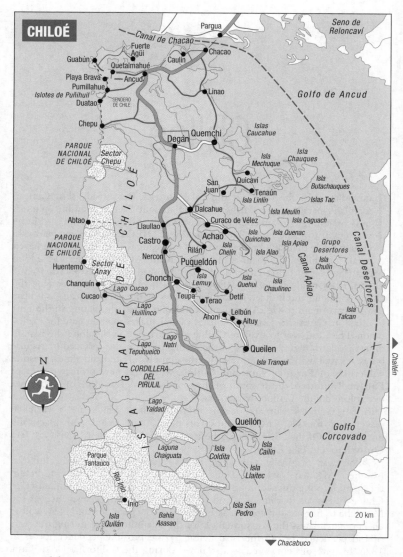

occurred here more than in other parts of South America, making today's
Chiloé more "pagan Catholic" than Roman Catholic.

Arriving in Chiloé

There are regular ferry services from Pargua, 59km southwest of Puerto Montt
on the mainland (daily every 30min; 35min; CH$600, cars CH$9000) to the
village of **Chacao** on Isla Grande's northern shore; the ferry price is included
in the price of the bus ticket to either Ancud or Castro. Scheduled ferry services
also criss-cross the gulf, linking Puerto Montt, Chaitén, and Quellón, though

since Chaitén is currently uninhabited, only people with their own transport cross over to the mainland there.

Caulín

After 9km along the Panamericana on the way to Ancud from Chacao, a turn-off to the right leads to the hamlet of **Caulín** on the edge of a windswept, kilometre-wide sandy beach, where you can often see locals collecting and laying out a stinking grey seaweed to dry. Called *pelillo* ("fine hair") because it resembles human hair, this alga has a dual purpose: agar-agar, a gelatinous substance used in the food and cosmetics industries can be extracted from it, or the seaweed can be woven into a fibre. Caulín is famous for its specific type of **oysters**, the likes of which are only found in New Zealand, and you can sample the delicacies at the fine *Ostras Caulín* restaurant (mobile ☎09/643 7005, ✉ostrascaulin@terra.cl, reputedly the best in the village. Stay at the *Hotel Caulín* (☎09/330 1220, 🌐www.caulinlodge.cl; ❹–❺), with cosy rooms and five-person *cabañas*. Buses Claudio del Río and Buses Andrade both run twice-daily to Ancud on weekdays.

Ancud

ANCUD is a pretty little seaside town and a lively fishing port, with an excellent **museum**. Founded in 1769 as a Spanish stronghold, after Peruvian independence in 1824 it became the crown's last possession in South America. Its forts resisted one attempt at capture, but finally fell in January 1826 when the lonely and demoralized Spanish garrison fled into the forest in the face of a small *criollo* attack. The remains of these Spanish forts – **Fuerte San Antonio** in the town and **Fuerte Agüi** on a peninsula to the northwest – can still be visited today. Ancud makes a good base for a day-trip to the penguin colony at Puñihuil, or for the exploration of the nearby Península Lacuy – the start of the Chiloé section of the Sendero de Chile (see p.363).

Arrival and information

Long-distance buses **arrive** in the new terminal on Los Carrera 850, a ten-minute walk from the Plaza de Armas, while the rural bus terminal, serving numerous villages, is on Colo Colo, above the Full Fresh supermarket. Ancud's main tourist information office is **Sernatur**, on the Plaza de Armas at Libertad 665 (Jan–Feb daily 8.30am–7pm; Mar–Dec Mon–Thurs 8.30am-5.30pm, Fri 8.30am-4.30pm; ☎65/622800, ✉infochiloe@sernatur.cl). It has information on the entire archipelago and very helpful staff. Helpful websites include 🌐www.chiloe.cl, www.ancudmagico.cl, www.interpatagonia.cl and www.patagoniainsular.cl.

Accommodation

Camping Arena Gruesa Constanera Norte 292 ☎65/623428. Large campsite with excellent sea views near the Arena Gruesa beach; picnic tables, hot showers and individual shelters with lights for each site are included (CH$3000 per person). There are also fully-equipped *cabañas* for four or six people, as well as a hostel with basic rooms. ❶–❸

Hostal Chiloé O'Higgins 274 ☎65/622869, ✉analuisaancud@hotmail.com. Family-run

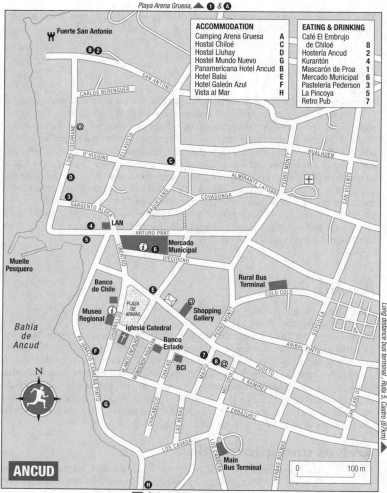

Playa Arena Gruesa, **1** & **A**

ACCOMMODATION
Camping Arena Gruesa	A
Hostal Chiloé	C
Hostal Lluhay	D
Hostel Mundo Nuevo	G
Panamericana Hotel Ancud	B
Hotel Balai	E
Hotel Galeón Azul	F
Vista al Mar	H

EATING & DRINKING
Café El Embrujo de Chiloé	8
Hostería Ancud	2
Kurantón	4
Mascarón de Proa	1
Mercado Municipal	6
Pastelería Pederson	3
La Pincoya	5
Retro Pub	7

Fuerte San Antonio

SAN ANTONIO
CARLOS BERENGUER
LORD COCHRANE
BELLAVISTA
O'HIGGINS
ALMIRANTE LATORRE
PEDRO MONTT
HUALHUÉN
COVADONGA
BAQUEDANO
SARGENTO ALDEA
SAN VICENTE
LAN
ARTURO PRAT
Mercado Municipal
LIBERTAD
DIECIOCHO
Muelle Pesquero
Rural Bus Terminal
COLO COLO
Banco de Chile
PLAZA DE ARMAS
Museo Regional
Iglesia Catedral
Shopping Gallery
RONCOLEA
CHORRILLOS
Bahía de Ancud
ANÍBAL PINTO
AV IGNACIO CARRERA PINTO
Banco Estado
BANCO IGLESIA
MONSEÑOR IGLESIA
CHACAO
BCI
MAIPÚ
MOCOPULLI
PUDETO
E. RAMÍREZ
N
CHACABUCO
LAS HERAS
F. ERRAZURIZ
SAN CARLOS
LOS CAVADA
LOS CARRERA
Main Bus Terminal
YERBAS BUENAS

Long distance bus terminal, Ruta 5, Castro (87km)

ANCUD

0   100 m

Península de Lacuy (15km)

---

guesthouse with several cosy rooms and a frilly living room; breakfast and internet included. **3**

Hostal Lluhay Lord Cochrane 458 ☎65/622656, ⊛www.hostal-lluhay.cl. Wonderfully plush en-suite rooms, a well-stocked bar, and breakfast and wi-fi included. Warm and welcoming owners offer home-made empanadas, and help to arrange tours. **3**

Hostal Mundo Nuevo Costanera 748 ☎65/628383, ⊛www.newworld.cl. Friendly, spotless *hostal* on the waterfront with a large garden and a sea-view terrace. Guests can use the kitchen facilities. Good breakfast is included and they offer bike rental. The helpful Swiss owner speaks English and German and can assist with arranging tours. **4**

Hotel Balai Pudeto 169 ☎65/622966, ⊛www.hotelbalai.cl. Unusual local art and trinkets lend this hotel plenty of character although some of its rooms are dark. Rooms have cable TV and internet; laundry service available and there's a restaurant on the premises. **4**

Hotel Galeón Azul Libertad 751 ☎65/622543, ⊛www.hotelgaleonazul.cl. The views across the Golfo de Quetalmahue from this vibrantly coloured hotel are staggering and the modern rooms all have high ceilings and private baths. **6**

Panamericana Hotel Ancud San Antonio 30 ☎65/622340, ℻65/622350, ⊛www.panamericanahoteles.cl. Built up on the peninsula just to the north, this is the priciest hotel in town, with a luxurious log-cabin feel and large picture windows overlooking the sea. The restaurant serving international cuisine is worth a try. ❼ **Vista al Mar** Av Costanera 918 ☎65/622617, Ⓦwww.vistaalmar.cl. This clean place is both a hotel and a youth hostel, with comfortable dorms, rooms and fully furnished apartments with a great sea view. The *Fogón Chilote* restaurant serves tasty Chilote dishes. ❸–❹

The Town

Ancud is built on a small, square promontory jutting into the Canal de Chacao and the Golfo de Quetalmahue. The centre of town is the pretty **Plaza de Armas**, which fills with craft stalls and street musicians in the summer.

Chilote mythology

The Chiloé islands have long been rife with myths and legends, especially in the remote rural regions, where tradition and superstition hold sway, with colourful supernatural creatures cropping up in stories throughout the archipelago.

Basilisco A snake with the head of a cockerel, the Basilisco turns people to stone with its gaze. At night, the Basilisco enters houses and sucks the breath from sleeping inhabitants, so that they waste away into shriveled skeletons. The only way to be rid of it is to burn the house down.

Brujo This is the general term for a witch; in Chiloé, there are only male witches and their legendary cave is rumoured to be near the village of Quicaví. To become a witch, an individual must wash away baptism in a waterfall for forty days, assassinate a loved one, make a purse out of their skin in which to carry their book of spells and sign a pact with the devil in their own blood, stating when the evil one can claim their soul. Witches are capable of great mischief and can cause illness and death, even from afar.

Caleuche This ghostly ship that glows in the fog travels at great speeds both above and below the water, emitting beautiful music, carrying the witches to their next destination. Journeying through the archipelago, it's crewed by shipwrecked sailors and fishermen who have perished at sea.

Fiura An ugly, squat woman with halitosis, she lives in the woods, clothed in moss. The coquettish Fiura bathes in waterfalls, where she seduces young men before driving them insane.

Invunche Stolen at birth by witches, and raised on the flesh of the dead and cats' milk, the Invunche was transformed into a deformed monster with one leg crooked behind his back. He feeds on goats' flesh and stands guard at the entrance to the legendary witches' cave, the Cueva de Quicaví, grunting or emitting bloodcurdling screams. If you're unlucky enough to spot him, you'll be frozen to that spot forever.

Pincoya A fertility goddess of extraordinary beauty, Pincoya personifies the spirit of the ocean and is responsible for the abundance or scarcity of fish in the sea. She dances half-naked, draped in kelp, on the beaches or tops of waves. If she's spotted facing the sea, the village will enjoy an ample supply of seafood. If she's looking towards the land, there will be a shortage.

Trauco A deformed and ugly troll who dwells in the forest, Trauco dresses in ragged clothes and a conical cap and carries a stone axe or wooden club, a *pahueldœn*. His breath makes him irresistible to women, and he is blamed for all unexplained pregnancies on the island.

Voladora The witches' messenger, the Voladora is a woman who transforms into a black bird by vomiting up her internal organs. The Voladora travels under the cover of night and can only be detected by her terrible cries, which bring bad luck. If the Voladora is unable to recover her innards at the end of the night, she is stuck in bird shape forever.

The colourful **Mercado Municipal**, one block to the north, is the place to grab a cheap meal or pick up fresh produce and some local crafts. A block to the west lies the hectic **fishing harbour**, a great place to watch the catch being hauled in. From the harbour, a crushed-shell promenade heads south, past half a dozen intriguing pieces of **sculpture**, while Calle Lord Cochrane follows the coast to the north to the reconstructed walls of the Spanish **Fuerte de San Antonio**, which affords a sweeping view over the Golfo de Quetalmahue and out to the Pacific Ocean. Its sixteen cannon, combined with the fifteen in Fuerte Agüi (on the Península Lacuy across the water) could sink any ship entering the Bahía de Ancud. Calle Bellavista, parallel to Cochrane, leads futher north to the **Balneario Arena Gruesa**, a popular swimming beach in summer, sheltered by high cliffs.

The Museo Regional

The **Museo Regional** is located on Libertad, one block south of the Plaza de Armas (Jan–Feb Mon–Fri 10.30am–7.30pm, Sat & Sun 10am–7.30pm; March–Dec Tues–Fri 10am–5.30pm, Sat & Sun, holidays 10am–2pm; CH$600). The outside patio houses a copy of the *Goleta Ancud*, a **schooner** which carried the first Chilean settlers down to the Magellan Strait in 1843. It was the culmination of a great tradition of Chilote boat-building, which included boats made from rough planks lashed together with vines and caulked with alerce bark. Also outside is an entire skeleton of a blue whale and a collection of rustic Chilote **mythological figures** (see box, p.361).

Inside the museum are excellent, partly interactive Spanish-language exhibits, covering various aspects of life in the archipelago, including Chiloé's natural environment and wildlife, European conquest, archaeology and religious art, with striking photographs illustrating the impact of the 1960 earthquake, which devastated much of the island.

Eating and drinking

Café El Embrujo de Chiloé Maipú at Ramírez, Local 3. A popular spot for coffee and cake or a beer.

Kurantón Prat 94. Excellent meat and fish dishes, as well as *curanto*, on offer in atmospheric surroundings.

Mascarón de Proa Baquedano s/n, on the premises of *Las Cabañas Las Golondrinas*. An unpretentious spot with a great sea view to the north of town, this restaurant cooks up ample servings of extremely fresh fish. The hake is excellent. Mains CH$5000.

Curanto – what's in a dish?

Chiloé's signature dish, *curanto*, has been prepared for several centuries using cooking methods very similar to those used in Polynesia. First, extremely hot rocks are placed at the bottom of an earthen pit; then, a layer of shellfish is added, followed by chunks of smoked meat, chicken, *longanisa* (sausage), potatoes, *chapaleles* and *milcaos* (potato dumplings). The pit is then covered with *nalca* (Chilean wild rhubarb) leaves and as the shellfish cooks, the shells spring open, releasing their juices onto the hot rocks, steaming the rest of the ingredients. Traditional *curanto* (*curanto en hoyo*) is slow-cooked in the ground for a day or two, but since traditional cooking methods are only used in the countryside, you will probably end up sampling *curanto en olla*, also known as *pulmay*, oven-baked in cast-iron pots. The dish comes with hot shellfish broth, known to the locals as "liquid Viagra", to be drunk with the *curanto*.

Mercado Municipal bordered by Prat, Dieciocho, Libertad and Blanco Encalada. The no-frills eateries at the market tend to be packed at lunchtime, all serving a variety of inexpensive fish and seafood dishes; try *Los Artesanos* or *Rincón Sureño*. Mains CH$3000–4000.

Panamericana Hotel Ancud San Antonio 30. The *hostería* has a good restaurant serving international food using fresh local ingredients. The scallops are excellent, but the food is overpriced for what it is. Mains CH$7000–9000.

Pastelería Pederson Lord Cochrane 470. Enjoy unbeatable harbour views as you tuck into a delicious, reasonably priced lunch or German-style *onces*. The *kuchen* are excellent; CH$1500.

La Pincoya Prat 61. The best place to eat *curanto* and ceviche, with a family-run atmosphere, low prices and excellent service. *Curanto* CH$4500.

Retro Pub Maipú 615. Decent burgers and pasta as well as palatable TexMex dishes are served in this dark bar which turns into a lively nightspot.

Listings

Banks and exchange There are ATMs at Banco de Chile (621 Chorillos) on the Plaza, as well as BCI (Chacao at Ramírez).
Hospital Almirante Latorre 301 ☎65/622356.
Internet Inside the gallery at Pudeto 276 or at Montt at Ramírez.
Post office Pudeto at Blanco Encalada.
Telephone centres Several near the market.
Tour operators Austral Adventures, Avenida Costanera 904 (☎65/625977 ⊛www.austral-adventures.com) caters to the more imaginative traveller, leading expertly guided trips not just to the standard attractions, such as the penguin colonies, but also on rugged hikes, and multi-day trips that allow immersion into Chilote culture; also available are multi-day boat trips in their own *Cahuella* to the northern part of Parque Pumalín as well as kayaking excursions. Viajes Nativa, at Los Carrera 850, Oficina 3 (☎65/622303 ⊛www.viajesnativa.cl), is a reputable operator offering day-trips to Parque Nacional Chiloé, to the penguin colonies, and to Península Lacuy, as well as a tour of some of the island's most famous churches.

Around Ancud

If you head west out of Ancud, you pass the turn-off towards Pumillahue at 14km, and shortly reach the edge of the **Península Lacuy**. Soon the road forks, with the left branch leading to the quiet white-sand beach of **Playa Guabún**, and **Faro Corona**, an isolated lighthouse on a remote promontory. The right fork deposits you, after 21km, below **Fuerte Agüi**, the last toehold of the Spanish Empire in Latin America. The rusting cannons are still in place, and from the ruins you get great views of the bay of Ancud and beyond. Minibuses Ahuí depart from Ancud's rural bus terminal for the fort up to four times on weekdays from 11.45am; last bus 6pm (CH$1200).

From the village of Guabún, part of the Sendero de Chile, a trail that is a mixture of coastal footpaths, stretches of beach, rural road and marked wooden walkways, runs all the way past Chepu Valley (see p.364) to the mouth of Río Lar. A twenty-kilometre stretch, half of it along the long, curving beach of Mar Brava, takes you to the village of Pumillahue. Just off the coast lies the rocky outcrop of the **Islotes de Puñihuil**, a **penguin colony** monitored and protected by the Fundación Otway (☎09/564 7866, ⊜otwafund@ctcinternet.cl). This thriving colony is unique to Chile in that it is visited by both Magellanic and Humboldt penguins in the breeding and rearing season, between December and March. The adults fish most of the day, so the optimum visiting time is early or late in the day. Several local operators have formed the "Ecoturismo Puñihuil" organization, which runs well-explained trips in zodiac dinghies to see the penguins and other marine fauna, including the delightful *chungungos* (sea otters). The excursions, if departing directly from the beach, cost around CH$5000 per person; CH$15,000 from Ancud, transportation included. *Restaurant Bahía Puñihuil* and *Restaurant El Rincón*, both on the beach, serve excellent seafood, including the tasty *empanadas de locos*. Buses Mar Brava runs three buses daily from Ancud every day except Sunday between 6.45am and 4pm (CH$1200).

From Pumillahue, it's a good six-to-eight-hour walk to the mouth of Río Chepu, and can be rather muddy in parts, though you are rewarded with splendid views of the unspoiled coast. Alternatively, a new dirt road runs through some farmland straight to the **Chepu Valley**. You'll see plenty of gently undulating pastureland, but the main attraction is a large stretch of **wetlands**, created in 1960 when the tsunami flooded a large section of coastal forest. Today, the sunken forest provides a thriving habitat for over a hundred different bird species, as well as ample ground for **kayaking** and fishing. *Mirador de Chepu* is a hillside eco-campsite that relies solely on power generated by the wind turbine and solar panels. Besides providing camping spaces with a fantastic view of the river and wetlands below, the welcoming owners hold barbecues and run Chepu Adventures (⊕09/93792482, ⓦwww .chepuadventures.com), organizing various nature outings, including the excellent "Kayaking at Dawn" trip, as well as walks along the coast to the large Ahuenco penguin colony, home to Magellanic and Humboldt penguins. Those who do not wish to camp can stay in basic *dormis* (❷) or the two en-suite *cabañas* (❹). The owners can also direct you to one of the two excellent *Agroturismo* homes (❸) in the area, run by friendly Chilote families, where you can eat ample amounts of home cooking and experience rural life firsthand.

Buses Yánez runs from Ancud to Chepu once daily at 4pm (2pm on Sat), excluding Sundays; it's also possible to take the Panamericana from Ancud and then the dirt road to Chepu from Km25 (4WDs only). If you don't have your own transport, go on any bus towards Castro, ask to be dropped off at the "cruce de Chepu", and arrange to be picked up by Chepu Adventures.

Quemchi

East from the Panamericana, 41km south of Ancud, a pictureque coastal road leads along the coast to Quemchi, an attractive little town with narrow, irregular streets sloping down to the water's edge. A couple of kilometres south, there's a tiny wooded island, **Isla Aucar**, only accessible by a 500-metre-long footbridge. Nestled on the island is a small wooden **church** with a duck-egg-blue roof and white walls.

Places to stay include the central, friendly *Hospedaje La Tranquera*, almost overhanging the sea at Yungay 40 (⊕65/691250; ❸), with clean, bare rooms and a picturesque view, or the simple yet homely *Hospedaje Costanera*, Bahamonde 141 (⊕65/691230; ❷). Eating options are limited, but the waterfront *El Chejo* is a good choice for inexpensive seafood. Buses Aucar runs six daily services from Ancud between 9am and 7pm, and there are twice-daily services by Expreso Quicaví. From Castro, Quemchi Bus has up to nine departures daily from 7am; fewer on weekends.

Castro and around

Built on a small promontory at the head of a twenty-kilometre fjord, lively **CASTRO** occupies an unusual position both physically and historically. Founded in 1567, it's the third-oldest city in Chile, but it never became strategically important because it's a terrible harbour for sailing ships, only

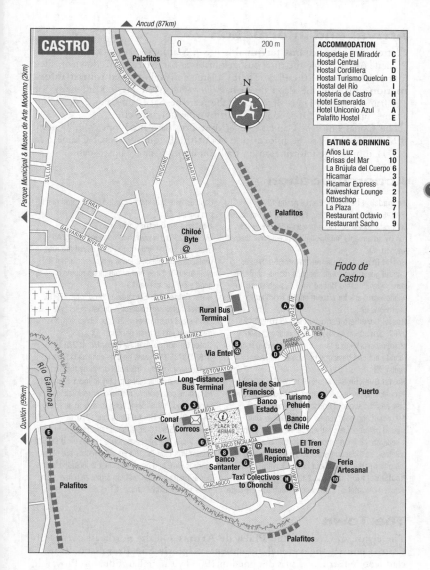

flourishing because the Jesuits chose to base their mission here. Castro has had its fair share of difficulties. It was sacked by the Dutch both in 1600 and then in 1643, destroyed by earthquake in 1646, by fire in 1729, by earthquake again in 1739, by fire again in 1890, by fire once more in 1936, and most recently by earthquake and tidal wave in 1960. Anyone else would have given up and moved long ago, but the Chilotes keep hanging on. Today, little remains of old Castro, though some buildings have miraculously survived, such as the groups of brightly coloured **palafitos** on the waterfront to the north and south of town.

Arrival and information

Castro's long-distance **bus terminal** is at San Martín 486, a block north of the Plaza de Armas, while the rural bus terminal is at San Martín 667, down an alley four blocks north of the Plaza. There's a large and well-stocked **tourist information** office on the Plaza de Armas (Dec–Feb Mon–Fri 9.30am–8pm, Sat 10.30am–8pm, Sun 11am–8pm; rest of the year Tue–Sat 10am–1pm, 3–6pm, Sun 11am–1pm, 3–6pm ☎65/633760; ✉turismo@municastro.cl).

The Conaf office at Gamboa 424 (Mon–Fri 10am–12.30pm & 2.30–4pm; ☎65/532501) has some information about the Parque Nacional Chiloé (see p.371), though the information on trail conditions is rarely up-to-date.

Accommodation

Hospedaje El Mirador Barros Arana 127 ☎65/633795, ✉maboly@yahoo.com. As the name suggests, this cosy house boasts a fine view. It's run by an amiable family who let guests use their kitchen. ❸

Hostal Central Los Carrera 316 ☎65/637026. Central guesthouse with spotless rooms, some en-suite, all with cable TV and wi-fi, though some are windowless; ask for a room on the top floor for the best view. ❸

Hostal Cordillera Barros Arana 175 ☎09/512 2767, ✉mpjtres@surnet.cl. Welcoming if slightly chaotic *hostal* with a large communal living room, roaring fire and basic rooms (some with very thin walls). ❸

Hostal Quelcún San Martín 581 ☎65/632396, ✉quelcun@telsur.cl. This excellent guesthouse not only has its own tour agency, but also lovingly decorated and cosy rooms, though those with shared bathroom are rather cramped. The rooms in a separate building across the garden are the quietest; breakfast, internet and wi-fi are some of the other perks. ❷ without bath, ❹ with.

Hostal del Río Thompson 232 ☎65/632223, ✉lola-1@surnet.cl. Large and comfortable en-suite doubles with breakfast included in a central family-run hostel. ❹

Hostería de Castro Chacabuco 202 ☎65/632301, ⓦwww.hosteriadecastro.cl. An oversized chalet with a strip torn out of the roof replaced with glass. It looks a bit bizarre, but it's well-furnished and half of the plush rooms have a good view out to sea. ❻

Hotel Esmeralda Esmeralda 266 ☎65/637900, ⓦwww.hotelesmeralda.cl. A decent hotel with good-sized rooms, bar with pool tables, top-floor restaurant and private parking. ❻

Hotel Unicornio Azul Av Pedro Montt 228 ☎65/632359, ⓦwww.hotelgaleonazul.cl. This unmissable, gaudy pink hotel down by the port is the most luxurious place to stay in town. Some of its quaint, comfortable rooms offer marvellous views, though the rooms tend to vary in size. ❻

Palafito Hostel Riquelme 1210 ☎65/531008, ✉palafitohostel@gmail.com. Brand-new friendly guesthouse on the west side of Castro in a *palafito*. The en-suite rooms are plush, there is wi-fi and good breakfast is included with home-made bread. Can help organize horse-riding in Parque Nacional Chiloé. ❸

The Town

The centre of Castro is the **Plaza de Armas**. On the northeast corner sits Castro's church, the national monument of **Iglesia San Francisco**. Its iron-clad wooden structure was designed in 1906 by the Italian Eduardo Provasoli, and the church's impressive interior is a harmonious blend of the island's native hardwoods.

Off the southeast corner of the Plaza de Armas, on Calle Esmeralda, is the **Museo Regional** (Jan–Feb Mon–Sat 9.30am–8pm, Sun 10.30am–1pm; March–Dec Mon–Sat 9.30am–1pm & 3–6.30pm; ☎65/635967; donations welcome), a small but well-laid-out museum displaying Huilliche artefacts and traditional farming implements, as well as photographs of the town, devastated by the 1960 earthquake.

Two blocks east of the plaza, down by the water, is the **Feria Artesanal**, a large covered market selling all manner of woolly goodies that the region is famous for. Behind the market there's a line of **palafitos** on the sea, which house bustling, inexpensive restaurants. You'll find more *palafitos* at the north end of Castro on Pedro Montt, with another cluster to the west of the promontory, along Ernesto Riquelme.

At the northeast end of town lies the **Parque Municipal**. In mid-February the park hosts an enormous feast, the culmination of the **Festival Costumbrista**, a celebration of traditional Chilote life, when *curanto* is cooked in great cauldrons, *chicha* (cider) flows freely and balls of grated potato – *tropón* – are baked on hot embers. The inevitable burnt fingers and resultant hot-potato juggling that results from picking them up is known as *bailar el tropón* (dancing the *tropón*).

Nearby is the **Museo de Arte Moderno** (Jan–Feb daily 10am–8pm; Nov, Dec & March Mon–Fri 11am–2pm; donation), a group of restored wooden barns that is home to a collection of modern art, including works by local artists.

Eating and drinking

Años Luz San Martín 309. This modern pub/restaurant serves excellent coffee and drinks from a fishing-boat converted into a bar. The food, including delicious crêpes, salads and cakes, is good too, if a little overpriced. Service can be leisurely.

La Brújula del Cuerpo O'Higgins 308. A bright café with a menu that's a bit laboured – dishes are given fire-related names – but it's inexpensive and lively, making it a pleasant spot for a drink and a sandwich.

Brisas del Mar Lillo 120, Cocinería no. 23. A bustling *palafito* restaurant behind the Feria Artesanal, popular with locals, and serving ample portions of fish, meat and *curanto* (CH$3500).

Hicamar Gamboa 413. Ambitious restaurant specializing in well-cooked meat dishes; try the wild boar or the signature steak. Mains CH$5500.

Hicamar Express Gamboa 435. Popular downscale sister option serving up large portions of fried chicken, burgers and hot dogs.

Kaweshkar Lounge Blanco 31. A trendy lounge with myriad cocktails, and also a decent spot to linger over a light meal. Live DJs some evenings; closed Mon.

Ottoschop Blanco 356. This bustling bar popular with a younger crowd gets busy in the evenings, and is a good spot for a Kunstmann beer or a quick meal. There is live music on weekends. Beers CH$1500.

Restaurant Octavio Montt 261. A smart family-run waterfront restaurant with a fine view over the sea, typical Chilean food and good service, though the prices are on the high side. The *curanto* is excellent. CH$5400.

Restaurant Sacho Thompson 213 ☎65/632079. The upstairs dining area offers excellent views across the fjord. The prices are higher than elsewhere, and the choice of fish seems to be limited to salmon and *congrio*, but even this cannot detract from the overall superb seafood menu, such as *carapacho* (crab), or anything clam-based. Mains CH$6500.

Listings

Airlines LAN, Blanco Encalada 299 ☎65/635254.
Banks and exchange There are ATMs around the Plaza de Armas, and Money Exchange at Chacabuco 286.
Bookshop El Tren Libros, Thompson 229.
Car rental Salfa Sur, Mistral 499 ☎65/630414, ⓦwww.salfasur.cl.
Internet access *Chiloé Byte*, Mistral 321 or Via Entel, Esmeralda 579.
Post office Plaza de Armas, O'Higgins 388.
Telephone centres Several along Esmeralda and Gamboa.

Tour operators Altué Expeditions Dalcahue ☎09/419 6809, ⓦwww.seakayakchile.com. Excellent outfit in Dalcahue that offers multi-day trips around the Chiloé archipelago, as well as multi-activity trips in the Lake District and Patagonia; pick-up from Castro available. Pehuen Expediciones, Blanco Encalada 208 (☎65/635254, ⓦwww.turismopehuen.cl) is an experienced outfit offering city tours (CH$10,000), trips to Isla Quinchao (CH$30,000) and excursions to the Parque Nacional Chiloé (CH$25,000). In summer they run boat trips, lasting from a day to a week, to the small, uninhabited islands of the Chilote archipelago. Turismo Quelcœn, San Martín 581 (☎65/632396, ⓔquelcun@hotmail.com), runs reliable tours of the Chilote archipelago at competitive prices (CH$15,000–25,000 for day-long outings, often with food included).

Dalcahue and around

The bustling historical town of **DALCAHUE** lies 20km from Castro via the turn-off at Llau-Llao and is famous for its thriving traditional boat-building industry and the Sunday Feria Artesanal, when artisans come from nearby islands to sell woollen crafts, wood carvings and hand-woven baskets. Dalcahue also provides the only link with nearby **Isla Quinchao** (see p.370), the second largest in the Chiloé archipelago.

Most of the action is centred around Dalcahue's attractive Plaza de Armas and the open-sided market building on the waterfront. On the plaza rises the imposing 1893 Iglesia de Nuestra Señora De Los Dolores, with a unique nine-arched portico, one of the UNESCO World Heritage sites.

You'll find some reasonable **accommodation** near the plaza. Right in the centre of town sits *Pensión Putemun*, Freire 340 (☎65/641330; ❷), with comfortable, if somewhat noisy, rooms. *Residencial La Playa*, Rodríguez 009 (☎65/641397; ❷), offers simple rooms with shared facilities above a restaurant, while the more upmarket *Hotel La Isla*, Elías Navarro 420 (☎65/641241; ❹),

Chilote churches

It is impossible to visit Chiloé and not be struck by the sight of the archipelago's **wooden churches**. In the early nineteenth century these impressively large buildings would have been the heart of a Chilote village. Several of the churches have been declared national monuments, an honour crowned in 2001 when UNESCO accepted sixteen of them on its prestigious World Heritage list.

The churches generally face the sea and are built near a beach with an open area, plaza or *explanada* in front of them. The outside of the churches is almost always bare, and the only thing that expresses anything but functionality is the three-tiered, **hexagonal bell tower** that rises up directly above an open-fronted portico. The facades, doors and windows are often brightly painted, and the walls clad with *tejuelas* (wooden tiles or shingles). All the churches have three naves separated by columns, which in the larger buildings are highly decorated, supporting barrel-vaulted ceilings. The ceilings are often painted too, with allegorical panels or sometimes with golden constellations of stars painted on an electric blue background.

Only the *pueblos* with a priest had a main church, or *iglesia parroquial*. If there was no church, the missionaries used to visit once a year, as part of their so-called *misión circular*. Using only native canoes, they carried everything required to hold a mass with them. When the priest arrived, one of the eldest Chilotes would lead a procession carrying an image of Jesus, and behind him two youths would follow with depictions of San Juan and the Virgin. They would be followed by married men carrying a statue of San Isidro and married women carrying one of Santa Neoburga. If the *pueblo* was important enough there would be a small *capilla* (bell tower) with altars to receive the statues. The building where the missionaries stayed was known as a *residencia*, *villa*, *casa ermita* or *catecera*, and was looked after by a local trustee called a *Fiscal*, whose function was somewhere between that of a verger and lay preacher. This honorary position still exists and, in Chiloé's remoter areas, the *Fiscal* commands great respect in his community. For more information on Chiloé's churches, check out the informative ⓦwww.interpatagonia.com/iglesiaschiloe.

▲ Chilote church

features large, plush rooms inside a smart shingled exterior and a decent breakfast.

The small and extremely popular eateries inside the large boat-shaped establishment next door to the Feria Artesanal are the best spot for lunch: *Doña Lula*, Puesto 8, does fabulous empanadas; *Tenchita*, Puesto 2, is a favourite for *curanto*, while *La Nenita*, Puesto 4, offers very fresh salmon ceviche. Across the street, *Restaurant Chiloé*, 120 Pedro Montt, serves large portions of *curanto* on Sundays, as well as more standard fish and meat dishes.

Numerous daily buses run from Castro to Dalcahue; it is served by Queilen Bus (☎65/632173) and Buses Dalcahue Expreso; Monday–Saturday there is a bus every fifteen minutes between 7.15am and 9.15pm; on Sundays, there are buses every 30 minutes.

Tenaún, Quicaví and Isla Mechuque

From Dalcahue, an attractive gravel road heads northeast towards Quemchi, following the coast. Thirty-seven kilometres along, a small road heads to the somnolent coastal village of **TENAÚN** with an attractive waterfront. Smiling down at the quaint little fishermen's cottages is Chiloé's arguably most extraordinary **church**, painted white with two huge pale blue stars daubed onto the wall above the entrance and three vibrant blue and red towers, founded in 1734 but rebuilt in 1861. The only place to stay is the *Red de Agroturismo*-affiliated *Hospedaje Vásquez Montaña* (☎09/647 6750; ❷) with four simple rooms and shared facilities; owners run excursions to Isla Mechuque. There are three buses from Castro daily between 1pm and 6pm with Buses Tenaún.

Six kilometres beyond Tenaún on the main road, a turn to the east leads, after 7km, to the tiny seafront village of **QUICAVÍ**, whose sleepiness belies its importance in Chilote mythology. It's said that somewhere along the nearby coast lies the legendary **Cueva de Quicaví**, where a Spanish warlock left a powerful book of spells for the resident *brujos* after being defeated in a magic duel. The Spanish Inquisition, and many others besides, have searched for the cave in vain (see p.315). Perhaps because of this wealth of superstition, the missionaries built a larger than usual **church** in Quicaví.

There's a daily **bus** to Quicaví from Castro (see p.364), leaving in the middle of the afternoon, and Bus JM has daily services to Quicaví from Ancud at 12.45pm, excluding Sunday.

Small launches depart from the jetties at Tenaún and Quicaví for the beautiful island of **ISLA MECHUQUE**, the largest and most easily accessible of the Chauques subgroup. Since a quorum of passengers is required, the surest way of making this magical trip past unspoiled island scenery is to go on an organized excursion from Castro in the summer. The highlight of such trips to the tiny village of Mechuque is a genuine *curanto en hoyo* prepared before your eyes in an outdoor pit.

Isla Quinchao

For some, **ISLA QUINCHAO** is the cultural heart of the whole of Chiloé. Rich in traditional wooden architecture, this island is a mere ten-minute ferry ride from Dalcahue (services every half-hour 7am–11pm; foot passengers free, cars Dec–Feb CH$3500 return, March–Nov CH$1000 return).

A paved road runs across Isla Quinchao through the only two towns of any size, **Curaco de Vélez** and **Achao**, both of which offer a taste of traditional Chilote life.

Curaco de Vélez

Twelve kilometres from the ferry terminal, **Curaco de Vélez** comprises a couple of streets of weather-beaten shingled houses set around a beautiful bay and bordered by gently rolling hills. The Plaza de Armas features an unusual sight – a decapitated **church steeple**, docked from the top of an old church, and a bust of locally-born hero Almirante Riveros, who commanded the fleet that captured the Peruvian ironclad *Huáscar* during the War of the Pacific (see p.501).

All buses to Achao call at Curaco de Vélez, but there is no accommodation and only a couple of places to eat: *Bahía*, an upmarket restaurant on the coastal road, across the small bridge from the Plaza, offers good shellfish and fish dishes, but can be unexpectedly closed, while *Ostras Los Troncos*, next door, is a great spot for slurping a few oysters around some rough-hewn wooden tables (CH$200–300 per oyster; bring your own wine).

Achao

Fifteen kilometres southeast of Curaco lies the fishing village of **ACHAO** with its scattering of houses clad in colourful *tejuelas* (shingles), set against a backdrop of snow-capped volcano peaks across the gulf. It is famous both for the oldest church in the archipelago and early February's *Encuentro Folklórico de las Islas del Archipiélago*, a folk festival that draws both musical groups from all over Chiloé as well as the simultaneous *Muestra Gastronómica y Artesanal*, which gives you a chance to sample traditional Chilote cuisine and pick up the handiwork of the archipelago's artisans.

Achao is a living museum of Chiloé's *cultura de madera* (woodworking culture). Dominating the Plaza de Armas, **Iglesia Santa Maria de Loreto**, dating back to 1764, is a prime example of a typical Chilote church and is thought to be the oldest one in the archipelago. The main framework is made from *ciprés de las Guaitecas*, and *mañío*, a tree still common in southern Chile. The original *alerce* shingles which covered the exterior have mostly been replaced with *ciprés* boarding. Restoration work is a constant and expensive necessity – if you look around the *luma* wood floorboards, you can see the church's foundations, a rare glimpse into the way these old buildings were constructed. All the joints have been laboriously fixed into place with wooden plugs and dowels made from *canelo*, another type of Chilean wood.

The town's not short of **places to stay**. The stand-out *Hostería La Nave*, overlooking the beach one block north of the boat ramp at Calle Prat on the corner of Calle Aldea (☎65/661219; ❷), rises on stilts over the beach and is furnished with lots of bright, cheery natural wood. The smart, modern *Hospedaje Sol y Lluvia*, Serrano and Jara (☎65/661383; ❸), offers spacious and comfortable rooms, while the friendly *Hospedaje Sao Paulo*, Serrano 52 (☎65/661245; ❷), has cheap no-frills rooms above a lively restaurant popular with locals. The best **restaurant** in town is at the *Hostería La Nave*, but *Mar y Velas*, overlooking the busy boat ramp, is better for people-watching and offers inexpensive fish and seafood dishes. Achao's **Terminal de Buses** (Miraflores at Zañartu), a couple of blocks east of the Plaza, has half-hourly departures to Castro via Dalcahue run by San Cristóbal between 7am and 7pm daily.

Parque Nacional Chiloé

PARQUE NACIONAL CHILOÉ, comprising over 420 square kilometres of dense woodland and rugged Cordillera de Piuchén, largely unexplored by man and harbouring flora and fauna unique to the archipelago, is divided into three parts, the most accessible of which is Sector Anay, 45km southwest of Castro.

Thirty kilometres **south** of Ancud is the northern section of the Parque Nacional Chiloé, **sector Chepu** (Dec–March daylight hours; CH$1000), noted for its **wetlands**, rich in bird life. The sector is difficult to get to, because there is currently no regular way of crossing the Río Lar estuary (try making arrangements with fishermen in the Chepu Valley), but rewards with a ruggedly beautiful four-hour hike along the densely wooded coast to the (generally closed) Conaf station, with likely sightings of *pudú* and native bird species.

Every summer, hordes of backpackers descend on the park's Sector Anay (daily: Jan–Feb 9am–8pm; March–Dec 9am–1pm & 2–7pm; CH$1000; ⓦwww.parquechiloe.com), keen to camp on its twenty kilometres of white-sand beach and to explore the dense forest. This section of the national park covers 350 square kilometres of the Cordillera de Piuchén, rising up to 800m above sea level and comprises vast chunks of native flora, including *coigüe* and *mañío* woodlands and the magnificent *alerce*. Besides potentially catching glimpses of the shy Chilote fox, otters, and a wealth of native birds, the depths of primeval Chiloé forest allow you to experience a sense of true wilderness.

Sector Anay is reached by a 25km dirt road that shoots west from a junction on the Panamericana, 20km south of Castro. At the end of the road is the

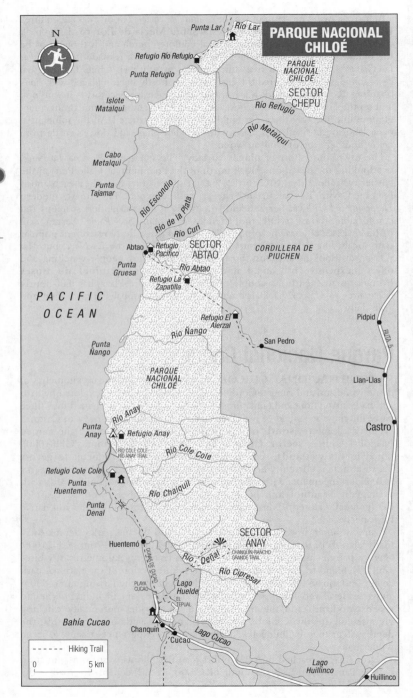

PACIFIC
OCEAN

N

Punta Lar   Río Lar

PARQUE NACIONAL CHILOÉ

Refugio Río Refugio

Punta Refugio

PARQUE NACIONAL CHILOÉ

SECTOR CHEPU

Islote Matalqui

Río Refugio

Río Metalqui

Cabo Metalqui

Punta Tajamar

Río Escondio

Río de la Plata

Río Curi

SECTOR ABTAO

CORDILLERA DE PIUCHEN

Abtao   Refugio Pacifico

Punta Gruesa

Río Abtao

Refugio La Zapatilla

Refugio El Alerzal

Pidpid

Río Ñango

San Pedro

RUTA 5

Punta Ñango

Llan-Llas

PARQUE NACIONAL CHILOÉ

Castro

Río Anay

Punta Anay   Refugio Anay

RÍO COLE COLE/ RÍO ANAY TRAIL

Río Cole Cole

Refugio Cole Cole

Punta Huentemo

Río Chaiquil

Punta Denal

SECTOR ANAY

Huentemó

DUNAS DE CUCAO

Río   Deñal

CHANQUÍN-RANCHO GRANDE TRAIL

Río Cipresal

PLAYA CUCAO

Lago Huelde

EL TEPUAL

Bahía Cucao

Chanquín

Lago Cucao

Cucao

Lago Huillinco

Huillinco

Hiking Trail

0   5 km

gateway to the park, Chanquín – a scattering of houses across the bridge from the ramshackle village of **Cucao**, where you can buy last-minute provisions. Proper exploration of the park requires at least four days, but there are several nice walks that you can do in a day, staying overnight in Chanquín. The German-owned ⚓ *Paradór Darwin* (☎09/799 9923 ❸) with attractive *cabaña* rooms and a small restaurant serving goulash, cakes, fish and clams, is the best spot to stay, and the owner can help organize horse-riding trips into the park; ownership is due to change soon, though. A little further up the road is *El Fogón de Cucao* (☎09/946 5685 ✉elfogondecucao@hotmail.com; ❹), a pleasant bed and breakfast that also organizes horse-riding and trekking expeditions; there is a separate restaurant, and a few spots for camping.

It is possible to explore parts of the park on horseback, but the quality of hire horses varies and not all of them are trained to carry beginners. *Palafito Hostel* in Castro can help organize trips with a reliable local guide (☎09/884 9552 or 09/8336 2706 🌐www.cahuelmapu.com).

Exploring the park

At the Conaf **Cucao Ranger Post** there's a **visitor centre** (daily: Jan–Feb 9am–8pm; March–Dec 9am–1pm & 2–7pm; ☎09/644 2489, ✉vidasur@telsur.cl) that explains the various environments you'll find in the park. You can stay at the *Camping Chanquín*, 200m past the visitors' centre on the banks of Lago Cucao, with twenty camping spots, fire pits, showers and picnic tables (CH$4000 per person).

A couple of short **hikes** start from the visitor centre. The first is the 770-metre "El Tepual" running through an area of the *tepu* forest, which thrives in this humid bogland; there are log walkways across the wetter sections of these enchanted-looking woods, with twisted moss-covered logs intertwined with other native species. The second hike is the Sendero La Playa, which leads you through patches of *nalca* (native rhubarb), and tunnels of dense vegetation, before emerging on the regenerating scrubland that takes you all the way across some sand dunes onto the exposed Pacific coast. A little more taxing is the three-kilometre (one-way) walk along the beach to Lago Huelde, technically outside the park boundary, where you pick up a nine-kilometre trail known as Sendero Rancho Grande along the Río Cipresal up to the edge of the tree line, revealing beautiful views below.

The park's longest hike is the beautiful twenty-kilometre (6hr) walk north along the coast and through dense, native evergreen forest to the Conaf *refugio* at **Cole Cole**; there is also a rustic campsite (CH$2000pp) overseen by the Huentemó community, and a Conaf ranger post that is only open in the summer. You can also continue another 8km north to the *Refugio Anay*, though the trail is rather difficult, as there is currently no shuttle across the Río Anay.

Further north but unconnected with Sector Anay lies Sector Abtao, technically reachable from the Panamericana; you can take a dirt road halfway between the villages of Llau-Llao and Pidpid to the hamlet of San Pedro, from where an 18km trail runs through swampland to the coast. The trail is difficult to follow and a local guide is essential; there are two *refugios* in various states of repair along the way before you reach Refugio Abtao on the coast.

At least four Expresos Interlagos **buses** a day run to Chanquín from Castro's rural bus station between 9am and 6pm, more during high season.

Chonchi

Twenty-three kilometres south of Castro lies the attractive working town of **CHONCHI**. Founded in 1767, the town thrived on timber exports and was home to the wood baron Ciriaco Alvarez, who earned the name *El Rey de Ciprés* (The Cypress King) by stripping the archipelago of almost all of its native forest. Lined around the most sheltered harbour on the island are the beautiful old wooden buildings, structures that have hardly changed since the eighteenth century. Calle Centenario, Chonchi's attractive and steeply curving main street, leads down to the harbour where you can see local women digging for razor clams at low tide.

The town's cheerfully painted **Iglesia San Carlos de Chonchi** rewards a visit; it has recently been restored to its full glory, and the Neoclassical facade is one of the island's finest.

A short way down the main street from the church is the informative **Museo de las Tradiciones Chonchinas**, Centenario 116 (Mon–Fri 9am–1pm, 2–6pm; Sat 9am–1pm; CH$500), a beautifully restored old traditional house filled with furniture, fittings and a large collection of photographs from the tree-felling heyday of *El Rey de Ciprés*.

Practicalities

A couple of doors along from the museum at Centenario 102 is one of Chonchi's best **places to stay**, *Hotel Huildín* (T65/671388, Wwww.hotelhuildin.com; ❸), a beautifully restored large wooden house with spacious airy rooms and fully-equipped *cabañas* available; breakfast costs CH$1500 extra. Slightly tucked away on the eastern end of the seafront, on Irarrázaval s/n, 🏃 *Esmeralda by the Sea* (T65/671328, Ecarlos @esmeraldabythesea.cl; ❷–❸) is a friendly *hospedaje* with comfortable rooms of various sizes and a helpful English-speaking owner who organizes land and sea tours and has a wealth of local knowledge. It offers a book exchange, use of kitchen, internet, bike rental and evening meals. You could also try *Posada El Antiguo Chalet*, on the western edge of town, just uphill from the harbour (T65/671221; ❺); it's a beautiful, natural-wood house set in large, well-kept grounds.

Eating well in Chonchi is not difficult; there are several restaurants that have been local institutions for years: *El Trebol*, Irarrázaval 187, at the southern end of the waterfront above the local market, and *La Quilla*, Andrade 183, both serve decent fish and seafood dishes, while the newcomer *Los Tres Pisos*, on the corner of Andrade and Esmeralda, is also promising.

There is a helpful little tourist office on the first floor of the Municipalidad building across the Plaza from the church (Jan–March daily 9am–7pm) and in February the town comes alive during the *Semana Verano Chonchi* – a folkloric festival featuring dancing, music, art and rodeo skills.

There are frequent **buses**, run by such operators as Cruz del Sur, Transchiloé, Expresos Interlagos and Queilen Bus (T65/253468), every half an hour from Castro to Chonchi; larger buses stop alongside the Plaza, while minibuses stop along the little triangular *plazuela* along Centenario.

Isla Lemuy

On the coast, a 4km walk south of Chonchi at **Huicha**, a ferry (daily 8am–8pm; Mon–Sat every 30min, Sun every hour; 20min; free) heads to **ISLA LEMUY** – a tranquil spot seldom visited by tourists. It's dotted with traditional rural settlements, each boasting just a few houses and in some cases a fine old church, **Puqueldón** being the island's main settlement. The most remote village of all is **Detif**, on an isolated, bleak headland at the far eastern end of the island, about 20km from Puqueldón. The only place to stay on the island is *Parque Yayanes* on the road from Puqueldón to Lincay (☎07/498 0655 or 08/861 6462, ✉yayaneslemuy@gmail .com), a unique lodging option which consists of two comfortable *cabañas*; the hospitable owners cook up a feast using fresh local seafood.

Buses Gallardo runs to Puqueldón from Castro (Mon–Sat five daily between 7.10am and 6.45pm; 9am departure Sun); the bus crosses to the island on the ferry.

The road from Chonchi to Queilén

Back on the mainland, the paved road to Queilén runs above a string of pretty little villages down by the sea. **Tepua** in particular is worth a visit to see its graveyard filled with *mausoleos*, traditional shelters that protect mourners from the elements when they visit the graves of the dead, some of which are splendidly ornate. You'll either need a sturdy vehicle to tackle the steep dirt paths leading to the villages, or be prepared for a lot of walking.

Forty-six kilometres from Chonchi, the road pulls into **QUEILÉN**, a sleepy little fishing town whose two main streets, Pedro Aguirre Cerda and Alessandri bisect the neck of a long, sandy peninsula. The western end of town is very pretty, lined with fishermen's houses built on a long beach sheltered by the nearby **Isla Tranqui**. In February the town hosts a craft fair in which all types of local products are sold, from handicrafts and farming equipment to traditional medicines.

If **staying**, try the *Hotel Plaza*, O'Higgins 93 (☎65/258271; ❷), with basic rooms with shared facilities, or the friendly *Hospedaje*, Calle Cerda 198 (no phone; ❷), opposite the Queilén Bus stop – similar facilities but no breakfast. The best place to **eat** fresh fish in the village is at *Restaurant Melinka*, at Alessandri 126, but the real find lies 11km out of town, on the way back to Chonchi: *Espejo de Luna* (☎74/313090, ⓦwww.espejodeluna.cl; ❻), unmissable due to its distinctive boat-shaped form, comprises an excellent restaurant and a plush nature retreat, with several individually designed *cabañas* offering both comfort and privacy, with a stunning sea view to boot.

Queilén Bus (☎65/632173) runs eleven **buses** daily to Queilén from Castro between 7.30am and 8pm; fewer on Sundays (CH$1500).

Quellón

From the junction with Chonchi and Queilén, the Panamericana heads south, culminating in **QUELLÓN** after 70km. Formerly a logging port, Quellón is now a scruffy commercial fishing port of growing importance, with few attractions for the visitor. It's based around three east–west streets that run parallel to the coast: the seafront *costanera* (Miramar and Pedro Montt); Ercilla, north of the *costanera*; and Ladrilleros, further north still. The main reason to come here is to catch a **ferry** across to Chaitén (see p.486) or down to Chacabuco (see p.394), or to organize transportation to Parque Tantauco (see p.376).

Practicalities

Hourly Cruz del Sur and Transchiloé **buses** from Castro (CH$1700) stop at the terminal a block west of the Plaza on Calle Cerda, while **ferries** from Puerto

Chacabuco and Chaitén – operated by Naviera Austral (☎65/682207, ◎www.navieraaustral.cl) at Costanera Pedro Montt 457, call at the harbour a block south. There's an **Oficina de Turismo** booth on the corner of Gómez García and Santos Vargas, a block north of the Plaza de Armas (Jan–Feb daily 9am–9pm; no phone). The extremely helpful Parque Tantauco office is at Av La Paz 68 (☎65/680066, ◎www.parquetantauco.cl).

Most **places to stay** are located along the Costanera, and include the *Hotel Melimoyu*, joined with the *Hostería Quellón*, Montt 369 (☎65/681310; ➍), with good en-suite rooms and a restaurant that specializes in good fish and seafood dishes. The *Hotel Chico Leo*, Montt 325 (☎65/681567; ➌–➍), has comfortable rooms with shared and private bathrooms, cable TV, and breakfast included, while the plush new *Hotel Patagonia Insular*, Ladrilleros 1737 (☎65/681610, ◎www.hotelpatagoniainsular.cl; ➑) overlooking the bay, is the most comfortable place to stay, with an international restaurant and airy, comfortable rooms, complete with cable TV. A number of restaurants along the Costanera offer inexpensive fresh fish and seafood, but the best lunch-time spot is the *Hostería Romeo Alfa*, in the *palafito* by the ferry port; the abalone dishes are excellent. *Café Isla Sándwich* on Ladrilleros 182 does a good variety of tasty sandwiches.

In January and February there are once-weekly ferry departures to Chaitén on Wednesdays at 8am (5hr; CH$19,700 per passenger, CH$25,000 for a reclining seat; see p.340) and for Puerto Chacabuco on Tuesdays at 4pm (10–15hr; CH$36,000). Ferries may be subject to delays and cancellations, so check with the Naviera Austral office in advance. Outside peak season there are fewer services.

Parque Tantauco

To the south of Isla Grande and to the east of Quellón lies **Parque Tantauco**, Chiloé's largest new natural attraction with nearly 1,200 square kilometres of unspoiled wilderness. The park, funded by the Fundación Futuro, is the brain-child of Sebastián Piñera, a Harvard-educated politician, self-made man and billionaire owner of LANChile. After Douglas Tompkins unveiled Parque Pumalín (see p.386), Piñera was inspired to start his own conservation project on Isla Grande. The project's goal is to "protect and conserve vulnerable ecosystems and species, and those at risk of extinction", as well as to restore a large chunk of the park's territory that was devastated by a forest fire in the 1940s, by replanting native forest in the affected area. The park is located on one of the world's 25 "Biodiversity Hotspots", given its unique ecosystems and wildlife habitats; it is home to such species as the Chilote fox, the *pudú*, the *huillín* (otter) and the blue whale.

Exploring the park

The park consists of Zona Sur and Zona Norte, with 150km of hiking trails that encompass both the coastal areas and Chilote rainforest. Zona Norte can be accessed by 4WDs along a dirt road branching off from the Panamericana, 14km north of Quellón, labelled "Colonia Yungay". If you don't have a vehicle of your own, the Quellón office (see above) can help you rent a 4WD at a cost of CH$40,000–45,000 for three or four people. The 18km drive brings you to the park administration office (permanently staffed Dec–March daily 9am–8pm) by Lago Yaldad, from where it's an additional 20km to Lago Chaiguata.

Chilean wildlife

Chile's diverse animal kingdom inhabits a landscape of extremes. The country's formidable natural barriers – the immense Pacific, lofty Andes and desolate Atacama – have prevented contact between its species and their counterparts on the rest of the continent, resulting in an exceptional degree of endemism. Indeed, one third of Chile's mammals are not found anywhere else in the world, including the nimble pudu, a miniature deer that darts though the woodlands of Chiloé. It's easy to build a trip – or multiple ones – around wildlife-spotting; what follows covers some of the more identifiable species you may see, from camelids and furry rodents to

Pudu deer ▲

Alpacas ▼

Puma ▼

Camelids of the altiplano

Camelids are prevalent throughout the highland regions of South America, and all four species of them can be found in Chile's barren **altiplano** (upland plateau). Best known is the shaggy **llama**, whose thick wool and remarkable strength as a beast of burden make it one of the continent's iconic animals. Its slightly smaller but even more hirsute cousin, the **alpaca**, is uniquely adapted to clambering up and down in these high altitudes, as it can rapidly increase the number of red blood cells in its body to facilitate oxygenation.

Unlike the llama and alpaca, the frail-looking **vicuña**, which also roams the altiplano, resists domestication. It has attracted the attention of hunters since pre-colonial times because of the exceptional fineness of its coat; indeed, only Inca royalty was allowed to wear the animal's highly prized fur. Thought to be the common ancestor of the other three South American camelids, the wild **guanaco**, also fawn in colour but far bigger than the vicuña, survives today in isolated herds above Arica and Iquique and down in Patagonia.

Wildcats and their prey

You'll have a harder time getting close to the wildcats – not that you'd want to. In the southern pampas and low savannahs, the **mara**, or **Patagonian cavy**, which resembles a hare, can break into a swift run, zigzagging at speeds of 45km per hour to escape humans and its habitual hunters such as the voracious **puma**, found in small numbers in the more remote corners of Patagonia and Aisén. Other wildcats, from the **colo-colo** to the **guiña**, also stalk these grasslands.

Birds

Newcomers to the southern hemisphere will encounter a curious mix of the familiar, like hummingbirds, and the lesser known. One unmistakable bird, the dandy-like Inca tern, sports scarlet legs and bill and a brilliant white forked moustache. Others are identified more by their calls: the shrill sounds of the chestnut-throated huet-huet and the chucao, furtive woodland foragers, ring through Chile's temperate rainforest, while the crested caracara, found on the edges of southern forests, sometimes hollers its greetings so heartily that it arches its head all the way onto its back.

Some of the more renowned species make their homes in the soaring mountains. One of the world's largest, the mighty Andean condor, with a wingspan of over three metres, wheels over Chile's magnificent peaks, buoyed by the upward thermals. High in the Andes

▲ Condor above the Andes

▲ Hummingbird

▼ Crested Caracara

Endangered furry rodents

An obvious target of predators, rodents abound in Chile's temperate grasslands and mountains. At the first sign of danger, the endemic mountain **vizcacha**, with its long furry ears and curly tail, emits a high-pitched whistle to alert the rest of the colony, who propel themselves to safety with their powerful hind legs. Its distant relative, the coastal or long-tailed **chinchilla** (which has the look of an overgrown hamster), used to be found in huge numbers, but its downfall has been its exceptionally soft, thick coat. Chinchillas were once trapped in their thousands, and remain extremely rare to this day.

near the Bolivian border, several species of flamingo gather at remote saltwater lakes, including the Chilean flamingo, recognizable for its grey-green feet with red joints. The most magnificently hued of the flamingoes, the James's flamingo has a delicate pinkish tinge that bursts into crimson at the base of the neck and gradually fades over the wings.

Darwin's rhea or ñandú also inhabits the highland regions and parts of the far south. Resembling the ostrich or emu, it hides its periscopic head and neck under its bushy feathers to blend in with the surrounding brush.

Flamingoes in Salar de Surire ▲

Penguins in Patagonia ▼

Sea birds from pelicans to penguins

With such bountiful nutritive supplies in the chilly Humboldt Current, Chile enjoys one of the richest and most varied populations of sea birds in the world. The **Peruvian pelican**, a dapper species with a pronounced yellow crest, is found only around the current, as is the **Humboldt penguin** and four species of the gawky-looking **storm petrels**, who swarm behind fishing boats awaiting the ejection of galley waste. But perhaps the most eye-catching is the largest of all the sea birds, the **albatross**, eight species of which migrate through Chilean waters.

To see more of Chile's penguins you'll need to head south. **Rockhopper penguins,** named for their peculiar, stuttering gait, congregate around the fjords and islets of Patagonia. **Magellanic penguins,** also called jackass penguins because of the braying noise they make, are found in numerous breeding sites along the southern Chilean coast. The **Emperor penguin** – the tallest, at over a metre – lives on the ice floes of Antarctica.

There you'll find a campsite with eight sites, with a fully-equipped indoor cooking area. Camping in the park is free. It's possible to visit Zona Norte in a day, as there are a couple of nice short hikes, such as the **Sendero Siempreverde**, an interpretive walk leading through evergreen forest, or the **Circuito Muelle**, that goes from *Camping Chaiguata* along the banks of Lago Yaldad. Alternatively, the **Sendero Lagos Occidentales** is a six-kilometre walk of moderate difficulty, leading you through evergreen forest from Lago Chaiguata to Lago Chaiguaco, where you can overnight at the *Refugio Chaiguaco* (bring own food and bedding).

As of 2008, it's possible to hike between Zona Norte and Zona Sur, the latter otherwise only accessible by boat; you must allow four days to a week for the hike, bring all the necessary gear, including waterproof clothing, and inform the park authorities. From *Refugio Chaiguaco*, the trail continues through the forest to *Refugio Piramide* (15km; 5hr), next to a tiny lagoon. From there it's possible to either head south, towards Caleta Inío, or to do a side trek to the coast along the river, stopping at the *Refugio Emerenciana* on the banks of the picturesque Laguna Emerenciana along the way (allow an extra three days for the detour).

A densely wooded trail heads south, reaching *Refugio Huillín* after six hours (14km). From there it's a further six or seven hours (15km) to Río Inío, passing **Mirador Inío** on the way – a watchtower which gives you a great overview of the landscape. It's possible to organize a boat in advance to take you along Río Inío to the fishing village of Caleta Inío – the entry point to Zona Sur. There is only one official boat per week leaving from Quellón, normally on a Friday but dependent on the weather (☏65/680066; confirm reservation 24hr before departure). If exploring the whole of the park, it's easier to hike from Zona Norte to Zona Sur and then catch a ride back to Quellón with one of the fishing boats.

At Caleta Inío, you can either spend the night at the designated campsite or stay in a friendly family home run by Señora Cadin, who has eleven beds available with shared facilities (full board CH$15,000 per person). You can buy some basic food supplies in the village, including fresh fish.

Around Caleta Inío, you can explore the coastal caves where the indigenous Chonos once resided, as well as the pristine beaches and little islets off the coast. There is also a beautiful circuit around the Inío headland, which takes in stunning viewpoints and stretches of beach and forest; you can overnight at the *Refugio Quilanlar* (16km; 12hr).

Taking a boat back to Quellón is an extremely rewarding experience, as you are likely to get glimpses of marine life, such as sea lions and possibly even blue whales, but the journey is dependent on the weather, so be prepared for a fairly bumpy ride in the Golfo Corcovado.

Travel details

Buses

Ancud to: Castro (every 15min; 1hr 15min); Caulín (4 daily; 30min); Chacao (every 15min; 30min); Península Lacuy and Fuerte Agüi (3 daily except Sun; 45min); Puerto Montt (every 30min; 1hr 30min–2hr); Quemchi (5–6 daily; 1hr); Quicaví (1 daily; 1hr 45min).

Castro to: Achao (every 30min; fewer on Sun; 1hr 50min); Ancud (every 15min; 1hr 15min); Chonchi (every 30min; 30min); Chanquín and the Parque Nacional Chiloé, sector Anay (4–6 daily; 1hr 45min); Curaco de Vélez (every 30min, fewer on Sun; 1hr 30min); Dalcahue (every 30min; 30min); Puerto Montt (every 30min; 3hr); Punta

Arenas, via Argentina (2 weekly, 32hr); Puqueldón (3 daily, 1 on Sun; 1hr 15min); Queilén (11daily; 1hr 30min); Quellón (hourly; 2hr 15min).

Puerto Montt to: Ancud (every 30min; 1hr 30min–2hr); Pargua (every 30min; 30min).

Ferries and Catamarans

Chaitén to: Quellón (1 weekly; 5hr).
Chacao to: Pargua (2–4 hourly; 30min).
Quellón to: Chaitén (1 weekly; 5hr); Puerto Chacabuco (1 weekly in summer; 10–15hr).

The Carretera Austral

CHAPTER 8

Highlights

* **Laguna San Rafael glacier** Be dazzled by the icy beauty of this gigantic tongue of ice with its own lagoon that may be gone by 2030. See p.394

* **Termas de Puyuhuapi** Soak your bones and gaze at the southern night skies at Chile's premier spa resort. See p.396

* **Ventisquero Colgante** Gawk at the suspended glacier that seems to defy gravity in Parque Nacional Queulat. See p.399

* **White-water rafting at Futaleufú** "Purgatory", "Hell" and "Terminator" are just three of the world-class rapids you can hurtle down on the "Fu". See p.401

* **Crossing Lago General Carrera** Bundle up before taking the thrilling ferry ride across the second-largest lake in South America. See p.403

* **Villa O'Higgins border crossing** Take up the challenge of crossing the border into Argentina on foot and by boat through spectacular scenery. See p.408

▲ Rafting at Futaleufú

8

The Carretera Austral

rom Puerto Montt, the **Carretera Austral**, or "Southern Highway", stretches over 1000km south through the wettest, greenest, wildest and narrowest part of Chile, ending its mammoth journey at the tiny settlement of Villa O'Higgins. Carving its path through tracts of untouched wilderness, the route takes in soaring, snow-capped mountains, Ice Age glaciers, blue-green fjords, turquoise lakes and rivers, and one of the world's largest swaths of temperate rainforest. Most of it falls into **Aisén**, Chile's "last frontier", the final region to be opened up in the early twentieth century. A hundred years on, Aisén remains very sparsely populated, and still has the cut-off, marginal feel of a pioneer zone.

The original inhabitants of this rain-swept land were the nomadic, hunter-gatherer **Tehuelche** of the interior, and the canoe-faring **Alcalufe**, who fished the fjords and channels of the coast, though now only a handful of the latter remain. In 1903, the government initiated a colonization programme that ultimately handed over thousands of hectares of land to three large livestock companies. At the same time, a wave of individual pioneers – known as **colonos** – came down from the north to try their luck at logging and farming, which resulted in massive deforestation and destruction of the natural environment. Like the livestock companies, the new settlements were totally dependent on Argentina for trade and communications.

Faced with the encroaching influence of its bigger and more powerful neighbour, the government set out actively to "Chileanize" this new zone. Over the years, the population grew, communities expanded and communications improved, but the perceived need for state control of the region did not diminish, and explains the rationale behind the construction of the Carretera Austral, initiated by earlier governments but with the greatest progress achieved under **General Pinochet**. Building the road was a colossal and incredibly expensive undertaking: the first section was finished in 1983, followed by two more stretches in 1988. Engineers completed the final 100km in 2000, from tiny Puerto Yungay to the frontier outpost of Villa O'Higgins, by the Argentine border. Further south, the mainland gives way to an impenetrable ice field bordered by a shredded mass of islets that thwart even the most ambitious of road-building schemes.

Due to the eruption of the Chaitén volcano (see box, p.386), it's easiest to begin your exploration of the area from the regional capital of **Coyhaique**, located roughly halfway down the Carretera Austral. The only exceptions are **Parque Nacional Alerce Andino**, and **Parque Nacional Hornopirén**,

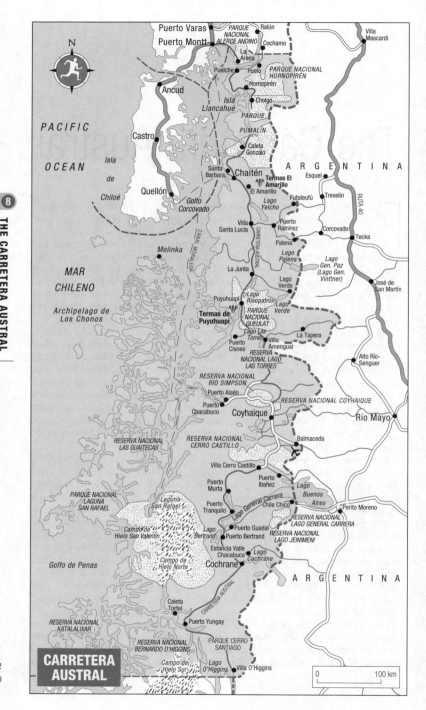

CARRETERA AUSTRAL

| 0 | | 100 km |

which are more easily accessed from Puerto Montt; and **Parque Pumalín**, whose north section is best accessed from either the Lake District or Chiloé.

Heading north up the Carretera from Coyhaique, you come to **Parque Nacional Queulat**, whose extraordinary hanging glacier and excellent trails make this one of the most rewarding places to get off the road. Don't miss the chance to soak your bones in the secluded hot pools of the nearby **Termas de Puyuhuapi**, the most luxurious thermal resort in Chile. Beyond, one branch of the road heads east, to the border village of Futaleufú, the top centre for **white-water rafting**, while the Carretera runs through the ghost town of Chaitén, before reaching the privately owned **Parque Pumalín**, where the Carretera cuts a passage through virgin temperate rainforest before reaching Caleta Gonzalo.

West of Coyhaique, the little port of **Puerto Chacabuco** is the principal starting point for boat excursions to the sensational **Laguna San Rafael glacier**, while south of Coyhaique, the road loops around South America's second largest lake, **Lago General Carrera**, blessed by a balmy microclimate supporting several lakeside farming villages, such as **Chile Chico**. The final stretch of the Carretera connects the little town of **Cochrane** to the isolated hamlet of **Villa O'Higgins**, with a road branching off to the unusual settlement of **Caleta Tortel**.

Getting around

"Doing" the Carretera Austral requires a certain amount of forward planning, and time should always be allowed for unexpected delays. A limited **bus** service does exist between the few main towns along the road, but it provides little opportunity for getting off along the way and exploring the backcountry. To get the most out of the region, you'll need your own transport, which for a growing number of visitors means a **mountain bike**, but for most others, a **4WD** or a sturdy pick-up truck to cope with the hard dirt road covered with loose gravel. There are sufficient **petrol** stations along the way to get by without carrying your own fuel, but it's always worth keeping a spare supply just in case.

The first part of the road, between Puerto Montt and Chaitén, is "bridged" by two ferry crossings; there is only limited service between Hornopirén and Caleta Gonzalo (Jan and Feb only), and there is no public transport between Hornopirén and Villa Santa Lucía. Therefore, to access the Carretera from the north, you could start or end the journey on the largely paved roads on the Argentine side of the border, with convenient border crossings at Futaleufú and Chile Chico (make sure you have the correct paperwork) or take one of the year-round ferries from Puerto Montt or Quellón to Chaitén, 200km down the Carretera Austral, or to Puerto Chacabuco, a further 420km south. Another option is to **fly** to Coyhaique and use it as a base for exploring the both the northern and southern part of the Carretera Austral.

If you're thinking of renting a vehicle in one part of the country and dropping it off in another, the only rental company that will allow you to do so is Hertz, whose outlets are found in all major cities. Note, though, that the drop-off fees, depending on the distance, can be pricey.

Parque Nacional Alerce Andino and around

Heading out of Puerto Montt, the Carretera Austral hugs the shore of the Reloncaví fjord, skirting wide mud flats and empty beaches. Some 40km down the road – just beyond the Puente de Lenca – a signed track branches left and leads 7km to the southern entrance of **PARQUE NACIONAL ALERCE ANDINO** (daily 9am–noon & 2–5pm; CH$2000), where you'll find a small **Conaf** hut, a ranger station and a **camping** area (CH$6000 per site). The park was created in 1982 to protect the region's ancient and rapidly depleting *alerce* forests, threatened with extinction by intense logging activity. Almost 200 square kilometres – half the park's land area – are covered by the massive *alerces*, mixed in with other native species like *coigüe* and *lenga*. This dense covering is spread over a landscape of steep hills and narrow glacial valleys dotted with dozens of lakes.

There's a good, long **day–hike** from the Conaf hut (at the southern entrance); the path follows the Río Chaica for 5km as far as the pretty **Laguna Chaiquenes**, surrounded by steep, forested hills. On the way, about an hour from the hut, you pass some impressive waterfalls, and twenty minutes later, a huge, 3000-year-old alerce tree. From Laguna Chaiquenes, the now deteriorating path heads north for a further 4km, as far as the long, thin **Laguna Triángulo**, where it peters out. Count on taking around three hours to get to Laguna Chaiquenes, and another three hours to get to Laguna Triángulo. There is a third entrance to the park, at Sargazo, via a dirt track running south from Correntoso. From the Conaf hut here, there are two good hikes: the hour-long ramble through the rainforest to the pristine **Laguna Sargazo**, and the longer, muddier trail that skirts the north side of the lagoon and continues on to the very remote Laguna Fría (6hr one way), passing by a thick stand of alerces.

Hornopirén-bound Buses Fierro (℡65/289024) from Puerto Montt (one daily) can drop you off at Chaica, from where it's a 4km walk to the Chaicas Conaf ranger station. It's also possible to take Buses Fierro to the tiny settlement

Alerce trees

The famed **alerce** trees – accorded national monument status by the government in 1976 – are endemic to southern Chile and Argentina and grow in high, soggy soil, usually on mountainsides between 600m and 800m above sea level. Among the **largest and oldest trees in the world**, they can rise to a height of 45m, with a trunk diameter of up to 4m, and live for over three thousand years. After shooting up rapidly during their first hundred years, they slow down dramatically, their diameter increasing just 1mm every three years. As they grow, they lose their lower branches, keeping only their top crown of dark-green, broccoli-like leaves. The lighter, lower leaves belong to parasite trees, which often prove useful to the ancient alerces, supporting them when they topple and keeping them alive. The trees' grey, papery bark conceals a beautiful, reddish-brown and extremely **valuable wood**; a large tree is worth tens of thousands of dollars. In the late-nineteenth and early-twentieth centuries, the trees were chopped down at random by early colonizers – sometimes to be used for telegraph poles or shingles, but often just to clear land which was later found to be useless for agriculture. Today, it's illegal to chop down an alerce due to their protected status, but it's not forbidden to sell the wood of dead trees. This leaves a lot of room for getting round the protection laws, as landowners have been known to find clever ways of causing premature death to their trees.

of Correntoso (2 daily), though from there it's a two-hour walk to the Correntoso Conaf hut.

The only place to stay in the park is the remote and exclusive **Alerce Mountain Lodge** (☎65/286969, ⓦwww.mountainlodge.cl), a sensitively designed timber lodge built around the alerces, and accessed via a steep and extremely rough jeep track (signed "Lodge") which branches north from the access track to the national park – best not attempted unless you have 4WD. Set in a small depression by a romantic lake, this is one of the most peaceful, beautiful and isolated places to stay in Chile, and makes for a memorable experience of the country's wilderness without roughing it. A three-night stay (the minimum) starts at CH$650,000 for a double room; this includes transfers to and from Puerto Montt, all meals and various excursions led by friendly guides, including short or long hikes through the forests, a stiff climb up to a panoramic viewpoint, and horseback treks. At day's end, you can relax in a sauna and Jacuzzi.

Hornopirén and around

The sheltered, sandy cove of **La Arena** lies 13km south of the turn-off to Parque Nacional Alerce Andino; it's the departure point of a **ferry** (9 per day; CH$9700 per car, passengers free; consult ⓦwww.tmc.cl for the updated schedule), which operates on a first-come, first-served basis. After the thirty-minute crossing, the ferry lands at tiny **Caleta Puelche**, from where the road winds through 58km of thickly forested hills, before arriving at the village of **HORNOPIRÉN**. Here you catch a Naviera Austral **ferry** to Caleta Gonzalo, where the Carretera continues, though you have to have your own transport (Jan & Feb only; Mon and Sat at 9am; 6hr; CH$7000 for passengers, CH$54,300 for cars; check ⓦwww.navieraustral.cl for updated schedules).

Perched on the northern shore of a wide fjord, at the foot of **Volcán Hornopirén**, the village enjoys a spectacular location. An important timber centre in the nineteenth century, with a currently thriving salmon industry, the village's prosperity has recently taken a blow in the form of the Chaitén volcano eruption, effectively turning the stream of visitors who would otherwise continue along the Carretera Austral into a trickle. Unless you have your own vehicle and are really determined to press on south, you will only come here to visit the Parque Nacional Hornopirén or to try and access the northern half of Parque Pumalín (see p.386) by hiring a fishing boat to take you to the Cahuelmó hot springs.

Good places to spend the night include the comfortable *Hostería Catalina*, Ingenieros Militares s/n (☎65/217359; ❸), and the inexpensive and charming *Hotel Hornopirén* on Ignacio Carrera Pinto 388 (☎65/217256; ❸), with basic rooms with shared bath, breakfast included. Popular with locals, the inexpensive *Monteverde*, on O'Higgins, serves typical Chilean fried fish and meat.

Buses Fierro (☎65/253022) runs daily to Puerto Montt; call to check the schedule.

Parque Nacional Volcán Hornopirén

To the east of Hornopirén unfold the 500 square kilometres of protected wilderness that make up **PARQUE NACIONAL VOLCÁN HORNOPIRÉN**. The park's namesake and centrepiece, 16km along a muddy track from the village, is the perfectly conical **Volcán Hornopirén**, whose steep slopes are

The eruption of Volcán Chaitén

On May 2, 2008, **Volcán Chaitén**, at the foot of which nestles its namesake town, **erupted** for the first time in over 9,000 years, taking the local residents completely by surprise, as the volcano was thought to be fully dormant. The town, and much of the surrounding area, had to be evacuated as the 19-mile (30-kilometre) plume of ash and steam from the volcano affected the local water sources. The ashfall drifted as far as some of the outlying Chiloé islands to the west and parts of eastern Patagonia, covering Futaleufú and even reaching Argentina's Esquél. On May 12, 2008, a lahar (**mudslide**), caused by the eruption, made the Río Blanco overflow, which flooded Chaitén and destroyed a large part of the town. Chaitén remains a vital part of the Carretera Austral, though, so reduced ferry services still run here from Puerto Montt and Chiloé's Quellón. Due to the continuing threat posed by volcanic activity, however, the Chilean government forbids travellers to stay in Chaitén; you may only pass through on the way to other Carretera Austral destinations. Some areas have recovered: Futaleufú can be accessed from Puerto Montt via Argentina, and also via the rerouted buses from Coyhaique. However, there is currently no public transport along the stretch of the Carretera Austral between Santa Lucía and Caleta Gonzalo.

densely forested, discouraging all but the most determined of hikers from reaching the 1572-metre summit. Five kilometres further along the track lies the seldom-visited **Lago General Pinto Concha**, with excellent fishing and stunning views onto the 2111-metre **Volcán Yate** (1hr one-way). From Lago General Pinto Concha, another track leads to the base of Volcán Yate (2hr one-way).

Back towards the village, a turn-off from the track leads south around the end of the fjord to a modern bridge over the turbulent **Río Blanco**, with a short trail to your left leading up to the impressive Salto del Río Blanco waterfall. A well-defined, eight-kilometre path follows the river upstream, passing through alternating patches of pastureland and forest before reaching a small farm. You'll encounter grand stands of *alerce*, *coigüe*, *tepa* and *lenga* around here, and if you continue on above the tree line, you'll enter a landscape of ice-covered peaks and glaciers. This makes a great **day-hike**, and you're unlikely to see another soul all day.

Parque Pumalín

North of the devastated town of Chaitén lies **PARQUE PUMALÍN**, the world's largest privately owned conservation area, covering 3,200 square kilometres (790,400 acres) of land. The Pumalín Project, founded by North American millionaire Douglas Tompkins to protect one of the world's last strongholds of temperate rainforest, has generated a considerable amount of controversy over the past few years, yet few would deny that the park represents a magnificent environmental achievement. It's a place of overwhelming natural beauty, with hauntingly calm lakes reflecting stands of endangered alerce trees, ferocious waterfalls gushing through chasms of dark rock, and high, snowy-peaked mountains. All accommodation is closed until further notice due to the still-active Chaitén volcano, although you can still access the trails if you have your own car. For the latest park conditions, contact Parque Pumalín's Puerto Varas office at Klenner 299 (℡65/250079, ⓦwww.parquepumalin.cl), or the

US Foundation for Deep Ecology office at Building 1062, Fort Cronkhite, Sausalito, CA 94965 (☎415/229 9339, ⓦwww.deepecology.org).

Exploring the park

Parque Pumalín falls into two sections, cut in half by a large chunk of land owned by ENDESA, the energy corporation. The **northern section** boasts the gloriously isolated **Termas de Cahuelmó**: a series of natural hot pools, carved out of the rock at the end of a steep, narrow fjord, accessible only by boat. You'll find a rustic camping area nearby, from where a five-kilometre trail leads to the crystal-clear **Lago Abascal**, surrounded by dramatic scenery. From the Vodudahue Valley, reachable by boat only, take the trail along the Río Vodudahue to the project farms adjacent to Parque Pumalín, where you can get advice on trail conditions. Following the trail to the confluence of Río

Douglas Tompkins and the Pumalín Project

In 1995 it was publicly announced that a North American millionaire, **Douglas Tompkins**, had used intermediaries to buy a 3000-square-kilometre chunk of southern Chile – marking the beginning of a five-year national soap opera that transformed Tompkins into one of the most controversial public figures in the country. In 1991, the 49-year-old Californian, deeply disillusioned with the corporate world, and increasingly committed to environmental issues, sold his fifty percent share in the Esprit clothing empire, bought an abandoned ranch on the edge of the **Reñihué fjord**, 130km south of Puerto Montt, and moved there with his wife and kids. Inspired by the "deep ecology" movement pioneered by the Norwegian environmentalist **Arne Naess**, Tompkins set out to acquire more of the surrounding wilderness, with the aim of protecting it from the threat of commercial exploitation. As he did so, he was seized with the idea of creating a massive, privately funded national park, which would ensure permanent protection of the **ancient forest** while providing low-impact facilities for visitors.

Over the next four years Tompkins spent more than US$14 million buying up adjoining tracts of land, in most cases hiding his identity to prevent prices from shooting up. His initial secrecy was to have damaging repercussions, however, for once his land acquisitions became public knowledge, he was engulfed by a wave of suspicion and hostility, fuelled by several right-wing politicians and the press, with his motives questioned by everyone. The biggest cause for alarm, it seemed, was the fact that Tompkins' land stretched from the Argentine border to the Pacific Ocean, effectively "cutting Chile in two".

Tompkins appeared on national television, explaining his intentions to create **Parque Pumalín**, a nature sanctuary with free access, slowly winning over some of the public. It was a long struggle to have his lands declared a Santuario de la Naturaleza; eventually, the government agreed to support Tompkins' aims to establish the park – on the condition that for one year he would not buy more than 7000 contiguous hectares (17,250 acres) of land in the south of Chile. Tompkins was also prevented from purchasing Huinay, a 740,000-acre property owned by the Catholic University of Valparaíso, separating the two separate chunks of his land, which was instead sold to ENDESA, Chile's largest energy corporation.

Ownership of Parque Pumalín was transferred to the US-based **Conservation Land Trust**, who in 2003 donated it to the Chilean Fundación Pumalín, whose board includes Tompkins and his wife. Tompkins, determined to save a little more unspoiled terrain from development, in 2001 purchased another chunk of land near the Termas del Amarillo, south of Chaitén, while his wife Kristine is currently working on the conservation project of **Estancia Valle Chacabuco** near Cochrane (see p.406).

Barcelo and Río Vodudahue, you'll have to cross over to the north side of the river in the boat provided. This easy trail takes around four or five hours and leads you through a beautiful valley hemmed in by tall peaks, with hanging glaciers visible along the way, before ending at a tranquil lagoon where Río Vodudahue and Río Libertadores meet; you can camp on the shores here. From the farm, you can also do the two- to three-day hike to the beautiful Cascadas de Vodudahue. The not-too-strenuous trail runs along the Río Vodudahue, passing stands of alerce trees before arriving at the falls; you can camp wild here. Check the weather forecast before attempting either of the hikes, as the rivers rise fast during heavy rain. Getting here is expensive, costing around CH\$80,000 per boat trip, which can be arranged in Hornopirén. The easier option is to join a multi-day kayaking adventure trip with either Alsur Expediciones (☎65/232300, ⓦwww.alsurexpeditions.com), Yak Expediciones (☎09/299 6487, ⓦwww.yakexpediciones.cl) or take a multi-day boat trip with Austral Adventures (☎65/625977, ⓦwww.austral-adventures.com).

The **southern section** has more infrastructure geared towards visitors. Near the ferry ramp at Caleta Gonzalo, the **Sendero Cascadas** climbs steeply through a canopy of overhanging foliage up to a fifteen-metre waterfall (3hr round-trip). Three other trails have been carved out of the forest, branching off from the Carretera Austral as it heads south through the park. Twelve kilometres down the road, **Sendero Laguna Tronador** is probably the most exciting, crossing a narrow gorge filled with a rushing, white-water stream, climbing up to a look-out point with fabulous views onto Volcán Michimahuida, and ending at a pristine lake with a camping area alongside (3hr round-trip). One kilometre south, across the Río Blanco, **Sendero Los Alerces** is an enjoyable twenty-minute circular route, dotted with information panels, through a grove of ancient, colossal alerces. Another kilometre down the road, the **Sendero Cascadas Escondidas** is an easy walk through the forest to several high, slender waterfalls; you reach the first one after 25 minutes or so, and the other two half an hour after that.

Coyhaique and around

After the smattering of small villages scattered along the Carretera Austral, Aisén's lively regional capital, **COYHAIQUE**, can be a welcome change. The city's fifty thousand inhabitants make up half the region's population, and it's the only place along the Carretera that offers a wide range of services, from pharmacies and banks to laundries and car-rental outlets. It's also a good launch pad for some great **day-trips** that will give you a taste of the region's wilderness – for more details see p.390.

Arrival and information

Most **buses** pull in at the central terminal on the corner of Lautaro and Magallanes, though a few arrive at and depart from their respective company offices. All Sky and LAN flights land at the **Aeropuerto de Balmaceda**, 55km south, and are met by **minibuses** that take passengers to their hotels for CH\$4000. Charter flights take off from the Aeródromo Teniente Vidal, 5km west of town.

You can pick up information on the city and the region at the helpful **Sernatur** office, at Bulnes 35 (Jan–Feb Mon–Fri 8.30am–8pm, Sat–Sun 10am–6pm; March–Dec Mon–Fri 8.30am–5.30pm; ☎67/231752, ⓦwww.patagoniachile.cl). During summer you'll also find an **information** kiosk on

COYHAIQUE

ACCOMMODATION

Camping Río Correntoso	A
HI Albergue Las	
Salamandras	K
Hospedaje Gladys	D
Hospedaje Natty	L
Hostal Belisario Jara	I
Hostal Bon	H
Hostería Coyhaique	F
Hotel Luís Loyola	J
Hotel Los Ñires	C
Hotelera San Rafael	E
Hotel El Reloj	G
Sra Herminia Mansilla	B

EATING & DRINKING

Café Alemana	3
Café Oriente	4
Café Ricer	9
Caramba	2
Casino de Bomberos	1
La Casona	7
La Olla	5
Pizzeria La Fiorentina	8
Piel Roja	10
El Reloj	6

the plaza. For more on Aisén's national parks and reserves, visit **Conaf**'s Oficina Patrimonio Silvestre at Av Ogana 1060 (Mon–Fri 8.30am–noon & 3–5.30pm; ☏67/212109).

Accommodation

HI Albergue Las Salamandras Carretera Teniente Vidal, Km 1.5 ☏67/211865 ⓦwww .salamandras.cl. Set in a wood by a river 1.5km along the road to Teniente Vidal, this popular hostel offers the use of a kitchen, ample common spaces, TV loft, laundry facilities, mountain-bike rental and a range of excursions, including cross-country skiing during Coyhaique's long winter. Camping possible. ❷–❸

Hospedaje Gladys Parra 65 ☏67/245288. Welcoming, quiet, central guesthouse with spotless mid-sized rooms, cable TV included. Some English spoken. Breakfast CH$1500 extra. ❸

Hospedaje Natty Almirante Simpson 417 ☏67/231047. Friendly guesthouse with clean rooms, though some have windows into the coridor, with a separate guest kitchen and eating area, space for a couple of tents and a handy laundry service next door. ❷

Hostal Belisario Jara Bilbao 626 ☏67/234150 ⓦwww.belisariojara.ltgo.com. Distinctively decorated, elegant guesthouse with airy wood-panelled en-suite rooms, and attentive staff. ❼

Hostal Bon Serrano 91 ☏67/231189. Small hotel with thin partition walls and a mixture of shared baths and en-suite rooms; a few are a little cramped. It's a friendly place, though, with a good restaurant that specializes in hearty *parrilladas*. ❹

Hostería Coyhaique Magallanes 131 ☏67/231137, ⓦwww.hotelsa.cl. Imposing gates give way to ample gardens and a relatively low-key four-star hotel with modern amenities; it's favoured by large tour groups. Offers a number of multi-day adventure tours, both in the nearby area and beyond. ❼

Hotel Luís Loyola Prat 455 ☏67/234200 Ⓔhotel-loyolacoyhaique@chile.net. A modern hotel with eighteen en-suite rooms, all with cable TV and central heating. Probably the best choice in this price range. **⑤**

🎿 **Hotel Los Ñires** Baquedano 315 ☎67/232261 ⓦwww.doncarlos.cl. One of the older hotels in town, and part of the Empresas Don Carlos that owns a bus and plane company. There's little character, but comfortable en-suite rooms and a popular restaurant. **⑥**

Hotelera San Rafael Moraleda 343 ☎67/233733 ⓔcsanrafael@patagoniachile.cl. Cheerful, spacious rooms with lots of light and modern amenities are popular with foreign travellers as well as locals. **⑥**

Hotel El Reloj Baquedano 828 ☎67/231108 ⓦwww.elrelojhotel.cl. Located in a former sawmill, the town's best hotel boasts spotlessly clean, comfortable en-suite rooms with cable TV and internet, as well as Coyhaique's best restaurant and a good buffet breakfast. **⑦**

Sra Herminia Mansilla 21 de Mayo 60 ☎67/231579. Popular with budget travellers, this neat and tidy *casa familiar*, slightly out of the centre, has light, airy rooms and a friendly owner who is very proud of the long list of foreign visitors in her guestbook. **②**

The Town

Coyhaique's most unusual (and confusing) feature is its large, five-sided **Plaza de Armas**, from which the main streets radiate; even with map in hand, travellers often find themselves wandering around in circles (or pentagons). On the southwest corner with Horn, the small **Feria de Artesanos** sells jewellery and leather goods, while just across the plaza on the corner with Montt, the **Galería Artesanal de Cema Chile** features a wide range of handicrafts, including knitwear, weavings, wooden carvings and ceramics.

At the junction of Montt with Baquedano, the city's main thoroughfare, the **Monumento al Ovejero**, a large sculpture of a shepherd and a flock of sheep, commemorates Aisén's pioneer farmers. Almost opposite the monument, within the Casa de Cultura, stands the **Museo Regional de la Patagonia** (Jan & Feb daily 9am–8pm; March–Dec Mon–Fri 9am–5.30pm; CH$500), where an informative collection of black-and-white photographs vividly captures the "Wild West" frontier atmosphere during the opening up of Aisén a century ago, as well as miscellaneous exhibits on the area's geology and natural history.

Eating and drinking

Café Alemana Condell 119. With its scrubbed pine tables and floral furnishings, this is an attractive place for a snack, though there's nothing remotely German about the menu, which offers the usual *lomos*, pizzas and sandwiches –

plus above-average pancakes and home-made ice creams.

Café Oriente Condell 201. This small, basic café (the oldest in town) serves up reasonable snacks and sandwiches as well as *kuchen*.

> ## Tours from Coyhaique
>
> The adventure companies listed below are established, experienced and come highly recommended. Andes Patagónicos, Horn 48 (☎67/216711, ⓦwww.ap.cl), is a good bet for arranging half-day and full-day **tours** to the nearby **lakes** (see p.392), to see local **rock art** and to **Reserva Nacional Cerro Castillo** (see p.392), among other destinations, as well as multi-day trips to the Northern and Southern Ice Fields. Geoturismo Patagonia, Balmaceda 334 (☎67/573460, ⓦwww.geoturismopatagonia.cl), offers a variety of excursions, from horseback riding in the area to rafting on Río Simpson, and **aerial tours** of Laguna San Rafael. Condor Explorer, Dussen 357 (☎67/573634, ⓦwww.condorexplorer.com), specializes in **mountaineering excursions**, trekking, horseback riding and ski treks in winter. Cochrane-based Patagonia Adventure Expeditions (☎67/411330, ⓦwww.adventurepatagonia.com) does multi-day expeditions to seldom-visited destinations, such as the "Ice to Ocean" eleven-day trip that involves hiking, rafting and horseback riding, as well as shorter rafting trips on the Río Simpson, Río Paloma or Río Mañihuales and horse trekking.

Moving on from Coyhaique

There have been major changes to **bus schedules** since the May 2008 eruption of Volcán Chaitén. Buses Queilén (℡67/240760) runs to **Osorno**, **Puerto Montt**, **Ancud** and **Castro** (Mon, Wed & Fri, 5pm; CH$30,000–35,000). Transaustral has similarly priced departures to Osorno and Puerto Montt on (Tues & Fri, 4.45pm) and to **Comodoro Rivadavia**, Argentina (Mon & Fri, 8am; CH$20,000). **Cochrane** is served by Buses Don Carlos, Subteniente Cruz 63 ℡67/211981 (Mon, Thurs, Sat; 9.30am; CH$11,000), Buses Sao Paolo ℡67/255726 (Tues, Thurs, Sat; 9.30am), and Buses Acuario 13 ℡67/255726 (Wed, Fri, Sun; 9.30am). Buses Sao Paolo also runs to **Puerto Aisén** (every 30min between 7am and 8.30pm; fewer on weekends; CH$1200), as does Buses Syray, Prat 265 (℡67/238387). Buses Don Oscar (℡67/232903) goes to **Puerto Cisnes**, **Puyuhuapi** (CH$8000), **La Junta** (CH$9000), **Santa Lucia**, **Palena** and **Futaleufú**, while Buses Daniela (℡67/231701) runs to Futaleufú via Puyuhuapi and La Junta (Tues & Thurs, 8am). Buses Acuario also runs to **Villa Cerro Castillo**, **Puerto Ibañez**, **Puerto Tranquilo**, **Puerto Guadal**, **Chile Chico**, **Puerto Bertrand**, **Cochrane** and **Caleta Tortel**. Patagonia Interlagos (℡67/2408400) has departures to Villa Cerro Castillo (CH$4500), Puerto Río Tranquilo (CH$7000), Puerto Guadal (CH$9000), Puerto Bertrand (CH$10,000), and Cochrane (CH$11,000). Buses Quelulat, at Parra 329 (℡67/242626) runs to **Chaitén** via La Junta and Santa Lucía, overnighting in La Junta, with a boat connection from Chaitén to Puerto Montt the following morning (Thurs & Sun, 8am).

LAN has **flights** to Santiago and Puerto Montt daily, and to Punta Arenas on Saturdays. Sky has daily flights to Santiago, Puerto Montt and Punta Arenas. Transportes Aéro Don Carlos has charter flights to Cochrane, Villa O'Higgins and Chile Chico; call for updated schedules. The Navimag **ferry** to Puerto Montt leaves once a week from Puerto Chacabuco during summer, less often in winter.

Café Ricer Horn 48. Just off the plaza, this bright and cheerful café attracts a lot of gringos, partly for its vegetarian dishes; Chilean standards are better than anything that sounds more adventurous. There's a more upscale restaurant upstairs, decorated with evocative photographs of the early pioneers, and knick-knacks from the early 1900s.
Casino de Bomberos General Parra 365. Slightly hidden away, Coyhaique's firemen's canteen – packed and lively – is one of the best places in town for lunch, with excellent-value set meals. Busy at lunchtimes.
La Casona Vielmo 77. Come to this upmarket spot for both Chilean staples and more elaborate meals; the lunchtime *menú ejecutivo* is good value. Particularly popular with locals.
Caramba Condell at Moraleda. Quality fast food burger and kebab joint, with a different special daily, and the food prepared in front of you. Meal CH$3200.

La Olla Prat 176 ℡67/234700. Run by a charming man from Extremadura, this cosy, old-fashioned restaurant does excellent paellas every Sunday (and through the week if you phone in advance) and first-class *estofado de cordero* (lamb stew) all at reasonable prices.
Piel Roja Moraleda 495. An excellent spot for a beer and snack, this lively pub with a quirky interior serves up good burgers and *quesadillas*. Strut your stuff on the dancefloor of the adjacent disco (bar and disco open until 4am). Beers CH$1200.
Pizzeria La Fiorentina Prat 230. Reliable Italian food – mostly pasta and pizza – served in pleasant surroundings makes this one of the most popular eateries in town. Mains CH$4500.
El Reloj Baquedano 828. Some of the tastiest (but pricey) food in town, such as lamb with rosemary, and excellent ceviche, is served in this sophisticated dining room tended by the friendly hoteliers.

Listings

Airlines Transporte Aéreo Don Carlos, Subteniente Cruz 63 ℡67/231981; LAN, General Parra 402 ℡67/231188; SKY, Prat 203, at Dussen ℡67/240825.

Banks and exchange The following banks have ATMs: Banco Santander, Condell 184, Banco de Chile, Condell 298 and BBVA, Condell 254. *Cambios*

include Turismo Prado de la Patagonia at 21 de Mayo 417 and Emperador at Freire 171.
Bike rental Figon at Simpson at Colón ☏67/234616.
Car rental Automundo AVR, Bilbao 510 ☏67/231621; Budget, Errázuriz 454 ☏67/255171; Traeger-Hertz, Gral Parra 280 ☏67/245780.
Ferry The Navimag office is at Horn 47.
Hospital The regional hospital is on Carrera s/n ☏67/231286.

Internet At the *centro de llamados* at Horn 51, or try Trapanda Cyber, Parra 86.
Post office Cochrane 202, near Plaza de Armas.
Outdoor equipment Condor Explorer, at Dussen 357, has a wide selection of camping, fishing and mountaineering gear, plus outdoor clothes.
Telephone centres Try the *centro de llamados* at Horn 51.

Reserva Nacional Coyhaique

Just 4km north of the city – about a 45-minute walk – the **RESERVA NACIONAL COYHAIQUE** (daily: April–Nov 8.30am–6.30pm; Dec–March 8.30am–9pm; CH$1500), huddled at the foot of towering Cerro McKay, is an easily accessible slice of wilderness, featuring areas of native forest, a couple of lakes and fantastic views down to Coyhaique and the Río Simpson valley.

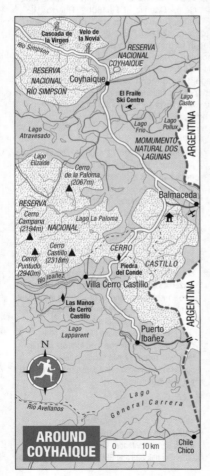

Sendero Los Leñeros leads almost 2km from the *guardería* by the entrance through native *lenga* and *ñire* trees to a **camping** area (CH$3500 per site), from where the path continues for another 1.8km through pine trees to **Laguna Verde**. From here, you pick up with a jeep track which, if you follow it north for a couple of hundred metres, will take you to the trailhead of **Sendero Las Piedras**, the best (and steepest) hike in the reserve, leading 13km up to and across a ridge, giving breathtaking views for miles around; allow four hours to complete. After descending at the other end, a side path branches off to **Lago Venus**, an attractive lake 1km beyond, reached by walking through dense native forest. Alternatively, keep on going another couple of hundred metres and you'll join up with **Sendero El Chucao**, which leads 2.6km back to the *guardería*.

Reserva Nacional Cerro Castillo

About an hour's drive south of Coyhaique, the Carretera Austral crosses the (unsigned) northern boundary of the **RESERVA NACIONAL CERRO CASTILLO**. Spread out below you is a broad river valley flanked by densely forested lower slopes that rise to a breathtaking panorama of barren, rocky peaks. Dominating the skyline is the reserve's eponymous centrepiece, **Cerro Castillo**, whose needlepoint spires loom over the valley like the turrets of a Transylvanian castle. Further down the road, you pass the *guardería* on your left (daily: April–Nov 8.30am–5.30pm; Dec–March 8.30am–9pm; CH$700), which has a basic **camping** area (CH$3500). Part of the Sendero de Chile, the rewarding forty-kilometre Sendero Cerro Castillo, which takes about three days to complete, branches right (west) from the road 6km south of the *guardería*, and follows the Río La Lima upstream to a 1,450m pass on the east side of Cerro Castillo (2,300m) through *coigüe* and *ñire* forest. On the way, you pass the stunning **Laguna Cerro Castillo**, at the foot of a glacier suspended from the mountainside, before descending to the village of **Villa Cerro Castillo** (see p.405). Note that the trail is very poorly marked; you should buy an IGM map in advance in Coyhaique and get more detailed route advice from the *guardaparque*, who should be informed before you set off. You can get here on any of the **buses** from Coyhaique to Villa Cerro Castillo.

West of Coyhaique

From Coyhaique, a paved section of the Carretera runs west towards the coast, to the nondescript **Puerto Aisén**, 65km away, formerly a port for shipping cattle, which literally became a backwater when its harbour silted up, forcing commercial vessels to use nearby **Puerto Chacabuco** from 1960.

The scenic route holds fast to the Río Simpson as it rushes through the **Reserva Nacional Río Simpson**, sandwiched between tall, craggy cliffs. Thirty-seven kilometres out of Coyhaique, a small wooden sign by the road points to the reserve's Conaf office and attached **museum** (daily: April–Nov 8.30am–5.30pm; Dec–March 8.30am–9pm; CH$500) on local flora and fauna, of which the best exhibit is the huge stump of a four hundred-year-old lenga tree in the garden. The reserve's main attractions are conveniently located right by the road: 1km on from the museum, you'll pass the **Cascada de la Virgen**, a tall, graceful waterfall that drops in two stages, separated by a pool of water with a shrine to the Virgin Mary next to it; a further 8km east thunders another waterfall, the **Velo de la Novia**, or "bride's veil", so named for its diaphanous spray. You can stay at the attractive *Camping San Sebastián*, 5km east of the Conaf hut, with sheltered sites and hot showers (CH$5000 per site); a better option is the *Camping Río Correntoso*, 24km west of Coyhaique, with its stunning riverside setting and rustic showers (CH$3000 per person). Any bus running between Coyhaique and Puerto Aisén can drop you off at the Reserva.

Puerto Aisén can be a useful overnight base before or after a journey to the San Rafael glacier; its long main street has ATMs, restaurants and guesthouses. Modern *Hotel Caicahues*, Michimalonco 660 (☎67/336633, ✉caicahue @patagoniachile.cl; ❺), has decent en-suite rooms, a restaurant and a bar, while *Hospedaje Mar Clara*, Caupolicán and Carrera (☎67/333030; ❹), offers basic clean rooms. The top spot for **eating** in town is the popular *Isla Verde*, Teniente Merino 710, specializing in fish and seafood.

Buses Acuario 13 has hourly departures for Coyhaique, just off the main street, while Buses Suray has four departures every hour along the main Sargento Aldea to neighbouring Puerto Chacabuco and half-hourly departures to Coyhaique.

Puerto Chacabuco

Fifteen kilometres west of Puerto Aisén, the busy port of **PUERTO CHACABUCO** sits dramatically on a natural harbour enclosed by craggy, jagged peaks brushed with snow. In contrast, the road is lined with ugly fish processing factories emitting a nauseating smell of fish. Your only reason for coming here would be to take a boat to the Laguna San Rafael glacier; as the boats set out early in the morning, and get back late, you might want to spend a night here before and after the trip.

Puerto Chacabuco also serves as the terminal for ferries to and from Puerto Montt and Quellón, operated by Naviera Austral (☎67/351144) whose office is on the road down to the ferry ramp, and Navimag cruises to Puerto Natales and Puerto Montt.

Just up the hill from the port, at José Miguel Carrera 50, sits the best hotel in the area: the attractive, and expensive, ⚑ *Hotel Loberías del Sur* (☎67/351115, ⓦwww .hoteloberiasdelsur.cl; ❼), with beautifully renovated, tastefully furnished en-suite rooms with king-sized beds, wi-fi, a gym, a sauna, a superb fish and seafood restaurant (try the salmon *cancato*), catamaran tours to Laguna San Rafael and an attractive private 250-hectare nature reserve nearby (ⓦwww.parqueaikendelsur.cl). Cheaper accommodation along the road down towards the ferry terminal includes *Residencial Moraleda*, O'Higgins 82 (☎67/351155; ❸), the best of a motley bunch, with neat, spartan **rooms**, whitewashed wooden walls, decent showers and a basic **restaurant** downstairs.

Minibuses run to Puerto Aisén every half an hour (CH$600); Buses Suray continues to Coyhaique.

Laguna San Rafael

From Puerto Chacabuco, a 200-kilometre boat ride through the labyrinthine fjords of Aisén brings you to the dazzling **San Rafael glacier**, spilling into the broad Laguna San Rafael. The journey is a spectacle in itself, as boats edge their way through narrow channels hemmed in by precipitous cliffs dripping with vegetation. After sailing down the long, thin Golfo de Elefantes, the boat enters the seemingly unnavigable Río Témpanos, or "Iceberg River", before emerging into the Laguna San Rafael. Floating in the lagoon are dozens of **icebergs**, fashioned by wind and rain into monumental sculptures, with such a vibrant electric-blue colour that they appear to be lit from within.

Sailing around these icy phantoms, you approach the giant **glacier** at the far end of the lagoon. Over 4km wide, and rearing out of the water to a height of 70m, it really is a dizzying sight. While the cruise boat keeps at a safe distance, to avoid being trapped by icebergs, you'll probably be given the chance to get a closer look on board an inflatable motor dinghy – but not too close, as the huge blocks of ice that calve off into the water with a deafening roar create dangerous waves. What you can see from the boat is in fact just the tip of the glacier's "tongue", which extends some 15km from its source.

The glacier is retreating fast, frequently by as much as 100m a year. Early explorers reported that, in 1800, the glacier filled three-quarters of the lagoon, and archive photographs from the beginning of the twentieth century show it as being far longer than it is today. It is estimated that by the year 2030, the glacier will be gone.

Stretching beyond the shores of the lagoon are the 4.2 million acres of land that make up **Parque Nacional Laguna San Rafael**. Almost half this vast area is covered by the immense ice field known as the **Campo de Hielo Norte**; it feeds eighteen other glaciers on top of this one and contains over 250 lakes and

The glacier is currently accessible *only* by boat or plane. **Flights** from Coyhaique in five-seater planes are offered by the Coyhaique-based **Aéreo Don Carlos** (Subteniente Cruz 630 ℡67/232981, 🌐www.doncarlos.cl) and **Transportes San Rafael** (℡67/233408), last ninety minutes each way and cost CH$100,000–120,000 per person – usually requiring a full plane. Flying over the icefield is indeed an unforgettable experience, but the most sensational views of the glacier are from the small **dinghies** that thread through the icebergs towards its base, usually included as part of a visit to the lagoon **by sea**. Two companies run day-trips to the glacier in high-speed **catamarans** (four or five hours each way): *Hotel Loberías del Sur*'s own **Catamaranes del Sur** (℡02/231 1902, 🌐www.catamaranesdelsur.cl; CH$150,000) and **Patagonia Connection** (℡02/225 6489, 🌐www.patagoniaconnex.cl; trips are combined with a 2-night stay at the *Termas de Puyuhuapi* hotel (see p.397) and one night in Puerto Chacabuco; rates start from around CH$570,000). All trips include three meals and operate an open bar – it is now a tradition to drink a whisky or cocktail containing "thousand-year-old ice cubes" chipped from an iceberg. The downside to catamaran trips is that you only get a couple of hours at the glacier. If you're after a more leisurely visit, you could opt for a multi-day cruise from Puerto Montt or Puerto Chacabuco, either with **Navimag** (Puerto Montt ℡65/253318; Coyhaique ℡67/233306; 🌐www.navimag.com; cruises all year round, from CH$230,000/245,000 per person) or the far more luxurious **Skorpios** (Puerto Montt ℡65/256619; Santiago ℡02/477 1900; 🌐www.skorpios.cl; 4-day/3-night journey from CH$380,000 and the seven-day/six-night journey from CH$570,000; cruises from Sept–May only).

lagoons. The 4058-metre **Monte San Valentín**, the highest peak in the southern Andes, towers over the frozen plateau. The CH$4000 park entrance fee is payable only if you land. A mere five hundred or so per year do so, most of them on the light aeroplanes that fly tourists over the glacier and touch down for a couple of hours. Those who arrange a longer stay at the park can stay in the Conaf-run *Casa de Huéspedes Laguna Caiquenes*, a *refugio* with hot water, kitchen facilities and electricity (CH$70,000 for six people) while the small *Camping Laguna Caiquenes* has three basic sites for CH$3000 per person; call ℡67/332743 to reserve. From the Conaf *guardería*, a seven-kilometre trail leads to a breathtaking viewpoint platform over the sprawling, icy tongue, taking around two hours up and slightly less coming down. A road is currently under construction from Puerto Río Tranquilo, on the Carretera, to Bahía Exploradores, which joins the Estero Elefantes, which may make the park more accessible in the near future.

Parque Nacional Queulat and around

One of Aisén's biggest attractions – **Parque Nacional Queulat**, with its stunning, rugged scenery and its namesake hanging glacier – lies north of Coyhaique along the Carretera Austral. The southwest edge of the park is bordered by the little town of **Puerto Cisnes**, a low-key, scenic detour from the Carretera Austral and the gateway to the little-explored **Isla Magdalena**. In the middle of Parque Nacional Queulat and some 90km from Puerto Cisnes you'll come across the charming village of **Puyuhuapi**, the departure point for excursions to the **Termas de Puyuhuapi**, and a convenient base for exploring **Parque Nacional Queulat**.

Puerto Cisnes

A small, quaint fishing village in a dramatic setting at the mouth of Río Cisnes, **PUERTO CISNES** sits at the end of a 35-kilometre side road that branches west from the Carretera Austral, just beyond the southern limit of Parque Nacional Queulat. Formerly a solitary sawmill, set up by a German pioneer in 1929, Puerto Cisnes with its colourful fishing boats makes for a peaceful detour; it is also the access point to the little-visited Parque Nacional Isla Magdalena (not to be confused with the penguin colony near Punta Arenas), a 1,580-square kilometre expanse of densely forested mountains and pristine rivers, with very little infrastructure and home to such fauna as the *pudú* and the *güiña* (wildcat). Negotiating passage to the island across the Canal Puyuhuapi is expensive (around CH$100,000), but worth it for independent travellers who really want to get away from it all; contact Héctor Parra (☎67/346548) or ask around in the village.

Accommodation in the village includes the comfortable *Hostería El Gaucho*, perched on the edge of a stream at Holmberg 140 (☎67/346514; ❸), with a good restaurant and bar, the fully-equipped *Cabañas Río Cisnes*, Costanera 101 (☎67/346404; ❻), which sleep four to eight people each; the owner runs fishing trips. *El Guairao*, near the bridge that links the two halves of the village, at Piloto Pardo 58 (☎67/346473; ❺), offers motel-style en-suite rooms with satellite TV and its restaurant is also the best place to **eat**; try the local speciality of *puyes*, similar to whitebait and absolutely delicious. The small fishermen's bars along the road by the sea are good for simple meals and snacks.

Buses Terraustral (☎67/254335) runs daily to Coyhaique, while Buses Don Oscar (☎67/232903) stops here four times weekly on the way to and from the northern Carretera Austral destinations.

Puyuhuapi

Squatting at the head of the narrow Ventisquero fjord, surrounded by steep, wooded hills, quaint little **PUYUHUAPI** is a great place to break your journey along the Carretera Austral in either direction – not only for the wild beauty of its setting, but also for its proximity to the most compelling attractions in the whole region, the **Termas de Puyuhuapi** and the **Parque Queulat**. Puyuhuapi's rambling streets and old timber houses offer a pleasing contrast to the utilitarian "villages" installed along the Carretera in the 1980s after the completion of the road.

The village was founded in the 1930s by four young German immigrants from Sudetenland (now in the Czech Republic), who married Chilean women. Many of their descendants still live in Puyuhuapi, which has an unmistakably Teutonic look with its steep-roofed chalets and well-tended gardens. Alfombras de Puyuhuapi, the local carpet factory (☎67/325131, ⊛www.puyuhuapi.com; Mon–Fri 8.30am–noon & 3–7pm; guided tours CH$1500), was founded in 1940 by textile engineer Walter Hopperdietzel, and is still flourishing, with handmade woollen carpets produced by dextrous Chilote women weavers. The town's premier attractions are the **Termas de Puyuhuapi** – an upmarket hot springs resort. Those not wishing to visit the plush *termas* (see opposite) can head instead to the more easily accessible **Termas Ventisquero** (daily 9am–11pm; CH$7000), 6km south of town along the Carretera, with two simple outdoor pools fed by thermal springs, a beautiful view and a decent café serving sandwiches and *kuchen*.

Practicalities

There is a small but helpful **tourist office** on Avenida Übel, in the centre of town (no phone; ⓦwww.puyuhuapi.org; Mon–Sat 10am–2pm & 6–9pm in summer only).

The best place to **stay** in Puyuhuapi is *Casa Ludwig* at Übel 850 (☎67/325220, ⓦwww.contactchile.cl/casaludwig; ❸ shared bath, ❺ en-suite), a delightful yellow chalet with comfortable rooms, excellent breakfast, a library and great views, run by a charming lady who speaks English and German and is a wealth of information on the area. Or, head to the recommended *Hostería Alemana* at Übel 450 (☎67/325118, ⓔhosteria-alemana@entelchile.net; ❺), a large, elegant timber house with comfortable rooms, set in a mature garden. Opposite, *Residencial Marily* (☎67/325201; ❸) is closer to the budget end with clean rooms, some en-suite, with comfortable beds.

In the village, you can tuck into excellent **meals** at the cute *Café Rossbach*, opposite the carpet factory, where wild berries are used in their mouth-watering *kuchen*; it gets very busy here at dinner time. Best of all, though, is the excellent 🍴 *Lluvia Marina*, next to *Casa Ludwig*, where you can get real coffee, home-made cakes and excellent, reasonably priced meals, including salmon ceviche, onion soup, pasta, pizza and meat dishes.

Puyuhuapi is served by at least one **bus** daily, running between Coyhaique and Futaleufú; northbound buses pass through around 2pm, while southbound ones tend to arrive between 3 and 5pm.

Termas de Puyuhuapi

The luxurious thermal baths, 🍴 lodge and spa at **TERMAS DE PUYUHUAPI** (☎67/325103; in Santiago, ☎2/225 6489, ⓦwww.patagonia-connection.com) enjoy a fantastic location, marooned on the edge of a peninsula on the opposite side of the fjord from the Carretera, reachable only by boat. Four times a day from December to March (call for updated schedule), and less frequently off-season, a motor launch collects passengers from a signposted wooden jetty 15km south of Puyuhuapi, and whisks them across the water on a ten-minute ride to the lodge.

The thermal baths used to be a handful of ramshackle cabins that were transformed into a series of low-lying, beautifully designed buildings made of reddish-brown alerce timber and lots of glass by the East German shipbuilding magnate Eberhard Kossman in the late 1980s. Apart from its spectacular location, the main reason to come here is to soak in the steaming **hot springs**, channelled into three outdoor pools reached by a short walk through the forest. Two of the pools are large enough to swim in, and sit right on the edge of the fjord, while the third one, containing the hottest water, is a small pond enclosed by overhanging ferns and native trees. There's a the state-of-the-art **spa**, specialising in a range of treatments and massage, whirlpools, a gym with an excellent view and a large indoor pool.

You don't need to be an overnight guest to visit, but you should phone ahead to book, and to make sure you're met by a launch: a **day visit** costs CH$15,000 for the outdoor pools, CH$25,000 for the use of the indoor pool and CH$10,000 for the round-trip boat ride (free to guests). The restaurant serves delicious three-course meals made with fresh local produce, though they fall short of gourmet cuisine.

Parque Nacional Queulat

PARQUE NACIONAL QUEULAT features a vast expanse of virgin forest, towering granite peaks and rumbling glaciers. The Carretera Austral enters the

Aisén is currently the most exciting fly-fishing region in Chile and is internationally renowned, drawing serious anglers, including a number of Hollywood stars. Here, local boatmen whisk fishermen through the bewildering maze of channels and islets to remote, hidden rivers, as clear as glass and teeming with fish.

The **season** varies slightly according to the area, but in general lasts from October or November to May. You need a **licence** to fish, which costs around CH$8000 and is widely available in town halls and sport-fishing shops. To find out more about fly-fishing in Chile, contact the **Servicio Nacional de Pesca** (a government agency) at Victoria 2832, Valparaíso (℡32/819441, ⍟www.sernapesca.cl).

The Carretera Austral has opened up the area to opportunities for anglers, and a number of first-class fishing lodges have sprung up around the region. Most lodges are of an extremely high standard, and charge between US$4000–7000 per person for a seven-night package including accommodation, fishing guide, all food and an open bar. Below, we have listed the pick of the bunch:

Futa Lodge near Futaleufú; ℡67/236402 or 800/628 1447, ⍟www.angleradventures .com. North American Jim Repine spent many years guiding in Alaska before coming down to the Futaleufú river valley. With guest capacity of six, and excellent food and wine, this is a small, intimate, relaxing lodge, especially geared towards couples. Rainbow and brown trout are most prevalent, with wading right at the front door; saltwater fishing in Parque Nacional Queulat is also possible. Friendly owners organize horseback riding and bird-watching excursions for non-fishing guests. Open November–April.

Heart of Patagonia Lodge 11km from Puerto Aisén ℡67/233701, ⍟www .heartofpatagonia.com. One of the more easily reached lodges, a remodelled 1930s home on the banks of the Río Simpson, this homely American-owned place caters to international guests. The restaurant serves good Chilean food and there are hiking and horseriding options for non-fishing guests.

Isla Monita Lodge ℡2/339 8465, ⍟www.islamonita.cl. English-owned, remote, deluxe lodge sitting on a tiny island in the middle of Lago Yelcho, with access to some of the most diverse fly-fishing conditions in the country. They offer dry and wet fly-fishing from wooden boats. The lake has abundant salmon and trout, and the national fly-fishing record was set here with a salmon of 17kg. There is room for just twelve guests, a homely atmosphere prevails, and the food is excellent.

El Patagón Lodge South of Futaleufú and Palena ℡65/212030, ⍟www .southernchileexp.com. Owned by the *Yan Kee Way Lodge* on Lago Llanquihue (see p.341), this remote lodge is located amidst temperate rainforest, with great access to the area's streams and lakes, filled with trout. The four rough-hewn wooden cabins house a total of eight guests; the restaurant is superb and the hot tub on the Río Figueroa an added plus.

Patagonia Baker Lodge Puerto Bertrand ℡67/411903, ⍟www.pbl.cl. *The* place for fly-fishing enthusiasts, sitting on the waterfront of the world-renowned Río Baker, which is teeming with brown and rainbow trout as well as good-sized salmon. Deluxe rooms have electric heating and private bathrooms as well as a stunning view of the Río Baker. The lodge also boasts two halls with open fireplaces and a gourmet restaurant. Open late-October–April.

southern boundary 55km south of Puyuhuapi and crosses the northern limit 15km north of the village. Just beyond the southern entrance to the park, there's a short trail leading west to a mighty waterfall, 40-metre-high **Saltos del Cóndor**. Five kilometres beyond, the road narrows and zigzags its way down the steep **Cuesta de Queulat**, through sheer-sided mountains crowned with glaciers. After you drive through the Portezuelo de Queulat pass, you will shortly pass a short staircase trail (Sendero Padre García) leading 200m down to the **Salto Padre García**, a powerful waterfall dropping 30m into the Río Queulat.

Twenty kilometres north lies by far the most popular sight in the park – the incredible **Ventisquero Colgante**, or "hanging glacier". Wedged between two peaks, forming a V-shaped mass of blue-white ice, the glacier indeed seems to hang suspended over a sheer rock face. Long fingers of ice feed two thundering waterfalls that plummet 150m down to a glacial lake. From the parking area by the Conaf information centre (daily: April–Nov 8.30am–6.30pm; Dec–March 8.30am–9pm; CH\$2000) follow the signposted trail 250m to a spectacular viewpoint. If you cross the suspension bridge over the river and turn right, a 600-metre **Sendero Río Guillermo** leads to the Laguna Los Témpanos through dense native forest, from where you get excellent views of the glacier. Left of the bridge, the steep **Sendero Ventisquero Colgante** climbs 3.5km to a higher viewpoint. There's a **camping** area (CH\$10,000 per site of up to six people) by Río Guillermo, on fairly hard ground with toilets and cold showers. Another trail, **Sendero Río Ventisquero**, starts at the car park and follows the southern bank of the Río Ventisquero Valley, but it is currently so overgrown in places that it's virtually impassable. There are plans to eventually extend the trail for a further 12km, leading to the foot of a glacier.

Other hikes in the park include the **Sendero Río Cascadas**, an easy but exhilarating hike (3hr 30min return), branching off to the left from the Carretera Austral just before the Portezuelo de Queulat, leading 1.7km through moss-covered ancient trees before ending at the Río Cascadas. From here, follow the river up the hill for another 800m, and you'll arrive at its source – a jade-green lake at the foot of a granite cliff, topped by a glacier and streaked by waterfalls. Beyond Puyuhuapi, in the northern sector of the park (Sector Panque), a track pulls off the road to the **Conaf** *guardería*, on the shores of the long, thin **Lago Risopatrón**. The lake, flanked by steep mountains jutting abruptly out of its deep-blue waters, is a lovely spot, and the **camping** area

▲ Ventisquero Colgante

(CH$10,000 per site) near the Conaf hut is one of the prettiest along the entire road; the sites have access to hot showers, picnic tables and barbecue area. Starting at the *guardería* by Lago Risopatrón, the **Sendero Laguna Los Pumas** (14km return; 5hr) starts with a steep ascent, climbing to 1100m. From the plateau at the top, you get sweeping views onto surrounding mountains and out to the fjord. The trail then descends through a pass, leading to the shimmering Laguna Los Pumas, bordered by a sandy beach.

There is no public transport to the park; you can get any bus to drop you off in the park, though it can be difficult catching a ride out. Several tour companies run day-trips to the Ventisquero Colgante during the summer months.

From Parque Nacional Queulat to Futaleufú Valley

Beyond the northern boundary of Parque Nacional Queulat, the Carretera Austral continues north, passing through **La Junta**, a depressing collection of tin houses established in 1983 as one of General Pinochet's "new towns", and home to a controversial unauthorized monument to the dictator. La Junta is the access point to the **Reserva Nacional Lago Rosselot**, whose namesake lake has gained popularity with the fly-fishing set. Also, from here, a new dirt road proceeds east towards the Argentine border, which will eventually help make the Aisén region more accessible. If you wish to stay here overnight, try *Hostal Espacio y Tiempo* (☎67/314141; ❻) with its appealing rustic interior, comfortable rooms, good restaurant serving Chilean staples, and fly-fishing excursions on offer, though it's rather overpriced. A more basic option is the family-run *Hospedaje Tía Letty* (☎67/314106; ❸), Calle Varas 596, while *Mi Casita de Té* is a good spot for inexpensive breakfast or lunch. Some 70km north of La Junta, you'll reach **Villa Santa Lucía**, a dull, modern settlement established in 1982, made up of regimented rows of prefabricated houses. Since the eruption of the Chaitén volcano, it has been getting more business; still, few people stop here, preferring to head east towards the Futaleufú Valley. From here, the Carretera runs north through the ghost town of Chaitén, and through Parque Pumalín to Caleta Gonzalo; there are no services for 140km, so you would only be heading that way if you have your own vehicle and onward ferry passage to Hornopirén or ferry booking for Puerto Montt or Quellón from Chaitén. Otherwise, you'll take the eastbound road which heads past the large glacial Lago Yelcho to the Futaleufú Valley.

The Futaleufú Valley

The 80-kilometre trip up the **FUTALEUFÚ VALLEY** is one of the most enjoyable diversions off the Carretera Austral. Heading east from Villa Santa Lucía, you first skirt the southern shore of Lago Yelcho for 30km, before arriving at Puerto Ramírez, where there is a fork in the road. The right turn goes to the quiet border village of **Palena**, while the left branch follows the turquoise **Río Futaleufú** for 17km through towering gorges, lush forests and snow-streaked mountain peaks to its namesake town.

Though the quiet village of Palena does not have Futaleufú's infrastructure, its late-January **Rodeo de Palena** showcases the local *huaso* culture and it's gaining popularity as a destination for outdoor enthusiasts. Palena is also the starting

Sendero de Chile: from Palena to Villa La Tapera

A new section of the Sendero de Chile stretches for over 100km from the village of Palena to the hamlet of **Villa La Tapera**, passing through some spectacular scenery along the way; some sections are best tackled with local guides, as it crosses terrain where the trail is not very well-marked. The first section runs through endemic forest of the **Reserva Nacional Río Palena**, skirting the beautiful Lago Palena, a popular fly-fishing destination, and finally arriving at the village of **Lago Verde**, by its namesake lake. From Lago Verde, the track leads south; having been used for generations by gauchos to move livestock from one place to another, it's not difficult to follow, passing through alternating landscapes of Patagonian steppes, covered in *coirón*, and thickly forested *lenga* and *coigüe* valleys, boxed in by the surrounding mountains. Halfway to Villa La Tapera, the trail climbs to the **Portezuelo Los Contrabandistas** (1,355m), which offers a spectacular view of the nearby mountains and their glaciers. The final section of the trail crosses Río Cisnes before arriving at Villa La Tapera, a small village reachable by dirt road from an eastbound turnoff from the Carretera, north of Coyhaique but before the westbound turnoff towards Puerto Cisnes. There are several *refugios* along the trail and it's possible to camp wild.

point for the Sendero de Chile trail section that runs through Reserva Nacional Lago Palena to the hamlet of Lago Verde (see box above) and, being only 8km from the Argentine border, makes for an easy (though slow) border crossing. Good accommodation here includes *Río Palena Lodge*, Costa Río Palena s/n (📧 jorge@riopalena.cl; ❼), with its all-inclusive packages comprising comfortable rooms, as well as fly-fishing, rafting and floating on the nearby rivers; the welcoming, family-run *Hospedaje El Americano*, Mendoza 780 (☎ 67/741243; ❸), with four cosy doubles and good breakfast; and *Hospedaje Bellavista*, at the confluence of Río Palena and Río Tranquilo (☎ 67/741263; ❸), a friendly B&B with clean, basic rooms with shared bathroom and serving good Chilean food; owners can organize horseriding tours. Guiado Don Emir (☎ 65/741263) is a recommended horse-riding tour operator offering excursions along the Sendero de Chile and Ruta Patrimonial Río Palena. Some buses between Coyhaique and Futaleufú stop in Palena; check updated bus schedules.

Futaleufú

Sitting on the Río Futaleufú, near its confluence with the Rio Espolón, and surrounded by forested, snowy peaks, Futaleufú more than earns the grandiose slogan – "A landscape painted by God" – coined by its inhabitants. With its big "explosion waves" and massive "rodeo holes", Río Futaleufú is regarded by many professional rafters and kayakers as the most challenging white-water river in the world. A growing number of Chilean and US operators offer **rafting** trips down the river, which begins by passing through a basalt gorge, known as the *Gates of Hell* and boasts over forty class IV–V rapids. An attractive little town, Futaleufú serves as a popular summer base primarily for rafting, though there is a shadow hanging over it in the form of the energy corporation ENDESA, which has plans to construct a dam and to build a hydroelectric plant on the river; the plan currently faces concerted opposition by locals, tourism operators and environmentalists.

Practicalities

In the summer, the helpful **tourist office** (☎ 65/721370) operates on the south side of the Plaza de Armas at O'Higgins 536, dishing out maps of local walks.

Outdoor activities around Futaleufú

Most people come to Futaleufú for the range of **outdoor activities**, including hiking, horse-trekking, mountain biking, fly-fishing, floating (drifting down a river on an inner tube), canyoning (abseiling down canyons) and canoeing, in addition to the obligatory rafting and kayaking trips. Various experienced outfits offer these activities, including **Centro Aventura Futaleufú**, run by the American Olympic team kayaker Chris Spelius, which operates out of the *Hostería Río Grande* (see below; Ⓦwww.pachile.com). **Futaleufú Explore** at O'Higgins 772 (☎65/721527, Ⓦwww.futaleufuexplore.com), **Expediciones Chile**, at Gabriela Mistral 296 (☎65/721386, Ⓦwww.exchile.com) and **Earth River Expeditions,** on a private ranch outside Futaleufú (☎800/643 2784, Ⓦwww.earthriver.com), also organize professional outings on the river. Expect to pay around CH$20,000 for a relatively simple run down the Río Espolón, CH$45,000 for a half-day excursion on the Río Futaleufú and CH$80,000 for a full day on the Futa that includes tackling Class V rapids; the above operators also offer all-inclusive week-long packages that cost between CH$1,300,000 and 1,500,000. The best horseback riding in the area is offered by **Rancho Las Ruedas** on Piloto Carmona 337 (☎65/721294, Ⓦhttp://rancholasruedas.shinranet.com/); horses cost around CH$5000 per hour or CH$15,000 per day; multi-day adventures available.

Plentiful **accommodation** includes *Hostería Río Grande*, O'Higgins 397 (☎65/721320, Ⓦwww.pachile.com; ❼), favoured by rafting enthusiasts, and one of the best hotels to stay for miles around, with its chic-rustic decor, quality en-suite rooms, fine restaurant and bar and multilingual owners who operate Centro Aventura Futaleufú (see above), out of the hotel. Groups are better off at the *Lodge Frontera Patagónica*, 5km south of town (☎65/721320, Ⓦwww.fronterapatagonica.com; ❼), the Dutch-Chilean-owned complex of handsome four-person cabins with wood-burning stoves, with breakfast included and fishing, kayaking and rafting trips available. *Hospedaje Adolfo*, O'Higgins 302 (☎65/721256, Ⓔhospedajeadolfo@hotmail.com; ❷), is a standout family-run budget choice, with comfortable rooms, good breakfast and reliable hot showers; also decent is the quiet *Posada Ely*, Balmaceda 409 (☎65/721205; ❹), with large rooms and shared bathrooms. For camping, try the peaceful *Camping Puerto Espolón* (open Jan–Feb only; CH$3000 per person), with its own beach and hot showers, on the southern edge of town adjacent to the Río Espolón.

There are a few good places to **eat**: *Hostería Río Grande*, O'Higgins 397, is one of the best places in town, with a European-influenced menu of meat and seafood dishes, stylish decor and young crowd, while *Hotel El Barranco*, O'Higgins 172, has an attractive dining room offering a menu of tasty meat dishes. *Martín Pescador*, on Balmaceda 603, serves particularly good salmon and a fine range of wines. For simpler fare, such as sandwiches and a lunchtime menu, try *Restaurant Encuentro* on O'Higgins 653. Budget travellers flock to *Sur Andes*, at Cerda 308, for the large hamburgers, snacks and fresh fruit juices, and there are hot-dog stands just north of the plaza in the evenings.

Thrice-weekly Transporte Cordillera **buses** (☎67/721248) head to the **Argentine border** at Paso Futaleufú at 8.45am and 6.15pm on Mondays, Wednesdays and Fridays for connections to the Argentine towns of Esquel and Trevelin. Buses Transaustral runs to Puerto Montt via Argentina, departing at 8.15am on Sundays (12hr; CH$26,000). Buses Daniela (☎67/231701) travels to Coyhaique on Wednesday and Friday mornings, while Buses Don Oscar runs similar twice-weekly services. Most buses depart from the plaza.

Across Lago General Carrera to Chile Chico

Just beyond the southern boundary of Reserva Nacional Cerro Castillo, a 31-kilometre side road shoots south from the Carretera Austral to the tiny village of **Puerto Ibáñez**, on the northern shore of **Lago General Carrera**. This lake, encircled by rocky, sharp-peaked mountains, is the second largest in South America, and stretches east into Argentina, where it is known as Lago Buenos Aires. Regular ferries connect Puerto Ibáñez with the small town of **Chile Chico**, on the opposite shore, making this an attractive alternative to following the Carretera Austral around the lake. From Chile Chico, a 128-kilometre road skirts the lake's southern shore, joining the Carretera just beyond the village of Puerto Gaudal.

Puerto Ibáñez

Sitting in a green, fertile plain, divided up by rows of soldier-like poplars, in sharp contrast with the barren hills around it, **PUERTO IBÁÑEZ** is a shrinking village, which you'll probably only pass through on the way to or from the ferry across Lago General Carrera. Once an important port, connecting Coyhaique with Chile Chico and the remote estancias on the lake's southern shore, it fell into decline with the construction of the Carretera Austral bypass. Nowadays, the village is a centre for vegetable growing, distinctive pottery and is the site of the largest Tehuelche cemetery in Patagonia.

Puerto Ibáñez has several places to **stay**: at San Salvador 593, *Hospedaje Don Francisco* (T67/423234; ❷) has simple but comfortable rooms; camping is possible (CH$3500) per person, and full board available; at no. 282, *Residencial Vientos del Sur* (T67/423208; ❷) is a clean, modern *casa familial*, offering decent set **meals** and offering various excursions; and the Swiss-owned 𝕏 *Cabañas Shehen Aike* at Risopatrón 55 (T67/423284, Ⓦwww .shehenaike.cl; ❹) offers large cabins and excellent food, as well as various tours. **Minibuses** travel from Coyhaique to Puerto Ibáñez; they leave from Calle Prat (opposite the shop Calaforte) or will collect passengers from their homes or hotels and get here in time for the ferry. Phone to book a place as far in advance as possible with Miguel Acuña, Manuel Rodríguez 143 (T67/251579 or 09/217 3520), Sixto Martínez (T67/423278) or Buses Carolina (T67/219009).

> ### Ferries across Lago General Carrera
>
> The **ferry** *El Pilchero*, operated by Mar del Sur, makes the crossing between Puerto Ibáñez and Chile Chico. Offices are in Coyhaique, at Baquedano 146A (T67/233466 and 67/231255) and in El Refugio on the pier in Chile Chico (T67/411864). The crossing takes 2hr 30min – be prepared for a rough ride as strong winds often whip up gigantic waves on this huge exposed lake – and costs CH$4000 for passengers, and CH$24,000 per vehicle. Ferries set off from Puerto Ibáñez at 10am on Tuesday, Wednesday and Friday, at 11am Saturday and 3pm Sunday, and from Chile Chico at 8am on Monday, 3pm on Tuesday and Friday, 1pm on Thursday and noon on Sunday. Check these times well ahead because they are subject to change; reservations are a must as space is limited. When buying your ticket in Chile Chico it's also a good idea to buy an onward minibus ticket to Coyhaique (CH$4000).

Chile Chico

Sitting on the southern shore of Lago General Carrera, the small agricultural town of **CHILE CHICO** has a deserted feel to it on Sundays, though otherwise it's a sunny place with an attractive Plaza de Armas, lined with apricot trees and pines, and is famous for its fruit festival at the end of January. The town was settled by farmers who crossed over from Argentina in 1909, causing a conflict known as the "Chile Chico war" when they refused to hand over land to the concessionaires given grants by the government. The new settlement depended entirely on Argentina until a road was built between Coyhaique and Puerto Ibáñez in 1952, after which Chile Chico's orchards became Coyhaique's main source of fresh fruit, though production was temporarily depressed by Volcán Hudson's 1991 eruption.

You can pick up a town map at the **Oficina de Turismo** (supposedly open Mon–Sat 10am–5pm; ☎67/411123) on main street O'Higgins, at the corner of Lautaro. Upstairs, a small **museum** (same hours) shows off a few Tehuelche artefacts and fossils of giant molluscs and other marine animals, reminders that thousands of years ago this area was covered by the sea.

Practicalities

Small supermarkets, internet cafés and call centres are found along O'Higgins. There is a single **ATM** at Banco Estado at O'Higgins and Baquedano; it only accepts MasterCard. **Accommodation** includes the friendly *Hotel Plaza* on the corner of O'Higgins and Balmaceda, with clean, basic rooms (☎67/411215; ❸) and the Belgian-Chilean *Hostería de la Patagonia* at Chacra 3-A (☎67/411337; ❹), a charming house with comfortable en-suite rooms, good home-cooked food, and outdoor excursions on offer, tucked away in a large garden on the eastern edge of town. Opposite, *Casa Quinta No Me Olvides* (☎09/833 8006; ❷)

▲ Chile Chico

is popular with backpackers, with seven basic, good-value rooms and space to camp in the large orchard. There are few **eating options**: *Café Loly y Elizabeth*, Gonzáles 25, facing the plaza, is the only place open on Sunday and serves basic meat and fish dishes, as well as empanadas; *Café Refer*, on O'Higgins 416, offers sandwiches and salmon dishes, while *Antu Mapu*, O'Higgins 366, dishes up pizza, hot dogs, sandwiches and ice cream.

Onward from Chile Chico

Moving on from Chile Chico, Transportes Ale, Rosa Amelia 820 (℡09/882 0753), operates a **bus** service down to Cochrane on Thursdays and Sundays. Nieves del Sur (℡67/412012 and 08/423 4459) runs to Puerto Guadál and Río Tranquilo on Mondays at 3pm and Tuesdays and Thursdays at 5pm, returning on Tuesdays, Thursdays and Fridays at 7am. There several minibuses daily to Los Antiguos, across the Argentine border (CH$3000), while La Unión runs to Los Antiguos and Perito Moreno on alternate days. Most bus services leave from in front of the Via Entel call centre at O'Higgins 426; check for updated schedules. There are weekly flights to Coyhaique (CH$30,000) with Aeréo Don Carlos (call the Coyhaique office for up-to-date schedules).

Around Lago General Carrera

Looping around the lake along the Carretera Austral offers spectacular panoramas – in this case of the grey-and-pink mountains west of the road, plus a few glimpses of the Campo de Hielo Norte. Nine kilometres on from the turn-off to Puerto Ibáñez, you pass **Villa Cerro Castillo**, a rather bleak pioneer settlement whose sole draw is the rugged hiking around Cerro Castillo (see p.393). You'll find some **places to stay** here, including friendly *Hospedaje El Rodeo* at Pedro Aguirre Cerda 281 (℡67/419200; ❸); the owner is a wealth of information on trekking in the area. Just across the bridge outside the town, a signed two-kilometre track leads steeply uphill to **Monumento Nacional Manos de Cerro Castillo**, a dense collection of over one hundred handprints, in three separate panels, at the foot of a sheer basalt rock face. The images, mostly negative prints against a red background, are thought to have been left by the Tehuelche people between 5000 and 8000 years ago. Between December and April, there's an admission charge of CH$500.

Some 25km south of the turn for Puerto Murta, a tiny cattle-farming community, you'll reach **Puerto Tranquilo**, a picturesque lakeside hamlet with basic services. The best place to stay here is the excellent *Hostal El Puesto*, Lagos 258 (℡2/196 4555, ⓦwww.elpuesto.cl; ❻), with comfortable en-suite rooms; the owners organize excellent tours of the area. In the nearby Valle Explora-dores, *Campo Alacalúf* (℡67/419500; ❺) is a secluded German-owned rustic house with a handful of rooms and home-cooked meals. A number of operators run boat trips across the lake to **Capilla de Mármol** ("Marble Chapel"), an impressive limestone cliff looming out of the water, streaked with blue-and-white patterns and gashed with caves which can be entered by boat, including *Bahía Mansa* (℡67/258168).

Thirty-five kilometres south of Puerto Tranquilo lies the outlet of **Lago General Carrera**, that drains into the adjacent Lago Bertrand. Shortly after-wards, you'll reach **Cruce El Maitén**, a fork in the road; the left road leads northeast along the southern edge of Lago General Carrera to Puerto Guadal, a picturesque little town with an excellent stretch of beach (free camping available) and Chile Chico. Good **accommodation** choices here include the highly recommended *Cabañas Mallín Colorado* (☎2/234 1843, ⓦwww.mallincolorado.cl; ❼), with cabins made of native timber that offer outstanding views of Lago General Carrera, superb food and excellent horseriding trips; and the *Terra Luna Lodge* (☎67/431263, ⓦwww.terra-luna.cl; ❹–❼), two kilometres along the road to Puerto Guadal, with attractive bungalows, a good restaurant, numerous excursions on offer and a Jacuzzi.

Twenty-five kilometres further south, you arrive at the charming little village of **Puerto Bertrand**, sitting near the head of the turquoise Río Baker. Patagonia Adventure Expeditions (☎67/411330, ⓦwww.adventurepatagonia.com) offers multi-day trekking, fishing and horse-riding plus kayaking trips in the pristine wilderness around the village. Several stylish spots offer **accommodation**: *Green Lodge Baker* (☎2/196 0409, ⓦwww.greenbakerlodge.cl; ❻), caters to anglers with five comfortable *cabañas*, while the more affordable *Hostería Bertrand*, Costanera s/n (☎67/419900; ❸), offers clean rooms with and without bath, and breakfast is included.

From Cochrane to Villa O'Higgins

The last major stop on the Carretera Austral, **COCHRANE** lies 50km south of Puerto Bertrand. The town's paved, orderly streets spreading out from the neat Plaza de Armas, and array of efficient services, make this a prime spot to rest up after the wildness of the Carretera Austral. You'll find an **information** kiosk on the plaza during the summer months (Mon–Sat 9am–1pm & 2.30–8pm; ⓦwww.cochranepatagonia.cl). The **Conaf** office at Río Neff 417 (☎67/522164) has the latest information on the nearby nature reserves.

Residencial Cero a Cero, at Lago Brown 464 (☎67/522158; ❸), is a friendly, cosy, family-run guesthouse that serves good breakfast, while *Hostal Latitude 47° Sur* (☎67/522280; ❸) on Lago Brown 564, offers similar services. Popular with cyclists tackling the Carretera Austral, *Residencial Rubio* at Teniente Merino 871 (☎67/522173; ❸) has clean and roomy en-suite twin rooms, breakfast included, while the pricier, inn-style *Hotel Último Paraíso* at Lago Brown 455 (☎67/522361; ❻) offers tastefully decorated rooms, and a good restaurant for guests only. One of the best **restaurants** is *El Fogón*, at San Valentín 651, which serves filling *parrilladas* and is the only place open in the off-season. *Café Ñirrantal*, on the corner of Avenida O'Higgins and Esmeralda, a block south of the Plaza de Armas, whips up excellent vegetarian crêpes and meat dishes.

While in town, you can make a day-trip to the **Reserva Nacional Tamango** (daily: April–Nov 8.30am–6.30pm; Dec–March 8.30am–9pm; CH$2000), 9km east of town, set on the banks of **Lago Cochrane**, a skinny, twisting lake that straddles the Argentine border. The reserve is notable for its population of around eighty *huemúl* (native deer); if you're lucky, you'll spot some on the five-hour guided walks with Conaf rangers (around CH$35,000 for up to six people). There are also several marked trails from the entrance leading to Laguna Tamanguito, Laguna Elefantina and up Cerro Tamango (1,722m) for excellent views of Campo de Hielo Norte to the west and the nearby lakes; bring windproof clothing.

Cochrane is an ideal base for those wanting to visit and volunteer for the ambitious conservation project of **Estancia Valle Chacabuco**, a 173,000-acre plot of land purchased by Kristine Tompkins (see box on Douglas Tompkins, p.387) in 2004 through the non-profit Conservación Patagónica foundation. The aim is to restore the heavily damaged grasslands and wetlands, home to diverse fauna such as the endangered *huemúl*, as well as guanacos and the four-eyed Patagonian frog, and turn it into a national park. Volunteers are mainly involved in land restoration, such as dismantling of wire fences, and the project takes place between October and May; for more information on the project, contact ℡67/970833 or check out Ⓦwww.conservacionpatagonica.org or www.patagonia.com).

Caleta Tortel

Beyond Cochrane, the paved road becomes a dirt-and-gravel track that makes its way through a dense carpet of evergreens and giant *nalca*. Just over 100km beyond Cochrane, you come to the embarcadero de Río Vagabundo. From here twelve-passenger launches (*lanchas*) and nine-passenger motorboats (*chatas*) ferry residents and visitors to the tiny, remote hamlet of **CALETA TORTEL**, located at the mouth of the Río Baker between the northern and southern ice fields. Besides flights from Coyhaique, these boats were the only means of getting to the town until 2002, when a twenty-kilometre road, following the course of the Río Baker, was opened.

Originally a logging spot for a lumber company interested in the dense forests of endemic **ciprés de las Guaitecas**, Tortel soon grew into a scattered settlement of quaint wooden houses, each with its own jetty and linked by a network of walkways and bridges made of fragrant cypress (slippery when wet); there are no streets here, and even the fire engine is a boat. Put on the map when Britain's Prince William worked on an Operation Raleigh project here before going to university, Tortel is also renowned for a mysterious incident that gave its name to a nearby island, the **Isla de los Muertos**, in which dozens of employees involved in the original timber-felling scheme a century ago suddenly died in unexplained circumstances. Officially the cause was an epidemic of some kind, possibly scurvy, but rumours suggested they were poisoned, maybe deliberately so that the company didn't have to pay their wages. You can visit this morbid but beautifully unspoiled place on a forty-minute boat-trip from Tortel. Also within easy reach by boat are two glaciers: Ventisquero Steffens, which originates from the northern ice field (2hr 30min walk, 3hr north by boat; speedboat CH\$50,000; *lancha* CH\$60,000), and Ventisquero Jorge Montt, an enormous bluish ice-wall that comes from the southern ice field (5hr by *lancha*; CH\$90,000; 2hr by motorboat; CH\$80,000), best done in a group, as the trip is charged per vessel.

To book **accommodation**, call the municipality (℡67/211876) or the public phone (℡67/234815). A handful of places in town offer basic but pleasant rooms, including *Hostal Constanera* (❸), and *Hospedaje Don Adán* (❸), opposite it on the boardwalk. *El Mirador*, at Sector Base, is good for simple yet super-fresh salmon dishes, while *Café Celes Salom* serves basic and very affordable Chilean dishes.

Bus Ale (℡67/522448) runs to Tortel at 2.30pm on Tuesdays, Thursdays, Fridays and Sundays (3hr); there's also a weekly bus in summer to Villa O'Higgins on Sundays (℡67/431821), and a bus to Coyhaique every other day, with connections in Cochrane. A monthly **ferry** also heads to the remote Puerto Edén, the last remaining Kawéskar settlement in the southern fjords. If you time it right, from Puerto Edén you can catch a Navimag ferry either to Puerto Natales or to Puerto Montt.

Villa O'Higgins and around

Tiny **VILLA O'HIGGINS** is reached via the very final – and particularly spectacular – 100-kilometre stretch of the Carretera beyond the small military camp of Puerto Yungay, 20km beyond the turn-off to Caleta Tortel, where you must cross the Estero Mitchell via ferry (3 daily Dec–March, more during Jan–Feb; check timetable locally; 45min; free) to continue south. Here the Carretera Austral narrows to a single lane, ribboning its way around hairpin bends as the terrain becomes even hillier, with sheer drops on the side of the track revealing spectacular vistas of glacial rivers cutting through endless forest, and distant mountains shrouded in mist.

Villa O'Higgins was built on a simple grid, with the Carretera Austral running along the western side all the way down to the Bahía Bahamondez on the enormous glacial **Lago O'Higgins**, 7km away. Half of the lake's spindly waterways lie in Argentine territory where it's called Lago San Martín, after Argentina's independence hero.

Most of the earliest settlers – who came at the beginning of the twentieth century, when it was most easily accessible from Argentina – were British. The first Chilean settlers did not arrive until the 1920s, and the town wasn't officially founded and given its present name until 1966. Until 1999, this cluster of wooden houses huddled against a sheer mountain face was reachable only by a small prop plane from Coyhaique or by boat from Argentina.

A footpath from Calle Lago Cisnes runs through Parque Cerro Santiago up to a *mirador* that offers an excellent view of the village; from here, the path continues on towards the ice "tongue" of the **Ventisquero Mosco**, the nearest hanging glacier, though the trail is sometimes impassable. Several glaciers, including Ventisquero O'Higgins, spill into Lago O'Higgins from the massive Campo de Hielo Sur – a titanic ice cap that blocks any further progress southwards of the Carretera. These can be visited by boat. From here, in the summer months (Dec–March), a cross-lake ferry travels to the Argentine side, from where it's possible to walk to Argentina's El Chaltén along a route increasingly popular with intrepid hikers and bikers (see box on lake crossing, opposite). The boat crosses over to the hamlet of Candelario Mansilla – the starting point for the rewarding 7km Sendero de Chile hike that climbs steeply through *lenga* forest to the Dos Lagunas pass, where you get sweeping views of the O'Higgins, Chico and Pirámide glaciers, before descending to the refugio by Lago O'Higgins' Brazo Sur, where you can arrange to be picked up by the boat that runs tours to the glaciers.

Practicalities

The youthful staff at the small **tourist office** on the plaza (open in summer only; Mon–Fri 9am–5.30pm; Ⓦ www.villaohiggins.com) are very helpful and provide plenty of information on the town and the surrounding area. Hielo Sur (Ⓣ 67/431821 Ⓦ www.hielosur.com), on a nameless side street off the west end of Calle Mosco, has up-to-date timetables for the Lago O'Higgins crossing (CH$20,000) and organizes boat trips to the Ventisquero O'Higgins and Ventisquero Chico (CH$25,000), as well as single and multi-day hikes and horseback riding excursions. The **library**, on the east side of the plaza, has several computers with swift **internet** connections; there's also small call centre towards the north end of town. Since there are no banks or ATMs, you'll have to bring plenty of cash with you; if you've just crossed the border from

To cross or not to cross?

The crossing between Villa O'Higgins and Argentina's El Chaltén is remote and challenging, yet more and more hardy travellers are prepared to take on the lake crossing, followed by a strenuous hike over the border. The sixty-passenger *Quetru*, connected to Villa O'Higgins by a private minibus (CH$1500), leaves Bahía Bahamóndez at 8.30am (Jan–Feb Mon, Wed & Sat; Dec–Feb Wed & Sat; CH$20,000) and arrives at the hamlet of **Candelario Mancilla** at around 11am. Here there are no-frills accommodation (CH$6000) and **camping spots** (CH$2000 per tent) and you will get your passport stamped by **Chilean border control**. Beyond, a wide gravel track runs slightly uphill through patches of woodland to the international border; on the way, you will have to either ford the shallow, glacial **Río Obstáculo**, or cross it on some rickety planks. Beyond the border, the 7.5-kilometre stretch of trail to the **Argentine Gendarmería** on the banks of the **Laguna del Desierto** becomes a narrow, muddy footpath snaking its way through hilly forest and scrubland; cyclists have to push and sometimes carry their bikes. After being stamped into Argentina, you can either pitch a tent at *Camping Laguna del Desierto* (CH$2000), catch the *Viedma* motor launch across the lake (daily at 1.30pm, 4.45pm & 6.30pm; 30–45min; CH$8000, bicycles CH$4000 extra) or hike the remaining 15km (5hr) along a thickly forested path on the left side of the lake, emerging at the *guardería* by the pier on the south side. Minibuses to **El Chaltén** meet the arriving boats, the last one leaving for town at 7.45pm (CH$5000). While it is possible to complete the border crossing in a day, boat schedules are weather-dependent; pack enough food for several days. To book a guide and packhorses (CH$15,000 per packhorse), and for up-to-date information on the trek, visit the helpful website, @www.villaohiggins.com.

Argentina and have a surplus of Argentine pesos but no Chilean currency, the owner of *Hostal El Mosco* acts as an unofficial money-changer.

Accommodation consists of modest guesthouses; most offer meals at extra cost. The family-run *Hospedaje Patagonia* at Río Pascua 191, on the plaza (T67/431818; ❷), has clean, basic rooms with shared bathroom; breakfast CH$1500 extra; lunch or dinner CH$3500. *Hospedaje La Cascada*, on Lago Salto at Río Mosco s/n (T67/431833; ❷), is another good budget accommodation choice; ample servings of delicious home-cooked food and its own bakery are a plus. *Hostal Runín*, Loto 5, Predio Angelita (T67/431870; ❹), is a tranquil and popular guesthouse with welcoming rooms, hot showers and tasty cooking. It's possible to camp at *Camping Los Ñires*, just south of *Hostal Runín*, a spacious, tree-lined campsite with a cooking hut and hot showers, though the ground can be muddy (CH$2500 per person). *Entre Patagones*, on the Carretera Austral at the north end of town, is an excellent family-run restaurant, busy after 8pm, serving tasty Patagonian favourites such as *asador patagónico* (spit-roasted lamb) and hearty *cazuela* in a homely environment.

Buses Don Carlos (T67/522150), leaving from the small Supermercado San Gabriel on Calle Lago O'Higgins (buy your ticket in advance in the supermarket), runs to Cochrane on Mondays and Thursdays (8am; 7hr; CH$11,000), returning the following day, whilst Aéreos Don Carlos operates a twice-weekly **flight** between Cochrane and Villa O'Higgins on Mondays and Thursdays (CH$150,000 return); only take this option if you are in a hurry and have a strong stomach.

Travel details

Buses

Coyhaique to: Futaleufú (1 daily; 12hr); Cochrane (4 weekly; 10hr); La Junta (4 weekly; 6hr); Puerto Aisén (15 daily; 1hr); Puerto Cisnes (1 daily; 4hr); Puerto Ibáñez (1 daily; 2hr 30min); Punta Arenas, via Argentina (1 weekly Jan & Feb; 24hr).
Cochrane to: Villa O'Higgins (2 weekly; 6–7hr).

Ferries and catamarans

Caleta Gonzalo to: Hornopirén (Jan & Feb 2 weekly; 6hr).
Caleta Puelche to: La Arena (9 daily; 30min).
Chaitén to: Puerto Montt (ferry: 1–3 weekly, 10hr); Quellón (1–2 weekly; 5hr).
Hornopirén to: Caleta Gonzalo (Jan & Feb only, 2 weekly on Mon & Sat; 6hr).

La Arena to: Caleta Puelche (9 daily; 30min).
Puerto Chacabuco to: Laguna San Rafael (ferry Dec–March 2 weekly; 16hr; catamaran several weekly in season, 5hr); Puerto Montt (2–4 weekly; 24hr); Quellón (1–3 weekly; 20hr).
Puerto Ibáñez to: Chile Chico (6 weekly; 2hr 30min).

Flights

Balmaceda (for Coyhaique) to: Puerto Montt (4 daily; 1hr); Punta Arenas (4 daily; 2hr); Santiago (4 daily; 3hr).
Cochrane to: Villa O'Higgins (2 weekly; 30min).
Coyhaique (aerodrome) to: Chile Chico (2 weekly; 40min); Cochrane (2 weekly; 1hr); San Rafael glacier (daily in season; 1hr 30min); Villa O'Higgins (2 weekly; 1hr 30min).

Southern Patagonia

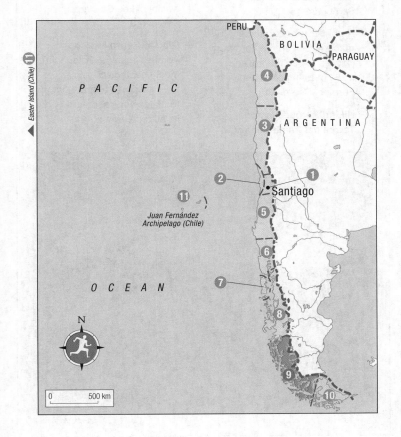

Easter Island (Chile) 11

PERU

BOLIVIA

PARAGUAY

4

PACIFIC

3

ARGENTINA

2

1

•Santiago

11

5

Juan Fernández
Archipelago (Chile)

6

7

OCEAN

8

N

9

10

0   500 km

CHAPTER 9

Highlights

✳ **Cemetery at Punta Arenas**
Visit this moving – and beautiful – memorial to the pioneers from Britain and Spain, Croatia and Italy.
See p.420

✳ **Penguins at Isla Magdalena**
Watch their comic antics on this island sanctuary.
See p.424

✳ **A boat trip to exquisite glaciers** Sail up the fjord from Natales to see the frozen flows of Balmaceda and Serrano. See p.430

✳ **Hiking Parque Nacional Torres del Paine** Set aside at least a few days to trek through this spectacular park, an unforgettable experience.
See p.431

✳ **Laguna de Los Tres**
Complete the most demanding and scenic of hikes in the Fitz Roy mountain range of Argentina's Parque Nacional Los Glaciares.
See p.440

✳ **Glaciar Perito Moreno**
Admire Argentine Patagonia's most spectacular glacier from afar, take a boat right up to its face or go ice-hiking on its surface. See p.441

▲ Penguins at Isla Magdalena

9

Southern Patagonia

Patagonia lies tucked away right at the southernmost tip of the Americas – indeed of the world's landmass, not counting Antarctica. Geographically ill-defined, "Patagonia" usually refers to the narrow triangle of land south of a line between Puerto Montt, in Chile, and Argentina's Península Valdés, while in Chile the term is usually reserved for **SOUTHERN PATAGONIA**. Much of Argentine Patagonia is flat rolling **pampa**, but in the western sliver of land shared by both countries, the Andes take a last, dramatic breath before plunging into the ocean.

Its very name holds a fascination for many travellers, but the reality can be harsh: Patagonia is cursed by a persistent wind, the *Escoba de Dios* (God's Broom); trees grow horizontally here, sculpted by the gales; winters are long and summers short.

These days large numbers of Chileans and non-Chilean visitors come to Patagonia principally to hike in the country's most famous and stunning national park, **Parque Nacional Torres del Paine**, a massif crowned with otherworldly granite towers. Others want to follow in the footsteps of the region's famous travellers, such as navigator Ferdinand Magellan, naturalist Charles Darwin, and author Bruce Chatwin, to come and gaze at the region's many spectacular **glaciers** or to visit the **penguin colonies**. Since the whole of this region is physically cut off from the rest of Chile by two vast ice caps, the only links with territory to the north are by air, water or through **Argentina**. The last option allows you to visit some of the latter's finest landscapes, including the **Parque Nacional Los Glaciares**, where the **Fitz Roy Massif**, near El Chaltén, offers incredible hiking and climbing opportunities, while the **Glaciar Perito Moreno**, accessible from the town of El Calafate, is visually stunning.

Chilean Patagonia, the site of the some of the continent's oldest human habitation, was originally populated by Tehuelche hunter-gatherers who stalked roaming guanacos in the interior, and the sea-faring Kawéscar who dove naked for shellfish in the frigid waters around the southern fjords. The first European to discover the area was **Ferdinand Magellan**, a Portuguese navigator who sailed through the strait now bearing his name. Spanish colonisation attempts failed catastrophically and no European tried to settle the place again for another two hundred and fifty years.

The voyages of the *Beagle*, from 1826 to 1834, the second one bearing young Charles Darwin, renewed interest in the area, prompting continued Chilean and Argentine attempts to colonize the area. In the 1870s the two narrowly avoided

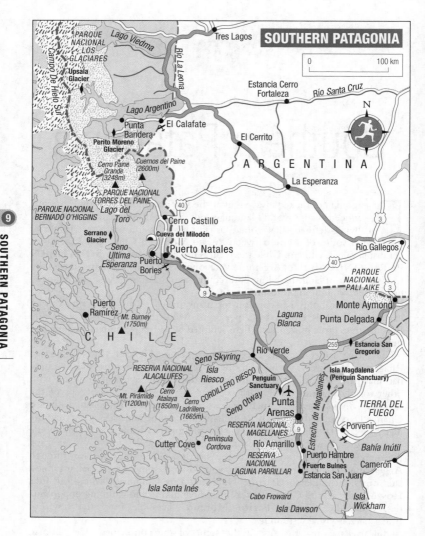

SOUTHERN PATAGONIA

0   100 km

Tres Lagos

Lago Viedma

Río La Leona

PARQUE
NACIONAL
LOS
GLACIARES

Campo De Hielo Sur

Upsala
Glacier

Estancia Cerro
Fortaleza

Río Santa Cruz

Lago Argentino

Punta
Bandera

El Calafate

El Cerrito

A R G E N T I N A

Perito Moreno
Glacier

Cerro Paine
Grande
(3248m)

Cuernos del Paine
(2600m)

La Esperanza

N

PARQUE NACIONAL
TORRES DEL PAINE

Lago del
Toro

40

PARQUE NACIONAL
BERNADO O'HIGGINS

Serrano
Glacier

Cerro Castillo

Cueva del Milodón

Puerto Natales

Río Gallegos

40

Seno
Ultima
Esperanza

Puerto
Bories

9

PARQUE
NACIONAL
PALI AIKE

3

Puerto
Ramírez

Mt. Burney
(1750m)

Laguna
Blanca

Monte Aymond

Punta Delgada

C H I L E

Seno Skyring

Río Verde

255

Estancia San
Gregorio

RESERVA NACIONAL
ALACALUFES

Isla
Riesco

CORDILLERO RIESCO

Penguin
Sanctuary

Isla Magdalena
(Penguin Sanctuary)

Mt. Pirámide
(1200m)

Cerro
Atalaya
(1850m)

Cerro
Ladrillero
(1665m)

Seno Otway

Punta
Arenas

Estrecho de Magallanes

TIERRA DEL
FUEGO

RESERVA NACIONAL
MAGELLANES

Porvenir

Cutter Cove

Península
Cordova

Río Amarillo

9

Bahía Inútil

RESERVA
NACIONAL
LAGUNA PARRILLAR

Puerto Hambre

Fuerte Bulnes

Cameron

Estancia San Juan

Isla Santa Inés

Cabo Froward

Isla Dawson

Isla
Wickham

war over the territory, not for the last time. From 1849, Punta Arenas was boosted by the California Gold Rush; while it didn't last long, the introduction of sheep farming created sprawling estancias (ranches) and brought great wealth to their owners in the late nineteenth century.

Wool has now been replaced by **oil**, commercial salmon farming and tourism as the region's main resources. The Chileans call the area the province of **Magallanes**, in the explorer's honour, and it's one of the least inhabited areas in Chile. The provincial capital is the lively city of **Punta Arenas**, and the only other town of any size is superbly located **Puerto Natales** in the northwest, gateway to Torres del Paine national park.

Chilean Patagonia

Chilean Patagonia can be divided up into four distinct areas: **Punta Arenas** and its surroundings; **Puerto Natales** and the unforgettable **Torres del Paine National Park**; the broad expanse of frigid grassland between the two towns, stretching to the Atlantic coast and taking in the desolately beautiful **Parque Nacional Pali Aike**; and the remote, hardly visited **islands** of the Pacific coast.

Punta Arenas and around

Seen from the air, **PUNTA ARENAS**, 3090km south of Santiago, seems lost in the flat barren plains and vast expanses of water that surround it, a sprawling patchwork of galvanized tin roofs struggling up from the shores of the Magellan Strait. On the ground, however, the city looks much more substantial and modern, especially in the centre where glass and concrete office buildings have replaced the ramshackle wooden houses, paid for in part by the oil that's been flowing into the city since the first wells started gushing in 1945.

Arenas started life 60km south of where it is now, at a place called **Fuerte Bulnes**, the first Chilean settlement along the Magellan Strait. It was founded in 1843 by Captain John Williams, a seaman from Bristol in the service of the Chileans, to forestall any other country's attempts at colonization. In 1848 the new settlement moved to a more suitable location to the north, named by an English sailor "Sandy Point", loosely translated into "Punta Arenas" in Spanish.

Punta Arenas blossomed in the nineteenth-century sheep boom, when thriving immigrant communities from Croatia, Germany and elsewhere sprang up and left their marks. Today Punta Arenas is enjoying another boom of sorts, with oil revenues flowing into the town and the **Zona Franca** ("duty-free zone") attracting shoppers.

As the only true city in the south, it's well-equipped with services, and a useful base for exploring both Chilean Patagonia and Tierra del Fuego. Nearby lie a couple of exciting local sights – the **penguin sanctuary** of **Isla Magdalena** and, to the west, the **Reserva Forestal Magallanes**.

Arrival and information

Most travellers arrive at the user-friendly **airport**, housed in a very handsome modern building, 20km north of town. It's quite a busy little place, with a bustling café, ATMs, internet access and car-rental desks. Taxis to the centre charge CH$7000, minibuses CH$3500 and buses – run by a company called Transfer (☏61/222241) – cost CH$2500; they all meet incoming flights, though be warned that the minibuses fill up quickly straight after the arrival of a flight and you can be waiting for transportation for a long time. Some buses stop by the airport on the way to **Puerto Natales** and **Torres del Paine**.

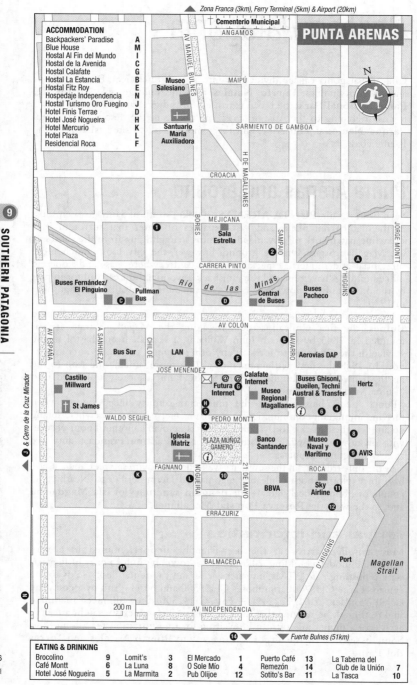

Zona Franca (3km), Ferry Terminal (5km) & Airport (20km)

Cementerio Municipal

PUNTA ARENAS

N

SOUTHERN PATAGONIA

9

◀ & Cerro de la Cruz Mirador

ACCOMMODATION

Backpackers' Paradise	A
Blue House	M
Hostal Al Fin del Mundo	I
Hostal de la Avenida	C
Hostal Calafate	G
Hostal La Estancia	B
Hostal Fitz Roy	E
Hospedaje Independencia	N
Hostal Turismo Oro Fuegino	J
Hotel Finis Terrae	D
Hotel José Nogueira	H
Hotel Mercurio	K
Hotel Plaza	L
Residencial Roca	F

ANGAMOS

AV MANUEL BULNES

MAIPÚ

Museo
Salesiano

Santuario
María
Auxiliadora

SARMIENTO DE GAMBOA

H DE MAGALLANES

CROACIA

JORGE MONTT

MEJICANA

BORES

Sala
Estrella

SAMPAIO

CARRERA PINTO

A

O'HIGGINS

Río   de   las   Minas

Buses Fernández/
El Pinguino

Pullman
Bus

Central
de Buses

Buses
Pacheco

B

AV COLÓN

AV ESPAÑA

A SANHUEZA

CHILOÉ

Bus Sur

LAN

NAVARRO

Aerovías DAP

JOSÉ MENÉNDEZ

Castillo
Millward

St James

Futura
Internet

Calafate
Internet

Museo
Regional
Magallanes

Buses Ghisoni,
Queilen, Techni
Austral & Transfer

Hertz

WALDO SEGUEL

PEDRO MONTT

H

Iglesia
Matriz

PLAZA MUÑOZ
GAMERO

Banco
Santander

Museo
Naval y
Marítimo

I

FAGNANO

NOGUEIRA

21 DE MAYO

ROCA

AVIS

BBVA

Sky
Airline

ERRÁZURIZ

BALMACEDA

O'HIGGINS

Port

Magellan
Strait

0   200 m

AV INDEPENDENCIA

Fuerte Bulnes (51km)

EATING & DRINKING

Brocolino	9	Lomit's	3	El Mercado	1	Puerto Café	13	La Taberna del	
Café Montt	6	La Luna	8	O Sole Mío	4	Remezón	14	Club de la Unión	7
Hotel José Nogueira	5	La Marmita	2	Pub Olijoe	12	Sotito's Bar	11	La Tasca	10

The town doesn't have a bus terminal as such, so different **bus companies** drop passengers at various points around town, though all within five blocks of the main Plaza Muñoz Gamero. You might also arrive at Punta Arenas by **ferry** from Porvenir, in Tierra del Fuego. The ferry terminal is a shortish *colectivo* (CH$700) or taxi ride (CH$2000) from downtown, along the Natales road to the north.

Punta Arenas has an excellent **Sernatur** office at Navarro 999 (Mon–Fri 8.15am–7pm, Sat 10am–6pm; ℡61/241330, ⊛www.puntaarenas.cl), with helpful staff and lots of information on both the city and the region. Should you find it closed, try the city tourist office, housed in a kiosk on the southern side of the plaza (Mon–Thurs 8am–5.30pm; Fri 8am–4.30pm; ℡61/200610). **Conaf**, at Bulnes 309, fourth floor (Mon–Thurs 8.30am–5.50pm, Fri 8.30am–4.50pm; ℡61/238554), is the place to pick up information on the area's national parks and reserves.

Accommodation

Punta Arenas boasts a wide range of hotels, hostels and *residenciales* in all price ranges. During the low season, hotels often offer reduced rates to fill their rooms.

Backpackers' Paradise Carrera Pinto 1022 ℡61/240104, ⓔbackpackersparadise @hotmail.com. The most popular backpackers' hostel in town, with 30 bunks in two open-plan rooms. Extras include cable TV, internet access and use of the kitchen. ❷

Blue House Balmaceda 545 ℡61/227006, ⓔcrigar73@hotmail.com. Half a dozen rooms with three to five bunks each, several shared bathrooms, a spillover house with inexpensive singles and doubles, a kitchen and internet use make this a good bargain. The hostel can also organize all manner of tours and book onward bus tickets for you; buses pick you up from in front of the hostel. ❷

Hostal Al Fin del Mundo O'Higgins 1026 ℡61/710185, ⊛www.alfindelmundo.cl. Clean rooms, which vary in size, and a dorm (with beds rather than bunks) in a central location; free breakfast, internet and wi-fi, kitchen use, pool tables, book exchange and a comfy lounge with massive TV and extensive DVD collection. ❸

Hostal de la Avenida Av Colón 533 ℡61/247543. Only a block or two from most bus companies, this cosy family home offers comfortable rooms with cable TV and American breakfast. ❹

Hostal Calafate Magallanes 926 ℡61/241281, ⊛www.calafate.cl. Central guesthouse boasts spacious rooms with cable TV, some with bathrooms, some without; wi-fi and attached cybercafé are a bonus, but the breakfast is unremarkable. Can help arrange tours. ❹

Hostal La Estancia O'Higgins 765 ℡61/249130, ⓔhostallaestancia@yahoo.com. Warm and hospitable, this *hostal* features high-ceilinged dorms on

the ground floor and bright rooms set around a communal landing on the first floor. Excellent breakfast is included and there's internet access; lots of information on the local area provided. ❸

Hostal Fitz Roy Navarro 850 ℡61/240430, ⓔhostalfitzroy@hotmail.com. Run by a former Torres del Paine guide, this large rambling house has spacious doubles and triples with cable TV; all share a bathroom. Home-cooked breakfast is included and the owner is an excellent source of local information. ❸

Hospedaje Independencia Independencia 374 ℡61/227572. Friendly young owners allow camping in the yard and can rent equipment, as well as organize tours of the area. Dorms and rooms are rather small, but warm; generous breakfast is included and kitchen and internet facilities available. ❷

Hostal Turismo Oro Fuegino Fagnano 356 ℡61/249401, ⊛www.orofuegino.com. parking. This attractive guesthouse beneath the city *mirador* boasts comfortable en-suite rooms with cable TV and telephone; some have skylights rather than windows; popular with groups. Breakfast is included. ❹

Hotel Finis Terrae Av Cristóbal Colón 766 ℡61/209100, ⊛www.hotelfinisterrae.com. Conveniently located, if pricey, hotel with spacious rooms featuring all manner of conveniences, including wi-fi. Good buffet breakfast is included and the on-site restaurant offers excellent views of the city. Discounts are available out of season. ❽

Hotel José Nogueira Bories 959 ℡61/711000, ⊛www.hotelnogueira.com. This lovely hotel boasts a prime location on the plaza, in the Palacio Sara Braun: some rooms are a little small but very stylish. Excellent service, a first-rate restaurant and a plethora of excursions on offer make this the best hotel in town. **❽**

Hotel Mercurio Fagnano 595 ☏61/242300, Ⓦwww.chileaustral.com/mercurio. Old-fashioned yet comfortable hotel near the Plaza de Armas, and with friendly staff. Rooms have television and telephones; there is internet access and a decent bar. **❺**

Hotel Plaza José Nogueira 1116 ☏61/241300, Ⓦwww.hotelplaza.cl. Large rooms with spacious

bathrooms on offer at this intimate hotel on the second floor of a traditional building on the Plaza de Armas. Cable TV and wi-fi are some of the amenities; tours can be arranged. **❹–❺**

Residencial Roca Magallanes 888, 2nd floor ☏61/243903, Ⓔfranruiz@entelchile.net. If you're looking for inexpensive central accommodation that isn't a hostel, this family-run guesthouse offers simple rooms with high ceilings on the second floor of an old building. Simple breakfast is included and there's reliable hot water in the shower. **❷**

The City

Set on a windy edge of the Magellan Strait, Punta Arenas faces eastward to the ocean. The city has four main streets; the north–south axes are **Avenidas España and Bulnes**, the east–west are **Avenidas Independencia and Colón**. Contained within them, the compact centre of town is focused around the central **Plaza Muñoz Gamero**. The main shopping street, **Bories**, runs north from the west of the plaza.

Around the Plaza

The tranquil **Plaza Muñoz Gamero**, featuring shady pathways under magnificent hundred-year-old Monterey cypresses, fills with strolling couples in the evening. In the middle rises an imposing **monument to Ferdinand Magellan**. If you touch (some say kiss) the toe of the Ona Indian, tradition has it that you'll return to Punta Arenas.

▲ View of Punta Arenas with the ocean beyond

Magellan, pioneer of global exploration

Fernoã Magalhães, known to English-speakers as **Ferdinand Magellan**, was born in about 1480 in northern **Portugal**, and had an adventurous early life: in his twenties he saw service with the Portuguese fleets in their wars against the Muslims of the Indian Ocean, and by 1515 he was a veteran of the campaigns in Morocco. In 1516, after being refused a rise in his pension by the king of Portugal, Magellan took his services to **Spain**.

Those days were the beginning of European exploration, prompted mainly by the desire to seek out new routes to the East and its valuable Spice Islands (the Moluccas of Indonesia). Magellan believed that the answer lay to the west, under or through the newly discovered American continents, and he asked the king of Spain, **Carlos I**, to fund his search. Charles agreed, eager to prove that the Spice Islands lay in the half of the New World that the pope had just assigned to Spain.

On September 20, 1519, Magellan sailed west as admiral of a fleet of five ships. They crossed the Atlantic Ocean, and started to search the coast of South America for the elusive passage. It was a long and hard hunt, and not all Magellan's fleet believed there was a strait: on Easter Day 1520, Magellan had to quash a mutiny by his Spanish captains. But on October 21, 1520, his flagship, the **Trinidad**, finally rounded Cabo Virgenes and entered the strait that now bears his name. Thirty-six days later the open seas of an ocean were sighted; they named the new ocean "the Pacific" for its calmness after the storms of the strait, and set out across it, not expecting it to be so wide.

They sailed for four months without seeing land. Their food and water ran out. Then Magellan himself was killed in a fight with the natives of Mactán Island, but the fleet didn't turn back, petrified of attempting to go through the straits at the bottom of South America for a second time. Three years after they'd set out, just one of Magellan's original five ships finally limped back to Spain. It was loaded with spices (cloves and nutmeg) and manned by only eighteen of the original crew, men wasted and half-dead. The voyage's chronicler said he could not imagine the journey ever being repeated.

Around the plaza rise several grand houses dating from the wool boom. The only one you can visit is the **Palacio Sara Braun** (Mon–Fri 10am–1pm & 6–8.30pm; CH$1000), on the northwestern corner, designed by a French architect, Numa Mayer, for Sara Braun, widow of one of the great sheep barons, and now divided between the *Club de la Unión* and the *Hotel José Nogueira*, with several elegant rooms that make up the small museum.

If you head north from the square along Calle Magallanes, you'll find another glorious house: the **Palacio Braun Menéndez**. The family residence had been donated to the nation some years ago to become the home of the **Museo Regional Magallanes** (May–Oct daily 10.30am–2pm; Nov–April Mon–Fri 10.30am–5pm, Sat & Sun 10.30am–2pm; CH$1000, free on Sun and holidays). You can visit the beautifully preserved private quarters, a time-capsule 1903 French family home. Lavishly decorated and filled with European furniture and paintings, the dining room, bedrooms and sitting rooms recall a wealthy middle-class lifestyle achieved by few who came to Patagonia in search of it.

Seven of the fourteen rooms in the museum are devoted to a permanent exhibition detailing the colonization of Patagonia and Tierra del Fuego, with pioneer articles, historical photos and bilingual displays on the maritime and farming history of the region, as well as the region's **native tribes** – the Kawéscar (Alacalufes) and the Selk'nam (Ona). Dusty old account books and documents reveal that the founding families controlled not only the sheep trade, but an immense range of other commercial activities. In effect, they *were* the city.

One and a half blocks east of the plaza, three blocks north of the port, sits the engaging **Museo Naval y Marítimo** at Pedro Montt 981 (March–Nov Mon–Fri 9.30am–12.30pm, Sat & Sun 3–6pm, Dec–Feb Mon–Sat 9.30am–5pm; CH$1000). It houses a collection of minutely detailed scale models of ships associated with the town's history, including Sir Ernest Shackleton's "Endurance", while the first floor is decked out as a ship, complete with nautical equipment and interactive displays.

Castillo Millward

In the days when the town was still called Sandy Point, and sterling widely accepted as currency, a leading member of the community was one **Charley Milward**, great-uncle of the author **Bruce Chatwin**. Chatwin wrote his travelogue *In Patagonia* about his trip here to learn more about Milward, ex-sea captain and adventurer, who helped discover a chunk of a deep-frozen prehistoric ground sloth in the Cueva del Milodón (see p.429). Around the corner at España 959 you can see Milward's old house (not open to the public), part Victorian parsonage, part castle. It was here, in 1914, that the famous explorer Sir Ernest Shackleton stayed and planned the rescue of his stranded crew after his ship, the *Endurance*, was crushed by ice in the Antarctic. (For a detailed account of Shackleton's expedition and rescue, consult ⓦwww.south-pole.com.)

If you cross Avenida España and climb some steps up to the **Mirador Cerro la Cruz**, you can enjoy a sweeping view of the city's multicoloured roofs and the Magellan Strait beyond.

Museo Salesiano Maggiorino Borgatello and around

Seven blocks north of the plaza, on the west side of the wide Avenida Manuel Bulnes, is the **Museo Salesiano Maggiorino Borgatello** (Tues–Sun 10am–12.30pm & 3–5.30pm; CH$2000) which covers the evangelisation of the natives of southern Patagonia and Tierra del Fuego by the Salesian order. The exhibits suggest that the missionaries acted as mediators between the locals and the settlers, failing to point out the evangelisers' roles in the demise of native culture. The best displays amongst natural history samples vividly depict the daily life of the Fuegian Indians and the weapons they used for hunting and fishing. Another excellent exhibit is the collection of photographs of the region, taken by the Italian mountaineering priest, Alberto de Agostini.

Two blocks north of the Museo Salesiano, on the other side of Avenida Bulnes, lies the city's magnificent **Cementerio Municipal** (daily: summer 7.30am–8pm; winter 8am–6pm; free), which covers four city blocks and is the most fascinating sight in Punta Arenas. Crisscrossed by a network of footpaths lined with immaculately clipped cypresses, this eclectic necropolis reflects the turbulent history of Patagonia in marble and stone, Croatian names mingling with English and Spanish ones and the colossal ostentatious mausoleums of Punta Arenas's wealthiest families overshadowing the modest graves of immigrant labourers.

Take one of the many buses or *colectivos* running north past the cemetery with "**Zona Franca**" written on the front and you'll arrive at Punta Arenas's **duty-free shopping** zone, 3km north of the centre of town – a good place to stock up on supplies.

Eating and drinking

Brocolino O'Higgins 1049. A must-stop for gourmets, this excellent restaurant may not look like much from the outside, but its classically trained chef Hector whips up such delights as "Aphrodisiac soup", using the freshest local fish, *centolla* (king crab) and sweetbreads in a champagne cream sauce. All dishes are imaginative, well-executed and reasonably priced. Mains CH$5000–7000.

Café Montt Pedro Montt 976. Cosy café with wi-fi access serving an excellent range of coffees, including the delectable *mochachino* with condensed milk (CH$1500). Closed Sundays.

Hotel José Nogueira Carlos Bories 959 ☏61/248840. Relax with a pisco sour or enjoy a reasonably priced steak with crab sauce in the hotel's restaurant housed in a beautiful vine-draped conservatory. Mains CH$7000.

Lomit's José Menéndez 722. This informal and popular fast-food place serves decent hamburgers and sandwiches; coffee and drinks make this a good meeting-place, especially since it stays open late.

La Luna O'Higgins 1017. One of Arenas's best eateries features fine fish and seafood dishes, a bright blue and yellow decor, Latin rhythms and friendly service. After a generous pisco sour, try the *chupe del día* or other well-cooked dishes (CH$6000). Don't forget to pin your place of origin on the maps decorating the walls.

La Marmita Plaza Sampaio 678. Known for its excellent vegetarian options, this intimate and welcoming restaurant also serves a wide range of well-executed regional dishes and hearty soups.

El Mercado Mejicana 617, second floor. If you're looking for first-class seafood, including moderately priced lunch menus, look no further: the calamari, razor clam and king crab dishes are particularly good. There's a full-size *centolla* mounted on the wall, so you can see just how big these crustacean monsters really are.

O Sole Mío O'Higgins 974. Popular with locals, this informal restaurant gets busy at lunch time. The size of the pasta dish portions and the decent pasta sauces make up for the fact that the pasta is not homemade. Mains CH$3000–4000.

Pub Olijoe Errázuriz 970. A cosy and popular pub with an upscale feel to it, great for drinks and snacks, with wooden panelling and a no-smoking area. Try *Glaciar*, the potent house special.

Puerto Café O'Higgins at Independencia. Located above a shop selling all manner of souvenirs and maps, this is a good place for a light meal, a tasty empanada or a beer.

Remezón 21 de Mayo 1469. One of the most imaginative (though expensive) places to eat in town, this upscale restaurant uses natural wild Patagonian ingredients to create exotic game dishes (guanaco, beaver, wild goose) and excellent seafood specialities. Try anything with krill or *centolla*.

Sotito's Bar O'Higgins 1138 ☏61/245365. The bare brick walls and starched linen of this local institution's tablecloths conjure up an elegant New York or London brasserie. Attentive waiters serve large portions of both meat and seafood, though it's the latter that's the restaurant's forté. Booking recommended in season.

La Taberna del Club de la Unión Plaza Muñoz Gamero 716. In the basement of the Palacio Sara Braun, this atmospheric upmarket venue, decorated with black-and-white maritime photographs, is a good place for a quiet drink or swapping travel tales.

La Tasca Plaza Muñoz Gamero 771. This Spanish-themed restaurant offers large helpings of quality dishes, but the real bargain is the lunch-time set menu (CH$4500).

Listings

Airlines DAP, O'Higgins at Menéndez ☏61/616100, ⓦwww.dap.cl; LAN, Bories 884 ☏61/241232, ⓦwww.lanchile.cl; Sky Airline, Roca 935 ☏61/710645, ⓦwww.skyairline.cl

Banks and exchange Most of the banks are clustered around the plaza, especially on its eastern side, and numerous *cambios* are found on Pedro Montt and Lautaro Navarro.

Bus companies Bus El Pingüino, Sanhueza 745 ☏61/221812; Bus Sur, Menéndez 552 ☏61/614224, ⓦwww.bus-sur.cl; Buses Fernández, Sanhueza 745 ☏61/221429, ⓦwww.busesfernandez.com; Buses Ghisoni, Queilen and Tecni Austral, Lautaro Navarro 975 ☏61/613420; Buses Pacheco, Av Colón 900 ☏61/242174, ⓦwww.busespacheco.co.cl; Buses Transfer, Lautaro Navarro 975 ☏61/617202; Turibús, Armando Sanhueza 745 ☏61/227970. Central de Buses, Colón and Magallanes ☏61/245811, sells tickets for various bus companies.

9

SOUTHERN PATAGONIA | Punta Arenas and around

Punta Arenas tour companies

Most tour companies offer trips to the Seno Otway penguin colony (CH$12,000), Fuerte Bulnes (CH$15,000), Parque Nacional Pali Aike (CH$45,000) and day-trips to Torres del Paine national park, though for the latter, you're better off travelling up to Puerto Natales and visiting a tour operator there (see p.430). To visit the penguin sanctuaries or any of the sights near Punta Arenas, it's cheaper to take a tour with Bus Sur, Buses Fernández and Buses Transfer. Below are reputable operators offering both standard and specialized excursions.

Arka Patagonia Manuel Señoret 1597 ☏61/248167, ⓦwww.arkapatagonia.com. Runs multi-day trips around Punta Arenas, Puerto Natales and Torres del Paine, and can help arrange adventures further afield – around Cape Horn and to Antarctica.

COMAPA Magallanes 990 ☏61/200200, ⓦwww.comapa.com. Takes bookings for the Navimag ferry from Puerto Natales to Puerto Montt and runs the *Melinka*, the boat that visits the Isla Magdalena penguin sanctuary for CH$25,000.

Turismo Cabo de Hornos Angamos 663 ☏61/614181, ⓦwww.turismocabodehornos .cl. Arranges all manner of multi-day tours, including boat trips to Antarctica, sailing around Cape Horn, tours of the Magellan Strait area, Torres del Paine and more.

Turismo Pali Aike Magallanes 619 ☏61/221987, ⓦwww.turismopaliaike.com. A variety of nature-watching trips, including daily trips to Isla Magdalena, and Seno Otway and Estancia Lolita safari, as well as full-day canopy trips, transfers to the nearby Reserva Nacional Magallanes and excursions to the historical Fuerte Bulnes.

Turismo Yámana Errázuriz 932 ☏61/710567, ⓦwww.turismoyamana.cl. Apart from running high-quality day tours to standard destinations around Punta Arenas, this longstanding specialist offers numerous trekking and exploration trips in Torres del Paine.

Car rental Avis (Emsa), Roca 1044 ☏61/229049 and at the airport; Hertz, O'Higgins 987 ☏61/248742 and at the airport.
Consulates Argentina, 21 de Mayo 1878 ☏61/261264; Brazil, Arauco 769 ☏61/241093; Netherlands, Magallanes 435 ☏61/248100; UK, Cataratas de Niagara 1325 ☏61/211535.

Hospital Hospital Regional, Angamos 180, between Señoret and Zenteno ☏61/244040.
Internet *Hostal Calafate*, Magallanes 926; Futura Internet, Menéndez 787.
Post office Bories 911.
Telephone offices There are phone centres at Bories 801A, Lautaro Navarro 931 & Nogueira 1116.

South of Punta Arenas

Forty-eight kilometres from Arenas along the main road, you'll see a large **white obelisk** – a monument to the geographical centre of Chile, which takes into account Chilean Antarctic territory right down to the South Pole. The road to the left of the obelisk leads 2km south to **Puerto Hambre** ("Port Famine"). One of the first two Spanish colonies on the Magellan Strait, Puerto Hambre is the site of the ambitious 1584 colony founded by Pedro Sarmiento de Gamboa, which ended in starvation of its colonists. All that's left is a plaque, a concrete dolmen and the ruins of a church, sitting forlornly on a little promontory exposed to the elements. The road to the right of the obelisk leads to **Fuerte Bulnes**, a 1940s reconstruction of the first Chilean settlement in the area. Fuerte Bulnes was founded in September 1843 by a boatload of sailors from Ancud in Chiloé, captained by one John Williams. They came to pre-empt colonization from Europe, and only just made it: a few hours after they arrived, a French warship, the *Phaeton*, turned up and planted the tricolour on the shore. After Williams protested, the French moved off and annexed Tahiti in the Pacific instead. There are a number of old cannons, sturdy but empty log cabins and a lookout tower, while standing slightly apart is a small wooden **chapel**, adorned inside with gifts and supplications left by visitors, giving it a shrine-like atmosphere. Ninety kilometres south of Punta Arenas lies **Cabo Froward**, the southernmost mainland point on the continent. No roads lead here, but the cape can be reached via a two-day wild hike along the cliffs by any reasonably fit individual. Besides impressive views of the Magellan Strait, you'll also see a giant cross, erected here in 1987 in anticipation of Pope John Paul II's visit. Join an Erratic Rock wilderness excursion (see box on Puerto Natales tour operators, opposite), or ask the Punta Arenas tour companies about guided hikes to the cape.

The Reserva Forestal Magallanes

The pretty **RESERVA FORESTAL MAGALLANES** (Nov to mid-April Mon–Fri 8.30am–8pm; CH$2500), 196 square kilometres of protected Magellanic forest, lies just 8km west of Arenas. The forest has two entrances, both of which provide wonderful views back over the city, across the Magellan Strait and towards Tierra del Fuego.

A road to the north leads to the reserve's main entrance, at a dense stand of native forest. You can embark on several hikes here, including the two-hour loop of **Sendero Mirador**, which crosses the ski area and offers panoramic views of the Strait and Tierra del Fuego beyond, and the **Sendero de Chile Tramo Bocatoma-Las Minas** (3km, 1hr), both of which meander through native *coigüe*, *lenga* and *ñire* trees, and the **Sendero Las Lengas** (3.5km, 1hr) to the **ski centre**, the site of the reserve's second entrance, also accessible from the road to the south; there is also a mountain bike circuit. Known as **Club Andino**, the ski centre has a *refugio* and a single chairlift, which you can ride to the top of Cerro Mirador year round (CH$10,000). From June to August, it's a good

> ### Moving on from Punta Arenas
>
> The *Melinka* **ferry** for **Porvenir** in Tierra del Fuego leaves from the ferry terminal at Tres Puentes, 5km north of town, Tuesdays through Saturdays mostly at 9am, and on Sundays at 9.30am to make the crossing (2hr 30min) to Bahía Chilota, 5km west of Porvenir. It returns from Bahía Chilota from Tuesday to Saturday at 2pm, on Sundays from September to April at 5pm and from May to August at 3.30pm. The timetable can change due to the weather, so it's worth checking in advance. Book a space for a car with Transbordadora Austral Broom at Bulnes 5075 (☎61/218100, ⓦ www.tabsa.cl). One-way fares are CH$4600 for a foot passenger and CH$29,000 for a car.
>
> Buses Transfer runs to the Punta Arenas airport. Buses Tecni Austral and Bus Sur serve **Ushuaia**, via Bahía Azul (daily 7/8am; 12hr; CH$30,000); book in advance in peak season. Bus Sur, Buses Fernández, Buses Pacheco and Buses Transfer go to **Puerto Natales** (15 daily; 3hr; CH$4000 one way; CH$6000 return). Bus El Pinguino, Buses Ghisoni and Buses Pacheco serve **Río Gallegos** with connections to Buenos Aires and Los Antiguos (several daily; 4hr; CH$7000), and Río Grande in Argentina (1 daily; 8hr; CH$20,000). Bus Sur, Buses Pacheco, Queilén, Pullman and Turibœs run to **Osorno, Puerto Montt and Chiloé** (daily 7.30/9.30am; 28–30hr; CH$35,000–40,000), with Turibús and Pullman continuing to **Santiago**. Remember that buses for anywhere north of Puerto Natales travel through Argentina.
>
> Scheduled **flights** leave Punta Arenas for Balmaceda, Puerto Montt and Santiago. In summer, **DAP** runs twice-daily flights (except Sun) to Porvenir (US$70 return), daily flights (except Sun) to Puerto Williams (US$150 return); LAN has twice and- weekly flights to Ushuaia (summer only; schedules subject to change).

9

SOUTHERN PATAGONIA | Punta Arenas and around

enough place to ski, with eleven runs, a ski-school and equipment for rent (CH$15,000 per day). To get here, you can walk, cycle, join a tour or take a taxi (around CH$8000).

Penguin colonies

There are two penguin colonies that make ideal day excursions from Punta Arenas. One of the largest penguin colonies in southern Chile, **MONUMENTO NATURAL ISLA MAGDALENA** is home to more than 120,000 Magellanic penguins (also called jackass penguins because of the braying noise they make). The small island, just one square kilometre and topped by a pretty red lighthouse, lies 35km northeast of Arenas, two hours away by boat. Fifteen-metre-high cliffs surround the island; they're covered in tufts of grass, under which the penguins dig their burrows. In October each year, the birds migrate back here and find their mate – they're monogamous and remain faithful to one partner all their lives. The female lays two eggs in the nest. When the chicks hatch, in November, both parents nurture the young, one adult remaining with the chick, the other going fishing. In late January, the chicks shed their baby feathers and get ready for their first trips into the ocean. By the end of March the penguins have returned to sea again.

You can get very close to the birds as they half hide in the waving grass, and lounge by the sea. Ungainly on land, they are surprisingly agile underwater, shooting by like miniature torpedoes, rapidly changing direction. If they start to cock their heads from side to side you're disturbing them; try not to upset the chicks in particular. You can reach Isla Magdalena by the *Melinka*, a passenger ferry operated by Turismo COMAPA (see p.422). It departs at 4pm every Tuesday, Thursday and Saturday in season (Dec–Feb). The five-hour round-trip, which includes one hour viewing the penguin nesting area, costs CH$25,000, and is worth it for the scenic ride alone, as you may well spot dolphins and other marine mammals.

An hour's drive north of Punta Arenas, across open pampa, lies the small **Seno Otway penguin colony** (mid-Oct to end March 8am–7pm; CH$4000). This nesting site of five thousand or so Magellanic penguins is best seen in the morning (before 10am) or evening (after 5pm), before or after they go fishing. You're not allowed on the beach itself, but ramshackle beach-front hides strung along an 1800-metre walkway let you watch the birds amble out of the water. Better still, go and see the far larger, better-cared-for colony on Isla Magdalena (see above).

There are no buses out here, so the easiest way to get here is to drive or join a tour, which takes three hours in all and costs CH$14,000.

Northeast to Chile's Atlantic coast

Forty-three kilometres north of Punta Arenas along Ruta 9, you can take a gravel road that loops along Seno Otway to Seno Skyring and *Estancia Río Verde* (open Nov–March ☎61/311123), where you can view some extremely well-maintained Magellanic architecture, as well as feast on the famous Sunday *parrilladas*, stay in comfortable and stylish rooms overlooking Isla Riesco and take part in horseback-riding excursions.

Back on Ruta 9, shortly after the gravel road turnoff lies a crossroads; the left (northwest) fork leads to Puerto Natales past Río Rubens; trout fishing enthusiasts can stay in the modest *Hotel Río Rubens* (☎09/640 1583), with a good restaurant and camping facilities.

The right-hand fork heads to the Atlantic and to the **Estancia San Gregorio**, once owned by José Menéndez, and part of his Sociedad Explotadora de Tierra del Fuego, which controlled 13,500 square kilometres of grazing land and owned two million sheep. All that's left are the weathered ochre bricks of the storehouses, shearing sheds and *huasos'* sleeping quarters, dating back to 1882, accompanied on the seashore by the ribs of the sailing barque *Ambassador* and the steamship *Amadeo*, skeletal reminders of the Menéndez fleet. The only maintained buildings include a pretty church – visible from the road but locked – and an old estancia house, at the end of a kilometre-long avenue of gale-blasted trees that were once delicate topiary.

Thirty kilometres further on you reach a junction, with the attractive *Hostería El Tehuelche* (T 61/198 3002; ➍) offering decent meals located by the turn-off leading to the Primera Angostura.

The Primera Angostura ("First Narrows") is the narrowest point of the Magellan Strait, and it's here that the **ferries to Tierra del Fuego** cross from the mainland. The ferries leave from the port of Punta Delgada, 16km from the main road. Two ferries, run by Transbordadora Austral Broom (W www.tabsa.cl), make the trip, running between Punta Delgada and Bahía Azul (April–Oct 8.30am–11.45pm; Dec–March 7am–1am; 20min; CH$1600 per person, CH$13,900 for a car). They leave about every forty minutes in summer, and every ninety in winter, except at **low tide**, when they don't run at all.

Parque Nacional Pali Aike

Eleven kilometres beyond the turning for the ferry is the small town of Punta Delgada and the road heading 18km north to Chilean Patagonia's seldom-visited **PARQUE NACIONAL PALI AIKE** (Oct–April daily 9am–6pm; CH$1500). The park's entrance looms up out of the barren rolling plains, green roof first; the sight explains its Tehuelche Indian name, meaning "desolate place of bad spirits". This is an area of flat heath land, with tussocks of beige grass and enormous skies. Strange volcanic formations dot the heath, and on either side of the road lies the occasional depression filled with evaporating water and ringed by white tidemarks, where you can occasionally spot flamingos.

There are four treks in the park, including a 1700m ascent through the fields of jagged black rock, the **Escorial del Diablo** ("Devil's slag heap"), to the **Morada del Diablo** ("Dwelling of the devil") rim; sturdy footwear a must. The best, though, is a nine-kilometre (2hr 45min) **walk** across flat, windy, exposed terrain (carry water) that leads from Pali Aike to remote, picturesque **Laguna Ana** to the northwest.

To the south of the Escorial unfolds a ridge of congealed lava, ten metres high; in this wall of rock, 8km from the park entrance, is **Pali Aike**, a 17m-deep cave excavated by the famous archaeologist Junius Bird in 1937, which contained evidence of prehistoric inhabitation, including bones of a milodón and an extinct American horse, dating from nine thousand years ago.

Wild camping is not permitted in the park and there's no public transport here, though several companies run full-day tours from Punta Arenas.

Puerto Natales and around

Chilean Patagonia's second city, **PUERTO NATALES**, 250km north of Punta Arenas, enjoys a stunning location at the edge of the pampa, sitting by a body of water fringed by tall peaks. The town is the gateway to the **Parque Nacional**

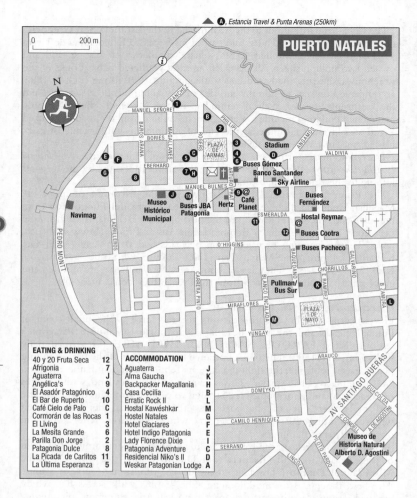

A, Estancia Travel & Punta Arenas (250km)

PUERTO NATALES

0   200 m

N

Stadium

Buses Gómez
Banco Santander
Sky Airline

Museo
Histórico
Municipal

Navimag

Buses JBA
Patagonia

Hertz

Café
Planet

Buses
Fernández

Hostal Reymar

Buses Cootra

Buses Pacheco

Pullman/
Bus Sur

PLAZA
DE
MAYO

Museo de
Historia Natural
Alberto D. Agostini

EATING & DRINKING	
40 y 20 Fruta Seca	12
Afrigonia	7
Aguaterra	J
Angélica's	9
El Asadór Patagónico	4
El Bar de Ruperto	10
Café Cielo de Palo	C
Cormorán de las Rocas	1
El Living	3
La Mesita Grande	6
Parilla Don Jorge	2
Patagonia Dulce	8
La Picada de Carlitos	11
La Última Esperanza	5

ACCOMMODATION	
Aguaterra	J
Alma Gaucha	K
Backpacker Magallania	H
Casa Cecilia	B
Erratic Rock II	L
Hostal Kawéshkar	M
Hostel Natales	G
Hotel Glaciares	F
Hotel Indigo Patagonia	E
Lady Florence Dixie	I
Patagonia Adventure	C
Residencial Niko's II	D
Weskar Patagonian Lodge	A

SOUTHERN PATAGONIA | Puerto Natales and around

Torres del Paine, and a useful base for visiting the nearby **Cueva del Milodón**, the glaciers of the **Parque Nacional Bernardo O'Higgins**, and, across the border in Argentina, the **Parque Nacional Los Glaciares**. Natales is also a good transport hub, home to the terminal of the **Navimag** ferry from Puerto Montt in the Lake District, and linked to Punta Arenas, Torres del Paine and Argentina by regular bus services.

Arrival and information

The Navimag ferry terminal is on Pedro Montt 308, or Costanera, five blocks west of the Plaza de Armas (☏61/411421, ⓕ61/411229). There's no main bus terminal, so each bus pulls in outside its company's offices, all a couple of blocks from the Plaza de Armas.

The helpful **Sernatur** office sits at Costanera Pedro Montt 19 (Mon–Wed & Fri 8.30am–8pm, Thurs 8.30am–9pm, Sat & Sun 9.30am–1pm & 3–6pm; ☏61/412125, ⓔinfonatales@sernatur.cl). You can also pick up information at

9

the **Oficina Municipal** in the museum (see p.428) at Bulnes 285 (☏61/411263). For information about Torres del Paine, visit Erratic Rock at Baquedano 719, where an informative talk is held every afternoon at 3pm.

Accommodation

There is ample accommodation to suit any budget in Natales, though it is wise to book ahead, especially for stays in January.

Aguaterra Bulnes 299 ☏61/412239, ⓦwww .aquaterrapatagonia.com. This stylish, central hotel has well-furnished en-suite doubles and triples and a cosy guest lounge with cable TV; the good restaurant/café is a bonus, as is the alternative therapy on offer. The staff are knowledgeable, and can organize all manner of tours. ❼

Alma Gaucha Galvarino 661 ☏61/415243, ⓔalmagauchacl@hotmail.com. Rustic hostel run by a genuine gaucho with clean dorms and kitchen facilities. Cowboy paraphernalia adorning the walls and Patagonian barbecue on the patio add to the atmosphere. ❷

Backpacker Magallania Tomás Rogers 255 ☏61/414950, ⓔmagallania@yahoo.com. Drawing a younger crowd, this relaxed central hostel offers clean, spacious dorms and doubles, breakfast, kitchen privileges and a common room with TV. ❷–❸

🏃 **Casa Cecilia** Tomás Rogers 60 ☏61/461 3560, ⓦwww.casaceciliahostel.com. A long-time traveller favourite, this warm, cosy *hospedaje* with a Swiss standard of hygiene has good beds, a decent breakfast and tasty, home-baked bread; guests have kitchen access. Also runs tours, rents bikes and camping equipment and is an excellent source of information; English, French and German spoken. ❸

Erratic Rock II Zamora 732 ☏61/414317, ⓦwww.erraticrock2.com. An offshoot of the original hostel, this warm, family-run guesthouse offers tastefully decorated en-suite doubles with cable TV and includes a sumptuous breakfast. Friendly owners organize tours into the surrounding area. ❸–❹

Hostal Kawéshkar Encalada 754 ☏61/414553. Incredibly laid-back backpacker haunt, run by the knowledgeable Omar. Kitchen privileges and lockers are included; it's possible to camp out back and Omar helps to organize all manner of trips. ❷

Hostel Natales Ladrilleros 209 ☏61/410081, ⓦwww.hostelnatales.cl. Spacious, light and beautifully decorated hostel with a tranquil lounge with fountain, numerous computers for use, comfy dorm beds, an adjoining travel gear shop and helpful staff. Ample breakfast CH$2000 extra; some dorms only have a window into the lounge. ❸

Hotel Glaciares Eberhard 104 ☏61/411452, ⓦwww.hotelglaciares.co.cl. Welcoming modern hotel with spacious doubles equipped with modern conveniences, plus a restaurant serving regional specialities, and a private transportation fleet to whisk you off to Torres del Paine. ❼

Hotel Indigo Patagonia Ladrilleros 105 ☏61/413609, ⓦwww.indigopatagonia.com. With its unique design and decor, Natales's plushest hotel has drawn both praise and criticism. Looking out over Last Hope Sound from one of its three rooftop hot tubs is nothing short of wonderful, though, and spa packages are available to non-guests as well (CH$40,000). Free wi-fi and comfortable rooms seal the deal. ❽

Lady Florence Dixie Bulnes 659 ☏61/411158, ⓦwww.chileanpatagonia.com/florence. A long-established central hotel, with spacious rooms, private baths and a slightly old-fashioned ambience. Off-season discounts are a real bargain. ❼

Patagonia Adventure Tomás Rogers 179 ☏61/415636, ⓦwww.apatagonia.com. Bright central hostel run by young owners; a good breakfast is included and other bonuses include internet, a camping gear outlet next door and the hostel's own adventure outfit for kayaking enthusiasts. ❸

Residencial Niko's II Phillipi 528 ☏61/411500, ⓦwww.nikostwoadventure.com. Sister building of the original on Ramirez; offers use of kitchen facilities, communal breakfast, a laundry service and internet access to mostly young backpacking guests. ❷–❸

🏃 **Weskar Patagonian Lodge** Ruta 9, Km 1 ☏61/414168, ⓦwww.weskar.cl. North of town lies Natales's most appealing hotel/eco-lodge, created by two fishing families. Fantastic location aside, the hosts are welcoming, the plush doubles are spacious, warm and light, the restaurant serves excellent regional cuisine and it makes a great base for exploration of the surrounding wilderness, though own transport is a boon. ❽

The Town

Puerto Natales sits on the lovely Seno Ultima Esperanza ("Last Hope Sound"), a turquoise channel with the remnants of a wooden pier bedecked with cormorants stretching into the distance. The channel's name comes from the 1557 explorer, Juan Ladrilleros, who came upon it when he was at the end of his tether while searching for the western entrance to the Magellan Strait. He found the strait, but almost all his crew died in the attempt.

Natales centres on the **Plaza de Armas**, which has an old **locomotive engine** formerly used in the nearby Puerto Bories abattoir as its centrepiece – an evening magnet for lovers and drunken teenagers.

A couple of blocks west of the plaza you'll find the small but well laid-out **Museo Histórico Municipal** at Bulnes 285 (Mon–Fri 8am–7pm, Sat 10am–1pm & 3–7pm; CH$1000), with attractively laid-out bilingual exhibits on the region's European settlement, natural history, the Milodón's cave and the native Aonikenk and Kawéshkar tribes, illustrated with black-and-white photos. A room is dedicated to the region's first settler, a rather fierce-looking German called Herman Eberhard; look out for his ingenious collapsible boat that turns into a suitcase.

Eating and drinking

Self-caterers can try the well-stocked Abu-Gosch **supermarket** on Bulnes between Baquedano and Ramírez, or the minimarkets along Baquedano.

40 y 20 Fruta Seca Baquedano 443. This shop is an excellent place to stock up on trail mix and all manner of dried fruit before heading to Torres del Paine. Try the dried mango.

Afrigonia Eberhard 343. Natales's best restaurant serves imaginative African-Patagonian cuisine. Every dish is expertly prepared, but standouts include the lamb and the ceviche with mango. As there is only one chef, come early, or be prepared for a leisurely dinner.

Aguaterra Bulnes 299. Attached to the hotel of the same name, this quirkily decorated café is a good spot for a light meal, including tasty Mexican-style fajitas (CH$3500).

Angélica's Eberhard 532. Mediterranean-style food served in elegant surroundings, with friendly service and excellent desserts. The mains are somewhat pricey but the quality is good.

El Asadór Patagónico Prat 158. On the eastern side of the plaza, this quality restaurant specializing in grilled meat and spit-roast lamb can easily be identified by the barbecue pit in the window.

El Bar de Ruperto Bulnes s/n. Currently the only pub in town, this English-run establishment has decent music (live at weekends), a well-stocked bar and a cybercorner.

Café Cielo de Palo Rogers 179. A good spot for freshly made soups, sandwiches, fresh fruit juices and light snacks, this café stays open late on most days.

Cormorán de las Rocas Sanchez 72. The view of the Last Hope Sound rivals the quality of the fish, meat and seafood dishes in this trendy new restaurant, though even if you don't come here to eat, try to have a drink or two.

El Living Smart wooden tables, soothing decor and pleasant tunes create a perfect setting for a drink and a snack or light meal. Cocktails, yoghurt drinks, real tea, coffee, excellent cakes, moderately priced salads and vegetarian dishes are the draw, and the book exchange is a bonus. The only downside is the early closing time (10pm), apart from Thursdays, when the Navimag ferry comes in.

La Mesita Grande Eberhard 508. The best place in town for a thin-crust pizza. Extremely popular with travellers and locals alike, encouraging socializing by having its diners sit in rows along the long wooden tables. Try the "Matavampiros" ("Vampire Killer") with roasted garlic CH$3800.

Parilla Don Jorge Bories 430. Another excellent place for carnivores, with ample portions of *asadór Patagónico* (spit-roasted lamb), though the fish and shellfish dishes are also well-executed. Lamb CH$6000.

Patagonia Dulce Barros Arana 233. For home-made chocolate, excellent *kuchen* and tasty ice cream (try the *calafate* berry flavour), head to this gingerbread house.

La Picada de Carlitos Blanco Encalada at Esmeralda. A budget traveller favourite, this perpetually busy restaurant serves ample portions of good if unremarkable, fish and meat dishes. The large sandwiches are good value (CH$2500).

La Última Esperanza Eberhard 354. A fairly formal, popular seafood restaurant, serving such classics as *chupe de locos* (abalone chowder) and the freshest fish. Mains CH$5000–6500.

Listings

Airlines Sky Airline, Bulnes 682 ☎61/410646.
Banks and exchange There's an ATM in Banco Santander, Bulnes 598, or Banco de Chile, Bulnes 544; there are several *cambios* along Blanco Encalada and Bulnes.
Books and maps Try *Café & Books Patagoniax*, Blanco Encalada 226.
Bus companies Buses Cootra, Baquedano 454 ☎61/412785; Buses Fernández, Ramírez 399 ☎61/411111; Buses Pacheco, Baquedano 500 ☎61/414800; Bus Sur, Baquedano 668 ☎61/614220; Buses Transfer, Baquedano 414 ☎61/412708; Turismo Zaahj, Arturo Prat 236 ☎61/412260; Buses Turis-Sur, Blanco Encalada 555 ☎61/415700; Buses JBA Patagonia, Prat 258 ☎61/410242.

Camping equipment Most of the tour operators rent equipment, but try Erratic Rock, Baquedano 732 or Mundo Sur, Bulnes at Rogers. To buy equipment, including gas canisters, go to La Maddera, Bulnes at Prat.
Car rental Motor Cars, Blanco Encalada 330 ☎61/413593; Hertz, Blanco Encalada 353 ☎61/414519.
Hospital Hospital Puerto Natales, Ignacio Carrera Pinto 537 ☎61/411582.
Internet *Hotel Indigo Patagonia*, Ladrilleros 105; *Coffee Planet*, Bulnes 555 and *Hostal Reymar*, Baquedano 420.
Post office Eberhard 429.

From Puerto Natales to Torres del Paine

From Natales, a fast 150-kilometre road runs through flat Patagonian scrubland to Torres del Paine national park, with the **Cueva del Milodón** (summer daily 8am–9pm, winter daily 8.30am–6pm; CH$3000), a standard stop after 21km.

The cave itself is pretty impressive – 30m high, 80m wide and 200m deep. In 1895, the German settler Herman Eberhard, who owned the land bordering the cave, discovered a large piece of skin from an unidentifiable animal. Over the next few years explorers systematically excavated the cave, and eventually traced more fragments of skin to a giant sloth called a milodón. This creature was thought to be long extinct, but the excavated skin looked so fresh that rumours

Moving on from Puerto Natales

Numerous bus companies ply the Puerto Natales-**Punta Arenas** route, while buses from Punta Arenas going on to other Chilean destinations, such as **Osorno, Puerto Montt, Castro** and **Santiago** call at Puerto Natales on the way. Punta Arenas-bound buses stop at the airport on the way – check when you buy your ticket. From October to April, Turismo Zaahj and Buses Cootra depart for **El Calafate**, Argentina (3 daily; 4–5hr; CH$11,000 one way; CH$18,000 return). Buses JBA Patagonia and other transfers leave for the **Torres del Paine** (daily 7–8am & 2–3pm; 3hr; CH$15,000 return). They stop at three places in the park itself – the park entrance at Laguna Amarga, *guardería* Pudeto and the park administration building.

The Navimag **ferry** to Puerto Montt leaves once a week during summer, less often in winter. For more details, see the box on ferries under Puerto Montt (p.353).

DAP (see Punta Arenas "Listings") operates a summer air-bridge service between Natales and Calafate (Mon–Fri; 1hr; CH$40,000).

Tour companies

Standard tours run by every one of the dozens of tour operators in town include a half-day trip to the **Cueva del Milodón** (CH$5000), see p.429; a day-trip to the Argentine town of **El Calafate** and **Parque Nacional Los Glaciares** (from CH$40,000, park entrance extra), mainly to witness the Glaciar Perito Moreno, see p.441; and a day-trip to **Torres del Paine** (CH$25,000, park entrance extra). Below are outfits offering more specialized activities.

Baqueano Zamora Baquedano 534 ☏61/613531, ⓦwww.baqueanozamora.com. This experienced outfit arranges horse-trekking in Torres del Paine (starting at around CH$30,000 an hour) as well as longer hikes of up to four days; they also run an estancia and a *hostería* in the park.

Big Foot Adventure Bories 206 ☏61/414611, ⓦwww.bigfootpatagonia.com. They specialize in climbing and kayaking, offering a day of ice-hiking on Glacier Grey (upward of CH$70,000) and one-, two-, and three-day ice-climbing seminars (CH$150,000–350,000.) They also run kayaking day-trips on the Eberhard Fjord, three-day kayaking tours down the Río Serrano and a four-day journey to the Tyndall Glacier.

Chile Nativo Eberhard 230 ☏61/411835, ⓦwww.chilenativo.com. Dynamic young outfit specializing in top-end bespoke trips including three- to eight-day horse-trekking tours of the region, visiting out-of-the-way locations, in addition to bird-spotting and photographic safaris.

Erratic Rock Baquedano 719 ☏61/410355, ⓦwww.erraticrock.com. Experienced Oregon operator offering advice on trekking in Torres del Paine, as well as running multi-day trekking trips in the wilderness to Cabo Froward, the southernmost point in Patagonia (summer only) and to Tierra del Fuego.

Mandala Andino Eberhard 161 ☏61/414143, Ⓔmandalaandino@yahoo.com. Not only is this one of the best places in town for a reasonably priced massage after hiking in the park, this operator arranges tours of the surrounding area (CH$28,000), sea kayaking day-trips (CH$70,000) and trekking to the Cueva del Milodón (CH$40,000), among other activities.

Onas Blanco Encalada 211 ☏61/614300, ⓦwww.onaspatagonia.com. Specializes in water-based activities, including trips up the Serrano River in a Zodiac inflatable boat (CH$75,000) and a two-day sea kayaking excursion (CH$180,000).

Turismo 21 de Mayo Eberhard 560 ☏61/411176, ⓦwww.chileaustral.com/21de Mayo. Organizes day-trips and sailing excursions to see the Balmaceda and Serrano Glaciers in Parque Nacional Bernardo O'Higgins on their private cutter, *21 de Mayo*, and yacht, *Alberto de Angostini*; day-trips include a BBQ lunch at the Estancia Perrales (CH$45,000). Zodiac up to the Serrano Glacier costs extra.

began to circulate that it might still be alive. In 1900 an expedition sponsored by London's *Daily Express* arrived to investigate, but no live creatures were found. The skin, it turned out, was so well preserved because it had been deep-frozen by the frigid Patagonian climate. Shortly after the 1900 expedition an unscrupulous gold prospector and Charley Milward (see p.420) dynamited the cave's floor, uncovering and then selling the remaining skin and bones. Two pieces made their way to Britain: one to the Natural History Museum in London, and the other to Charley Milward's family. On-site there is a good **Museo de Sitio** (daily 8am–8pm) with detailed information on the park and a decent restaurant.

To the northwest of the cave, the Seno Ultima Esperanza continues on for about 100km until it meets the Río Serrano, which, after 36km, arrives at the **Balmaceda** and **Serrano glaciers**. A boat trip here is one of the most beautiful in the entire area. It takes seven hours and you pass a colony of cormorants and a slippery mass of sea lions. The glaciers themselves make an impressive sight, especially when a chunk of ice the size of a small house breaks off and crashes into the water. They form the southern tip of **Parque Nacional Bernardo O'Higgins**, the largest and least visited national park in the whole of Chile. The east of the park is almost entirely made up of the Campo de Hielo Sur (the Southern Ice Field); the west is comprised of fjords, islands and untouched forest.

Parque Nacional Torres del Paine

Nothing really prepares you for your first sight of **PARQUE NACIONAL TORRES DEL PAINE** (daily 8.30am–8pm; summer CH$15,000; winter CH$5000). One of the world's stunning geographical features is the **Paine Massif**, the unforgettable centrepiece of the park, which suddenly appears behind the salt-encrusted turquoise **Laguna Amarga** after a couple of hours' drive through largely featureless scrubland. The finest views of it are from the south bank of Lago Nordenskjöld, whose waters act as a great reflecting mirror.

What you see is a set of mountains, the main body of which is made up of the twin peaks of **Monte Almirante Nieto** (2668m and 2640m). On the northern side are the soaring, unnaturally elegant **Torres del Paine** ("Paine Towers"), the icon of the park, and further west, the dark-capped, sculpted **Cuernos del Paine** ("Paine Horns"), which rise above the **Valle del Francés** ("Frenchman's Valley"). To the west of the park is the broad ice river of **Glaciar Grey**, and on the plains at the mountains' feet large herds of **guanacos** and the odd *ñandú* still run wild, which you are more likely to spot than the park's elusive fauna: pumas and the *huermúl* deer.

If you're coming here to taste true wilderness, you may be disappointed, as this popular park is fully equipped with *refugios*, campsites and hotels, though the good infrastructure makes the park very accessible.

Arrival and information

The only entrance to the park for those coming by bus is 117km from Natales at **Laguna Amarga**, where you pay the park fee at the Conaf station. From here, you can either take a minibus that runs to the *Hostería Las Torres* (CH$2000) or walk for about 1hour 30minutes before reaching the start point of the treks. The buses from Natales continue along Lago Nordenskjöld for another 19km to the **guardería Pudeto**, near the impressive cataract of Salto Grande and the departure point for the catamaran to *Paine Grande Lodge*. The road continues beyond here, past *Hostería Pehoé*, *Camping Pehoé* and *Hotel Explora*, opposite Salto Chico, to reach the **Park Administration Centre** (daily 8.30am–8pm; ✆61/691931) after 18km, around which there's a visitor centre, a refuge, a grocery store, a *hostería* and even a post office.

From the *guardería* Pudeto, a **catamaran** runs across Lago Pehoé (Nov to mid-March daily at 9.30am, noon and 6pm; from mid- to late-Oct and from mid- to late-March, at noon and 6pm; the rest of year daily at noon; CH$11,000 one-way; CH$18,000 return; tickets sold on board. Return trips from *Paine Grande Lodge* are half an hour later and are met by buses heading back to Puerto Natales. From the park administration there are regular buses to Puerto Natales, the last leaving at 6.30pm.

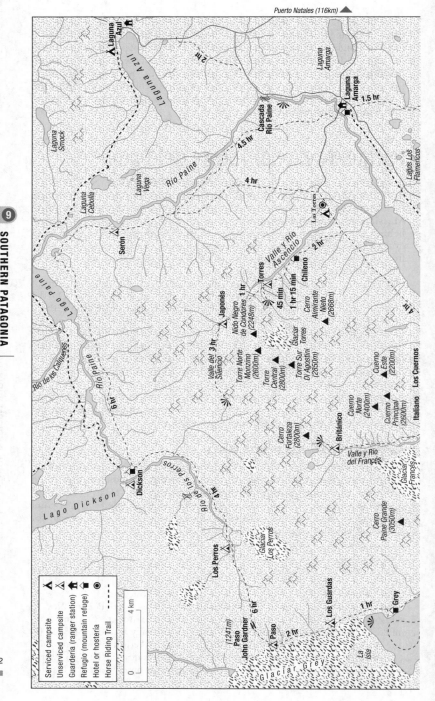

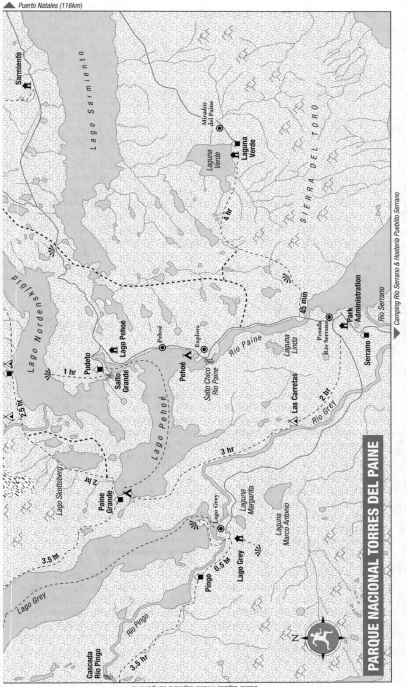

PARQUE NACIONAL TORRES DEL PAINE

▶ Camping Río Serrano & Hostería Pueblito Serrano

▼ Glaciar Zapata, Mirador Zapata & Campamento

433

The best place for general **information** is the Park Administration Centre, although all the *guarderías* can provide information about the state of the trails. You'll be given a basic overview map of the park when you pay your entrance fee. To **climb** in the park, you'll need to get a permit from the Dirección de Fronteras y Límites (see Basics, p.56, for details), and Conaf; the latter costs CH$60,000 and covers any ascent.

In January and February the park is crammed with holidaymakers, so the **best months to visit** are November and December or March and April. Although in winter (June–Sept) temperatures can fall to -10°C (14°F) or even lower, freezing lakes and icing over trails, and there's the possibility of snow, the small numbers of visitors, lack of wind and often clear visibility can also make this another good time to come – just wrap up warmly.

Come prepared for inclement weather, even in summer, and stick to the signposted trails, as it is possible to get lost and the only means of rescue is by boat or on horseback. Follow park guidelines regarding lighting **fires** (an unauthorized campfire in 2005 unwittingly led to the destruction of 15,000 hectares) and carry all your rubbish back to Puerto Natales, including toilet paper. If camping, take your own food (the small shops attached to *refugios* and campsites have a limited selection and are overpriced); drinking water, however, can be collected from most streams. Bring a sturdy waterproof tent, hiking poles and all necessary camping equipment, though it is possible to rent tents and sleeping bags from most *refugios*.

Accommodation

You'll find several different types of accommodation in the park: unserviced (free) campsites, serviced campsites, *refugios*, and *hosterías*, the last two being rather expensive. Wild camping isn't permitted.

Hosterías

Hostería Lago Grey ☎61/410172, ⊛www .turismolagogrey.com. This *hostería* has beautiful views of Lago Grey, though the plush rooms are on the small side. A conventional boat run by the *hostería* makes a three-hour return trip twice daily to Glaciar Grey at 9am and 3pm; they also run dinghy runs on Lago Grey (CH$80,000) as well as down the Ríos Pingo and Grey (CH$55,000 per person). The guides are excellent. ❽

Hostería Mirador del Payne ☎61/228712, ⊛www.miradordelpayne.com. Beautifully located on Laguna Verde, this is a colonial-style house with a veranda and eight *cabañas*; excellent Patagonian cuisine on offer. The location isn't very convenient for the exploration of the park; you'll need your own transport. Excursions offered. ❽

Hostería Pehoé ☎61/411390, ⊛www.pehoe .com. Sits on a small island in Lago Pehoé looking out to the highest peaks of the Paine Massif. There's a warm bar and restaurant and numerous excursions on offer. ❽

Hostería Las Torres ☎61/363636, ⊛www .lastorres.com. Excellent location, beautiful,

comfortable rooms and a good restaurant (open to non-guests as well) make this a top choice. Numerous (though pricey) excursions available, including horse-riding trips of varying length (prices start at CH$30,000 for three hours). There's also a spa in which to pamper yourself. ❽

Hotel Explora ☎61/411247, ⊛www.explora.com. This is the most extravagant and exclusive hotel in the park, set near the Salto Chico, with incredible views from every room. Swimming pool, gym, excellent meals and twenty-five tours with knowledgeable bilingual guides are included, from day treks to horseriding. ❾

Posada Río Serrano ☎61/613531, ⊛www .baquedanozamora.com. Comfortable *hostería* housed in an attractive old structure on the site of the first estancia. Run by Baqueano Zamora (see p.430), this *posada* has comfortable rooms with or without bath, with cable TV. The good restaurant is a bonus, as are the numerous horse-riding excursions on offer. ❻–❼

Refugios and campsites

The **refugios** in the park are usually open from September to May and are generally closed by the weather during the rest of the year. Six are run by two companies, Fantástico Sur (℡61/226054, ⊛www.fantasticosur.com) and Vértice Patagonia (℡61/414300, ⊛www.verticepatagonia.cl); these are well-equipped, offer hot meals and equipment rental and charge CH$20,000 for a bunk bed, CH$5000 for a sleeping bag and CH$5000/7000/10,000 for breakfast/lunch/dinner. Discount available if you pay in US dollars; foreigners are exempt from IVA (tax). In peak season, book *refugio* beds in advance. Conaf also operates a number of free *refugios* throughout the park (Zapata, Pingo, Laguna Verde, Laguna Amarga, and Pudeto) although these are very basic and frequently in a poor state of repair.

The **unserviced campsites** (Campamento Las Torres, Japonés (climbers only), Italiano, Británico, Lstets Guardas and Paso on the Torres del Paine Circuit are free and are just a flat patch of land and a *fogón* (some have toilets). All the **serviced campsites** are listed below.

Campamento Los Perros (Vértice Patagonia). Last campsite before the John Gardner pass, situated in a wooded area, with a small shop, cold showers and a cooking hut (CH$4000 per person).

Campamento Serón (Estancia Cerro Paine). A pleasant campsite (CH$4000 per person) with picnic tables, cold shower and a small shop in a pleasant meadow setting at the bottom of the northeast corner of the massif.

Camping Lago Pehoé (Turismo Río Serrano) ℡61/266910, ⊛www.campingpehoe.com. Campsite with a shop, a restaurant, a picnic area and hot showers on the eastern edge of Lago Pehoé beneath a couple of excellent *miradores*. CH$12,000 for up to six people.

Camping Laguna Azul ℡61/411157. On the shores of a little-visited lake to the northeast of the park with hot showers. CH$12,000 for a site for up to six people, CH$3500 to picnic.

Camping Río Serrano (Turismo Río Serrano) ⊛www.campingchile.com. Out of the way, south of the park administration building, this campsite with cold showers (CH$12,000 for up to six people) is on a bend in the Río Serrano and accessible from the road. It's possible to organize excellent horse-riding tours from here and Patagonian barbecue can be arranged for groups.

Camping Las Torres (Estancia Cerro Paine). Near the park entrance at Laguna Amarga and the *Hostería Las Torres*, with hot showers, fire pits and firewood available for purchase; access to *Refugio Las Torres* for hot meals and a small shop. (CH$4000 per person).

Paine Grande Lodge and Camping (Vértice Patagonia). This new, modern structure is a firm favourite for its scenic location and modern comforts, including a café, eatery and small store within the lodge. You can camp in the adjoining grassy fields (CH$4000 per person). There is a separate toilet, hot showers and cooking hut for campers.

Refugio Dickson (Vértice Patagonia). Quiet and peaceful, this is the most remote refuge (CH$18,000 per person) in the park, on the shores of Lago Dickson on the northern part of the Circuit; the staff are friendly and there's a well-stocked shop here. Camping also possible (CH$3500 per person).

Refugio y Camping Chileno (Fantástico Sur). It's halfway up the Valle Ascencio, at the foot of the Torres del Paine. CH$20,000 per person at the refuge.

Refugio Grey (Vértice Patagonia). A popular *refugio* (CH$18,000 per person) thanks to its position by Glaciar Grey; has facilities for ice-climbing.

Refugio Las Torres (Fantástico Sur). Near the park entrance at Laguna Amarga and the *Hostería Las Torres*, this place has a small shop, gear rental and cafeteria(CH$20,000 per person).

Refugio y Camping Los Cuernos (Fantástico Sur). A modern hut (CH$20,000 per person) in a clearing beneath the Cuernos del Paine, on the northern shore of Lago Nordenskjöld, with a cafeteria and campsite (CH$4000 per person). Campers may use a small stove in the *refugio* to cook after 10pm.

Exploring the park

The two most, popular hikes are the "**W**", so-called because the route you follow looks like a "W", up three valleys, taking you to the "stars" of the park – Las Torres, Valle del Francés and Glaciar Grey, and the "**Circuit**", which leads

▲ Parque Nacional Torres del Paine

you around the back of the park and encompasses the "W"; allow seven-ten days for the "Circuit" and at least four for the "W".

The Circuit

The best way to tackle the "Circuit" is anticlockwise, as it also means you'll have excellent views of Glacier Grey in front of you rather than behind you when you come to tackle the most challenging part of the hike – the Paso John Gardner.

You can either start from the *guardería* at Laguna Amarga, in which case you have a straightforward 10km (4.5hr) walk over largely flat terrain to *Campamento Serón* on your first day. If you start from the *Hostería Las Torres*, you can either head to *Serón*, which entails an easy four-hour walk up and down gentle inclines, crossing vast fields of giant daisies, or tackle the climb up Valle Ascencio first, depending on whether or not you want to save the Las Torres highlight, til last or not.

If you arrive at the base of Valle Ascencio by 5.30pm, in the summer you have enough daylight hours to make it to the top of the valley by dusk. From the *Hostería Las Torres*, go west along the foot of the massif. Just after a bridge you head uphill along a dirt trail strewn with scree; after a relatively steep two-hour climb, it's possible to spend the first night at the so-so *Refugio y Camping Chileno*. From *Chileno*, the trail continues up and down exposed inclines (beware of sudden gusts of wind), and then through *lenga* brush, crossing a stream, to the wooded *Campamento Torres*; allow ninety minutes. This is a free campsite by another stream at the foot of the track up to the **Torres** themselves. You can camp overnight here, leave your gear and then tackle the knee-popping forty-five minute climb up uneven boulders in order to reach Las Torres just before daybreak. If the weather is clear you are treated to a stunning postcard view across Laguna Torres up to the three strange statuesque towers that give the park its name – **Torre Monzino** (2600m), **Torre Central** (2800m) and **Torre D'Agostini** (2850m), at their most gorgeous when bathed in the first rays of the sun.

An alternative trek from *Campamento Torres* is to press on north for an hour or so, guided by cairns, to the *Campamento Japonés*, a climbers-only campsite. Along the way the path crosses a couple of icy brooks and some massive rock falls. At *Japonés* you'll find the beautiful **Valle del Silencio** that heads west. It's much less visited than the Torres and a great place to escape the crowds.

After descending back to *Hostería Las Torres*, you can then press on to *Serón* the same day. From *Serón*, it's a five- or six-hour hike to *Refugio Dickson*, with a flat trail along Río Paine, which then climbs steeply uphill as you pass a small horseshoe-shaped lagoon. The trail meanders on west, with sweeping views of Lago Paine on your right-hand side, ducking into patches of vegetation and crossing several streams. A boggy section of the trail is partially covered with wooden boardwalks. Finally, the trail descends steeply to *Refugio Lago Dickson* in its scenic setting at the southern end of iceberg-flecked Lago Dickson.

You can spend the night here, or press on to *Campamento Los Perros*, another four hours' hike from *Dickson*, bearing in mind that the trail runs largely uphill. This scenic trail snakes through dense forest for most of the way; you may have to clamber over several fallen trees. You cross two bridges over large glacial streams and pass a pretty waterfall, before emerging at the exposed, rocky section of the trail, which treats you to a fabulous view of Glaciar Los Perros above a round lagoon, before continuing to a patch of forest which partially shields the campsite from icy blasts of wind.

Here you'll need to wait for the weather to be in your favour before starting on a three- to four-hour climb to the top of **Paso John Gardner** (1241m) following cairns and orange markings that are sometimes covered by snow, as it is too dangerous (and often impossible) to cross the pass in gale-force wind or during a snowstorm. From *Los Perros* you'll have to cross a stream using a rickety wooden bridge, after which the trail deteriorates into dozens of muddy paths, involving an hour's trudge through ankle-deep mud. Above the tree line, it's a straightforward uphill slog along the rock-strewn slope, and patches of snow, before reaching the exposed pass. The reward for all this is the sudden, staggering view over the icy pinnacles of **Glaciar Grey**, more than 7km wide at its largest point, and the vast immaculate expanse of the **Campo del Hielo Sur** – over ten thousand square kilometres of ice cap and one of the largest ice fields outside the poles.

On the other side of the pass the scree-strewn path descends steeply into *lenga* forest, and can be very muddy. Much of the trail has been made into crude steps, to facilitate the descent, and for the most part, you have handrails or taut rope to hold on to. It takes a couple of hours from the top of the pass to reach the small and basic *Campamento Paso*, where there is a toilet, a *guardería* and a shelter for cooking; a stream nearby provides drinking water. Faster trekkers can press on down to the extremely basic, unserviced (except for a toilet) *Campamento Los Guardas* (also free), two hours' trek away, with the trail climbing in and out of ravines. In two places, you will have to ascend or descend along metal ladders attached to vertical slopes. From *Campamento Los Guardas*, it's a further hour's descent through the forest to *Refugio y Camping Grey*, beautifully sited on the beach at the foot of Glaciar Grey.

Just before you reach it, a short side path leads to a *mirador* overlooking the snout of the glacier. To go ice-hiking on the glacier, buy tickets at the camp office, or organize it beforehand in Puerto Natales with Big Foot Adventure, see p.430).

From *Refugio y Camping Grey*, the path runs alongside the lake, before the largely exposed trail almost doubles back on itself, climbing steeply, after which it runs mostly uphill alongside Lago Grey through the **Quebrada de los Vientos** ("Windy Gorge"), with some rather steep sections, and several viewpoints from which to admire the lake and the house-sized bits of ice bobbing in the water. It then ducks into some *ñire* glens, crossing several small streams and heading away from the lake, passing the small Laguna Los Patos on the right-hand side, and descending through a green valley to the *Paine Grande Lodge* and campsite, situated on the bank of the stunning glacial Lago Pehoé, three and a half hours later. From here you can continue along the "Circuit"; this is also the ideal place to start the "W".

The "W"

Like the "Circuit", it's best to do the "W" anti-clockwise, leaving the steepest hike to Las Torres until last, by which time you will have consumed most of your supplies. The first leg of the "W" is the hike there and back from *Paine Grande Lodge* to Glaciar Grey, described above. You can leave your gear at the lodge. The following day, take the signposted trail that runs along the southern side of the Paine Grande massif, passing the picturesque Lago Skottsberg and a couple of smaller lagoons on the right-hand side, before crossing a suspension bridge across Río del Francés and bringing you to the free *Campamento Italiano* (unserviced except for toilets); you can leave you gear here before heading north up the Valle del Francés.

It takes two and a half hours of hiking along, some of it rather steep, but with great views of the **Glaciar del Francés** and waterfalls cascading from it along the way, to reach another campsite, *Campamento Británico* (free, with drinking water but no toilets). It takes another hour through enchanted-looking *lenga* woods and across a bare patch of granite scree to reach a viewpoint at the head of the valley, from where you can admire **Paine Grande**, the massif's highest peak at 3050m, to your west, and the **Cuernos del Paine**, a set of incredibly carved towers capped with dark rock peaks, guarding the entrance to the valley to the southeast.

Back at the foot of the valley, you can then either spend the night at *Campamento Italiano*, or better yet, carry on for another two and a half hours along the pale blue waters of the icy Lago Nordenskjold to the *Refugio y Camping Los Cuernos*, which nestles in a clearing in the shadow of Los Cuernos. Much of the trail is a steep downhill descent (beware of loose scree) before emerging on the beach with gently lapping waves.

From *Los Cuernos*, it takes an easy four hours to reach the *Hostería Las Torres*, as the trail runs along gentle inclines through low shrubbery and then along green hills. The only tricky part is having to cross a glacial stream partway; there used to be wires strung across it to hold onto, but as they are currently in disrepair, you'll have to wade across or hop from rock to rock. Shortly before reaching the *Hostería Las Torres*, you will see the signposted trail leading up Valle Ascencio, and depending on whether or not you have already paid a visit to the park's last highlight, you either head uphill, or complete your trek up ahead.

Other trails

The two most popular walks by no means exhaust the park. There's a three-and-a-half-hour signposted walk from Guardería Laguna Amarga to **Laguna Azul**, a secluded and little-visited lake in the northeast. From Laguna Azul there's a mostly gentle four-hour walk past Laguna Cebolla to **Lago Paine**, where there's an unserviced refuge (now closed). From here, it used to be possible to hike to Lago Dickson and cross the narrowest part of the lake to *Refugio Dickson*, but the boat is no longer functioning, though if you are on horseback, you can wade across Río Paine and continue along this trail to a viewpoint overlooking Glaciar Dickson, at the north end of Lago Dickson.

Laguna Verde is another remote lake, five hours' walk through *lenga* forest; the trail starts to the east of the park administration building, which is also served by a spur from the Torres del Paine–Puerto Natales road. The fact that so few people come here encourages an abundance of wildlife (guanacos, foxes, hares, rheas and loads of birds), the main reason for doing this trail.

Another seldom-trod path takes you up to **Mirador Zapata**, six to seven hours from *Guardería Lago Grey* at the southern tip of Lago Grey, itself a four-and-a-half-hour walk from the park administration building. It's a steep climb, rewarding you with views of all the park's lakes plus the ice cap and a magnificent glacier, Glaciar Pingo. You'll find the unserviced *Campamento Pingo* half an hour into the trek, and *Campamento Zapata* an hour and a half from the *mirador*, making it an ideal overnight stop. There is also a steep, signposted one-hour trek up the hill behind the *guardería* to Mirador Ferrier, with excellent views.

Into Argentina: Parque Nacional Los Glaciares

Just over the easily crossed border in Argentina are two of the region's star attractions: the trekkers' and climbers' paradise of the **Fitz Roy Sector** in the north of the **Parque Nacional Los Glaciares**, accessed from relaxed **El Chaltén**; and, to the south, the craggy blue face of the **Glaciar Perito Moreno**, regularly cited as one of the world's natural wonders, situated near the touristy town of **El Calafate**, only five hours by bus from Puerto Natales.

The Fitz Roy Massif and El Chaltén

The northernmost section of Argentina's **Parque Nacional Los Glaciares** contains the **FITZ ROY MASSIF**, boasting some of the most breathtakingly beautiful mountain peaks on the planet. Two concentric jaws of jagged teeth puncture the Patagonian sky, with the 3445-metre incisor of **Monte Fitz Roy** at the centre.

The base for **trekking** in this area is **EL CHALTÉN**, which has expanded since it was established in 1985 and has a good infrastructure for a town of four hundred, with a pleasant and relaxed atmosphere and a good mix of Argentines and foreign visitors.

All buses currently call in at the **national park information centre**, about 800m before the village (daily 9am–8pm; ☎02962/493004, ⓦwww.elchalten .com), where visitors are given an informative talk on hiking in the park and receive trail maps. Climbers *must* register here, as should anyone planning to stay at the Laguna Toro *refugio* and campsite to the south. There are short films on the area daily at 2pm. El Chaltén has one ATM (Lago del Desierto s/n) but don't rely on it; bring plenty of cash to cover your stay. Chaltén Travel and Taqsa buses stop outside Rancho Grande, while Cal Tur stops outside the *Fitz Roy Inn*. Buy your bus ticket out of town in advance, as spaces are limited.

Stay at *Hostería Los Ñires*, Lago del Desierto s/n (☎02962/493009, ⓦwww .elchalten.com/losnires; ⑤), a comfortable family-run guesthouse with a good restaurant and views of Fitz Roy; alternatively, try *Senderos*, Perito Moreno s/n

(☎02962/493258, ⓦwww.senderoshosteria.com.ar; ⑨), with a welcoming propri-etress and cosy rooms inside an attractive wooden house; wine-tasting is held in the evenings here. Other good choices include the plush *El Pilar*, owned by an experienced mountain guide, in a spectacular setting out of town along Lago del Desierto (☎02962/493002, ⓦwww.hosteriaelpilar.com.ar; ⑧) – an excellent base for exploration of the northern part of the park. El Huermúl transfers from town (☎02962/493312; AR$35) drop people off at *El Pilar* if they want to hike to Piedras Blancas and Laguna de los Tres without having to retrace their steps.

Backpackers can stay at the welcoming HI-affiliated *Albergue Patagonia*, San Martín 493 (☎02962/493019, ⓦwww.patagoniahostel.com.ar; ❷–❸), with cosy dorms and doubles, restaurant and bike hire, or the huge *Rancho Grande*, San Martín s/n (☎02962/493005, ⓔchaltenrancho@yahoo.com.ar; ❷) which offers cheap meals, internet access and sells onward bus tickets for Chaltén Travel; it is one of only two places open in winter.

Splurge on imaginative fare, including venison ragout, at *Ruca Mahuida* on Lionel Terray, just off San Martín. Alternatively, try *El Bodegón*, San Martín s/n, the perpetually popular microbrewery drawing all with its tasty pizza and *locro* (thick stew); *Domo Blanco*, Costanera at De Agostini, for home-made ice cream; *Del Bosque*, San Martín 640, for excellent cakes and good lunches, or *Patagon-icus*, Güemes at Madsen, for delicious home-made pasta and pizza. Buy bread in *panaderías* all along San Martín and stock up on supplies at the El Gringuito **supermarket**, on the corner of San Martín and Lago del Desierto.

Trekking in the park

The area's claim to be the trekking capital of Argentina is justified, and the closer you get to the mountains, the clearer their beauty becomes. Early mornings are the best time for views and photography. Adequate outdoor clothing is essential at all times of the year, as snowstorms are possible even in midsummer. One of the beauties of this park is that those with limited time can still make worthwhile **day walks**, using El Chaltén as a base, and thus not have to lug around heavy rucksacks. For those who enjoy sleeping in the wild, there are free basic campsites at Laguna Torre, Laguna Capri, Laguna Toro and Poincenot, with Río Blanco reserved from climbers only. The most popular day hike takes you to the stunning Laguna de Los Tres, with Fitz Roy looming directly behind it (8hr return); all the peaks you see in front of you have been scaled by someone at some time. If you make it this far, go around the corner to take in the equally spectacular Laguna Sucia. From Poincenot, the last hour's scramble up is steep and rocky and if it's too windy, you'll have to detour to Piedras Blancas, for an alternative view of Fitz Roy. Again, from Poincenot, you can take the Laguna Madre e Hija trail (2hr 30min) to connect with the other popular day hike to Laguna Torre to view Cerro Torre (4hr from El Chaltén). If hiking to Laguna Toro (7hr one way), you'll have to stay overnight. For short hikes, from the north end of town, it's an hour's walk to Chorillo del Salto (waterfall), while from the national park information centre, take the Los Condores or Las Aguilas trails; even if you don't see condors or eagles, you will get a panoramic view of El Chaltén and the plains stretching towards El Calafate. If you exhaust your hiking options in the immediate vicinity of El Chaltén, take Las Lengas transfer to the nearby Lago del Desierto (daily at 8.30am & 3pm; AR$80; reserve in advance) and do the day hike to the icy expanse of Glaciar Huermúl, among others, or even take on the challenging border crossing to Chile's Villa O'Higgins (see box, p.409). For those looking for alternative adventure activities, Fitz Roy Expedi-ciones (☎02962/493017, ⓦwww.fitzroyexpediciones.com.ar) organizes kayaking and ice-hiking on Cerro Torre's Glaciar Grande and Glaciar Viedma, while Walk

Patagonia (☎02962/493275, Ⓦwww.walkpatagonia.com) offers hikes around El Chaltén, led by knowledgeable bilingual guides, with an emphasis on the park's history, flora and fauna.

El Calafate

EL CALAFATE is the centre of the tourist network in the deep south of mainland Argentine Patagonia. The main thoroughfare, Avenida Libertador, is where you will find most restaurants, along with an ATM and numerous souvenir shops and internet cafés.

All **buses** stop at the terminal on Avenida Julio Roca, on the hillside one block above Avenida Libertador to which it is connected by a flight of steps. The helpful **tourist office** is situated in the terminal (daily: April–Oct 8am–8pm; Nov–March 8am–10pm; ☎02902/491090, Ⓦwww.elcalafate.gov.ar) and can help track down accommodation. The **national park information office**, at Libertador 1302 (Mon–Fri 7am–2pm, ☎02902/491755, Ⓔlosglaciares@apn .gov.ar), has some useful maps, sells fishing licences, and will give you the latest information on campsites near the glacier.

Of the plentiful **accommodation**, *Los Alamos*, Gob. Moyano and Bustillo (☎02902/492424, Ⓦwww.posadalosalamos.com; ⑧) is the most luxurious, with wood-panelled rooms, an excellent restaurant, a pool and a spa. You'll find cheaper accommodation to suit most people at *Los Dos Pinos*, 9 de Julio 358 (☎02902/491271; ❷–❹), with clean dorms, spacious rooms with/without bath and shared kitchen areas; wi-fi is a bonus. *Hostel del Glaciar Pioneros*, Los Pioneros 251 (☎02902/491243, Ⓦwww.glaciar.com; ❷–❹), is El Calafate's original hostel and boasts clean, four-bed rooms, plus kitchen, free shuttle to and from the bus terminal, a good-value restaurant and travel services; more expensive private rooms with en-suite bathroom are available. An attractive sister hostel, *Hostel del Glaciar Libertador*, Av Libertador 587 (☎02902/491792, Ⓦwww.glaciar.com; ❷–❹) offers similar services but the dorm rooms have en-suite bathrooms and are set around a courtyard; HI members are entitled to a 15 percent discount.

For **food**, try *La Cocina* at Libertador 1245, where tasty home-made pasta is the star of the show; try the spicy *putanesca*. *Casimiro*, Libertador 963, is an excellent choice for steak and their plate of Patagonian appetizers, such as smoked trout and deer salami, is superb. Carnivores should head for *Mi Viejo*, Libertador 1111, for serious portions of expertly prepared steak and other meaty delights, such as *mollejas* (sweetbreads). *Pura Vida* at Libertador 1876 serves up traditional food with a modern touch as well as tasty vegetarian dishes in an A-frame cabin.

Glaciar Perito Moreno

The main sightseeing area of the **Parque Nacional Los Glaciares**, the part containing the glaciers that give it its name, is the southern sector within reach of El Calafate. Here you'll find one of Argentina's leading attractions, the **GLACIAR PERITO MORENO**; head a little more than 30km past the park's **main gate** (AR$35 per person) to the series of **boardwalks** from where you can view the spectacle. The glacier sweeps down off the ice cap in a great curve, a jagged mass of crevasses and towering, knife-edged obelisks of ice (seracs), almost unsullied by the streaks of dirty moraine; it's marbled in places with streaks of muddy grey and copper sulphate blue, whilst at the bottom the pressu-rized, de-oxygenated ice has a deep blue, waxy sheen. When it collides with the southern arm of Lago Argentino, vast blocks of ice, some weighing hundreds of tonnes, detonate off the face of the glacier with the report of a small cannon and come crashing down into the waters below. These frozen depth-charges then come surging back to the surface as icebergs, sending out a fairy ring of smaller lumps that form a protecting reef around the berg, which is left to float in a mirror-smooth pool of its own. The glacier tends to be more active in sunny weather and in the afternoon. You can take one of the hourly boats up close to the face of the glacier for a greater appreciation of its vastness (AR$35).

Park practicalities

Guided day-excursions to the glacier are offered by virtually all agencies in El Calafate allowing around four hours at the ice face, the minimum required to appreciate this spectacle. The excursions run by *Hostel del Glaciar* and *Hostel del Glaciar Libertador* (AR$150) are highly recommended, as is their two-day Chaltén glacier trekking trip (AR$550). Chaltén Travel at Libertador 1174 also offers good trips with knowledgeable guides. The recommended Hielo y Aventura at Libertador 935 (T02902/491053, Wwww.hieloyaventura.com) offers numerous ice-related adventures, including trekking on the glacier. If you don't want to be restricted to a tour, you can catch a twice-daily shuttle bus services run by both Taqsa and Cal-Tur (AR$40 each way) that depart El Calafate at 7am and 3.30pm, returning at 12.30pm and 6pm, rent a car (around AR$350 per day), or hire a *remise* taxi with other people (AR$300; be sure to negotiate the amount of waiting time before setting out). Remember that the glacier lies a long way from the park entrance itself (over 30km).

The even larger Upsala (50km long and 10km wide) and Spegazzini glaciers can only be reached by boat from **Puerto Bandera** (a tiny harbour at the mouth of the Canal de los Témpanos, in the northern reaches of the Península de Magallanes), 45km west of El Calafate. Boat trips are run as a park's concession by Renée Fernández Campbell, using a fleet of modern catamarans and launches; choose the biggest one with the greatest deck space for the best views. Prices are the same at all the agencies (AR$350 plus AR$35 park entrance) or you can buy direct from Fernández Campbell at Libertador 867 (T02902/491155). Trips run throughout the year, with daily departures on popular routes in high season.

Travel details

Buses

Puerto Natales to: Cerro Castillo (4 weekly; 1hr 30min); El Calafate, Argentina (4 daily; 5hr); Parque Nacional Torres del Paine (12 daily; 2hr 30min–3hr 30min); Punta Arenas (hourly; 3hr); Río Gallegos, Argentina (3 weekly; 5hr); Ushuaia, Argentina (3 weekly; 13hr).
Punta Arenas to: Puerto Natales (hourly; 3hr); Río Gallegos, Argentina (1 daily; 7hr); Río Grande, Argentina (2 daily; 8hr 30min); Ushuaia, Argentina (Mon–Sat 2 daily; 12hr).

Ferries

Puerto Natales to: Puerto Montt (1 weekly; 70hr).

Punta Arenas to: Porvenir (1 daily except Mon; 2hr 30min–3hr); Puerto Williams (Nov–March 4 monthly; 36hr).
Punta Delgada to: Bahía Azul, Tierra del Fuego (every 1hr 30min, except at low tide; 30min).

Flights

Puerto Natales to: El Calafate, Argentina (5 weekly in summer; 1hr).
Punta Arenas to: Balmaceda (2 daily; 1hr); Porvenir (Mon–Sat 1 daily; 15min); Puerto Montt (2 daily; 2hr); Puerto Williams (summer 6 weekly, winter 3 weekly; 1hr 30min); Santiago (several daily; 4hr); Ushuaia, Argentina (2 weekly in summer; 1hr).

Tierra del Fuego

CHAPTER 10

Highlights

✳ **Parque Nacional Tierra del Fuego** Explore this little-visited and fascinating chunk of jagged mountains, beech forest, bogs, tundra and beautiful coast in a 4WD. See p.447

✳ **Isla Navarino** Fly or sail to Puerto Williams, the most southerly town on earth or tackle the Dientes de Navarino hiking circuit. See p.450

✳ **Cape Horn** Even if you don't kayak around it, consider rounding the tip in a ship or viewing its harsh beauty from the air. See p.451

✳ **Winter sports at Ushuaia** Zip down the slopes of the winter sports resort dramatically located at the end of the world or go sledging with huskies. See p.457

✳ **Boat trip along the Beagle Channel** Spot sea lions and penguins, cormorants and albatrosses, and maybe even killer whales. See p.458

▲ Cape Horn

10

Tierra del Fuego

At the bottom end of the South American continent, and split between Chile and Argentina, **TIERRA DEL FUEGO** ("Land of Fire") holds nearly as much fascination for travellers as Patagonia, from which it is separated by the Magellan Strait. Though comprising a number of islands, it's more or less the sum of its most developed part, the **Isla Grande**, the biggest island in South America. Argentina possesses the easternmost half of **Isla Grande**, plus Isla de los Estados (Staten Island) and a smattering of tiny islets to the south; the rest is Chilean territory.

On the **Chilean side**, you'll find the nondescript main town of **Porvenir**, which huddles on the Magellan Strait, and a string of oil settlements. Flat plains cover much of northern and central Isla Grande, but further south, hills appear and the countryside becomes less barren, with thick woodland and crystalline rivers near little **Camerón**, stretching towards a number of exquisite lakes to the southeast, including the aptly named **Lago Blanco**, principally favoured by anglers. In the far south, the densely forested 2000-metre peaks of the Cordillera Darwin, the Andes' tail-end, make Chilean territory all but inaccessible, as do the remote Fuegian Channels, where the sea winds its way between hundreds of uninhabited islands. South of Isla Grande, across the Beagle Channel, lies **Isla Navarino**, home to the surprisingly welcoming naval base of **Puerto Williams**, the southernmost permanently inhabited place in the world, plus one of the best hiking trails in the archipelago, the **Los Dientes Circuit**. Beyond Navarino are the **Islas Wollaston**, whose southerly tip is **Cabo de Hornos** (Cape Horn), the land's end of the Americas, accessible only by sea or air.

In the Argentine sector, by far and away the leading tourist attraction is the well-known city of **Ushuaia** on the south coast of **Argentine** Tierra del Fuego; it is *the* base for visiting the tremendous **Beagle Channel**, rich in **marine wildlife**, the lakes, forests and tundra of nearby **Parque Nacional Tierra del Fuego**, the historic **Estancia Harberton** along the coast to the east, and, of course, **Antarctica**. A colourful, if rather chaotic town, it's also Tierra del Fuego's main tourist destination, with winter skiing and summer trekking high on the list of activities. Also in Argentine Tierra del Fuego, you'll find the scenic **Lago Fagnano**, and the village of **Tolhuin** at its eastern end. From Tolhuin to the 2985-metre **Paso Garibaldi**, the gateway to Ushuaia by road, you'll travel through patches of low, transitional lichen-festooned **Fuegian woodland**. Much of the area's beauty, together with its isolated estancias, are only really accessible to those with their own transport, as public transport is infrequent.

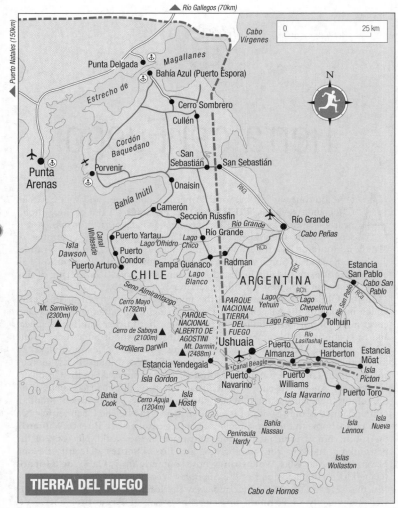

Río Gallegos (70km)

Puerto Natales (150km)

Cabo
Vírgenes

0   25 km

Punta Delgada   Magallanes

Bahía Azul (Puerto Espora)

Estrecho de

Cerro Sombrero

Cullén

Cordón
Baquedano

San
Sebastián   San Sebastián

Porvenir

N

RN3

Punta
Arenas

Onaisin

Bahía Inútil   Camerón

Sección Russfin   Río Grande

Río Grande   Río Grande

Canal
Whiteside   Puerto Yartau   Lago Ofhidro   Lago
Chico   Cabo Peñas

Isla
Dawson   Puerto
Condor   RCb

Puerto Arturo   Pampa Guanaco   Radman

CHILE   Lago
Blanco   A R G E N T I N A   Estancia
San Pablo

Cabo San
Pablo

Seno Almirantazgo

Cerro Mayo
(1792m)   PARQUE
NACIONAL
TIERRA
DEL
FUEGO   Lago
Yehuin   Lago
Chepelmut   RCh

Mt. Sarmiento
(2300m)

Cerro de Saboya
(2100m)   PARQUE
NACIONAL
ALBERTO DE
AGOSTINI   Lago Fagnano   Tolhuin

Cordillera Darwin   Mt. Darmin
(2488m)   Ushuaia   Río
Lasifashaj   Estancia
Harberton

Puerto
Almanza   Estancia
Möat

Estancia Yendegaia   Canal Beagle   Puerto
Navarino   Puerto
Williams   Isla
Picton

Isla Gordon

Bahía
Cook   Cerro Aguja
(1204m)   Isla
Hoste   Isla Navarino   Puerto Toro

Península
Hardy   Bahía
Nassau   Isla
Lennox   Isla
Nueva

Islas
Wollaston

Cabo de Hornos

TIERRA DEL FUEGO

People tend to visit Tierra del Fuego between December and February, when Ushuaia in particular gets very busy. However, in March and April the country-side is daubed with the spectacular autumnal colours of the southern beech, while springtime (Oct to mid-Nov), before the tourist season gets going, is also a great time to come, though it can be even windier than normal. Temperatures rarely plummet way below freezing as they can on the mainland, and in January temperatures over 20°C (68°F) are not uncommon. Sunscreen is vital as the ozone layer is treacherously thin here.

Chilean Tierra del Fuego

The settlement of **Porvenir** sits on the Magellan Strait across from Punta Arenas. Flat plains cover much of northern and central Isla Grande, but the southern reaches, especially the virtually inaccessible Cordillera Darwin, are characterized by dramatic, snow-capped mountains. The dense forests and crystalline rivers southeast of **Camerón** stretch towards a series of lakes, including the beautiful **Lago Blanco**. To the south of Isla Grande, across the Beagle Channel, is **Isla Navarino**, home to the quirky little **Puerto Williams**, with the turbulent waters around **Cabo de Hornos** (Cape Horn) lying beyond.

Porvenir and around

A collection of brightly painted corrugated iron houses set in a narrow bay of the same name, **PORVENIR** (optimistically meaning "future") lies 35km east of Punta Arenas across the Magellan Strait and 147km west of the border crossing at San Sebastián. The town gives off the impression of order stamped on nature, with neat topiary leading down the main street, Philippi, from an immaculate Plaza de Armas. On the seafront the Parque del Recuerdo sports a curve of flagpoles, the painted skeleton of a steam engine and the mounted stern of a boat. The harbour teems with all manner of sea birds, such as cormorants and kelp geese and a twenty-minute walk along the coast takes you to Cerro Mirador, from where you get an excellent view of the town.

Porvenir started life in 1883 as a police outpost during the Fuegian gold rush and has since been settled by foreigners: first came the British managers of sheep farms, and then refugees from Croatia after World War II. You can read the history of the town in the names of the dead at the **cemetery** (daily 8am–6pm) four blocks north of the plaza, where English names mingle with Spanish and Croatian ones. The only other site of interest in Porvenir is the **Museo de Tierra del Fuego Fernando Cordero Rusque** on the north corner of the Plaza (Mon–Fri 9am–5pm, Sat & Sun 10.30am–1.30pm & 3–5pm; CH$800), with photographs of miners and machinery, a collection of cine cameras from the early days of Chilean film, natural history exhibits, and Selk'nam skulls and mummies. The museum also doubles as a tourist office of sorts (☎61/581800, ⓔmuniprovenir@terra.cl).

Practicalities

Ferries from Punta Arenas arrive at Bahía Chilota, 5km to the west of Porvenir along the bay, where a taxi into town costs CH$3000, and a *colectivo* CH$1000. **Buses** pull in to the corner of Riobo and Sampaio, a couple of blocks northeast of the Plaza and leave for the ferry an hour before departure. The **aerodrome** sits 5km north of town, and flights are met by taxis that charge CH$4000 to take you into Porvenir; DAP runs a cheaper door-to-door shuttle.

There are a number of reasonable **places to stay**. The modern *Hostería Yendegaia*, Croacia 702 (☎61/581665; Ⓦwww.turismoyendegaia.com; ❹) offers spacious en-suite rooms with cable TV, while *Hotel España*, Croacia 698 (☎61/580160; ❸–❹), a deceptively large old building run by a formidable woman, features both basic rooms with shared bathrooms and plush en-suite doubles. At the cosy 🦐 *Hotel Rosas*, Philippi 296 (☎61/580088; ❹), the knowledgeable owner has lots of information on the region. At the high end of the market and the far western end of Teniente Merino, at no. 1253, the comfortable refurbished *Hostería Los Flamencos* (☎61/580049, Ⓦwww .hosterialosflmencos.com; ❺) enjoys harbour views, has comfortable rooms and a decent restaurant.

There are several **places to eat** in town, and the best is probably the lively waterfront *Club Croata*, Señoret 542, serving well-prepared standard Chilean fare. The restaurant in the *Hotel Rosas* (see above) offers generous portions of well-prepared seafood dishes and the *Puerto Montt*, Croacia 1169, near *Los Flamencos*, has moderately priced seafood. *Hotel España* does good sandwiches and bargain set lunches.

You can **change money** at the Banco del Estado, Philippi 265, where there's also an ATM, and use the internet at Philippi 375; there's a post office on the plaza at Philippi 176.

Currently there is limited bus service from Porvenir to Cerro Sombrero with the privately-owned Jorge Bastian's minibus (three departures weekly; CH\$3500; ☎61/345406 or 09/8503 3662) from the Porvenir Municipalidad. To go to Argentina, or back to Punta Arenas, you would have to call the specific bus company and request that they stop at Cerro Sombrero.

You can buy tickets for the **ferry** back to Punta Arenas from Tabsa in a kiosk on the Costanera (Calle Señoret s/n, Sector Costero ☎61/580089; Mon–Fri 9am–noon & 2–6.30pm, Sat 9am–noon & 3–6pm). If that's shut, the restaurant at Bahía Chilota sells tickets for the ferry an hour before it leaves (departures Tues–Sat 2pm & Sun 5pm, but again, check times well ahead). The airline DAP, whose offices are in the same building as Tabsa on Calle Señoret (☎61/580089), sells **plane** tickets to Punta Arenas (departures Mon–Sat, twice daily; CH\$35,000 with a maximum of 10kg luggage).

Northeast to Cerro Sombrero and Bahía Azul

The first 20km out of Porvenir heading north is lined with large shallow lakes, ranging in colour from turquoise to sapphire and often adorned with dazzling pink flamingos. Eighty-six kilometres later you reach the turning to the right that leads to Chilean Tierra del Fuego's other town, **CERRO SOMBRERO**, a small oil town looming up out of the moonscape, snugly ensconced on the top of a small flat hill and bristling with TV aerials. It's a helpful place to stop if you need petrol or just want a break. There are a couple of places to stay, the best of which is 🦐 *Hostería Tunkelén*, at Arturo Prat 101, which sits at the bottom of the hill (☎61/345001; ❸). This pleasant truck stop, run by a hospitable family, has a quality en-suite room in the main house, and a large outside block of rooms with one shared bathroom; there is also a good (though somewhat overpriced) restaurant serving typical Chilean fare.

Forty-three kilometres north of Cerro Sombrero (139km from Porvenir), the **ferry** that crosses the Primera Angostura departs from a place known locally as **BAHÍA AZUL**, but usually marked "Puerto Espora" on maps. There's nothing at the ferry terminal except a telephone and a couple of buildings, one of them a café serving snacks. During the crossing, if you're lucky you may see schools of dolphins leaping out of the water alongside the ferry.

East across the Baquedano Hills to the border

A little-used road heads east from Porvenir across the **BAQUEDANO HILLS**, where most of the region's gold was discovered. It starts with a beautiful view, 20km outside Porvenir, looking back down to the town and across the strait to Punta Arenas. All around, the landscape bears the reminders of the gold that was mined here – 41km from Porvenir you pass a gold washer, and then the road crosses the Río del Oro (Gold River), where you'll see the rusting remains of an original dredge. You'll also pass rudimentary grass shelters belonging to a few individuals who still pan for gold here. After a steep descent, you come to the main Porvenir–San Sebastián road, and after another 84km of rolling pampas beneath a leaden sky you reach the **San Sebastián frontier**. There are two San Sebastiáns – the Chilean border post and a fully-fledged village further on in Argentina. All there is on the Chilean side is a hotel, *Hostería La Frontera* (☎61/224731; ⑤), with basic rooms and a restaurant serving good onion soup, and the crossing post (daily: April–Oct 8am–10pm; Nov–March 24hr), where you can expect fairly lengthy delays. Ten kilometres southeast of San Sebastián lies "Las Onas" hill, the site of the oldest inhabited place on the island, estimated to be 11,880 years old.

South to Lago Blanco

While the north of Isla Grande is flat, bleak grasslands, in the south, around beautiful **LAGO BLANCO**, you'll find forest where you can trek, fish and camp.

With little traffic down here, the only realistic means of travelling is in a rental car, though an erratic bus service does run between Porvenir and Camerón. The prettiest road is the one that follows the coast, starting along the northern shore of **Bahía Inútil**, a wide bay that got its name by being a useless anchorage for sailing ships. After 99km you reach a crossroads; turn south, and a little past the village of Onaisin you pass a little **English cemetery**. The gravestones have short inscriptions in English that hint at tragic stories: "killed by Indians", "accidentally drowned" and "died in a storm".

The coast road then skirts around the south of Bahía Inútil, giving beautiful views across to **Isla Dawson**. It passes the occasional small cluster of bare fishermen's huts – keep an eye out for the windlasses used to keep the small boats out of the reach of the furious sea, but be careful of taking photos here, as the whole area is a military zone. When the tide's out, you can see a more ancient way of catching fish – underwater stone *corrales* (pens) built by the Selk'nam Indians to trap fish when the tide turned. Just before the village of **Camerón**, the road turns inland and leaves the bay, while a dirt track carries on south along the coast, passing the sawmills at Puerto Yartou, the beginning of Río Condor, which is excellent for salmon fishing (Erratic Rock in Puerto Natales sometimes runs trips here; see p.430) and ends at Puerto Arturo, a small stockbreeding settlement with numerous penguin nests nearby.

Camerón was once a Scottish settlement, hence the name, and is built on either side of the Río Shetland. Once it was a thriving town, the centre of the largest sheep farm on the island, but nowadays all that's left are some neat little workers' houses and a large shearing shed.

From here, the land begins to lose its Patagonian severity, and as you travel inland you'll see dense forest. Thirty-seven kilometres in, you pass another rusting reminder of the gold rush – a 1904 dredge, now preserved as a national monument – as well as several isolated estancias. Some 20km later, the road forks north to San Sebastián, and south to a place called Sección Río Grande, where an iron bridge crosses the river. You are now surrounded by Magellanic forest, occasionally interspersed with open grassland, where you are likely to see roaming guanacos.

Twenty-one kilometres further lies **Lago Blanco** itself, majestic and brooding, surrounded by steeply forested hills and snow-covered mountains, where you'll find plenty of wilderness in which to trek, fish and camp. Currently the only place to stay in the area is the high-end *Refugio Isla Victoria* on an island in Lago Blanco itself (☎61/241197; open Sept–March; ❸). From Lago Blanco the road continues further south, past Lago Deseado, currently ending at the majestic Lago Fagnano, part of Parque Nacional Tierra del Fuego. There is an ongoing project to pave the horse trail that runs south to the remote Estancia Yendegaia and there are plans to turn the highly photogenic landscape around **Bahía Yendegaia** into a destination aimed at adventure tourism, but at present, you can only reach it on horseback or by cruise ship from Punta Arenas to Ushuaia.

Isla Navarino

Apart from tiny **Puerto Williams** and a few estancias along the northern coast, **ISLA NAVARINO**, the largish island to the south of Isla Grande, is an uninhabited wilderness studded with barren peaks and isolated valleys. Covering about four thousand square kilometres, virtually unspoilt and mostly inaccessible, Navarino is dominated by a dramatic range of peaks, the **Cordón Dientes del Navarino** through which weaves a 70-kilometre hiking trail called the **Los Dientes Circuit**. What has spoilt some of the landscape, especially the woodland, however, is the devastation brought about by feral **beavers**, originally introduced from Canada for fur-farming in the 1940s.

The quickest and most reliable way to get to Isla Navarino is to **fly** (CH\$56,000 one-way) with DAP from Punta Arenas to Puerto Williams (see p.448), a spectacular journey when the weather is good, and bumpy when it's bad. In summer, flights depart at 3pm Tuesday to Saturday. In winter, there are flights Tuesday, Thursday and Saturday. A **ferry** travels from Punta Arenas once a week; it departs Punta Arenas Wednesdays at 6pm and returns from Puerto Williams on Saturdays at 10pm (around 36hr; fares start at US\$175). COMAPA (see p.422) also runs a four-day luxury cruise on the *Mare Australis* and the *Via Australis* (ⓦwww.australis.com), from US\$1700 per person. You might be lucky and catch a ride on a private boat crossing from Ushuaia; make enquiries at the Yacht Club.

Puerto Williams

PUERTO WILLIAMS nestles in a small bay on the north shore of Isla Navarino, 82km due east and slightly south of Ushuaia along the Beagle Channel. Although Ushuaia loudly proclaims its "end of the world" status, that title rightfully belongs to tiny Puerto Williams, home to just over two thousand people, founded as a military outpost and officially the capital of Chilean Antarctica. The compact, windblown town has a somewhat desolate quality to

Having come this far south, many travellers like to go the whole hog and "round the Cape", which is the biggest ship graveyard in the Americas. This is no easy feat, especially if you follow earlier madmen and try and do it in a kayak (not recommended). Ask around in Puerto Williams about **boat trips** to the most southerly point of the world's land mass, barring Antarctica – SIM travel agency (see p.452) is a good place to start. Weather permitting, you disembark on a shingle beach, climb a rickety ladder and visit the tiny Chilean naval base, lighthouse and chapel; a statue of an albatross overlooks the stormy waters beyond. DAP (see p.448) and the local flying clubs also run fairly expensive 30-minute flights from both Punta Arenas and Puerto Williams that do a loop over the headland and return without landing. These air excursions treat you to incredible views of Isla Navarino and the Darwin peaks. As always, weather is a vital factor.

it even in the height of the brief summer; the streets appear deserted and few businesses open before 4pm. In contrast to the ferocious weather, the people of Puerto Williams are exceptionally warm and welcoming; you get a real sense of a close-knit community, brought together by isolation from the rest of Chile. Most businesses are concentrated in the **Centro Comercial**, by the Plaza O'Higgins, with a few **guesthouses** scattered nearby. Calle Yelcho leads west to the colourful **cemetery**, uphill from the seaside Avenida Costanera, which takes you past a cluster of beached fishing boats and a rusted hulk of a half-sunken barge loaded with *centolla* traps, towards the indigenous community of **Villa Ukika**. In the other direction, it leads towards the airport, past the **Mirador Plaza Costanera**, the bright-red pier leading up to the channel's cold blue waters, from which you get a wonderful view of the town against a backdrop of forest-covered jagged peaks of **Los Dientes** beyond.

At the professional **Museo Martín Gusinde**, Aragay 1 (Mon–Fri 9am–1pm & 2.30–7pm, Sat–Sun 2–6pm; donations), named after a clergyman and anthropologist who spent a great deal of time among the native tribes of Tierra del Fuego, you'll find well-laid-out photographs and maps that chart the history and exploration of the region, from the days of the Fuegian Indians, through the gold rush, to the commercial shipping of today. There's also a collection of knick-knacks donated by modern kayakers who've paddled around Cape Horn, only 120km south of here, and an informative display of the island's geology, flora and fauna.

Practicalities

On **arrival** at the midget airport, you'll be met by at least one private car acting as a makeshift taxi that will take you into town. If coming by boat from Ushuaia, you will disembark at Puerto Navarino on the east side of the island, where you must pass through Chilean customs before an hour's ride in a minibus to Puerto Williams. The booth that provides **tourist information**, including photocopied maps of the Dientes de Navarino Circuit, is located at the main entrance to the Centro Comercial, and is perpetually closed. Go to the nearby yellow bakery and ask the proprietress to open it. **Accommodation**, mostly basic but decent, is clustered in the centre. Try *Hostal Bella Vista*, Teniente Muñoz 118 (℡ 61/621010; Ⓦ www.victory-cruises.com; ❸–❹), a new hostel run by an American-Chilean family, and featuring incredible views of the Beagle Channel as well as warm rooms, some en-suite, laundry service and wi-fi. The excellent *Refugio Coirón*, Maragaño 168 (℡ 61/621227; Ⓦ www.hostalcoiron.cl; ❸) has shared rooms with bunks, private en-suites, kitchen open to guests and plenty of advice on local trekking by the owner. The plushest accommodation on the island is the excellent *Lakutaia*, 2km west of town (☎61/621721, ⓦwww .lakutaia.cl; ❾), with every modern convenience, but the major draw are the trips it runs, from helicopter flights over Cape Horn to multi-day wilderness excursions around the island. The top budget choice, however, is the friendly *Hostal Pusaki* at Piloto Pardo 222 (☎61/621116, ⓦwww.hostalpusaki.com; ❸), a perpetual traveller favourite with a warm family atmosphere and excellent home-cooked food. Even if you are not staying here, you can arrange to come for dinner, provided you give Patty a couple of hours' warning; *centolla* night is best. At the small, friendly *Los Dientes del Navarino*, Centro Comercial Sur 14, you'll probably have to settle for the Chilean *menú del día* or whatever's in the kitchen. Head to the well-stocked Supermercado Simón y Simón to buy delicious bread, empanadas and amazingly good wine. There is not much in the way of **nightlife** here: to while away your evening, visit the *Club de Yates Micalvi*, an ex-Navy supply ship with a markedly "old salt" atmosphere and a well-stocked bar where you can chat and drink until the early hours with local sailors, fellow travellers and Antarctic explorers. Alternatively, try *Café Ángelus*, Centro Comercial Norte 151, a popular place day and night for a beer, with a range of alcoholic coffees, cakes and decent sandwiches and pasta. The friendly proprietress is a good source of local information and speaks fluent English and French.

Banco de Chile, located down a narrow passageway from the Centro Comercial towards the seafront, has an **ATM** and can exchange US dollars ($100 minimum) but not traveller's cheques. A **post office** and two **telephone centres** are on the main plaza as well. The **internet café** by the yellow bakery in the Centro Comercial has several slow and expensive computers; entrance through the grocery store. *Cape Horn Cyber Net Café*, at Teniente Muñoz 118, has newer computers, though still slow.

The main **tour agency** is SIM (Sea and Ice and Mountains Adventures) on the main plaza (☎61/621227, ⓦwww.simltd.com); ask the intrepid German-Venezuelan operator for details of treks around the island and yacht excursions down to Cape Horn. Other agencies include Shila Turismo Aventura, Atamu Tekena s/n (☎61/621366 or 09/123 3179, ⓦwww.turismoshila.com); Luis and family run hiking trips around Isla Navarino and fishing excursions to Lago Windhond, Lago Navarino and Laguna Rojas. Victory Adventure Expeditions at Teniente Muñoz 118 (☎61/621010, ⓦwww.victory-cruises.com) specialize

The Yámana, the Selk'nam and the Kawéskar

The unforgiving lands of Tierra del Fuego and Isla Navarino were originally home to three tribes, the Yámana (Yahgan), the Selk'nam (Ona) and the Kawéscar (Alacaluf). The latter inhabited the Magellan Strait and the western fjords, and the former two resided on and around Isla Navarino. The Yámana and the Kawéskar were both "Canoe Indians", who relied on their catch of fish, shellfish and marine animals, while the Selk'nam were hunter-gatherers who subsisted almost entirely on a diet of guanaco meat. Though dismissed by European explorers as savages (Charles Darwin famously commented that the "Canoe Indians" were "among the most abject and miserable creatures I ever saw"), and now largely culturally extinct, the tribes had complex rituals. The Selk'nam, for example, performed a sophisticated male initiation ceremony, the *Hain*, during which the young male initiates, or *kloketens*, confronted and unmasked malevolent spirits that they had been taught to fear since their youth, emerging as *maars* (adults). Father Martín Gusinde was present at the last **Hain ceremony** in 1923, and managed to capture the event in a series of remarkable photographs, copies of which circulate as postcards today.

in sailing trips to Ushuaia and voyages to Cape Horn. **DAP** has its offices at the Centro Comercial Sur 151 (℡61/621114). Tabsa, at Costanera 435 (℡61/621015), sells tickets for the Punta Arenas-bound ferry. Minibuses pick you up at your *hospedaje* to take you to Puerto Navarino to catch a boat back to Ushuaia (weather permitting).

The Los Dientes de Navarino circuit

Most travellers come to Puerto Williams to complete the **Los Dientes de Navarino Circuit** challenge, a strenuous four- to seven-day hike in the Isla Navarino wilderness, where there is no infrastructure whatsoever, and you are faced with unpredictable weather as well as the rigours of the trail. Follow Vía Uno west out of town; the trail starts behind the statue of the Virgin Mary in a grassy clearing. The road leads uphill to a waterfall and reservoir, from where a marked trail climbs steadily through the *coigüe* and *ñire* forest. It is a two-hour ascent to **Cerro Bandera**, a *mirador* with a wonderful view of the town, the Beagle Channel and the nearby mountains; this climb is part of the Sendero de Chile and definitely worthwhile, even if you're not thinking of doing the circuit. The rest of the trail is not well-marked; there are thirty-eight trail markers (rock piles) spread out over the 53km route, which entails crossing four significant passes and negotiating beaver dams in between. The trail leads you past the starkly beautiful **Laguna El Salto**, and then you can either cross a fairly steep pass and do a detour to the south, to the remote expanse of Lago Windward, or head west to **Laguna de los Dientes**. Continue west past Lagunas Escondido, Hermosa and Matrillo before reaching the particularly steep and treacherous descent of **Arroyo Virginia**; beware of loose rocks. The trail markers end before Bahía Virginia, and you have to make your own way over pastures and through scrubland to the main road. The trail officially finishes 12km out of town, behind a former estancia owned by the MacLean family which has been developed into a *centolla*- and shellfish-processing factory, from where you follow the main road back to Puerto Williams or hitch a lift. You can pick up rudimentary photocopied maps of the trail at the tourist kiosk, but it's far better to get the JLM Beagle Channel Trekking Map no. 23 in Punta Arenas or Santiago and 000) or the Tierra del Fuego & Isla Navarino satellite map by Zagier & Urruty Publications in Ushuaia. Before setting out, make sure you have plentiful food and water supplies, sunscreen and warm and waterproof outdoor gear, and remember that water on the island is not drinkable due to the giardia carried by the beavers. Be prepared for inclement weather, as it can snow even in summer, and inform people in town of your plans before leaving.

Around Puerto Williams

Near the start of the Los Dientes trail, 3km west of Puerto Williams, is the entrance to the experimental **Parque Etnobotánico Omora** (daylight hours; donation; Ⓦwww.cabodehornos.org), named for the world's southernmost hummingbird. A part-state, part-private enterprise, the park plays an educational and environmental role, protecting the *ñire* and *lenga* forest by, among other things, encouraging locals to cull beavers for their meat. Native birds, including the red-headed Magellanic woodpecker (*lana*) and the ruffed-legged owl (*kujurj*), are monitored, along with other endangered species of flora and fauna.

Thirty-two kilometres east of Cerro Bandera, at Mejillones, there is a Yámana graveyard and memorial, while on the western tip of the island is Puerto Navarino, home to a handful of Chilean marines and their families. A twenty-minute coastal walk east along Costanera Ukika from Puerto Williams brings you to the hamlet of **Villa Ukika**, home to the last remaining descendants of the Yámana people. The only object of note here is the replica of a traditional Yámana dwelling – the **Kipa–Akar** (House of Woman) – which is uninhabited. From Ukika, the road continues, giving beautiful views across the Beagle Channel before ducking into the forest and heading inland. It emerges once again at **Puerto Toro**, a tiny fishing post frequented by *centolla* fishermen. Beyond lies the cold expanse of the Atlantic Ocean, the treacherous Cape Horn, and Antarctica – the final frontier.

Argentine Tierra del Fuego

Argentina possesses the easternmost half of **Isla Grande**, plus Isla de los Estados and a smattering of tiny islets to the south. Also way down south lies **Ushuaia**, meaning "westward-looking bay" in the indigenous Yámana tongue. It's Tierra del Fuego's main tourist destination, with winter skiing and summer trekking high on the list of activities. A colourful, if rather chaotic town, it occupies a stunning mountain-backed location on the **Beagle Channel**, along which you can observe all manner of **marine wildlife**, from penguins to sea lions. Ushuaia makes for an ideal base to explore the wilds of southern Isla Grande, including the **Parque Nacional Tierra del Fuego**, a very short distance to the west, and the historic **Estancia Harberton**, along the coast to the east.

Ushuaia and around

Dramatically located between the mountains and the sea, **USHUAIA** tumbles down the hillside to the wide, encircling arm of land that protects its bay from the southwesterly winds and occasional thrashing storms of the icy **Beagle Channel**.

In 1869, Reverend Waite Stirling became Tierra del Fuego's first white settler when he founded his **Anglican mission** amongst the Yámana here. Stirling stayed for six months before being recalled to the Falklands Islands to be appointed Anglican bishop for South America. Thomas Bridges, his assistant, returned to take over the mission in 1871, after which time Ushuaia began to figure on mariners' charts as a place of refuge in the event of shipwreck. In 1896, in order to consolidate its sovereignty and open up the region to wider colonization, the Argentine government used a popular nineteenth-century tactic and established a **penal colony** here, eventually closed by Perón in 1947.

Arrival and information

The international **airport**, Malvinas Argentinas, sits 4km southwest of town; a **taxi** to the centre costs about AR\$15. **Buses** arrive and depart from their companies' respective offices (see "Listings", p.458).

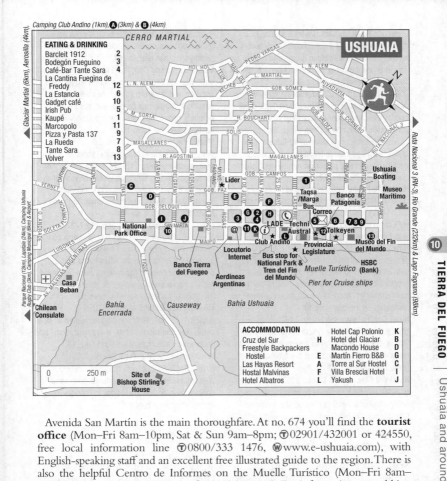

EATING & DRINKING

Barcleit 1912	2
Bodegón Fueguino	3
Café-Bar Tante Sara	4
La Cantina Fuegina de Freddy	12
La Estancia	6
Gadget café	10
Irish Pub	5
Kaupé	1
Marcopolo	11
Pizza y Pasta 137	9
La Rueda	7
Tante Sara	8
Volver	13

ACCOMMODATION

Cruz del Sur	H	Hotel Cap Polonio	K
Freestyle Backpackers Hostel	E	Hotel del Glaciar	B
Las Hayas Resort	A	Macondo House	D
Hostal Malvinas	F	Martín Fierro B&B	G
Hotel Albatros	L	Torre al Sur Hostel	C
		Villa Brescia Hotel	I
		Yakush	J

Avenida San Martín is the main thoroughfare. At no. 674 you'll find the **tourist office** (Mon–Fri 8am–10pm, Sat & Sun 9am–8pm; ☎02901/432001 or 424550, free local information line ☎0800/333 1476, ⓦwww.e-ushuaia.com), with English-speaking staff and an excellent free illustrated guide to the region. There is also the helpful Centro de Informes on the Muelle Turístico (Mon–Fri 8am–9.30pm, Sat & Sun 9am–7.30pm; ☎02901/437666). For information on trekking and climbing, contact the **Club Andino**, Fadul 50 (Mon–Fri 10am–noon & 3–8.30pm; ☎02901/422335 ⓦwww.clubandinoushuaia.com.ar); register with them before you make any trek or climb. **Oficina Antártica** at the Muelle Turístico (Mon–Fri 9am–7pm; ☎02901/423340 ⓔantartida@tierradelfuego.org .ar) provides information on Antarctica, including a list of approved International Association of Antarctica Tour Operators (ⓦwww.iaato.org), for those interested in taking a cruise to the world's remotest continent; costs start from US$3000.

Accommodation

Ushuaia offers a good range of hotels and hostels, most on the first four streets parallel to the bay. From December through February, you should book **accommodation** in advance, even for hostels.

Cruz del Sur Gob. Deloqui 636 ☎02901/423110, ⓦwww.xdelsur.com.ar. Ushuaia's best backpacker haunt, with clean dorms, decent kitchen, wi-fi and free internet access and a fun ambience. The owner is very well-travelled and knowledgeable about the local area. ❷

Freestyle Backpackers Hostel Gob. Paz 866 ☎02901/432874, ⓦ www.ushuaiafreestyle.com. A well-run hostel with clean dorms and rooms, spacious common area and laundry service. ❷–❸

Las Hayas Resort Luis Martial 1650 ☎02901/430710, Ⓕ02901/430719, ⓦwww .lashayas.com.ar. Five-star hotel: luxurious, quiet and high up, 4km from centre. Most of the stylish, commodious rooms enjoy sea views. Singles are almost the same price as doubles; there are no triples. Facilities include a health spa, a Jacuzzi, excellent buffet and indoor swimming pool. Shuttle bus to port and centre. ❽

Hostal Malvinas Gob. Deloqui 615 ☎02901/422626, Ⓔ hostalmalvinas@speedy.com .ar. If you're looking for a quiet central place to stay with clean spacious rooms and decent baths, this is it. Few extra amenities, though. ❺

Hotel Albatros Maipú 505 ☎02901/423206, ⓦwww.albatroshotel.com.ar. Well-appointed hotel with all modern conveniences and a superb seafront location, although oddly none of the rooms have sea views. There is a good, though overpriced, restaurant on the premises. ❼

Hotel Cap Polonio San Martín 746 ☎02901/422131, Ⓔ cappolonio@tierradelfuego .org.ar. Comfortable hotel with spruce rooms and pleasant bathrooms. Also runs the *Marcopolo* restaurant next door. ❹

Hotel del Glaciar Luis Martial 2355 ☎02901/430640, ⓦ wwwa.hoteldelglaciar.com. A large four-star hotel at the foot of the Glaciar Martial chair lift, 5km up the steep mountainside

from the centre (free shuttle bus). Choose between a mountain or sea view. Single rooms cost only slightly less than doubles. ❾

Macondo House Gob. Paz 1410 ☎02901/437576, ⓦ www.macondohouse.com. Ideal for self-caterers as well as travellers passing through, this guesthouse has stylish, uniquely decorated comfortable rooms with kitchenettes and cable TV. ❺

Martín Fierro B&B 9 de Julio 175 ☎02901/430525, Ⓔ javiersplace@hotmail.com. This guesthouse offers small spotless rooms with shared bathrooms, two "aparthotel" rooms which sleep up to four people each, and comfortable lounge areas. Bathrooms rather small, but good breakfast is a bonus. ❹–❺

Torre al Sur Hostel Gob. Paz 1437 ☎02901/430745, ⓦwww.torrealsur.com. Popular, friendly HI-affiliated hostel that gets extremely busy in summer, when it can be cramped and noisy. It has recently been revamped, has kitchen access, great views, inexpensive meals available and cheap internet access. ❷

Villa Brescia Hotel San Martín 1299 ☎02901/431397, Ⓔ info@villabrescia.com.ar. One of the best mid-range hotels, with bright rooms and panoramic views from the second floor. ❺

Yakush San Martín at Piedrabuena ☎02901/435807, ⓦ www.hostelyakush.com.ar. Welcoming central hostel with large dorms and doubles. Kitchen use, good book exchange, library and internet are a bonus. ❸

The Town

Start your explorations by the pier, the Muelle Turístico, on the seafront avenue, Maipú, at the corner with Lasserre. The 1920s **Provincial Legislature** overlooking the sea is one of the town's most stately buildings. Northeast of here you'll find the small, edifying **Museo del Fin del Mundo**, at Maipú 175 (daily 9am–8pm; AR$20), with exhibits on the region's history and wildlife, including the serene polychrome figurehead of the *Duchess of Albany*, a ship wrecked on the eastern end of the island in 1893, and a rare example of the Selk'nam–Spanish dictionary written by the Salesian missionary, José María Beauvoir.

You can visit the former **prison** to see the **Museo Marítimo** (daily 9am–8pm; AR$45), two blocks further along the seafront and two more inland, at Yaganes and Gobernador Paz. It houses a motley collection of exhibits, including scale models of famous ships from the island's history, with the central draw being the sprawling prison building itself, whose wings radiate out like spokes from a half-wheel. The most celebrated prisoner to stay in the cells was the early twentieth-century anarchist Simón Radowitzsky, whose miserable stay and subsequent brief escape in 1918 are recounted by Bruce Chatwin in *In Patagonia*.

East of the centre, at Perito Moreno 2564, you'll find the Ushuaia Acuario (daily noon–8pm; AR$25); the aquarium has interesting exhibits of Beagle Channel fauna, worth a visit just to see the live *centolla* moving around their tanks.

Winter sports

To **ski** at the end of the world, come some time from late May to early September and head to either the small Club Andino, 3km from town, or the ski run by Glaciar Martial (see below). Equipment rental costs between AR$20 and $60 a day. You'll also find excellent cross-country and several downhill skiing options in the modern Cerro Castor centre (ⓦwww.cerrocastor.com), 26km from town, the only centre for Alpine skiing in the area, boasting powder snow, and 24km of ski runs. Tierra Mayor (ⓣ02901/423240), 20km from Ushuaia, has excellent terrain for cross-country skiing and snowshoeing, and offers half- and full-day husky sledging excursions. In the same valley you'll come across the *Valle de los Lobos*, 18km out of Ushuaia (ⓣ015/612319 for reservations). This breeding centre for seventy or so baying huskies (husky rides available in the winter; open for visits in the summer) is part of the owner's dream to take part in Alaska's challenging 1800km Iditarod race; rustic *refugio*-style **accommodation** is on offer (bring sleeping bags; AR$25 per person plus AR$10 for breakfast).

Head 7km behind the town to the hanging **Glaciar Martial**, with magnificent views of the Beagle Channel and Isla Navarino. To get here, walk or take one of several buses (four companies offering ten daily departures; AR$10) from the corner of Maipú and Fadul up to the *Hotel Del Glaciar*, and then climb or take the **chair lift** (9.30am–6.30pm daily; AR$35) from behind the hotel. The climb takes two hours without the chair lift; the latter halves the climbing time. Beware of loose rocks on the steep middle section of the trail.

Eating and drinking

Ushuaia is crammed with eateries and restaurant of all kinds. Self-caterers will find all they need at one of two **supermarkets** in town: La Anónima on the corner of Gob. Paz and Rivadavia and another at San Martín and Onas.

Barcleit 1912l Fadul 148. Friendly, family-run restaurant serving hearty portions of pasta and pizza as well as good steak with a variety of sauces.

Bodegón Fueguino San Martín 859. Very central spot popular with young gringos, tempted by the home-brewed beer, melt-in-your-mouth lamb and a wide range of wine.

Café-Bar Tante Sara San Martín 701. This lively offshoot of the popular *Tante Sara* is a good spot for a drink, coffee or a generous breakfast.

La Cantina Fuegina de Freddy San Martín 518. Quality *centolla* and *merluza negra* dishes at this popular restaurant, though the rice and seafood stews tend to be on the bland side. Mains AR$35–75.

La Estancia San Martín 253. A good option for carnivores, with excellent steak and a reasonably priced *tenedor libre* (AR$60).

Gadget Café San Martín 1260. Open until 2am daily, this little place serves up delicious cake and coffee as well as the town's best ice cream in a plethora of flavours.

Irish Pub San Martín at Roca. Lively joint popular with travellers and locals; unexceptional food, but it's a good spot for a beer or three.

Kaupé Roca 470 ⓣ02901/422704. Hands down the best restaurant in Ushuaia, with friendly service, top-notch food, including excellent shellfish and *centolla*, and unpretentious decor in what is essentially just a family home with a fabulous view. Mains AR$70–90.

Marcopolo San Martín 748, in the *Cap Polonio* hotel. This bright restaurant serves breakfast, lunch, tea and dinner, including trout stuffed with crab, and juicy *parrillas*.

Pizza y Pasta 137 San Martín 137. Trendy restaurant with friendly service offering excellent home-made pasta and pizza, as well as a wide range of empanadas, including vegetarian options.

La Rueda San Martín 193. One of the town's best options for meat-eaters, serving a full *parrillada* at knock-down prices. *Tenedor libre* AR$56.

Tante Sara San Martín 137. Excellent and perpetually busy restaurant specializing in pasta dishes with imaginative sauces, as well as salads and light meals. Service is slow when the restaurant is full.

Volver Maipú 37. Atmospheric waterfront spot serving excellent seafood and fish dishes. While the *centolla* dishes are not their forté, the Beagle Channel mussels are superb and the *merluza negra* dishes expertly prepared.

Listings

Airlines Aerolineas Argentinas, Maipú 823 ☎02901/422267; LADE, San Martín 542 ☎08108/105233; various travel agencies sell LAN tickets.

Banks and exchanges ATMs at most banks, most of which are along San Martín, as is the main *casa de cambio*, at no. 788.

Bus companies Líder, Gob. Paz 921 ☎02901/436421; Tecni Austral; book through Tolkar at Roca 157 ☎02901/431408. Pacheco; book through Comapa at San Martín 350 ☎02901/430727; Marga/Taqsa, Godoy 41.

Car rental Hertz, San Martín 245 ☎02901/437529; Wagen Rent a car, San Martín 1222 ☎02901/430739.

Telephone centres Several *locutorios* along San Martín; the one at no. 840 has reliable high-speed internet.

Beagle Channel

No visit to Ushuaia is complete without a journey on the **BEAGLE CHANNEL**, the majestic, mountain-fringed sea passage to the south of the city. Most **boat trips** start and finish in Ushuaia, and you can enjoy the best views of town looking back at it from the straits. The standard tours visit Les Eclaireurs Lighthouse – previously thought to be the Lighthouse at the End of the World from the Jules Verne novel, though he actually meant the one on Isla

Tours from Ushuaia

Ushuaia is Tierra del Fuego's outdoor activity centre and there are a number of companies which offer everything from conventional city tours and boat outings on the Beagle Channel to rock climbing, 4WD adventures, horse-riding and diving. Here's a pick of the best:

All Patagonia Fadul 40 ☎02901/433622, ⊛www.allpatagonia.com. Specialist in ice-climbing, trekking and trips to Cape Horn and Antarctica.

Centro Hípico Ruta 3, Km 3021 ☎02901/443996, ⊛www.centrohipicoushuaia.com .ar. Excellent horse-riding centre with free transfers from town. Choose from half- and full-day excursions (the latter with *asado*); multi-day trips also available on request.

Canal Fun 9 de Julio 118 ☎02901/437395, ⊛www.canalfun.com. Recommended operator offering trekking, 4WD excursions, riding and canoeing.

Comapa San Martín 245 ☎02901/430727, ⊛www.comapa.com. Agency offering conventional tours; also sells bus tickets and tickets for Cruceros Australis cruises and arranges trips to Antarctica.

Compania de Guías de Patagonia San Martín 628 ☎02901/437753, ⊛www .companiadeguias.com.ar. Experienced agency runs multi-day trekking trips in Tierra del Fuego, arranges ice- and rock-climbing and offers dives in the Beagle Channel as well as sailing and horse-riding excursions.

Rumbo Sur San Martín 350 ☎02901/422275, ⊛www.rumbosur.com.ar. Arranges flights, bus tickets, conventional tours and Antarctic expeditions.

Tolkar Roca 157 ☎02901/431412, ⊛www.tolkarturismo.com.ar. Sells bus and plane tickets, and runs conventional tours, as well as mountain biking to Lago Fagnano.

Tolkeyen San Martín 1267 ☎02901/437073, ⊛www.tolkeyenpatagonia.com. Specializes in catamaran trips and excursions to Parque Nacional Tierra del Fuego as well as selling bus and flight tickets.

▲ Beagle Channel

de los Estados (Staten Island), which lies off the peninsula's eastern point, Isla de los Pájaros and Isla de los Lobos. Estancia Harberton, the penguin colony on Isla Martillo and Parque Nacional Tierra del Fuego are other popular destinations. The main draw of these excursions is the chance to spot the **marine wildlife** that lives along the channel, including albatrosses, giant petrels, skuas, cormorants, South American terns and Magellanic penguins; resident sea mammals are sea lions, Peale's dolphins, minke whales and, if you're lucky, you'll see killer whales. Boats depart from the pier, **Muelle Turístico**, where you'll find a huddle of agents' booking huts. Try the *Barracuda* (☎02901/437233), offering three-hour tours (9.30am & 3pm; AR$160); or Héctor Monsalve's trips for small groups on the quiet motorized sailboat, *Tres Marías* (☎02901/421897 ⓦwww.tresmariasweb.com; Nov–Easter 9.30am & 3pm; 4hr; AR$180), which includes a stop at Isla H, with archeological sites and a plethora of bird life. *Canoero Catamaranes Ushuaia* (☎02901/433893; 9am; AR$210) pays a visit to Estancia Harberton and gives the option of returning via land, stopping to see the famous *Árboles banderas* ('banner' trees, bent low by unremitting wind) and the huskies at the *Valle de los Lobos*, while *Pira-Tour* is the only company authorized to offer a walk with the penguins on Isla Martillo.

Estancia Harberton

Eighty-five kilometres east of Ushuaia along the scenic RCj lies **ESTANCIA HARBERTON**, an ordered assortment of whitewashed buildings on the shores of a sheltered bay (daily 9am–7pm; ☎02901/422742, ⓔngoodall @tierradelfuego.com.ar). This farmstead, built in 1886 by the Reverend Thomas Bridges, author of the Yámana–English dictionary, served as a voluntary refuge for groups of Yámana, Selk'nam and Mannekenk. It is now run by his great-grandson, Tommy Goodall, and Goodall's wife, Nathalie, a renowned biologist

From Ushuaia there are frequent **flights** to Río Grande, Río Gallegos, El Calafate and Buenos Aires; there are also twice-weekly flights with LAN to Punta Arenas in the summer, as well as several flights weekly to Puerto Williams with the Aeroclub de Ushuaia (Base Naval ☎02901/421717; ⓦwww.aeroclubushuaia.org.ar). Frequent Tecni Austral, Líder and Marga/Taqsa **bus services** run to Río Grande (AR$60) with daily services to Río Gallegos (AR$90), via Chile, while Pacheco and Tecni Austral also run to Punta Arenas on alternate days (AR$180; departures around 8am); all long-distance bus rides entail a short **ferry** ride at Primera Angostura (see p.448). In peak season it's a good idea to book your bus or plane ticket well in advance, as demand outstrips supply. Cruceros Australis (ⓦwww.australis.com) runs two **luxury cruise ships** to Punta Arenas; check with Comapa for details. Ushuaia Boating, Deloqui at Godoy (☎02901/436153; ⓔushuaiaboating@argentina.com.ar), due to move to a new location imminently, operates daily boat crossings to Isla Navarino (weather permitting; AR$270 one way).

who oversees the impressive marine mammal museum, **Museo Acatushún** (daily 9am–7pm, ⓦwww.acatushun.com; AR$15), with excellent tours in English. Entrance to the estancia proper at Harberton is by **guided tour** only (45min–1hr 30min; mid–Oct to mid–April 10am–7pm; last tour 5.30pm; AR$25), which includes the sampling and identification of local flora and the viewing of the estancia's cemetery. The *Mánacatush* **tearoom** is the only part of the main building open to the public: you can enjoy afternoon tea, with large helpings of cake, delicious home-made jams and hearty soup. It is possible to spend a night here, either in the *Old Shepherd's House* (AR$360 per person, includes breakfast), the *Old Cook's House* (AR$280 per person), or at one of the estancia's three **campsites** with the owners' permission.

While at Harberton you can cross (four times daily in summer; 1hr 30min; AR$180) to the Reserva Yecapasela on Isla Martillo, also known as **Penguin Island**, home to Magellanic and Gentoo penguins and a large shag colony.

Several companies run buses from the corner of Maipú and Fadul to Harberton, departing at 9.30am or 10am, with one daily service at 3pm, returning at 2pm, 4pm and 8pm; the return fare is AR$180.

Parque Nacional Tierra Del Fuego

The **PARQUE NACIONAL TIERRA DEL FUEGO**, a mere 12km west of Ushuaia, protects 630 square kilometres of jagged mountains, intricate lakes, southern beech forest, swampy peat bog, sub-Antarctic tundra and verdant coastline. The park stretches along the frontier with Chile, from the Beagle Channel to the **Sierra de Injugoyen** north of Lago Fagnano, but only the southernmost quarter is open to the public, accessed by the RN-3 from Ushuaia. The park is broken down into three main sectors: Bahía Ensenada and Río Pipo in the east; Lago Roca further to the west; and the Lapataia area to the south of Lago Roca, which includes Lago Verde and, at the end of RN-3, Bahía Lapataia on the Beagle Channel. While here you may see **birds** such as Magellanic woodpeckers, condors, torrent ducks, steamer ducks, upland geese and buff-necked ibises, and **mammals** such as guanacos, the rare sea otter, Patagonian grey foxes, and their larger, endangered cousin, the native Fuegian fox, once heavily hunted for its pelt. The park offers several relatively unchallenging though beautiful **trails**, ideal for short excursions or day hikes.

Practicalities

The most common (and cheapest) access to the park is along the good dirt-and-gravel road from Ushuaia (sometimes cut off briefly by snowfalls in late May to early Oct); frequent buses run from Ushuaia's waterfront between 8am and 7pm (AR$60) You can also come via the rather expensive, gimmicky tourist railway of **El Tren del Fin del Mundo** (AR$85 one way; AR$90 return; Ⓦwww.trendelfindelmundo.com.ar), which departs from a station 8km west of Ushuaia. The 4.5km trip to the park takes fourty minutes. You must pay an entrance fee of AR$30 at the main park gate, except in winter. You will be given a map of the park, and if you're planning to come back the following day, let the staff know, and you won't have to pay the park fee twice.

You'll find four main areas for **camping** in the park: Bahía Ensenada and Río Pipo are currently free, but you're better off heading to the paying sites of the Lago Roca and Lago Verde areas. The latter boasts the two most beautifully sited campsites in the park, right next door to each other and encircled by the Río Ovando: *Camping Laguna Verde* (☎02901/421433, Ⓔlagunaverde@tierradelfuego.ml.org; AR$5 per person), with a tiny toilet block and sink, a shop, and tent rental (AR$20 a day, sleeping bags included); and *Camping Los Cauquenes* (pay at *Lago Verde*; AR$5 per person) just across the road. *Camping Lago Roca* (☎02901/433313, Ⓔlagoroca@speedy.com.ar; AR$10 per person), boasts hot showers, a little shop, tent rental, a rustic hostel and the *La Cabaña El Bosque* restaurant.

Ushuaia (RN-3)(12km)

Exploring the park

The small **BAHÍA ENSENADA**, 2km south of the crossroads by the Tren del Fin del Mundo train station, is where you'll find the jetty for boats to Lapataia and the Isla Redonda. It's also the trailhead for one of the most pleasant walks in the park, the highly recommended **Senda Costera** (7km; 3hr). The not-too-strenuous route takes you through dense coastal forest of evergreen beech, Winter's bark, and *lenga* while affording spectacular views from the Beagle Channel shoreline. On the way, you'll pass grass-covered mounds that are the ancient campsite **middens** of the Yámana. These mounds are protected archeological sites and should not be disturbed.

Another recommended, if tiring trek, is the climb up **CERRO GUANACO** (8km; 3hr), the 970-metre-high mountain ridge on the north side of Lago Roca. Remember that, at any time of the year, the weather can be capricious, so bring adequate clothing even if you set out in glorious sunshine. Take the Hito XXIV path from the car park at Lago Roca and after ten minutes you'll cross a small bridge over a stream. Immediately afterwards, the path forks: to the left, **Senda Hito XXIV** runs along the northeastern shore of Lago Roca to an obelisk that marks Argentina's border with Chile (5km; 1hr 30min). To the right, **Senda Cerro Guanaco** runs right up the slope to the summit of its namesake peak. The path up the forested mountainside is steep but not hazardous, but after rain you're sure to encounter some slippery tree roots and muddy patches, especially during the boggy part of the trail. The view from the crest to the south is memorable: the tangle of islands and rivers of the Archipiélago Cormoranes, Lapataia's sinuous curves, the Isla Redonda in the Beagle Channel, and across to the Chilean islands, Hoste and Navarino, separated by the Murray Narrows.

Travel details

Buses

Porvenir to: Cerro Sombrero (Mon, Wed, Fri; 2hr).
Punta Arenas to: Ushuaia, Argentina (daily in summer; 12hr).
Ushuaia to: El Calafate (1 daily; 14hr); Punta Arenas (1 daily; 12hr); Puerto Natales (4 weekly via Punta Arenas; 14hr); Río Gallegos (Mon–Sat 1 daily; 9hr).

Ferries

Puerto Williams to: Ushuaia (summer: 1 daily in the afternoon; 45min–1hr).
Punta Arenas to: Porvenir (1 daily except Mon; 2hr 30min–3hr); Puerto Williams (4 monthly on Sat; 36hr).
Punta Delgada to: Bahía Azul (Puerto Espora), Tierra del Fuego (every 1hr 30min, tides permitting; 20–30min).

Ushuaia to: Puerto Williams (summer: 1 daily in the morning; 45min–1hr).

Flights

Puerto Williams to: Punta Arenas (1 daily except Sun Nov–March; otherwise 3 weekly; 1hr 30min); Ushuaia (summer: several weekly; 10min).
Punta Arenas to: Porvenir (at least one daily; 15min); Puerto Williams (1 daily except Sun Nov–March; otherwise 3 weekly; 1hr 30min); Ushuaia (3 weekly; 1hr).
Ushuaia to: Buenos Aires (2–4 daily; 3hr 30min); El Calafate (at least one daily; 2hr 15min, longer if stopover at Río Gallegos); Puerto Madryn, Argentina (6 weekly; 2hr); Puerto Williams (summer: several weekly; 10min); Punta Arenas (3 weekly; 1hr); Río Gallegos (6 weekly; 1hr).

Easter Island and the Juan Fernández Archipelago

✳ **Tapati** If you are here late January–early February, discover the mysterious roots of Easter Island's ancient culture at its carnival, featuring everything from traditional dancing and singing to hurtling down volcanic slopes on banana trunks. See p.472

✳ **Ahu Tongariki** Fifteen impeccably restored moai (giant statues) line up to be admired against a backdrop of green cliffs and roaring waves. See p.475

✳ **Rano Raraku** This mighty mountain at the heart of Rapa Nui is where the moai were quarried – and some, too big to move, never left the rock where they were hewn. See p.475

✳ **Orongo** Imagine the mindboggling rituals of the birdman cult as you gaze out at craggy islets in a sapphire-blue ocean or inwards to a reed-filled crater at one of the island's most breathtaking natural sites. See p.480

✳ **Hike Robinson Crusoe Island** See the island landscape change dramatically from desert to dense forest as you make your way along the coastline from the airstrip to San Juan Bautista via the Mirador de Selkirk. See p.482

✳ **Juan Fernández flora and fauna** Frolic underwater with fish and sea lions, watch the antics of hummingbirds and observe dozens of endemic species of plant on this treasure island of unique (and painfully fragile) wildlife. See p.585

▲ Sea lions and sea birds on Juan Fernández

Easter Island and the Juan Fernández Archipelago

C hile is the proud possessor of two remote island territories, mysterious **EASTER ISLAND** and the virtually unknown **JUAN FERNÁNDEZ ARCHIPELAGO**, collectively referred to as the Islas Esporádicas ("Far Flung Isles"). Both are classified as national parks, and each has been singled out by UNESCO for special protection. Neither is easy to get to and most visitors to Chile never do, but those who make the journey will find their effort and expenditure richly rewarded with a set of tantalizingly enigmatic statues and one of the world's most precarious ecosystems, respectively.

Lost in the vastness of the ocean, tiny **Easter Island** remains a world unto itself, surrounded on all sides by huge expanses of empty ocean, its closest inhabited neighbour being Pitcairn Island, 2250km northwest. Spanning just 23km at its longest stretch, the island is triangular in shape, with low-lying extinct volcanoes rising out of each corner. Scattered between these points are dozens of **moai**, among the most arresting and intriguing ancient sculptures in the world, the monolithic stone **statues** that have made this little island universally famous.

Much closer to the mainland, at a mere 675km due west of Valparaíso, but still relatively unknown, the **Juan Fernández Archipelago** is, ironically, far more difficult to reach. With their sharp, jagged peaks soaring dramatically out of the ocean, coated in a thick tangle of lush, deep-green foliage, the islands boast a topography that counts among the most spectacular in the whole of Chile.

The archipelago's largest and only inhabited island – **Isla Robinson Crusoe** – started out as a pirates' refuge. Notorious freebooters like Bartholomew Sharp and William Dampier used it as a watering spot during their raids on the Pacific seaboard in the seventeenth century. In 1709 the faraway island was brought to public attention when the Scottish seaman Alexander Selkirk was rescued from its shores after being marooned there for more than four years. Selkirk's story was used by Daniel Defoe as the basis for his classic novel, *The Adventures of Robinson Crusoe* (see p.482). These days, the island's small community milks the

Crusoe connections to death in an attempt to boost the tourist trade, but the Juan Fernández Archipelago remains an adventurous destination, well off the beaten track.

Easter Island

One of the most remote places on earth, tiny **EASTER ISLAND** is home to some four thousand islanders. Two thirds are indigenous (called *pascuenses* in Spanish), with the rest being mainly *continentales* (Chilean immigrants). The Rapa Nui have fine-boned Polynesian features and speak their own Polynesian-based language (also called Rapa Nui) in addition to Spanish. Virtually the entire population lives in the island's single settlement, **Hanga Roa**, and just about all the islanders make their living from tourism, which has been growing steadily ever since an airstrip was built here in 1968.

Most points of interest are found within **Parque Nacional Rapa Nui**, which comprises much of the island, and there's open access to all the park's land at all times. The island's highlights include **Rano Kau**, a huge volcanic crater and site of the ceremonial village of **Orongo**; the **Rano Raraku** quarry, where almost all the *moai* were carved; and the largest *ahu* (platform) on the island, **Ahu Tongariki**, which boasts fifteen *moai*. Archeological treasures aside, Easter Island has a great deal to offer outdoor enthusiasts, from diving in waters with arguably the best visibility in the world to surfing major waves off the island's south coast.

The weather is fairly constant year-round, with an average temperature of 23°C (73°F) in January and February, and 18°C (64°F) in July and August. Late January and early February is the busiest time and also the most exciting, as the islanders put on an extravagant display of singing, dancing and feasting during their annual two-week **Tapati Rapa Nui festival**.

Getting to Easter Island is possible only with LAN, which flies here from Santiago's international airport two or three times a week. The standard fare is about CH$400,000 round-trip; lower fares are sometimes available, especially if you book a ticket in conjunction with a long-distance LAN flight outside of Chile or if you purchase your ticket directly at a Chilean LAN office. Most flights from the mainland continue to Papeete, Tahiti.

Post-contact history

Easter Island was "discovered" and named by Dutch naval commander **Jacob Roggeveen** on Easter Sunday, 1722. In the absence of any written records left by the islanders, Roggeveen's **log** is the earliest written account we have of the island. His party spent only a single day on land, long enough to observe the "particularly high erected stone images."

After their departure, it was another 48 years before Easter Island was revisited, this time by the Spanish commander **Felipe González**, who mapped the island and claimed it for King Carlos III of Spain during a six-day stay. Four years later, **Captain Cook** anchored here in the hope of restoring the health of his scurvy-ridden crew. He, too, observed with incredulity the "stupendous figures" erected

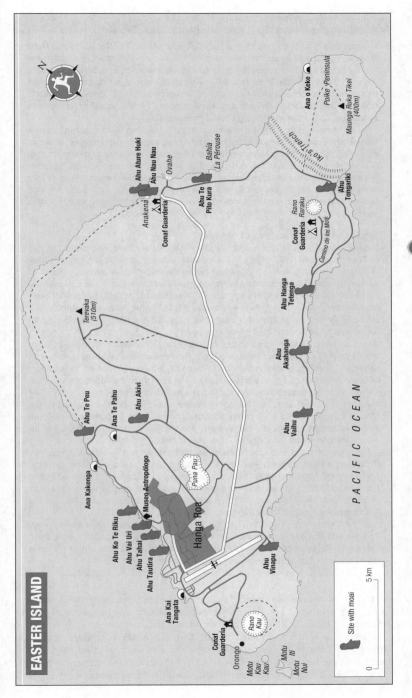

EASTER ISLAND

Ana o Keke

Poike Peninsula

▲ *Maunga Ruka Tikei (400m)*

Ahu Ature Huki

Ahu Nau Nau

Ovahe

Anakena

△⌂ Conaf Guarderia

Bahía La Pérouse

Ahu Te Pito Kura

Ahu Tongariki

Rano Raraku

Conaf Guarderia △⌂

Camino de los Moai

Ahu Hanga Tetenga

▲ *Terevaka (510m)*

Ahu Akahanga

Ahu Te Peu

Ana Te Pahu

Ahu Akivi

Ahu Vaihu

PACIFIC OCEAN

Ana Kakenga

Museo Antropólogo

Puna Pau

Ahu Ko Te Riku

Ahu Vai Uri

Ahu Tahai

Hanga Roa

Ahu Tautira

Ahu Vinapu

Ana Kai Tangata

Conaf Guarderia

Rano Kau

Orongo

Motu Kau Kau

Motu Iti

Motu Nui

N

0 — 5 km

▭ Site with moai

Where did the Rapa Nui come from?

The islanders' oral history claims that the original colonizer of Easter Island was **Hotu Matu'a**, a great *ariki henua*, or chief, who lived possibly in Polynesia, or perhaps the Marquesas. It had been revealed to Hotu Matu'a's tattooist in a dream, or "spirit voyage", that an island with craters and fine beaches awaited his master, so the chief dispatched a reconnaissance party to find this promised land, following on some time later with his family, servants and fellow colonists. He arrived safely on Anakena beach, just as his wife was giving birth to their first son.

As *ariki henua*, Hotu Matu'a's role was not that of political leader, but rather of a revered and important person in possession of great supernatural qualities, or *mana*. Accordingly, he and the place where he lived were *tapu*, or sacred and untouchable, and so Hotu Matu'a and his family lived at Anakena while the rest of his party dispersed around the island, where their families expanded and eventually grew into eight separate kin-groups, each with its own *tangata honui*, or leader. As time passed, these groups became more sophisticated and stratified, made up of a diverse collection of priests, fishermen, farmers and craftsmen.

What the experts say: east or west?

Central to any discussion of Easter Island's settlement are the controversial theories of **Thor Heyerdahl** (1906–2002), the Norwegian explorer-archeologist whose widely publicized expeditions and best-selling books generated an enormous amount of academic interest in the island's history. Heyerdahl was convinced that Easter Island had been colonized by settlers from South America and, in 1948, he proved, quite spectacularly, that such a voyage was indeed possible when he and five companions successfully sailed a traditionally constructed balsa raft (the *Kon Tiki*) from Peru to an island east of Tahiti in a 101-day voyage.

He backed up his theory with some persuasive but highly selective details, concentrating on the fact that winds and currents in the Pacific move in a westward, not an eastward, direction; on the presence in Polynesia of the sweet potato, indisputably of South American origin; on the resemblance between the close-fitting stonework of some Easter Island platforms and some types of Inca masonry; and on the ancient Peruvian custom of artificially extending the ear lobes, just like the islanders at the time of European contact. He failed to explain, however, the total absence of South American pottery and textiles in Polynesia, and the fact that no trace of any indigenous South American language had been found there.

The view of most experts, however, is that Easter Island was colonized by Polynesians from the west – an opinion backed by linguistic evidence, physical anthropology, including bone analysis, and the proliferation on Easter Island of Polynesian plants such as taro, yam, bananas and sugarcane. Which precise part of Polynesia these settlers came from is still open to debate, though the **Marquesas** is thought to be the most likely point of departure.

As for the date of the settlers' arrival, all we can be sure of is that they were constructing *ahu* (ceremonial platforms) by 800 AD. No one knows for sure if this culture developed in complete isolation, or if another wave of colonists arrived at a later date, as suggested in some of the oral traditions.

on the island, though he noted that some lay strewn on the ground, toppled from their platforms. Later visitors reported an increasing number of **fallen statues**, and by 1825, all of the *moai* on Hanga Roa bay had been destroyed.

In 1805 the island was raided by the first of the **slave traders**, when an American schooner captured twelve men and ten women to be used as seal hunters on the Juan Fernández Islands. After three days at sea, the prisoners were allowed onto the deck, whereupon they promptly threw themselves overboard and drowned in a desperate attempt to swim back to the island. Between 1862 and 1864, Peruvian sailors landed on the island and attacked and captured over 2500 people, who were shipped off to work as slaves in the Peruvian guano mines. After many of the islanders had died from disease and appalling work conditions in the mines, the Bishop of Tahiti, Tepano Jaussen, finally managed to persuade the Peruvian government to repatriate the remaining prisoners – most of whom died on the return voyage home. Tragically, the sixteen who made it back infected the rest of the islanders with smallpox and TB, reducing the population to near one hundred. Critically, the loss of life was accompanied by the loss of a crucial part of the island's culture and collective memory, for the last *ariki henua* (high chief), *moari* (keepers of sacred knowledge), and *tangata rongo rongo* (specialist readers) were among those who perished.

A certain degree of stability came when the first missionary, **Eugène Eyraud**, arrived on the island in 1864 and set to converting its people to Christianity, a mission fully accomplished by the time of his death, four years later. The peace was disrupted, however, when a French plantation owner, **Jean-Baptiste Onésime Dutrou-Bornier**, bought up large tracts of land and proceeded to run the island as his personal ranch, paying the islanders a pittance for their hard labour and resorting to violence when they wouldn't co-operate. When the missionaries opposed Doutrou-Bornier's exploitation of the islanders, he instigated armed attacks on their missions, forcing them to evacuate the island. He dealt a further blow to the island's slowly recovering population by sending all but a hundred islanders to Tahiti to work on his partner's plantation, before finally being murdered in 1877 by the oppressed islanders.

The **Chilean government** acquired the lands that had belonged to Doutrou-Bornier, and went on to purchase most of the remaining land on the island, leaving only the village of **Hanga Roa** in the possession of the islanders. Then, on September 9, 1888, the Chilean Navy – apparently with the islanders' consent – officially **annexed** Easter Island, declaring it Chilean

Rongo rongo

In 1864, the French missionary **Eugène Eyraud** wrote of "tablets or staff of wood covered with hieroglyphics" that he'd come across in the islanders' homes. This was the first the outside world had heard of *ko hau motu mo rongo rong* or "lines of script for recitation". Predictably, the *rongo rongo* tablets remained firmly beyond the grasp of the scholars who came to study them, for none of the islanders knew how to read them. Almost 140 years later, no one has succeeded in deciphering them.

The script consists of tiny, tightly packed symbols carved in straight lines across the wooden boards. The symbols, which include representations of people, animals, birds and plants, are upside down on each alternate line, requiring the reader to turn the board around at the end of each line. Late nineteenth-century oral testimonies suggest that the tablets contained records of genealogies, creation myths, wars and deaths, and religious hymns.

Some modern scholars believe that the script was developed after the first European contact, inspired by the written documents that the Spaniards made the island's chiefs sign in 1770, while others believe that it is only one of four written languages in the world to have developed entirely independently of outside influence. The most widely accepted theory is that, rather than representing grammatical sentences, the symbols were **mnemonics** for use in recitals and chanting.

Today, only 29 *rongo rongo* tablets, which deserve equal attention as works of art as of repositories of lost information, remain in existence, all of them spirited off to overseas museums in Santiago, Rome, London, and Washington, D.C.

territory. Chile then leased it off to Williamson Balfour, a British wool-trading company, which virtually governed the island according to its own needs and interests. In 1953, the company's lease was revoked and the Chilean Navy stepped in to resume command, though the islanders were given no say in the running of the island.

It was not until 1964, eighty years after annexation, that they were allowed outside Hanga Roa (let alone off the island), and granted full citizenship and the right to vote. Since the return to democracy, the management of most local affairs, especially education, which is now bilingual, has finally been transferred to the islanders.

Hanga Roa

Arrival and information

The **airport** is on the southern edge of Hanga Roa, about 1km from the centre. It's a good idea to arrange your accommodation beforehand during busy times such as Tapati, the Easter Island carnival; otherwise, you can negotiate with the *residencial* representatives on arrival at the airport.

Sernatur has a helpful office down towards the *caleta Hanga Roa*, at Tu'u Maheke and Policarpo Toro (Mon–Fri 8.30am–1.30pm & 2.30–5.30pm; ☏32/100255, ✉ipascua@sernatur.cl). Staff provide detailed information on the island's attractions and can help organize camping and activities such as horseriding and vehicle rental; some English and French spoken.

HANGA ROA

PACIFIC OCEAN

ACCOMMODATION

Aloha Nui Guest House	H	Explora Casas Rapa Nui	J
Ana Rapu	B	Hotel Irona	D
Apina Tupina	C	Hotel Manavai	F
Cabaña Chez Cecilia	G	Residencial Kona Tau	I
Camping Mihinoa	A	Hotel Taura'a	E

Caleta Hanga Piko

Caleta Hanga Roa

Orca Diving Center

Mike Rapu Diving Center

Cemetery

Entel

Banco Estado

Feria Municipal

@ Atanet

Kare Taui Moni

Mercado Artesanal

LAN

Hospital

Rano Kau

Tahai & Museo Antropológico

Ahu Akivi

AV. APINA

AV. PONT

AV. POLICARPO TORO

AV. POLICARPO TORO

AV. ATAMU TEKENA

AV. ATAMU TEKENA

AV. AVAREIPUA

AV. HOTU MATUA

AV. PONT

TU HAKE HE VARI

TUUKOIHU

MOLINA

LUCO

SIMON PAOA

ARA ROA RAKEI

HEWA

EATING, DRINKING & ENTERTAINMENT

Aloha	7
Banana Pub	10
Café Tatvai	11
Cinema	6
Kai Mana	8
Kari Kari	9
Kono Ai O Te Kai	12
La Taverne du Pêcheur	1
Merahi Ra'a	4
Piditi	13
Restaurant Pea	2
Toroko	3
Vai Mata	5

Aeropuerto Mataveri

0   500 m

Anakena   J

Conaf's administration centre is on Rano Kau s/n, south of Hanga Roa (Mon–Fri 8.30am–6pm; ☎ 322/100236, ⓦ www.conaf.cl). You can make reservations for Conaf-run campgrounds here. Conaf ranger stations are found at Rano Raraku, Anakena Beach and Orongo ceremonial village.

Accommodation

Easter Island has accommodation to suit every budget, though since many *residenciales* do not accept credit cards, you have to bring plenty of cash from the mainland. US dollars are widely accepted. There are two Conaf-run campsites on the island, equipped with cold showers and fire pits, at Rano Raraku and Anakena Beach; reserve at the Conaf office. Many *residencial* owners allow camping in their gardens, charging around CH$5000 per tent or per person.

Aloha Nui Guest House Atamu Tekena s/n ☎ 322/100274, ⓔ haumaka@entelchile.net. Excellent guesthouse with comfortable en-suite rooms in a tropical garden setting. Knowledgeable owners speak English and German and run a variety of excursions around the island. ❺

Ana Rapu Apina Iti s/n ☎ 322/100540, ⓦ www.anarapu.cl. Airy rooms, some en-suite, in a very popular guesthouse set amidst lush vegetation, presided over by a knowledgeable hostess. Includes kitchen privileges and good breakfast; camping is possible and horseriding can be arranged. ❷–❹

Apina Tupina Policarpo Toro s/n ☎ 322/100763, ⓦ www.apinatupuna.com. Oceanside *residencial* with bright rooms, decorated with the owner's own artwork, popular with younger travellers. Breakfast and fully-equipped kitchen included; camping allowed. ❷–❹

Cabaña Chez Cecilia Atamu Tekena s/n ☎ 322/100499, ⓦ www.rapanuichezcecilia.com. Cosy en-suite rooms, along with six-person *cabañas* and garden camping; rates include breakfast, and dinner can also be arranged. Good for organizing multilingual guided tours of the island as well as diving excursions. ❷–❹

Camping Mihinoa Pont s/n ☎ 322/551593, ⓦ www.mihinoa.com. Large campsite with an excellent ocean view, run by a friendly family. Showers, kitchen facilities, dining room, internet access and car, scooter and bike rental; lack of shade is the only drawback. Adjoining guesthouse has basic, clean rooms and a five-bed dorm; it's also possible to rent tents (CH$5000). ❷–❸

Explora Casas Rapa Nui Te Miro Oone sector, 5.6km from Hanga Roa; reservations ☎ 2/206 6060 or US toll-free 1/866-750-6699, ⓦ www .explora.com. Comfortable guesthouses with luxurious common areas, outdoor pool, open-air Jacuzzis, a massage salon, a bar, a cosy dining area serving fusion cuisine, plus an outdoor barbecue area. Each of the 30 rooms has the creature comforts you would expect from the luxury chain, and the rates include daily excursions with knowledgeable bilingual guides. ❽–❾

Hotel Iorana Ana Magaro s/n, ☎ 32/100608; reservations ☎ 2/695 2058, ⓦ www.ioranahotel.cl. Though the rooms are somewhat overpriced, the secluded location, looking down to the ocean, is unbeatable. As well as a regular outdoor pool, there's a "natural" pool enclosed by rocks and filled with seawater, the restaurant comes recommended and there are several tours on offer. 15min walk from town. ❽

Hotel Manavai Te Pito O Te Henua 1945 ☎ 322/100670, ⓦ www.hotelmanavai.cl. Central hotel with attractive en-suite veranda rooms built primarily from local wood, overlooking a lush tropical garden with a swimming pool. Includes a decent restaurant. ❼

Hotel Manutara ☎ 322/100297, ⓦ www .hotelmanutara.cl. A short walk from the airport, this friendly, well-run place has spacious, comfortable rooms spread across extensive grounds, with a pool, filling tropical breakfasts, internet and wi-fi, massage salon and lots of peace and quiet. Visits of the main sites are on offer through Aku Aku Tours, one of the better agencies. ❼

Hotel O'Tai Av Te Pito Te Henua s/n ☎ 322/100250, ⓦ www.hotelotai.com. Smart, well-furnished bungalow rooms with patio doors, set in a large, flower-filled garden, run by a friendly family. Superior rooms have a/c; the restaurant serves tasty island cuisine and guests have use of a swimming pool. A number of tours are on offer, as well as cultural shows. ❼

Hotel Taura'a Atamu Tekena s/n ☎ 32/100463, ⓦ www.tauraahotel.cl. This central hotel boasts spacious, airy rooms and an attractive garden. Tropical breakfast is included; English and French spoken, and the congenial owners run one of the island's best tour agencies. Highly recommended. ❻

Residencial Kona Tau Avareipua s/n
ⓣ322/100321, ⓦwww.hostelz.com/hostel/44363
-Kona-Tau. HI-affiliated hostel in a large family
home with a friendly atmosphere, with sixteen
comfortable dorm beds, as well as basic en-suite
rooms set in a mango-strewn garden; large
breakfast a bonus. Close to the airport but
somewhat inconvenient for the rest of town. ❷–❹

The Village

Hanga Roa has been the island's only residential sector since the 1860s, when
Catholic missionaries relocated the islanders here to facilitate their conversion.
Its long, sprawling, unpaved streets are lined with single-storey houses and
fragrant eucalyptus trees, giving the place the unfinished feel of a recently
settled frontier town.

Atamu Tekena is the main road, lined with small supermarkets, souvenir
shops, **internet** cafés, eateries and tour agencies. Most of the action is centred
around the Caleta Hanga Roa harbour, overlooked by Ahu Tautira, the only
moai site in the town proper. Restaurants and eateries stretch from here along
oceanside Policarpo Toro, parallel to Atamu Tekena. East–west Te Pito O Te
Henua connects the two, ending at the church, where islanders still congregate
every Sunday morning for an unforgettable rhapsody of joyful Polynesian
hymns. Just south of the pier lies tiny Playa Pea, where a rock pool safe for
swimming is cordoned off from the stretch of ocean popular with surfers and
body boarders.

Eating, drinking and entertainment

Hanga Roa offers a good selection of cafés and restaurants. You can dine on truly
exceptional fresh fish at a number of high-end restaurants, or you can just as
easily survive on empanadas and sandwiches, offered by several informal cafés.

Aloha Atamu Tekena s/n at S. Englert. Trendy bar-
restaurant serving excellent (though pricey) fish
dishes; a good spot for a beer and snacks, such as
Japanese *gyoza* dumplings. Evening service can be
leisurely. Fish dishes CH$6000.
Café Tatvai Atamu Tekena s/n. Small, informal
spot serving sandwiches and fresh fruit juices.
Sandwich CH$3500.
Cinema At *Hotel Manavai*, Te Pito O Te Henua s/n.
Has twice-weekly screenings of the Hollywood
view of Rapa Nui.
Kai Mana Atamu Tekena s/n, opposite Tuki Haka
He Vari. Ignore the unexceptional pizza on the

menu and go for the succulent fish dishes.
Leisurely service. Grilled fish CH$7000.
Kari Kari Atamu Tekena s/n, opposite Tuku Haka
He Vari. Extremely entertaining and worthwhile
traditional dance-and-music show, featuring
talented young dancers and musicians in elaborate
costumes. Three shows weekly. Entry CH$10,000.
Kono Ai O Te Kai Plaza Policarpo Toro. Handy
takeaway spot serving hot dogs, pizza and
excellent empanadas in the evenings. Empanada
CH$2000.
La Taverne du Pêcheur Te Pito O Te Henua s/n.
Hanga Roa's most expensive restaurant serves

Easter Island festivals

To witness the island's culture at its best, time your visit so that it coincides with one
of the festivals. **Tapatai Rapa Nui** is a ten-day cultural celebration held in late
January or early February. Famous for celebrating Rapa Nui culture, tradition and
history, the festival features dancing, body painting, statue carving, choral recitals,
surfing displays, canoe races, re-enactments of old legends and huge *curanto* feasts.
Semana Santa (Easter week) features lively celebrations at Hanga Roa's Iglesia
Parroquial de la Santa Cruz. The **Ceremonia Culto al Sol** is a feast that takes place
on June 21 for the winter solstice, while **Día de la Lengua Rapa Nui**, a celebration
of the Rapa Nui language, is held in late November.

The easiest, most hassle-free choice is to take an **organized tour**, but while this ensures you get to see a large number of sites, with guided commentary, you can feel you're on a sightseeing conveyer belt. Tours usually cost around CH$25,000 for a full day, and CH$15,000 for a half-day. Recommended **tour companies** on the island include: Aku Aku Turismo at Av Tu'u Koihu s/n (T 322/100770, W www .akuakuturismo.cl) and Kie Koe Tour, Atamu Tekena s/n (T 322/100852, W www .kiakoetour.cl), both offering bilingual archeological tours of the island. Haumaka Archaelogical Tours on Puku Rangi Uka s/n (T 322/100274, W www.haumakatours .com) offers guided tours of the island's archeological sites in English, French and German, as well as horse-riding tours and diving trips, and can also organize traditional Rapa Nui meals, including *curanto*. Finally, Taura'a Tours on Atamu Tekena s/n T 322/100463 offers full-day, small-group tours of the south coast, including Anakena Beach as well as the principal sites, or the west coast, incorporating the inland *moai* site of Ahu Akivi; English and French spoken. If you want more solitude and independence, you can hire a **jeep** or a **scooter** (see "Listings", below). This is a very popular option, so you should book your vehicle as soon as you can after arrival (or even before), before the rest of your plane beats you to it. **Horseback riding** can be an excellent way of seeing the sites as well. A day's horse riding can set you back CH$38,000 or so and your best bet is to contact a reputable operator listed with Sernatur. These include Cabalgatas Pantu (T 322/100577, W www .pantupikerauri.cl), offering half- and full-day horseback tours of the west and north coasts, including the ascent of Maunga Terevaka, the island's highest point, and a lunch of either grilled fish cooked in the traditional Rapa Nui manner, or traditional *curanto* for groups. Alternatively, try Piti Pont (T 322/100664 or 09/5740582), a renowned guide who runs various horse-riding trips around the island. Finally, you could consider visiting some sites on a **mountain bike** or **on foot**, though walking around the whole island would be quite a challenge.

large platters of well-cooked fish with sides of sweet potato, taro, and other island tubers. The chocolate cake is excellent, too. Fish platter CH$10,000; cake CH$5000.

Merahi Ra'a Te Pito O Te Henua s/n. This is *the* place for large servings of expertly prepared fish and the local speciality of *rape rape* (spiny lobster), as well as melt-in-your-mouth tuna ceviche. Ceviche CH$7000; *rape rape* CH$25,000.

Piditi Av Hotu Matua s/n, by the airport. Smaller club that gets packed with an older crowd on weekends; action kicks off after midnight. Open until 6am.

Restaurant Pea Policarpo Toro s/n, next to Playa Pea. The delicious seafood empanadas and other fishy offerings are compliemented by the view of the surfing action. Empanada CH$1500.

Toroko Av Policarpo Toro s/n, near the cemetery. Popular disco with a mellow atmosphere that seems to draw all the young islanders on a Saturday night; it may be a bit daunting for foreigners at first.

Vai Mata Te Pito O Te Henua s/n. Inexpensive eatery serving sandwiches and light meals. Sandwich CH$3000.

Listings

Airline LAN, Atamu Tekena at Av Pont
T 322/100279.
Banks and exchange There is only one bank on the island: Banco Estado, on Tu'u Maheke s/n (Mon–Fri 9am–1pm), with an adjoining ATM that only accepts MasterCard. You can also get a cash advance inside the bank, but you may only withdraw CH$200,000 at a time with a CH$2000

commission charge. There is another Banco Estado ATM at the gas station, at the west end of Avenida Hotu Matu'a. *Hare Tani Moni*, towards the north end of Av Atamu Tekena, changes foreign currency at poor rates. Best bet is to bring pesos from the mainland.
Camping As you can't bring fuel on the plane, you'll need to buy it on the island. White gas

(*bencina blanca*) is hard to come by, but is usually stocked at Kai Nene supermarket on Atamu Tekena. Make sure your tent is ant-proof. *Camping Mihinoa* has some tents for rent.

Car rental In addition to the car-hire firms, many souvenir shops and even supermarkets on Atamu Tekena hire jeeps as a sideline, usually with just a couple of vehicles available. Outlets include Insular Rent a Car ⓣ322/100480; Oceanic Rent a Car ⓣ322/100985; Kia Koe Tour ⓣ322/100852. Typical rate CH$35,000 per 12hr. There is no car insurance on the island.

Hospital Hospital Hanga Roa on Simón Paoa s/n (ⓣ322/100183), southeast of the church, has basic medical facilities.

Internet access and telephone centre Internet cafés in Hanga Roa tend to be expensive, charging upwards of CH$2000 per hr. At@net (Akamu

Tekena s/n; Mon–Sat 9am–10pm; Sun 10am–10pm) doubles as a call centre; cheap calls to mainland Chile, very expensive to rest of world.

Mountain bikes Several shops on Atamu Tekena, including Kodak and Via Mona; compare state of bikes and prices. Typical rate CH$8000 per 24hr.

Post office Opposite *Hotel O'Tai*.

Scuba diving The established and reputable Orca Diving Centre (ⓣ322/550877 or 322/550375, ⓦwww.seemorca.cl) and Mike Rapu Diving Centre (ⓣ322/551055, ⓦwww.mikerapu.cl) both offer a range of dives (CH$30,000–40,000).

Surfing schools Surfing schools Hakangaru (no phone) and Makohe (no phone) at the Caleta Hanga Roa offer lessons to beginners, and Hare Orca, next to the Orca Diving Centre, rents surf and boogie boards (CH$10,000/7,000).

The southeastern circuit

The loop formed by the sixteen-kilometre southern coast road and the thirty-kilometre paved road from Anakena to Hanga Roa lends itself to a convenient sightseeing route that takes in some of the island's most impressive sights – including **Vinapu**, **Ahu Tongariki**, **Rano Raraku** and **Anakena**.

Vinapu

From Hanga Roa, follow Avenida Hotu Matu'a down to the southern coast road then turn right, just after the white oil containers, and you'll reach **VINAPU**, the site of two large *ahus*, with *moai* lying in fragments behind the platforms. Anyone who's seen Macchu Pichu or other Inca ruins will be amazed by the similarity of the masonry of Vinapu's main *ahu*, made of huge, mortarless blocks of stone "fitted carefully to one another without a crack or a hole". Close to this platform, known as Vinapu I, is another *ahu*, Vinapu II, whose stonework is vastly inferior to its neighbour.

Heyerdahl's expedition was the first to excavate the site and, with radiocarbon dating, concluded that the precisely carved Vinapu I was among the earliest built on the island, and that Vinapu II was a much later construction, suggesting that the island's first settlers imported the highly specialized stone-carving techniques of Peru, and that later platforms were built by "far less capable architects, who were no longer masters of the complicated Inca technique". Modern archeologists, however, believe that this impressive masonry is simply a perfected example of a style developed locally on Easter Island, and more recent radiocarbon tests have given Vinapu I a new date of 1516 AD, and Vinapu II a date of 857 AD – the reverse of Heyerdahl's sequence.

Along the southern coast

Back on the coast road, the first site you pass is **Vaihu**, where eight tall statues lie face-down on the ground, their red stone topknots strewn along the coast. Three kilometres further along, **Ahu Akahanga** presents an equally mournful picture of a row of fallen *moai*; according to some oral traditions, it's also the burial place of Hotu Matu'a. Further up the coast, **Ahu Hanga Tetenga** is the site of the largest *moai* – 9.94m – ever transported to a platform

Just beyond Ahu Hanga Tetenga, the road forks. The left-hand branch (**Camino de los Moai**), leads to the quarry of Rano Raraku. It's thought to have been the main roadway along which the statues were transported from the quarry. The right-hand branch continues up the coast to the magnificent Ahu Tongariki.

Ahu Tongariki

The fifteen colossal *moai* lined up on **AHU TONGARIKI** make a sensational sight. This was the largest number of *moai* ever erected on a single *ahu*, which, at 200m long, was the largest built on the island. It was totally destroyed in 1960 when a massive tsunami, caused by an earthquake in Chile, swept across this corner of the island, dragging the platform blocks and the statues 90m inland – a remarkable distance, given that the statues weigh up to thirty tonnes each.

In November 1988, Sergio Rapu, former Governor of Easter Island, was being interviewed for a **Japanese television programme**, and said that if they had a crane they could save the *moai*; a Japanese man watching the show decided to act and a committee was set up in Japan. The restoration of the *ahu* involved Chilean archeologists Claudio Cristino and Patricia Vargas, a group of forty islanders, specialists from the Nara Institute of Japan and recognized international experts in stone conservation. The project took five years and was finally completed in 1995.

Rano Raraku

North of Tongariki, **RANO RARAKU** rises from the land in a hulking mass of volcanic stone. This crag is where almost all of the island's statues were produced, carved directly from the "tuff" (compacted volcanic ash) of the crater's outer slopes. The first surprise, on approaching the crater from the car park, are the dozens of **giant heads** sprouting from the ground. They are, in

▲ Moai statues at Ahu Tongariki

The enduring symbol of Easter Island always has been, and doubtless always will be, the monolithic *moai* that line its shores. A Neolithic statue cult on this scale would impress in any location, but the fact that it developed in total isolation on a tiny island in the middle of the Pacific almost defies belief. There are some four hundred finished statues scattered around the island, and almost as many in the statue quarry, in varying stages of completion.

The *moai* range in height from 2m to about 20m, and all are carved in the same highly stylized manner. Their bellies are gently rounded, and their arms are held tightly by their sides, with their strange, long-fingered hands placed across their abdomens. Their heads are long and rectangular, with pointed chins; prominent, angular noses; and thin, tight lips. According to the assertions of the islanders, which are consistent with widespread Polynesian tradition, these figures represented important **ancestors**, such as chiefs and priests, and were erected on the ancestral land of the kin-group these individuals belonged to, which they would watch over and protect with their *mana* (almost all the moai are looking inland, rather than gazing out to sea). Archeologists have proposed tentative dates of around 1000 AD for the carving of the early statues, and around the fifteenth century for the bulk of the statues, when production was at its peak. The unfinished statues in Rano Raraku demonstrate quite clearly how their forms were chiselled out of the rock face until they were attached to it by only a thin keel running down their spine. When all was completed but their eye sockets, they were freed from their keel and slid down the slope of the quarry, then temporarily erected in a pit until they were transported to their ahus.

Transporting the moai

The island's oral histories offer no clues as to how the 20–25 tonne statues were moved, claiming that the statues' *mana* enabled them to walk a short distance each day until they reached their platforms. Modern theories have included horizontal swivelling and vertical swivelling, but since it was established in the 1980s that the island was once densely covered by two species of tree – the shrublike *toromiro* and a large palm closely related to *Jubae chilensis* – it's been assumed that they were dragged either on wooden sledges, or on top of rollers.

Raising the moai

How the statues were **erected** onto their platforms in the absence of any type of machinery is another enigma, though in 1955, Thor Heyerdahl challenged the island's mayor to raise a fallen, 25-tonne statue at Anakena Beach and, under the mayor's supervision, twelve islanders raised the statue in eighteen days, using two levers and slipping layer after layer of stones underneath the horizontal statue. Little by little, it was raised on the bed of stones until it was level with its platform; at this point, the

fact, finished *moai* brought down from the quarry, which were probably placed in shallow pits (that gradually built up) until they could be transported to their *ahu*. One of them bears an image on its chest of a three-masted sailing ship, suggesting that they were carved after European contact.

Among this mass of shapes, still attached to the rock face, is **El Gigante**, the biggest *moai* ever carved, stretching over 20m from top to bottom. Experts believe that it would have been impossible to transport, let alone erect.

The east end of the trail culminates in the kneeling, round-headed **Moai Tukuturi**, the only one of its kind, discovered by Thor Heyerdahl's expedition in 1955. To the west, the trail winds its way up between wild guava trees into the crater itself, with several dirt paths running through knee-high shrubbery alongside the large reed-strewn, freshwater lake. If you follow the trails all the layers of pebbles were placed only under its head, until the statue was nearly vertical and could be slipped into place. Archeologists agree that this method is highly likely to have been used to raise the statues. In contrast, no one has been able to demonstrate how the large, heavy "topknots" were placed on the raised statues' heads – a monumental feat, achieved only with the use of a crane in modern times.

The statue-carvers

Easter Island society was based around independent clans, or **kin-groups**, each with its own high-ranking members. The statue-carvers were highly revered members of a privileged class who were exempt from food production and were supported by farmers and fishermen on the island. Such a system must have involved a great deal of economic co-operation, which appears to have been successfully maintained for hundreds of years. Then, in the later stages of the island's prehistory, the system collapsed. Groups that had worked peacefully, if competitively, alongside each other at Rano Raraku withdrew from the quarry and exchanged their tools for weapons, as the island became engulfed by internal strife and warfare. The island's archeological record reveals a sudden, dramatic proliferation of obsidian **weapons** during the eighteenth century, as well as the remains of violently beaten skulls, and evidence of the widespread use of caves as refuges. In several locations archeologists have found possible evidence of cannibalism – something that features prominently in the island's oral traditions. The most dramatic testimony of this period of conflict, however, is provided by the hundreds of fallen statues littering the island, deliberately and systematically toppled from their platforms as enemy groups set out to desecrate each other's sacred sites.

So what went wrong on Easter Island?

It seems likely that the seeds of social collapse lay in the extremes that the statue cult was taken to by the islanders. As the impulse to produce moai required more and more hands, the delicate balance between food distribution and statue-carving was destroyed. This situation was profoundly aggravated by the growing scarcity of food brought about by overpopulation, and deforestation, following centuries of logging for boat-building, fuel consumption and statue-transportation. This must have had a catastrophic effect on the islanders' ability to feed themselves: deep-sea fishing became increasingly difficult, and eventually impossible, owing to the lack of wood available for new canoes, and even land cultivation was affected, as the deforestation caused soil erosion. In this climate of encroaching deprivation, the farmers and fishermen were no longer willing or able to pool their spoils – and the Easter Island civilization descended into anarchy, dragging its majestic monuments with it.

way up to the crater's eastern rim (avoid treading on the toppled *moai* right at the top) you are rewarded with unparalleled views of the bay and Ahu Tongariki in the distance.

The Poike Peninsula

East of Rano Raraku, the seldom-visited **POIKE PENINSULA** is a green, gently rounded plateau bound in by steep cliffs. Poike's main interest lies in the myths and legends associated with it. One tells of the **cave of the virgins**, Ana o Keke, where a number of young girls were confined for months on end so that their skin would remain as pale as possible. Another one, more famous, is of the battle of the **"Long Ears"** and **"Short Ears"**. This battle is supposed

The myth of the "Long Ears" and the "Short Ears"

An oft-repeated oral tradition has it that the island's population, in the time just before the toppling of the statues, was divided into two principal groups, **the "Short Ears" and the "Long Ears"**. In fact, the whole myth is based on a mistranslation. The word *epe* means "ear" in the Rapa Nui tongue, and it seems that the two clans were really the *Hanau eepe* ("short and stocky people") and the *Hanau momoko* ("tall and slim people"); the strange mix-up came from mistranslating *eepe* – short and stocky – as "ear".

The "Long Ears", who saw themselves as more aristocratic, were extremely domineering, and the "Short Ears" resented them intensely. The "Short Ears" rebelled when forced to clear rocks off the land, forcing the "Long Ears" to retreat to the **Poike Peninsula** at the eastern end of the island. Here the "Long Ears" dug a series of deep ditches separating the peninsula from the rest of the island, and filled them with branches and grass, intending to force their enemies inside and set them alight. However, a "Short Ears" woman who was married to one of the "Long Ears" alerted her people to this scheme, and, with a secret signal, allowed them to pass into the peninsula and surround their enemies while they were sleeping. When the "Short Ears" attacked, the "Long Ears" had nowhere to run but straight into their own ditch, which the "Short Ears" gleefully set fire to. The "Long Ears" roasted to death in the pits, but three of them escaped, and fled into hiding. Two of them were caught and executed, but one, a certain **Ororoina**, was allowed to live, and went on to father many children – whose descendants, to this day, are proud of their *Hanau momoko* heritage.

to have taken place in the 3.5-kilometre-long ditch separating the peninsula from the rest of the island, known as Ko te Ava o Iko, or "Iko's ditch".

You can walk round the edge of the peninsula in about four hours, but there's no shade, no path, while access to Ana o Keke is treacherous and should not be attempted without a local guide.

North to Anakena

From the southern coast, the road turns inland, cutting past the Poike Peninsula, and leads directly to Ovahe and Anakena. On the way, look out for **Ahu te Pito Kura**, down by Bahía La Pérouse (signposted). This is the site of **Paro**, probably the largest *moai* successfully erected on a platform, at 9.8m tall. Paro is thought to have been one of the last *moai* to be moved and erected, and is estimated to weigh a staggering ninety tonnes. No one has attempted to restore and re-erect the giant, which still lies face down before its *ahu*, surrounded by rubble.

Further north, **Ovahe** is a tiny, secluded and exquisitely beautiful beach, its white sands lapped by crystal-clear waters at the foot of a large volcanic cliff, very popular with locals who come here to picnic, swim and snorkel. It's best earlier in the day, before the cliff blocks the afternoon sun. A little further up the coast, **Playa Anakena** is much larger, and presents a picture-postcard scene of powdery golden sands fringed by swaying palm trees, great for an afternoon of swimming or sunbathing. You can camp by the **Conaf** office across from the beach, which offers shade and limited water; multiple snack stands offer drinks and sandwiches, so you don't need to bring all your food and water with you.

ANAKENA has a special place in Rapa Nui oral history, which holds it to be the landing site and dwelling place of Hotu Matu'a, the island's first colonizer (see box, p.468). It's also home to the splendid *moai* of **Ahu Nau Nau**, which were so deeply covered in sand until their restoration, led by local archeologist Sergio Rapu Haoa in 1978, that they were largely protected from the effects of weathering. What makes these *moai* really striking, though, are the large, gleaming white eyes inserted into their eye sockets, fixed in a slightly up-turned gaze towards the sky. Archeologists had always assumed that the statues' eye sockets had remained empty, but when fragments of white coral and a circular red pebble were discovered here in 1978, it was found that they fitted together to form an oval eye with a red iris. It's not known if all the statues on the island had such eyes, as the only other fragments found have been at Vinapu.

Just up the hillside by the beach you'll find the squat and rather corpulent *moai* of **Ahu Ature Huki**. This was the first *moai* to be re-erected on the island in the experiment carried out by Thor Heyerdahl in 1955, when twelve strong islanders showed they could raise a 25-tonne statue in eighteen days (see box, p.476).

The northern circuit

Although the triangle formed by Vinapu, Tongariki and Anakena contains the densest concentration of sites, the western and northern parts of the island are also well worth exploring. Attractions include the impressive *moai* of **Tapai** and **Ahu Akivi**, plus a network of underground **caves**.

Tapai and around

If you walk north from the *caleta* past the cemetery, taking the road that hugs the coast, after about ten minutes you will reach the ceremonial centre of **TAPAI**, composed of three *ahus*, a favourite spot for viewing colourful sunsets. The first, **Ahu Vai Uri**, supports four broad, squat *moai*, two of which have badly damaged heads, and the stump of a fifth statue. In front of the *ahu* is the outline of a flattened esplanade, presumed to have been used as a ceremonial site. Archeological remains suggest that some individuals – possibly chiefs and priests – used to live near these ceremonial sites, in several locations on the island, in stone, oval houses called *hare paenga* that looked like an upturned canoe. You can see the foundations of one of these houses near Ahu Vai Uri. The second platform is **Ahu Tapai** itself, topped by a lone, weathered *moai*. Finally, **Ahu Kote Riku** is the site of a well-preserved *moai* fitted with white, glinting eyes, and a red topknot.

About half a kilometre further north, set well back from the coastal path, the excellent **Museo Antropológico "Sebastián Englert"** (Tues–Fri 9am–12.30pm & 2–5.30pm, Sat & Sun 9.30am–12.30pm; CH\$1500; ☎322/551020, ⓦwww.museorapanui.cl) is not to be missed, as it gives a thorough introduction to the island's geography, history, society, **birdman cult** and the origins and significance of the *moai*. The well-labelled displays are in Spanish, with English handouts, and include a very evocative collection of black-and-white photographs of islanders from about 1915 onwards, a rare female *moai* and replica *rongo rongo* tablets.

Dos Ventanas Caves and Ahu Te Peu

Back on the coastal road, continue north for about 3km – until you reach the point where you're standing opposite two little islands out at sea – and look out for the stone cairn by the left-hand side of the road signalling a track down towards the cliffs; it's not very easy to spot. At the end of the track, a tiny opening in the ground is the entrance to a pitch-black passage (take a torch), which continues 50m underground to the adjoining Ana Kakenga (**DOS VENTANAS CAVES**). Both caves are flooded with light streaming in from the "windows", or gaping holes, that open out of the cliff wall. Prepare for a rush of adrenaline as you approach the edges, as both drop vertically down to a bed of sharp rocks and pounding waves many metres below.

About 1km further up the coast you reach **AHU TE PEU**. The *moai* that once stood on the *ahu* still lie flat on the ground, left as they were during the period of warfare. Scattered around the *ahu* are the remains of many boat-shaped *hare paenga*, including one that's sixty metres long. It's thought that this was the site of the village of the Miru clan, the direct descendants of Hotu Matu'a.

At Ahu Te Peu, most people join up with the inland road and head back to Hanga Roa via Ahu Akivi. You can, however, continue north, either heading up the gentle volcanic cone of **Terevaka**, where you'll be rewarded with fine views across the island from its 510-metre summit, the highest point of the island (no path; 1hr up), or else follow the coastline round to Playa Anakena (4–5hr). Sunscreen is absolutely essential and you must take plenty of water.

On the way, you'll pass many fallen *moai*, none of them restored, as well as the ruins of stone houses and chicken pens.

Inland to Puna Pau, Ahu Akivi and Te Pahu Caves

From Hanga Roa, heading up the inland road to Ahu Akivi (first left from the paved road to Anakena) you'll pass a signed track branching left to **PUNA PAU**, a low volcanic crater made of rusty-coloured rock, known as "scoria", where the islanders carved the **pukao** – the cylindrical "topknots" worn by up to seventy of the *moai* standing on *ahu*. No one knows for sure what these cylinders represented, though suggestions include topknots (of hair) and feather headdresses. Up in the quarry, and along the track to the top, you can see thirty or so finished *pukao* lying on the ground.

Back on the road, continue north and you'll reach **AHU AKIVI**, whose seven *moai* are the only ones to have been erected inland, and the only ones that look towards the sea. It's been discovered that they are oriented directly towards the rising summer solstice, along with several other *ahu*, suggesting that solar positions were of significance to the islanders. The Ahu Akivi *moai* were raised in 1960 by William Mulloy and Gonzalo Figueroa, two of the archeologists recruited by Heyerdahl in 1955, both of whom went on to devote their entire careers to Easter Island.

From Ahu Akivi, the road turns towards the coast, where it meets Ahu Te Peu. On the way, a second path branches left from the main road, leading towards the **TE PAHU CAVES**. If you clamber down, you'll see some tall bamboo trees growing in a magical underground garden, along with sweet potatoes, taro, avocados, lemons and sugarcane. This cave is connected to another huge cave (once used as a dwelling place) by a long lava tube.

Rano Kau and Orongo

South of Hanga Roa, a dirt road climbs steeply past a *mirador* offering an excellent view of Hanga Roa up to one of the most awe-inspiring spots on the island – the giant crater of the extinct **RANU KAU** volcano, and the ceremonial village of **ORONGO**, perched high on its rim. The dull waters of the volcano's reed-choked lake contrast sharply with the brilliant blue of the Pacific,

The birdman ceremony

The ritual of the birdman took place each year at the September **equinox**, when the chiefs of the various kin-groups on the island assembled at Orongo to take part in a ritual competition. The object of this competition was to find the first egg laid by the sooty tern (a migratory bird) on Motu Nui, the largest of three islets sitting opposite Orongo, 2km out to sea. Each chief would choose a representative, or *hopu*, who would then scale down the sheer cliff to the ocean and swim through shark-infested waters out to the islet. It could take several weeks for the egg to be found; meanwhile, the chiefs would remain in Orongo, where they participated in ritual dances, songs and prayers. Once the sacred egg was finally found, its discoverer would bellow the name of his master across the sea, and then swim back to the island with the egg tucked into a headband. The victorious chief now became the new *tangata manu*, or **birdman**. The new birdman would first have all the hair shaved off his head, including eyebrows and eyelashes; he would then live in strict seclusion for a whole year in a sacred house at the foot of Rano Raraku, eating only certain foods prepared by a special servant, and forbidden to bathe or cut his nails. His kin-group, meanwhile, was endowed with a special, high status, which was often taken as an excuse for members to dominate and bully their rival groups.

stretching as far as the eye can see, visible where a great chunk of the crater wall is missing. Just before you reach Orongo, a path disappears into the lush vegetation around the crater's edge; it is possible to follow this around the crater as a leisurely day's walk, but bring plenty of water. Orongo is easily reached from Hanga Roa, either by car or taxi in ten minutes, or on foot in about an hour. Either way, you'll end up at the Conaf hut at the top, where you're supposed to pay your park fee (unfixed hours; CH$5000). The village, a short distance beyond, consists of the partially restored remains of some 48 low-lying, oval-shaped huts made of thin stone slabs, each with a tiny entrance just large enough to crawl through (don't try). A few steps from the houses, on the face of some basalt outcrops looking out to sea, you'll find a dense group of exquisitely carved **petroglyphs** depicting curled-up human figures with birds' heads and long curved beaks. These images honour an important annual ceremony dedicated to the **cult of the birdman**. A great deal is known about this ceremony, as it was practised right up to 1878.

The Juan Fernández Archipelago

The **JUAN FERNÁNDEZ ARCHIPELAGO** is made up of three islands and numerous rocky islets. The archipelago is named for **João Fernandes**, the Portuguese sailor who discovered it on November 22, 1574, while straying out to sea to avoid coastal winds and currents in an attempt to shorten the journey between Lima and Valparaíso. The more easterly of the two main islands was called **Más a Tierra** ("Nearer Land"), while the other, 187km further west, was known as **Más Afuera** ("Farther Out"). Fernandes made a brief attempt to colonize the three uninhabited islands, introducing vegetables and goats, which multiplied in great numbers (the third, smallest, island was later known as Goat Island, officially as Isla Santa Clara). These were still flourishing when British buccaneers started making occasional calls here to stock up on water and fresh meat between their raids on the mainland.

Following Alexander Selkirk's much-publicized rescue, more and more buccaneers began calling here, prompting the Spanish Crown to take official possession of the archipelago in 1742, building a series of forts around Más a Tierra. The island was then used as a **penal colony** for many years, and it wasn't until the mid-nineteenth century that a mixture of Chilean and European colonizers formed a permanent settlement here. In 1966, with an eye on the islands' potential as a tourist destination, the Chilean government changed Más a Tierra's name to **Isla Robinson Crusoe**, while Más Afuera became **Isla Alejandro Selkirk**, seasonal home to lobster fishermen and very difficult to reach. Today, only a few hundred tourists make it out here each year, arriving between October and March, when the climate is warm and mostly dry, and the seawater is perfect for bathing.

Isla Robinson Crusoe

Twenty-two kilometres long, and 7km at its widest point, **ISLA ROBINSON CRUSOE** is the archipelago's only permanently inhabited island. Most of the five hundred or so islanders – some of them descendants of the Swiss Baron de Rodt and his compatriots who settled the island at the end of the nineteenth century – live in the little village of **San Juan Bautista**, on the sheltered Bahía Cumberland. The main economic activity is trapping **lobsters**, and one of the highlights of a stay here is accompanying a fisherman, for a small cost, out to haul in his catch – most trips include a fresh-as-it-comes lobster supper, prepared over a small stove on the boat. Lobsters aside, the island's two principal attractions are the sites associated with the famous castaway **Alexander Selkirk**

Alexander Selkirk

Daniel Defoe's story of Robinson Crusoe, the world's most famous literary castaway, was inspired by the misadventures of the real-life Scottish mariner **Alexander Selkirk**, who was marooned on Isla Robinson Crusoe (then Más a Tierra) in 1704 while crossing the Pacific on a privateering expedition. Unlike Crusoe, who was shipwrecked, Selkirk actually asked to be put ashore following a series of quarrels with his captain. The irascible sailor regretted his decision as soon he was deposited on the beach with a few scanty supplies, but his cries from the shore begging to be taken back onboard were ignored. Selkirk spent four years and four months on the island, with only his Bible and dozens of wild goats for company. During that time he was transformed into an extraordinary athlete, as he hunted the goats on foot, and a devout Christian. Following his rescue by a British ship in 1709, however, Selkirk reverted to his buccaneering ways, joining in attacks on Spanish vessels all the way home. Back in Fife, the former castaway became something of a celebrity and threw himself into a life of drink and women. Fourteen years after his rescue, Selkirk finally met his end when he took up the seafaring life once more, set off on another privateering expedition, and died of fever in the tropics.

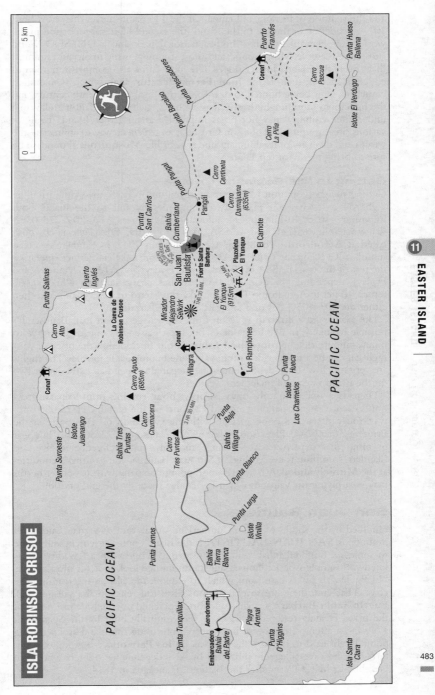

ISLA ROBINSON CRUSOE

PACIFIC OCEAN

PACIFIC OCEAN

0   5 km

N

Punta Suroeste

Islote Juanango

Bahía Tres Puntas

Punta Lemos

Cerro Chumacera ▲

Cerro Aguado (685m) ▲

Cerro Tres Puntas ▲

3 HR 30 MIN

Punta Tunquillax

Embarcadero Bahía del Padre

Aerodromo ✈

Bahía Tierra Blanca

Playa Arenal

Punta O'Higgins

Isla Santa Clara

Islote Vinilla

Punta Larga

Punta Blanco

Bahía Villagra

Punta Baja

Conaf ⛺ Villagra

Los Ramplones ●

Islote Los Chamelos

● **Punta Hueca**

Punta Salinas

△

Conaf ⛺ ▲ *Cerro Alto* △

La Cueva de Robinson Crusoe

Mirador Alejandro Selkirk ✳

Cerro El Yunque (915m) ▲

1 HR 30 MIN

△ **Plazoleta El Yunque**

30 MIN

● El Camote

Puerto Inglés △

Punta San Carlos

Bahía Cumberland

San Juan Bautista

Fuerte Santa Bárbara

Cerro Damajuana (635m) ▲

● Pangal

▲ *Cerro Centinela*

Punta Pangal

Punta Bacalao

Punta Pescadores

Cerro La Piña ▲

Conaf ⛺ *Puerto Francés*

Punta Hueso Ballena

Islote El Verdugo ○

▲ *Cerro Pascua*

11

EASTER ISLAND

483

and the richness of its flora and fauna. Of the 146 plant species that grow here, 101 are endemic or unique to the island (the second highest proportion in the world after Hawaii), which is both a national park and a UNESCO World Biosphere Reserve. Most prolific, and most stunning, is the luxuriant rainforest that covers the island's higher slopes. The local fauna also comprises numerous endemic species, such as the **Juan Fernández fur seal**, which is making a comeback after being hunted to near-extinction in the eighteenth century, and the Firecrown hummingbird, as well as sea birds, such as the giant petrel. While underwater visibility may not be as impressive as on Easter Island, diving at various sites around Isla Robinson Crusoe is an excellent way to appreciate the wealth and diversity of its abundant underwater life. **Mosquitoes** abound, so be sure to bring plenty of repellent.

Getting to Isla Robinson Crusoe

Getting to Isla Robinson Crusoe is an adventure in itself, involving a bumpy flight on a seven-seater plane. Two companies fly out to the island, both imposing a strict 10-kilo luggage allowance. Aerolíneas ATA (⊕2/275 0363, Ⓦwww.aerolineasata.cl) and LASSA (⊕2/273 5209, Ⓔlassa@terra.cl), both based at **Aeródromo Tobalaba**, Avenida Larraín 7941, in Santiago's eastern suburb of La Reina, fly twice weekly in peak season; a skeletal service operating the rest of the year; LASSA on Tuesdays and Fridays and ATA on Mondays and Fridays, depending on demand. Both airlines charge around CH$400,000 return. To get to Aeródromo Tobolaba, take the Metro to Plaza Egaña and then either the 403/403C bus or a taxi east along Av Larraín.

The island's little **airstrip** is 13km from the village of San Juan Bautista; it's possible to hike it in five hours or so, but most passengers opt for the fifty- to ninety-minute ride by **motorised fishing boat** (included in the price of your flight); it can be a rough ride, coming after the bumpy plane journey. The flights are very much weather-dependent, so be prepared to spend an extra day or two on the island in case of inclement weather.

There is a once-monthly **navy supply boat** coming from Valparaíso; 24 hours each way and spending around 72 hours on the island; CH$25,000 one-way. You can try and book passage with the Comando de Transporte at the Primera Zona Naval, Plaza Sotomayor 592, Valparaíso (⊕322/506354), but bear in mind that departure dates change monthly, and preference is given to islanders, so timing is everything. In San Juan Bautista, you can make enquiries at the **Municipalidad**. A new private shipping company with passenger berths may start plying the Valparaíso-Juan Fernandez route by the end of 2009.

San Juan Bautista

Huddled by the shores of Bahía Cumberland, at the foot of a green curtain of mountains, **SAN JUAN BAUTISTA** is the island's only settlement and home to some six hundred inhabitants. A spread-out village with a few dirt streets lined with simple wooden houses, and an unfinished look to it, for most people, "El Pueblo" is just a base from which to explore the island's interior and the coast. That said, there are several curious historical relics in the village itself. **Fuerte Santa Barbara**, a small stone fort, is perched on a hillside just north of the plaza. Heavily restored in 1974, it was originally built by the Spanish in 1749 in an attempt to prevent buccaneers from using the island as a watering point. Right next to the fort, the **Cuevas de los Patriotas** is a group of seven fern-covered caves allegedly inhabited by 42 independence fighters who were banished to Más a Tierra after the Battle of Rancagua in 1814.

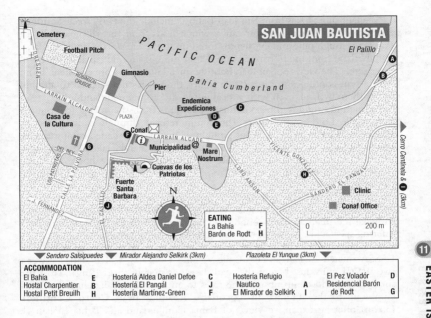

EATING
| La Bahía | F |
| Barón de Rodt | H |

0   200 m

ACCOMMODATION

El Bahía	E	Hostería Aldea Daniel Defoe	C	Hostería Refugio		El Pez Volador	D
Hostal Charpentier	B	Hostería El Pangál	J	Nautico	A	Residencial Barón	
Hostal Petit Breuilh	H	Hostería Martínez-Green	F	El Mirador de Selkirk	I	de Rodt	G

Down on the shore, follow the path to the north end of the bay and you'll reach the cliffs of the **Punta San Carlos**, embedded with unexploded shells fired by British warships at the German *Dresden* during World War I. The Germans surrendered, but sank their ship rather than let it go to the British, and the wreck still lies 70m under the sea, in Bahía Cumberland. Nearby you'll find the graves of the naval battle's casualties in the island's **cemetery**, next to the lighthouse. At the **Casa de la Cultura** (Mon–Fri 10am–1pm & 4–8pm, Sat 11am–1pm & 5–8pm; donation welcome), there are some interesting historic **photos**, primarily of the World War I incident. At the southern end of the bay, a five-minute walk from the village, the small rocky beach of **El Palillo** is good for swimming and diving, and has a few picnic tables.

Exploring the island

There are numerous good hikes around the island, though some are not marked; you will need local guides for all hikes in the eastern half of the island, as well as between Bahía Inglés and Puerto Vaquería. Some destinations are reached by **boat** with local fishermen, who can drop you off in the morning and pick you up at the end of their day's work. You can also hire a boat to circumnavigate the island; though this is a pricey option, it will allow you to view otherwise inaccessible areas.

A fifteen-minute boat ride from the village lies **Bahía Inglés**, where you'll find a mock-up of the cave where Selkirk took refuge and a good camping spot. Other boat destinations include **Puerto Vaquería**, west of Bahía Inglés, a popular spot to snorkel with seals and the site of a Conaf *refugio*; **Puerto Francés**, in the eastern part of the island, where there are ramparts overlooking the sea, built by the Spanish to deter French pirates; and **Playa Arenal**, the island's only sandy beach with warm, transparent waters, which lies two hours and thirty minutes by boat through islets and seal colonies, just south of the airstrip.

Excellent short hikes from San Juan Bautista include the fairly steep **Sendero Salsipuedes** ("Get out if you can"), which leads from the village's Calle La Pólvora through pine and eucalyptus forest up to the *mirador* overlooking Bahía Cumberland from the northwest side. Allow an hour's roundtrip and beware of loose scree. The views of San Juan Bautista spread out below are excellent. From here, a trail continues towards Bahía Inglés, though it's not advised to attempt to get there by land, even with a local guide, due to frequent landslides.

A sometimes muddy three-kilometre trail leads from the village (continuing from Calle Lord Anson; allow 1hr 30min return) through native forest to **Plazoleta El Yunque**, a lookout point and an attractive shaded campsite with picnic tables at the foot of Cerro El Yunque, the island's tallest mountain at 915m. The stone ruins near the site are the remains of the house of Hugo Weber, the "German Robinson Crusoe", who spent twelve years living as a hermit here after escaping from the *Dresden* in 1915. From the campsite, the pleasant trail loops through native vegetation, including giant *nalca* (rhubarb) and ferns, before finishing back at the campsite. From the Plazoleta, it is possible to make the steep ascent through thick native forest to **El Camote**, the peak offering spectacular views of the island, though this requires a local guide.

A 45-minute walk from the south end of San Juan Bautista brings you to the LASSA-owned El Pangál; take Calle Vicente Gonzáles, which starts between two WWII guns. Just before the road descends steeply to El Pangál, cross the small stream and climb up past the trees to an animal corral; behind it, a trail climbs up to the antenna on top of the oceanside peak, **Cerro Centinela** (362m) offering expansive views of Bahía Cumberland and Bahía El Pangál. From here, an unmarked trail zigzags its way along the coast to Puerto Francés, only to be attempted with a knowledgeable local.

The island's **best hike** runs from the airstrip to San Juan Bautista, via the Mirador de Selkirk. Arrange to be dropped off by a fisherman at the Bahía del Padre, the launching place for the boat that picks you up from the airstrip, which is home to a large colony of fur seals. Outside breeding season, they are not dangerous and you can swim and snorkel with them. The largest fur seal colony lies at **Bahía Tierras Blancas**, the first bay you come to along the trail.

Follow the road uphill and take the well-marked trail running from the airstrip. Bring plenty of water and allow at least five hours to take in the spectacular coastal scenery. The trail skirts the zigzagging coastline, with turquoise bays appearing around every corner, the barking of sea lions echoing from below and the landscape gradually changing from arid desert-like hills with their vividly multi-coloured soil to steep pasture land to jagged mountains covered in dense endemic vegetation. For the most part, the track is wide enough to take a vehicle, ascending very gradually until you reach **Villagra**, a couple of houses with a corral for animals, where the rodeo is held in February. Here the track divides; take the rocky footpath overgrown with vegetation, which climbs steeply uphill until it reaches the **Mirador Alejandro Selkirk**, the famous lookout point where, according to a now-disputed story, Selkirk lit his daily smoke signals and scoured the horizon for ships. Here you'll be rewarded with stunning panoramic views of most of the island. Note the two metal memorial plaques set in the rocks, one donated by the officers of *HMS Topaze* in 1868, the other by one of Selkirk's descendants in 1983, pledging to remember his forefather "Till a' the seas gang dry and the rocks melt i' the sun".

If you do not have the time to do a cross-island hike, you can reach the *mirador* from the village, though that way it's a steeper climb, taking about ninety minutes; the path starts north of the plaza, extending from Subida El Castillo, snaking through lush native forest, dense with overhanging ferns. The descent to the village takes around an hour.

Isla Alejandro Selkirk

Those with plenty of time and an even greater sense of adventure may consider trying to reach the even more remote and ruggedly mountainous **Isla Alejandro Selkirk**. During the October–May lobster season, it's home to around fifty people, as well as a small team of conservationists from the US and some feral goats. Bring all necessary food and gear with you, including a tent. An infrequent supply boat serves the island, and fishermen ply the waters between the two islands, so you can enquire at the Municipalidad about passage (17hr; around CH$60,000); if you don't arrange a return trip, you may find yourself marooned for some time.

Accommodation, eating and drinking

San Juan Bautista's guesthouses offer half-board or full board. If you want to eat somewhere other than your *residencial*, let them know in advance. Fresh fruit and vegetables are a luxury, so your diet will consist principally of local fish. Food in the few small shops by the plaza is expensive and limited.

El Bahía Larraín Alcalde s/n. More of a watering hole than a restaurant, this spot next to *El Pez Volador* has erratic opening hours, but is known to occasionally serve excellent fish and lobster.
Hostal Charpentier Ignacio Carrera Pinto 256 ⊤ 322/751020, ⊛ www.hostalcharpentier.cl. Friendly guesthouse offering beautiful en-suite doubles with floor-to-ceiling glass windows as well as a fully-equipped *cabaña*. The restaurant is another good choice for fresh fish; full- and half-board available. ❻
Hostería Martínez-Green Larraín Alcalde s/n ⊤ 322/751039. Comfortable rooms with TV, just off the plaza, run by a lobster fisherman and his wife. Full- and half-board available and owners can help organize tours. ❺
Hostería El Pangál ⊤ 02/273 1458 (reservations); no phone in hotel itself. Attractive hotel owned by LASSA; package deals with flight are available. Bonuses include great views from the deck, outdoor swimming pool, hot tub and massage. The secluded setting and the 45min walk to the village are drawbacks. Credit cards accepted. ❽
Hostería Refugio Náutico Ignacio Carrera Pinto s/n, towards El Palillo ⊤ 322/751077, ⊛ www .islarobinsoncrusoe.cl. With its own sea access, plus kayaks, boats and diving equipment, as the outfit's name suggests, this guesthouse is oriented towards, but not exclusively for, people interested

in spending time on or under the water. The food and pisco sours are generally very good, with expertly cooked fish straight from the ocean. ❼
El Mirador de Selkirk El Castillo 251 ⊤ 322/751028, ⊜ mfernandeziana @hotmail.com. Attractive B&B with three cosy rooms and with ocean views from the deck. The friendly proprietress, a third-generation islander happy to discuss her family history, also cooks excellent fish dishes as well as lobster empanadas. Restaurant open daily. Take the street running up along the right side of Fuerte Santa Barbara to get here. ❹
El Pez Volador Larraín Alcalde s/n ⊤ 322/751227, ⊛ www.endemica.com. The unique-looking building south of the plaza, flying the Jolly Roger, is the guesthouse run by Endémica Expediciones (see p.442), with three attractive wood-panelled rooms and an excellent restaurant. Half-board available. Try the curried lobster or the ceviche. ❺
Residencial Barón de Rodt La Pólvora s/n ⊤ 322/751109, ⊜ baronderodt@yahoo.es. Small, friendly family-run guesthouse belonging to the great-granddaughter of the Baron himself. There are only two en-suite doubles, so booking's essential. The restaurant serves superbly fresh local *vidriola* fish, *chupe de cangrejo*, seafood empanadas and lobster. ❸

Listings

Airline LASSA, Larraín Alcalde s/n, on the plaza (⊤ 322/100279). ATA does not have an office, but you can get the latest information on flights at the internet shack.

Banks There are no banks or *cambios* on the island, and few places accept credit cards, so you have to bring plenty of cash from the mainland to cover your stay here, bearing in mind that poor weather may delay your flight by a day or two.

Conaf To find out more about the island's trails, wildlife and local guides and to register and pay your park entrance fee (CH$3000 valid for a week), visit the kiosk on the main square (daily in peak season 9am–1pm & 2–6pm) or the Conaf Centro de Información Ambiental at Sendero El Pangal 130 (Mon–Thurs 8am–12.50pm & 2–6pm; Fri 8am–12.50pm & 2–5.50pm; ☎322/751022).

Hospital The government-run Posta Rural on Vicente Gonzáles s/n (☎322/751067) deals with minor medical emergencies; anyone requiring serious treatment has to be flown to the mainland.

Internet access and telephone centre There is an internet hut with four computers on Larraín Alcalde s/n, near the Conaf office; CH$500 for 30min. International calls can be made from a single phone here. internet access at Casa de la Cultura also.

Post office Larraín Alcalde 352-A, on the south side of the plaza.

Tour agencies Endémica Expediciones (see *El Pez Volador*, above) offers diving, snorkelling, hiking and fishing excursions around the island, as do the Refugio Náutico (see listing) and Mare Nostrum Expediciones (☎322/751080, ⓦwww.marenostrumexpediciones.com).

Tourist information The Municipalidad (Mon–Fri 8.30am–1pm; ☎322/701045 or 322/751067, ⓦwww.comunajuanfernandez.cl), off the southwest corner of the plaza, hands out accommodation lists, maps and leaflets.

Contexts

Contexts

History

Enveloped by the Andes, the Atacama Desert and the Pacific Ocean, Chile has evolved almost as an island, relatively undisturbed by the turbulence that has raged through much of South America's history. Though inhabited by indigenous groups for millennia, the country's actual recorded history dates from the sixteenth-century arrival of the Spaniards. The colonial society that emerged and the ensuing struggle for independence resemble that of the whole continent, but, from its early days as a republic, Chile took on its own political shape, distinct from that of its neighbours. With its largely ordered, constitutional model of government, and a healthy respect for the law, Chile earned itself the sobriquet of "the England of South America" in the nineteenth century. More recently, however, it returned to the attention of the outside world with the repressive military regime of General Augusto Pinochet in the 1970s and 1980s. Today, with democracy firmly back in place, Chile is an outward-looking nation boasting political and economic stability, albeit with some serious social inequalities and unresolved political legacies lurking beneath the surface.

The beginnings

Chile's anthropological record, like that of all the Americas, began when the first groups of Asians crossed the land bridge connecting Siberia to Alaska before the end of the last Ice Age, when the sea level was 70–100m lower than it is today. Archeologists are unable to tell us exactly when this **first migration** occurred, but it's generally thought to have been between 25,000 and 40,000 years ago.

What *is* known is that by 12,000 BC the descendants of these people, supplemented by further waves of migration from Asia, had spread down the whole of North and South America as far as the southern tip of Patagonia. While some devoted themselves to fishing, the majority were probably nomadic hunters living off the animals that inhabited the region at the time – mastodons (prehistoric elephants), mammoths, giant armadillos and wild horses. When the last Ice Age came to an end around 11,000 BC, the climate changed abruptly and many of these animals became extinct. The hunters were forced to adapt, supplementing their diet by gathering fruits and seeds. Eventually this led to the deliberate cultivation of foodstuffs and the domestication of animals, and along with these incipient agricultural practices came more stable communities and important developments, such as pottery and burial customs. Slowly, distinct cultural groups emerged, shaped by their very different environments and the resources available to them.

The pre-Columbian cultures

In the absence of written records, archeologists have had to piece together information about Chile's **pre-Columbian cultures** from what these groups have left behind, principally funerary offerings found in burial sites and domestic objects left in former dwelling places. The strata in which the remains are buried (plus the use of radiocarbon dating) indicate the chronology in which these developments took place. However, variations in Chile's geography from north to south present unequal conditions for the preservation of artefacts and have led to a far greater knowledge of the cultures of the north than of the south.

El Norte Grande

More is known about the pre-Columbian cultures of Chile's Norte Grande – the Far North – than of any other part of the country. The extreme dryness of the Atacama Desert preserved archeological remains for thousands of years. One of the earliest groups of people to leave its mark was the **Chinchorro culture**, a collection of nomadic fishing communities that lived along the desert coast some 8000 years ago. By 5000 BC, the Chinchorro had developed the practice of **mummifying their dead** (see box, p.243) – two thousand years earlier than the Egyptians. Their technique, which involved removing internal organs and tissues and replacing them with vegetable fibres and mud, survived for 4000 years and is the oldest known in the world.

By around 500 BC, life in El Norte Grande was based largely on agriculture, supplemented by fishing in the coastal areas, and herding llamas and alpacas in the Andean highlands. Although vast tracts of the region are taken up by barren desert, a number of oases provided fertile land where agricultural communities were able to dedicate themselves to the cultivation of maize, beans, squash, chillies and potatoes. They lived in permanent dwellings, usually consisting of circular huts surrounding a shared patio, and often with a cemetery nearby.

Among the most important (and longest-lasting) of these early agricultural groups was the **San Pedro culture** (also known as the Atacameño culture), which settled along the salt-flat oases around San Pedro de Atacama around 500 BC. They produced ceramics, textiles, and objects in copper and stone, along with delicately carved wooden snuff tablets and tubes used for inhaling hallucinogenic substances – a custom probably introduced by the **Tihuanaco culture** around 300 AD. This latter was a powerful religious state based near the southern shores of Lake Titicaca in present-day Bolivia, and its influence extended over most of northern Chile and much of Peru for many centuries. The Tihuanaco impact was most visible in the spread of its ceramics and textiles, often decorated with images of cats, condors and snakes, which probably had religious significance. The Tihuanaco also fostered an active trading system, encouraging the exchange of goods between regions, bringing about increased social stratification, with those at the top controlling the commercial traffic.

Sometime between 900 and 1200 AD, the Tihuanaco culture declined and collapsed, for reasons unknown today. The regional cultures of the Norte Grande were then free to reassert their individual authority and identity, expressing their independence with a series of *pukarás* (fortresses) dotted around the altiplano. This period of *desarrollo regional* ("regional development"), as it is known, was halted only by the arrival of the Inca in the late fifteenth century.

El Norte Chico

Around 300 AD, when the peoples of the Norte Grande had been living in fixed agricultural communities for several centuries, those of the Norte Chico were just beginning to abandon their lives of hunting and gathering, and turn to cattle herding and farming. The resulting **El Molle culture** was composed of communities that settled along the river valleys between Copiapó and Illapel, where they developed a system of artificial irrigation to cultivate maize, beans, squash and possibly cotton. They also herded llamas, a practice recorded in numerous petroglyphs, and produced the first ceramics of the Norte Chico. Between 700 and 800 AD the El Molle culture declined and was replaced by a new cultural group known as **Las Animas**, which probably originated in the Argentine highlands. The changes introduced by this culture included rapid developments in metalworking; new, more decorative, styles of pottery; and – most curiously – the custom of ritual sacrifice of llamas.

Towards 1000 AD an important **Diaguita culture** appeared in the Norte Chico, dominating the region over the next five centuries until the Spanish invasion. The Diaguita tended to live in large villages along the river valleys, presided over by a chief and a shaman. Each valley was divided into two sections: a "lower" section, towards the coast, which was ruled by one chief, and a "higher" section, towards the mountains, ruled by another. Their economy was based on agriculture, herding, mining and metalworking, and was supplemented by fishing on the coast, aided by the invention of inflated sealskin rafts. The Diaguita's greatest achievement, however, was their outstandingly fine pottery, characterized by intricate white, black and red geometric patterns.

Central Chile

The first agricultural groups to settle in central Chile were the **El Bato** and **Llolleo** peoples, from around 300 AD. The El Bato group occupied the zone between the Río Choapa (near Illapel) and the Río Maipo (south of Santiago); its highly polished monochrome pottery indicates that it was strongly influenced by the El Molle culture from the Norte Chico. The Llolleo settlements were spread along the coastal plains between the Río Aconcagua (just north of Santiago) and the Río Maule (near Talca). One of the most striking characteristics of this culture was their custom of burying their dead under their own houses, with small children buried in clay urns.

Later, around 900 AD, the Aconcagua emerged as the dominant culture in Central Chile; these people lived in houses made of branches and mud and dedicated themselves to growing beans, maize, squash and potatoes; they also developed far more specialized ceramics than had previously existed in the region.

Araucania

While relatively little is known about the development of the cultures of the south of Chile, owing to a paucity of archeological remains, it's generally agreed that the first group to adopt cultivation was the **Pitrén culture**, around 600 AD. This comprised small family groups spread between the Bío Bío and Lago Llanquihue, where they grew maize and potatoes on a small scale, as well as hunting and gathering. They also produced ceramics, often decorated with zoomorphic and anthropomorphic images, which they usually buried with their dead.

Around 1000 AD a new community, known as **El Vergel**, emerged in the region between Angol and Temuco. Its economy combined hunting and gathering with the cultivation of potatoes, maize, beans and squash, and it is likely that its people were the first to domesticate guanacos. Other practices these people brought to the region included burying their dead in ceramic urns, which they decorated with red and white paint. They also developed a very beautiful style of pottery, now known as Valdivia pottery, characterized by parallel zigzag lines and shaded triangles.

Sometime in the fourteenth century a group of nomadic hunters called the *moluche* ("people of war") arrived from Argentina and occupied the land between the Itata and Toltén rivers. They absorbed the existing Pitrén and El Vergel cultures to form a new entity called **Mapuche** ("people of the land"). While engaging in fishing, hunting and gathering, their lifestyle was based principally on herding and farming – labour was divided between the sexes, with men responsible for preparing the fields, and women for sowing and harvesting. The basic social unit was the family clan, or "lov", which were independent from each other and autonomous. Its isolation meant the Mapuche culture didn't develop any further until forced to unite in the face of the Spanish invasion.

The far south

The narrow channels, fjords, impenetrable jungles and wild steppes of the far south have never encouraged communities to settle in one place. Accordingly, the peoples that inhabited this region led a more primitive lifestyle than those further north – they could not adopt agriculture as their main economy, and so maintained their tradition of hunting and fishing in nomadic groups. Groups like the **Selk'nam** and the **Tehuelche** hunted guanaco and rhea on the Patagonian steppes, and lived in temporary wigwam-like structures covered in guanaco skins. The **Yámana** and **Chono** people hunted seals, otters, birds and gathered shellfish in their canoes, constantly moving from place to place. None of the Patagonian or Fuegian groups produced ceramics, manufacturing instead bows, arrows, lassos, baskets and warm skin capes. Their understanding of the world was rich in mythology and symbolism – the Selk'nam, for instance, believed that many birds and animals were spirits that had once been human; they also practised elaborate initiation rites marking the passage from boyhood into manhood, involving physical tests and secret ceremonies. Unlike the other native peoples of Chile, these groups were never incorporated into Spanish colonial society, and their lifestyles remained virtually unchanged until the twentieth century, when the clash with seal hunters and sheep farmers led to their disappearance.

The Inca conquest

While the native peoples of Chile were developing relatively simple communities based on agriculture, herding and fishing, a great civilization was emerging further to the north – that of the **Inca**. This people arrived in Cusco around 1200 AD and by the fifteenth century had developed a sophisticated and highly organized society that boasted palaces, temples and fortresses of great architectural sophistication. In 1463, the Inca emperor, Pachacuti, initiated a period of massive **expansion** that saw the conquest of lands stretching north to modern-day Quito and south as far as the Río Maule in Chile, where its progress was halted by the fierce resistance of the Mapuche.

The impact of the Inca in Chile was considerable: they constructed a breathtaking network of roads connecting the conquered lands to the capital of the empire in Cusco (later very useful to the Spanish conquistadors), and forced the subjugated peoples to pay tribute to the Inca ruler and to use **Quechua** as their official language. While the Inca tolerated indigenous cults, they required their subjects also to adopt the **cult of the sun**, a central tenet of the Inca religion. Sun worship usually took place at altars built on high mountain peaks where the sun's first rays were received; it sometimes involved human sacrifice, but more commonly animals or objects like silver figurines were offered as substitutes. Remains of Inca worship sites have been found on numerous mountains in Chile, the most famous being Cerro El Plomo, near Santiago, where the frozen body of a small child, undoubtedly offered as a sacrifice, was discovered in 1954. The Inca occupation of Chile spanned a relatively short period of time – about seventy years in the Norte Grande and perhaps just thirty in Central Chile. It was interrupted first by civil war in Cusco, caused by the struggle between two rivals over succession to the throne. Then, in 1532, the Spanish arrived in Peru, marking the beginning of the end of the Inca empire.

The Spanish conquest

It was while seeking a westward route to Asia across the Atlantic that **Christopher Columbus** inadvertently "discovered" the Americas in 1492. His patron, Queen Isabella of Spain, supported him on two further expeditions, and sent settlers to colonize the Caribbean island of Hispaniola (site of today's Haiti and Dominican Republic). It gradually became apparent that the islands were not part of Asia, and that a giant landmass – indeed a whole continent – separated them from the East. After colonizing several other islands, the explorers and adventurers, backed by the Spanish Crown, turned their attention to the mainland, and the period of conquest began in earnest. In 1521 **Hernán Cortés** defeated the great **Aztec Empire** in Mexico and then in 1524 **Francisco Pizarro** and his partner **Diego de Almagro** set out to find the rich empire they had been told lay further south. After several failed attempts, they finally landed on the coast of **Peru** in 1532, where they found the great **Inca Empire** racked by civil war. Pizarro speedily conquered the empire, aided by advanced military weapons and tactics, the high morale of his men, their frenzied desire for gold and glory and, most significantly, the devastating effect of Old World diseases on the indigenous population. Within a few years, Peru was firmly in Spanish hands.

Diego de Almagro was entrusted with the mission of carrying the conquest further south to the region named **Chile**, spoken of by the Peruvian natives as a land rich in gold and silver. In 1535, Almagro and his four hundred men set off from Cusco and followed an Inca road down the spine of the Andes as far as the Aconcagua Valley, suffering extreme deprivation and hardship along the way. To make matters worse, the conquistador found none of the riches the Peruvians had spoken of. Bitterly disappointed, Almagro returned to Cusco, where his deteriorating relations with Pizarro led to armed combat and death at the hands of Pizarro's brothers.

Three years later, **Pedro de Valdivia** (one of Pizarro's most trusted officers) was granted licencse to colonize Chile. Owing to its lack of gold and the miseries of the first expedition, Chile was not an attractive destination, and so it was with just ten compatriots, a group of native porters and his mistress, Inés Suarez, that Valdivia set off from Cusco in 1540. Almost a year later, having picked up 150 extra men en route, Valdivia reached the Río Mapocho in the Aconcagua Valley, where he founded **Santiago de la Nueva Extremadura** on

February 12, 1541. The new "city" was hastily put together, with all the trappings of a colonial capital, including church, prison, court and *cabildo* (town council), which elected Valdivia as governor. It was a humble affair, regularly attacked and destroyed by local Picunche, but the new colonists were determined to stay and did not return to Peru.

Over the next decade, Valdivia attempted to expand the colony, founding the cities of **La Serena** in the north in 1544 and **Concepción** in the south in 1550, followed by a handful of other centres in the south. It was here that the Spaniards faced the fierce resistance of the **Mapuche** (known by the Spanish as the Araucanians), who successfully prevented the spread of colonization south of the Bío Bío River, which became known as **La Frontera**. It was in a confrontation with the Mapuche that Valdivia met his death in 1553, at the hands of the famous chief **Lautaro**. The details of Valdivia's execution are believed to be particularly grisly – some versions claim he was forced to swallow molten gold, others that he was lanced to death by a crowd of warriors, one of whom sliced through his breast and ripped out his heart.

In the panic caused by Valdivia's death, the southern colonists retreated to Santiago, leaving only Concepción as a garrison outpost, occupied mainly by soldiers guarding La Frontera. A new governor – Don García Hurtado de Mendoza – was dispatched from Peru, and by the time his term of office ended, in 1561, the natives in the central region had been subjugated and colonization was effectively complete.

Colonial society

The new colony was a marginal, isolated and unprofitable addition to Spain's empire in the Americas, which revolved around the viceroyalties of Mexico and Peru. The need to maintain a standing army to guard La Frontera, and the absence of large quantities of precious metals to fund it, meant that Chile ran at a deficit for most of the colonial period. Administratively, it was designated a "**captaincy-general**", ruled by a governor with the help of an *audiencia* (a high court, whose function included advising the governor). All high officials were sent from Spain as representatives of the king, whose authority was absolute, and whose instructions were communicated via the *Consejo de Indias* (Council of the Indies). Chile, however, received little attention and, enclosed within the mighty barriers of the Atacama desert and Andean cordillera, was more or less left to its own devices.

Growth was very slow, amounting to no more than five thousand settlers by 1600. Most of these lived from the farming of land handed out by the governor in grants known as **mercedes de tierra**, spreading over the valleys near Santiago and in the Central Valley. At the same time, large "grants" of indigenous people were given to the colonists in what was known as the **encomienda** system – the *encomienda* being the group of natives allocated to an *encomendero*. In theory, the *encomenderos* were supposed to look after the wellbeing of their charges and convert them to Christianity in exchange for tribute (by means of work) offered to the Spanish Crown. In reality, the system simply provided the colonists with a large slave workforce that they could treat however they pleased, which was often appallingly. From the very beginning, then, the *mercedes de tierra* and *encomiendas* established a pattern that was to dominate Chile's rural society until modern times: namely, large estates owned by seignorial landlords at the head of a dependent, disempowered workforce.

During the **seventeenth century** this pattern became more clearly defined with the emergence and economic dominance of the **hacienda**. Enclosed within thick, protective walls, haciendas were self-sufficient, self-contained entities, whose buildings – arranged around numerous courtyards – comprised workshops, wine *bodegas*, dairies, a chapel and the *casa patronal*, the landowner's home. Initially the workforce was provided by *encomiendas*, but, with tragic inevitability, the indigenous population rapidly decreased through exposure to Old World diseases. In its place there sprang up a new generation of **mestizos**, the result of miscegenation between the Spanish colonists (almost exclusively male in the early years) and indigenous women.

In time, a more or less homogeneous *mestizo* population came to make up the bulk of the Chilean workforce, presided over by a ruling, landowning elite made up of **peninsulares** (Spaniards born in Spain) and **criollos** (those of Spanish blood born in the colony). Most *mestizos* were incorporated into the haciendas either as peons or as **inquilinos** – labourers allowed to farm a small plot of land in return for year-round service (a practice that continued until the twentieth century). The main activities on the haciendas were livestock raising and the cultivation of cereals and fruit. Production was healthy but never reached particularly high levels, owing to Spanish trading restrictions, which prevented the colonies from trading freely with each other or with Spain.

Along with the haciendas, the other main shaping force in Chilean society was the **Catholic Church**. From the colony's earliest days, missionaries from most orders poured into Chile and embarked on a zealous programme of conversion in the farthest flung corners of the territory, erecting chapels and crosses wherever they went. Their success was rapid and set the seal on the "pacification" of the Indians, who were less likely to cause trouble if they could be incorporated into the Hispanic culture and their sense of separate identity diminished. The Catholicism that emerged wasn't an altogether orthodox version, as many indigenous elements of worship – such as ritual dancing and sacrificial offerings – were incorporated into this new religion, and even now survive in Chile's more remote communities, especially in the north. Nonetheless, both *indígenas* and *mestizos* embraced the symbolic elements of the Catholic faith with enthusiasm, and several cults sprang up around supposedly miraculous icons, such as the **Cristo de Mayo** in Santiago, believed to have bled real blood after an earthquake in 1647.

The most influential element of the Church was the **Jesuit order** (Compañía de Jesús), which arrived in Chile in 1593 and quickly established itself as one of the colony's largest landowners. In a paternalistic arrangement, the Jesuits gathered hundreds of indigenous families to their missions, where they were fed, clothed, converted, taught Spanish and instructed in many skills from weaving to glass manufacturing. As a result, the order's numerous workshops were the most productive and profitable in the country, as was the case throughout Spanish America – until the Jesuits were suddenly expelled from the Spanish Empire in 1767, when the Crown was persuaded that they had become too powerful to tolerate.

The first half of the **eighteenth century** saw little real advance in Chile's development. Patterns that had been established earlier on were simply reinforced: the *mestizo* population grew, and the dominance of the great landed estates (known as *latifundia*) was bolstered by the creation of **mayorazgos**, a system of entailment that allowed (at a price) the wealthiest landowners to pass on their property without having to divide it among their heirs. The bulk of the population was rural and attached to the estates, principally spread between the Aconcagua and the Maule valleys, with only a very limited urban population outside of Santiago.

Things did change noticeably, however, with the reign of **Charles III**, from 1759 to 1788. The most progressive of the Bourbon monarchs (who had replaced the Habsburg dynasty in Spain in 1700), the king set about improving the management of the American colonies and increasing their productivity, so as to augment revenues. Among his reforms was the relaxation of the stifling trade restrictions that had hampered economic growth throughout much of Spanish America. Suddenly, the colonies were able to trade freely with each other and with Spain. There was no overnight miracle, but Chilean trade did expand considerably, particularly with neighbouring Río de la Plata (future Argentina).

At the same time, imports soared, and the need to pay for them in gold or silver stimulated a small **mining boom** in the Norte Chico. Settlements sprang up around the mining centres, and some, such as Copiapó, Vallenar and Illapel, were granted official city status. All in all, there was an emerging spirit of change and progress, which gave a sense of empowerment to Chile's *criollos*, who had always been barred from the highest colonial offices. But while Chile's commercial horizons were widening, the king's administrative shake-ups – which involved sending a number of *intendants* to the colonies to tighten up administration and eradicate abuses of local power – were experienced as unwanted interference. The resulting tension would soon find a more focused channel.

The struggle for independence

Chile entered the **nineteenth century** with a burgeoning sense of its own identity. The *criollo* elite, while fiercely loyal to the Spanish king, was becoming increasingly alienated from the *peninsulares* dispatched from Spain to administer the colony, and the gap between them was widening with each successive generation. *Criollo* aspirations of playing a more active role in government (and thus of looking after their own interests, not just the Crown's) were given a sudden, unexpected opportunity for fulfilment when Napoleon invaded Spain in 1808 and deposed Ferdinand VII. **Local juntas** sprang up in Spain's main cities to organize resistance to Napoleon, and they were soon followed by a number of locally elected juntas in the American colonies. In Chile, over four hundred leading citizens gathered in Santiago on September 18, 1810, and elected a six-man **junta**, made up of Chileans. It must be stressed that the junta's initial objective was to "preserve the sovereignty of Ferdinand VII" in the absence of legitimate authority, and few entertained thoughts of independence at this stage. The junta did, however, go on to implement several far-reaching reforms: trade was liberalized; a Congress was elected; and the *real audiencia* (royal court) was replaced by a tribunal with Chilean judges.

Soon, a minority of *criollos* began to seek a far greater degree of autonomy for the colony, and whispers of independence grew. This small tide was given dramatic impetus in November 1811, when **José Miguel Carrera**, a member of one of the wealthiest and most influential *criollo* families in Chile, seized power, dissolving Congress and appointing himself head of a new, more radical, junta. His actions were swift and bold, and included the creation of a Chilean flag and the drafting of a provisional constitution that declared all rulings issued outside Chile to be illegitimate. Greatly alarmed, the viceroy of Peru – where the colonial machinery remained intact – sent troops in early 1813 down to the old-guard strongholds of Chiloé and Valdivia to prepare for an assault on Santiago. In response, Carrera charged down to confront them with Chilean troops (whose generals numbered one Bernardo O'Higgins, the son of a former viceroy of Peru), and war was effectively declared. Loyalties were now thrown sharply into focus with the **Royalists** on one side, made up of Spaniards and pro-Spanish Chileans, and the **Patriots** on the other, made up of *criollos* who supported some form of self-government.

Bernardo O'Higgins and José de San Martín

When Carrera's military leadership did not produce impressive results, the junta voted to replace him with **Bernardo O'Higgins**, who proved far more adept at holding off the Royalist forces. In July 1814, the power-hungry Carrera returned to Santiago and overthrew the government once more, reinstating himself at its head and causing considerable upheaval. In October of that year, Royalist troops, taking advantage of the chaos, began to advance on Santiago. O'Higgins mounted a desperate and heroic defence at Rancagua, attempting to hold them back, but Carrera's promised reinforcements never arrived, and the Patriots were overwhelmingly defeated. The "**Disaster of Rancagua**", as it is known, marked the end of La Patria Vieja (the name given to the fledgling independent nation) and its leaders fled across the Andean border to Mendoza in Argentina, as the Royalist troops marched triumphantly into Santiago.

The victory coincided with the defeat of Napoleon in Spain and the restoration of Ferdinand VII, who immediately set out to crack down on all insurgent elements in his American colonies. In Chile, some forty Patriot *criollos* were exiled to the Juan Fernández Islands, where they were to live in caves, and every reform instigated by the junta was reversed. The Spanish Crown's attempt to turn back the clock and revert to a centralized, interventionist colonial government was felt as repressive and authoritarian by *criollos* throughout the continent.

Just as the great general **Simón Bolívar** was preparing anti-Spanish campaigns in Venezuela that would liberate the northern half of the continent, **José de San Martín**, the Argentine general, was drawing plans for South American emancipation from his base in Mendoza, near the Chilean border. San Martín knew that independence could never be assured until the Spanish were ejected from their heartland in Peru, which he planned to achieve by first liberating Chile, from where he would launch a naval attack on Lima. To this end, San Martín was rigorously recruiting and training an army – known as the **Army of the Andes** – whose numbers were considerably increased by the Chilean Patriots who fled across the border after their defeat at Rancagua. With O'Higgins in command of the Chilean division, San Martín's army scaled the cordillera over four different passes in February 1817. On the twelfth, Patriot forces surprised the Spaniards and defeated them at the Battle of Chacabuco, just north of Santiago. The Royalists fled to the south, and the Patriots entered the capital in triumph. Fighting continued after Royalist reinforcements were sent from Peru, but when San Martín inflicted devastating losses on their army at the Battle of Maipú in April 1818, the Patriot victory was complete, setting the final seal on Chilean independence. Leadership of the new country was offered to San Martín, but he declined – instead, the job went to Bernardo O'Higgins, who was elected Supreme Director by an assembly of Chile's leading *criollos*.

O'Higgins' immediate task was to put together a national navy with which to clear the southern coast of remaining Royalist troublemakers and launch the seaborne attack on Peru. A flotilla was equipped and placed under the command of a British admiral, **Lord Thomas Cochrane**, who successfully captured

Callao, the port of Lima, in 1820. With the colonial nerve centre effectively toppled, the days of the Spanish Empire in the Americas were numbered. Turning his attention from liberation to government, however, O'Higgins was confronted with a whole set of new problems, not least the near bankruptcy caused by crippling war costs. Resentment at the stiff taxes imposed to recoup these costs caused widespread discontent, and after five years of difficult rule O'Higgins was forced to step down. The former hero exiled himself in Peru, where he remained until his death in 1842, leaving the new republic of Chile with the challenge of building itself into a nation.

The early republic

The transition from colony to republic was not smooth. In its first thirteen years of independence, Chile got through five constitutions and eleven changes of government, marked by continual tussles between **Liberal** and **Conservative** factions. Then, in 1829, the Conservatives, with the support of the army, imposed an authoritarian-style government that ushered in a long period of political stability, making Chile the envy of Latin America. The chief architect of the regime was **Diego Portales**, who never stood for presidency, preferring to run the show from various cabinet posts. Convinced that Chile could only move forward under a strong, centralist government able to maintain rigorous order, Portales designed, in 1833, the **Constitution** that was to underpin Chilean government for 92 years. It granted enormous powers to the president, allowing him, for instance, to veto any legislation passed by Congress, and protecting him from impeachment until his term of office had expired (two five-year terms were allowed). Portales was not, however, without his detractors, and in 1837, in protest at the government's invasion of Peru (which had been forcibly annexed by the Bolivian president), he was brutally gunned down by political opponents. This atrocity led to increased support for the government, which went on to defeat the Peru-Bolivia Confederation – to the great pride of Chilean citizens.

The growing self-confidence of the nation, added to the political and social stability within it, created conditions that were favourable to growth. Between the 1830s and 1870s international trade took off rapidly, with hugely increased wheat exports fuelled by the Californian and Australian gold rushes, and, more significantly, **a silver- and copper-mining boom** in the Norte Chico. At the same time, advances in technology and communications saw railways, roads, steamships and telegraphs opening up the country. Its populated territory expanded, too: a government programme encouraged Europeans to come over and settle the lakeland region of the south, which was duly cleared and farmed by some four thousand German immigrants. Meanwhile, Santiago and Valparaíso were being transformed – with avenues, parks, palaces and mansions, and an ever-expanding population. Only the countryside in the Central Valley heartland showed no real change, dominated as it was by haciendas whose owners frequently neglected their estates in favour of other business interests.

In time, the nation began to tire of the authoritarian model of government established by Portales, and the influence of Liberal politics began to gain ground. In 1871 the election of **Federico Errázuriz Zañartu** as president marked the beginning of twenty years of Liberal government. Many of the Liberals' reforms were aimed at reducing the undiminished power of the

Church: they legalized free worship in private places; they introduced civil cemeteries, where persons of any faith could be buried; and they instituted civil marriages and registries. The Liberals also went some way towards reducing the individual power of the president, and giving Congress a stronger role in government. The breath of fresh air and sense of optimism produced by these reforms suffered a deathblow, however, when a world recession between 1876 and 1878 sent copper and silver prices tumbling and brought wheat exports to a virtual halt, plunging Chile into economic crisis.

The War of the Pacific

Rescue was at hand in what at first appeared to be yet another calamitous situation. Ever since the 1860s, when two enterprising Chileans started exploiting the vast nitrate deposits of the Atacama desert, Chilean capital and labour had dominated the region's growing **nitrate** industry (see box, p.229). Most activity took place on the pampas around Antofagasta, which Chile had formally acknowledged as Bolivian territory in 1874 – following lengthy border disputes – in exchange for an assurance from Bolivia that export tariffs would not be raised for 25 years. Many of Chile's most prominent politicians had shares in the nitrate companies, so when Bolivia flouted its agreement by raising export taxes in 1878 – directly hitting shareholders' pockets – they were up in arms, and determined to take action.

With tension mounting, Chilean troops invaded Antofagasta in February 1879 and soon took control of the surrounding coastal strip. Within two weeks Chile and Bolivia were at war, with Peru drawn into the conflict on Bolivia's side within a couple of months. It soon became clear that success would depend on **naval supremacy** – Bolivia did not have a navy, leaving Peru and Chile pitted against each other, and fairly evenly matched. Following a series of early losses, Chile secured an overwhelming maritime victory in August 1879, when it captured Peru's principal warship, the *Huáscar*. The coast was now clear for the invasion of Peru's nitrate territories, and the emphasis shifted to land fighting. Casualties were heavy on both sides, but by June 1880 Chile had secured control of these areas with a resounding victory at El Morro, Arica.

With the nitrate fields theirs, the Chilean government would doubtless have been happy to bring the war to a close, but the public was clamouring for blood: it wanted Peru brought to its knees with the capture of Lima. In January 1881

Arturo Prat

Nothing has captured the Chilean imagination like the heroic, and tragic, efforts of **Arturo Prat** in the Battle of Iquique. On the morning of May 21, 1879, the *Esmeralda* – an old wooden boat under Prat's command – found itself under attack from Peruvian artillery on one side, and from the ironclad warship, the *Huáscar*, on the other. The two vessels could not have been more unevenly matched: the *Huáscar* boasted 300lb cannon, while those of the *Esmeralda* were only 40lb. When the *Huáscar* rammed the *Esmeralda*, Prat refused to give in, instead leaping aboard the enemy's vessel, sword in hand, determined to fight to the end. The gesture was futile, and Prat was killed on the warship's deck, but the commander's dignity and self-sacrifice have made him Chile's favourite national hero, in whose honour a thousand avenues and squares have been named.

Peru's humiliation was complete when Chilean troops occupied the capital. Peru was still not ready to give up, though, and the war dragged on for two more years, resulting in heavy human loss and exhausting both sides. Eventually, Peru accepted defeat, sealed by the **Treaty of Ancón** in October 1883 (an official truce with Bolivia was not signed until April the following year).

By the conclusion of the war, Chile had extended its territory by one-third, acquiring the Peruvian province of Tarapacá, and the Bolivian littoral (thus depriving Bolivia of sea access). Its new, nitrate-rich pampas yielded enormous, almost overnight wealth, refilling government coffers and restoring national confidence.

Civil War and the Parliamentary Republic

Unfettered by war, the nitrate industry began to boom in earnest, and by 1890 export taxes on nitrates were providing over fifty percent of government revenue. With national confidence running high and the economy in such good shape, the government's position looked unassailable. Within a short time, however, cracks began to appear in the constitutional framework, expressed by mounting tension between the legislature (Congress) and the executive branch (chiefly the president).

The conflict came to a dramatic head under the presidency of **José Manuel Balmaceda** (1886–1891), a Liberal but autocratic leader who believed passionately in the president's right to run a strong executive branch – an approach jarringly at odds with the political trend of the previous couple of decades. One of the unifying objectives of the various Liberal parties was the elimination of electoral intervention, and when Balmaceda was seen to influence Congressional elections in 1886, many Liberals were outraged and withdrew their support. Equally polarizing was the president's determination to insist on his right to pick and choose his cabinet, without the approval of Congress – whose response was to refuse to pass legislation authorizing the following year's budget until Balmaceda agreed to appoint a cabinet in which they had confidence.

Neither side would give way, and as the deadline for budget approval drew close, it became obvious that Balmaceda would either have to give in to Congress's demands, or act against the Constitution. When he chose the latter option, declaring that he would carry the 1890 budget through to 1891, Congress revolted, propelling the two sides into war. Balmaceda held the army's support, while Congress secured the backing of the navy. Operating out of Iquique, where they established a junta, Congress was able to use nitrate funds to recruit and train an army. In August that year, its troops landed near Valparaíso, where they defeated Balmaceda's army in two long, bloody battles. The president, whose refusal to give in was absolute, fled to the Argentine embassy, where he wrote poignant farewell notes to his family and friends before shooting himself in the head.

The authoritarian model of government established by Diego Portales in the 1830s, already undermined over the previous two decades, had now collapsed. Taking its place was a system – dubbed the **Parliamentary Republic** – based on an all-powerful legislature and an extremely weak executive. Now it was Congress who imposed cabinets on the president, not the other way round, with frequent clashes and constantly shifting allegiances seeing cabinets formed and dissolved with breathtaking frequency – between 1891 and 1915 the government got through more than sixty ministries. This chronic instability seriously hampered government action, although, ironically, the one arena where great progress was made was the public works programme vigorously promoted by Balmaceda, which saw rapid construction of state railways, roads, bridges, schools, hospitals, prisons and town halls.

The advent of industrialization

All this was taking place against a background of momentous social and economic change that the government, bound up with its continual infighting, seemed scarcely aware of. One of the by-products of the nitrate industry was increased **industrialization** elsewhere in Chile, as manufacturing stepped up to service increased production in the north. This, combined with the growth of railways, coal mining, education, construction and banking, saw a period of rapid **social diversification**. A new group of merchants, managers, bureaucrats and teachers formed an emerging middle class, while the increasingly urban workforce – usually living in dire poverty – formed a new working class more visible than its counterpart on the large rural estates.

It was in the nitrate fields of the north that an embryonic **labour movement** began to take root, as workers protested against the appalling conditions they were forced to live and work in. With no political representation to voice these grievances, **strikes** became the main form of protest, spreading from the mining cities of the north to the docks of Valparaíso. The government's heavy-handed attempts to suppress the strikes – reaching a peak of brutality when almost two hundred men, women and children were shot dead in Iquique, in 1907 – were symptomatic of its inability to deal with the social changes taking place in the country. When the nitrate industry entered a rapid decline with the outbreak of World War I in 1914, leaving thousands of workers unemployed and causing inflation to soar, Chile's domestic situation deteriorated further.

1920–1970

The first leader committed to dealing with the republic's mounting social problems was **Arturo Alessandri**, elected in 1920 on the strength of an ambitious reform programme. The weakness of his position, however, in the face of an all-powerful and obstructive Congress, prevented him from putting any of his plans into action, and after four years hardly anything had been achieved. Then, in 1924, a strange set of events was set in motion when an army junta – frustrated by the lack of government action – forced the cabinet to resign and had Alessandri appoint military men to key cabinet positions. The president appeared quite willing to accommodate the junta, which used its muscle to ensure that Congress swiftly passed a series of social reform laws, including legislation to protect workers' rights. After several months, however, the relationship between the president and his military cabinet began to unravel and Alessandri fled to Argentina in exile.

More drama was to follow when, on January 23, 1925, a rival junta led by Colonel **Carlos Ibañez** staged a coup, deposed the government and invited Alessandri to return to Chile to complete his term of office. With Ibañez's weight behind him, Alessandri set about redrafting the Constitution, with the aim of restoring authority to the president and reducing the power of Congress.

This was achieved with the **Constitution of 1925**, which represented a radical departure from the one of 1833, incorporating protective welfare measures among other reforms. Despite this victory, however, tensions between Ibañez and Alessandri led to the president's resignation. The way was now clear for the military strongman, Ibañez, to get himself elected as president in May 1927.

Ibañez's presidency was a curious contradiction, at once highly autocratic, with severe restrictions on freedom of expression, and refreshingly progressive, ushering in a series of badly needed reforms promoting agriculture, industry and education. His early years were successful, bringing about improvements in living standards across all sections of society, and stimulating national prosperity. But when the Wall Street crash of 1929 sparked off a worldwide Depression, Chile's economy collapsed virtually overnight, producing deep social unrest. Faced with a wave of street demonstrations and strikes, Ibañez was forced to resign in July 1931. The task of restoring stability to the nation fell to the old populist, Alessandri, who was re-elected in 1932.

Military interference in government affairs was now at an end (for a few decades, at least), and the country settled down to a period of orderly political evolution, no longer held back by a weak executive. What emerged was a highly diverse multi-party system embracing a wide spectrum of political persuasions. After 1938, the government was dominated by the **Radical Party**, a centre-right group principally representing the middle classes. Radical presidents such as Pedro Aguirre Cerda, Juan Antonio Ríos and Gabriel González Videla took an active role in regenerating Chile's economy, investing in state-sponsored steelworks, copper refineries, fisheries and power supplies. In the 1950s, left-wing groups gained considerable ground as the voting franchise widened, but old-guard landowners were able to counter this by controlling the votes of the thousands of peasants who depended on them for their survival, thus ensuring a firm swing back to the right. Nonetheless, it was by a very narrow margin that the socialist Salvador Allende was defeated by the Conservative Jorge Alessandri (son of Arturo) in the 1958 elections, causing widespread alarm among the wealthy elite. As the next election approached in 1964, the upper classes, with the discreet backing of the USA (still reeling from the shock of the Cuban missile crisis), threw all their efforts into securing the election of **Eduardo Frei**, the candidate of the rising young **Christian Democrat Party**.

In power, Frei turned out to be a good deal more progressive than his right-wing supporters could have imagined, initiating – to their horror – bold **agrarian reforms** that allowed the expropriation of all farms of more than 180 hectares. The other memorable achievement of the Frei administration was the "Chileanization" of the **copper industry**, which had replaced nitrates as the country's dominant source of revenue, and which was almost exclusively in the hands of North American corporations. Frei's policy gave the state a 51 percent stake in all the major copper mines, providing instant revenues to fund his social reform programme. These included the introduction of a minimum wage and impressive improvements in education, and made Frei's government popular with the working classes, though his reforms were unable to keep pace with the rush of expectations and demands. At the same time, Conservative groups became increasingly alarmed at the direction in which Frei was steering the country, prompting Liberals and Conservatives to join forces and form the new **National Party**, aimed at putting a check on reform. As Chile approached the 1970s, its population grew sharply polarized between those who clamoured for further social reform and greater representation of the working class, and those to whom this was anathema and to be reversed at all costs.

Salvador Allende and the Unidad Popular

On September 4, 1970, **Salvador Allende** was elected as Chile's first socialist president, heading a coalition of six left-wing parties, known as the **Unidad Popular** (UP). His majority, however, was tiny, and while half the country rejoiced, full of hopes for a better future, the other half feared a slide towards communism. Allende was passionately committed to improving the lot of the poorest sectors of society, whose appalling living conditions had shocked him when he had encountered them in his training as a doctor. His government pledged, among other things, to nationalize Chilean industries, to redistribute the nation's wealth, to increase popular participation in government, and to speed up agrarian reform, though there were disagreements as to how fast these changes should be made. Within a year, over eighty major companies had been nationalized, including the copper mines, which were expropriated without compensation. The following year, radical agrarian reform was enforced, with over sixty percent of irrigated land – including all haciendas with more than 80 hectares – taken into government hands for redistribution among the rural workforce. In one fell swoop, the *latifundia* system that had dominated rural Chile for more than four hundred years was irrevocably dismantled.

In the short term, Allende's government was both successful and popular, presiding as it did over a period of economic growth, rising wages and falling unemployment. But it wasn't long before strains began to be felt. For a start, government expenditure soon exceeded income by a huge margin, creating an enormous deficit. The looming economic crisis was dramatically accelerated when the world copper price fell by some 27 percent, cutting government revenue still further. Inflation began to rise uncontrollably, with wages unable to keep pace, and before long food shortages became commonplace.

Part of the UP's failure stemmed from the sharp divisions within the coalition, particularly between those who, like Allende, were in favour of a measured pace of reform, and those pressing for rapid, revolutionary change. The internal disunity led to a lack of coordination in implementing policy, and an irreversible slide towards political chaos. Making matters worse were the extremist far-left groups outside the government – notably the Revolutionary Left Movement, or **MIR** – which urged the workers to take reform into their own hands by seizing possession of the haciendas and factories where they worked.

Opposition to the government rose sharply during 1972, both from political parties outside the coalition (such as the Christian Democrats, who had previously supported Allende) and from widening sectors of the public. Panic was fuelled by the right-wing press and reinforced behind the scenes by the CIA, who, it later emerged, had been given a US$8 million budget with which to destabilize the Allende government. Strikes broke out across the country, culminating in the truckers' stoppage of October 1972, which virtually paralysed the economy. By 1973, with the country rocked by civil disorder, it was clear to all that the government could not survive for much longer.

The military coup

On the morning of September 11, 1973, tanks rolled through the capital and surrounded the presidential palace, La Moneda, marking the beginning of the **military coup** that Chile had been expecting for months. La Moneda was evacuated and Salvador Allende was offered a safe passage to exile. He refused, and in an emotional speech broadcast live on radio from the palace, vowed that he would never give up, and that he was ready to repay the loyalty of the Chilean people with his life. In this unique moment of history, citizens heard their president declare "I have faith in Chile and in its destiny. Other men will overcome this dark and bitter moment…You must go on, safe in the knowledge that sooner rather than later, the great avenues will open once more, and free men will march along them to create a better society…These are my last words, but I am sure that my sacrifice will not be in vain." Shortly afterwards, the signals were cut short, and jets began to drop their bombs. At the end of the day, Allende was found dead in the ruins of the palace, clutching a submachine gun, with which, it is widely believed, he had killed himself.

The Pinochet years

The coup was headed by a four-man junta of whom **General Augusto Pinochet**, chief of the army, quickly emerged as the dominant figure. Although Chile had seen military intervention in government affairs on two occasions in the past, these had been the exception to a highly constitutional norm. Nothing in the country's political history prepared its people for the brutality of this operation. In the days and weeks following the takeover, at least seven thousand people – journalists, politicians, socialists, trade union organizers and so on – were herded into the national football stadium, where many were executed, and still more were tortured. Curfews were imposed, the press was placed under the strict control of the junta, and military officers were sent in to take charge of factories, universities and other seats of socialist support. Before long, Congress had been dissolved, opposition parties and trade unions banned, and thousands of Chileans had fled the country.

General Pinochet saw his mission – and it was one in which he was supported by a sizeable portion of the population – as being that of rescuing Chile from the Left and, by extension, from the economic and political chaos into which it had undoubtedly fallen. To achieve this, he planned not to hand the country over to a right-wing political party of his approval, but to take it into his own hands and rule it himself. His key strategy was to be the adoption of a radical **free-market economy**, which involved a complete reversal of Allende's policies and a drastic restructuring of government and society. In this he was influenced by a group of Chilean economists known as "the Chicago boys", who had carried out postgraduate studies at the University of Chicago, where they'd come into contact with the monetarist theories of Milton Friedman. Almost immediately, price controls were abolished, government expenditure was slashed, most state-owned companies were privatized, import tariffs were reduced, and attempts were made to liberalize investment and attract foreign capital.

Such measures would take time to work, and called for a period of intense austerity. Sure enough, unemployment soared, wages plummeted, industrial output dropped, and the lower and middle classes became significantly poorer. At the same time, as Pinochet strove to reduce the role of the state in society, social welfare became increasingly neglected, particularly health and education. By the late 1970s, the economy was showing signs of growth and inflation was finally beginning to drop – from an annual rate of 900 percent in 1973 to 65 percent in 1977 and down to a respectable 9.5 percent in 1981.

Soon, there was talk of the Chilean "economic miracle" in international circles. The boom did not last, however, and in 1982, Chile found itself, along with much of Latin America, in the grip of a serious **debt crisis** which swept away the previous advances: the country was plunged into recession, with hundreds of private enterprises going bankrupt and unemployment rising to over 30 percent. It wasn't until the late 1980s that the economy recovered and Pinochet's free-market policies achieved the results he sought, with sustained growth, controlled inflation, booming, diversified exports and reduced unemployment. This prosperity, however, did not benefit all Chileans, and 49 percent of Chile's private wealth remained in the hands of 10 percent of its population.

Pinochet's free-market experiment had only been possible with the tools of ruthless repression at his disposal. His chief instrument was the secret police known as the **DINA**, which carried out surveillance on civilian (and even military) society, brutally silencing all opposition. Although the wholesale repression that followed the coup diminished in scale after the first year, regular "disappearances", torture and executions continued throughout Pinochet's regime. The regime was actively, if clandestinely, supported by the US, through the CIA, which even helped with the elimination of dissidents. In the absence of any organized political opposition, only the Catholic Church spoke out against the government's human rights violations, providing assistance and sanctuary to those who suffered, and vigilantly documenting all reports of abuse. Pinochet held the country in such a tight, personal grip – famously claiming "there is not a leaf that stirs in Chile without my knowing it" – that it doubtless became difficult for him to conceive of an end to his authority. The Constitution that he had drawn up in 1980 – ratified by a tightly controlled **plebiscite** – guaranteed him power until 1988, at which point the public would be given the chance to either accept military rule for another eight years, or else call for elections.

From the mid-1980s, **public protest** against Pinochet's regime began to be voiced, both in regular street demonstrations and with the reformation of political opposition parties (still officially banned). Open repression was stepped down as international attention became increasingly focused on the Chilean government's behaviour, and the US (a major source of foreign investment) made clear that it favoured a return to democracy. In this climate, the opposition parties were able to develop a united strategy in their efforts to oust the dictator. As the referendum in which Chile would decide whether or not to reject military rule drew closer, the opposition forces banded together to lead a highly professional and convincing "no" campaign. Pinochet remained convinced of his own victory, and with control of all media, and the intimidation tactics of a powerful police state at his disposal, it is easy to see why. But when the plebiscite took place on **October 5, 1988**, 55 percent of the nation voted "no" to continued military rule.

After sixteen years in power, the writing was on the wall for Pinochet's dictatorship. Much to everyone's surprise, he accepted his defeat without resistance and prepared to step down. But the handover system gave him one more year in power before democratic elections would be held – a year in which he hastily prepared **amnesty laws** that would protect both himself and the military from facing any charges of human rights abuses levied by the new government, and that would make his constitutional model extremely difficult to amend. A year later, on December 14, 1989, the Christian Democrat Patricio Aylwin, at the head of a seventeen-party centre-ground coalition called the **Concertación de los Partidos por la Democracia**, became Chile's first democratically elected president in seventeen years.

Return to democracy

The handover of power was smooth and handled with cautious goodwill on all sides, including the military. **Patricio Aylwin** was in the fortunate position of inheriting a robust economy and an optimistic public. Yet he faced serious challenges, including the need to channel substantial funds into those areas neglected by the previous regime while sustaining economic growth, and to address human rights abuses without antagonizing the military and endangering the transition to democracy.

Pinochet's **economic** model was barely contested, and was vigorously applied in an effort to promote "growth with equity" (the Concertación's electoral slogan). Foreign investment poured into the country and exports continued to rise, keeping economic growth at high levels and allowing Aylwin to divert resources into health and education. He was also felt to be making genuine efforts to alleviate the problems faced by the poorest members of society.

On the matter of **human rights** issues, progress was more difficult. One of the new government's first actions was the establishment of a **National Commission for Truth and Reconciliation** to investigate and document the abuses committed by the military regime. The commission's 1991 report confirmed 2279 executions, disappearances, and deaths caused by torture, and listed a further 641 suspected cases. But although compensation was paid to the families of the victims, the few attempts made to bring the perpetrators to justice were unsuccessful, owing to the protective **amnesty laws** passed by Pinochet before he relinquished power.

After a successful four-year term, the Concertación was in 1993 once again elected to power, headed by the Christian Democrat **Eduardo Frei** (son of the 1964–70 president). Frei's policies were essentially a continuation of his predecessors', with a firmer emphasis on tackling human rights issues and eradicating severe poverty. His success was mixed. His National Programme for Overcoming Poverty, established in 1994, was seen as inconsistent and ineffective. More progress was made on **human rights**, with courts finally willing to find ways of getting round Pinochet's amnesty laws. In 1995, there were breakthrough convictions of six former *carabineros*, two former DINA (secret police) agents, and most significantly, of General Manuel Contreras and Brigadier Pedro Espinoza, these last sentenced to life imprisonment in "Punta Peuco", a jail built purposely for high-profile human rights criminals.

In its last couple of years, Frei's government ran into unexpected problems. Firstly, the Asian economic crisis of 1998 had serious repercussions on the Chilean economy, hitting exports, foreign investment (much of which came from Southeast Asia) and the value of the peso, which has been sliding gradually ever since. At the same time, the unresolved tensions over lack of justice for Pinochet erupted afresh when the general retired from his position of commander-in-chief of the army in early 1998 but immediately took up a seat in Congress as life senator. Pinochet was dramatically thrust into the spotlight once more when he was arrested in a London hospital on October 16, 1998, following a request for his **extradition** to Spain to face charges of murder and torture. The arrest provoked strong reactions in Chile: families of Pinochet's victims rejoiced euphorically; supporters of the general were outraged, burning British flags in the streets; while the government, in a difficult position, denounced the arrest as an affront to national sovereignty and demanded Pinochet's immediate return to Chile – whereupon, they claimed, his alleged crimes would be dealt with in the Chilean courts.

After a protracted and complex legal battle, during which the British judiciary ruled in Pinochet's favour and against him, in April 1999 Britain's Home Secretary, **Jack Straw**, announced that proceedings could go ahead. They again got bogged down, this time over whether the former dictator was fit to stand trial, with the British minister holding the final decision.

The Lagos years

In December 1999, the first round of presidential elections left two front-runners neck and neck in the second round: the Concertación's candidate, socialist **Ricardo Lagos**, a former education minister under Aylwin who had famously voiced criticism of Pinochet in the late 1980s, and **Joaquín Lavín**, who had served under the general and was standing on a firmly right-wing platform. Lagos pulled off an eleventh-hour victory on January 16, 2000, beating his opponent narrowly – 51 percent to 49.

The **Pinochet affair** dogged the newly elected president and has repeatedly reared its ugly head since. Britain finally decided to send Pinochet back to Chile in early March 2000, just before Lagos was sworn in at La Moneda. There was an international outcry when he was welcomed back with pomp and circumstance by the armed forces, and Congress granted all former heads of state **lifelong immunity** from prosecution. Even Lagos expressed support for such a move, to quell any stirrings in the military. Yet the former dictator was stripped of his immunity in June and faced charges for kidnapping opponents before Christmas 2000. At the beginning of 2001 he was judged mentally fit for trial, and, at the end of January Chilean judge **Juan Guzmán** ordered Pinochet's house arrest. But within months the case fizzled out yet again, and in July 2001 all charges against Pinochet were dropped after a Santiago court decided he was, after all, unfit to stand trial. Nevertheless, like the former tyrant himself, the case would not lie down and die. Further appeals and counter appeals meant that the affair dragged on for one more year. Finally the country's Supreme Court ruled, in early July 2002, that Pinochet was indeed prevented from standing for trial on mental-health grounds. He responded by resigning as life senator from Chile's Congress and was reported as saying that he did so "with a clear conscience", unleashing a furore among his opponents.

Spectre-like, Pinochet returned to the fore amid a **financial scandal** in 2005. Though the ex-dictator had always claimed that, unlike many of his peers, his only interest was the wellbeing of his country and not of his pocket, it transpired that he and/or his relatives had creamed off tens of millions of dollars in murky wheeling and dealing and carefully stashed the laundered booty in US bank accounts, one of them at Riggs; cooperation with the US financial authorities revealed the existence of the funds, a very generous nest egg for his family. In February 2005, the Riggs Bank donated $8 million to a pension fund set up for the families of three thousand victims of human rights abuses under the general's regime. In June 2005 the courts decided that he was fit to stand trial to answer the corruption charges.

Human rights and the military regime continued to haunt the political arena. Several more cases resulted in prison sentences for violators, but the government controversially approved measures aimed at imposing a time limit on human rights investigations, which some claimed were dragging on excessively. In spectacular circumstances, former secret police chief **Manuel Contreras**, who had already served part of an earlier life sentence, was arrested in early 2005 on fresh charges – he allegedly tried to shoot the officers who went to his house to detain him.

In the meantime the highly popular Lagos implemented an ambitious programme based on reforming the State. Lagos was determined to continue with his predecessors' overhaul of two main areas of social policy: **health and education**. Universal free medical care is the eventual goal but hospitals and other services, mostly in a pitiful state after years of neglect, have been improved. After compulsory schooling, shortened to the bare minimum by Pinochet, was dramatically lengthened, plans to recruit more teachers, improve their training and raise their salaries have been implemented. **Divorce** was finally legalized in late 2004 (leaving only Malta and the Philippines divorce-free), despite opposition by the Church, which has said it will do all it can to obstruct the new, democratically enacted law – but abortion remains utterly taboo.

Lagos also tried to tackle the thorny issue of **indigenous peoples' rights**, handing back large tracts of land to the Mapuche and others early on in his presidency. This backfired somewhat, with emboldened *indígenas* demanding even more of their land back, resulting in some ugly clashes with the police in early 2002, when demonstrators tried to block the construction of a new road through land claimed by Mapuche; there have been several similar incidents in recent years.

International relations, in particular with the country's neighbours, were decidedly rocky as Lagos headed towards the end of his term of office. His dismissive remarks plus chauvinistic Chilean media coverage following the arrest of two young Chileans, accused of defacing an ancient wall in the Inca city of Cusco, did little to smooth relations with **Peru**, Chile's traditional rival to the north. Chile's refusal to negotiate a guaranteed ocean access for landlocked **Bolivia** further soured relations with another long-time foe. And **Argentina**'s decision to prioritize its domestic gas demand, at the risk of cutting supplies to Chile, increased trans-Andean tensions.

To the present day

Since March 2006, Chile has had a woman president, socialist **Michelle Bachelet**, elected by a comfortable margin in the second-round run-off on January 15 of that year. She had stood against charismatic businessman Sebastián Piñera, of the centre-right National Renewal Party, in the *balotaje* (decisive second round). Piñera, who is the billionaire owner of the TV channel Chilevisión, and president of LAN, the national airline, has been likened to Italy's Silvio Berlusconi – not least by Lavín supporters, furious at Piñera's decision to run and split the right-wing vote. Bachelet, a physician, went into exile in Australia and East Germany in the 1970s after her father, a moderate Air Force general, was assassinated under Pinochet. In her victory speech she said that a **feminine touch** was needed to smooth international relations and promised to work for greater friendship between Chile and its neighbours, particularly Argentina.

Her election as Chile's first female Head of State also makes her the first woman to be directly and democratically elected in South American history. Indeed, one of outgoing President Lagos' stated aims had been to reduce the acute **gender inequality** in the country, and he appointed Chile's first female ministers for defence (Bachelet herself) and foreign affairs (her erstwhile rival in the presidential race, Soledad Alvear). The number of women in the principal judicial bodies has also gone up while the House of Deputies had two woman Speakers at the beginning of the millennium.

Criticized during the campaign for her vague policies and indecision, Bachelet nevertheless started her presidency with a strong mandate, a supportive parliament and many expectations. She promised a new, participatory style of government that would continue pro-market economic policies begun under the dictatorship of Augusto Pinochet, but with an accent on empowering ordinary Chileans. The fact that she was detained and tortured, along with her mother, in the early Pinochet years before her family was allowed to leave the country, enhanced her popularity on the Left; but her **progressive stance** on delicate issues such as divorce, human rights and religion (she is a professed agnostic) and the fact that she is separated from her husband and did not marry the father of her third child put off many traditional voters even in her own camp. That said, she was staunchly opposed to abortion and gay marriage (but not to some kind of official recognition of same-sex couples).

Although Bachelet enjoyed 62 percent approval shortly after taking office, in little time, labour protests, social unrest from students complaining about the poor quality of public education and a botched overhaul of Santiago's transport caused her public standing to plummet. During the first two and a half years of her presidency, Chile's economy ticked along nicely, thanks largely to Asian demand delivering booming revenues for Chile's chief export, copper. But amid the **global financial crisis** that took hold in mid-2008, the price of copper halved in the space of four months. Bachelet is set to begin her final year in office burdened by the pressures of rising inflation, banks cutting back on credit and the devaluing of Chilean pensions hit hard by the fall in world stock markets.

As for **Pinochet**, once more passions were polarized over the general, this time following his death after a heart attack in December 2006, symbolically on international Human Rights' Day. On his death, he was under house arrest and facing trial over charges in Chilean courts relating to one financial enquiry and five human rights cases. In October of that year, an appeal court had dropped corruption charges brought against his wife and five children who had been accused of sending state funds illegally to foreign bank accounts in the US. They say that for Chileans there's no middle ground on Pinochet – they either love him or hate him. This never appeared so true than in the days following his death. While jubilant opponents danced in the centre of the capital, his supporters mourned outside the military hospital where he died, loving the man they insisted had saved the country from Marxism and put Chile on the path of strong economic growth. Bachelet refused to authorize the type of state funeral normally granted to former presidents, saying it would be "a violation of my conscience" to do so. Instead, he was allowed only military honours as a former head of the Chilean army. For many, there is still anger and frustration that the former dictator never faced trial for his crimes. Though it may be little solace, in the words of Uruguayan writer Mario Benedetti: "formal justice may remain incomplete, but history has judged him and condemned him."

In a country with fewer **women** in the workforce than anywhere else in Latin America, Bachelet promised to champion the woman's cause and, in her first year, delivered not only the breast-feeding law but also set up hundreds of nurseries and shelters for victims of domestic violence. By presidential decree, and to the disgust of the Catholic Church, she made the **morning-after pill** available free to girls as young as 14.

Bachelet aimed to focus foreign policy on improving **international relations** with Chile's neighbours. In a move seen as a chance to improve strained ties between Bolivia and Chile, Bachelet made a rare trip to **Bolivia** in 2007 for talks with President Evo Morales and the president of Brazil in La Paz. There they agreed to build a highway by 2009 that will link the Atlantic and Pacific coasts of South America from Santos in Brazil to Iquique in Chile, a plan that promises to be economically advantageous for all parties. However, though the countries might appear friendlier towards each other, the border dispute still rumbles on. The same old tensions continue to shape relations between Chile and **Argentina**, but, since the election of President Cristina Kirchner, a friend of Bachelet, diplomatic relations are better now than they have been for a long while. The two countries, though, have still not formally agreed on borders separating them. In 2007, during one of South America's coldest winters, Argentina cut supplies of natural gas along pipelines to Chile, a move that led inevitably to frostier relations between the two. Bachelet is keen to emphasize Chile's long-term energy option of diversifying its energy supplies thereby reducing future dependence on Argentina for fuel. Relations with **Peru** soured in 2008, when it filed a lawsuit at the International Court of Justice in a bid to settle the long-standing dispute over maritime boundaries.

With just over a year to go before the next **presidential election**, the main opposition to Bachelet's governing party, the right-wing Alliance for Chile coalition, gained ground in local elections. It won mayoral contests in a number of key cities so that, for the first time, the right has more mayors in office than the ruling coalition. Led by **Sebastián Piñera** – who narrowly lost to Bachelet in 2006 – the Alliance hopes to translate these gains into success in the next presidential poll. Bachelet's coalition party, the Concertación, has been in power since the return of democracy in 1990 and remains the largest bloc in Chilean politics. But, its seeming invincibility is under threat. With just a year before the next election, it is without an obvious candidate to stand for president. Under the constitution, Bachelet cannot seek a second successive term and her party faces a potentially damaging leadership battle over the coming year.

In contrast, the right-wing coalition has largely united behind Piñera. If he does win in 2009, it will mark the end of an era for Chile – the end of nearly two decades of moderate left-wing rule in which the country has emerged from the Pinochet years, healed some of the wounds of the past and re-established its democratic credentials. The billionaire businessman hailed the local election results as a "great triumph" and as evidence that Chileans are ready for a change. Only when Chileans go to the polls again in December 2009 will it become clear if he is right or not.

Landscape and the environment

One of South America's smaller countries, Chile is roughly the same size as France and Britain combined – but stretched over the equivalent distance of Vancouver to Panama. This sliver of land, on average just 180km across, spans 4350km from the desert of the north to the subantarctic ice-fields in the south, and encompasses almost every kind of natural habitat along the way.

Geography

Geographically, Chile is divided into a number of latitudinal **zones**, each of which shows clear differences in terms of climate, vegetation and fauna. These zones only tell part of the story, though, with Chile's three principal landforms – the Andes, the central depression and the coastal range – all having a significant impact on the local ecology. The **Andes**, in particular, straddles all of Chile's disparate regions. Characterized by precipitous slopes with ravines cut deep into the rock, at points the range acts as a great, impenetrable wall dividing Chile from neighbouring Argentina and Bolivia. Scores of **volcanoes**, many topping 6000m, line these borders, where episodic eruptions and seismic activity are everyday realities. The country's highest peak, Ojos del Salado (6893m), is also the world's highest active volcano; Aconcagua (6959m), the globe's tallest peak outside the Himalayas, lies a few kilometres over the Argentine border.

In the far north, the **Norte Grande** region stretches from the Peruvian border over 1000km south to the Copiapó river valley. Covering the central depression between the Andes and the coastal range lies the **Atacama Desert**, thought to be the driest place on earth. Surprisingly, the desert is unusually temperate, due to the moderating influence of the Humboldt Current, a cold-water sea current just off the coast. While thick fog banks, known as *camanchaca*, accumulate along the coast where the cold water meets the warm air, a high-pressure zone prevents the cloud from producing rain and moving inland.

A search for wildlife is a pretty fruitless activity in these barren northern wastes. The frustrated ornithologist A.W. Johnson remarked that the desert was "without doubt one of the most completely arid and utterly lifeless areas in the whole world". It's a very different story, however, up in the Andes bordering the Atacama, where a high plateau known as the **altiplano** is home to a diverse wildlife population and an otherworldly landscape of volcanoes, lakes and salt flats.

The semi-arid **Norte Chico**, bounded roughly by the Copiapó Valley and the Aconcagua Valley, just north of Santiago, forms a transitional zone, where the inhospitable northern desert gives way to scrubland and eventually forests further south, as precipitation levels increase. The heat of the sun here is tempered by air humidity, making the land suitable for irrigation farming. The crops of tobacco and cotton that predominated in the colonial era have since been replaced by more lucrative exotic fruits, such as papaya and *cheirimoya*.

Throughout the north mining has also long been prevalent, thanks to the high levels of nitrates, copper, silver and other minerals in the soil.

Beyond Santiago, the region known as the **Central Valley** extends south to the Bío Bío river. Mineral-rich earth coupled with warm dry summers and short humid winters have provided ideal conditions here for growing grapes, peaches, pears, plums, mangoes, melons and apricots. As the country's primary agricultural zone, as well as a major centre of industry, it is no surprise that this region is home to around eighty percent of the country's population, almost half based in the capital.

Towards the southern end of the Central Valley, forests signal a marked increase in precipitation levels. Systematic **afforestation**, begun over a hundred years ago in Arauco province, has seen the introduction of a variety of foreign trees, such as eucalyptus and Australian myrrh. No species has flourished as well as the radiata pine, however, which far exceeded the rate of development normal in its native California; concern is mounting that its success is damaging Chile's fragile endemic forest habitats.

In the **Lake District**, between Temuco and Puerto Montt, precipitation reaches 2300mm a year, allowing luxuriant native forests to predominate over the rolling foothills of the coastal range. To the east, azure lakes, remnants of the last glacial age, are backed by conical, snowcapped **volcanoes**. Amongst the many volcanoes still active, both Villarrica and Llaima have erupted ten times in the last hundred years. On May 2, 2008, the Chaitén volcano, situated further south on the mainland across from Chiloé, began erupting for the first time in nine thousand years. The Chilean government evacuated 4,200 residents from the nearby town of Chaitén and the surrounding area as a huge column of smoke and ash rose into the sky coating the land around the volcano and reaching into neighbouring Argentina.

Beyond Puerto Montt, the central depression submerges into the sea, while the tops of the coastal mountains nudge through the water in a mosaic of **islands** and **fjords**. It is here, in this splintered and remote region, that continental Chile finally runs out of dry land: the Carretera Austral, the highway that runs south from Puerto Montt, is cut short after 1000km by two massive ice fields, the largest in the southern hemisphere outside Antarctica. **Southern Patagonia** is a mostly inhospitable place, with continual westerly winds roaring off the sea and dumping up to seven metres of snow, sleet, hail and rain on the western slopes every year. Even so, the glaciated scenery, with its perfect U-shaped valleys and rugged mountains, has an indisputable grandeur. In stark contrast, the monotonous grasslands of the Patagonian pampa, which lies in the rain shadow on the eastern side of the Andes, describe the beginning of a quite different habitat.

Tierra del Fuego ("Land of Fire") is an archipelago separated from mainland Chile by the Magellan Strait. Mountains and forests dominate the south of the region, while the north hosts little more than windswept grasses. From Cape Horn, South America's southernmost point, Antarctica is a mere 1000km away.

Flora

Extraordinary diversity of altitude, latitude and precipitation inevitably leads to an extraordinary diversity of flora. Only humid tropical forest fails to feature in Chile's rich and varied ecology. The tropical area in the far north is stricken with aridity too severe to support most plant life, except at higher altitudes, where **xerophytes** ("dry growers"), such as **cacti**, begin to appear. Ninety percent of Chile's vascular plants are from the cactus family, many of them endemic and endangered. On the altiplano, **tough grasses** and **brush** associated with minimal rainfall support the herds of grazing alpaca.

Moving south towards Central Chile, where the climate is more balanced and water less scarce, **sclerophyllous** ("rigid leaf") shrubs and trees feature leathery leaves that help them retain water. As rainfall increases towards the south, these plants begin to blend with **temperate rainforests**. In the heavily populated areas of this central region, such woodlands have suffered widespread deforestation as land has been cleared for farming and housing, and only patches remain. In Parque Nacional La Campana near Santiago, for example, stands the last forest of endangered **Chilean palm** (*Jubaea chilensis*), sole reminder of a time when millions of the trees covered the area, favoured as they were for the flavour of their sap.

Further south the **temperate rainforests** have fared a little better, constituting almost a quarter of this type of habitat worldwide. Over 95 percent of the fifty tree species found here are endemic, including the **araucaria** (*Araucaria araucana*), known in English as the **monkey puzzle**, Chile's national tree, and rare **southern beeches** (*Nothofagus*) – principally *coïgue*, *ñire*, *raulí* and *lenga* – which vie for sunlight, towering up to 40m into the air to break clear of the canopy. The **alerce**, or **Chilean false larch** (*Fitzroya cupressoides*), a relative of the North American sequoia, takes several hundred years to reach maturity and can live for four thousand years, providing the loggers don't get there first. The tree is best seen in the areas around Puerto Montt.

In Chilean Patagonia, **evergreen beeches** (*Nothofagus betuloides*) grow in the sheltered areas bordering the great fields of ice, while their **deciduous** cousins *Nothofagus pumilio* and *antarctica* prefer the drier eastern flanks of the Andes. Where the canopy is broken, dazzling scarlet *embothrium*, yellow *berberis* bedecked with mauve berries, and deep-red *Pernettya* emblazon the ground. Rare **orchids** and pink **oxalis** interweave in a tapestry of colour. Such brilliant displays are impossible on the coastal Magellanic **moorland**, where high levels of precipitation drown all but the sphagnum **bog** communities and **dwarf shrubs**. Here, the wind-beaten **Magellanic gunnera** grows only a few centimetres high, a tiny fraction of what its relatives are capable of in the Valdivian rainforest. Meanwhile, the rain shadow effect on the eastern Patagonian steppe supports little more than coarse tussocks of *festuca* grasses.

Environmental Issues

The slow destruction of Chile's environment was set in motion by the Spanish in the sixteenth century, though it wasn't until the early twentieth century, with widespread settlement and increased industrialization, that the scale reached damaging levels. Today, although Chile has suffered less environmental degradation than most other countries with comparable resources, there are few habitats that have not been affected in some way by human activity, and it's debatable whether the government is prepared to prioritize future protection over financial exploitation.

There was little interest in environmental issues in Chile until large-scale disruption caused by the appalling **smog in Santiago**, considered by Greenpeace to be the third most polluted city in Latin America, mobilized public concern. Most years the capital's schools are suspended for days on end and people are warned to stay indoors as a dense cloud of toxic gases hangs over the capital, caught between the two surrounding mountain ranges. The problem is worsened in dry weather, when the concentration of contaminated air is not dissolved by rain. Pressure from the urban middle class has forced the government to introduce (many say weak) measures to lessen air pollution in Santiago and has encouraged politicians to include environmental elements to their policies.

The most important **new environmental law**, following a guarantee in the 1980 Constitution that all Chileans have "the right to live in an environment free of pollution", is the Environmental Act of 1994, which has standardized procedures for assessing environmental damage, while encouraging public involvement by allowing citizens to bring charges against violators, even if they have not been directly affected by them. One successful application of this new law occurred in 1997, when the Chilean Supreme Court overturned a government-approved project involving the logging for woodchips of centuries-old, endangered forests of native lenga, a cherry-like beech found in Tierra del Fuego.

Chile's precious **temperate rainforests** have been threatened for many years by intensive logging and the introduction of harmful foreign species, with large tracts razed in the free-for-all scramble to colonize remote areas. The worst damage occurred in the prewar years, but illegal clearance is still common today. The alerce, an evergreen with a life span of four thousand years, has been a target of international campaigning as it continues to be logged because of the high commercial value of its wood, despite a law passed in 1976 making it illegal to cut live alerces. Yet landowners burn the trees or strip their bark to kill them first, thus evading the hands of the law. Many thousands of hectares of alerce forest are wiped out in this manner every year.

Meanwhile in the central regions native trees have been wiped out to make space for the commercial planting of more profitable foreign species. In many areas the practice has left only islands of indigenous forest in an ocean of introduced eucalyptus and radiata pine. The result is genetic isolation of both flora and fauna, leaving many mammals with distinct ecological needs imprisoned in small pockets of native woodland. The few thin strips that connect such pockets are the only way for many species to maintain communication with the rest of their population. If these corridors are destroyed, countless endemic organisms face extinction.

In the north **mining** is a major cause of environmental concern. Chuquicamata, near Antofagasta, is the biggest open-pit copper mine in the world and continues to grow. Now visible from space, the giant pit has effectively swallowed up the town that grew with it, as 600,000 tons of rock are dug up every day, spewing arsenic-rich dust into the air. Workers at the mine and their families have now been relocated from Chuquicamata to nearby Calama. The plume from the smelting works carries 200km to San Pedro de Atacama, a pre-colonial village in the east. The country's mines consume vast quantities of water, often contaminating it in the process. In tandem with agricultural irrigation, reckless water usage is taking its toll on wildlife, as animals find the search for drinking places increasingly difficult. Even the human population has been put out, relying in some northern villages on an ingenious invention that turns fog into drinking water.

Overexploitation of the land and sea has brought further problems. Incompetent or negligent farming, either through overgrazing or the clearing of vegetation, has resulted in extensive **desertification**, particularly in the north. Meanwhile, careless practices in the fishing industry are upsetting the

Nature's footnote to the end of the millennium, the **1997–98 El Niño** wreaked havoc with global climate patterns and brought chaos to the world. In parts of Chile, Peru and Ecuador, floods and landslides engulfed people and animals, houses, farms and factories, while torrents swept away bridges, roads and railways. Elsewhere, severe droughts scorched the earth, drying up forests and bushland and creating the tinderbox conditions that sparked off raging fires. Clouds of poisonous smoke billowed into the atmosphere, affecting seventy million people in Southeast Asia, while millions of others risked starvation following widespread crop failure. As the Pacific countries affected by El Niño picked up the pieces, conservative estimates of the cost of reparation put it at around US$20 billion.

In Chile, **flooding** was the worst it had been for a decade, as 80,000 people were made homeless in June 1998 alone. The warm coastal water associated with El Niño drove fish stocks to cooler places, crippling the fishing industry and killing millions of marine animals. But while some watched their crops and livestock drown, the rains also filled irrigation basins that had been at a critically low level for years, and water surges saved the hydroelectric companies from having to ration their power output. In the Atacama Desert, freak rainfall woke up the barren soil, causing it to burst into blossom.

The El Niño phenomenon is no new thing. Records document such events over four hundred years ago, but it was only in the 1960s that the Norwegian meteorologist Jacob Bjerknes identified the processes that lead to such an event. He saw that the El Niño (meaning "the Little Boy" or "the Christ Child", a name given by Peruvian fishermen to the body of warm water that would arrive around Christmas) was intimately connected to extremes in the so-called **Southern Oscillation**, a feature where atmospheric pressure between the eastern equatorial Pacific and the Indo-Australian areas behaves as a seesaw, one rising as the other falls.

In "normal" years easterly trade winds blow west across the Pacific, pushing warm surface water towards Indonesia, Australia and the Philippines, where the water becomes about 8°C warmer and about 50cm higher than on the other side of the ocean. In the east, the displacement of the sea allows cold, nutrient-rich water, known as the Humboldt or Peru Current, to swell up from the depths along the coast of South America, providing food for countless marine and bird species.

An El Niño event occurs when the trade winds fall off and the layer of warm water in the west laps back across the ocean, warming up the east Pacific and cooling the west. Consequently, air temperatures across the Pacific begin to even out, tipping the balance of the atmospheric pressure seesaw, which further reduces the strength of the trade winds. Thus the process is enhanced, as warm water continues to build up in the eastern Pacific, bringing with it abnormal amounts of rainfall to coastal South America, while completely starving other areas of precipitation. The warm water also forces the cold Humboldt Current and its microorganisms to deeper levels, effectively removing a vital link in the marine food chain, killing innumerable fish, sea birds and mammals. Meanwhile, the upset in the Southern Oscillation disturbs weather systems all around the world, resulting in severe and unexpected weather.

Since 1980 or so, El Niño-Southern Oscillation (ENSO) events seem to have become stronger, longer and more frequent, leading many to suggest that human activity, such as the warming of the earth's atmosphere through the greenhouse effect, could well be having an influence. If this is true, failure to cut emissions of greenhouse gases may in the end cost the lives and livelihoods of millions of people across the world.

A relatively mild El Niño in early 2002 meant that while the ski season was one of the best in the last ten years, torrential rains in central Chile left fifty thousand people homeless and killed nine.

fragile balance of Chile's **marine life**. A leaked government report shows that some fish stocks were depleted by as much as 96 percent between 1985 and 1993.

On a global level, many believe human-induced climate change to be a leading cause of the **El Niño phenomenon**, which has badly damaged Chile's fisheries, agriculture and marine species (see box, p.517). Moreover, the expansion of the hole in the ozone layer over Antarctica has put many people, especially in Patagonia, on guard against the harmful ultraviolet rays that seep through it.

Chile has been more effective than most Latin American countries in its opposition to the damage brought about by the excesses of unfettered capitalism, and awareness of the delicacy of the country's habitats and its unique species is growing. The Lagos government seemed to take ecological issues very seriously. However, environmentalists continue to bemoan the lack of concerted pressure, claiming that many merely respond occasionally and emotionally to images churned out in the media rather than pushing consistently for action and reform.

Chilean music: Nueva Canción

C hile has produced a wide range of music genres, from cueca to bolero, but none has been so important and influential as **Nueva Canción**, the "New Song" movement that developed in Chile in the 1960s, along with parallel movements in Argentina, Uruguay and also Cuba. A music rooted in the guitar traditions of the troubadour, the songs could be love lyric or chronicle, lament or call to action, and, as such, they have played a part in Latin America's political and cultural struggles. It was brought to international attention, above all, through the lyrical songs of Chilean theatre director and singer-songwriter Víctor Jara, who was murdered for his art by Pinochet's thugs during the 1973 coup d'état, while groups like Inti Illimani were forced into exile. In an extract taken from the *Rough Guide to World Music*, Jan Fairley looks at the history and legacy of this music of "guitar as gun".

Pity the singer...

Pity the singer who doesn't risk his guitar and himself...who never knew that we were the seed that today is life.

Cuban Pablo Milanés *"Pobre del cantor"*

Nueva canción as a movement spans a period of over thirty years, from the early 1960s, when its musicians became part of the political struggle to bring about change and reform in their own countries. As a result of their activities, many of their number were arrested or forced into exile by dictatorships which through murder, torture and disappearance wiped out so much of a generation. The sense of a movement grew as the musicians involved met one another at festivals in Cuba, Nicaragua, Peru, Mexico, Argentina and Brazil, visited each other's countries, and occasionally sang each other's songs. At the end of the 1990s, with the return to democracy on the continent, the singers continued to pursue their careers in different ways, while maintaining long-term friendships and exchanges.

The 1960s was a time of politics and idealism in South America – far more so than in Europe or North America. There was a stark challenge presented by the continent's obvious inequalities, its inherited power and wealth, its corrupt regimes, and by the denial of literacy and education to much of the population. It is within this context that nueva canción singers and writers must be understood. With voice and guitar, they composed songs of their own hopes and experiences in places where many of those involved in struggles for change regularly met and socialized.

It is a music that is now, in some ways, out of date: the revolutionary past, the 1960s rhetoric of guitar as gun and song as bullet. Yet the songs – poems written to be performed – are classic expressions of the years of hope and struggle for change, their beauty and truth later nurturing those suffering under dictatorship, and those forced into exile. They are still known by heart by audiences throughout the continent and exiled communities in Europe.

Nueva canción was an expression of politics in its widest sense. It was not "protest song" as such. The musicians involved were not card-carrying members of any international organization and were often independent of political parties – although in the early 1970s the Chilean musicians were closely linked with the Popular Unity government of Salvador Allende, the first socialist president and government to be legitimately elected through the ballot box.

What linked these and other musicians of the movement was an ethical stance – a commitment to improve conditions for the majority of people in Latin America. To that end they sang not only in concerts and clubs but in factories, in shanty towns, community centres and at political meetings and street demonstrations. People in protest the world over have joined in the Chilean street anthems *El Pueblo Unido Jamás Sera Vencido* (The People United Will Never Be Defeated) and *Venceremos* (We Will Win).

Yupanqui and Violeta Parra

The roots of the nueva canción movement lie in the work of two key figures, whose music bridged rural and urban life and culture in the 1940s and 50s: the Argentine **Atahualpa Yupanqui** (1908–92) and the Chilean **Violeta Parra** (1917–67). Each had a passionate interest in his or her nation's rural musical traditions, which had both an Iberian and Amerindian sensibility. Their work was in some respects paralleled by the Cuban Carlos Puebla.

Atahualpa Yupanqui spent much of his early life travelling around Argentina, collecting popular songs from itinerant *payadores* (improvising poets, Chile's indigenous rappers) and folk singers in rural areas. He also wrote his own songs, and during a long career introduced a new integrity to Argentine folk music – and an assertive political outlook which ultimately forced him into exile in Paris.

Violeta Parra's career in Chile mirrored that of Yupanqui. She travelled extensively, singing with and collecting songs from old *payadores* and preserved and popularized them through radio broadcasts and records. She also composed new material based on these rural song traditions, creating a model and repertoire for what became nueva canción. Her songs celebrated the rural and regional, the music of the peasant, the land-worker and the marginalized migrant.

Musically, Parra was also significant in her popularization of **Andean or Amerindian instruments** – the armadillo-shelled *charango*, the *quena* (bamboo flute) and panpipes, and in her enthusiasm for the **French chanson** tradition. She spent time in Paris in the 1960s with her children Angel and Isabel, where they met Yupanqui, Edith Piaf and the flautist Gilbert Favre, who was to found the influential Andean band, Los Jaivas, and with whom Violeta fell in love. Returning to Buenos Aires, she performed in a tent in the district of La Reina, which came to be called the Carpa de La Reina (The Queen's Tent). However, with a long history of depression, she committed suicide in 1967.

Parra left behind a legacy of exquisite songs, many of them with a wry sense of humour, including the unparalleled *Gracias a la vida* (Thanks to life), later covered by Joan Baez and a host of others. Even her love songs seem informed by an awareness of poverty and injustice, while direct pieces like *Qué dirá el Santo Padre?* (What will the Sainted Pope Say?) highlighted the Church's responsibility to take action. As Parra wrote (in the form she often used in her songs) in her autobiography:

I sing to the Chilean people
if I have something to say
I don't take up the guitar
to win applause
I sing of the difference there is
between what is certain
and what is false
otherwise I don't sing.

The movement takes off

Nueva canción emerged as a real force in the mid-1960s, when various governments on the continent were trying to effect democratic social change. The search for a Latin American cultural identity became a spontaneous part of this wider struggle for self-determination, and music was a part of the process.

The first crystallization of a nueva canción ideal in Chile emerged with the opening of a crucial new folk club. This was and is the legendary crucible of nueva canción, the **Peña de los Parra**, which **Angel and Isabel Parra**, inspired by the Paris *chanson* nightclubs, opened in downtown Santiago in 1965. Among the regular singer-songwriters who performed here were Víctor Jara and Patricio Manns. Their audiences, in the politically charged and optimistic period prior to the election of Allende's government, were enthusiastic activists and fellow musicians.

Víctor Jara

The great singer-songwriter and theatre director **Víctor Jara** took nueva canción onto a world stage. His songs, and his life, continue to reverberate, and he has been recorded by rock singers like Sting, Bruce Springsteen, Peter Gabriel and Jackson Brown, and (memorably) by the British singer Robert Wyatt. All have been moved by Jara's story and inspired by his example.

Jara was born into a rural family who came to live in a shanty-town on the barren outskirts of Santiago when Víctor's father died; he was just eleven. His mother sang as a *cantora* for births, marriages and deaths, keeping her family alive by running a food-stall in the main Santiago market. It was from his mother and her work that Jara gained his intuitive knowledge of Chilean guitar and singing styles.

He began performing his songs in the early 1960s and from the beginning caused a furore. During the government of Eduardo Frei, for example, his playful version of a traditional piece, *La Beata* – a send-up of the desires of a nun – was banned, as was his accusatory *Preguntas por Puerto Montt* (Questions for Puerto Montt), which accused the minister of the interior of the massacre of poor landless peasants in the south of Chile. Working with Isabel Parra and the group **Huamari**, Jara went on to create a sequence of songs called *La Población*, based on the history and life of Santiago's shanty-town communities. His great gift was a deceptively simple and direct style applied to whatever he did.

One of his best-loved songs, *Te recuerdo Amanda* (I remember you, Amanda), is a good example of the simplicity of his craft. A hauntingly understated love song, it tells the story of a girl who goes to meet her man, Manuel, at the factory gates; he never appears because of an "accident", and Amanda waits in vain. In many of his songs, Jara subtly interwove allusions to his own life with the experiences of other ordinary people – Amanda and Manuel were the names of his parents.

Jara's influence was immense, both on nueva canción singers and the Andean-oriented groups like **Inti Illimani** and **Quilapayún** (see opposite), whom he worked with often, encouraging them to forge their own new performance styles. Enormously popular and fun-loving, he was nevertheless clear about his role as a singer: "The authentic revolutionary should be behind the guitar, so that the guitar becomes an instrument of struggle, so that it can also shoot like a gun." As he sang in 1972 in his song *Manifiesto*, a tender serenade which with hindsight has been seen as his testimony, "I don't sing just for love of singing, but for the statements made by my guitar, honest, its heart of earth, like the dove it goes flying…Song sung by a man who will die singing, truthfully singing his song".

Like many Chilean musicians, Jara was deeply involved with the Unidad Popular government of Salvador Allende, who in 1970, following his election, had appeared on an open-air stage in Santiago surrounded by musicians under a banner saying "There can be no revolution without song". Three years later, on September 11, 1973 – along with hundreds of others who had legitimately supported the government – Jara was arrested by the military and taken to the same downtown stadium in which he had won the First Festival of New Chilean Song in 1969. Tortured, his hands and wrists broken, his body was found with five others, riddled with machine-gun bullets, dumped alongside a

Plegaria aun Labrador (Prayer to a Labourer)

Stand up and look at the mountain
From where the wind comes, the sun and the water
You who direct the courses of the rivers
You who have sown the flight of your soul
Stand up and look at your hands
So as to grow
Clasp your brother's, in your own
Together we will move united by blood
Today is the time that can become tomorrow

Deliver us from the one who dominates us
through misery
Bring to us your reign of justice and equality
Blow like the wind the flower of the canyon
Clean like fire the barrel of my gun
Let your will at last come about here on earth
Give to us your strength and valour so as to fight
Blow like the wind the flower of the canyon
Clean like fire the barrel of my gun

Stand up and look at your hands
So as to grow
Clasp your brother's, in your own
Together we will move united by blood
Now and in the hour of our death
Amen.

Victor Jara

wall of the Metropolitan Cemetery; his face was later recognized amongst a pile of unidentified bodies in one of the Santiago mortuaries by a worker. He was just 35.

Jara left behind a song composed during the final hours of his life, written down and remembered by those who were with him at the end, called as a poem of testimony *Estadio Chile* (Chile Stadium). It was later set a cappella to music as *Ay canto, que mal me sales*, by his friend and colleague Isabel Parra.

Exiles and Andean sounds

After Pinochet's coup d'état anything remotely associated with the Allende government and its values came under censorship, including books and records, whose possession could be cause for arrest. The junta issued warnings to musicians and folklorists that it would be unwise for them to play nueva canción, or indeed any of the Andean instruments associated with its sound – *charangos*, panpipes and *quenas*.

It was not exactly a ban but it was menacing enough to force the scene well underground – and abroad, where many Chilean musicians lived out the junta years in exile. Their numbers included the groups Inti Illimani and Quilapayún and later Illapu (see p.524), Sergio Ortega, Patricio Manns, Isabel and Angel Parra, and Patricio Castillo. They were not the only Latin Americans forced from their country. Other **musician exiles** of the 1970s included Brazilian MPB singers Chico Buarque, Caetano Veloso and Gilberto Gil; Uruguay's nueva canción singer Daniel Viglietti; and Argentina's Mercedes Sosa.

In Chile, the first acts of musical defiance took place behind church walls, where a group of musicians who called themselves **Barroco Andino** started to play baroque music with Andean instruments within months of the coup.

It was a brave act, for the use of Andean or Amerindian instruments and culture was instinctively linked with the nueva canción movement. Chilean groups like **Quilapayún** and **Inti Illimani** wore the traditional ponchos of the peasant and played Andean instruments such as panpipes, bamboo flutes and the *charango*, and the maracas and shakers of Central America and the Caribbean. That these were the instruments of the communities who had managed somehow to survive slavery, resist colonialism and its aftermath had a powerful symbolism. Both the "los Intis" and "los Quilas", as they were familiarly known, worked closely with Víctor Jara and also with popular classical composers Sergio Ortega and Luis Advis.

In 1973 both groups travelled to Europe as official cultural ambassadors of the Allende government, actively seeking support from governments in Europe at a time when the country was more or less besieged economically by a North American blockade, its economy being undermined by CIA activity. On September 11 when General Pinochet led the coup d'état in which Salvador Allende died, the Intis were in Italy and the Quilas in France. For the Intis, the tour ("the longest in history", as Intis member Jorge Coulon jokes) turned into a fifteen-year and fifty-four days European exile for the group, an exile which put nueva canción and Amerindian music firmly on Europe's agenda of Latin American music.

The groups were the heart and soul of a worldwide Chilean (and Latin American) solidarity movement, performing almost daily for the first ten years. Both also recorded albums of new songs, the Intis influenced

Nueva canción has had a raw deal on **CD** – it peaked in the decades before shiny discs – and for many classics, you'll need to search second hand stores for vinyl. If you travel to Chile, you can also obtain **songbooks** for the music of Víctor Jara (the Fundación Víctor Jara publishes his complete works), while most other songs of the period are featured in *Clásicos de la Música Popular Chilena Vol 11 1960–1973* (Ediciones Universidad Católica de Chile).

Compilations

Music of the Andes (Hemisphere EMI, UK).
Despite the title, this is essentially a nueva canción disc, with key Chilean groups Inti Illimani, Quilapayún and Illapu to the fore. There is also an instrumental recording of *Tinku* attributed to Víctor Jara.

Artists

Illapu
Illapu, with a track record stretching back over 25 years, and a big following in Chile, play Andean instruments – panpipes, *quenas* and *charangos* – along with saxophones, electric bass and Caribbean percussion. Their music is rooted in the north of the country where most of the band hails from.

Sereno (EMI, UK).
This enjoyable collection gives a pretty good idea of what Illapu have got up to over the years and includes strongly folkloric material, as well as dance pieces influenced by salsa, romantic ballads and the earlier styles of vocal harmony.

Inti Illimani
The foremost Chilean "new song" group, who began as students in 1967, bringing the Andean sound to Europe through their thousands of concerts in exile, and taking European influences back home again in the late 1980s. The original band, together for thirty years, featured the glorious-voiced José Séves.

Lejan'a (Xenophile, US).
The focus is on Andean themes in this celebration of their thirtieth anniversary and their original inspiration.

Arriesgaré la piel (Xenophile, US).
A celebration of the music the Intis grew up with, from creole-style tunes to Chilean *cuecas*, most lyrics by Patricio Manns with music by Salinas. This was the final album to be made with the core of the original band before Séves left.

Grandes Exitos (EMI, Chile).
A compilation of seventeen songs and instrumental pieces taken from the band's thirty-year history.

Quilapayún
This key Chilean new-song group worked closely in their early years with Víctor Jara and in 1973 – the year of the coup – they split into multiple groups in order to get

by their many years in Italy, creating some beautiful songs of exile, including the seminal song *Vuelvo*, with key singer-songwriter and musician **Patricio Manns**.

The impact of their high-profile campaigning against the military meant that the Intis were turned back on the airport tarmac long after politicians and trade union leaders were repatriated. They eventually returned on September 18, 1988, Chile's National Day, the day of one of the biggest meetings of supporters of the "No" vote to the plebiscite called by Pinochet to determine whether he should stay in office. Going straight from the airport to sing on a huge open-air stage and to dance the traditional *cueca* (Chile's National Day dance), the group's homecoming was an emotional and timely one. In 1998, after ten years of their message across on as many stages as possible. They co-authored, with Sergio Ortega, the street anthem *El Pueblo Unido Jamás Sera Vencido* (the People United Will Never Be Defeated). Although they disbanded in the late 1990s, their influence lives on.

Santa María de Iquique (Dom Disque, France).

Chilean composer Luis Advis's ground-breaking Cantata, composed for Quilapayún, tells the emblematic and heroic tale of the murder of unarmed nitrate workers and their families in 1907.

Víctor Jara

The leading singer-songwriter of his generation, Víctor Jara was murdered in his prime by Pinochet's forces in September 1973. His legacy is an extraordinary songbook, which can be heard in his original versions, as well as a host of Latin and western covers.

Manifesto (Castle, UK).

Reissued to mark the 25th anniversary of his death, this is a key disc of nueva canción, with *Te recuerdo Amanda*, *Canto libre*, *La Plegaria a un Labrador* and *Ay canto*, the final poem written in the Estadio Chile, before his death. Includes Spanish lyrics and English translations.

Vientos del Pueblo (Monitor, US).

A generous 22-song compilation that includes most of the Jara milestones, including *Te recuerdo Amanda* and *Preguntas por Puerto Montt*, plus the wonderful revolutionary romp of *A Cochabamba me Voy*. Quilapayún provide backing on half the album.

Víctor Jara Complete (Plane, Germany).

This four-CD box is the definitive Jara, featuring material from eight original LPs. Plane have also released an excellent single-disc selection of highlights.

La Población (Alerce, Chile).

Classic Jara: a project involving other musicians, but including most of all the lives and experiences of those celebrated here, who lived in various shanty towns (*poblaciones*) including the one where Jara himself grew up.

Violeta Parra

One of South America's most significant folklorists and composers, Violeta Parra collected fragments of folklore from singers, teaching them to the next generation and influencing them with her own excellent compositions. Parra's songs have also been superbly recorded by Argentinian Mercedes Sosa.

Canto a mi América (Auvidis, France).

An excellent introduction to Parra's seminal songs.

Las Ultimas Composiciones (Alerce, Chile).

A reissue of Parra's 1965 release which turned out to be her last as well as latest songs ("Ultimas" means both in Spanish).

rebuilding their lives, making music and supporting various projects, including the Víctor Jara Foundation, the group's personnel, almost unchanged since 1967, is now adapting to the amicable departure of Max Berri and Jose Séves to pursue other projects.

The Andean instruments and rhythms used by Quilapayún (who disbanded in the 1980s) and Inti Illimani have been skilfully used by many other groups whose music is equally interesting – groups like **Illapu**, who remained popular throughout the 1980s (with a number of years in forced exile) and 1990s.

The Future and Legacy

Times have changed in Chile and in Latin America generally, with revolutionary governments no longer in power, democracy restored after dictatorships, and even Pinochet placed under arrest. The nueva canción movement, tied to an era of ideals and struggle, and then the brutal years of survival under dictatorship, would seem to have lost its relevance.

Its musicians have moved on to more individual concerns in their (always poetic) songwriting. But the nueva canción form, the inspiration of the song as message, and the rediscovery of Andean music and instruments, continues to have resonance and influence. Among a new generation of singers inspired by the history of "new song" are **Carlos Varela** in Cuba and the Bolivian singer **Emma Junaro**.

And there will be others. For Latin America, nueva canción is not only music but history. As the Cuban press has said of the songs of Silvio Rodriguez: "We have here the great epic poems of our days." Or as the Dominican Republic's merengue superstar Juan Luis Guerra, put it, "they are the master songwriters – they have influenced everyone."

Books

U nfortunately, a number of the best and most evocative books written on Chile have long been out of print, but we include some of them – mainly travel narratives or general accounts – below (marked by o/p in the parentheses after the title), as they can often be found in public libraries or on the internet. Modern publications are inevitably dominated by analyses and testimonies of the Pinochet years, much of which makes compelling reading. There are relatively few up-to-date general histories of Chile in English, with those available focusing more on the academic market than the general reader. Chilean fiction, meanwhile, is not very widely translated into English, with the exception of a handful of the country's more famous authors. Its poetry, or more specifically the poetry of its famous Nobel laureate Pablo Neruda, has been translated into many languages and is widely available abroad. Note that in the list below, where two publishers are given, these refer to UK/ US publishers respectively. If just one publisher is listed, and no country is specified, the book is published in both the UK and the US. Highly recommended books are preceded by 🟊. UP is University Press.

Impressions, travel and general accounts

General introductions

Stephen Clissold *Chilean Scrapbook* (Cresset; o/p). Beautifully and evocatively written, taking you from the top to the bottom of the country via a mixture of history, legend and anecdote.

Augustin Edwards *My Native Land* (Ernest Benn; o/p). Absorbing and vivid reflections on Chile's geography,

history, folklore and literature; particularly strong on landscape descriptions.

Benjamin Subercaseaux *Chile: A Geographic Extravaganza* (New York; o/p). This seductive, poetic meander through Chile's "mad geography" is still one of the most enjoyable general introductions to the country, if a little dated.

Recent travel/accounts

Tim Burford *Chile and Argentina: The Bradt Trekking Guide* (Bradt Travel Guides). Fantastically detailed account of how to access and climb the Andes from Atacama to Tierra del Fuego. Plenty of trail maps and practical advice from the original South American explorers.

Bruce Chatwin *In Patagonia* (Vintage/Penguin). The cult travel

book that single-handedly enshrined Patagonia as the ultimate edge-of-the-world destination. Witty and captivating, this is essential reading for visitors to Patagonia, though unfortunately concentrates far more on the Argentine side.

Ariel Dorfman *Desert Memories* (National Geographic). Vivid depiction of desert life gleaned from Dorfman's travels through Chile's Norte Grande, which weaves past and present, memoir and meditation, history and family lore to provide an engaging chronicle of modern Chile.

Toby Green *Saddled with Darwin* (Phoenix). One hundred and sixty-five years after Charles Darwin embarked on the journey that produced the most radical theory of modern times, Green set out to retrace his footsteps on horseback. The result is an epic journey across six countries, including Chile, which paints an incisive portrait of change across the southern section of the continent.

Brian Keenan and **John McCarthy** *Between Extremes: A Journey Beyond Imagination* (Black Swan/Corgi/Transworld Pub Inc.). Five years after Keenan and McCarthy were released from captivity in Beirut, the pair set off to fulfil a dream they'd shared as hostages to journey down the spine of Chile, from Arica to Tierra del Fuego. This account of their journey, told in alternating narratives, is as much an homage to their friendship as it is a description of the landscapes and people of Chile.

John Pilkington *An Englishman in Patagonia* (Century; o/p). A fun-to-read and sympathetic portrayal of Patagonia and its people. Includes some wonderful black-and-white photographs.

Rosie Swale *Back to Cape Horn* (Collins; o/p). An extraordinary account of the author's epic 409-day journey on horseback from the Atacama Desert down to Cape Horn – which she'd last visited while sailing around the world ten years previously in 1972.

Patrick Symmes *Chasing Che* (Robinson/Vintage Books). The author undertakes an epic motorbike trip through South America – including hundreds of miles of Chile – following the route taken by a young Che Guevara back in 1952, as chronicled in *The Motorcycle Diaries* (see below). A great mix of biography, history, politics and travel anecdotes, this is a sharply written and highly entertaining read.

Sara Wheeler *Travels in a Thin Country* (Abacus/Modern Library). A pacy, amusing account of the author's six-month solo journey zigzagging the entire length of Chile in the early 1990s.

Nineteenth- and early twentieth-century accounts

John Arons and Claudio Vita-Finzi *The Useless Land* (Robert Hale; o/p). Four Cambridge geography students set out to explore the Atacama Desert in 1958 and relate their adventures along the way in this highly readable book.

Charles Darwin *Voyage of the Beagle* (Penguin/Wordsworth Editions Ltd). This eminently readable (abridged) book contains some superb, evocative descriptions of nineteenth-century Chile, from Tierra del Fuego right up to Iquique.

Maria Graham *Journal of a Residence in Chile During the Year 1822* (o/p). The classic nineteenth-century travel narrative on Chile, written by a spirited, perceptive and amusing British woman.

Che Guevara *The Motorcycle Diaries* (Fourth Estate/Verso Books). Comic, picaresque narrative taken from the diaries of the future revolutionary as he and his buddy, both just out of medical school, travelled around South America – including a large chunk of Chile – by motorbike.

Useful addresses

Canning House Library 2 Belgrave Square, London SW1X 8PJ ☏020/7235 2303 (ext. 208), ✉library@canninghouse.com, ⍟www.canninghouse.com/library.htm. An exhaustive collection of books on Chile (and other Hispanic countries). Also produces a quarterly bulletin detailing new publications on Latin America and Brazil.

Latin American Bureau 1 Amwell St, London EC1R 1UL ☏020/7278 2829, ✉contactlab@lab.org.uk, ⍟www.lab.org.uk. Publishers of books on Latin America, available by mail order along with a wide selection of titles produced by other publishers.

South American Explorer 126 Indian Creek Rd, Ithaca, NY 14850, US ☏607/277-0488, ✉explorer@saexplorers.org, ⍟www.samexplo.org. Among its mountain of resources on South America, this long-established organization produces a free catalogue containing a wide choice of books available by mail order. The service can be used by members and non-members alike.

Auguste Guinnard *Three Years Slavery Among the Patagonians* (Tempus Publishing). This is the account of Guinnard's capture and often brutal enslavement by Tehuelche Indians at war with the European colonizers in 1859, his surprising enlightenment and eventual escape.

E.B. Herivel *We Farmed a Desert* (o/p). Entertaining account of the fifteen years spent by a British couple on a small farm in the Huasco Valley in the 1930s and 1940s.

Alistair Horne *Small Earthquake in Chile* (Macmillan; o/p). Wry description of a visit to Chile during the turbulent months leading up to the military coup, written by a British journalist.

Bea Howe *Child in Chile* (o/p). A charming description of the author's childhood in Valparaíso in the early 1900s, where her family formed part of the burgeoning British business community.

W.H. Hudson *Idle Days in Patagonia* (Tempus Publishing). Drawn by the variety of fauna and the remarkable birdlife, the novelist and naturalist W. H. Hudson travelled to Patagonia at the tail-end of the nineteenth century and wrote this series of charming, gentle observations.

George Musters *At Home with the Patagonians* (Tempus Publishing). Remarkable account of time spent living with the Tehuelche Indians at the end of the nineteenth century that explodes the myth of the "noble savage" and provides a historically important picture of their vanishing way of life.

History, politics and society

General

Leslie Bethell (ed) *Chile Since Independence* (Cambridge UP). Made up of four chapters taken from the *Cambridge History of Latin American History*, this is rather dry in parts, but rigorous, comprehensive and clear.

Nick Caistor *In Focus: Chile* (Latin American Bureau/Interlink Books). Brief, potted introduction to Chile's history, politics and society, highlighting the social problems bequeathed by Pinochet's economic model.

Simon Collier and William Sater *A History of Chile, 1801–1994* (Cambridge UP). Probably the best single-volume history of Chile from independence to the 1990s; thoroughly academic but enlivened by colourful detail along with the authors' clear fondness for the country and its people.

John Hickman *News from the End of the Earth: A Portrait of Chile* (Hurst & Co./St Martin's Press). Written by a former British ambassador to Chile, this concise and highly readable book makes a good (if conservative) introduction to Chile's history, taking you

from the conquest to the 1990s in some 250 pages.

Brian Loveman *Chile: the Legacy of Hispanic Capitalism* (Oxford UP). Solid analysis of Chile's history from the arrival of the Spanish in the 1540s to the 1973 military coup.

Sergio Villalobos *A Short History of Chile* (Editorial Universitaria, Chile). Clear, concise and sensible outline of Chile's history, from pre-Columbian cultures through to the past decade, aimed at the general reader with no prior knowledge of the subject. Available in Santiago.

The Pinochet years

Andy Beckett *Pinochet in Piccadilly: Britain and Chile's Hidden History* (Faber and Faber). A fascinating political travelogue that connects the past to the present as it explores the relationship between the two nations.

Sheila Cassidy *Audacity to Believe* (Darton, Longman & Todd; o/p). Distressing account of the imprisonment and horrific torture of a British doctor (the author) after she'd treated a wounded anti-Pinochet activist.

Pamela Constable and Arturo Valenzuela *A Nation of Enemies* (W.W. Norton & Company). Written during the mid- to late 1980s, this is a superb look at the terror of everyday life in Chile at that time and the state apparatus used to annihilate free thinking and initiative in Chile. Essential to understanding contemporary Chile.

Marc Cooper *Pinochet and Me: A Chilean Anti-Memoir* (Verso Books). First-hand account of life under Pinochet in the early days of the coup, written by a young American who served as Allende's translator and barely escaped the death squads. Followed up by accounts of his periodic visits to Chile over the next quarter century.

John Dinges *The Condor Years: How Pinochet and His Allies Brought Terror to Three Continents* (New Press). Exhaustively researched book that examines the creation and use of international hit squads by the Pinochet regime. The chilling accounts of multi national agreements to execute "enemies of the state" are recreated by author Dinges, an internationally recognized investigative reporter and professor at Columbia University.

Paul Drake (ed) *The Struggle for Democracy in Chile* (University of Nebraska Press). Excellent collection of ten essays examining the gradual breakdown of the military government's authority. The pieces, which offer contrasting views both in support of and opposition to the regime, were written in 1988, during the months around the plebiscite.

Diana Kay *Chileans in Exile: Private Struggles, Public Lives* (Longwood Academic). Although written in a somewhat dry, academic style, this is nonetheless a fascinating study of Chilean exiles in Scotland, with a strong focus on women. The author looks at their attempts to reconstruct their lives, their sense of dislocation, and the impact exile has had on

C

CONTEXTS | Books

their attitude to politics, marriage and the home.

Hugh O'Shaughnessy *Pinochet: The Politics of Torture* (Latin America Bureau; New York UP). Covering everything from the arrest of Pinochet in London to Pinochet's secret plans to distribute sarin nerve gas to Chilean consulates abroad, this book provides an overview of the most influential man in Chilean politics from 1973 to 1998.

Patricia Politzer *Fear in Chile, Lives Under Pinochet* (New Press). Award-winning account of the lives of Chileans during the dictatorship, another classic account of the repressive apparatus used to subdue Chileans.

Grino Rojo and John J Hasset (ed) *Chile, Dictatorship and the Struggle for Democracy* (Ediciones Hispamérica). A slim, accessible volume containing four essays written in the months approaching the 1988 plebiscite, in which the country would vote to reject or continue with military rule. Contains contrasting analyses of the impact of the dictatorship on the country and its people.

Jacobo Timerman *Chile: Death in the South* (Vintage Books; o/p). Reflections on the Pinochet years by an Argentine journalist, written thirteen years into the military regime. Particularly compelling are the short personal testimonies of torture victims that intersperse the narrative.

Thomas Wright and Rody Oñate *Flight from Chile: Voices of Exile* (University of New Mexico Press). Detailed and affecting account of the exodus after the 1973 coup, when over 200,000 Chileans fled their homeland.

Special-interest studies

George McBride *Chile: Land and Society* (Kennikat Press; o/p). A compelling and exhaustively researched examination of the impact of the hacienda system on Chilean society, and the relationship (up to the mid-twentieth century) between landowners and peasants.

Colin McEwan, Luis Borrero and Alfredo Prieto (eds) *Patagonia: Natural History, Prehistory and Ethnography at the Uttermost End of the Earth* (British Museum Press/Princeton UP). Brilliant account of the "human adaptation, survival and eventual extinction" of the native peoples of Patagonia, accompanied by dozens of haunting black-and-white photographs.

Nick Reding *The Last Cowboys at the End of the World: The Story of the Gauchos of Patagonia* (Crown). A brutally honest and at times brutal look at the end of the gaucho era in Patagonia. Excellent exploration of how in the mid-1990s the gaucho culture crashed headlong into the advance of modern society.

William Sater *The Heroic Image in Chile* (University of California Press; o/p). Fascinating, scholarly look at the reasons behind the near-deification of Arturo Prat, the naval officer who died futilely in battle in 1879, described by the author as "a secular saint".

Richard W Slatta *Cowboys of the Americas* (Yale UP). Exhaustively researched, highly entertaining and lavishly illustrated history of the cowboy cultures of the Americas, including detailed treatment of the Chilean *huaso*.

Chilean women

Marjorie Agosin (ed) *Scraps of Life: Chilean Arpilleras: Chilean Women and the Pinochet Dictatorship* (Zed Books/Red Sea Press). A sensitive portrayal of the women of Santiago's shanty towns who, during the dictatorship, scraped a living by sewing scraps of material together to make wall hangings, known as *arpilleras*, depicting scenes of violence and repression. The *arpilleras* became a symbol of their protest, and were later exhibited around the world.

Jo Fisher *Out of the Shadows* (Latin American Bureau/Monthly Review Press). Penetrating analysis of the emergence of the women's movement in Latin America, with a couple of chapters devoted to Chile.

Elizabeth Jelin (ed) *Women and Social Change in Latin America* (Zed Books). A series of intelligent essays examining the ways women's organizations have acted as mobilizing forces for social and political change in Latin America.

Fiction and poetry

C

CONTEXTS | Books

Fiction

Marjorie Agosin (ed) *Landscapes of a New Land: Short Fiction by Latin American Women* (White Wine Press). This anthology includes four short stories by Chilean women authors, including the acclaimed Marta Brunet (1901–67) and María Luisa Bombal (1910–80). Overall, the book creates a poetic, at times haunting, evocation of female life in a patriarchal world. Also edited by Agosin, *Secret Weavers: Stories of the Fantastic by Women of Argentina and Chile* (White Wine Press; o/p) is a spellbinding collection of short stories interwoven with themes of magic, allegory, legend and fantasy.

Isabel Allende *The House of the Spirits* (Black Swan/Bantam Books). This baroque, fantastical and best-selling novel chronicles the fortunes of several generations of a rich, landowning family in an unnamed but thinly disguised Chile, culminating with a brutal military coup and the murder of the president. Allende's *Of Love and Shadows* (Black Swan/Bantam Books) is set against a background of disappearances and

dictatorship, including a fictional account of the real-life discovery of the bodies of fifteen executed workers in a Central Valley mine. The author is a relative (niece) of Salvador Allende.

José Donoso *Curfew* (Picador/Grove Atlantic). Gripping novel about an exiled folk singer's return to Santiago during the military dictatorship, by one of Chile's most outstanding twentieth-century writers. Other works by Donoso translated into English include *Hell Has No Limits* (Sun and Moon Press), about the strange existence of a transvestite and his daughter in a Central Valley brothel, and *The Obscene Bird of Night* (Godine), a dislocated, fragmented novel narrated by a deaf-mute old man as he retreats into madness.

Ariel Dorfman *Hard Rain* (Readers International). This complicated, thought-provoking novel is both an examination of the role of the writer in a revolutionary society, and a celebration of the "Chilean road to socialism" – not an easy read, but one that repays the effort. Dorfman later became internationally famous for his play *Death and the Maiden* (Penguin), made into a film by Roman Polanski. Dorfman has also written an account of the effort to prosecute Pinochet in *Exorcising Terror: The Incredible Unending Trial of Augusto Pinochet*.

Alberto Fuguet *Bad Vibes* (o/p; St Martin's Press). Two weeks in September 1980 as lived by a mixed-up Santiago rich kid. A sort of Chilean *Catcher In the Rye* set against the tensions of the military regime.

Alicia Partnoy (ed) *You Can't Drown the Fire: Latin American Women Writing in Exile* (Virago/Cleis Press). Excellent anthology bringing together a mixture of short stories, poems and essays by exiled Latin American women, including Veronica de Negri, Cecila Vicuña, Marjorie Agosin and Isabel Morel Letelier from Chile.

Luis Sepúlveda *The Name of a Bullfighter* (Allison & Busby Ltd). Fast-paced, rather macho thriller set in Hamburg, Santiago and Tierra del Fuego, by one of Chile's leading young novelists.

Antonio Skármeta *The Postman* (Hyperion), formerly *Burning Patience* (Minerva). Funny and poignant novel about a postman who delivers mail to the great poet Pablo Neruda, who helps him seduce the local beauty with the help of a few metaphors. It was also made into a successful film, *Il Postino*, with the action relocated to Capri. Also by Skármeta, *I Dreamt the Snow Was Burning* (Readers International) is a tense, dark novel evoking the suspicion and fear that permeated everyday life in the months surrounding the military coup, while *Watch Where the Wolf is Going* (Readers International) is a collection of short stories, some of them set in Chile.

Poetry

Vicente Huidobro *The Selected Poetry of Vicente Huidobro* (W.W. Norton & Co./New Directions). Intellectual, experimental and dynamic works by an early twentieth-century poet, highly acclaimed in his time (1893–1948) but often overlooked today.

Gabriela Mistral *Selected Poems* (Johns Hopkins UP). Mistral is far less widely translated than her fellow Nobel laureate, Neruda, but this collection serves as an adequate English-language introduction to her quietly passionate and bittersweet poetry, much of it inspired by the landscape of the Elqui Valley.

Pablo Neruda *Twenty Love Poems and a Song of Despair* (Jonathan Cape/

Penguin); *Canto General* (French & European Publications/University of California Press); *Captain's Verses* (New Directions). The doyen of Chilean poetry seems to be one of those poets people love or hate – his work is extravagantly lyrical, frequently verbose, but often very tender, particularly his love poetry. Neruda has been translated into many languages, and is widely available.

Nicanor Parra *Emergency Poems* (W.W. Norton & Co./New Directions). Both a physicist and poet, Parra pioneered the "anti-poem" in Chile during the 1980s: bald, unlyrical, often satirical prose poems. A stimulating read.

Biography and memoirs

Isabel Allende *My Invented Country – A Nostalgic Journey Through Chile* (HarperCollins). A memoir that is an enthralling mix of fiction and biography and which describes her life in Chile up until the assassination of her uncle, president Salvador Allende. She provides a very personal view of her homeland and exhaustively examines the country, its terrain, people, customs and language.

Fernando Alegria *Allende: A Novel* (Stanford UP). Basically a biography, with fictional dialogue, of Salvador Allende, written by his former cultural attaché, who was busy researching the book while the president died in the coup. Also of note by Alegria is *The Chilean Spring*, a fictional diary of a young photographer coming to terms with the coup in Santiago.

Ariel Dorfman *Heading South, Looking North* (Hodder & Stoughton/Penguin). Memoir of one of Chile's most famous writers, in which he reflects on themes such as language, identity, guilt and politics. Intelligent and illuminating, with some interesting thoughts on the causes of the Unidad Popular's failures.

Joan Jara *Víctor: An Unfinished Song* (Bloomsbury; o/p).

Poignant memoir written by the British wife of the famous Chilean folksinger Víctor Jara, describing their life together, the Nueva Canción movement (see p.519) and their optimism for Allende's new Chile. The final part, detailing Jara's imprisonment, torture and execution in Santiago's football stadium, is almost unbearably moving.

R.L. Mégroz *The Real Robinson Crusoe* (Cresset Press; o/p). Colourful biography of Alexander Selkirk, who spent four years and four months marooned on one of the Juan Fernández Islands, inspiring Daniel Defoe to write *The Adventures of Robinson Crusoe*.

Luis Muñoz *Being Luis* (Impress Books). Account of a childhood spent growing up in 1960s–70s Chile that reflects recent history and leads to Muñoz's development as a left-wing activist, his arrest and torture by the military regime and eventual exile to England.

Pablo Neruda *Memoirs* (Penguin). Though his occasional displays of vanity and compulsive name-dropping can be irritating, there's no doubt that this is an extraordinary man with a fascinating life. The book also serves as a useful outline of Chile's political movements from the 1930s to the 1970s.

Pacific Islands

Paul Bahn and John Flenley *Easter Island, Earth Island* (Thames & Hudson; o/p). Richly illustrated with glossy photographs, this scholarly but accessible book provides an up-to-date and comprehensive introduction to

the island's history and archeology. Interestingly, it also suggests that Easter Island could be a microcosm representing a global dilemma – that of a land so despoiled by man that it could no longer support its civilization.

Sebastian Englert *Island at the Centre of the World* (Hale; o/p). Based on a series of lectures broadcast to the Chilean Navy serving in Antarctica, this is perhaps the clearest and most accessible (though now somewhat dated) introduction to Easter Island, written by a genial German priest who lived there for 35 years from 1935.

Thor Heyerdahl *Aku Aku* (George Allen & Unwin; o/p). This account of Heyerdahl's famous expedition to Easter Island in 1955 makes a cracking read, with an acute sense of adventure and mystery. Dubious as the author's archeological theories are, it's hard not to get swept along by his enthusiasm. In contrast, his *Reports of the Norwegian Archeological Expedition to Easter Island and the East Pacific* is a rigorous and respected documentation of the expedition's findings.

Alfred Métraux *Easter Island* (André Deutsch; o/p). Key study of Easter Island's traditions, beliefs and customs by a Belgian anthropologist, based on exhaustive research carried out in the 1930s. Métraux's *The Ethnology of Easter Island*, published in periodical format, is available from Periodicals Service Company, 11 Main St, Germantown, NY, USA (℡518/537-5899).

Catherine and Michel Orliac *The Silent Gods: Mysteries of Easter Island*

(Thames & Hudson; o/p). Pocket-sized paperback, densely packed with colour illustrations and surprisingly detailed background on the island's explorers, statues, myths and traditions.

Katherine Routledge *The Mystery of Easter Island* (Adventures Unlimited Press). Recently back in print, this compelling book chronicles one of the earliest archeological expeditions to the island, led by the author in 1914. Routledge interviewed many elderly islanders and recounts their oral testimonies as well as the discoveries of her excavations.

Diana Souhami *Selkirk's Island* (Phoenix/Harcourt) This gripping account of the misadventures of Alexander Selkirk – the real life Robinson Crusoe, who spent four years marooned on a Chilean Pacific island – includes some vivid and evocative descriptions of what's now known as Isla Robinson Crusoe. Deservedly won the Whitbread Biography Award in 2001.

Ralph Lee Woodward *Robinson Crusoe's Island* (University of North Carolina Press; o/p). There's a good deal more drama to the Juan Fernández islands' history than the famous four-year marooning of Alexander Selkirk, all of it enthusiastically retold in this lively book.

Flora and fauna

Sharon R. Chester *Birds of Chile* (Wandering Albatross). First-rate, easy-to-carry guide with over 300 colour illustrations of the birds of mainland Chile.

Claudio Donoso Zegers *Chilean Trees Identification Guide/Arboles Nativos de Chile* (Marisa Cïneo Ediciones, Chile). Handy pocket guide to Chile's main native trees,

with commentary in Spanish and English. Produced for Conaf (Chile's national parks administration), and part of a series that includes *Chilean Bushes*, *Chilean Climber Plants* and *Chilean Terrestrial Mammals*. Available in Conaf's information office in Santiago.

Language

Language

Chilian Spanish

To get by in Chile, it's very helpful to equip yourself with a bit of basic Spanish. It's not a difficult language to pick up and there are numerous books, cassettes and CD-ROMs on the market, teaching to various levels – *Teach Yourself Latin American Spanish* is a very good book-cassette package for getting started, while for an old-fashioned, rigorous textbook, nothing beats H. Ramsden's *An Essential Course in Modern Spanish*, published in the UK by Nelson.

The snag is that Chilean Spanish does not conform to what you learn in the classroom or hear on a cassette, and even competent Spanish-speakers will find it takes a bit of getting used to. The first thing to contend with is the dizzying **speed** with which most Chileans speak; another is **pronunciation**, especially the habitual dropping of many consonants. In particular, "s" is frequently dropped from the end or middle of a word, so *dos* becomes *do*, *gracias* becomes *gracia*, and *fósforos* (matches) becomes *fohforo*. "D" has a habit of disappearing from past participles, so *comprado* is *comprao*, while the "gua" sound is commonly reduced to *wa*, making the city of Rancagua *Rancawa*. The *–as* ending of the second person singular of verbs (*estás*, *viajas*, and so on) is transformed into *–ai*: hence *¿cómo estás?* usually comes out as "comehtai"; the classic *"¿cachai?"* ("get it?") is the second person singular form of the slang verb *cachar*, meaning to understand.

Another way in which Chilean differs from classic Castilian Spanish is its borrowing of words from indigenous languages, mainly Quichoa, Aymara and Mapuche, but also from German (*küchen*, for cake) and even English ("plumber" in Chile is inexplicably *el gasfiter*). Adding to the confusion is a widespread use of **slang** and **idiom**, much of which is unique to Chile. None of this, however, should put you off attempting to speak Spanish in Chile – Chileans will really appreciate your efforts, and even faltering beginners will be complimented on their language skills.

Pronunciation

The rules of **pronunciation** are pretty straightforward and, once you get to know them, strictly observed. Unless there's an accent, words ending in d, l, r, and z are **stressed** on the last syllable, all others on the second last. All **vowels** are pure and short.

A somewhere between the "a" sound of back and that of father.

E as in get.

I as in police.

O as in hot.

U as in rule.

C is soft before E and I, hard otherwise: *cerca* is pronounced "serka".

G works the same way, a slightly guttural "h" sound (between an aspirate "h" and the ch in loch) before e or i, a hard G elsewhere – *gigante* becomes "higante".

H is always silent.

J is guttural: *jamón* is pronounced "hamón".

LL sounds like an English Y: *tortilla* is pronounced "torteeya".

N is as in English unless it has a tilde over it (ñ), when it becomes NY: *mañana* sounds like "manyana".

QU is pronounced like an English K (the "u" is silent).

R is rolled, RR doubly so.

V sounds more like B, *vino* becoming "beano".

X is slightly softer than in English – sometimes almost SH – except between vowels in place names where it has an "H" sound – for example México (Meh-Hee-Ko).

Z is the same as a soft C, so *cerveza* becomes "serbessa".

On the following page we've listed a few essential words and phrases, though if you're travelling for any length of time a dictionary or phrase book is obviously a worthwhile investment. If you're using a **dictionary**, bear in mind that in Spanish CH, LL, and Ñ count as separate letters and are traditionally listed in a special section after the Cs, Ls, and Ns respectively, though some new dictionaries do not follow this rule.

Words and phrases

The following should help you with your most basic day-to-day language needs; a menu reader and list of slang terms follows on.

Basics

yes, no	sí, no
please, thank you	por favor, gracias
where, when?	dónde, cuándo
what, how much?	qué, cuánto
here, there	aquí, allí
this, that	este, eso
now, later	ahora, màs tarde
open, closed	abierto/a, cerrado/a
with, without	con, sin
good, bad	buen(o)/a, mal(o)/a
big	gran(de)
small	pequeño/a, chico
more, less	más, menos
today, tomorrow	hoy, mañana
yesterday	ayer

Greetings and responses

Hello, Goodbye	Hola, adiós (ciao/chau)
Good morning	Buenos días
Good afternoon	Buenas tardes
Good evening/night	Buenas noches
See you later	Hasta luego
Sorry	Lo siento/discúlpeme (perdón)
Excuse me	Con permiso/perdón
How are you?	¿Como está (usted)?
I (don't) understand	(No) Entiendo

Not at all/You're welcome	De nada
Do you speak English?	¿Habla (usted) inglés?
I (don't) speak Spanish	(No) Hablo español
My name is...	Me llamo...
What's your name?	¿Cómo se llama usted?
I am English	Soy inglés(a)
...Irish	...irlandés (a)
...Scottish	...escocés (a)
...Welsh	...galés (a)
...American	...norte-americano(a)
...Australian	...australiano (a)
...Canadian	...canadiense
...New Zealander	...neozelandés (a)

Accommodation and transport

I want	Quiero...
I'd like	Quisiera...
Do you know...	¿Sabe...?
I don't know	No sé
There is (is there?)	(¿) Hay (?)
Give me...	Deme...
...(one like that)	...(uno así)
Do you have...	¿Tiene...?
...the time	...la hora
...a room	...una habitación

...with two beds/ double bed	...con dos camas/ cama matrimonial	Is there a hotel nearby?	¿Hay un hotel aquí cerca?
...with private bath	...con baño privado	How do I get to...?	¿Por dónde se va a...?
It's for one person (two people)	es para una persona (dos personas)	Left, right, straight on	Izquierda, derecha, derecho
for one night (one week)	para una noche (una semana)	Where is...?	¿Dónde está...?
It's fine,	Está bien,	the bus station	el terminal de buses
how much is it?	¿cuánto es?	the train station	la estación de ferrocarriles
It's too expensive	Es demasiado caro	the nearest bank	el banco más cercano
Don't you have anything cheaper?	¿No tiene algo más barato?	the post office	el correo
Can one...?	¿Se puede...?	the toilet	el baño
camp (near) here?	acampar aquí (cerca)?	Where does the bus to... leave from?	¿De dónde sale el bus para...?

Useful transport vocabulary

Ticket	Pasaje	Is this the train for Santiago?	¿Es éste el tren para Santiago?
Seat	Asiento	I'd like a (return) ticket to...	¿Quisiera un pasaje (de ida y vuelta) para...
Aisle	Pasillo		
Window	Ventana		
Luggage	Equipaje	What time does it leave (arrive in...)?	¿A qué hora sale (llega en...)?
Left luggage	Custodia		
Car	Auto	How long does the journey take?	¿Cuánto tiempo demora el viaje?
Car rental outlet	Rentacar		
To rent	Arrendar	What is there to eat?	¿Qué hay para comer?
4WD	Doble tracción or cuatro por cuatro (4x4)		
		What's that?	¿Qué es eso?
Non-4WD	Tracción single or dos por dos (2x2)	What's this called in Spanish?	¿Como se llama esto en español?
Unlimited kilometres	Kilometraje libre		

Numbers and days

Insurance	Seguro
Damages excess	Deducible
Petrol	Bencina
Petrol station	Estación de bencina
Jerry can	Bidon
Highway	Carretera
Pick-up truck	Camioneta

1	un/uno/una
2	dos
3	tres
4	cuatro
5	cinco
6	seis
7	siete
8	ocho
9	nueve
10	diez
11	once
12	doce
13	trece
14	catorce
15	quince

Chilean road signs

Danger	Peligro
Detour	Desvío
Slippery surface	Resbaladizo
No overtaking	No adelantar
Dangerous bend	Curva peligrosa
Reduce speed	Reduzca velocidad
No hard shoulder	Sin berma

16	dieciséis	200	doscientos (as)
17	diecisiete	201	doscientos (as) uno
18	dieciocho	500	quinientos (as)
19	diecinueve	1000	mil
20	veinte	2000	dos mil
21	veintiuno	first	primer(o)/a
30	treinta	second	segundo/a
40	cuarenta	third	tercer(o)/a
50	cincuenta	Monday	lunes
60	sesenta	Tuesday	martes
70	setenta	Wednesday	miércoles
80	ochenta	Thursday	jueves
90	noventa	Friday	viernes
100	cien(to)	Saturday	sábado
101	ciento uno	Sunday	domingo

Food: a Chilean menu reader

Basics

Aceite	Oil
Ají	Chilli
Ajo	Garlic
Arroz	Rice
Azúcar	Sugar
Huevos	Eggs
Leche	Milk
Mantequilla	Butter
Mermelada	Jam
Miel	Honey
Mostaza	Mustard
Pan	Bread
Pimienta	Pepper
Sal	Salt

Some common terms

A la parrilla	Grilled
A la plancha	Lightly fried
A lo pobre	Served with chips, onions and a fried egg
Ahumado	Smoked
Al horno	Oven-baked
Al vapor	Steamed
Asado	Roast or barbecued

Asado al palo	Spit-roasted, barbecued
Crudo	Raw
Frito	Fried
Pastel	Paste, purée, mince
Picante	Spicy hot
Pil-pil	Very spicy
Puré	Mashed (potato)
Relleno	Filled or stuffed

Meals

Agregado	Side order
Almuerzo	Lunch
Cena	Dinner
Comedor	Dining room
Cuchara	Spoon
Cuchillo	Knife
Desayuno	Breakfast
La carta	The menu
La cuenta	The bill
Menú del día	Fixed-price set meal (usually lunch)
Once	Afternoon tea
Plato vegetariano	Vegetarian dish
Tenedor	Fork

Meat (carne) and poultry (aves)

Bistec	Beef steak
Carne de vacuno	Beef
Cerdo	Pork
Chuleta	Cutlet, chop (usually pork)
Churrasco	Griddled beef, like a minute steak
Conejo	Rabbit
Cordero	Lamb steak
Escalopa Milanesa	Breaded veal escalope
Filete	Fillet steak
Jamón	Ham
Lechón, cochinillo	Suckling pig
Lomo	General term for steak of indiscriminate cut
Pato	Duck
Pavo	Turkey
Pollo	Chicken
Ternera	Veal
Vienesa	Hot-dog sausage

Offal (menudos)

Chunchules	Intestines
Guatitas	Tripe
Pana	Liver
Lengua	Tongue
Patas	Feet, trotters
Picante de conejo	Curried rabbits' innards
Riñones	Kidneys

Fish (pescado)

Albacora	Albacore (a small, white-fleshed tuna)
Anchoveta	Anchovy
Atún	Tuna
Bonito	Pacific bonito, similar to tuna
Ceviche	Strips of fish Marinated in lemon juice and onions
Congrio	A large, superior member of the cod family known as conger eel
Corvina	sea bass (not the same as Chilean sea bass, which is under boycott)
Lenguado	Sole
Merluza	Hake
Reineta	Similar to lemon sole
Salmón	Salmon
Trucha	Trout
Vidriola	Firm-fleshed white fish from the Juan Fernández archipelago

Seafood (mariscos)

Almeja	Clam, cockle
Calamar	Squid
Camarón	Prawn
Centolla	King crab
Choro, chorito	Mussel
Erizo	Sea urchin
Langosta	Lobster
Langosta de Isla de Pascua	Spiny lobster
Langosta de Juan Fernández	Crayfish, rock lobster
Langostino	Crayfish, red crab
Loco	Abalone
Macha	Razor clam
Mariscal	Mixed shellfish, served chilled
Mejillones	Mussels
Ostiones	Scallops
Ostras	Oysters
Paila marina	Thick fish and seafood stew
Picoroco	Giant barnacle with a single crab-like claw
Piure	Scarlet-red, kidney-shaped animal with hair-like strands that lives inside a shell
Pulpo	Octopus

Vegetables (verduras)

Aceitunas	Olives
Alcachofa	Artichoke

Cebolla	Onion
Champiñón	Mushroom
Choclo	Maize, sweetcorn
Chucrút	Sauerkraut
Espinaca	Spinach
Lechuga	Lettuce
Palmito	Palm heart
Palta	Avocado
Papa	Potato
Papas fritas	Chips (French fries)
Poroto verde	Green, French, runner bean
Tomate	Tomato
Zapallo	Squash

Soups and stews

Caldillo	Vegetables cooked in meat stock; between a stew and a soup
Caldo	Quite bland, simple meat stock with loads of added salt
Charquicán	Meat stew with lots of vegetables
Chupe	Thick fish stew, topped with butter, breadcrumbs and grated cheese
Crema	Creamy soup thickened with flour or egg yolks
Zarzuela	Seafood stew (like bouillabaisse)

Salads (ensaladas)

Ensalada chilena	Tomatoes, shredded onion and vinaigrette
Ensalada primavera	Hard-boiled eggs, sweetcorn, peas, carrot, beetroot
Ensalada rusa	Diced vegetables and peas mixed in a thick mayonnaise
Ensalada surtida	Mixed salad
Palta reina	Avocado filled with tuna

Sandwiches (sanwiches)

Ave mayo	Chicken and mayonnaise
Ave sola	Chicken
Barros Jarpa	Ham and melted cheese
Barros Luco	Beef and melted cheese
Churrasco solo	Griddled beef, like a minute steak
Completo	Hot dog, sauerkraut, tomato, mayonnaise
Diplomático	Beef, egg and melted cheese
Especial	Hot dog with mayonnaise
Hamburguesa	Hamburger

Fruit (frutas)

Albaricoque	Apricot
Cereza	Cherry
Chirimoya	Custard apple
Ciruela	Plum
Durazno	Peach
Frambuesa	Raspberry
Frutilla	Strawberry
Higo	Fig
Limón	Lemon
Lúcuma	Native fruit often used in ice cream and cakes
Manzana	Apple
Membrillo	Quince
Mora	Mulberry
Naranja	Orange
Pera	Pear
Piña	Pineapple
Plátano	Banana
Pomelo	Grapefruit
Sandía	Watermelon
Tuna	Prickly pear
Uva	Grape(s)

Dessert (postres)

When fruit is described as being "in juice" (*al jugo*) or "in syrup" (*en almíbar*), it will be out of a tin.

Flan	Crème caramel
Helado	Ice cream
Küchen	Cake

Macedonia	Fruit salad
Manjar	Very sweet caramel, made from condensed milk
Panqueques	Pancakes
Torta	Tart

Drinks and beverages

Note that, owing to the Chileans' compulsive use of the diminutive (*ito* and *ita*), you'll hardly ever be asked if you want a *té* or *café*, but rather a *tecito* or *cafecito*, which tends to throw people at first.

Alcoholic drinks

Cerveza	Beer
Champán	Champagne
Chicha (or sidra)	Cider
Vino (tinto/blanco/ rosado)	Wine (red/white/rosé)

Hot drinks

Café	Coffee
Descafeinado (rarely available)	Decaff
Chocolate caliente	Hot chocolate
Té de hierbas	Herbal tea
Té	Tea

Soft drinks

Bebida (en lata/botella) (de máquina)	Fizzy drink (in a can/bottle) (draught)
Jugo natural	Juice (pure)
Néctar	Juice (syrup)
Agua	Water
Agua mineral (con gas) (sin gas)	Mineral water (sparkling) (still)

Idiom and slang

As you travel through Chile you'll come across a lot of words and expressions that crop up again and again, many of which aren't in your dictionary, or, if they are, appear to have a different meaning from that given. Added to these day-to-day **chilenismos** is a very rich, exuberant and constantly expanding vocabulary of slang (*modismos*). Mastering a few of the most common examples will help you get by and raise a smile if you drop them into the conversation.

Everyday words and expressions

Some of the words and expressions listed below are shared by neighbouring countries, while others are uniquely Chilean. As well as these peculiarities, we've listed a few other expressions you're likely to encounter very frequently.

Al tiro "right away", "immediately" – though this can mean anything up to several hours.

Boleta as Chilean law requires that customers must not leave shop premises without their *boleta* (receipt), you will frequently hear "*su boleta!*" yelled at you as you try to leave without it.

Calefónt (pronounced calefón) water heater; not a real Chilean word, but one you'll need on a daily basis if you're staying in budget accommodation, where you'll have to remember to light the *calefónt* with *fósforos* (matches) before you take a shower.

Carné identity card.

Cédula interchangeable with *carné*.

Ciao (chau) by far the most common way of saying "goodbye" among friends; in slightly more formal situations, *hasta luego* is preferred over *adiós*.

Confort (pronounced "confor") A brand name but now the de facto word for toilet paper (which is correctly *papel higiénico*).

De repente in Spain this means "suddenly"; in Chile it means "maybe", "sometimes" or "occasionally".

Flojo "lazy", frequently invoked by northerners to describe southerners and southerners to describe northerners.

Guagua (pronounced "wawa") baby, derived from Quichoa.

Harto "loads of" (for example *harto trabajo*, loads of work); a more widely used and idiomatic alternative to *mucho*.

Listo literally "ready", and used as a response to indicate agreement, or that what's been said is understood; something like "sure" or "right".

Plata literally "silver" but meaning "money", used far more commonly than *dinero*, except in formal situations.

Qué le vaya (muy) bien "May everything go (very) well for you", frequently said when saying goodbye to someone you probably won't see again.

Rico "good", "delicious", "tasty", usually to describe food and drink.

Ya Chilean equivalent of the Spanish *vale*; used universally to convey "OK", "fine", "sure" or (depending on the tone) "Whatever", "Hmm, I see".

Slang

The few examples we give below barely scrape the surface of the living, constantly evolving lexicon of Chilean slang – for a crash course, get hold of the excellent *How to Survive in the Chilean Jungle* by John Brennan and Alvaro Baboada, published by Dolmen and available in the larger Santiago bookshops.

Buena onda "cool!"

Cachar "to understand"; hence "*¿cachai?*", "are you with me?", scattered ad nauseam through conversations.

Cocido drunk.

Cuico yuppie (especially in Santiago).

Huevón literally "huge testicle", meaning something like "asshole" or "fucker", but so commonly and enthusiastically used it's no longer particularly offensive. More like "jerk" or "idiot".

Los pacos the police.

Pololo/a boyfriend, girlfriend.

¡Sale! emphatically used to mean, "bullshit!" or "not a chance!"

Sí, po abbreviation of *sí, pues*, meaning "yeah", "sure" ("po" is tacked onto the end of just about every phrase, hence "*no po*", "*no sé po*").

Taco traffic jam.

Glossary

Adobe Sun-dried mud.

Altiplano High plateau region in the Andes of the far north.

Apu Mountain god.

Arriero Muleteer, or horseman.

Ayllu Kinship group or clan.

Barrio District, quarter or suburb.

Bofedal Spongy green grass or peat bog in the altiplano.

Cabaña chalet, log cabin.

Camanchaca Coastal mist.

Carabineros police.

Casa patronal Hacienda-owner's house.

Cerro hill, mountain, peak.

Chicha Cider; fermented grape or maize drink.

Colectivo Shared taxi.

CONAF National parks administrative body.

Cordillera Mountain range.

Costanera waterfront, promenade.

Criollo "Creole": used historically to refer to a person of Spanish blood born in the American colonies, but nowadays as an adjective to describe something (such as food or music) as "typical" or "local".

Cuadra city block.

Encomendero Possessor of an *encomienda*.

Encomienda A grant of indigenous labourers to landowners during colonial times.

Estancia Ranch, or large estate.

Fundo Estate or farm.

Hacienda Large estate.

Hoja de coca Coca-leaf.

Huaso Chilean "cowboy", or mounted farm worker.

Junta A ruling council; usually used to describe small groups who have staged a coup d'état.

Latifundio Huge estate.

Llareta Deep-green, rock-hard woody plant in the altiplano.

Local "Unit" or "shop" in shopping centre or mall.

Mayorazgo Entailment system of large estates.

Mestizo Person of mixed Spanish and indigenous blood.

Micro City bus.

Pampa Plain.

Peña Restaurant or nightclub where live folk music is performed.

Población Poor suburb.

Portazuela Mountain pass.

Pukará Fort.

Puna Quichoa word referring to barren Andean heights, sometimes used interchangeably with the Spanish word *altiplano*.

Quebrada Ravine, dried-out stream.

Seno gulf, inlet, estuary.

Soroche Altitude sickness.

Tábanos Horseflies.

Travel store

ROUGH GUIDES Complete Listing

D: Rough Guide
DIRECTIONS for
short breaks

Available from all good bookstores

ROUGH GUIDES

Stay In Touch!

Subscribe to Rough Guides' **FREE** newsletter

News, travel issues, music reviews, readers' letters and the latest dispatches from authors on the road. If you would like to receive roughnews, please send us your name and address:

UK and Rest of World: Rough Guides, 80 Strand, London, WC2R 0RL, UK
North America: Rough Guides, 4th Floor, 345 Hudson St,
New York NY10014, USA
or email: newslettersubs@roughguides.co.uk

"The most accurate maps in the world"

San Jose Mercury News

ROUGH GUIDE MAP

France

1:1,000,000 · 1 INCH: 15.8 MILES · 1CM: 10KM

CITY MAPS 25 titles
Amsterdam · Athens · Barcelona · Berlin
Boston · Brussels · Chicago · Dublin
Florence & Siena · Frankfurt · Hong Kong
Lisbon · London · Los Angeles · Madrid
Marrakesh · Miami · New York City · Paris
Prague · Rome · San Francisco · Toronto
Venice · Washington DC
US$8.99   Can$13.99   £4.99

COUNTRY & REGIONAL MAPS 48 titles
Algarve · Andalucía · Argentina · Australia
Baja California · Brittany · Crete
Croatia · Cuba · Cyprus · Czech Republic
Dominican Republic · Dubai · Egypt · Greece
Guatemala & Belize · Iceland · Ireland
Kenya · Mexico · Morocco · New Zealand
Northern Spain · Peru · Portugal · Sicily
South Africa · South India · Sri Lanka
Tenerife · Thailand · Trinidad & Tobago
Tuscany · Yucatán Peninsula and more.
US$9.99   Can$13.99   £5.99

Plastic waterproof map
ideal for planning and touring

waterproof • rip-proof • amazing value
BROADEN YOUR HORIZONS

ROUGH GUIDES

Visit us online
www.roughguides.com
Information on over 25,000 destinations around the world

- **Read** Rough Guides' trusted travel info
- **Access** exclusive articles from Rough Guides authors
- **Update** yourself on new books, maps, CDs and other products
- **Enter** our competitions and win travel prizes
- **Share** ideas, journals, photos & travel advice with other users
- **Earn** points every time you contribute to the Rough Guide community and get rewards

BROADEN YOUR HORIZONS

Small print and
Index

A Rough Guide to Rough Guides

Published in 1982, the first Rough Guide – to Greece – was a student scheme that became a publishing phenomenon. Mark Ellingham, a recent graduate in English from Bristol University, had been travelling in Greece the previous summer and couldn't find the right guidebook. With a small group of friends he wrote his own guide, combining a highly contemporary, journalistic style with a thoroughly practical approach to travellers' needs.

The immediate success of the book spawned a series that rapidly covered dozens of destinations. And, in addition to impecunious backpackers, Rough Guides soon acquired a much broader and older readership that relished the guides' wit and inquisitiveness as much as their enthusiastic, critical approach and value-for-money ethos.

These days, Rough Guides include recommendations from shoestring to luxury and cover more than 200 destinations around the globe, including almost every country in the Americas and Europe, more than half of Africa and most of Asia and Australasia. Our ever-growing team of authors and photographers is spread all over the world, particularly in Europe, the USA and Australia.

In the early 1990s, Rough Guides branched out of travel, with the publication of Rough Guides to World Music, Classical Music and the Internet. All three have become benchmark titles in their fields, spearheading the publication of a wide range of books under the Rough Guide name.

Including the travel series, Rough Guides now number more than 350 titles, covering: phrasebooks, waterproof maps, music guides from Opera to Heavy Metal, reference works as diverse as Conspiracy Theories and Shakespeare, and popular culture books from iPods to Poker. Rough Guides also produce a series of more than 120 World Music CDs in partnership with World Music Network.

Visit www.roughguides.com to see our latest publications.

Rough Guide travel images are available for commercial licensing at www.roughguidespictures.com

Rough Guide credits

Text editor: AnneLise Sorensen
Layout: Ankur Guha
Cartography: Jasbir Sandhu
Picture editor: Mark Thomas
Production: Rebecca Short
Proofreader: Stewart J Wild
Cover design: Chloë Roberts
Photographer: Tim Draper
Editorial: Ruth Blackmore, Andy Turner, Keith Drew, Edward Aves, Alice Park, Lucy White, Jo Kirby, James Smart, Natasha Foges, Róisín Cameron, Emma Traynor, Emma Gibbs, Kathryn Lane, Christina Valhouli, Monica Woods, Mani Ramaswamy, Harry Wilson, Lucy Cowie, Helen Ochyra, Amanda Howard, Lara Kavanagh, Alison Roberts, Joe Staines, Peter Buckley, Matthew Milton, Tracy Hopkins, Ruth Tidball; **Delhi** Madhavi Singh, Karen D'Souza, Lubna Shaheen
Design & Pictures: **London** Scott Stickland, Dan May, Diana Jarvis, Chloë Roberts, Nicole Newman, Sarah Cummins, Emily Taylor; **Delhi** Umesh Aggarwal, Ajay Verma, Jessica Subramanian , Pradeep Thapliyal, Sachin Tanwar, Anita Singh, Nikhil Agarwal, Sachin Gupta
Production: Vicky Baldwin

Cartography: **London** Maxine Repath, Ed Wright, Katie Lloyd-Jones; **Delhi** Rajesh Chhibber, Ashutosh Bharti, Rajesh Mishra, Animesh Pathak, Karobi Gogoi, Alakananda Bhattacharya, Swati Handoo, Deshpal Dabas
Online: **London** George Atwell, Faye Hellon, Jeanette Angell, Fergus Day, Justine Bright, Clare Bryson, Aine Fearon, Adrian Low, Ezgi Celebi, Amber Bloomfield; **Delhi** Amit Verma, Rahul Kumar, Narender Kumar, Ravi Yadav, Debojit Borah, Rakesh Kumar, Ganesh Sharma, Shisir Basumatari
Marketing & Publicity: **London** Liz Statham, Niki Hanmer, Louise Maher, Jess Carter, Vanessa Godden, Vivienne Watton, Anna Paynton, Rachel Sprackett, Libby Jellie, Laura Vipond, Vanessa McDonald; **New York** Katy Ball, Judi Powers, Nancy Lambert; **Delhi** Ragini Govind
Manager India: Punita Singh
Reference Director: Andrew Lockett
Operations Manager: Helen Phillips
PA to Publishing Director: Nicola Henderson
Publishing Director: Martin Dunford
Commercial Manager: Gino Magnotta
Managing Director: John Duhigg

Publishing information

This fourth edition published August 2009 by
Rough Guides Ltd,
80 Strand, London WC2R 0RL
14 Local Shopping Centre, Panchsheel Park, New Delhi 110017, India
Distributed by the Penguin Group
Penguin Books Ltd,
80 Strand, London WC2R 0RL
Penguin Group (USA)
375 Hudson Street, NY 10014, USA
Penguin Group (Australia)
250 Camberwell Road, Camberwell, Victoria 3124, Australia
Penguin Group (Canada)
195 Harry Walker Parkway N, Newmarket, ON, L3Y 7B3 Canada
Penguin Group (NZ)
67 Apollo Drive, Mairangi Bay, Auckland 1310, New Zealand
Cover concept by Peter Dyer.

Typeset in Bembo and Helvetica to an original design by Henry Iles.

Printed and bound in Singapore by SNP Security Printing Pte Ltd

© Melissa Graham and Andrew Benson 2009

No part of this book may be reproduced in any form without permission from the publisher except for the quotation of brief passages in reviews.

568pp includes index

A catalogue record for this book is available from the British Library

ISBN: 978-1-84836-175-1

The publishers and authors have done their best to ensure the accuracy and currency of all the information in **The Rough Guide to Chile**, however, they can accept no responsibility for any loss, injury, or inconvenience sustained by any traveller as a result of information or advice contained in the guide.

1   3   5   7   9   8   6   4   2

Help us update

We've gone to a lot of effort to ensure that the fourth edition of **The Rough Guide to Chile** is accurate and up-to-date. However, things change – places get "discovered", opening hours are notoriously fickle, restaurants and rooms raise prices or lower standards. If you feel we've got it wrong or left something out, we'd like to know, and if you can remember the address, the price, the hours, the phone number, so much the better.

Please send your comments with the subject line "**Rough Guide Chile Update**" to ©mail @roughguides.com. We'll credit all contributions and send a copy of the next edition (or any other Rough Guide if you prefer) for the very best emails.

Have your questions answered and tell others about your trip at
Ⓦcommunity.roughguides.com

ROUGH GUIDES

SMALL PRINT

Acknowledgements

Anna Khmelnitski: Thanks to everyone who assisted me during my travels, including all the Sernatur and Conaf staff whose assistance proved invaluable, with Sernatur in Coyhaique deserving a special mention; Britt, Carlos and Alan for their local knowledge of Chiloé; Fernando and Amory for their boundless hospitality; Sarah and Cristian in Pucón for being my "home away from home" and plying me with information and *asado*; the good folk of Erratic Rock for being a sheer treasure trove of insider knowledge; Pierre for the conversation at the end of the world; Christina and Simon, for the cheerful companionship on Rapa Nui and on the Carretera Austral; all the hospitable folk on Juan Fernández, including Pedro for the diving and the help, and Willy for the fishing at sunrise; Nikolai for tackling the Torres del Paine Circuit with me; Mike, Pete and Zoe of JLA for the tireless advice, memorable meals and nature outings; and everyone at Rough Guides involved in the project, AnneLise in particular for the opportunity, the patience and the scrupulous editing. I dedicate my research to Pete – a constant source of inspiration.

Shafik Meghji: *Muchas gracias* to all the tourist office staff, travellers and locals who helped along the way. A special thank you must go to: Malcolm Coad, for his help and expertise; Cath Collins, for her invaluable insider's take on Santiago; Juan Eduardo and Juan Carlos Torres, for their insight into Valpo and the Central Coast; Cristian Leon and Cristian Lopez, for their recommendations; Veronica Morgado, for her information on the Maule Valley; Jean, Nizar and Nina Meghji, for their love and support; Carlos Reyes-Manzo, for his suggestions and contacts; Catherine O'Rourke, for her input into the Santiago chapter; James Smart, for his flexibility with schedules; and AnneLise Sorensen, for the initial commission and her advice and support throughout.

The editor would like to thank Shafik, Anna and Charlotte for their excellent updating, perseverance and passion for Chile. And, as always, it was a true pleasure to work with the Delhi typesetting and cartography teams, Ankur Guha, Katie Lloyd-Jones, Mark Thomas, Stewart J Wild and Mani Ramaswamy.

Readers' letters

Thanks to all the readers who have taken the time to write in with comments and suggestions (and apologies if we've inadvertently omitted or misspelt anyone's name):

Vince Biondo, Michiel Cappendijk, Gloria Ulloa Castillo, José Fliman, Cécilia Gourlaouen, Barbara Knapton, Sally Kondziolka, Annika Lindkvist, Fabian Märkl, Nadia Muñoz, Daniela Papadatos, Oliver Potart, Barry Ress, Christophe De Scheemaecker, Daan Steijnen, Luca Toscani, Emily Walker, Doug Young

Photo credits

All photos © Rough Guides except the following:

Introduction
Easter Island © Tim Draper

Things not to miss
02 Laguna Verde © Imagebroker/Alamy
07 Paragliding © Design Pics/Alamy
11 Pablo Neruda © Macduff Everton/Corbis
16 Chinchorro mummies © Ivan Alvarado/Corbis
17 Lapis lazuli © Phil Degginger/Alamy
18 Dancer at the Tapati Festival, Easter Island
   © Marla Lampert/Alamy
22 Curanto © Wolfgang Kaehler/Corbis
24 Sea lions in the Beagle Channel © Visions of
   America/Alamy

Chilean wildlife colour section
Puda © Arco Images GmbH/Alamy
Puma © Blickwinkel/Alamy
Condor © Skip Brown/Getty Images
Hummingbird © Chile DesConocido/Alamy
Caracara © Chris Mattison/Alamy

Adventure sports colour section
Skiing © Stockshot/Alamy
Paragliding © Design Pics Inc/Alamy
Aerial view of the Andes © Martin Harvey/Alamy
Sand dunes © Imagebroker/Alamy
Hiking in Torres del Paine © Keith Drew

Black and whites
p.281 Kayaking, Río Bío Bío © Imagebroker/
   Alamy
p.291 Parque Nacional Nahuelbuta © Fabian
   Gonzalez/Alamy
p.298 Parque Nacional Conguillío © June
   Morrissey/Alamy
p.314 Landscape around Pucón © Robert
   Harding/Alamy
p.326 Valdivia © Jon Arnold/Alamy
p.418 Punta Arenas © Robert Harding/Alamy
p.436 Torres del Paine © Bruce Perry/Alamy
p.444 Cape Horn © M Timothy O'Keef/Alamy
p.464 Sea lions on Juan Fernández © WorldFoto/
   Alamy
p.475 Moai statues, Easter Island © Tim Draper

Selected images from our guidebooks are available for licensing from:
ROUGHGUIDESPICTURES.COM

Index

Map entries are in colour.

INDEX

INDEX

564

INDEX

565

BABYLON PUBLIC LIBRARY

3 0610 00127 4059

Map Symbols

maps are listed in the full index using coloured text

------	International boundary		🏠	*Guardería* (ranger station)
-----	Chapter boundary		🏠	*Refugio* (mountain lodge)
48	Motorway		⬆	Customs post
	Major road		⛷	Skiing area
	Minor road		🍇	Vineyard
	Pedestrianized road		🏛	Monument
IIIIIIIIII	Steps		♟	Museum
------	Path		🏊	Swimming pool
	Unpaved road		⛪	Church (regional maps)
	Railway		🔭	Observatory
	Waterway		⚔	Battle site
	Tunnel		⛩	Picnic area
	Bridge		Ⓜ	Metro station
✈	International airport		★	Bus stop
✈	Domestic airport		Δ	Campsite
♦	Point of interest		⊞	Hospital
♜	Castle		☎	Telephone office
∴	Ruins		ⓘ	Information office
☼	Viewpoint		✉	Post office
⌂	Cave		@	Internet access
▲	Mountain peak		◉	Accommodation
⚞	Mountain range		■	Restaurant
⩵	Mountain passes		●—●	Cable car
12	Cliffs		▨	Building
⋀	Volcano		⊞	Church
🜊	Waterfall		☐	Market
⋀	Spa/hot springs		⬭	Stadium
⋙	Surf area		▨	Park
⚓	Port/harbour		▨	Beach
🕯	Lighthouse		⊟	Salt pan
/|\	Hill shading		▨	Glacier/icefield
�★	Swamp		⊡	Cemetery

AUG 1 9 2009

New York Times **bestselling author**
FAYE KELLERMAN

"A master of mystery."
—*Plain Dealer* (Cleveland)

"She does for the American cop story
what P.D. James has done for the British mystery,
lifting it beyond genre."
—*Richmond Times-Dispatch*

MOON MUSIC

"Irresistible."
—*Mary Higgins Clark Mystery Magazine*

"Anyone who likes mysteries salted with the gothic
will eat up this tale."
—*Atlanta Journal-Constitution*

"An energizing, terrifying, thought-provoking introduction
to the Las Vegas of Romulus Poe. . . . You'll want to go back often
and stay late. . . . Faye Kellerman's talent for deeply complex
characters, riveting action, and thorough research keeps us
on the edge of our seats, wide awake late at night."
—*BookPage*

"Go find a favorite reading spot and enjoy."
—*San Francisco Examiner*

And praise for Faye Kellerman's award-winning
Peter Decker/Rina Lazarus Mysteries:

SERPENT'S TOOTH

"Readers will be frantically flipping pages."
—*People*

"A shocker. . . . A bang-up whodunit. . . .
The phenomenally popular Kellerman
has produced another sure winner."
—*Booklist*

"One of the best."
—*San Francisco Examiner*

"A page-turner. . . . Lots of action, an intricate plot,
and credible, multi-dimensional characters."
—*Publishers Weekly*

PRAYERS FOR THE DEAD

"First-rate . . . fascinating. . . .
An unusually well-written detective story."
—*Los Angeles Times Book Review*

"A real gem . . . brilliant and stunning. . . .
Kellerman proves once again that she is a master storyteller."
—*Chattanooga Free Press*